THE EUROPEAN COMPOSITE ADMINISTRATION

THE EUROPEAN COMPOSITE ADMINISTRATION

Oswald Jansen and
Bettina Schöndorf-Haubold (eds.)

intersentia
Cambridge – Antwerp – Portland

Intersentia Ltd
Trinity House | Cambridge Business Park | Cowley Road
Cambridge CB4 0WZ | United Kingdom
mail@intersentia.co.uk

Distribution for the UK:
Hart Publishing Ltd.
16C Worcester Place
Oxford OX1 2JW
UK
Tel.: +44 1865 51 75 30
Email: mail@hartpub.co.uk

Distribution for the USA and Canada:
International Specialized Book Services
920 NE 58th Ave. Suite 300
Portland, OR 97213
USA
Tel.: +1 800 944 6190 (toll free)
Email: info@isbs.com

Distribution for Austria:
Neuer Wissenschaftlicher Verlag
Argentinierstraße 42/6
1040 Wien
Austria
Tel.: +43 1 535 61 03 24
Email: office@nwv.at

Distribution for other countries:
Intersentia Publishers
Groenstraat 31
2640 Mortsel
Belgium
Tel.: +32 3 680 15 50
Email: mail@intersentia.be

The European Composite Administration
Oswald Jansen and Bettina Schöndorf-Haubold (eds.)

ISBN 978-94-000-0098-8
D/2011/7849/29
NUR 823

PREFACE

From the outset the European Union has been a community of public administrations. In this community national administrative bodies cooperate in numerous policy areas with the European Commission as well as national administrative bodies of other EU Member States. More recently agencies and EU-institutions form an administrative structure which at its own turn is building administrative cooperative relations at the EU level. Next to the distinction between direct and indirect application and implementation (*direkter und indirekter Vollzug*) a composite of national public administrations and EU-administrations has arisen. In this European Composite Administration (*Europäischer Verwaltungsverbund*) the national borders become less important both from the perspective of citizens as from the perspective of administrative bodies. The Lisbon Treaty will make this composite even more dense.

Administrative activity in this European Composite Administration brings us specific legal questions on which the contributions in this collection are focused. The idea to undertake this project is related to the cooperation in research between legal scholars from Utrecht and Heidelberg in which these colleagues discussed each others research projects, conducted common research projects and exchanged ideas and results between each other. It all started with a coincidental meeting of two legal scholars: Hans-Christian Röhl and Oswald Jansen.

The research cooperation rested upon three pillars. The first pillar consists of a long-range research project on the legal aspects of administrative cooperation (*Europäisches Verwaltungskooperationsrecht*) on the initiative of Eberhard Schmidt-Aßmann of Heidelberg University. The project was granted by the German Research Foundation (*Deutsche Forschungsgemeinschaft* (DFG)). This research project has resulted in numerous publications and PhD theses. In 2005 the results were collected and published in German by Mohr Siebeck entitled Schmidt-Aßmann and Schöndorf-Haubold (eds.), *Der Europäische Verwaltungsverbund*. The present volume contains the English translation of the majority of the German contributions in *Der Europäische Verwaltungsverbund*. In this way the outcome of this important research project will be better accessible to the non-German speaking or reading scientific community.

The second pillar of the research cooperation between the Heidelberg and Utrecht scholars consists of (a part of) the Utrecht research project 'Transnational law enforcement in the European legal area' which was granted by the Dutch

Research Foundation (NWO), initiated by Rob Widdershoven and John Vervaele and coordinated by Oswald Jansen. The third pillar of this research cooperation is formed by the cooperative research project jointly granted by both the German and the Dutch Research Foundation entitled *Transnational Law Application and Enforcement in the European Legal Area* on the initiative of Oswald Jansen.

In short, in this book the translated German results of the first pillar of the research cooperation are combined with the Utrecht results of the second pillar of this cooperation, and the third pillar of the cooperation made it all possible.

The combined research results of the German and Dutch legal scholars offer a wide range of insights in specific legal areas and deliver valuable in depth analyses related to their common perspective and focus on common or comparable issues of European administrative cooperation. The numerous studies of specific legal areas which are in many cases based upon the results of more detailed and extensive PhD research of the author involved within that specific area offer rich substantive materials of reference to the scholarship and the ongoing study and development of the system of general administrative law in both the national and the European level of the European Composite Administration.

After a general introduction to the concept of European Composite Administration (*Europäischer Verwaltungsverbund*) by Eberhard Schmidt-Aßmann, the contributions are distributed in three parts of the book.

In the first part ten fields of European Administrative Law are analysed: Structural Funds (Schöndorf-Haubold), European Environmental Law (Sommer), and the Law on Plant Protection Products (Keessen), Financial Services and more specifically the Law on Insider Dealing (Luchtman), European Veterinary and Food Law (Knipschild), European Aviation Law (Riedel), the Law on Police and Customs Cooperation (Harings), European Product Safety Law (Röhl), Transnational Water Management (Hey and Van Rijswick), and Public Access to Documents (Duijkersloot).

The second part covers contributions that focus on acts and procedures in the European Composite Administration. Ruffert presents an in depth analysis of the Transnational Administrative Act, whereas Wettner focuses on the general law of procedure of Mutual Administrative Assistance in the European Union. Vogt presents an analysis of the Administrative Decision as a means of normative law making, and David gives us the results of her study of the role of Inspections as an instrument of implementation in European Administrative Law. Schenk finishes this part of the book with his analysis of EC Grant Management.

The third and last part of this book ends with some contributions on administrative structures and legal protection. Röhl analyses the Voidable Decision as a Form of Legal Protection, Hofmann examines the system of Legal Protection and Liability in EU law. Van Hoek and Luchtman present the results of their study of the role of Human Rights in the Transnational Cooperation in

Criminal Matters, and Vervaele concludes the volume with his contribution on the transnational ne bis in idem Principle.

We would like to thank all colleagues and assistants involved for their effort to publish their work in a non native language and their patience with the sometimes headache causing procedure leading to this result. All translators involved, and especially Maris van der Laak, cannot underestimate the value of their work to this book. We also would like to thank Intersentia for their willingness to publish this book, and Kris Moeremans and Isabelle Van Dongen for their valuable contribution and patience.

Due to the fact that this volume is a collection of the translated versions of previously published contributions, the manuscripts of the articles in large part were finished by the end of 2008. Except for a small number of contributions, modifications by the Lisbon Treaty and subsequent developments could not be taken into account in the volume.

Heidelberg and Utrecht
Summer 2010
Oswald Jansen and Bettina Schöndorf-Haubold

SHORT TABLE OF CONTENTS

CONTENTS

A. FIELDS OF LAW

LIST OF ABBREVIATIONS

AB	AB Rechtspraak Bestuursrecht
AFM	Authority for the Financial Markets (NL)
AG	Advocate General
AO	Abgabenordnung (D)
AöR	Archiv des öffentlichen Rechts
Awb	Algemene wet bestuursrecht (General Administrative Law Act – GALA – NL)
Awr	Algemene wet inzake rijksbelastingen (NL)
BAFin	Bundesanstalt für Finanzdienstleistungsaufsicht (D)
BEHG	Bundesgesetz über die Börsen und den Effektenhandel (CH)
BSE	Bovine Spongiform Encephalopathy
BVerfGE	Entscheidungen des Bundesverfassungsgerichts (Decisions of the Federal Constitutional Court – D)
CAP	Common Agricultural Policy
CBb	College van Beroep voor het bedrijfsleven (administrative law court of appeal – NL)
CE	Conseil d'Etat (F)
CESR	Committee of European Securities Regulators
cf.	confer
CFI	Court of First Instance
CFS	Community Support Framework
CIS	Customs Information System
CISA	Convention implementing the Schengen Agreement
CMLR/CMLRev.	Common Market Law Review
CONSOB	Commissione nazionale per le società e la borsa (I)
CS	Certification Specifications
Dir.	Directive
DNB	De Nederlandsche Bank (NL)
DÖV	Die Öffentliche Verwaltung
DV	Die Verwaltung
DVBl.	Deutsches Verwaltungsblatt
e.g.	exempli gratia (for example)
E.L.Rev.	European Law Review
EAGGF	European Agricultural Guidance and Guarantee Fund

EASA	European Aviation Safety Agency
ECHR/ECtHR	European Court of Human Rights
ECJ	European Court of Justice
ECMACM	European Convention on Mutual Assistance in Criminal Matters
ECR / E.C.R.	European Court Reports
ECSC	European Coal and Steel Community
ECT	European Community Treaty
ed.	edition/editor
eds.	editors
EEA	European Environment Agency
EEB	European Environmental Bureau
EEC	European Economic Community
EELR	European Environmental Law Review
EEW	European Evidence Warrant
EFSA	European Food Safety Authority
EGGVG	Einführungsgesetz zum Gerichtsverfassungsgesetz (German introduction law of the Constitution of the Courts – D)
EGTC	European Grouping of Territorial Cooperation
EIB	European Investment Bank
EMEA	European Medicines Agency
ERDF	European Regional Development Fund
ESF	European Social Fund
esp.	especially
et seq.	et sequens (and the following)
ETS	European Treaty Series
EU	European Union
EUDUR	Handbuch zum europäischen und deutschen Umweltrecht
EuR	Europarecht
EuZW	Europäische Zeitschrift für Wirtschaftsrecht
FAA	Federal Aviation Authority (USA)
f./ff.	folgende (et seq.)
FG	Festgabe
FIFG	Financial Instrument for Fisheries Guidance
FINDAG	Finanzdienstleistungsaufsichtsgesetz (D)
FIOD-ECD	Fiscale Inlichtingen- en Opsporingsdienst - Economische Controledienst (NL)
fn.	footnote
FR 2002	Financial Regulation 2002
FS	Festschrift

FVO	Food and Veterinary Office
GDP	Gross Domestic Product
GG	Grundgesetz (D)
GPR	Zeitschrift für Gemeinschaftsprivatrecht
GRURInt	Gewerblicher Rechtsschutz und Urheberrecht Internationaler Teil
GS	Gedächtnisschrift
Handelingen NJV	Proceedings of the Nederlandse Juristenvereniging (the Dutch Union of Lawyers)
HbEUWiR	Handbuch des EU-Wirtschaftsrechts
HR	Hoge Raad (High Council – NL)
i.e.	id est
IACS	Integrated Administration and Control System
ibid.	ibidem
IOSCO	International Organization of Securities Commissions
IRG	Gesetz über die internationale Rechtshilfe in Strafsachen (D)
ISPA	Instrument for Structural Policies for Pre-Accession
JAR	Joint Aviation Requirements
JB	Jurisprudentie Bestuursrecht
JbUTR	Jahrbuch des Umwelt- und Technikrechts
JEEPL	Journal for European Environmental and Planning Law
JEPP	Journal of European Public Policy
JHA	Justice and Home Affairs
JIT	Joint Investigation Teams
JöR	Jahrbuch des öffentlichen Rechts der Gegenwart
Jura	Juristische Ausbildung
JZ	JuristenZeitung
MenR	Milieu en Recht
MJ	Maastricht Journal
mn.	marginal number
NJ	Nederlandse Jurisprudentie
NJB	Nederlands Juristenblad
NJW	Neue Juristische Wochenschrift
NuR	Natur und Recht
NVwZ	Neue Zeitschrift für Verwaltungsrecht
NWVBl	Nordrhein-Westfälische Verwaltungsblätter
OECD	Organisation for Economic Co-operation and Development
OJ	Official Journal
OLAF	Office Européen de lutte anti-fraude (European Anti-Fraud Office)

OM	Openbaar Ministerie (NL)
OP	Operational Programme
OVG	Oberverwaltungsgericht (D)
OWiG	Ordnungswidrigkeitengesetz (D)
p.	page
para.	paragraph
PGC	German Dutch Transboundary Water Commission
POP	persistent organic pollutant
pp.	pages
RASFF	Rapid Alert System for Foodstuffs
RECIEL	Review of European Community and International Environmental Law
Reg.	Regulation
SEC	Securities and Exchange Commission (USA)
SEW	Tijdschrift voor Europees en economisch recht
SIS	Schengen Information System
SPD	Single Programming Document
StaasWiss. und StaatsPr.	Staatswissenschaften und Staatspraxis
StPO	Strafprozessordnung (D)
StVj	Steuerliche Vierteljahresschrift
TEC	Treaty establishing the European Community
TEU	Treaty on European Union
TFEU	Treaty on the Functioning of the European Union
UNSC	United Nations Security Council
VerwArch	Verwaltungsarchiv
VG	Verwaltungsgericht (D)
vol.	volume
VVDStRL	Veröffentlichungen der Vereinigung der Deutschen Staatsrechtslehrer
VwGO	Verwaltungsgerichtsordnung (D)
VwVfG	Verwaltungsverfahrensgesetz (D)
WED	Wet economische delicten (NL)
WFD	Water Framework Directive
Wft	Wet op het financieel toezicht
Wob	Wetopenbaarheid van bestuur
WpHG	Wertpapierhandelsgesetz (D)
Wte	Wet toezicht effectenverkeer (NL)
ZaöRV	Zeitschrift für ausländisches öffentliches Recht und Völkerrecht
ZEuS	Zeitschrift für europarechtliche Studien
ZLR	Zeitschrift für das gesamte Lebensmittelrecht
ZPO	Zivilprozessordnung (D)

I. INTRODUCTION: EUROPEAN COMPOSITE ADMINISTRATION AND THE ROLE OF EUROPEAN ADMINISTRATIVE LAW*

Eberhard SCHMIDT-AẞMANN

1. EUROPEAN COMPOSITE ADMINISTRATION: DATA EXCHANGE, DECISION-MAKING AND CONTROL

Community Law is, as a rule, implemented by the administrations of the Member States. The Community itself possesses only limited executive powers and instruments of its own. This first common statement on the issue of 'administration and administrative law in the European Community' emphasises the *organisational* aspect of Community law enforcement, distinguishing between the administrative entities involved: either the Member States or the Community. Such an approach reflects only *one* side of the executive challenge, however. In order to establish a complete picture, the functional constituent must be added which is characterised by cooperation rather than separation. Effective enforcement of Community law presupposes a functioning cooperation of national administrations.[1] This is the *second* common statement of undisputed validity. Separation *and* incorporation, exclusive competence *and* cooperation are essential components of Community law implementation.

The cornerstones of this concept are laid down in Articles 5 and 10 ECT: the principles of limited powers and of subsidiarity on the one hand, and the general duty of mutual loyalty among the Member States and the Community institutions on the other. The subjects of the regulation are the numerous interacting national and Community institutions, authorities, offices, bodies and other legal entities

* Revised and updated version of my contribution to the Festschrift for H. Steinberger (Berlin et al., 2002), p. 1375 ff; first version (in German) was published in Eberhard Schmidt-Aßmann and Bettina Schöndorf-Haubold – translation by Lenka Dzurendova, Institute for German and European Administrative Law.

1 Schmidt-Aßmann, *Das allgemeine Verwaltungsrecht als Ordnungsidee*, (2nd ed. 2004), p. 381 et seq.

that are duly authorised to implement EC law as well as the laws of the individual Member States passed according to EC requirements. Although performing the latter task separately, according to their national competency provisions, they are united by the common aim of effective and uniform administration. All these actors taken together shall be referred to as the *European Composite Administration* (*Europäischer Verwaltungsverbund*) or shortly *European Administration*. This term is not restricted to the administrative entities of the Community, the so called 'direct implementation' or 'EC administration', but rather comprises the Community *and* the Member State administrations, which ought to be regarded as 'co-dependent organisms'.[2]

1.1. FUNCTIONS OF EUROPEAN ADMINISTRATION

Since their very beginnings, the European Communities have to some extent assumed the function of administrative bodies. European administration has taken the shape of manifold activities of national and EC authorities implementing EC Law on a daily basis,[3] involving the administrative tasks inherent to the national law such as in the fields of taxation, public security, the steering of behaviour patterns and granting benefits. A more detailed analysis would require an examination of relations emanating from the interplay of the individual administrative tasks, the character of the law to be implemented and the responsible executive structures. Here, only a brief outline can be drawn:

- *Tax administration* (Abgabenverwaltung) represents a major part of the European administration due to the mere fact that the Community was founded as a customs union, and as such has called for extensive administrative activities. In this field, European administration is a decentralised administration carried out by national customs authorities.[4] A sufficient level of uniformity has been reached through the application of common implementation rules, the Community Customs Code, and through abidance by the uniform requirements of the Common Customs Tariff according to Article 26 ECT. The extraordinary importance of the

---

2 Cassese, *Der Einfluß des gemeinschaftsrechtlichen Verwaltungsrechts auf die nationalen Verwaltungsrechtssysteme*, (1994) 33 *Der Staat*, p. 25 at 26; likewise v. Bogdandy, in: Grabitz/Hilf (eds.), *Das Recht der Europäischen Union*, original Vol. I, Art. 5 ECT, par. 43.

3 For a demonstrative description, see the contributions on the respective policy fields in Dauses (ed.), *Handbuch des EU-Wirtschaftsrechts* (HbEUWiR), (Loose-leaf version, last update May 2004); Reich, *Europäisches Verbraucherrecht*, (4th ed. 2003); on environmental law, in particular, Rengeling (ed.), *Handbuch zum europäischen und deutschen Umweltrecht* (EUDUR), 2 Volumes (2nd ed. 2003); on social law Haverkate/Huster, *Europäisches Sozialrecht* (1999). On the political science perspective, see the contributions in Wallace/Wallace (eds.), *Policy-Making in the European Union* (1996).

4 Witte/Wolffgang, *Lehrbuch des europäischen Zollrechts* (4th ed. 2003).

cooperation in customs matters is underlined in Article 135 ECT. At the same time, tax administration has had positive effects on the development of further administrative regulatory tasks.[5]

- *Public security administration* (Ordnungsverwaltung) is multifaceted within the Community framework: on the one hand, it serves the purposes of the prevention of specific dangers, with product security being the most important field of action. Harmonised EC law is implemented mainly decentrally, involving self-regulative mechanisms of certification and accreditation over broad areas.[6] In distinct cases, however, such processes may be subject to administrative supervision and special authorisation.[7] European public security administration also serves the purpose of market regulation. In this function it has assumed the shape of competition and state aid supervision, which lie largely or even completely within the competence of the European Commission. The activities of national authorities in the deregulated fields of power supply, telecommunications and rail and air traffic[8] constitute another part of the market regulation administration.
- *Regulatory administration* (Lenkungsverwaltung) exerts its steering function partly through enactment of prohibitive and prescriptive rules and partly by giving financial impetus, that is to say by granting subsidies and levying taxes. The most important area in this respect is the Common Agricultural Policy (Articles 32–38 ECT).[9] The respective executive procedures lie within the competence of the national authorities but each procedure is embedded in a complex network of legal and financial regulations. The cooperation between the administrations of the Member States and the Community is particularly close in this field. Joint monitoring of checks and the financial clearance process are among the interesting schemes integrated into this cooperation. A new function of regulatory administration has emerged in the field of the common fisheries policy, a part of CAP, which can be described as 'sustainable development administration'.
- *Grant administration* (Leistungsverwaltung) is a type of European administration which aims at regulating the allocation of budgetary commitments for Structural Funds.[10] Political requirements on the funding

---

5 Grabitz/v. Bogdandy/Nettesheim, *Europäisches Außenwirtschaftsrecht* (1994).

6 For basic information, see Röhl, *Akkreditierung und Zertifizierung im Produktsicherheitsrecht* (2000); idem, in this vol., p. 205 et seq.

7 See e.g. Royla, *Grenzüberschreitende Finanzmarktaufsicht in der EG* (2000); Wagner, *Europäisches Zulassungssystem für Arzneimittel und Parallelhandel* (2000); Schlag, *Grenzüberschreitende Verwaltungsbefugnisse in EG-Binnenmarkt* (1998).

8 Eifert, *Grundversorgung mit Telekommunikationsleistungen im Gewährleistungsstaat* (1998); Schneider, *Liberalisierung der Stromwirtschaft durch regulative Marktorganisation* (1999).

9 See Priebe/Mögele, in Dauses, *HbEUWiR* (fn. 3), Section G.

10 See Oppermann, *Europarecht* (2nd ed. 1999), section 968 et seq.; Schöndorf-Haubold, *Die Strukturfonds der EG* (2005); idem, in this vol., p. 25 et seq.; generally on grant administration Schenk, in this vol., p. 389 et seq.

> criteria and the volume of financial aid are subject to multilateral negotiations, which form the basis, for decisions on the allocation of funds. Concrete budgetary commitments are taken in accordance with a bilateral administrative allocation scheme, which uses the instruments of common programme planning, evaluation and control. This sphere is dominated by the notion of a 'mixed administration'. Research funding, a second sector of European grant administration (Articles 163–173 ECT), can be named as an example of EC direct implementation.[11] Funding decisions are met by the Commission itself following direct communication with the institutions to be funded, often involving private organisations acting as executive agencies.

As a result, the scope of tasks to be carried out by the European administration reaches far beyond the matters that are usually attributed to direct implementation.[12] However, they are not quite identical with the field of the much discussed 'Europeanisation of Administrative Law' either.[13] Europeanisation even covers some areas that are almost exclusively executed by national authorities, without any involvement in cooperation networks. This applies, for example, to public procurement law. Environmental policy, too, emerged initially as a policy for harmonisation of national rules, without developing its own administrative dimension. This changed recently with the creation of the European Environment Agency.[14] Nowadays, manifold tasks of administrative cooperation pervade environment law.[15]

1.2. 'CO-DEPENDENT' ADMINISTRATIVE ACTION

A specific trait of European administration constitutes the embedding of its activities in joint information, support and coordination processes between the administrations involved.[16] Such cooperation is a prerequisite for an effective 'administration of the Community territory'. Numerous examples prove this assumption. If the EC Commission had to dispense with the assistance of

---

11 See Oppermann, *Europarecht* (fn. 10), section 1941 et seq.; Spannowsky, in: Rengeling, *EUDUR* (fn. 3), §86; in detail Pfeiffer, *Die Forschungs- und Technologiepolitik der Europäischen Gemeinschaft als Referenzgebiet für das europäische Verwaltungsrecht* (2003).

12 Cf. Schwarze, *Europäisches Verwaltungsrecht* (Vol. 1, 1988), p. 25 et seq.

13 For a basic treatise on this topic, see v. Danwitz, *Verwaltungsrechtliches System und Europäische Integration* (1996); Kadelbach, *Allgemeines Verwaltungsrecht unter europäischem Einfluß* (1999); Schoch, (2000) *DV* supplement 2, p. 135 et seq.

14 Ladeur, (1997) NuR, p. 7 et seq.

15 Cf. Sommer, *Verwaltungskooperation am Beispiel administrativer Informationsverfahren im Europäischen Umweltrecht* (2001); idem, in this vol., p. 55 et seq.

16 Cf. Schmidt-Aßmann/Hoffmann-Riem (eds.), *Strukturen des Europäischen Verwaltungsrechts* (1999); cf. also Scheuing, in Hoffmann-Riem/Schmidt-Aßmann (eds.), *Innovation und Flexibilität des Verwaltungshandelns* (1994), p. 289 at 331 et seq.; Kahl, (1996) 29 *DV*, p. 341 at 373 and 379 et seq.; Sydow, *Verwaltungskooperation in der Europäischen Union* (2004).

national administrations, it would be unable to fulfil its supervisory function as regards compliance with EC competition and State aid laws by the Member States. National authorities would lack the necessary information if they had no EC-wide accessible centralised system of environment or product information data at their disposal. Uniform implementation of EC law on external trade and customs over the entire Community territory can be achieved only through uniform action of the national administrations.

The structure of the cooperation processes is partly *vertical*, between the EC authorities and the Member States and partly *horizontal*, between the Member States' administrations. In some cases, the cooperation ceases after a single contact, but, often, it evolves into permanent ties. Bilateral cooperations are just as common as tri- and multilateral forms. Occasionally, the cooperation has been extended to an EC-wide structure of high complexity that connects information, coordination and decision-making processes, individual and joint decisions and executive acts and control schemes with each other. One example of this is EC pharmaceutical legislation, comprising different forms of local and central marketing authorisation and supervision.[17]

Cooperation fulfils several tasks in EC law, its major function being to provide the national administrations involved with the necessary information (*informational cooperation*). This includes the cases of one-off and occasional data exchange as well as the creation of central networks, with the composition and submission of reports and statistics being its special forms (Article 285 ECT). Second, cooperation has assumed the manifold shapes of the mutual provision of information, coordination of action and the joint conduct of proceedings (*procedural cooperation*). Such duties as the mutual recognition of diplomas and the certification of new products, for example, can be practically imposed only if relevant procedures are available that provide for flexible solution schemes in cases of urgency or dispute. Finally, cooperation can be also carried out by agencies set up for that very purpose (*institutional cooperation*). As examples, one can name the management boards of European agencies and the highly developed network of committees at EC level, with the comitology system in particular (see also 3.3.). In its entirety, European Administration can be described as a network of administrations on data exchange, decision-making and control.

[17] Wagner, *Europäisches Zulassungssystem* (fn. 7), esp. at p. 169 et seq. and 233 et seq.

2. SHAPING EUROPEAN ADMINISTRATION: BETWEEN COOPERATION AND HIERARCHY

2.1. INTRODUCTION

Administrative law fulfils *two* regulatory tasks: first, it regulates citizen-state relations, and, second, inter-administrative relations.[18] In national administrative law, the emphasis has traditionally laid on the first objective since, historically, this had developed from efforts to enhance the accountability of an existing administration for infringements of civic liberties according to the rule of law. The evolution of European administration has been a different one: the 'Administration of Community territory' was only established gradually, after some resistance on the side of the Member States had been overcome. This phenomenon led to the emergence of the effet-utile case law aiming at a uniform implementation of EC law.[19] With the growing integration and increasing executive activity in relation to EU citizens and companies, it has become essential to accomplish this jurisdiction by (even) stricter application of administrative procedures according to the rule of law. Nonetheless, solving *inter-administrative* conflicts will remain an outstanding challenge to be coped with by means of European Administrative Law in the future also. The legal structures of this novel administrative system have only just begun to evolve.

2.2. THE CONCEPT OF COMPOSITE ADMINISTRATION ("VERWALTUNGSVERBUND")

It is not easy to categorise administrations integrated into multilevel systems, by using the typical state and administrative law schemes and mechanisms. Terms like *Weisung* (instruction), *Fachaufsicht* (supervision of a given sector) or *Selbsteintrittsrecht* (the right of a superordinate authority to step into/take over the execution process carried out by a subordinate authority) do not fit into the existing European administrative structures: similarly the terms *Staatenbund* (Federation of Nation States) and *Bundesstaat* (Federal State) do not express the true nature of the Community in its entirety. That is not to say that the analytic and explanatory potential of the traditional theories should be left unused. Law enforcement in multilevel systems is by no means a product of spontaneous, accidental or irregular actions, but rather a result of regular processes which must be put into relation with each other and be given a legal framework. The term *Composite Administration* will make this possible. *Verbund* expresses a

---

18 Schmidt-Aßmann, *Ordnungsidee* (fn. 1), p. 1 et seq.; on European administrative law *ibid.* at p. 377 et seq.

19 For its interpretation cf. Ladeur, (1995) *EuR*, p. 227 at 236 et seq.

systemic notion which creates the necessary entity through interlinking with each other the two organisational principles – the principle of cooperation and the principle of hierarchy. The "*Verbund*"-concept implies likewise the notions of sovereignty, respect and the ability to undertake joint action. The meaning of the term varies depending on the context: the Federal Constitutional Court has used it in the creation of the term *Staatenverbund* (Federation of Nation States), clearly stressing the legitimation of the Nation States.[20] Legal scholars have meanwhile used the term *Verfassungsverbund* (European Constitutional Order) and thus laid greater emphasis on the integrative component.[21]

Both forms indicate a rather unstable state which – if a one-way solution is to be avoided – should be regulated and stabilised by applying contradictory systemic approaches.[22] The most valuable source in this respect undoubtedly is the federal state doctrine that adopts a comparative method. Its results, once again, cannot be applied to a European Administration without adjustment. However, its approaches can facilitate the analysis of emerging problems, and its structures and methods can help in finding novel 'federative' regulatory instruments since the major issues remain the same[23]: the gaining momentum of differing interests, the existence of centrifugal and centripetal forces and the relation between 'integration and subsidiarity'.[24]

At EC level, law must tackle the singular trias of roles performed by the Member States – as 'Masters of the Treaties', 'Partners of the Commission' and 'Addressees of supervisory measures subject to control'. The tensions arising out of this functional interplay can be shown in the example of state aid supervision according to Articles 87–89 ECT. This finding makes quite clear that any simplifying legal concept would be misplaced. Taken together, the regulatory mechanisms of European Administrative Law must aim at combining the following three elements:

- The *intergovernmental* element is represented by the Council of Ministers whose political opinion is formed along federal negotiation patterns targeted at reaching a compromise or balance of interests.[25] This element constitutes the framework of the European Administration and specifies the tasks to be executed. However, some traits of intergovernmental decision-making can be

20 Bundesverfassungsgericht, Judgement of 12. October 1993, E 89, p. 155 at 182 et seq.; Kirchhof, in: Isensee/Kirchhof (eds.), *Handbuch des Staatsrechts*, Vol. 7 (1992), §183 para. 39 et seq.

21 Pernice (1999) 48 *JöR*, p. 205 et seq.; for a recent polemic view, see Jestaedt, in: *GS für W. Blomeyer* (2004), p. 637 et seq.

22 See v. Bogdandy, *Supranationaler Föderalismus als Wirklichkeit und Idee einer neuen Herrschaftsform* (1999); Badura, in: *Festschrift for Leisner* (1999), p. 695 et seq.

23 Cf. Giegerich, *Europäische Verfassung und deutsche Verfassung im transnationalen Konstitutionalisierungsprozeß: Wechselseitige Rezeption, konstitutionelle Evolution und föderale Verflechtung* (2003), esp. p. 304 et seq.

24 Cf. Oeter, *Integration und Subsidiarität im deutschen Bundesstaatsrecht* (1998).

25 For an example from the regional structural policy, see Benz, in: Schmidt-Aßmann/ Hoffmann-Riem (eds.), *Strukturen* (fn. 16), p. 45 et seq.

found even in individual actions of extraordinary political importance. Occasionally, the Council also performs executive functions. The comitology system, in particular, shows a tendency towards a weakened intergovernmental steering of executive processes at the middle level.

- The *integrative* element guarantees a centrally defined state of 'common welfare' throughout the Community as far as EC legislature and effective implementation of EC law are concerned. The Council's policy of negotiation is therefore opposed by an approach aiming at effective decision-making. As far as European Administration is concerned this approach is taken by the Commission and the highly specialised European agencies and bureaus. The European Court of Justice had also assumed this position for a considerable period of time and acted as a 'driving force of integration'. In its recent judgements, however, the Court has outlined a more distinct division of powers within the Community, thus indicating that it will assume a rather neutral position between the two options in future.
- The *Nation-State* element avoids the cumulative action of the Member States being mistaken for the interests of the individual Nation States. This has been stated accurately for the purposes of the federal state doctrine.[26] It applies at least with the same force in the field of European Administration. The individual Member States, which provide major parts of the administrative apparatus, still differ considerably in their organisational structures, administrative traditions and conception of themselves.[27] Owing to this very fact, the 'Nation-State' element has gained extraordinary importance. In addition, it has been confirmed by law in a series of safeguard clauses and reserved rights.[28] The effectiveness of decision-making is also the leading principle here; the decision based on the isolated Nation-State perception needs to be transferred into the Community system by means of cooperation schemes.

2.3. INSTRUMENTS OF SEPARATION OF POWERS

2.3.1. Introduction

Is it at all possible to speak of an 'Administration' at EC level considering that the Community does not follow the rules of the traditional separation of powers?[29] In national administrative law, the principle of separation has proven to be the major cornerstone of structure building regardless of its manifold variations in

26 Lerche, *Aktuelle föderalistische Verfassungsfragen* (1968).

27 Cf. Schwarze, *Europäisches Verwaltungsrecht* (fn. 12), p. 33 et seq.; Stettner, in: Dauses, *HbEUWiR* (fn. 3), Section B III.

28 See Pühs, *Der Vollzug von Gemeinschaftsrecht* (1997), p. 186 et seq.

29 Cf. Steinberger, (1991) 50 *VVDStRL*, p. 9 at 29 et seq.; Möllers, *Gewaltengliederung. Legitimation und Dogmatik im nationalen und übernationalen Rechtsvergleich*, Heidelberger Habilitationsschrift (2004), §7.

individual constitutional orders.[30] By differentiating between law making (*Gesetzgebung*) and law execution (*Gesetzesvollzug*), it guarantees the steering role of the parliament as well as parliamentary accountability according to the rule of law, and makes both subject to judicial control. In this way, it remodels the requirements of the rule of law and the principle of democracy into a form manageable by the instruments of administrative law. The picture is more complex in the multilevel system of the European Union: a number of legislative bodies at Community and national level stand *vis-à-vis* numerous institutions that fulfil executive tasks, at least to some extent. On abstract examination, it is undeniable that here lies a considerable potential for steering and control. However, the questions to be dealt with are the following. Is it possible to make a clear differentiation between the various functions in the concrete power relations? Can the individual functions be attributed to the respective bodies in charge, which are sufficiently independent in order to prevail over the *Verbund*-schemes and their negotiation patterns with the necessary distance and transparency? This question can be answered in the positive with some certainty, with regard to the supervision function (2.3.2.). The major difficulties concern the legislation and concomitantly the differentiation of the executive functions (2.3.3.).

2.3.2. Supervisory tasks

'Among all structural elements of the Community it is the judiciary that differs the least in its nature compared to judiciaries of constitutional states'.[31] *Judiciary control* is carried out by the European Court of Justice and the national courts which insofar act as 'Community courts'.[32] The European Court of Justice is on the one hand 'Administrative Court' insofar as it is (also) authorised to supervise the executive decisions of the Community organs, judging on actions for annulment and for failure to act according to Articles 230 and 232 ECT. The supervision of national administrations is carried out by the national administrative courts that assess the lawfulness of administrative action according to the standards of national and EC law. By referring a case under the preliminary ruling procedure laid down in Article 234 ECT, the national courts can make an indirect contribution to securing the legality of EC legal acts.[33]

The European Court of Justice also plays an important role in the settlement of conflicts concerning supervision arising between the EC organs and the

---

30 See Schmidt-Aßmann, *Ordnungsidee* (fn. 1), p. 179 et seq.

31 Steinberger, (1991) 50 *VVDStRL*, p. 9 at 37.

32 Burgi, *Verwaltungsprozeß und Europarecht* (1996), p. 58 et seq.; Kadelbach, in: Schmidt-Aßmann/Hoffmann-Riem (eds.), *Verwaltungskontrolle* (2001), p. 205 et seq.

33 For a detailed treatise on 'Legal protection in European Administrative Law', see Dörr, in: Sodan/Ziekow (eds.), *Nomos-Kommentar zur Verwaltungsgerichtsodnung* (Loose-leaf-coll., last update January 2003), Vol. 1.

Member States. Such a settlement, also found in federal state law, is achieved mainly by means of infringement proceedings initiated by the Commission against a Member State under Article 226 ECT.[34] So far, these extensive proceedings have been primarily triggered against national legislatives, particularly upon their failure to implement a directive. However, it is also available for the purposes of supervising administrative procedures, e.g. highly interesting cases on public procurement and the location of enterprises as well as discriminatory decisions in permit procedures in the domain of telecommunications.[35] In full compliance with the intertwined-competency model, Article 227 ECT provides for a parallel type of infringement procedure which allows a Member State to sue another Member State. From this point of view, the judicial control system shows the complexity of EC administrative structures. The reoccurring deficiencies of legal protection[36] do not indicate the unsuitability of the system as such. These are caused more by the swift changes of the executive action schemes in the Community Administration. What is still lacking are satisfying structural solutions in matters of legal protection at horizontal administrative level. National courts, which have been held solely responsible so far, have adopted a principle of separation which, however, has not quite met all the challenges resulting from the horizontal cooperation between the national administrations.[37]

Budget and cost effectiveness supervision rest with audit courts and institutions of a comparable status in terms of autonomy. This supervisory function has been enhanced recently, resulting in the present recognition of the Court of Auditors as an organ of the Community according to Article 7 in conjunction with Articles 246–248 ECT.[38] The new budget laws make additional provisions to be applied in a series of internal control and budget revision procedures.[39] Conferring independent status on the European Anti-Fraud Office (OLAF) is also part of this same context. This act has demonstrated the essential importance of an autonomous supervisory authority transcending the administrative levels

---

34 Pühs, *Vollzug* (fn. 28), p. 220 et seq.

35 Cf. Seventeenth annual report on monitoring the application of Community law – 1999, [2001] OJ C30/01 at 23 et seq.; for breaches of contract in general, see ibid. p. 67 et seq.; Twentieth annual report on monitoring the application of Community law – 2002, of 21.11.2003, COM(2003)669 final.

36 Cf. just the divergent decisions on legal protection against regulations, Case T-177/01, *Jégo-Quéré* [2002] ECR II-2635; Case C-50/00 P, *Unión de Pequeños Agricultores* [2002] ECR I-6677; Case C-263/02 P, *Jégo-Quéré*, (2004) *NJW*, p. 2006; Röhl, (2003) *Jura*, p. 830 et seq.; idem, (2004) *GPR*, p. 178.

37 See Schmidt-Aßmann, in: *Festschrift for Bernhardt* (1995), p. 1238 et seq.; Burgi, *Verwaltungsprozeß* (fn. 32), p. 55 et seq.; Ehlers, *Die Europäisierung des Verwaltungsprozeßrechts* (1999), p. 8 et seq., 14 et seq.; in detail now Jens Hofmann, *Rechtsschutz und Haftung im Europäischen Verwaltungsverbund* (2004); Cf. also idem, in this vol., p. 447 et seq.

38 Cf. Declaration No 21 on the Maastricht Treaty.

39 Cf. Schöndorf-Haubold, in this vol., p. 25 et seq.

and being capable of exerting influence on the interlinked administrative procedures.[40]

One issue which still remains is that of *parliamentary control*. Its weakening on the national level has only been compensated by the enhanced supervisory powers of the European Parliament over Community actions to a limited extent but it would be false to claim that parliamentary control has been worn away by EC administrative structures. Recently, the establishment of temporary committees under Article 193 ECT has proven to be a perfectly effective instrument in various cases, since it has actually been applied for purposes of supervision, rather than as a means in the struggle for political power, which was the case in the misguided German political scene. The resignation of the Santer Commission has shown that the Parliament is capable of effective administrative control. This crisis was not so much one of high politics but was more one of an 'administrative' character.

2.3.3. Executive tasks

The differentiation between executive and legislative tasks has caused greater difficulties.[41] Even at national level a simple solution to this issue has not been found yet. The dual function of the administrative regulation as a means of constitutive law and of administrative law serves as the best example. It shows that 'executive power' means more than carrying out strict statutory instructions or effecting administrative acts by applying the juridical techniques of subsumption.[42] The traditional administrative law doctrine has nonetheless been founded on such a *basic notion* of a simplistic and hierarchical implementation, since attributing administrative actions to general laws makes them politically acceptable, and shaping administrative decisions into the form of individual acts guarantees their assessment according to the rule of law.

The dividing lines are even less distinguishable at EC level.[43] The Council, being the legislative organ, also takes individual decisions (although just occasionally); the Commission as the executive organ participates intensively in the legislative process; and the national executives even create through their involvement in the Council the legal bases that are actually to provide them with the legitimation necessary for their executive activity. Finally, the intransparency is increased by the fact that the range of legal forms available at EC level, according to Article 249 ECT, bears little resemblance to the clear distinction to be found between a national legislative act and a national administrative act. The apparent mixture of power positions and institutional functions at EC level

40 Mager, (2000) *ZEuS*, p. 177 et seq.; Uerpmann, (2000) 125 *AöR*, p. 551 at 566 et seq.; also Wolffgang/Ulrich, (1998) *EuR*, p. 616 et seq.
41 See Winter (ed.), *Sources and Categories of European Union Law* (1996), p. 38 et seq.
42 See Schmidt-Aßmann, *Ordnungsidee* (fn. 1), p. 198 et seq.
43 Steinberger, (1991) 50 VVDStRL, p. 9 at 31 et seq.

influences the entire Community territory, and hence, affects the national administrative level, too. Therefore, working out the structures of the separation of powers and the specific administrative function, in particular, constitutes a real challenge.[44] It shall nevertheless be attempted as far as the following three aspects are concerned:

- An individual examination of the various fields of European administrative action described above shows clearly that, despite unclear border lines, it is undoubtedly possible to discern administrative procedures of traditional executive character in large fields of activity. This applies to national customs authorities implementing the Community Customs Code and the Customs Tariff, as well as to decisions of the Commission in matters of state aid and competition law, for example. The application of legal terms that require extensive interpretation and involve definition margins has been common to national administrative law as well and hence the fact that they occur at Community level cannot lead to the activities mentioned being classified as executive measures.
- A further major field of action is made up of inter-administrative relations, which include, in particular, the multifaceted activities of cooperation on data exchange. These activities can also be classified as executive measures in a broader sense, provided that they possess a minimum procedural determination and that their adoption is not subject to the proceedings according to Article 249(4) ECT, which are determined mainly by the principle of the rule of law.
- Lastly, the existing complexities have been simplified by the increase in competence of the European Parliament. The *basic legal acts of secondary EC law*, basic regulations and framework directives, have hereby assumed an independent political profile and have continually evolved into a European 'legislature'[45] capable of effecting the legitimation achieved in essence by the rule of separation of powers. According to the European Court of Justice, basic legal acts concern the 'basic elements of the matter to be dealt with'.[46] The only provisions that can be classified as essential are those 'which are intended to give concrete shape to the fundamental guidelines of Community policy'.[47] Such an approach differs from the German *Wesentlichkeitslehre* – a constitutional doctrine saying that any essential (*wesentliche)* decisions, that is, decisions relevant in terms of fundamental rights and freedoms, must be taken by parliament. The Court's understanding allows for *implementing*

44 In detail Möllers, *Gewaltengliederung* (fn. 29).
45 Winter, *Sources* (fn. 41), p. 22 et seq.
46 Case C-25/70, *Einfuhr- und Vorratsstelle für Futtermittel v. Köster*, [1970] ECR 1161, para. 6.
47 Case C-240/90, Germany v. Commission [1992] ECR I-5383, par. 37.

powers to be conferred on the Commission according to Article 202 ECT.[48] "The concept of implementation for the purposes of that article comprises both the drawing up of implementing rules and the application of rules to specific cases by means of acts of individual application'.[49] Among the implementation rules applied by the Commission, there are numerous regulations and directives which would, from the point of view of German administrative law, classify as *Allgemeinverfügung* (administrative act directed at a discernible group of addressees) rather than as legislative acts. At any rate, a considerable part of the implementation legislation belongs to the administrative sphere.[50] However, there still remain implementation rules that fill in broad definition margins and thus resemble in effect legislation rather than executive acts. It is these very acts, in fact, that constitute a real challenge under the principles of democracy and rule of law, and hence require further legal concretion.

2.4. LINKING DIVERGENT STRUCTURAL PRINCIPLES

European administration in its function as a network for data exchange, decision-making and control rests upon the same interconnection of hierarchical and cooperative elements like the concept of composite administration ("*Verbund*") in its entirety.[51] Since it acts within a given framework and on the basis of preset implementation rules, it might be referred to as a 'hierarchy with a cooperative cushioning', in which the core function of the Commission becomes apparent. Although the Commission has only few direct executive powers, it controls the switch-points of the EC executive system. An extensive cooperative cushioning is necessary in order to respond to the demands at intergovernmental as well as at national level, as a result of which all regulatory mechanisms and procedures of European administration have been structured as *combinations* of the two principles. The core, consisting of hierarchical and cooperative implementation, is surrounded by a wide range of further elements following contradictory principles. Individual decisions are embedded into communication structures; negotiation rounds are combined with reservations of rights to final decisions. Consequently, it is not possible to transfer the legal forms which are known in national administrative law into European administrative law on a

48 Cf. Möllers, in: Schmidt-Aßmann/Schöndorf-Haubold (eds.), *Der Europaïsche Verwaltungsverbund* (2005), p. 293 et seq.

49 Case 16/88, Commission v. Council [1989] ECR 3457, para.11.

50 Cf. the statistical figures on legal acts published in the Official Journal provided by Falke, in: Joerges/Falke (eds.), *Das Ausschußwesen der Europäischen Union* (2000), p. 43 et seq.

51 For similar considerations on a 'fusion administration' from the perspective of political science, see Wessels, in: Jachtenfuchs/Kohler-Koch (eds.), *Europäische Integration* (2. ed. 2003), p. 353 et seq.

'one-to-one' basis nor is it necessary to develop them completely anew. The basic guidelines remain the same, since even as far as administrations in multilevel systems are concerned the applicable legal principles must follow a certain order, the mutual confidence of the authorities involved must be secured and the expenditure of common financial means must be dealt with prudently. Legal rules of a *European administrative law* are needed at least in respect of the following points:

- hierarchy of legal sources,
- autonomy and involvement modes for participation in the establishment of executive structures,
- informational cooperation and mutual control of the administrative authorities involved,
- schemes and procedures for formation of common political opinions and joint decision-making,
- reservations of rights to decision in cases of urgency and emergency as well as of rights to a final decision,
- accountability for matters of legal protection and liability issues.

European administrative law as a law of codependent administrations in a European multilevel system aims mainly at decision-making and establishment of organisational structures.[52] Therefore, it must provide a range of solutions for these issues, define the elements which, according to the requirements of EC and national constitutional laws, shape the European administration and arrange them in accordance with the necessities of the latter. In the process, it will become apparent that the solutions provided by federal state law, such as those regarding the German administration laid down in the *Grundgesetz* (Federal Constitution), do not necessarily constitute the utmost possible limit of the influence exercised by the central authority. Showing a lower degree of federalisation in its foundations, the concept of composite administration requires stricter steering and control mechanisms in individual spheres as a means of compensation for its flexible structure.

---

52 Cf. Hoffmann-Riem, in: Schmidt-Aßmann/Hoffmann-Riem (eds.), *Strukturen* (fn. 16), p. 317 at 331 et seq.

3. STRUCTURAL ELEMENTS OF EUROPEAN ADMINISTRATION

3.1. INTRODUCTION

An analysis of EC secondary legislation in various policy fields, for example, environmental and agricultural law as well as product liability and tax law, shows that numerous structures have been applied in several cases. At first sight, their features are determined by the material issues of the respective policy areas. Upon a closer look, however, far-reaching similarities appear/are revealed so that these structures can be considered as a general expression of typical functional mechanisms inherent to the concept of composite administration. Three types of such structural elements shall be analysed: the informational networks (3.2.), the comitology procedures (3.3.) and some EC supervision schemes (3.4.).

3.2. INFORMATIONAL NETWORKS

The administration of the Community territory has been in the first place an administration of data-exchange processes. It is hardly possible to assess the number of provisions of secondary EC law conferring on the Member States duties to submit reports and transmit information to the Commission as well as to supply each other with information, and on the EC organs to provide information to the Member States.[53] In this respect, European law outdoes by far the degree of regulation regarded as necessary in German federal law. Herein, the major conceptual challenge of European Administration is expressed, namely, that uniformity must first be created and uniformity means primarily a uniform level of information. The basic notion of European administrative informational law lies in the mutual dependency of all executive authorities involved in the accessibility of information throughout the whole EC territory. Its basic structure, therefore, relies on the principle of *reciprocity.* Considering the critical importance of the informational system, it is not surprising that, in this field, spontaneous and punctual forms of data exchange have been subject to increasing institutionalisation. Here, one can distinguish between two forms: the highly integrated information agencies and the informational cooperations established on the horizontal level.[54]

Information agencies are, for example, the Copenhagen-based European Environment Agency (EEA) and the European Monitoring Centre for Drugs and

---

53 For a systematic analysis on environmental law, see Sommer, *Verwaltungskooperation* (fn. 15), p. 73 et seq.; idem, in this vol., p. 55 et seq.

54 For an in-depth analysis, see v. Bogdandy, in: Hoffmann-Riem/Schmidt-Aßmann (eds.), *Verwaltungsrecht in der Informationsgesellschaft* (2000), p. 133 at 172–193.

Drug Addiction (EMCDDA) in Lisbon.[55] Being independent administrative units endowed with legal personality, these agencies collect and process data in order to provide the policy-makers with sound and evidence-based information. They have been conferred a certain degree of autonomy in order to grant objectivity of data acquisition. From the structural point of view, they make up a part of the EC direct administration, but they are not subordinate organs. As far as their inner structure is concerned, it is the Member States who exert the decisive influence in the administrative boards while the role of the Commission has decreased. Nonetheless, information agencies are considered to be highly aggregate institutions. The major structural feature characteristic of these agencies is centralisation, which has been put into effect by establishing a system of data networks. The system follows uniform procedures and the respective national informational networks are a priori integrated therein.

A looser form of Europeanisation is represented by the *trans-European networks for the interchange of data* (*Informationsverbünde*) between administrations. By way of example, one can name the Integrated Administration and Control System, IACS, established in the course of the agricultural reform in 1992 for the purposes of recording and assessing data obtained on the basis of the aid applications, and the Customs Information System, CIS. IACS does not fulfil the function of a common data acquisition system, but rather confers on the Member States the duty to collect and transfer data whilst via CIS data gathered by the Member States are saved on a central computer. The organisational issues lie within the competence of the EC Commission. Legal matters, however, are decided by an executive committee consisting of Member States representatives.[56] Matters of liability and judicial review are subject solely to national law.

3.3. COMMITTEE SYSTEM: COMITOLOGY AND BOARDS OF EXPERTS

3.3.1. Introduction

The widely structured system of committees constitutes a characteristic feature of European administration.[57] Committees are institutionalised forms of data

55 On agencies in general, see Fischer-Appelt, *Agenturen der Europäischen Gemeinschaft* (1999), on informational agencies q.v. p. 55 et seq. On EEA, see also Brenner, in: Rengeling, *EUDUR* (fn. 3), vol. 1, §20 par. 7 et seq.; Kahl, (1996) 36 *JbUTR*, p. 119 et seq.; On European Aviation Safety Agency, see Riedel, in this vol., p. 157 et seq.

56 Cf. Harings, *Grenzüberschreitende Zusammenarbeit der Polizei- und Zollverwaltungen und Rechtsschutz in Deutschland* (1998), p. 100 et seq.

57 For basic information, see Joerges/Falke, *Ausschußwesen* (fn. 50), providing statistical figures at p. 76 et seq.; Winter, *Sources* (fn. 41), p. 541 et seq.

exchange and communication processes that require constant reshaping at EC level, while those at national level have developed gradually, which has given them a more permanent character. The committee system allows for activation of information and data resources that could not be maintained by the EC institutions due to their limited manpower. Comitology also serves the specific purpose of providing a discussion forum for intergovernmental negotiations. Committees consist largely of public servants, but there are also expert boards and mixed bodies involving both, public officers and experts. Recently, it has been justly pointed out that the committee system, which was initially given little attention from the legal perspective, to some extent bears a constitutional dimension in relation to European administration.[58] In its context, major issues concerning legitimacy, transparency and accountability can be shown with particular clarity.

3.3.2. Comitology procedure

Comitology plays the most important role in the system of committees.[59] It is connected to conferring executive tasks on the Commission according to Article 202 ECT. For a long time, it has been the regular practice of the Council to reserve the right to exert some influence on the measures implementing the basic legal acts it had passed for itself. This influence has been secured through committees provided for in the relevant legal acts, and which consist of Member States' representatives and a Commission representative who presides over the committee. Since the ruling of the European Court of Justice in the *Köster* case, this practice has been acknowledged as lawful.[60] Committees as such have no consenting powers, but they have considerable procedural importance. Their negative vote on a proposal brought forward by the Commission triggers, according to the three procedures available, diverse participation modes of the Council in the legislative process. Nonetheless, the political weight lies with the committees as such. The figures from the agricultural sector show that in the period between 1973 and 1994 statements were requested from the 'comitology' committees in more than 50,000 cases, 90% of which had a successful outcome. In total, the Council made use of its decision-making powers in as few as 47 cases.[61] Even allowing for a higher number of conflict cases in other spheres, such as in environmental law, comitology must be still regarded as a major factor in amicable decision-making. However, despite this fact, comitology has become subject to criticism founded on the assumption that the Commission formulates its proposals a priori in a 'committee-friendly' way. In general, legal doctrine had

58 Joerges, in: Joerges/Falke, *Ausschußwesen* (fn. 50), p. 349 et seq.

59 See Falke, in: Joerges/Falke, *Ausschußwesen* (fn. 50), p. 5 et seq.

60 Case Case C-25/70, *Einfuhr- und Vorratsstelle für Futtermittel v. Köster*, [1970] ECR 1161, paras. 9, 13 et seq.

61 Cf. Demmke/Haibach, (1997) *DÖV*, p. 710 at 712 et seq.

long regarded comitology as an intransparent and bureaucratic-technocratic form of governance.[62] Recent studies have, however, pointed out its positive functions.

Setting up rules for comitology is a major issue of administrative law. At least as far as organisational matters and issues of accountability are concerned, today, there is unanimity concerning the attribution of the committees to the sphere of the Commission[63] rather than classifying them as bodies assisting the Council or being EC institutions of their own. Whenever basic legal acts require involvement of the Council in the executive process, the respective procedures must be, according to Article 202 ECT, 'consonant with the principles and rules to be laid down in advance by the Council, acting unanimously on a proposal from the Commission and after obtaining the opinion of the European Parliament'. The Council Decision on Comitology of 28 June 1999 was a reaction to a part of this criticism.[64] It reduced the number of procedures available for adoption of basic legal acts to just three: the advisory, the management and the regulatory procedure. To this extent, the legislative bodies are free, but are also obliged to choose one of these procedures. Moreover, Article 2 of the Decision sets up guidelines for the choice of a procedure. Accordingly, the management procedure is envisaged for adoption of measures implementing the Common Agricultural and the Common Fisheries Policy as well as for implementing programmes of substantial budgetary implications, while the regulatory procedure is regarded as appropriate for measures of general scope designed to apply essential provisions of basic instruments, including measures concerning the protection of health or safety of humans, animals or plants. This implies that the regulatory procedure is especially applicable for the adoption of implementation measures that belong, as stated above, in the border area between legislative and administrative law-making. It is quite understandable, therefore, that the Council has the ambition to secure itself a lasting influence in this area. However, such competency splitting and involvement of intergovernmental negotiation practices exert negative effects on a clear separation of powers. A positive view should, therefore, be taken of the strengthening of the role played by the Commission in the regulatory procedure, as effected by the Council Decision.[65] The previous criticism concerning the lack of transparency of procedure is now countered by making the 'comitology' committees subject to

---

62 Demmke/Haibach, (1997) *DÖV*, p. 710 at 712 et seq.; Mensching, (2000) *EuZW*, p. 268 at 269 et seq. with further references; Hofmann/Töller, (1998) StaatsWiss. und StaatsPr., p. 209 et seq.

63 On access to documents, see Case T-188/97, *Rothmans International BV v. Commission* [1999] ECR II-2463, par. 58 et seq.

64 Council Decision 1999/468 [1999] OJ L 184/23. Cf. the comments by Falke, in: Joerges/Falke, *Ausschußwesen* (fn. 50), p. 101 et seq.

65 Cf. Mensching, (2000) *EuZW*, p. 268 at 270.

Community rules on free access to documents applicable to the Commission.[66] All in all, the 'comitology' committees have proven to be a constitutive part of the above mentioned concept of 'hierarchical administration with cooperational cushioning'.

3.3.3. Scientific committees

This part of the committee system possesses a weaker legal structure. Experts in this area are leading scientists as well as representatives of interest groups. The European Court of Justice has repeatedly underlined the significance of decision-making founded on scientific data and classified a due consultation of a scientific committee as a mandatory procedural requirement.[67] Expert committees play an essential role, especially in the sphere of risk management.[68] At the same time, even these spheres have shown the weak points of the older committee practice, which was almost entirely lacking in provisions on personnel and procedural issues, in particular. The BSE crisis revealed the seriousness of the then situation.[69] In the aftermath of this crisis, significant improvements have been undertaken. Legal scholars have spurred on the development of legal structures[70] by requesting that legal provisions are established, stating the criteria for appointment of committee members, selection procedures, formation of opinions within the committees (involving the right to dissenting opinion) and grants of autonomy. The comitology system is the best indicator of the critical importance of a systematically developed European administrative law, which must in the first place cope with organisational and procedural issues.

3.4. COMMUNITY SUPERVISION

Supervision and control have always been issues of EC law.[71] Major topics have concerned, on the one hand, the control of national legislation implementing EC

---

66 The same Art. 7(2) of the Council Decision 1999/468; ECJ arriving at the same result already in: Case T-188/97, *Rothmans International BV v. Commission* [1999] ECR II-2463, par. 62 et seq.

67 Case C-212/91, *Angelopharm GmbH v Freie Hansestadt Hamburg* [1994] ECR I-171 (par. 31 et seq.); Cf. also Case C-269/90, *Technische Universität München v. Hauptzollamt München-Mitte* [1991] ECR I-5469, paras. 14 et seq.

68 Cf. Knipschild, (2000) *ZLR*, p. 693 et seq.; Schlacke, *Risikoentscheidungen im europäischen Lebensmittelrecht* (1998); Neyer, in: Joerges/Falke, *Ausschußwesen* (fn. 50), p. 257 et seq.

69 Cf. Falke, in: Joerges/Falke, *Ausschußwesen* (fn. 50), p. 108 et seq., 117: 'The BSE crisis is at the same time a crisis of the European comitology system.'

70 For basic information, see Knipschild, (2000) *ZLR*, p. 693 at 706 et seq.; Joerges, in: Joerges/Falke, *Ausschußwesen* (fn. 50), esp. p. 363 et seq.

71 Ipsen, *Europäisches Gemeinschaftsrecht* (1972), p. 220 et seq., 677 et seq.; Hatje, *Die gemeinschaftsrechtliche Steuerung der Wirtschaftsverwaltung: Grundlagen, Erscheinungsformen, verfassungsrechtliche Grenzen am Beispiel der Bundesrepublik Deutschland* (1998),

directives and, on the other, the control of EC direct implementation carried out by the European Parliament, the Court of Auditors and the European Courts. While it has been increasingly accepted that the *Administration of the Community territory* is a common task to be dealt with by the administrations on the EC *and* on the national level,[72] it has also become even more obvious that the great variety of novel cooperative relations between the administrations would inevitably bear consequences on the control concept of EC law.

The supervision of EC administration cannot be arranged in advance following a preset hierarchical supervision system, such as might be possible in a centralised nation state. EC control systems constitute a pluralistic structure that has to absorb manifold influences. At first sight, this structure looks like a complex mixture of instruments and institutions. However, a closer examination shows that it is the very absence of a hermetical control scheme that could be helpful even with regard to a review of the national control systems. Concerning all these aspects, the main objective has been first of all to use combined control competencies to create *mutual trust* in the incorruptibility, expertise and efficiency of all the administrations involved. Hence, control relations do not evolve just top down, but rather they make use of the counter-current principle, as well. Moreover, they also embrace the horizontal interconnections among the national administrations. Special attention shall be paid to the following elements:

- *State aid supervision* according to Articles 87–89 ECT is a control scheme designed to monitor the Member States' practice of granting subsidies.[73] From the German perspective, this scheme constitutes a badly needed extension of the so far insufficient regulation of the scope and control of subventions generously granted by the State. Judicial control in this sphere has only seldom proven to be sufficiently effective. The courts are not in a position to provide satisfactory legal assessment of the pending cases, let alone the necessary far-reaching control of effectiveness. This is not only due to the high requirements made of the filing of a complaint, but also due to the lack of willingness of competing undertakings to proceed openly against the State aid administration. Conferring aid supervision powers on the EC Commission puts the competitors into an intermediary position, which

p. 154 et seq.; Pühs, *Vollzug* (fn. 28), p. 307 et seq.; Scheuing, in: Hoffmann-Riem/Schmidt-Aßmann, *Innovation* (fn. 16), p. 335; Kahl, (1996) 29 *DV*, p. 341 at 361 et seq.; Albin, *Die Vollzugskontrolle des europäischen Umweltrechts* (1999), esp. p. 237 et seq.; Suerbaum, *Die Kompetenzverteilung beim Verwaltungsvollzug des Europäischen Verwaltungsrechts in Deutschland* (1998), p. 184 et seq.; cf. also the contributions in Streinz (ed.), *Die Kontrolle der Anwendung der europäischen Wirtschaftsrechts in den Mitgliedstaaten* (1998).

72 On the concept and the structure of this administration, cf. Schmidt-Aßmann, in: Schmidt-Aßmann/Hoffmann-Riem (eds.), *Strukturen* (fn. 16), p. 12 et seq.

73 Rodi, *Die Subventionsrechtsordnung* (2000), p. 141 et seq., also 752 et seq.

allows them to avoid an open conflict with the national administrations and, hence, creates a new control potential.

- The *procedure for the clearance of the accounts* applicable in agricultural law allows the Commission to examine in detail at the end of the year, whether the agricultural subsidies granted by the Member States during that year were in compliance with proper procedure; in this the Commission relies on the material submitted to it. In this way, the Commission is also able to oversee the administrative law enforcement.[74] During this process, dominant hierarchical elements alternate with stages of striving for mutual consent. By assuming a practice of negative corrections (*Anlastungen*), this procedure has turned into effective indirect legal supervision[75] and its application is now being considered for structural funds also.
- *Inspections* (on-site checks) are concrete supervision measures used by the EC Commission for the purposes of risk prevention in food and veterinary legislation, protection of resources in fisheries legislation and protection of budgetary Community interests in agricultural law.[76] They concern both administrative authorities of Member States and private persons. They are often designed as system reviews. In order to utilise external expertise and strengthen mutual trust, these reviews are carried out not only by EC officials, but also by public servants from the Member States.
- *Self-executive control schemes* in the Member States: In view of its extremely limited personnel resources, the EC Commission is keen on promoting the establishment of autonomous supervision schemes in the Member States, which are either activated from an own need for control, or which at least guarantee a sufficient level of independency from the national administrations. This aim has been pursued by creating independent agencies in the Member States which have been provided for in some EC legal acts. The primary target, though, has been to activate the public to become a means of control in EC law enforcement. In environmental law, for example, a cornerstone of self-executing administrative control has been laid with the introduction of 'the model of informed public' (*Modell der informierten Öffentlichkeit*).[77]

---

74 Mögele, *Die Behandlung fehlerhafter Ausgaben im Finanzierungssystem der gemeinsamen Agrarpolitik* (1997), p. 209 et seq.

75 Hatje, *Wirtschaftsverwaltung* (fn. 71), p. 167.

76 See David, *Inspektionen im Europäischen Verwaltungsrecht* (2003), pass.; idem, in this vol., p. 363 et seq.; also Ulrich, *Kontrollen der EG-Kommission bei Wirtschaftsbeteiligten zum Schutz der finanziellen Interessen der Gemeinschaft* (1999).

77 See Schmidt-Aßmann/Ladenburger, in: Rengeling, *EUDUR* (fn. 3), vol. 1 §18 paras. 4 et seq.; Scherzberg, *Die Öffentlichkeit der Verwaltung* (2000), p. 255 et seq. Cf. also Rossen-Stadtfeldt, in: Schmidt-Aßmann/Hoffmann-Riem (eds.), *Verwaltungskontrolle* (fn. 32), p. 117 et seq.

3.5. EUROPEAN ADMINISTRATIVE LAW – LEGAL STRUCTURE FOR AN INSTITUTIONAL NETWORK

European Composite administration is an network which consists of informational, decision-making and control elements and which comprises the activities of EC and Member States' administrative authorities. This structure has no central regulation. However, it is made up not merely of spontaneous cooperative actions, but has rather persistent patterns which combine hierarchical and cooperative elements in themselves. The negotiation practices adopted by the collegiate bodies and the decision-making rationale of central and local executive authorities alternate in the course of the implementation process: decisions agreed on in negotiations pass on requirements to the decision-making process in the following stages. Decisions are embedded into processes of data exchange and mutual consultation. The establishment of a legal structure for the regulatory schemes shaped in this way constitutes the greatest challenge to be dealt with by European administrative law, but shaping this law will require more than taking over the schemes and principles applicable in national administrative law. Nonetheless, legal comparison of the existing administrative law systems constitutes an important stage in its development.[78] The peculiarities of the *Verbund*-administration must also be taken into consideration. The resemblance of the tasks with which the Community has to cope to those facing national administrations (see 1.1. above) is proportionate to the divergences of their organisational structures. Since the organisational arrangements represent, in fact, the most characteristic feature of European Composite Administration, European administrative law must be shaped – to a far greater extent than national administrative law – as a law of organisation and of inter-administrative procedures. Procedural and organisational law have developed to major regulatory tools[79] in the sphere of European administration.

---

[78] Cf. just Ladenburger, *Verfahrensfehlerfolgen im französischen und im deutschen Verwaltungsrecht* (1999); Maier, *Befangenheit im Verwaltungsverfahren* (1998); Trantas, *Akteneinsicht und Geheimhaltung im Verwaltungsrecht* (1998); idem, *Die Anwendung der Rechtsvergleichung bei der Untersuchung des öffentlichen Rechts* (1998).

[79] See the contributions in Schmidt-Aßmann/Hoffmann-Riem (eds.), *Verwaltungsorganisationsrecht als Steuerungsressource* (1997).

A. FIELDS OF LAW

II. COMMON EUROPEAN ADMINISTRATION: THE EUROPEAN STRUCTURAL FUNDS*

Bettina Schöndorf-Haubold

1. INTRODUCTION

The law on the European Structural Funds represents an important reference field of European administrative law. Since one third of the European Union's budget is spent on granting aid in the framework of Structural Funds, their practical bearing is considerable. Hence, the legal regime underpinning the Structural Funds, laid down mainly in the Council Regulation on general provisions on Structural Funds (EC) No. 1260/1999,[1] constitutes an example of an extensive procedural codification of the Common European Administration.[2]

---

* This contribution is based upon my dissertation "*Die Strukturfonds der Europäischen Gemeinschaft – Rechtsformen und Verfahren Europäischer Verbundverwaltung*", C.H. Beck, München 2005. A first version is published (in German) as "Gemeinsame Europäische Verwaltung: die Strukturfonds der Europäischen Gemeinschaft", in: Eberhard Schmidt-Aßmann/Bettina Schöndorf-Haubold, *Der Europäische Verwaltungsverbund*, Tübingen 2005, p. 25 et seq. The main focus of the article is on the programme period 1999–2006.

1 Council Regulation (EC) No 1260/1999 of 21 June 1999 laying down general provisions on the Structural Funds (OJ L 161, 26.6.1999, p. 1), as last amended by Regulation (EC) No 1105/2003 of 26 May 2003 (OJ L 158, 27.6.2003, p. 3); for the next generation of programmes see Council Regulation (EC) No 1083/2006 of 11 July 2006 laying down general provisions on the European Regional Development Fund, the European Social Fund and the Cohesion Fund and repealing Regulation (EC) No 1260/1999 (OJ L 210, 31.7.2006, p. 25) and Commission Regulation (EC) No 1828/2006 of 8 December 2006 setting rules for the implementation of Council Regulation (EC) No 1080/2006 and of Regulation (EC) No 1080/2006 of the European Parliament and of the Council on the European Regional Development Fund (OJ L 371, 27.12.2006, p. 1).

2 In German scholarship, however, the Structural Funds have not received much attention; cf. Holzwart, *Der rechtliche Rahmen für die Verwaltung und Finanzierung der gemeinschaftlichen Strukturfonds am Beispiel des EFRE*, 2003; Schöndorf-Haubold, *Die Strukturfonds der Europäischen Gemeinschaft – Rechtsformen und Verfahren Europäischer Verbundverwaltung*, 2005; for other Member States see Monti, *I fondi strutturali per la coesione europea*, 1996; Ordóñez Solís, *Fondos estructurales europeos*, 1997; Comijs, *Europese structuurfondsen*, 1998; Evans, *The E.U. Structural Funds*, 1999.

Granting aid under the Structural Funds is characterised by high complexity of administrative procedures and a detailed legal regulation at Union level. It is carried out in close collaboration between the Commission and the national and regional authorities. This type of intensified administrative cooperation can be referred to as Common Administration (2). The administrative procedure can be divided into a planning phase and an implementing phase, in which the Commission and the Member State concerned interact bilaterally and in various ways (3). It is characteristic of the Common European Administration to use common modes of action and organisation, as is demonstrated by the joint programmes established consensually and the mixed Monitoring Committees (4).

2. THE STRUCTURAL FUNDS' ADMINISTRATION AS COMMON EUROPEAN ADMINISTRATION

2.1. THE STRUCTURAL FUNDS

The structural political measures of the Community are based mainly on granting of joint aid. A major tool represent the *Structural Funds*.[3] According to Article 159(1), third subparagraph ECT (see now Article 175(1) TFEU), Structural Funds included the European Regional Development Fund (ERDF), the European Social Fund (ESF) and the Guidance Section of the European Agricultural Guidance and Guarantee Fund (EAGGF). In addition, there is the Financial Instrument for Fisheries Guidance (FIFG), which is also explicitly mentioned as a Structural Fund in Article 2(1) of the Council Regulation on the Structural Funds.[4] In the present period, only the ERDF and the ESF are referred to as the Structural Funds, and the Cohesion Fund, which has not belonged to the Structural Funds so far, is incorporated into the legal regime.[5]

In general, the Structural Funds of the European Union can be described as permanent financial instruments designed to assist the Commission and the Member States in setting up, implementing and financing the structural policy of the Union. They are, hence, European funds pursuing a specific structural political objective, however, not limited to merely providing financial means. The Funds are used to assist development projects in the Member States according to the principles and procedures established in joint plans and programmes in

3 The aims of the adjustment policy are also followed by the European Investment Bank (EIB) through the selective grant of loans and by the other existing Financial Instruments such as the European Investment Funds, e.g.

4 Council Regulation (EC) No 1260/1999 (fn. 1).

5 Article 1 of the Council Regulation (EC) No 1083/2006 (fn. 1). In addition, a new legal instrument will be introduced by Regulation (EC) No 1082/2006 of the European Parliament and of the Council of 5 July 2006 on a European grouping of territorial cooperation (EGTC) (OJ L 210, 31.7.2006, p. 19).

cooperation with the Member States. The assistance is effected primarily by granting community aids, which are, first of all, to supplement national funding. In the period between 2000 and 2006 the overall sum available to the 15 old Member States amounted to about 195 billion euro.[6] In addition, already in this period 47 billion euro were provided to assist the new accession countries in carrying out necessary structural measures, while 7 billion euro were spent since 1.1.2000 in the Instrument for Structural Policies for Pre-Accession (ISPA). The Structural Funds' expenditure thus amounts to about one third of the annual EU budget.[7]

The individual funds are based on different provisions of primary law and, in their beginnings, evolved independently.[8] What they have in common, however, is their legal framework: They lack their own legal personality and are not furnished with a separate budget, but constitute a part of the general budget, within which they are specified separately. They are financed out of the general income of the Union. All Funds are administered by the Commission.[9] Since the basic reform in 1988,[10] the administration of the three and later four Funds (FIFG was added in 1993) has been conducted under a uniform legal framework. The characteristics of each single Fund indicating the target pursued within the common objective of cohesion are laid down in special regulations on the individual funds.

2.2. OBJECTIVES AND PRINCIPLES OF FUNDING

2.2.1. Introduction

Since the reforms in 1988, the fundaments of fund administration have essentially remained the same. The funding process abides by some basic principles and is regulated in detail by secondary law. The provisions of primary law are, on the contrary, formulated in general terms and represent a political agenda rather than legally binding principles of planning.

---

6 Cf. European Commission, *Structural Political Measures 2000–2006*, 3, as well as the indicative annual breakdown of the Structural Funds resources in the table of the annex to the Regulation on Structural Funds (fn. 1); 308 billion Euros between 2007 and 2013.

7 In comparison with this, the expenses of the common agricultural policy (EAGGF) amount to about 41 billion (in 2000) which is about 44.5% of the entire budget. See European Community, *The Community Budget: The facts in figures 2000*, 81.

8 For the development of the European Adjustment Policy see Holzwart, *Strukturfonds* (fn. 2), 25 et seq. with further references.

9 This was expressly regulated only for the ESF, see Article 147(1) ECT (now Article 163(1) TFEU).

10 Further reforms were made by the end of a programming period in 1993 and 1999. For the reform in 2007, see Council Regulation (EC) No 1083/2006 (fn. 1).

2.2.2. *Objectives*

The function of Structural Funds was and is laid down in primary law. Article 158 ECT (now Article 174 TFEU) bestows them with the so called cohesion objective, i.e. the target of reaching economic and social cohesion. This target is to be reached in particular by reducing disparities between the levels of development of the various regions and the backwardness of the least favoured regions (Article 158(2) ECT; Article 174(2) TFEU). Formulated as a task pertaining to all sectors of economy and social life it has to receive due attention by the Community and the Member States even when they act in the scope of other policies.

A concretisation of these wide and rather vague outlines set by primary law is provided for in secondary law. The general Council Regulation on Structural Funds (EC) No. 1260/1999[11] states three major objectives that are to be pursued by allocating the Structural Funds' means. Objective 1 contributes to the development and structural adjustment of regions whose development is lagging behind. Objective 2 consists in promoting economic and social conversion of regions facing structural difficulties. Objective 3 aims at adapting and modernising policies and systems of education, training and employment.[12] These three objectives are flanked by the two policy fields of rural development and adjustment of fisheries' structures that follow similar procedures.[13]

The functions of the individual funds are specified in more detail in the respective regulations:[14] The main task of the ERDF is to reduce the disparities of development between the regions within the European Union. The ESF

11 Fn. 1.

12 The funding under Objective 1 and Objective 2 has a regional orientation. According to Article 3(1) of the Council Regulation No 1260/1999 on Structural Funds, the per capita GDP needs to be less than 75% of the Community average. Article 4 of the Regulation states criteria for the regions to be covered by Objective 2; these criteria are established by the Commission upon recommendation by the Member States. During the 2007–2013 period, the ERDF, the ESF and the Cohesion Fund will contribute to three objectives: convergence, regional competitiveness and employment and European territorial cooperation; see Article 3 of the Council Regulation (EC) No 1083/2006 (fn. 1).

13 For an overview on the agricultural structural policy see Priebe, in Dauses (ed.), *Handbuch des EU-Wirtschaftsrechts*, loose-leaf May 2004, G mn. 137 et seq.

14 Regulation (EC) No 1783/1999 of the European Parliament and of the Council of 12 July 1999 on the European Regional Development Fund (OJ L 213, 13.8.1999, p. 1); Regulation (EC) No 1784/1999 of the European Parliament and of the Council of 12 July 1999 on the European Social Fund (OJ L 213, 13.8.1999, p. 5); Council Regulation (EC) No 1257/1999 of 17 May 1999 on support for rural development from the EAGGF (OJ L 160, 26.6.1999, p. 80), amended by Council Regulation (EC) No 583/2004 (OJ L 91, 30.3.2004, p. 1); Council Regulation (EC) No 1263/1999 of 21 June 1999 on the Financial Instrument for Fisheries Guidance (OJ L 161, 26.6.1999, p. 54); see now Regulation (EC) No 1080/2006 of the European Parliament and of the Council of 5 July 2006 on the European Regional Development Fund and repealing Regulation (EC) No 1783/1999 (OJ L 210, 31.7.2006, p. 1); Regulation (EC) No 1081/2006 of the European Parliament and of the Council of 5 July 2006 on the European Social Fund and repealing Regulation (EC) No 1784/1999 (OJ L 210, 31.7.2006, p. 12) and Council Regulation

contributes to the improvement of employment opportunities in the Union. The EAGGF Guidance Section is involved, first, in co-financing of national support for agriculture and, second, in the development and diversification of rural areas. The Financial Instrument for Fisheries Guidance (FIFG) is to promote the structural political agenda in the sphere of fisheries, which is the restructuring of the fisheries sector.

Features common to objectives of all four Funds are their non-exclusive contents and broad scopes of interpretation which are explicated only in the planning phase by the Commission and the Member States.

2.2.3. Principles

The management of the Structural Funds has been based since the reforms in 1988 on four and later five basically unchanged principles.[15]

- The allocation of means is carried out according to common *programming* set up jointly by the Commission and the Member States for a period of several years. The programming is the core of the Structural Funds management. The programming periods (e.g. from 2000 until 2006) are aligned with the respective Financial Perspectives, which indicate the financial frame for the entire Union budget.
- All reforms of the Structural Funds' regime have been marked by the effort to reach the highest possible *concentration* of the allocated means. It is ensured in three ways that the promotion measures reach the most underprivileged regions: First, a topical concentration is effected by following the three Objectives mentioned above. Within the Objectives 1 and 2 the funding is additionally concentrated in geographic terms to certain regions. Finally, financial focus is put on Objective 1: 69.7% of the Structural Funds budget is allocated to regions whose per capita GDP is less than 75% of the Community average and which are therefore rated as such with the greatest need.[16]

(EC) No 1084/2006 of 11 July 2006 establishing a Cohesion Fund and repealing Regulation (EC) No 1164/94 (OJ L 210, 31.7.2006, p. 79).

15 See descriptions in European Commission, *Structural Political measures 2000–2006*, 9; Priebe, in Schwarze (ed.), *EU-Kommentar*, 2000, Art. 161 EGV mn. 6 et seq.; Puttler, in: Magiera/Sommermann (eds.), *Verwaltung in der Europäischen Union*, 2001, 171 (174 et seq.); for earlier regulations Priebe, in: Randelzhofer/Scholz/Wilke (eds.), *Gedächtnisschrift für Grabitz*, 1995, 551 (558 et seq.). On the principles and the meaning of the funding by structural funds Mehde, *NWVBl.* 2002, 178; Jung/Hassold, *DÖV* 2000, 190 (194); Holzwart, *Strukturfonds* (fn. 2), 160. Without important modifications of the content, the principles in the new Regulation are now: complementarity, consistency, coordination and compliance (Article 9 of the Council Regulation (EC) No 1083/2006 (fn. 1)).

16 Article 3(1), first subparagraph and Article 7(2) of the Council Regulation No 1260/1999 on Structural Funds. The new Regulation on Structural Funds continued this concentration on the areas of Objective 1 under the new name "Convergence Objective"; cf. Article 3, point (2a)

- Next, the management abides by the *principle of partnership*, which is an important procedural and organisational principle in all phases. The term is legally defined in Article 8(1) of the Council Regulation on Structural Funds as "close consultation (...) between the Commission and the Member State, together with the authorities and bodies designated by the Member State within the framework of its national rules and current practices, namely the regional and local authorities and other competent public authorities; the economic and social partners and any other relevant competent bodies within this framework".[17]
  This principle represents a legal cooperation rule that prescribes the cooperation between the Commission and a Member State, both, during the planning and the implementation phase.[18] Addressing not only the Member States as the traditional interaction partners of the Commission, the principle, also includes private actors and establishes direct contacts between the Commission and the national authorities in charge, which are usually to be found on the regional level. Therewith, the partnership causes a breakthrough of the Community level to the subordinate levels of the Member States' administrations.[19]
- According to the principle of *additionality* or *complementarity*, the Community funding represents only a contribution to the public expenditure by the Member States but may not substitute it nor take its place.[20] Together with the principle of co-financing, the principle of additionality leads in each case of funding to mixed financing by community, national and, as the case

---

and Article 5 of the Council Regulation (EC) No 1083/2006 (fn. 1). Since the per capita GDP has diminished as a consequence of the accession of new Member States, the scenery of the development area has changed significantly.

17 Now Article 11 of the Council Regulation (EC) No 1083/2006 (fn. 1). On partnership in general Priebe, in Schwarze, *EU-Kommentar*, Art. 161 EGV mn. 16 et seq.; *id.*, in: Hill/Pitschas (eds.), *Europäisches Verwaltungsverfahrensrecht*, 2004, 337 (346); Poth/Mögele, *Prinzip der Partnerschaft*, 1993; Monti, *Fondi strutturali* (fn. 2), 66 et seq.; Ordóñez Solís, *Fondos estructurales* (fn. 2), 72 et seq.; Gil Ibáñez, *Commission Tools for the Supervision and Enforcement of EC Law*, Jean Monnet Working Papers, No. 12/1998, under 6; Hummer, in: *Festschrift für Schwind*, 1993, 269, considers the Principle of Partnership to be a special aspect of the principle of subsidiarity.

18 On the level of primary law, this principle derives from the principles of subsidiarity and of cooperation, without being a general legal principle at the same time, see Schöndorf-Haubold, *Strukturfonds* (fn. 2), 437 et seq., 456 et seq. It seems that the model of partnership as established by the Regulation on Structural Funds, has not yet been applied to other areas, see Gil Ibáñez, *Supervision and Enforcement of EC Law* (fn. 17), 6.1 et seq.

19 Schöndorf-Haubold, *Strukturfonds* (fn. 2), 455; Puttler, in: Magiera/Sommermann (eds.), *Verwaltung in der EU* (fn. 15), 171 (181).

20 This is already expressed in Article 159(1) ECT (now Article 175(1) TFEU), which considers the cohesion objectives to be tasks of the Member States, additionally supported by the Community. See Article 15 of Council Regulation (EC) No 1083/2006 (fn. 1).

may be, private means[21], herewith establishing a financing coalition between the Union and the Member State in question.

The principle of highest possible *effectiveness* was expressly formulated as such only in 1999 although it had been of importance also in the course of earlier reforms.[22] For reaching optimum effectiveness of interventions the Council Regulation No 1260/1999 on Structural Funds provides tools of regular guidance, monitoring and evaluation. A new addition has been the so-called performance reserve.[23] After an interim evaluation of the programmes, a retained reserve of 4% of all financial means originally assigned to one Member State is distributed to those programmes which prove to be particularly efficient in respect to achieving their objectives, their administration and financial handling. This way, the European Union initiates a competition, though not among the administrations of the Member States, but among the programmes and, hence, usually also among the regions of one Member State.

2.3. LEGAL REGIME

There are but few primary law provisions on allocation of Structural Funds' means. The European Treaties include only general aims and legal bases for the Funds and the Regulations on the funding procedure. Article 158 ECT (now Article 174 TFEU) states the cohesion objective and constitutes thereby the "structural political general clause".[24] Further primary law provisions concerning Structural Funds can be found in Article 34(3) ECT (EAGGF), Articles 146–148 ECT (ESF) and Articles 159–162 ECT (now Articles 40(3), 162–164 and 175–178 TFEU).

The legal regime for the management of the Structural Funds in the examined period followed from the Council Regulation (EC) No. 1260/1999 of 21 June 1999, which layed down general provisions on the Structural Funds[25] and from the implementing regulations of the Commission based on it. Apart from these, some very few particular provisions were and are stipulated in the regulations on

21 Holzwart, *Strukturfonds* (fn. 2), 188.

22 Recital No 25 of the Regulation on Structural Funds says: "Effectiveness should be regarded as a fundamental principle." The principle of effectiveness is qualified as a legal principle in the sense of an "imperative to optimise" by Hoffmann-Riem, in: Hoffmann-Riem/Schmidt-Aßmann (eds.), *Effizienz als Herausforderung an das Verwaltungsrecht*, 1998, 11 (23); Schmidt-Aßmann, *ib.*, 245 (248): "Effizienz als Entscheidungsregel für die Ressourcenallokation"; on the basis of this principle in EC Law see *ib.*, 245 (257).

23 Article 44 of the old Council Regulation on Structural Funds (fn. 1).

24 Priebe, in Schwarze, *EU-Kommentar* (fn. 17), Art. 158 EGV mn. 7; Borchardt, in: Lenz/Borchardt (eds.), EUV/EGV, 3rd edition, 2003, Art. 158 mn. 9 et seq.; Stabenow, in: Grabitz/Hilf (eds.), *Das Recht der Europäischen Union*, loose-leaf 2004, Art. 158 mn. 3.

25 OJ L 161, 26.6.1999, p. 1 (fn. 1), now Council Regulation (EC) No 1083/2006 (fn. 1).

the individual Funds. The implementing provisions enacted by the Commission in the Comitology procedure concern to the greater extent the management modalities such as implementation and control systems, financial corrections, information and publicity measures, the usage of the Euro and even some details on the eligibility of specific expenditure.[26] They contribute essentially to an extensive codification of the administrative procedure. Particularly, the numerous procedural and organisational rules applicable to the national administrative authorities constitute an exception within the EU legal system since the Union is, as a rule, denied the authority to interfere with the organisational sovereignty of the Member States under reference to the subsidiarity principle of Article 5(2) ECT (now Article 5(1) and (3) TEU) or to the principle of procedural and organisational autonomy of the Member States.[27] However, due to the fact that the state and administration systems of the individual Member States differ significantly it is difficult to find detailed organisational provisions that can be applied in all national legal systems. Therefore, open formulations and restrictions of powers prevail, leaving the choice of the authority that is to carry out the assigned task to the Member States. It is nonetheless questionable, whether refraining from the assignment of a concrete national authority in charge is sufficient and beneficial for securing the alleged national autonomy, keeping in mind the often very detailed regulation of duties by the Commission.

Below the level of primary and secondary law, the Structural Funds regulations are amended and specified by a variety of Commission's guidelines, issues papers and staff working documents.[28] They serve the Commission in guiding the administrative action of the Member States in the framework of administrative cooperation. The binding character of the individual types of texts is vague and varies regarding their possible addressees. Usually, they address the Member States in a non-binding way, but sometimes also the

---

26 See, e.g. Commission Regulation (EC) No 438/2001 of 2 March 2001 laying down detailed rules for the implementation of Council Regulation (EC) No 1260/1999 as regards the management and control systems for assistance granted under the Structural Funds (OJ L 63, 3.3.2001, p. 21), as amended by Commission Regulation (EC) No 2355/2002 (OJ L 35, 28.12.2002, p. 42); detailed analysis in Schöndorf-Haubold, *Strukturfonds* (fn. 2), 86 et seq.; a codification of most of these implementation rules is now provided for in Commission Regulation (EC) No 1828/2006 (fn. 1).

27 See Kadelbach, *Allgemeines Verwaltungsrecht unter europäischem Einfluß*, 1999, 110 et seq.; v. Danwitz, *DVBl* 1998, 421 (esp. 429 et seq.).

28 E.g. Guidelines for programmes in the period 2000 to 2006 (OJ C 267, 22.9.1999, p. 2); Working Paper 2 "*The Ex-Ante Evaluation of the Structural Funds Interventions*" (http://ec.europa.eu/regional_policy/sources/docoffic/working/doc/exante_en.pdf; January 2010). For the 2007–2013 period, the priorities of the European Community regarding programme-planning are laid down in the Council Decision of 6 October 2006 on Community strategic guidelines on cohesion (OJ L No 291, 21.10.2006, p. 11); cf. also Working Paper 1 "Indicative Guidelines on Evaluation Methods: Ex ante Evaluation" (http://ec.europa.eu/regional_policy/sources/docoffic/2007/working/wd1_exante_en.pdf; January 2010).

Commission itself. Only in exceptional cases are they legally binding due to an explicit provision ordering their binding nature, or due to the self-commitment of the Commission. However, they exert a considerable actual guidance effect on the planning and implementation of the Structural Funds' interventions. Therefore, they represent typical instruments of soft control in the European Composite Administration.[29]

2.4. COMMON ADMINISTRATION AS A MODEL FOR EUROPEAN ADMINISTRATION

The administration of the Structural Funds is characterised by the constant close cooperation between the Commission and the administrations of the Member States. The joint financing asks for extensive cooperation, leads to common programming and finally also to a, in vast parts, common programme management. Therefore, it can be referred to as a Composite Planning, Financing and Operating Administration (*"Planungs-, Finanzierungs- und Verwaltungs-verbund"*).

The administrative collaboration is not limited to informal co-operation owing to practical requirements for the purpose of information exchange.[30] The general Regulation No 1260/1999 on Structural Funds rather stated a cooperation regime that makes the cooperation obligatory and, at the same time, provided for its legal structure, procedure and institutional frame. First signs of evolving common legal instruments can be discerned.

This administrative model of a cooperative, tiered allocation of subventions does no longer fit into the conventional categories of direct and indirect implementation.[31] With regard to the Structural Funds' administration it seems more appropriate to talk of a Common Administration between the European Union and the Member States. This development is at the same time connected to a gain in influence and guidance powers of the Union, resulting in limited

---

29 The legal character of atypical Commission documents and their intended regulatory effect is discussed in detail in Schöndorf-Haubold, *Strukturfonds* (fn. 2), 399 et seq. with further references.

30 On the origins of administrative cooperation and on the law of administrative cooperation Schmidt-Aßmann, *EuR* 1996, 270; for an outline of the development *id.*, in this volume, p. 1; *id.*, in: *Festschrift für Häberle*, 2004, 395; Sommer, *Verwaltungskooperation am Beispiel adminstrativer Informationsverfahren im europäischen Umweltrecht*, 2003; *id.*, in this volume, p. 55.

31 This finding is not limited to the area of Structural Funds: see Schmidt-Aßmann, *Das allgemeine Verwaltungsrecht als Ordnungsidee*, 2nd edition 2004, 7/7; Chiti, *Diritto Amministrativo Europeo*, 1999, especially 113 et seq., 125 et seq., 176 et seq., 331 et seq. The intermediate categories developed by P.M. Huber, in: *Festschrift für Brohm*, 2002, 127 (134 et seq.) do not adequately describe the Structural Funds administration.

supervision powers of the Commission, or at any rate, in the emergence of sectoral supervision-like structures.[32]

3. PROCEDURE OF GRANTING AIDS UNDER THE STRUCTURAL FUNDS

3.1. INTRODUCTION

The administration of the Structural Funds, i.e. the allocation of the Structural Funds' resources by the Commission and the Member States, can be divided into two phases. In the initial planning phase, a strategic concept for the use of the resources is set up in close collaboration and, in the second implementing phase, it is put into reality by the Member States acting *vis-à-vis* the beneficiaries who are the addressees of the funding. The allocation of means under the four Funds, pursuing the three Objectives, is to a large extent subject to the uniform procedure rules laid down in the general Regulation on Structural Funds and the implementing regulations by the Commission.

The division into two phases can be traced back to the complex structure of the funding. From the Union's point of view the model is, despite the manifold ways of collaboration with the national authorities, still one of indirect funding: those involved are the Commission, the Member State in question and the final beneficiary, i.e. a public or private entity carrying out the project. Direct relations exist only between the Commission and the Member State or the national authority in charge, and between the Member State and the final beneficiary, but not between the final beneficiary and the Commission. The whole procedure is preceded by decisions of financial and geographical nature on the distribution of resources to the Member States and regions, which are made by the Commission according to preset criteria.[33]

3.2. PLANNING PHASE

3.2.1. Introduction

According to the principle of programming, the assistance by the Structural Funds is not based on the promotion of single projects but on the elaboration of

---

32 *Infra* 3.3.2 and 3.3.3.

33 This concerns multilateral decisions about the allocation of resources to the Member States and bilateral decisions about the eligible areas of a Member State within the scope of Objective 1 and Objective 2. Whereas the latter are defined by more or less clear criteria in the Regulation on Structural Funds, the procedures and criteria about the allocation of resources to the various Member States is hardly transparent, which is astonishing considering the importance of the decision; on this problem Schöndorf-Haubold, *Strukturfonds* (fn. 2), 144 et seq.

programmes into framework of which concrete national support measures have to fit. The subventions are allocated on the basis of comprehensive planning by the Community and the Member State in question. With the help of the subsequent procedural steps, a gradual problem diversification and plan refinement is reached in close cooperation between the Commission and the participating national and regional authorities.

3.2.2. Procedure of programming

In the examined period, the planning is carried out, according to the general Regulation on Structural Funds, in a three-stage or a simplified two-stage procedure. The basic model consists of three planning stages: the Member State submits to the Commission a Regional Development Plan that serves as a draft for the Community Support Framework. The latter is then transformed into Operational Programmes. The simplified procedure combines the Community Support Frameworks and Operational Programmes into Single Programming Documents. Both forms of planning are extended by amendments to programming.

Community Support Framework (CFS)

First, the Member State has to present to the Commission a draft of a support framework, the so-called *Regional Development Plan*. This plan contains, based on a socio-economic analysis of the region concerned, a rough concept of the support planned for this region following one of the three objectives of the structural policy. Based on this plan, a so-called *Community Support Framework* (CSF) is developed by the Commission in cooperation with the Member State, which is to include on basis of partnership the regions and social partners concerned. Accordingly, CSF is the approved plan, matching the expectations of the Commission, that is to say, the consented rough concept of the support for a certain region.

As to the content, the Community Support Frameworks entail, besides an account on the initial level of development of a region, a proposal for a support strategy focused on reaching the defined targets and a designation of the intended priority, without specifying measures and concrete projects for their implementation.[34] To ensure the greatest possible efficiency, a first ex-ante evaluation of the support strategy is made in this programming phase and integrated into the programme.[35] Next to an indicative financing plan, which

---

34 Critical about the altogether "lyrical" language of the Regulation Priebe, in: Schwarze, *EU-Kommentar* (fn. 15), Art. 158 mn. 4. For the 2007–2013 period, the CSF has been replaced by national strategic reference frameworks, presented by the Member States in dialogue with the Commission (Article 27 and 28 of the Council Regulation (EC) No 1083/2006 (fn. 1)).

35 See Article 41 of the Council Regulation No 1260/1999 on Structural Funds (fn. 1).

includes details on the annual contributions by the individual Funds to the intended priorities and on national co-financing, the programmes also contain provisions on procedures and competences in the implementation phase as well as an overview of the Operational Programmes intended for the implementation of the CSF.[36]

After submitting the plan, the Commission and the authorities in charge of the Member State concerned[37] enter into a dialogue, which comes to an end with the consensual agreement on the final CSF and the authorisation by the Commission. The Funds' committees are consulted in the comitology procedure and the EIB can also be involved if necessary.

Following the participation of the committees, the Commission makes the final decision on the CSFs according to Article 249(4) ECT (now Article 288(4) TFEU). According to Article 15(4), first subparagraph, third sentence of the Regulation No 1260/1999 on Structural Funds, the Commission takes the decision at the latest five months after the submission of the regional development plan, provided the plan entails all information required. The Commission's decision represents an explicit approval of the CSF. The decision is addressed only to the Member State concerned and is binding solely in the language of this state. Upon request, it is transmitted together with the approved programmes to the European Parliament for information purposes.[38] The decision is published in the Official Journal of the EU.[39]

As far as legal effects are concerned, a distinction has to be made between the Commission's decision approving a CSF and the CSF as a planning document itself.[40] Only the Commission's decision on the participation of the Funds, as

---

36 Articles 16 and 17 of the Regulation No 1260/1999 on Structural Funds (fn. 1); according to Article 9, point (h) of the Regulation, priority means "one of the priorities of the strategy adopted in a Community Support Framework or assistance"; e.g. the German CSF "Ziel 1 und Ziel 1-Übergangsunterstützung in Deutschland 2000–2006", 12.6.2000, 9 ff. (http://ec.europa.eu/regional_policy/funds/prord/document/gfk_de.pdf; January 2010); details about the content and the development of the CSF in Schöndorf-Haubold, *Strukturfonds* (fn. 2), 174 et seq.

37 This will often be a ministerial authority, e.g. for the German Objektiv-1-CSF (fn. 36) the Federal Ministry of Economy and the Federal Ministry of Finance.

38 See also No 1.1 of the Code of Conduct on the implementation of structural policies by the Commission, Annex II to the protocol of the meeting of the European Parliament of 6.5.1999 (OJ C 279, 1.10.1999, p. 488), where the Commission declares its willingness to forward the plans submitted by the Member States in connection with the various Objectives of the Funds to the Parliament as soon as the Commission has received them.

39 Article 15(7) of the Regulation No 1260/1999 on Structural Funds (fn. 1). The particular CSF is not published in the Official Journal of the European Community. See the Commission's decision of 19 June 2000 approving the CSF for Community structural assistance in the regions falling under Objective 1 or qualifying for transitional support under Objective 1 in Germany, C(2000) 1475 (OJ L 156, 14.6.2002, p. 1), as amended by the Commission Decision of 29 March 2001, C(2001) 800 (OJ L 156, 14.6.2002, p. 54). In the present planning period, the national strategic reference frameworks fall within the responsibility of the Member States, so that an approval decision by the Commission will no longer be required.

40 Different opinion by Holzwart, *Strukturfonds* (fn. 2), 207, who qualifies "the CSF and OP as decisions requiring approval and being addressed at the Member States, in terms of

published in the Official Journal, has the character of a formal decision in terms of Article 249(4) ECT (now Article 288(4) TFEU).[41] The support concept does not acquire the power of a formal decision upon approval. The concept in its entirety is neither the object of the formal decision, nor is it published in the Official Journal. Although the programmes in themselves have only a limited binding effect and are not being decisions in a formal sense, they nonetheless have to be complied with by the Member States during the further planning and the implementation of the interventions. Their implementation cannot be enforced positively.[42] However, sanctions can be imposed as punishment of infringements of the programmes within the scope of the implementation.[43]

Operational Programme (OP)

Each CSF is implemented by one or several so-called *Operational Programmes* (OP).[44] This specifying planning phase is not left to the Member States, but takes place on the basis of co-operation between the particular Member State and the Commission, as well.

According to Article 9, point (f) of the Regulation No 1260/1999 on Structural Funds, an Operational Programme "means the document approved by the Commission to implement a Community Support Framework and comprising a consistent set of priorities comprising multi-annual measures and which may be implemented through recourse to one or more Funds, to one or more of the other existing financial instruments and to the EIB." Regarding their content, the Operational Programmes lean closely on the respective underlying Community Support Frameworks, whose strategy and priorities they assume and specify for a particular issue or region.[45] Unlike the CSF, the Operational Programmes provide a summary and an evaluation of measures to be taken in order to

---

Article 249(4) of the Treaty establishing the European Community"; similarly Comijs, *Europese structuurfondsen* (fn. 2), 146 et seq., who is of the opinion that programme and programme approval cannot be separated.

41 On the legal qualification as decision and on the differentiation to a contractual agreement see Schöndorf-Haubold, *Strukturfonds* (fn. 2), 387 et seq. Contents of the formal decision are the basic elements of the CSF such as the particular priorities, the total costs numbered in the indicative financing plan, the amount of the participation of the Structural Funds and the national funding requirement resulting from this.

42 Also Holzwart, *Strukturfonds* (fn. 2), 191.

43 On the legal character of the programmes Schöndorf-Haubold, *Strukturfonds* (fn. 2), 392 et seq.; on sanctions within the scope of the implementation *ibid.*, 332 et seq.

44 Within the scope of Objective 1 CSF nine Operational Programmes were adopted, including six Regional Programmes (which are administered by the authorities of the Länder concerned and in East Berlin) and three Multi-regional Programmes (transport, human resources and farm-fishing); see *Inforegio Newsletter* No. 76 (July 2000), 1.

45 For the content of the Operational Programmes see Article 18(2) of the Regulation No 1260/1999 on Structural Funds (fn. 1); Articles 37 and 38 of the Council Regulation (EC) No 1083/2006 (fn. 1).

implement the priorities. Thereby, measures are not to be understood as single actions, but as whole sets of actions, such as a national aid programme.[46]

The procedure for approving an Operational Programme is similar to that for approving a CSF: The Member State[47] submits to the Commission a draft of the Operational Programme as an application for intervention in terms of Article 28 of the Regulation on Structural Funds.[48] Since the decision on the programme – such as the decision on the Community Support Frameworks – can only be made in consensus with the Member State, the Commission, after verifying the drafts, enters into negotiations with the Member State. Only an involvement of the Funds' committees is not intended at this planning stage.[49]

When the decision about the Operational Programme is taken, the budget is also committed at Community level and allocated thereby to a particular activity.[50] According to Article 15(4), second subparagraph and Article 28(1) of Regulation No 1260/1999 on Structural Funds the Commission's decision is essential with regard to the financial contributions from the individual Funds since it states for each intervention priority the maximum contribution provided by the Funds.[51] Subject to the Commission's decision are the major elements of the programmes, first of all, the extent of the co-financing of the particular priorities by the European Union.

Single Programming Document (SPD)

In the course of the reform of 1993 an optional shortened and simplified model was introduced, which consists only of two planning stages, thanks to melting the regional development plan and the draft for the Operational Programmes into a single programme. Accordingly, the Member States can submit just one

46 In Article 9, point (j) of Regulation No 1260/1999 on Structural Funds (fn. 1), *measures* are defined as means by which a priority is implemented over several years which enables operations to be financed; aid schemes in terms of Article 87 ECT (now Article 107 TFEU) are mentioned explicitly as examples.

47 Also in Germany, the Länder submit their plans for Operational Programmes to the Commission through the Federal Government (the Federal Ministry of Finance).

48 The procedure has been maintained in the new Regulation; see Articles 28(3) and 32 of Council Regulation (EC) No 1083/2006 (fn. 1). The elaboration of the programme drafts usually takes place for regional programmes within the region itself, for sectoral programmes on the level of the Member State concerned. In Germany, the Operational Programmes within the scope of Objective 1 for the individual Länder were mostly established by the regional ministries for economy, while the sectoral programmes were drafted by the federal ministry which was responsible for the relevant sector.

49 Only details of the programmes remain to be negotiated. The negotiation is officially made by the Member State; off the record, the drafts are often discussed directly with the regions concerned.

50 The first of the annual commitments in terms of Article 31(2), first subparagraph of Regulation No 1260/1999 on Structural Funds (fn. 1) is made automatically with the Commission's approval.

51 Article 28(1) second subparagraph of Regulation No 1260/1999 on Structural Funds (fn. 1).

draft of a programme that includes the elements of CSF and OP. After the negotiations with the Commission are concluded, this document, referred to as *Single Programming Document* (SPD) becomes the basis of the funding.[52]

SPDs represent the second major form of intervention, next to the Operational Programmes. They are applied mainly in the scope of the Objectives 2 and 3.[53]

Both, the planning guidelines and the procedures, correspond largely with the approval procedure of the CSF. Following the consultation of the Commission and the Funds' committees, the SPDs are also authorised by the Commission in a formal decision.

Programme Complement

In 1999, the so-called *Programme Complement* was introduced, which is an annex to the programming. The plans themselves are still quite abstract. They include no concrete measures, but only the support strategy and priorities. Therefore, the Member States work out, in order to inform the Commission, a so-called programme complement, in which the potential beneficiaries and the measures planned are specified. The planning is, hence, increasingly specified as it passes the stages from the CSF as a framework programme over the OP to the programme complement, or from the SPD to the complement documents. With the programme complement, the planning phase comes to an end.[54]

The planning phase of the Structural Funds' administration can be characterised in brief as common planning with strategic participation of the Commission and, at the same time, a decisive involvement of the Member State concerned, or simply as common decision making.

3.2.3. The function mode of the plans and programmes

The planning phase is the creative core element of the Structural Funds' administration. Here, the basic concepts of the support are laid down in a co-operative programme planning consisting of central and de-central elements. The individual subsequent stages of decision-making have a legal frame and

---

52 A Single Programming Document according to Article 9, point (g) of Regulation No 1260/1999 on Structural Funds (fn. 1) is "a single document approved by the Commission and containing the same information to be found in a Community Support Framework and Operational Programme". The simplified procedure under the new Regulation no longer provides for the SPD.

53 In practice, Single Programming Documents are used almost exclusively within the scope of Objective 2 and to a large extent within the scope of Objective 3.

54 According to Article 32(3), point (a) of Regulation No 1260/1999 on Structural Funds (fn. 1), the complement documents can also be prepared during the implementing phase. Accordingly, the interim payments of the Commission require that the complement documents exist. The planning procedure under Council Regulation (EC) No 1083/2006 (fn. 1) no longer contains programme complements.

feature different participants depending on their content.[55] In its core, the planning is carried out consensually between the Member State concerned and the Commission. The other Member States are involved only thanks to their representation in the committees. The Commission has an influential position in the planning phase since it has the last word on the Member States' plans.

The programming includes planning of tasks and resources. Based on an analysis of the present situation a target state is drafted at reaching of which the support aims whereby Union and national or regional structural policies are coordinated and adjusted to each other coherently. The planning on the substance inevitably involves also decisions on finances. In the plans, financial decisions are linked with substantial decisions and the individual financial contributions are decided on in general and in detail. Both, the substantive and the financial planning, have an important guidance effect on the support to be provided. Though only the Commission's authorisation decisions, but not the programmes themselves, exert binding legal effects, the programmes become significant guidelines for the actions of the national administrations, owing to their partial juridification through duties stated in secondary law and the possibility of imposing sanctions.

Taking the several procedural steps, a gradual problem diversification and plan refinement is reached with growing level of concretion: the objectives set in the Regulation on Structural Funds are furnished with strategies and priorities. These, in turn, are first specified by sets of measures and filled with concrete proposals only at the level of programme complement. The decision as to which concrete projects are to be funded is left to the implementation stage. By presetting single substantive elements, the national planning process is also structured and subjected to qualified legal requirements: An account on the socio-economic situation on which the planning is based is to be provided, a strategy developed, and priorities determined. At the same time, the planning process has to be evaluated ex-ante, that is to say, it is to be tested as to its conclusiveness and alternatives. Each element has to be explicitly documented in the plan. The structuring effects of the planning process facilitate the agreement of interests between the Union and the Member States, hence, result in greater rationality, transparency and improve the revisibility of the planning results.[56] This way, plans and programmes are created that provide flexible and consensus-oriented instruments for reaching both, the EU cohesion objective and the Member States' objectives in the sphere of regional policy.

55 The complexity of the planning is one of the items reviewed by the European Court of Auditors in their special report No. 7/2003 about the implementation of the programming for the Structural Funds' interventions within the period of 2000–2006 (OJ C 174, 2003, p. 1).

56 For planning in Germany, see Schmidt-Aßmann, in: *Festschrift für Schlichter* 1995, 3 (6); these considerations can also be applied to European planning; see also Holzwart, *Strukturfonds* (fn. 2), 198; for the rationalising aspect of planning see Schmidt-Aßmann, *Ordnungsidee* (fn. 31), 2/75 et seq.

3.3. IMPLEMENTING PHASE

3.3.1. Introduction

The final allocations of funds to the beneficiaries are a question of implementation of the programmes by and within the Member States. The rules applicable to them are mainly such of the respective national law on subventions. The EU co-operative planning is thus realised within the framework of the national funding regimes.

3.3.2. Procedural elements of implementation

Implementation in the narrow sense of the word

As a rule, Structural Funds' resources are used to co-finance national aid, which has to match with the programmes. In Germany, for example, part of the Structural Funds' resources is spent to co-finance the German regional support within the scope of the European Union task "Improvement of the regional economic structure".

The resources are allocated according to the German law on subsidies and state aid. The applications are to be submitted to the national authority in charge so that contacts with the beneficiaries exist only on the national or regional level.

From the Union's point of view, the Structural Funds' support follows in the implementing phase an indirect support model: European resources are forwarded to the beneficiaries by the Member States, who make the concrete decisions on the allocation. There are no direct legal relations between the European Union and the beneficiaries of the EU funding. They exist only in a triangle, between the Commission and the national authorities and between the national authorities and the beneficiaries. However, the Commission is involved also in the implementing phase through various participation modes. In addition, it has at its disposal a whole range of soft and hard means, mainly of cooperative steering and supervision, in the shape of participation rights or explicit control and supervision powers.

Guidance and evaluation

The implementing phase includes, apart from project specification and financial management, also guidance, evaluation and control of the interventions, i.e. measures of efficiency, financial and legal control. By providing guidance and carrying out evaluations of the programme implementation a flexible after-regulation of the planning is reached. A part of this procedural concept are, on the one hand, regular evaluations,[57] and on the other, continuous monitoring, which has been ensured, procedurally, by imposing annual duties to report and, institutionally, by setting up specialised boards, the so-called monitoring committees. In order to achieve a convincing and comparable evaluation it is crucial to carry out continuous and systematic collection, documentation and scanning of significant developments and results of an intervention according to preset substantive and financial indicators. Such an evaluation can lead, together with the comments and well-founded recommendations submitted by the Commission in dialogues or arbitration procedures, to an adjustment of the Member State's administration.[58]

The concept of guidance and evaluation, which leads, similar to administrative controlling, to constant assessment of the performance of the Structural Funds' administration, integrates, hence, elements of modern administration in the procedure. A steady self-reflection shall lead to an efficiency increase of the administrative actions by sustained learning that opens possibilities of revision. Also in this context belongs the new instrument of a performance-bound reserve, which aims at promoting competition among the most successful programmes for further Structural Funds' resources.

Control and financial corrections

With regard to the division of authorities during the implementing phase, referred to as "*shared management*" in the Council Regulation on the Financial Regulation applicable to the general budget of the EU[59], Article 53(5) of this Financial Regulation obliges the Commission to check, with help of control and financial correction schemes, whether the funds are used in accordance with the applicable rules.[60] The control structures resemble strongly the cooperation

57 Ex-ante evaluation during the planning, mid-term evaluation of the programme implementation and ex-post evaluation at the end (Articles 40–43 of Regulation No 1260/1999 on Structural Funds (fn. 1); Articles 47–49 of the Council Regulation (EC) No 1083/2006 (fn. 1)).

58 See Article 34(2), second subparagraph of Regulation No 1260/1999 on Structural Funds (fn. 1). These "soft instructions" are not legally binding, but they may not be disregarded by the Member States and may – under certain circumstances – lead to the suspension of mid-payments, see Schöndorf-Haubold, *Strukturfonds* (fn. 2), 293 and 320 et seq.

59 Article 53 b) Council Regulation (EC, Euratom) No 1605/2002 of 25 June 2002 on the Financial Regulation applicable to the general budget of the European Communities (OJ L 248, 16.9.2002, p. 1), amended by Council Regulation (EC, Euratom) No 1995/2006 (OJ L 390, 30.12.2006, p. 1); for details see Schenk, in this volume, p. 389; Craig, *ELRev* 2003, 840 (856 et seq.).

60 An analogous parallel correction mechanism can be found in the Common Agricultural Policy (CAP) with the clearance-of-accounts procedures. For this see Pache, *Der Schutz der finanziellen Interessen der Europäischen Gemeinschaften*, 1994, 278 et seq.; Mögele, *Die Behandlung fehlerhafter Ausgaben im Finanzierungssystem der gemeinsamen Agrarpolitik*, 1997, 15 et seq., 68 et seq.

structures. Parallel to the responsibility for the implementation of the programmes, the major burden of executing control lies on the Member States, while the Commission reviews the administrative systems of the Member States by means of so-called control of the control. Accompanying instruction-like competences as well as the authority to impose on the Member States financial corrections in the shape of reductions and cancellations justify talking about the emergence of a Community supervision in the scope of Common Administration.

While the national authorities are obliged to review the proper usage of the resources by the beneficiaries (*first-line control*), the Commission cannot simply forgo its own checks since, according to Article 274 ECT (now Article 317 TFEU), it is its own responsibility to implement the Community budget. Due to the division of powers, the checks by the Commission are, however, limited to the control of control (*second-line-control*).[61] This system of shared control authority, which occurs also in other spheres of Community law,[62] leaves untouched the Commission's responsibility for the EC budget: Even though the execution of concrete controls is left, for the most part, to the Member States the Commission cannot claim grievances within the single Member States to elude its own budget responsibility. It has, rather, to ensure, by introducing system controls, that the Member States establish adequate control schemes. To guarantee a certain minimum standard of the national control systems, the Community law in general, but also the law on Structural Funds in particular, provides a multitude of normative harmonising provisions.[63]

In view of financial corrections that are to be imposed in case of irregularities, the competence is also divided. Similar to the financial controls, the Member States are responsible in relation to the beneficiaries, while the Commission imposes sanctions on the Member States in case of malpractice, using the instrument of financial correction in shape of reductions or cancellation of the allocated funds. A financial correction is preceded by a procedure of bilateral

61 On the system of the control responsibilities see David, *Inspektionen im Europäischen Verwaltungsrecht*, 2003, 117 et seq. with further references; *id.*, in this volume, p. 363; Vervaele, in: *id.* (ed.), *Compliance and Enforcement of European Community Law*, 1999, 361 (364). On the control structures especially within the frame of the Structural Funds' administration see Holzwart, *Strukturfonds* (fn. 2), 289 et seq.; Schöndorf-Haubold, *Strukturfonds* (fn. 2), 298 et seq.

62 See the examples in David, *Inspektionen* (fn. 61), 30 et seq.

63 Jans/de Lange/Prechtal/Widdershoen, *Inleiding tot het Europees bestuursrecht*, 1999, 243 et seq.; David, *Inspektionen* (fn. 61), 124 et seq., Lühmann, *DVBl* 1999, 752 (759 et seq.). For the Structural Funds, the Commission especially enacted Commission Regulation (EC) No 438/2001 (fn. 26). Bilateral administrative agreements (the legal effect of which is unclear) allow the coordination of the controls; on this Schöndorf-Haubold, *Strukturfonds* (fn. 2), 302 et seq. These rules are supplemented by an informal manual of the Commission on the audit of management and control systems, Audit Manual for the Structural Funds – Financial Controls in the Member States, 12.5.1999 (XX/28/99-EN) (http://ec.europa.eu/employment_social/esf2000/working_documents/financial_control/en.pdf; January 2007).

mediation between the Commission and the Member State concerned, aiming at finding a consensual solution first.[64]

3.3.3. Co-operation and supervision

The diversity of co-operative relations and instruments, which have attained a procedural and organisational frame, militate in favour of characterising the Structural Funds' administration as Common European administration. The mediation procedures provided by the Regulation on Structural Funds constitute a way of handling situations of different evaluation by co-operating partners. Dialogue and conflict solution are legally pre-structured. Hereby, the traditional contact pattern Community – Member State has stepped back in favour of direct contacts between the Commission and the national authority in charge. These regulations are, therefore, characteristic for legal settlement of long-term co-operative relations and for the transition into the European Composite Administration. At the same time, structures of a European supervision can be discerned in the partly asymmetric distribution of control and sanction competences. These structures are, unlike those in a national context, characterised by a combination of hierarchic and co-operative elements.[65]

Interaction of instruments of co-operation and supervision

An example constitutes the complex system of legal and financial control, which avails itself of supervising and of co-operative elements. The traditional instruments of financial correction and issuing directives are flanked by schemes of co-operation. In addition to the duties of granting access to the documents, notification and reporting as the typical means of information exchange, the secondary law on Structural Funds requires common checks involving rights of participation, as well as regular informal meetings and adjustment of interests in bilateral control agreements.

The direction of the financial corrections from the Commission to the Member States predetermines also the orientation of the supervision structures. The Member States on their part can only conduct corrections in relation to the beneficiaries of the Community funding. Something similar applies to the instructions or instruction-like orders issued by the Commission *vis-à-vis* the Member States, which enable the Commission to exert considerable punctual influence. Their character as soft law merely precludes their binding effect, but hardly narrows their guidance potential, given the financial corrections in the background. Both instruments are embedded in an adjustment or dialogue

64 Article 39(2) and (3) of Regulation No 1260/1999 on Structural Funds (fn. 1); Articles 70–74 and 98–102 of the Council Regulation (EC) No 1083/2006 (fn. 1).

65 Schmidt-Aßmann, in this volume, p. 1 et seq.

procedure, which is to facilitate a consensual solution. Only in case of its inconclusiveness, financial correction and instructions make up a preliminary endpoint of the procedure. Hence, they lead to a partly subordinate role of the Member States *vis-à-vis* the Commission, without at the same time presupposing the definite hierarchy of a uniform administration.

Community or Union supervision

These findings might be characteristic of Community or Union supervision in the spheres of Common Administration. Definite hierarchies are alien to the multi-level system of the European Union.[66] However, the Union structure is not opposed to punctual exertion of directive powers in co-operative procedures. On the contrary, the ECT and now the TFEU provide explicitly for directive powers of the Commission in the shape of decisions addressed to the Member States.[67]

The development of a – selective or sectoral – Union supervision, in addition to the infringement procedure under Article 226 ECT (now Article 258 TFEU), is compatible with primary law provisions, even though it is subject to the strict requirements of the Treaty.[68] This is true even considering the almost unanimous opinion that neither a general instruction power of the Commission nor fixed hierarchies between the Commission and the Member States exist.[69] However, with regard to the broad sphere of Structural Funds' administration, the statement that instruction powers of the Commission are exceptional[70] is not generally valid any more.

Standards and limits

The primary law standards to be met by Community or Union supervision are, first of all, the principle of limited powers and the principle of subsidiarity according to Article 5(1) and (2) ECT (now Article 5 TEU).

What has no limiting effect is the so-called principle of organisational and procedural autonomy of the Member States, which represents merely a summary

---

66 On the European Union as a multi-level system see Benz, in: Schmidt-Aßmann/Hoffmann-Riem (eds.), *Strukturen des Europäischen Verwaltungsrechts*, 1999, 45, and the references cited in Schöndorf-Haubold, Strukturfonds (fn. 2), 44 et seq.

67 On the legitimacy of authority in the shape of state-directed decisions within the Community v. Bogdandy/Bast/Arndt, *ZaöRV* 62 (2002), 77 (97); Mager, *EuR* 2001, 661 (esp. 677).

68 Van Rjin, in: Curtin/Heukels (eds.), *Institutional Dynamics of European Integration*, 1994, Vol II, 409 (412 et seq.); Lühmann, *DVBl* 1999, 752 et seq.

69 See Kadelbach, *Allgemeines Verwaltungsrecht* (fn. 27), 110; Scheuing, in Hoffmann-Riem/Schmidt-Aßmann (eds.), *Innovation und Flexibilität des Verwaltungshandelns*, 1994, 298 (334); Sommer, *Verwaltungskooperation* (fn. 30), 508 et seq.; Kahl, *DV* 1996, 341 (360).

70 Scheuing, in: Hoffmann-Riem/Schmidt-Aßmann, *Innovation und Flexibilität* (fn. 69), 289 (335); Pühs, *Der Vollzug von Gemeinschaftsrecht*, 1997, 295.

of the relevant jurisprudence, but has not been anchored in primary law.[71] This principle can neither inhibit passing detailed organisational or procedural regulations of secondary law, such as usual in the sphere of controlling, nor is it opposed to instruction powers by the Commission provided for in secondary law and allowed for by primary law. If such a principle is acknowledged it can in the end reach only as far as is allowed by the principle of limited powers and the principle of subsidiarity.

In contrast, considerations of rule of law ask for an examination of the legally based and really existing hierarchies in certain contexts and, at the same time, for an enhancement of the Member States' authorities oriented at a balanced Common Administration. A transparent Union supervision would be preferable even in respect to the soft-law guidance concepts and open formulations of secondary law quite often found in the context of decentralisation.[72] These might represent flexible instruments for adjustment to the diverse national administrative structures, but they partly hide the real schemes for exerting influence by claiming the existence of not given margins of discretion. Hence, they are rather harmful in terms of transparency and legal certainty.

It is therefore essential to outline, in the first step, a clear division of control powers and, in the second step, to establish an explicit supervision and instruction authority of the Commission leaned on the financial correction schemes, which is to replace the soft guidance instruments that in their actual effects resemble legally binding directives, not least due to their regulation by secondary law. If the effects are practically the same a model that abides by the rule of law has to be given precedence.

In turn, instead of an illusory opening to scopes of Member States' discretion, clear-cut forms of participation must be introduced in shape of concrete evaluation authorities and margins of discretion, which are to be subject to control by the European Courts, but not the Commission.[73] Such margins of discretion, even if concerning just individual issues, would allow for a problem diversification and regulation structure that are not attainable by the currently applied model of decentralisation based on the principle of subsidiarity.[74]

---

71 Gil Ibañez, *The Administrative Supervision and Enforcement of EC law*, 1999, 211 et seq.; different opinion v. Danwitz, *DVBl* 1998, 421 et seq.; Kadelbach, *Allgemeines Verwaltungsrecht* (fn. 27), 110 et seq.; left open in Sommer, *Verwaltungskooperation* (fn. 30), 501 et seq.; Pühs, *Vollzug* (fn. 70), 96, 100. Nehl, *Europäisches Verwaltungsverfahren und Gemeinschafts-verfassung*, 2002, 76, considers the concession of direct controlling authority within the framework of the Structural Funds administration to be "remarkable" from the perspective of the Member States' autonomy.

72 Different opinion by Pühs, *Vollzug* (fn. 70), 298.

73 Similarly Gil Ibañez, *Administrative Supervision* (fn. 71), 211 et seq.

74 The mistrust in the national administrations – which is not diminishing with the increase of decentralisation – seems to be founded in the principle of separation, a principle which remains opposed to a control of Member State actions to implement the Community interest. From the Community perspective, however, real discretion in rule-making could be granted to the Member States in specific areas "without risk", if it were submitted to a European judge;

4. COMMON MODES OF ACTION AND ORGANISATION AS CHARACTERISTICS OF COMMON ADMINISTRATION

4.1. INTRODUCTION

The administration of the European Structural Funds represents, as a complex Common Administration of funding, a basic type of European administration. Its legal regime has provided, by developing characteristic forms of action and organisation, a contribution to the advancement of European administrative law.[75] Of particular interest for a European doctrine on legal instruments are common forms of action characterised by the co-operation of the Community and the Member States. The co-operation within the Composite Administration attains legal organisational framework by purposeful application of committees. The principle of partnership goes even further than the common form of institutionalised co-operation: this principle results in involving regional authorities and social actors in all stages of the procedure, which is safeguarded by organisational and procedural provisions. It represents a basic structural element of the Structural Fund's administration.

4.2. PROGRAMMES AS A COMMON MODE OF ACTION

4.2.1. Introduction

The administration of the Structural Funds is characterised by a variety of actions by the participating administrations and a high procedural complexity. Decisions and negotiation results, such as the plans and programmes, are often composed of single contributions by different actors and can only partly be attributed to the legal instruments provided for by the ECT respectively the TFEU. Nonetheless, these actions exert effects in the relationship between the Union and the Member States. If those effects do have legal relevance, the principle of legality valid also in the Community or Union framework, demands the effects to be defined precisely and the actions to be subjected to a fixed and predictable legal regime.

---

for approaches to overcome the principle of separation see Oliver, in: Heukels/McDonell (eds.), *The Action for Damages in Community Law*, 1997, 285 et seq.; Hofmann, *Rechtsschutz und Haftung im Europäischen Verwaltungsbund*, 2004, 190 et seq.

75 On the need for a more distinctive doctrine of forms of action in European administrative law Schöndorf-Haubold, *Strukturfonds* (fn. 2), 351 et seq.; Röhl, in this volume, p. 415 et seq.; Vogt, in this volume, p. 341 et seq.

The principle of legality asks for clarity, certainty and predictability of the applicable legal regime as well as legally binding power in respect to all actions of the EU organs.[76] Therefore, independent from particular internal or external effects, the rule of law requires that the doctrine on legal instruments results in disciplining not only of the national, but also of the EU legal order.[77] The acting organs are to make a clear decision in favour or against the binding character of their actions by choosing a certain action mode or legal instrument, which would automatically imply the applicability of particular standards.

Common forms of action by the Commission and the Member States, apart from treaties or institutionalised committee procedures preceding a Commission's decision, have so far constituted the exception in the system of legal instruments of the European Community.[78] Anyhow, the Structural Funds' administration contains some actions, which are conducted only in direct co-operation of the Commission and the Member States. For example, the planning phase, which foots on a bilateral dialogue between the Commission and the Member State in question, is concluded when a consensual agreement on a programme has been reached. Hereby, the Commission and the Member State participate in the establishment of the programme and in the final decision. As already mentioned, the programmes as such are to be distinguished from the programme authorisation. Subject to the decision are merely the basic elements of the programmes, first of all, the allocations of commitments. Therefore, their legal classification is to be made separately.[79]

4.2.2. A consensual decision as a co-operative action mode

Since the regulatory effects of the authorisations of the Member States' programmes, which are formal decisions in the sense of Article 249(4) ECT (now Article 288(4) TFEU), are attributed to the Commission alone, only EU law is applicable. The co-operation between the Commission and the respective Member State has been furnished with a legal shape of the strongly consensus-

---

76 On the importance of the principle of law Schmidt-Aßmann, *Ordnungsidee* (fn. 31), 7/28 et seq.; v. Bogdandy, in: *id.*/Bast (eds.), *Europäisches Verfassungsrecht*, 2nd ed. 2009, 13 (36 et seq.): "*Herrschaft des Rechts*" (supremacy of law). Chiti, *Diritto Amministrativo Europeo* (fn. 31), 307 et seq.

77 For German law see Schmidt-Aßmann, *Ordnungsidee* (fn. 31), 6/37; for Community law *ibid.*, 7/48 et seq.; Chiti, *Diritto Amministrativo Europeo* (fn. 31), 156: "Nell'attesa di una sistemazione della materia, necessaria per assicurare alle istituzioni un corretto funzionamento, e per garantiere adeguatamente le situazioni giuridiche di soggetti coinvolti, [...]"; Bast, in: v. Bogandy (ed.), *Europäisches Verfassungsrecht*, 2003, 479 (537): "Die Reform der Handlungsformen bleibt eine wissenschaftliche Daueraufgabe, der eine Renaissance zu wünschen ist". See also Pitschas, in: Hill/Pitschas (eds.), *Europäisches Verwaltungsverfahrensrecht* (fn. 17), 301 et seq.

78 Oliver, in: Heukels/McDonnell, *Action for Damages* (fn. 74), 285 (303).

79 *Supra* 3.2.2.

oriented procedure provided by the Regulation on Structural Funds.[80] Due to the requirement of approval by the Member States the co-operation is also reflected in the outcome of the procedure. The final result, however, is *not* a *common decision* by the Commission and the Member State.[81]

Nevertheless, these decisions requiring approval represent a further form of legally shaped administrative co-operation in the Composite Administration. Even though the result can be qualified only as a one-sided action, the outlay of the procedure leading to this result is based on co-operation.

This action mode does justice to the principle of legality, within the scope of the Composite administration, by avoiding legal uncertainty in respect to liability and choice of legal order. At the same time, it brings about a gain in efficiency, by ensuring the later implementation by and within the Member States due to the assent given by the Member State in the procedure.[82]

4.2.3. Plans and programmes between legally binding and informal administrative actions

Like in the case of authorisation decisions, the same questions on the choice of legal instrument, non-/binding character, authorship and legal regime arises in respect to the programmes, i.e. the Community Support Frameworks, Operational Programmes and Single Programming Documents. The fact that the authorisation decision and the programme as such are distinguished shows that the regulatory effect of the programmes is weaker than of the formal decisions by the Commission.

The programmes do not constitute a defined legal instrument of EU law, but rather a non-binding atypical form of action characterised by a co-operative set-up procedure. The plans do not exert obligatory effects in terms of a command to implement these plans. However, they provide for a frame for the later implementation measures, an orderly implementation of which requires compliance with the particular programme. Only the authorisation decision of the Commission following the planning has a legally binding power.

---

80 Comijs, *Europese structuurfondsen* (fn. 2), 153 ("communautair genormeerd onderhandelings-proces"). On the legal definition of consensual administration procedures in German law see Schmidt-Aßmann, *Ordnungsidee* (fn. 31), 6/113; Schultze-Fielitz, *DVBl* 1994, 657 (660 et seq.).

81 The approval of the programmes within the structural policy is considered an effective means of supervision of the Commission by Priebe, in: Schmidt (ed.), *Öffentliches Wirtschaftsrecht II*, §11 mn. 102. By the need for approval and by the mandatory negotiation procedure, this supervision is compensated to a large extent by an aspect of cooperation; see also Mögele, in: Dauses, *Handbuch des Europäischen Wirtschaftsrechts* (fn. 13), G mn. 179.

82 Pointing out the "peacemaking objectives and effects of cooperation, consensus and acceptance" Schoch, in: Hoffmann-Riem/Schmidt-Aßmann, *Innovation und Flexibilität* (fn. 69), 199 (231). This finding also applies to EC law.

The programmes represent a specific form of action sui generis with a concept character.[83] They provide the EU and the Member Sates, in situations when complex decisions are needed, with intermediate, non-mandatory concretisations of objectives on an abstract-concrete mid-level. These concretisations require, in turn, implementation by schemes provided for in the programme. In the programmes, the Commission and the Member State concerned specify jointly how the EU objective of economic and social cohesion is to be reached in a certain region. Due to the open formulation of the secondary law provisions, the Commission and the Member States can take a broad scope of actions. The programming proceeds as a dynamic set of negotiations open to development and with constant participation of the relevant actors. Such procedure serves the co-ordination of the targeted administration of funding by the Commission and the Member States.

Distinctive elements of this form of action, lacking a basis in primary law, thus, are its future orientation, attribution to concrete measures, affinity to procedure and openness to development, co-operation and non-binding character.[84]

4.3. THE PRINCIPLE OF PARTNERSHIP AND MONITORING COMMITTEES

A traditional instrument of multilateral institutional administrative co-operation constitute committees at the EU level manned by the Member States. The Commission makes use of them not only when passing the implementing legislation,[85] but also during the implementation of EU law itself. In addition, the law on Structural Funds provides also for the so-called partnership as a further form of organised administrative co-operation: the principle of partnership represents a sub-constitutional organisational standard, leading to extensive vertical co-operation between the Commission and the national and, in particular, regional authorities, in which private and social partners are also involved.[86]

---

83 On the concept of programmes as a form of action to be differentiated from planning see Müller, *Konzeptbezogenes Verwaltungshandeln*, 1992, esp. 255 et seq.; on the idea of concept in European administrative law Koch, *Arbeitsebenen der EU*, 2003, 62.

84 Programmes are also used in other areas of European administration with completely different objectives; see the examples in Rengeling, in: *Festschrift für W. Hoppe*, 2000, 883 (887); Kadelbach, *ibid.*, 879 (898 et seq., 911 about co-operative forms of planning). On the necessity of a European planning law see Wahl, *ibid.*, 913 et seq.

85 On this Möllers, in: Schmidt-Aßmann/Schöndorf-Haubold (eds.), *Der Europaïsche Verwaltungsverbund*, 2005, p. 293 et seq.

86 On partnership as a principle *supra* at 2.2.3 and, more in detail and with further references, Schöndorf-Haubold, *Strukturfonds* (fn. 2), 437 et seq.

The principle of partnership has received an organisational specification with the creation of so-called monitoring committees at the respective programme level. The monitoring committees are institutionalised bodies in which all "partners" in the sense of the principle are represented. The main task of these committees is the constant revision of the implementation of a programme, in order to ensure the greatest efficiency possible.[87]

The administrative co-operation in the EU, which is in general limited to the Commission and the Member States, has not only been extended, by the establishment of the monitoring committees, vertically and horizontally, but in addition, also institutionalised de-centrally.[88] Vertically, it has been extended to the sub-national, i.e. regional and local level. Horizontally, there is at least the facultative option of including economic and social partners or other relevant institutions.[89] The de-central institutionalisation takes place at the respective national or sub-national programme level. Therefore, the monitoring committees differ from the comitology committees, which are attached to the Commission, not only in terms of their tasks but also in terms of their structure for the latter distinguish themselves by the participation of all Member States and by a scope of activity that can be described as rather preventive.

The monitoring committees are established on the national level and are subject to the law of the respective Member State. Nevertheless, the Commission is represented by an employee of the responsible directorate-general. However, according to the Regulation on Structural Funds, this representative neither holds the presidency, nor does he have a voting right. The participation of the Commission is of a purely consultative nature. The monitoring committees, hence, cannot be considered as EU institutions despite the participation of the Commission.[90]

On the one hand, the participation of the Commission in the monitoring committees at the national and regional level makes it possible that the EU interest is articulated and exercised directly at these levels, without the necessity of a central intermediary. On the other hand, the Commission gains this way a direct insight into the administrations of the Member States, first through the

---

87 See Article 35 of the Regulation on Structural Funds (fn. 1); Article 63 of the Council Regulation (EC) No 1083/2006 (fn. 1). For details about the composition, the tasks and functions of the monitoring committees see Schöndorf-Haubold, *Strukturfonds* (fn. 2), 450 et seq.

88 Priebe, in: *Gedächtnisschrift Grabitz* (fn. 15), 551 (567); Lang/Schwab/Wollmann, *VerwArch* 91 (2000), 100 et seq.

89 According to Tömmel, *PVS Sonderheft 23/1992*, 185 (191) "mixed" committees.

90 This had also been a concern of the reform; cf. the 38th recital of Regulation No 1260/1999 on Structural Funds (fn. 1). During the past programming period, the authorities of the individual members of the monitoring committees had been defined less clearly, which had led to difficulties, on the one hand, in classifying these bodies and, on the other hand, in answering the emerging questions of legal protection; see Comijs, *Europese structuurfondsen* (fn. 2), 139 et seq., 261 et seq. as well as *infra* fn. 92.

evaluation of the interventions, which is the main task of the monitoring committees, and second, through the direct participation of the responsible national authorities in the committees. Hereby, the fulfilment of other tasks by the Commission in the sphere of evaluation and control is also facilitated.[91]

In the previous programming periods, the Commission also had a voting right. This mixed representation caused problems concerning the attribution of the decisions taken by the monitoring committees.[92] Therefore, Regulation No 1260/1999 on Structural Funds specifies explicitly that the monitoring committees shall act under the authority and within the jurisdiction of the Member States (Article 35(1), third subparagraph of the Regulation on Structural Funds). The representative of the Commission participates in the committee meetings only as a consultant.[93] The problem of the attribution of action was thereby solved in favour of the Member States.[94]

Similar difficulties followed from the fact that all adjustments and amendments adopted by the monitoring committees under the previous Regulations on Structural Funds had to be confirmed by the Commission, which also complicated their attribution to one of the legal systems (national or European). A confirmation of a decision made by a monitoring committee is no longer required, or a substantive decision amending the programme is made either by the administrative authority or the Commission respectively. On the other hand, the fact that, according to the wording of the Regulation on Structural Funds, amending decisions by the Commission require the approval of the monitoring committee[95] is without prejudice to the clear attribution of these Commission decisions to the EU level.

---

91 On the funtion of the Commission's participation see also Bernard, *Multilevel Governance in the European Union*, 2002, 122 et seq.

92 According to an oral information in the Commission, both the European Court and a national court of the Member State declared themselves as not competent to find on the appeal against a decision of the monitoring committee after having qualified the decision as national resp. community decision. On these problems of legal protection (which are also known in the jurisdiction of the European Court of Justice, see Case C-97/91, ECR 1992, I-06313 ff. – Borelli), see also Jans/de Lange/Prechal/Wid-dershoven, *Europees bestuursrecht* (fn. 63), 109; Comijs, *Europeese structuurfondsen* (fn. 2), 128 et seq., esp. 139 et seq., 261 et seq.; *id.*, in: Vervaele, *Compliance and Enforcement* (fn. 61), 301 (313 et seq.); Nehl, *Europäisches Verwaltungsverfahren* (fn. 71), 432 et seq. They cannot be solved by the traditional principle of separation. On the principle of transparency of binding legal consequences, Schmidt-Aßmann, in: *Festschrift für Häberle* (fn. 30), 395 (407); on the importance of clarity on the recourse to courts see J. Hofmann, *Rechtsschutz und Haftung* (fn. 74), 296; *id.*, in this volume, p. 447 et seq.

93 According to the old Regulations, the representative of the Commission in the monitoring committees also had a voting right: Article 25(3) of the Implementing Regulation (EEC) No 4253/88 as amended by Regulation (EEC) 2982/93.

94 Questions concerning attribution as problems of partnership are also mentioned by Bernard, *Multilevel Governance* (fn. 91), 100; generally Hofmann, *Rechtsschutz und Haftung* (fn. 74); *id.*, in this volume, p. 447 et seq.

95 Article 34(3) of Regulation No 1260/1999 on Structural Funds (fn. 1).

5. COMMON ADMINISTRATION: A CONCLUSION

Common Administration, such as found in the sphere of Structural Funds, represents an administration model for the European Composite Administration. By including all levels of administration in the European administrative area, national borders have been increasingly vanishing. Thereby, Common Administration has more and more become a part of the complex Composite Administration.

It is an efficient model for the administration in the European multi-level system. Manifold forms of co-operation between various actors mark the different stages of the procedures. The co-operational network between the Community and the Member States pertains to planning, financing and administration: common programming, additionality and co-financing are the primary pillars of the action under the Structural Funds. Even the implementation of the programmes by national and sub-national authorities is influenced by the Commission that avails itself of numerous binding and non-binding regulatory instruments and schemes of substantive, procedural and organisational nature. The Commission's capacity to exert guidance action results, not last, from its budget responsibility and implies supervisory authority without presupposing hierarchies in the traditional sense of the word.

Unlike the early, overcome forms of co-operation, the Common Administration under Structural Funds does not foot primarily on a co-operation arising out of informal, practical needs, but is to a great extent preset through procedural and organisational rules. Even though flexible and open to the different legal systems of the Member States, the law on the administration of the Structural Funds constitutes an extensive codification of administrative rules valid in this sphere, especially in terms of procedure and organisation, which is best proven by the provisions on common planning, guidance and evaluation, the regime of data exchange and the harmonised control. Another typical feature of the Common Administration is the development of forms of joint action and organisation, which will expectedly lead to the emergence of further common legal instruments, apart from the contract.

The Common Administration model has acquired additional support from the principle of partnership that has expanded the co-operation especially to the sub-national levels and has turned these into co-operation partners of the European Union. As a secondary legal organisational standard under secondary law, this principle roots in the primary legal principles of subsidiarity and co-operation. It is the latter principles that require rather than prohibit Common Administration, which is a model between direct EU administration and indirect administration by the Member States. Hence, in EU law, there is no general prohibition of a mixed administration spanning various levels, comparable to that in German law.

Barriers to Common Administration result from the primary legal standards of limited powers, subsidiarity and proportionality, which must be obeyed by in all actions of the EU, but which are not opposed to Common Administration in general. The principle of rule of law subjects the administrative action in the EU context to further requirements such as the establishment of a strict doctrine on legal instruments and a clear accountability for actions within the administrative co-operation. This is a challenge to be coped with by the European Administrative Law also in future.

III. INFORMATION COOPERATION PROCEDURES – WITH EUROPEAN ENVIRONMENTAL LAW SERVING AS AN ILLUSTRATION*

Julia Sommer

1. INTRODUCTION

The Constitution for the European Union[1] provided for a proper section on administrative cooperation, stating: "1. Effective implementation of Union law by the Member States, which is essential for the proper functioning of the Union, shall be regarded as a matter of common interest. 2. The Union may support the efforts of Member States to improve their administrative capacity to implement Union law. Such action may include facilitating the exchange of information and of civil servants as well as supporting training schemes. No Member State shall be obliged to avail itself of such support. European laws shall establish the necessary measures to this end, excluding any harmonisation of the laws and regulations of the Member States".[2]

The Constitution was the first explicit mention of the necessity of the exchange of information between the administrations and indicates that administrative cooperation is closely intertwined with the implementation of the law of the European Union. Nonetheless, an array of different types of administrative cooperation has long been part of the daily routine of the

* Note: this contribution is based on the authors phd research which was published as Julia Sommer, Verwaltungskooperation am Beispiel administrativer informationsverfahren im Europäischen Umweltrecht, Springer, Berlin 2003. A first version of this contribution has published (in German) in Eberhard Schmidt-Aßmann and Bettina Schöndorf-Haubold, Der Europäische Verwaltungsverband, Mohr Siebeck, 2005, p. 57–85. The contribution was not updated as to the references and the research since then.

1 Treaty establishing a Constitution for Europe (OJ EU 2004 No. C 310, p. 1), not ratified. In general on the Constitution see Oppermann, DVBl. 2003, 1165 et seq. and 1234 et seq., Ruffert, EuR 2004, 166 et seq.; Wuermeling, EuR 2004, 217 et seq. and Einem, EuR 2004, 202 et seq.

2 Title III, Chapter V, Section 7 "Administrative Cooperation", Art. III-285 (1) and (2).

European and national administrations.[3] The Article cited encompasses only measures of the European Union supporting the Member States in the implementation of European law but does not prohibit the enactment of greater and more far-reaching cooperation and information obligations on the basis of other provisions of the Treaty establishing the European Community (in the following "EC Treaty" or "EC") in the future.[4]

For lack of a genuine administrative basis, over the years, the European Community has created very subtle steering methods by means of a host of different procedures of administrative cooperation and, in particular, information cooperation, thus replacing the non existing power to advise the administrations of the Member States like a supervising authority.[5] Nevertheless, the implementation of norms is to some extent more like a continuing "negotiation and communication procedure" between the authorities involved, even within administration structures which provide for supervising powers, with the subordinate authority bringing its advanced knowledge of the facts to bear.[6] In this way, the implementation of legal norms is always dependant on the cooperation and the exchange of information by the authorities involved.

Owing to the formal separation of the administrations of the Member States and of the European Community, the authorities depend more than ever upon cooperation when it comes to the implementation of European law. *Schmidt-Aßmann* speaks in this context about the "separation principle" which must be supplemented by the "principle of cooperation" and the "principle of functional differentiation".[7] The creation of a joint European administrative area necessarily depends on the integration of information from all or, as the case may be, at least a number of Member States. The European Administration first of all is an "administration of information".[8] In the light of so called transnational administrative orders (*transnationaler Verwaltungsakt*)[9] which are also legally

---

3 For an overview of the cooperation structures see Schmidt-Aßmann, in: *Festschrift für Peter Häberle*, 2004, 395 et seq. Schmidt-Aßmann differentiates the categories "(simple) cooperation", "vertically organised decision making", "horizontally organised decision making" and "institutionalised cooperation" (*ibid.*, 397 et seq.). See also his Introduction: European Composite Administration (*Verwaltungsverbund*) and the role of European Administrative Law, in this vol., p. 1 et seq. and his contribution in: *Festschrift für Helmut Steinberger*, 2002, 1375 (1380).

4 In this sense explicitly Article III-285(3) of the Constitution (fn. 1).

5 More in detail: Sommer, *Verwaltungskooperation am Beispiel administrativer Informationsverfahren im Europäischen Umweltrecht*, 2003, 508 et seq. with further references.

6 Compare Garlichs, *Politikformulierung und Implementation im föderativen Staat*, in: Mayntz, *Implementation politischer Programme*, 1980, 20 (25 et seq.); see in more detail in: Sommer (fn. 5), 48 et seq.

7 Schmidt-Aßmann, in: FS Häberle (fn. 3), 395 (397 and 407 et seq.); see also his contribution in this vol., p. 1 et seq.

8 Schmidt-Aßmann in: FS Steinberger (fn. 3), 1375 (1391).

9 For the concept of the transnational administrative order see Schmidt-Aßmann, DVBl. 1993, 924 (935 et seq.); in more detail Neßler, *Europäisches Richtlinienrecht wandelt deutsches*

effective in the other Member States, irrespective of which Member State has enacted them, it is not only the European Union, but also the Member States, that depends on information cooperation procedures. The principle of the "control of the country of origin" according to which the Member State is in charge of the control of the legal conformity of a product on whose territory it has been produced, requires an atmosphere of mutual trust because all other Member States must be able to rely on such controls. Trust, again, relies upon open communication – communication is the minimal content of each cooperation and at the same time enhances the willingness to cooperate.[10]

2. A SYSTEMATIC INVENTORY OF INFORMATION COOPERATION PROCEDURES

2.1. INTRODUCTION

Administrative cooperation is a collective noun for various forms of interaction. One important part is the exchange of information. Information cooperation consists of very diverse elements. These elements are currently used in the legislation of the European Community and are paraphrased by exceedingly varied notions without a consistent systematic use. Moreover, the legal implications of these provisions cannot always be discerned due to the usage of ever new and unspecific terms.[11] A consistent wording and usage of well defined legal terms would help to discern the legal content of the information obligations in legislation of the European Community. Legal terms laying down details on the trigger of the obligation, the timeline, the extent and the medium to be used are crucial for legal certainty, and thus promote the implementation of Community law. When they exist, clearly specified legal terms are judiciable, making both law-making and judicial control easier and pointing to possible

Verwaltungsrecht, 1994, 5 et seq.; the *same*, NVwZ 1995, 863 et seq.; see also Ruffert, DV 2001, 453 et seq.

10 Storm, Report of the working group "Begriffe 'Information', 'Konsultation', 'Verhandlung', 'Kooperation', 'Abstimmung'" in: Bothe/Prieur/Ress, *Rechtsfragen grenzüberschreitender Umweltbelastungen*, 1984, 279 (282); Bohnet/Frey, *Ist Reden Silber und Schweigen Gold? Eine ökonomische Analyse, Zeitschrift für Wirtschafts- und Sozialwissenschaften 1995*, 169 et seq. Also Schmidt-Aßmann, *Verwaltungskooperation und Verwaltungskooperationsrecht in der Europäischen Gemeinschaft, EuR 1996*, 270 (290). See the same, *Strukturen des Europäischen Verwaltungsrechts: Einleitende Problemskizze*, in: Schmidt-Aßmann/Hoffmann-Riem, *Strukturen des Europäischen Verwaltungsrechts*, 1999, 9 (19 et seq.).

11 Examples are Article 9 and 10 of Regulation (EC) No. 850/2004 of 29 April 2004 on persistent organic pollutants (OJ EU 2004 No. L 158, p. 7), mentioning a "close cooperation" and the "facilitation" of the exchange of information. For an amusing description of the technique of the European Union in drafting legal acts see Walter, *Entwurf einer Richtlinie zur sprachlichen Gestaltung europarechtlicher Texte*, NJW 2004, 582 et seq.

means and methods of regulating a situation.[12] Ascribing certain administrative processes to certain key words gives an abstraction and generalisation which is, according to *Schmidt-Aßmann*, the memory capacity of administrative law.[13]

From a *de lege ferenda* perspective, the Community could enact standards for the different types of communication procedures in the sense of a catalogue of potential procedural components with detailed procedural provisions from which the legislature may choose when enacting information procedures, and to which the executive branch may refer when implementing information procedures. Such a standards catalogue could be enacted on the basis of Article 284 EC as an internal framework decision, in a similar way to Council Decision 1999/468/EC on the types of committee procedures to be used in European law-making.[14] An internally binding framework decision would leave enough leeway for testing new procedures and allow for variations according to the necessities of the case in question.[15] In line with this, the European Convention provided that the framework and the further conditions for the collection of information and the carrying out of checks by the Commission shall be set forth in a European regulation or decision.[16] Moreover, the Commission, the European Parliament and the Council have now enacted an Interinstitutional Agreement on better law-making, according to which the European Parliament and the Council undertake to adopt all suitable measures in order to prevent inaccuracies and inconsistencies.[17]

When standardising the components of information cooperation, one may distinguish between the main categories of *duties to collect information*, i.e. information procurement obligations and *communication procedures*, i.e. where information is passed on to another entity. The structure of the latter can be horizontal, i.e. between the Member States of the European Community, or vertical, i.e. between a Member State and an organ of the European Community. There is also a star-shaped structure of information exchange. This is the case when the Community forwards information simultaneously to all Member States.

---

12 Compare Schmidt-Aßmann, DVBl. 1989, 533 et seq.; the same, in: *Festschrift für Peter Lerche*, 1993, 513 et seq. and the same, in: FS Häberle (fn. 3). Schmidt-Aßmann hints at the importance of tying a particular form of action to a particular legal consequence in order to be able to steer legal provisions and thus also the activity of administrations. As to the systematic standardisation in administrative law v. Danwitz, in: Schmidt-Aßmann/Hoffmann-Riem, *Strukturen des Europäischen Verwaltungsrechts* (fn. 10), 171 et seq., as well as Hoffmann-Riem, *ibid.*, (fn. 10), 317 et seq.

13 Schmidt-Aßmann, DV 1994, 137 (139). See also the *same* in: FS Häberle (fn. 3), 395 (404 et seq.).

14 Decision 1999/468/EC laying down the procedure for the exercise of implementing powers conferred on the Commission (OJ EC 1999 No. L 184, p. 23).

15 For a more detailed analysis see in: Sommer, *Verwaltungskooperation* (fn. 5), 82 et seq. with further references.

16 Article III-428 of the European Convention (fn. 1).

17 Interinstitutional Agreement of the European Parliament, the Council and the Commission (OJ EU 2003 No. C 321, p. 1), paragraph 31.

2.2. COMMUNICATION PROCEDURES

Communication procedures consist, first, of the duty to *provide information upon a specific request*, a reactive information procedure concerning the inquiry on single events. Second, the proactive *notification* procedures belong to this category. They are triggered through a certain event upon which the obliged administration or person must pass on the respective information to another person or authority. One may say that notification procedures in their most ancient form are warnings in emergency cases between neighbouring countries, which were part of public international law from an early date. Within the European Community, warning obligations are now being outnumbered by the numerous notification obligations about statutory provisions that transform Community law into national law or that might be considered an obstacle to the freedom of the movement of goods and services, as well as notification obligations in the framework of registration and permission procedures for products and installations. The more comprehensive *reporting duties* covering a longer time span also belong to the communication procedures. A fourth category is *consultation duties* implying a bilateral or multilateral exchange of information to be used for problem solving. Last but not least, the obligation on a state to passively endure an *inspection* by another authority on its territory also belongs to those procedures of passing on information by allowing someone else to collect the information.

The duty to provide *information upon request* on a single event is the least intrusive and least burdensome form of an information duty. The trigger of the more proactive *notification duty*, by contrast, lies within the sphere of responsibility and (potential) knowledge of the person subject to the obligation. Sometimes, content and form of the information to be provided in a notification are precisely regulated and the non-fulfilment of such duty implies legal consequences. This is often the case in international treaties involving the transfer of dangerous goods or the occurrence of an accident with repercussions on other states. Consequently, the respective provisions of the European Community transposing these treaty provisions into European law also contain these formal procedures.

There are administrative notification obligations that are triggered by a prior notification to third parties – mostly the population of the respective state – and therefore shall be called *accessory notification duties*. They can be accessory in terms of time and/or extent, i.e. the other state or authority must be notified at the same time or shortly after the population of the state incurring the notification obligation has been informed and the content of the communication must encompass at least the information that has been forwarded to its own population. For example, the *IPPC Directive* provides that permission applications for the installations covered by the directive shall be submitted to the neighbouring states at the same time they are submitted to the state's own population if the operation of an installation is likely to have significant negative effects on the environment of another Member State.[18]

The Community constantly extends the information obligations of the Member States *vis-à-vis* the public and, thus, indirectly also the accessory information obligations between the Member States.[19] In the context of such information access rights of the public, one could argue that the Member States could, on the basis of Article 10 EC, always refer to the information access rights having been conferred on their own populations *vis-à-vis* other Member States, e.g. under *Directive 90/313/EC on the freedom of access to information on the environment* (now under Directive 2003/4/EC), even without a special information right conferred on the respective Member State in the inter-state relationship, thus demanding equal treatment with their own population.[20] Although the directive is not designed to empower other Member States, the latter could in fact make use of one of its citizens in order to request the respective information – a procedure which is not only cumbersome but also has the touch of unlawful spying on another Member State. Even if such an accessory information access right of the Member States is granted, this would not make special administrative information rights and procedures superfluous. Inter-administrative information procedures are generally less formal and faster than the public's rights of access to information, with the requesting Member State bearing no costs in relation to this. Moreover, in relation to another Member State, there are often fewer possibilities of denying access to information of another Member State for secrecy reasons because the secrecy interest can partly be taken due account of in the confidentiality obligation of the other Member State.

---

18 Article 17(1) of Directive 96/61/EC of 24 September 1996 concerning integrated pollution prevention and control (OJ EC 1996 No. L 257, p. 26).

19 E.g. by Directive 2003/35/EC of 26 May 2003 providing for public participation in respect of the drawing up of certain plans and programmes relating to the environment (OJ EU 2003 No. L 156, p. 17), as well as by Directive 2003/4 /EC of 28 January 2003 on public access to environmental information and repealing Council Directive 90/313 (OJ EU 2003 No. L 41, p. 26). Before these directives by Directive 90/313/EEC of 7 June 1990 on the freedom of access to information on the environment (OJ EC 1990 No. L 158, p. 56). The extension of the information and participation rights of the public under Directive 2003/35/EC, again, lead to an extension of the accessory information rights of the IPPC Directive (Directive 96/61/EC, see *supra*), with Directive 2003/35/EC now providing, *inter alia*, in Article 15 that the competent authority shall inform the public according to a procedure which is further set forth in the directive and shall provide access to certain, further named information. Consequently, pursuant to Article 17(1) of the IPPC Directive, a Member State must now provide the other Member States at the same time with the same information. See also in general with regard to the access rights of the public to information on the basis of EC law Nowak, DVBl. 2004, 272 et seq., as well as with regard to an array of issues Kloepfer, *Informationsrecht 2002*.

20 The nationality of those requiring access to information is disregarded under Directive 90/313/EC, thus empowering also the nationals of other Member States to request access to information (compare *Röger*, UIG, Commentary, 1995 §4, annotation 7).

More recently, traditional obligations to provide information upon request or under notification duties have often been made superfluous or have been replaced by *information systems* using electronic data storage and access tools.[21] Information on specific cases is often fed into such systems, which may be accessed online by the Commission, other Member States or even particular corporate or public stakeholders. Increasingly, the Commission feeds relevant information on to the internet, accessible for anybody.

Reporting duties imply a systematic observation covering a longer time period and are more comprehensive than notification duties because they encompass a longer period in time and are often important for monitoring the implementation of European law. Reports are, however, prone to an euphemistic description of the facts whenever administrations have to describe their own activities.[22] In addition, the costs can easily outgrow the benefits of a report. A special directive, *Directive 91/692/EEC standardising and rationalising reports on the implementation of certain Directives relating to the environment* ensures a standardisation of the reporting of the Member States on implementation measures taken by them.[23] In addition, the single directives often contain special reporting obligations.

Inter-administrative *consultation obligations* imply a reciprocal information exchange which is open as to its final result. They have their origin in public international law and often govern neighbouring relationships. They exist where there is a lack of binding sovereign power to decide the problem in question for the parties involved and therefore are often horizontal in structure. In the framework of the European Union, however, the European Commission is often granted a right to join a horizontal consultation procedure, thus enlarging it into a triangle structure.[24] Often, the Commission's task is to ensure that the material

---

21 The new version of the so called Seveso II Directive (Directive 96/82/EC of 9 December 1996 on the control of major-accidents hazards involving dangerous substances, OJ EC 1997 No. L 10, p. 13 as amended by 16 December 2003, OJ EU 2003 No. L 345, p. 97), e.g., explicitly provides for a database in which the data provided by the Member States is stored (Article 19(1a)), whereas the previous version provided for the installation of a not further specified "register and information system" (Article 19(2). For further details see Sommer, *Verwaltungskooperation* (fn. 5), 208 et seq.

22 Haunschild/Opitz, NdsVBl. 1996, 104 et seq. provide for an unmasking description of the administrative reality in this regard.

23 Directive 91/692/EEC of 23 December 1991 (OJ EC 1991 No. L 377, p. 48). The Member States must issue so called sectoral reports to the Commission every three years, covering all pertinent European directives of the respective sector. The reports shall be drawn up on the basis of a questionnaire or outline drafted by the Commission and are to be submitted nine months after the end of the three-year period covered by the report.

24 For a detailed analysis and further references see *Sommer, Verwaltungskooperation* (fn. 4), 136 et seq. Horizontal consultation obligations with a right of the Commission to step in are set forth, *inter alia*, in the Groundwater Directive (Article 17 of Directive 80/68/EEC of 17 December 1979 on the protection of groundwater against pollution caused by certain dangerous substances, OJ EC 1980 No. L 20, p. 43, several times amended). The directive will be repealed by the Water Framework Directive (fn. 27) as of 21 December 2013.

standards of European law are met by the consulting parties when discussing the solution of the problem in question.

When there are gaps, neighbouring States can often resort to the duties and procedures provided by public international law. Consultation obligations are a consistent part of international treaties and are often regulated here in more detail than in the respective European law. Some of the European directives even refer to the "bilateral relationships", i.e. international public law, when it comes to the consultation procedure.[25] Thus, the *Ozone Directive 2002*, for example, provides that as soon as the ozone concentration exceeds the target values provided for in the directive "due largely to precursor emissions in other Member States, the Member States concerned shall cooperate, where appropriate, in drawing up joint plans and programmes in order to attain the target values". The Commission shall support such efforts and shall "develop guidance for implementing this Directive".[26] The setting up of joint plans and programmes implies consultations between the Member States on the basis of the rules that govern their bilateral relationship. This is, as far as the law of the Community does not provide for such rules, public international law. Horizontal consultation obligations, however, seem to be decreasing in the framework of the European Community in favour of either unspecified information systems and networks set up by the respective directives and regulations of the Community, or, alternatively, a more centralised, detailed regulation of the specific topic and the respective dispute resolution procedures.

The parties to a consultation procedure have considerable discretion with regard to the form, the extent and the timeframe of the information exchange implied in consultation procedures. In this sense, the *Water Framework Directive* provides in Article 12 such a broad and – as to its legal obligation – unclear wording that *Reinhardt* called it "the institutionalising of a social counselling therapy".[27] A consultation procedure always implies that the parties must insure that they do not unilaterally produce given facts or *faits accomplis* before the end

---

25 E.g. Article 17 of the IPPC Directive (fn. 18) and Article 7 of the first version of the EIA Directive (Directive 85/337/EEC of 27 June 1985 on the assessment of the effects of certain public and private projects on the environment, OJ EC 1985 No. L 175, p. 40). Comprehensive provisions on the consultation procedure are contained in the EIA-Convention (Convention on Environmental Impact Assessment in a Transboundary Context, Espoo, 25 February 1991, BGBl. II 2002, 1406 [publication including an English version]) and the Convention on the Transboundary Effects of Industrial Accidents, Helsinki, 17 March 1992, BGBl. II 1998, 1527 [publication including an English version]). The new version of the EIA Directive (Directive 97/11/EC, OJ EC 1997 No. L 73, p. 5) contains a proper consultation procedure which shall partly implement provisions of the EIA Convention. The convention, however, still contains more detailed procedural rules than the EIA Directive.

26 Article 8 and Article. 12(1) of Directive 2002/3/EC of 12 February 2002 relating to ozone in ambient air (OJ EC 2002 No. L 67, p. 14).

27 Directive 2000/60/EC of 23 October 2000 establishing a framework for Community action in the field of water policy (OJ EC 2000 No. L 327, p. 1); *Rheinhardt*, DVBl. 2001, 145 (154). The citation reads in German: "*Institutionalizierung sozialpädagogischer Gesprächstherapie*".

of a consultation procedure. This would make the consultation process useless because the information exchanged and the solutions considered within this process could no longer be taken into account. The parties to a consultation procedure must take the information provided by the other party seriously into account.

Community law increasingly provides for *inspections* on the spot. They are few in the key areas of European environmental law but are proliferating in European fisheries law, in the control of state aid, in anti-fraud provisions and in European agricultural law.[28] Inspection rights seriously interfere with territorial sovereignty, and therefore have to meet high standards with regard to their appropriateness and proportionality. Generally, they can only be carried out in those cases where there is a factual basis for suspicion of some wrongdoing. Inspections of the territory can, to a certain extent, be substituted by satellite remote sensing, i.e. the observation of the soil and vegetation with satellites from outer space.[29] Pictures taken by satellite can be very precise. They can also provide a factual basis for carrying out further controls such as in-depth inspections on the spot.

2.3. DUTIES TO COLLECT INFORMATION

"Decisions taken by administrations never are better than the data basis on which they are taken".[30] This underlines the importance of the obligations of the Member States to collect information for an effective administration of the common market.

---

28 Regulated in detail, e.g., in food law by Regulation (EC) No. 882/2004 of 29 April 2004 on official controls performed to ensure the verification of compliance with feed and food law, animal health and animal welfare rules (OJ EU 2004 No. L 165, p. 1). See also Article 20 and Article 21 of Regulation (EC) No. 1/2003 of 16 December 2002 on the implementation of the rules on competition laid down in Articles 81 and 82 of the Treaty (OJ EC 2003 No. L 1, p. 1), which in comparison to its predecessor, Regulation No. 17, contains even more detailed provisions on the inspection procedure of the Commission; Article 2 of Regulation (EC) No. 659/1999 of 22 March 1999 laying down detailed rules for the application of Article 93 of the EC Treaty (OJ EC 1999 No. L 83, p. 1), as well as Regulation (Euratom, EC) No. 2185/96 of 11 November 1996 concerning on-the-spot checks and inspections carried out by the Commission in order to protect the European Communities financial interests against fraud and other irregularities (OJ EC 1996 No. L 292, p. 2). In detail with regard to inspection rights of the European Community David, *Inspektionen im Europäischen Verwaltungsrecht*, 2003 and her Inspections as an instrument of the execution control in the European Composite Administration in this vol., p. 363 et seq.

29 The preparation of the pictures from the raw data of the satellite is very labour-intensive but it is only after processing that this information about imminent natural catastrophes or the usage of agricultural territory, for example, can be recogniszed on the pictures. Often, private firms take over these tasks. In more detail see Sommer, *Verwaltungskooperation* (fn. 5), 662 et seq.

30 Schmidt-Aßmann, in: FS Häberle (fn. 3), 395 (413).

The main type of information procurement obligations are *environmental monitoring* duties. This duty encompasses the obligation to continuously observe and measure the environmental medium and its components such as air, water and soil, in order to gather data on the state of the environment. To ensure the comparability and the objectiveness of the data gained, environmental monitoring duties are often accompanied by the regulation of the methods of measuring, analysing and reporting on the data obtained, which in the following shall be called "informational framework data". Informational framework data counters the problem of an information overload. Such an overload appears when there is a lot of information on a topic but the relevance, validity and the concrete message with regard to the problem in question is not clear, and therefore exceeds the capacity of the recipient to process this information.

In addition to monitoring obligations, *registration and permission procedures* are used for the collection of information. Registration and permission procedures are often used in the context of environmental protection against pollution emanating from products and installations, independent of an actual danger but relating to potentially dangerous activities. As part of the preventive control of danger, the information is to be gathered by companies or individuals in order to enable the administration to control the due implementation of the underlying material obligations. Thus, according to *Schmidt-Aßmann* and *Ladenburger*, they are part of the process of privatising administrative procedures that have formerly been fulfilled entirely by the administration.[31] These preventive information procedures enable the national administration and the Commission to have basic information at hand in case of a concrete danger, in particular in case of an emergency. In the framework of a permission procedure, the obliged individuals are highly motivated to fulfil their information obligations as the permission they seek would not be granted without their rendering all the required information. This mechanism counteracts the tendency to hide information, known as "hidden information" and "prisoners' dilemma" from the economic game theory. Registration and permission procedures are, *inter alia*, set forth in relation to dangerous substances, biotechnology, (dangerous) installations, as well as the transboundary movement of goods. The procedure on the permission of installations was harmonised in 1996 by means of the *IPPC Directive*.[32]

Another important part of the information procurement duties are the supervision or *control duties* of the Member States. Those obligations relate to potential sources of contamination, i.e. the pollutants released by a production facility, in contrast to the environmental monitoring obligations that relate to the

---

31 Schmidt-Aßmann/Ladenburger, *Umweltverfahrensrecht*, in: Rengeling (ed.), *Handbuch zum europäischen und deutschen Umweltrecht (EUDUR)*, instalment 1, 2nd ed. 2003, §18 annotation 31.

32 See fn. 18. In more detail see in: Sommer, *Verwaltungskooperation* (fn. 5), 157 et seq.

potential object of contamination, that is the environmental medium such as soil, water or air. Control obligations have a trust-building function. Within the European internal market, product controls are primarily carried out by the country of origin. In this way, the country of origin also proceeds as a proxy for the other Member States, who must be able to rely upon the quality of these controls. This means that the country of origin bears a particular responsibility *vis-à-vis* the other Member States and the European Community for the investigation of the facts when it comes to the inspection and control of goods that will circulate freely within the European Community. Some of the European directives and regulations, therefore, request that the national control structures are made transparent to the other Member States and the European Community itself. They also lay down legal standards for the quality of the controls, such as frequency, methods and even the required personnel and technical means of the authority that is in charge of the controls.[33] Some of the standards to be applied to controls can also be derived from Article 10 EC Treaty. On the basis of the duty of loyalty which provides that the Member States "shall take all appropriate measures, whether general or particular, to ensure fulfilment of the obligations arising out of this Treaty [...]", the Member States first have to set up control systems.[34] Furthermore, they must regulate the frequency and the modalities of the controls, the supervision of the authority in charge of controls, as well as the necessity of drafting a report after the controls have been carried out.[35]

Under certain circumstances – mostly when the Community could administer the respective European law by itself, such as in the areas of third country commerce or of fraud protection with regard to the Community funds – the European Commission is allowed to order that specific examinations be carried out by the authorities of the Member States.[36] The competition law of the

33 Regulated in a very detailed manner in the Regulation on Food Control No. 882/2004 (fn. 28), Article 4 et seq., which even contains provisions on the financing of the controls (Article 26 et seq.). See also Council Decision 97/101/EC of 27 January 1997 establishing a reciprocal exchange of information and data from networks and individual stations measuring ambient air pollution within the Member States (OJ EC 1997 No. L 35, p. 14), as well as Council Resolution 94/C 179/01 of 16 June 1994 on the development of administrative cooperation in the implementation and enforcement of Community legislation in the internal market (OJ EC 1994 No. C 179, p. 1), in which the Council urges the Member States to inform the Commission about the structure of their respective administrations.

34 See only ECJ Case 50/76 (Amsterdam Bulb/Produktschap voor Siergewassen), ECR 1977, 137 (paragraph 32); Case 49/83 (Luxemburg/Commission), ECR 1984, 2931 (paragraph 20); similarly Case 68/88 (Commission/Greece), ECR 1989, 2965 (paragraph 23); Case 33/76 (Rewe/Landwirtschaftskammer Saarland), ECR 1976, 1989 (paragraph 5).

35 For further references and an analysis of the respective case law see Sommer, *Verwaltungskooperation* (fn. 5), 437 et seq.

36 See, *inter alia*, Article 20(3) of Regulation (EC) No. 2037/2000 of 29 June 2000 on substances that deplete the ozone layer (OJ EC 2000 No. L 244, p. 1): "The competent authorities of the Member States shall carry out the investigations which the Commission considers necessary under this Regulation". Article 40(3) *lit.* b of the Regulation on Food Control No. 882/2004 (fn. 28) provides that the Commission may request the competent authority of the Member

EC is the most important section where such examinations are ordered; Member States must carry out all investigations which the Commission may deem necessary.[37] With regard to product controls, the Member States themselves may even be allowed to request of the Member State in charge that a certain product be examined.[38]

However, the European Commission does not have the power of a supervisory authority with regard to the authorities of the Member States.[39] Nor does the Commission have a general, unwritten power to order a state authority to do what it deems useful. If this power was conferred on the Commission with regard to a specific question, it must be stated explicitly and clearly in the respective legal act. In addition, since the Member States principally enjoy institutional autonomy[40] and have the right, as well as the duty, to implement and administer the provisions of Community law, they have to be left with enough leeway with regard to the establishment of their own administrative structures and procedures, even when implementing Community law.

Community law often obliges the Member States to identify certain areas of importance for environmental protection and to set up plans and programmes called "emergency plans", "recovery plans" or "implementation programs", for example. *Identification duties* – predominantly the identification of environmentally sensitive spots – and *planning duties* imply that Member States must collect and assess the respective environmental data, thereby having a certain discretionary power. These duties afford a comprehensive and correct investigation of the facts and are judiciable mainly with regard to the correct establishment and restatement of the facts.[41] Participation rights help to gather information from all parties concerned and procedural rules compensate for the very broad discretionary power of the authorities. Member States frequently do

---

State of dispatch to intensify relevant official controls. For further examples see in: *Sommer*, Verwaltungskooperation (fn. 5), 181 et seq.

37 Now regulated in Article 22(2) of Regulation (EC) No. 1/2003 (fn. 28).

38 See Article 12(3) of Directive No. 97/68/EC of 16 December 1997 on the approximation of the laws of the Member States relating to measures against the emission of gaseous and particulate pollutants from internal combustion engines to be installed in non-road mobile machinery (OJ EC 1998 No. L 59, p. 1, amended several times).

39 Common understanding, see only Zuleeg, JöR 1971, 3 (42 et seq.); Rengeling, EuR 1974, 216 (231 et seq.); Hatje, *Die gemeinschaftsrechtliche Steuerung der Wirtschaftsverwaltung*, 1998, 156 et seq.; v. Bogdandy, *Rechtsfortbildung mit Art. 5 EG-Vertrag*, in: GS Grabitz, 1995, 17 (24).

40 See only *v. Danwitz*, DVBl. 1998, 421 (429 et seq.); Rengeling, VVDStRL 53, 1994, 202 (231).

41 The European Court of Justice requires such correctness, however without making it an explicit subject of the legal evaluation, see ECJ Case C-384/97 (Commission/Greece), ECR 2000, I-3823 (paragraph 41) and Case C-207/97 (Commission/Belgium), ECR, 1999, I-275 (paragraph 39 et seq.); compare also Joined Cases C-232/95 and C-233/95 (Commission/Greece), ECR 1998, I-3343 et seq. (paragraph 31 et seq.). For the quality requirements as to plans and programmes see in more detail Sommer, *Verwaltungskooperation* (fn. 5), 424 et seq. with an analysis of the respective case law.

not fulfil their planning obligations to the satisfaction of the Commission. Often, plans and programs are not specific enough and are submitted too late. The lack of concreteness, however, is partly due to the instructions given in the pertinent European legal provisions. Nonetheless, it is this lack of specific instructions and the broad discretionary power of the planning authority in particular that is characteristic of identification and planning obligations.

The European Court of Justice has given some guidelines with its series of judgments on Article 7 of the *Water Protection Directive*. As a rule, plans and the more specific programmes must contain a schedule, as well as specific, quantified measures that are part of a coordinated system.[42] Furthermore, the ECJ decided in relation to the waste management plans to be established under *Waste Directive* 75/442/EEC that such plans must contain either a geographic map which shows the exact location of the waste installations or sites, or sufficiently exact criteria in order to be able to determine such locations. However, the permissions granted for such waste installations or sites are not null and void if the respective plans do not conform to such requirements.[43]

With regard to *identification obligations*, the ECJ acknowledges that the Member States wield a discretionary power as to the selection of the most suitable area.[44] However, no other criteria than those which may be derived from the relevant legislative act may be taken into account by the Member States when determining the respective areas.[45] Furthermore, the Member States may not refer to their discretionary powers to change at will the nomination of areas which had been identified as in need of special protection, once these areas have been notified to the European Community, because otherwise the Member States could evade the obligations emanating from the nomination of such areas.[46]

---

42 See ECJ Case C-207/97, *ibid.* and Joined Cases C-232/95 and 233/95, *ibid.*, both relating to the requirement of specifying the objectives in quantitative terms, as well as Case C-255/93 (Commission/France), ECR 1994, I-4949 (paragraph 24 et seq.), in relation to Art. 3 of Directive 85/339/EEC on containers of liquids for human consumption (meanwhile repealed) which had not provided any quantified targets. See ECJ Case C-384/97, *ibid.*, paragraph 40 and Case C-214/96 (Commission/Spain), ECR 1998, I-7661 et seq. (paragraph 27 and 30) with regard to the requirement of a "consistent framework", respectively an "organised and coordinated system"; see also Case C-184/97 (Commission/Germany), ECR 1999, I-7837 (paragraph 56) referring to a "comprehensive and coherent approach".

43 ECJ, Joined Cases C-53/02 and C-217/02 (Commune de Braine-le-Château and Michel Tillieut and Others/Région wallonne), ECR 2004, I-3251, paragraph 35 and 46.

44 ECJ Case C-57/89 ("Leybucht"), ECR 1991, I-883 et seq. (paragraph 20); see also Case C-166/97 (Commission/France), ECR 1999, I-1719 et seq. (paragraph 11 et seq.); compare judgement of the German Federal Administrative Court, BVerwG, NuR 2001, 382 (383).

45 ECJ Case C-371/98 (First Corporate Shipping Ltd.), ECR 2000, I-9235 (paragraph 23 et seq.).

46 ECJ "Leybucht" (fn. 44), *ibid.*

2.4. INFORMAL INFORMATION COOPERATION AND MIXED NATIONAL-EUROPEAN PROCEDURES

A substantial part of the information exchange occurs informally. In particular, it takes place inside *committees* and during the course of other meetings, including those with outside experts, thus internalising external expertise. The expertise of the national civil servants in the committees improves the quality of EC law and its implementation while making the national officers more sensitive to the interests of the Community, while at the same time, however, implying a certain dependence of the Commission on such expertise. The Commission is not vested with the unwritten legal authority to issue directives *vis-à-vis* the civil servants; it has, in particular, no authority to oblige national civil servants to render specific information to the Commission in circumvention of their respective governments. Nonetheless, a trustworthy and open working climate is more important for the exchange of information in such committees than the existence of information duties.[47]

In the form of personalised *networks*, committees help to coordinate numerous actors in situations of insufficient information, building up a generalised trust that, in turn, will reduce the necessity of controls and the related transaction costs.[48] Networks counter the problems of the lack of information and lack of motivation that occur, according to the findings of organisational theory, particularly in hierarchical organisations. Networks can develop a quasi joint administration through the easy and flexible exchange of information and the structures of mutual trust. Network structures, however, are not suited for standard routine tasks.[49]

In the context of *mixed national and European administrative procedures*, the European Community, in particular the Commission, takes over the function of a supervisory authority without having the general status of such an authority,

---

47 In detail *Schmitt v. Sydow*, EuR 1974, 64 et seq.; the *same*, Die Kommission, 1980, 154, 160 et seq.

48 Transaction costs are the costs for economic activities such as the entering into contact with other actors (see in detail Posner, *Economic Analysis of Law*, 1999, 427 et seq.; the concept has been founded by Coase, *The Economic Nature of the Firm*, Economica 4, 1937, 389 et seq.). Information costs are said to be one of the main parts of transaction costs which together amount to around 50–70% of gross national income (see only Richter, *Institutionen ökonomisch analysiert*, 1991, 5 et seq.).

49 Apart from networks within committees, there are also more *ad hoc* and loose forms of information cooperation. Informal bilateral talks and "package meetings" between the Member States and the Commission often precede a formal procedure for breach of the EC Treaty. They support the investigation of the facts. There are also unspecific cooperation duties set forth in European secondary law. Those cooperation duties contain, as a minimum, the exchange of information and may be specified by the European Commission, laying down the procedures to be followed. Training and the exchange of the civil servants of the Member States also foster trust among the administrations of the Member States by generating some understanding of the circumstances and the background of other national authorities.

by regulating questions that would normally be regulated by a superior authority by way of binding orders and administrative directives. The Community compensates the lack of European administrative bodies involved in the collection of data on the level of the Member States, i.e. the lack of a subordinated European bureaucracy by instructing the Member States in detail on the collection, analysis and description of data needed in the form of the above-mentioned here so-called *informational framework data* which are set forth in detail in directives, regulations and decisions.[50]

Mixed inspections, i.e. inspections consisting of representatives of the Commission and civil servants of the respective Member State compensate for a lack of European powers of investigation or – in the case the Commission has or could be conferred the power to investigate – ease the administrative burden of the Commission which is ill-equipped for such tasks. Such inspections are regularly based on investigatory procedures and powers of the participating national authorities.[51] The Community furthermore is informed on the implementation of Community law via *approval procedures* in the context of national administrative procedures and can thus participate in the – national – decision-making. *Interpretation and implementation guidelines*, in fact, allow the Commission to take over the function of a supervisory authority in the guise of so-called "information memos".

Administrative dispute settlement procedures which are embedded in comprehensive information procedures often consist of a series of notification duties and the star-shaped passing on of the information by the Commission to the other Member States.[52] They often exist in connection with transnational administrative orders, i.e. orders having a transboundary effect.[53] All of these procedures are subtle ways of influencing and steering the implementation of Community law within the Member States in the context of vertical and horizontal information cooperation. In the light of the requirement to attribute responsibilities clearly to the authorities involved as elaborated by *Schmidt-*

---

50 The respective examples are manifold. See only the Ozone Directive 2002 (fn. 26) whose declared purpose it is "to ensure that common methods and criteria are used to assess concentrations of ozone and, as appropriate, ozone precursors [...] in ambient air in the Member States" (Article 1 *lit.* b).

51 The most renowned examples include the inspections of competition law, Article 20(5) and Article 22 of Regulation No. 1/2003 (fn. 28).

52 See e.g. Article 10(2) of Regulation (EC) No. 648/2004 of 31 March 2004 on detergents (OJ EU 2004 No. L 104, p. 1). For more examples see Sommer, *Verwaltungskooperation* (fn. 5), 287 et seq. Compare Caspar, DVBl. 2002, 1437 et seq. on the so called multistage administrative order (*mehrstufiger Verwaltungsakt*) implying a "Communitisation" (*Vergemeinschaftung*) of administrative procedures.

53 As to the transnational administrative order see above, fn. 9; with regard to product safety procedures see also Röhl, *Akkreditierung und Zertifisierung im Produktsicherheitsrecht*, 2000 and his Conformity assessment in European Product Safety Law in this vol., p. 205 et seq. See also Schlag, *Grenzüberschreitende Verwaltungsbefugnisse im EG-Binnenmarkt 1998*.

Aßmann (Gebot der Verantwortungsklarheit),[54] such procedures should be analysed with regard to every single administrative act implied.

There is a tendency towards personalised or electronic *information networks* with information procedures, which, despite being comprehensive, are unspecific, partly replacing more specific information obligations contained in former directives and regulations. To some extent, information exchange systems set forth in secondary law are called "information systems" in order to be able to leave the details of the procedure open. The organisation of the flow of information is then often vested with the Commission.[55] Moreover, in line with the new transparency policy and the *Information Access Directive* 90/313/EEC, and 2003/4/EC,[56] participation in such information systems is being extended more and more to so-called stakeholders, i.e. to the industry, persons affected, partly also concerned associations and NGOs, or even to the public as such. In this sense, the *Register and Information System of* the second *Seveso Directive* ("*Seveso II Directive*") developed from the register of major accidents of the first *Seveso Directive,*[57] now provides very broad access for "government departments of the Member States, industry and trade associations, trade unions, non-governmental organisations in the field of the protection of the environment and other international or research organisations working in the field".[58] The information system also contains information on "organisations able to provide advice or relevant information on the occurrence, prevention and mitigation of

---

54 Schmidt-Aßmann, EuR 1996, 270 (296 et seq.); in detail as to the problem of the current cooperation structures against the background of legal protection of the European citizens see Nehl, *Europäisches Verwaltungsverfahren und Gemeinschaftsverfassung, 2002*, as well as Schmidt-Aßmann, in: FS Häberle (fn. 3), 395 (403 et seq.) as to the principles of democracy and the rule of law.

55 See, e.g., the Ozone Directive 2002 (fn. 26) under which the Commission can draft guidelines for the implementation of the directive (Article 12(1)), encompassing the information obligations set forth in the directive, *inter alia*, the duty of the Member States to elaborate joint short-term action plans which cover neighbouring zones in different Member States and which ensure that the neighbouring Member States receive "all appropriate information" (Article 8(2)). When the thresholds set forth in the directive (so called "information threshold" and "alert threshold") are exceeded in areas close to national borders, "information should be provided as soon as possible to the competent authorities in the neighbouring Member States concerned in order to facilitate the provision of information to the public in those States" (Article 8(3)), also constituting an unspecific information obligation in need of further clarification as to the timeline and the content of the information.

56 See fn. 19.

57 Directive 82/501/EEC of 24 June 1982 on the major-accident hazards of certain industrial activities (OJ EC 1982 No. L 230, p. 1). The register will contain a summary of the major accidents which have occurred within the territory of the Member States, including an analysis of the causes of such accidents, experience gained and measures taken (Article 12).

58 Article 19(3) of Directive 96/82/EC (fn. 21). After the amendment of Directive 2003/105/EC (OJ EU 2003 No. L 345, p. 97) the Commission will now set up a database containing the information of the Member States and update the database accordingly. Access to the database, however, is restricted to persons who have been authorised by the Commission or the competent authorities of the Member States (Article 19 (1a *lit.* b) new version of the Seveso II Directive).

major accidents".[59] This enables the creation of an *informal network* between the stakeholders and the authorities in charge of the prevention and remediation of accidents. It remains to be seen to what extent these unspecific information systems are more useful for the exchange of information than specific procedural obligations. During a discussion programme on the management of the internal market, however, some of the national authorities expressed the need for more specific procedural rules for the exchange of information.[60]

Nonetheless, even this unspecific information exchange does not take place outside any legal order. Those procedures are governed by the legal guidelines which can be derived from the duty of loyalty (Article 10 EC Treaty), as well as the general principles of European law, including the principle of subsidiarity and proportionality, and the protection of business secrets and personal data.[61]

3. AN EXCERPT ON THE LEGAL ASPECTS OF INFORMATION COOPERATION

3.1. INTRODUCTION

The instruments of information cooperation raise numerous legal questions of which only a small number can be touched upon in the context of this article. The instruments of administrative cooperation are only auxiliary; they are not an end in themselves. They are used in order to effectively transpose and implement the policies of the Community, in environmental protection or the free movement of goods, for example. Administrations are held responsible for avoiding obstacles to the free movement of goods – such as controls – via the cooperation of the national authorities (see 3.3). The standards for the due implementation of information obligations are not yet entirely clarified (see 3.4). In relation to the legal consequences of a violation of certain information duties, however, there is now a body of case law from the European Court of Justice motivating the Member States to see that such obligations are met (see 3.5).

To begin with, the first question which arises before legal norms are enacted for access to information is whether there is free access to such information within the European Community, as a rule, and whether this freedom is then restricted by legal norms or whether there is, by contrast, no such freedom and a need for special information access rights to be enacted on some sort of a legal basis.

---

59 Article 19 (2 *lit.* d); see also Article 15(3).

60 Report of the Commission to the Council and the European Parliament of 29 January 1996 on cooperation between administrations for enforcement of internal market law – a progress report, COM (96) 20 final, p. 6 (No. 11).

61 See under 3 and 4. For a more detailed analysis and relevant case law and literature see Sommer, *Verwaltungskooperation* (fn. 5), 424 et seq. and 681 et seq.

3.2. THE SOVEREIGNTY OF INFORMATION AND THE LEGAL BASIS FOR INFORMATION DUTIES

There is no special law of administrative cooperation in the sense of an independent legal order. The law of interstate administrative cooperation is part of the existing legal order of the European Community and public international law.

The sovereignty of states, the basic rule of public international law, also sets the legal framework for the collection and the exchange of information. On the basis of the concept of territorial sovereignty, states are vested with a sovereign right with regard to the collection of information, the so called "sovereignty of information"[62] since restrictions upon the independence of states cannot be presumed.[63] Similar to the domestic right of a landlord, the principle of territorial sovereignty prohibits the unauthorised collection of information in the territory of one state for public purposes of either another state or an organ of sovereign power like an international organisation. The Member States of the European Community did not give up their territorial sovereignty when they joined the Community. This may be viewed differently once they can be considered to have become a fully integrated organisation with a single constitution which is, however, for the present not yet the case. The EC is not vested with the right of territorial sovereignty; this remains vested in the Member States. Nor is the EC vested with a so called competence-competence which is the power to decide on the extent of its own legislative, administrative and judicial powers.[64]

The European Community has been vested with enumerative powers but not with a general law-making and acting power that is typical of states. In accordance with the principle of conferred powers, the European institutions may only act within the framework of the powers conferred on them. Therefore, the Community needs a specially conferred power as a legal basis, provided for

62 For an analysis of the literature, in particular as to which acts of investigation and information gathering are prohibited and which may be allowed and respective references see Sommer, *Verwaltungskooperation* (fn. 5), 343 et seq. Some even go so far as to prohibit the mere official presence of civil servants of another State without the consent of the other State (however excluding their presence for private purposes), see Okresek, *Hoheitsakte auf fremdem Staatsgebiet*, ÖzöRV 1985, 325 (343).

63 The so called rule *in dubio mitius* which is based on the *Lotus Ruling* of the Permanent International Court of Justice (Affaire du "Lotus", Judgement No. 9, PCIJ Serie A, No. 10, 1927, 18).

64 See, e.g., Breitenmoser, *Die Europäische Union zwischen Völkerrecht und Staatsrecht*, ZaöRV 1995, 951 (988 et seq.); Constantinesco, L., *Das Recht der Europäischen Gemeinschaften*, Instalment 1 1977, 169; Isensee, *Integrationsziel Europastaat?*, in: Festschrift für Everling, 1995, 567 (577); Kraußer, *Das Prinzip begrenzter Ermächtigung im Gemeinschaftsrecht als Strukturprinzip des EWG-Vertrages*, 1991, 63; Steinberger, *Die Europäische Union im Lichte der Entscheidung des Bundesverfassungsgerichts vom 12. Oktober 1993*, in: Festschrift für Bernhard, 1995, 1313 (1321 et seq.); v. Borries, *Kompetenzveteilung und Kompetenzausübung*, in: EUDUR (fn. 31), Instalment 1 1998, §25, paragraph 10.

in the treaties on the foundation of the European Community, to be empowered to prescribe duties and procedures for the collection and the exchange of information.[65] Although literature implies differently to some extent,[66] the Member States are not subject to implicit all-encompassing and directly applicable information duties, neither on the basis of the duty of loyalty, i.e. the principle of *bona fide* laid down in Art. 10 of the EC Treaty, nor on the basis of Art. 284 EC. To an even lesser extent is there an unwritten, immediately applicable and all encompassing legal duty for the administrations of the Member States to mutually assist each other in all types of questions – in some Member States called "administrative aid (*Amtshilfe*)" – that would imply the duty to collect and exchange information whenever the European Community or another Member State requests so. Those duties must be discerned from the legal provisions of the European Community with regard to the specific information requested, with most information duties having been laid down in the secondary law of the EC, i.e. in directives, regulations and decisions.

There are various provisions in the EC Treaty that can serve as a legal basis for the enactment of duties on information collection and exchange, as, for instance, Articles 284,[67] 285 and 175 EC. Information procedures are an annex to the respective material provisions on the subject.[68] Because of the diverse provisions on the enactment procedure, such as the majorities required, and the unequal requirements for an allowed deviation from those provisions by the Member States, the legal basis needs to be carefully chosen in each single case. Information procedures that are closely tied to the regulation of the material subject, e.g. the water or air pollution regime, must be based on the legal basis governing the respective community policy, such as Article 175 EC for the protection of the environment or Article 95 EC with regard to the free movement of goods in order to prevent the circumvention of the procedural prerequisites laid down in the specific legal basis. This is predominantly the case for notification and permission procedures, as well as identification and planning duties which are closely intertwined with the respective substantive provisions and which cannot be severed from the latter without losing their meaning and comprehensibility.

---

65 For an analysis of the pertinent case law, the literature and respective references see Sommer, *Verwaltungskooperation* (fn. 5), 359 et seq.

66 Cf. Segond, *Ermittlungsbefugnisse der EG-Kommission im Vollzug des Umweltrechts*, in Ladeur/Winter, *Verfassungsprobleme der Europäischen Gemeinschaft*, 1991, 93 (98 et seq., 104 et seq.).

67 In this respect see in particular ECJ Case C-426/93 (Germany/Council) "Business Registers", ECR 1995, 3723 et seq. on using this Article as a legal basis for the enactment of an information collection regulation, Council Regulation No. 2186/93 of 22 July 1993 on Community coordination in drawing up business registers for statistical purposes (OJ 1993 No. L 196, p. 1).

68 Compare in relation to the European Coal and Steel Community ECJ Case 9/61 (Netherlands/High Authority), ECR 1962, 433 (479). In more detail see Sommer, *Verwaltungskooperation* (fn. 5), 384 et seq.

Article 284 EC, on the other hand, is a general provision – a *lex generalis* – that may be taken as legal basis for information duties whenever the information duties do not pursue one of the specially regulated community policies of the EC Treaty. This Article is not a *lex specialis* for all kinds of information cooperation but rather a general norm not obstructing the enactment of information procedures on the basis of special legal norms governing the respective community policy.[69] In particular, it can serve as a legal basis for information duties covering more than one community policy equally. Most of those information duties which cover an array of subjects and purposes at the same time include statistics, which are now covered by Article 285 EC as *lex specialis* having been inserted by the *Treaty of Amsterdam*. Article 284 EC may not be used as a legal basis to enact substantive law, i.e. provisions that go directly or indirectly beyond information duties and procedures. This would mean a circumvention of the more stringent prerequisites for law-making as set forth for the specific community policy in the respective part of the EC Treaty.

Apart from the enactment of information duties in secondary law, on the basis of the case law of the European Court of Justice the duty of loyalty set forth in Article 10 of the EC Treaty already implies some specific information duties.[70] In order to discern specific information duties that are immediately applicable, Article 10 EC needs to be complemented by more concrete provisions of Community law, providing a guideline on the conditions and the extent of the information duty. The duty of loyalty also implies certain quality standards such as completeness, clearness and trueness of the information provided. Without giving any further legal reasoning, the European Court of Justice implicitly assumes those standards when reviewing whether Member States have fulfilled their obligations.[71] In addition, information obligations must be fulfilled within a time limit that is adequate with regard to the problem in question. If the European Commission is involved in the implementation of the information duty, the Commission may set adequate time limits for the compliance of the Member States. The Commission may, however, not create information duties themselves solely on the basis of Article 10 EC. The duty of loyalty neither transforms non-binding acts of the organs of the Community into binding duties nor does it constitute a legal basis for the enactment of secondary law.

---

[69] Compare ECJ Joined Cases 188 through 190/80 (France, Italy and the United Kingdom/ Commission), "Transparency Directive", ECR 1982, 2545 (paragraph 10).

[70] For an analysis of this case law see Sommer, *Verwaltungskooperation* (fn. 5), 393 et seq.

[71] Compare ECJ Case 248/83 (Commission/Germany) "Non discrimination of men and women", ECR 1985, 1459 et seq. (paragraph 38), Case 6/71 (Rheinmühlen/Einfuhr- und Vorratsstelle Getreide), ECR 1971, 823 et seq. (paragraph 8); Case C-435/92 (Association pour la protection des animaux sauvages and others), ECR 1994, I-67 et seq. (paragraph 2); ECJ Case 96/81 (Commission/Netherlands) "Bathing Water Directive", ECR 1982, 1791 (annotation 8); Case 97/81 (Commission/Netherlands) "Drinking Water Directive", ECR 1982, 1819 (annotation 8); Blanquet, L'Article 5 du Traité C.E.E., 1993, 160; Lück, *Die Gemeinschaftstreue als allgemeines Rechtsprinzip im Recht der Europäischen Gemeinschaft*, 1992, 33 et seq.

3.3. ADMINISTRATIVE COOPERATION IN ORDER TO AVOID IMPEDIMENTS TO THE FREE MOVEMENT OF GOODS

The European Court of Justice has derived administrative cooperation duties, in particular horizontal information obligations from Articles 28 and 30 EC Treaty, i.e. the rules on the free movement of goods.[72] The cooperation duties emanate indirectly from the obligation of the Member States not to restrict this freedom disproportionately, as has long been established by the case law of the Court. A measure is, *inter alia*, not proportionate when it can be avoided by the exchange of information between the national authorities. Administrative cooperation in this context is primarily horizontal in nature, i.e. taking place between the Member States with the national authorities exchanging product information and the results of controls. This part of administrative cooperation cannot be sued for directly before the courts; rather, the legal consequence of a denial of such cooperation would be the establishment of a violation of Article 28 EC Treaty.

For instance, administrations must exchange existing documents – i.e. which the State of the exporter has acquired in the context of a registration or permission procedure – instead of forbidding the import of goods for missing documents as long as this information exchange is not unreasonably burdensome. The administrations of the European Member States have to mutually exchange and recognise documents and administrative controls as being equivalent as long as there is no indication that the national standards of protection differ substantially. Thus, the administration of the importing country may not demand from importers that they repeat costly controls that have already been carried out in the country of origin or that they have to provide documents that could be more easily attained by the administration itself.

After a series of judgments on this subject, starting with *De Peijper*[73] over *Denkavit*[74] to *Biologische Producten*,[75] *Holzbearbeitungsmaschinen*,[76] *Brandsma*,[77] *Harpegnies*[78] and *Canal Satélite Digital*,[79] this can now be deemed

---

72 For a detailed analysis and further references see Sommer, *Verwaltungskooperation* (fn. 5), 439 et seq.

73 ECJ Case 104/75, ECR 1976, 613.

74 ECJ Case 251/78, ECR 1979, 3369.

75 ECJ Case 272/80, ECR 1981, 3277. The authorities of the Member States "are not entitled unnecessarily to require technical or chemical analyses or laboratory tests where those analyses and tests have already been carried out in another Member State and their results are available to those authorities, or may at their request be placed at their disposal" (paragraph 14).

76 ECJ Case 188/84, ECR 1986, 419.

77 ECJ Case C-293/94, ECR 1996, I-3159.

78 ECJ Case C-400/96, ECR 1998, I-5121.

79 ECJ Case C-390/99 (Canal Satélite Digital SL/Administración General del Estado and Distribuidora de Televisión Digital SA), ECR 2002, I-607 et seq. (paragraph 36 et seq.); see

to be established case law.[80] Documents on the goods to be imported may only be rejected in the case of material faults, not for minor problems with regard to the form. In addition, the Member States must notify each other whenever they want to change a longstanding administrative practice regarding the importation of goods. Systematic controls of the goods may only be carried out in the case of suspicious facts and all measures must be taken in a timely manner. The authorities must become active and eventually request relevant documents from the authorities of other Member States – they may not passively wait until the documents are presented to them. Defects must be remedied in cooperation with the administration of the other Member States. This is particularly true where there is a legal and institutional framework for the cooperation,[81] in the framework of committees, for example.

3.4. THE IMPLEMENTATION OF INFORMATION OBLIGATIONS AND THE INSTITUTIONS INVOLVED

When considering the implementation of European law one must distinguish between the formal transposition of the norms into national law and its execution during the day-to-day activity of the authorities. The *transposition* of European information duties into national law must be done by a formal legal provision binding beyond the administration in the case that the information duty has a direct or indirect effect on individuals. This legal norm must be at least as concrete as the underlying provision of Community law.[82] If the European provisions contain specific standards for the investigation of the facts, the Member States cannot refer to a general principle in national administrative law requiring that all facts be investigated *ex officio* by the authority in charge, even if this principle is combined with yet more specific, but only internally binding, administrative orders which have no binding effect outside the administration.

With regard to mere inner-administrative duties, however, an inner-administrative order should suffice, since such an order is binding upon the authorities in question. The rulings of the ECJ are not entirely clear in that respect. Often, the court just stresses the fact that rights and duties of individuals have to be foreseeable and actionable.[83] But only the administrations are affected

also ECJ Case C-388/00 and C-429/00 (Radiosistemi Srl/Prefetto di Genova), ECR 2002, I-5845 et seq. (paragraph 45).

80 See now a similar explicit provision in Article 10(1) of the Regulation on Detergents (fn. 52).

81 See ECJ Case 42/82 (Commission/France), ECR 1983, 1013 et seq. with regard to the importation of Italian wine.

82 Similar but without referring to information obligations Rengeling/Gellermann, JbUTR 1996, 1 (21 et seq.). For a detailed analysis with respective references see Sommer, *Verwaltungskooperation* (fn. 5), 480 et seq.

83 ECJ Case C-131/88 (Commission/Germany), ECR 1991, I-825 (paragraph 6); Case C-361/88 (Commission/Germany) "TA Luft", ECR 1991, I-2567 (paragraph 15); Case C-59/89

with regard to mere inner-administrative information duties, so there is no need for a formal legal transposition. A formal legal transposition is necessary when individuals must be enabled to institute judicial proceedings in the case that the authorities infringe upon their rights or impose duties on them. Individuals have, however, no judicial standing with regard to mere inner- or inter-administrative information procedures which have no effect upon them. Community law does not confer upon the individuals the status of an *advocatus populus* overseeing the correct transposition and implementation with regard to inner-administrative information procedures nor does it require the Member States to do so. Other Member States or the Commission who are adversely affected, on the other hand, may institute proceedings before the European Court of Justice for breach of the EC Treaty and its secondary law in the case that those information duties are not transposed or implemented. There is no need for a formal provision of national law in order to institute proceedings with the ECJ whereas the other Member States and the Commission have no standing in the national courts, in any case, when aiming to sue the respective Member State itself. It is, however, not always easy to distinguish mere inner-administrative information duties from those having an effect upon individuals. Respective guidelines can be taken from the judgements *CIA Security*, *Enichem Base* and *Sydhavenens Sten*.[84]

With regard to the implementation, i.e. the real execution of the information duties, there is an array of institutions of the Community involved in them. One should think that the main role lies with the *European Environmental Agency* (EEA).[85] The Agency, however, is only equipped with very narrow powers relating to the management of environmental information.[86] The Agency has been conferred neither law-making nor implementation powers in relation to the information duties of the Member States. In particular, the EEA has so far not been vested with the repeatedly requested powers of inspection. With the

(Commission/Germany) "Air pollution – lead", ECR 1991, I-2607 (paragraph 18); Case C-58/89 (Commission/Germany) "Surface water", ECR 1991, I-4983 (paragraph 13).

84 ECJ Case C-194/94 (CIA Security/Signalson and Securitel), ECR 1996, I-2201 et seq.; Case 380/87 (Enichem Base and others/Commune di Cinisello Balsamo), ECR 1989, 2517 (paragraph 19 et seq.); Case C-209/98 (Sydhavenens Sten & Grus), ECR 2000, I-3805 et seq. (paragraph 96 et seq.).

85 Regulation (EEC) No. 1210/90 of 7 May 1990 on the establishment of the European Environment Agency and the European Environment Information and Observation Network (OJ EC 1990 No. L 120, p. 1, amended by Regulation No. 933/1999 of 29 April 1999, OJ EC 1999 No. L 117, p. 1, as well as by Regulation No. 1641/2003 of 22 July 2003, OJ EU 2003 No. L 245, p. 1).

86 For a more detailed analysis see Sommer, *Verwaltungskooperation* (fn. 5), 519 et seq. with further references. Kahl therefore classifies the Agency as a "consultative type" (JbUTR 1996, 119 et seq., 129). V. Bogdandy calls the EEA an "Information Agency" (in: Schmidt-Aßmann/Hoffmann-Riem, eds., Verwaltungsrecht in der Informationsgesellschaft 2000, 133, 172 et seq.); also Schmidt-Aßmann, in: FS Häberle (fn. 3), 395 (401); similarly Brenner, *Besondere Einrichtungen*, in: Rengeling, EUDUR (fn. 31), §20, annotation. 12 et seq. See also Riedel, in this vol., p. 157 et seq.

revision of the statute in 1999, the Agency can at least participate in the monitoring of the implementation, but only upon the request of the respective Member State.[87] The regulations establishing the Agency neither explicitly nor implicitly delegate decision making powers or other authoritative powers to the Agency. A delegation of such powers cannot be assumed if not stated in the respective founding acts. According to the so called *Meroni* case law of the ECJ, such powers must have been sufficiently explicitly set forth in the respective act.[88] Moreover, discretionary powers may in no case be delegated by the organs of the Community since this would change the responsibility for the decisions taken – the discretionary power which had been vested in the organs of the Community may not be replaced by the discretion of the entity onto which such power had been delegated. This is to prevent the undermining of the decision of the founding treaties of the EC as to which organ may decide which question in which procedure.[89] This is particularly true when third countries participate in the organisation established by the organs of the Community, which is the case with regard to the EEA.[90] A delegation of powers must be clear and may not encompass discretionary powers; the Agency may in no case take discretionary, material decisions.

The Agency must therefore rely on the information that is passed on to it by the Member States voluntarily or on the basis of specific legal provisions. The modalities can be laid down in agreements with the Agency.[91] Therefore, the EEA is more a service institution for the European Union and the Member States than a real administrative authority. The EEA also serves as a contact point between the European Union and third countries or other international organisations and bodies.[92] The main purpose of its activities is the precautionary

87 The EEA shall "advise individual Member States, upon their request [...] on the development, establishment and expansion of their systems for monitoring of environmental measures", however, "provided that such activities do not endanger the fulfilment of the other tasks established by this Article". Moreover, the EEA shall "assist" the Member States with the "monitoring of environmental measures through appropriate support for reporting requirements". This only relates to the implementation of the reporting duties of the Member States in which the EEA may participate setting up the respective questionnaires, helping with the reports of the Member States and disseminating the respective results. The goal of assistance by the EEA is the coordination of the reporting, not the empowerment of the Agency with the right to independently collect information nor to supervise the Member States. See Article 2 No. ii second and third hyphen of Regulation No. 1210/90 as amended by Regulation No. 933/1999 (fn. 85).

88 ECJ Case 9/56 (Meroni/High Authority), ECR 1958, 11 (42).

89 ECJ Case 10/56 (Meroni/High Authority), ECR 1958, 53 (81).

90 When the Agency was founded, Norway, Bulgaria, Island, Liechtenstein, Romania and Turkey participated. Although Bulgaria and Romania have meanwhile joined the EU, the other countries remain third countries.

91 Article 5 of Regulation No. 1210/90 (fn. 85).

92 For instance, the Agency has published the European Pollutant Emission Register (EPER) on the internet together with the Commission showing the emissions of certain industrial installations and the pollution of the air and water (www.eper.ec.europa.eu/eper). The EPER

collection of information. The Agency serves the other organs of the European Community as well as the Member States but cannot enact orders on the basis of a proper discretionary power which would impose obligations on the Member States, individuals or even other organs of the Community.

In line with *March* and *Feldman* it may be assumed that the EEA has been construed as a symbol for the environmental competence of the European Union and the legitimacy of its environmental law-making.[93] Such an institutionalised symbol can develop its own dynamics and emerge into a strong player that can force its "parent organisation" to adopt stricter rules by disseminating information.[94] Whether this will happen with the EEA remains to be seen. As for now, the Agency at least constitutes a forum for a network between the authorities of the Member States and can help establish so called *epistemic communities* – a community of knowledge and belief in times of uncertainty about present and future circumstances – through the analysis and interpretation of the collected environmental data.[95]

The main organ for the management of information within the European Union is still the *European Commission*. This is confirmed by directives and regulations enacted after the establishment of the European Environmental Agency which assign the power to collect, manage and decide with regard to information procedures to the Commission, and not to the EEA.[96] The Agency is barely mentioned there.

---

originates from an obligation of the Commission to publish an inventory on the most important emissions and their sources on the basis of the information provided by the Member States according to Article 15(3) of the IPPC Directive (fn. 18).

93 Feldman/March, *Information and Organisations as Signal and Symbol*, in: March (ed.), *Decisions and Organisations*, 1988, 409 et seq.

94 Cf. Feldman/March, *ibid.*, 421 et seq.

95 For epistemic communities see Hampson/Hart, *Multilateral negotiations: Lessons from Arms Control, Trade and the Environment*, 1995, 349 et seq.

96 See e.g. Article 12 of the Ozone Directive 2002 (fn. 26), according to which the Commission is to develop guidelines with regard to the implementation of the directive and hereby "will" (only) "call upon the expertise available in the Member States, the European Environment Agency and other expert bodies, as appropriate". Article 4(3) of the Decision on monitoring greenhouse gas emissions of 2004 (Decision No. 280/2004/EC of 11 February 2004 concerning a mechanism for monitoring Community greenhouse gas emissions and for implementing the Kyoto Protocol, OJ EU 2004 No. L 49, p. 1) sets forth that the EEA "shall provide assistance to the Commission" with regard to setting up a Community inventory system on greenhouse gases. Furthermore, the Commission shall, according to Directive 2001/81/EC of 23 October 2001 on national emission ceilings for certain atmospheric pollutants (OJ EC 2001 No. L 209, p. 22), establish inventories and projections of the pollutants covered by the directive "assisted by the European Environment Agency" and "in cooperation with the Member States" (Article 7(3)). The Decision on Measuring Ambient Air Pollution of 1997, the Air Quality Directive of 1996 and the Water Framework Directive of 2000 confer the respective implementation powers only on the Commission. The Commission is to revert to the EEA "in order to benefit from the experience acquired by the European Environment Agency" (Article 1(2) in connection with Article 7 of Decision 97/191/EC of 27 January 1997 establishing a reciprocal exchange of information and data from networks and individual stations measuring ambient air pollution within the Member States, OJ EC 1997 No. L 35,

But even the Commission has no general law-making power with regard to the management of information. The Commission often tries to direct the application of Community law by the Member States through so called "communications". Since only the European Court of Justice has the power to bindingly interpret the law of the European Community, those communications are not binding and can be challenged before the Court, which can annul them for lack of a legal basis in the case that the Commission intended to enact a binding directive.[97] The Commission, however, can enact binding rules if it has been conferred relevant regulation and implementation powers by the directive or regulation in question. This is done increasingly explicitly in secondary law in relation to the details of the administrative information procedure.[98] In this way, the *Directive on Trade in Greenhouse Gases* gives the Commission the power to enact guidelines for monitoring and reporting. Subsequently, the Commission issued a decision encompassing 74 pages, containing general standards, as well as details on the measuring methods.[99] The general standards set out the principles of monitoring and reporting, citing subjects like completeness, consistency, transparency, accuracy, cost effectiveness, materiality and faithfulness.

Law making powers as to the implementation of Community law can also be conferred implicitly by assigning the Commission a general competence relating to the implementation of the respective legislative act, as well as by naming the Commission as the body in charge of the organisation of the procedures resulting from the rules of the directive or regulation.[100] In addition, the Commission can request information about Member States on the basis of Article 10 EC Treaty in connection with Article 226 EC[101] and also, to a certain extent, in connection

p. 14), "will call upon as necessary the expertise available in the European Environment Agency" (Article 11 No. 3 of Directive 96/62/EC of 27 September 1996 on ambient air quality assessment, OJ EC 1996 No. L 296, p. 55) or will "take account of recommendations from" a number of actors, *inter alia* the European Environment Agency (Article 15 para. 5 of Directive 2000/60/EC, fn. 27).

97 ECJ Case 74/69 (Hauptzollamt Bremen/Krohn), ECR 1970, 451 (paragraph 9); Case 229/86 (Brother Industries/Commission), ECR 1987, 3757; Case 325/85 (Ireland/Commission), ECR 1987, 5041 (paragraph 17).

98 An explicit power to enact directives relating to the implementation of secondary European law is contained, e.g. in the Ozone Directive 2002 (fn. 26), Art. 12(1), as well as in Art. 14(1) of Directive 2003/87/EC of 13 October 2003 establishing a scheme for greenhouse gas emission allowance trading within the Community and amending Council Directive 96/61/EC (OJ EU 2003 No. L 275, p. 32) and Articles 3(3), 4(2), 5(6) and 8 (3) of Decision No. 280/2004 (fn. 96).

99 Directive 2003/87/EC, *ibid.*, and Commission Decision 2004/156/EC of 29 January 2004 establishing guidelines for the monitoring and reporting of greenhouse gas emissions pursuant to Directive 2003/87/EC (OJ EU 2004 No. L 59, p. 1). Similarly Commission Decision 2005/166/EC of 10 February 2005 (OJ 2005 No. L 55, p. 57), enacted on the basis of Decision No. 280/2004 (*ibid.*).

100 See for a detailed analysis as to the respective competencies of the Commission, Sommer, *Verwaltungskooperation* (fn. 5), 549 et seq.

101 This has been established by the Court in a series of judgments against Greece, ECJ Case 192/84 (Commission/Greece), ECR 1985, 3967 (paragraph 19); Case 240/86 (Commission/Greece), ECR 1988, 1835 (paragraph 26 et seq.); ECJ Case 272/86 (Commission/Greece), ECR

with Article 284 EC. The Commission must act thereby within the boundaries that are drawn by the directive or regulation in question, as well as by the general principles of Community law. Inspection powers conferred on the Commission, are as a rule to be interpreted restrictively, and are to be regarded as supplementary to national procedural law.

Last but not least, on the basis of Article 10 EC Treaty, the European Commission is obliged to share its knowledge with the Member States when they are dependant on this knowledge for the implementation of Community law. This *information assistance obligation* of the Commission has been stated by the ECJ in its *Zwartfeld* ruling.[102]

3.5. INAPPLICABILITY OF PROVISIONS IN CASES OF NON-NOTIFICATION

Self-implementing sanctions like the direct applicability of Community law can only be effective where individuals are affected and could sue the Member States if the latter fail to fulfil their obligations.[103] Mere inner-administrative information procedures with no effect on individuals, however, do not confer an individual a standing before the German administrative courts. With regard to such provisions Member States can only be sued before the ECJ by the Commission or another Member State.

A potential means of punishing the non-notification of norms and measures taken or planned by the Member States is to declare them inapplicable as long as they have not been notified. An example of this is the *Directive on the Notification of Technical Standards.* According to this directive, the Member States must notify the draft for national technical standards and regulations whenever the subject is not harmonised by European secondary law.[104] Detailed stand-still

1988, 4875 (paragraph 30 et seq.); ECJ Case C-35/88 (Commission/Greece), ECR 1990, I-3125 (paragraph 42 et seq.). In the framework of Community law, the Member States are not entitled to claim the principle of *nemo tenetur, i.e.* they can be obliged to provide information against themselves, assisting the Commission to establish whether Community law has been infringed.

102 ECJ Case C-2/88 Imm. (J.J. Zwartveld and others), ECR 1990, I-3365 et seq.

103 Only the duties to provide information upon request and specific notification duties are, as a rule, directly applicable as only they are sufficiently clear and unconditional according to the demands of the doctrine of the direct effect of Community law. State liability is the second means widely used by the ECJ as a way of penalising disrespect of Community law, but this is hardly applicable with regard to information procedures since there will seldom be quantifiable material damage caused by the violation of information obligations.

104 Article 8(1) of Directive 98/34/EC of 22 June 1998 laying down a procedure for the provision of information in the field of technical standards and regulations (OJ EC 1998 No. L 204, p. 37, amended by Directive 98/48/EC of 20 July 1998, OJ EC 1998 No. L 217, p. 18), which is a new codification of Directive 83/189/EEC of 28 March 1983 laying down a procedure for the provision of information in the field of technical standards and regulations (OJ EC 1983 No. L 109, p. 8, several times amended, in particular by Directive 94/10/EC, OJ EC 1994, No. L 100,

periods for the Member States follow during which the Commission is able to check the compatibility of these norms with European provisions on the free movement of goods.

With a number of judgments rendered by the ECJ have since given sufficient legal certainty with regard to the legal implications of such stand-still clauses. In the case *CIA Security*, the Court confirmed the legal opinion which had long been held by the Commission, according to which a lack of notification entails the ineffectiveness or at least the inapplicability of the national norm in question.[105] According to the case *Unilever/Central Food*, this is even valid when the technical standard has first been notified but the stand-still period set out in the *Directive on the Notification of Technical Standards* has not been met.[106] In its reasoning, the ECJ mainly refers to the argument of the effectiveness (*effet utile*) of the directive.[107] The Court, however, did not consider in its reasoning that the "simple" notification obligations might hereby be given a disproportionate effect, in the end exceeding the purpose of the *Directive on the Notification of Technical Standards* which neither regulates the enactment, nor the material lawfulness of those national norms.

The case *CIA Security* has had its effect. Since then, the number of notifications of technical standards has risen sharply;[108] risen has also the appetite of individuals for filing suit against unpleasant national technical standards on the grounds that they have not been duly notified to the Community.[109] The Court finally applied the emergency brake when a defendant in a criminal procedure claimed that the evidence was flawed because the national norm on the application of the breathalyser test was not notified to the Community. According to the *Lemmens* ruling, the missing notification of a national technical standard only prevents a restriction of the free movement of goods with regard to products which do not conform to such norm.[110] The application of a technical standard which has not been notified by the national

---

p. 1 which had explicitly extended the directive to technical standards relating to the protection of the environment). As to the procedure see v. Bogdandy, in: Schmidt-Aßmann/ Hoffmann-Riem, *Verwaltungsrecht in der Informationsgesellschaft* (fn. 86), 133 (151 et seq.).

105 ECJ Case C-194/94 (fn. 84), paragraph 40 et seq. The Commission now often refers to this judgment in its publication of notified technical standards in the Official Journal (see, e.g. OJ EC 2000, No. C 281, p. 2).

106 ECJ Case C-443/98 (Unilever/Central Food), ECR 2000, I-7535 (paragraph 37 et seq.).

107 See also the detailed analysis of this judgment by v. Bogdandy, in: Schmidt-Aßmann/ Hoffmann-Riem, *Verwaltungsrecht in der Informationsgesellschaft* (fn. 86), 133 (160 et seq.).

108 According to v. Bogdandy, notifications doubled in the year 1997 compared to the years before the ruling (*ibid.*, 162).

109 See only the rulings Unilever/Central Food (fn. 106); Case C-33/97 (Colim/Bigg's Continent Noord), ECR 1999, I-3175 et seq., as well as Joined Cases C-425/97, C-426/97 and C-427/97 (Criminal proceedings against Albers, van den Berkmortel and Nuchelmans), ECR 1999, I-2947 et seq.

110 ECJ Case C-226/97 (Criminal proceedings against Johannes Martinus Lemmens), ECR 1998, I-3711 (paragraph 35 et seq.).

authorities and which does not hinder the use or marketing of a product which is not in conformity with this is not hindered under European law.

It remains to be clarified how such infringements of European law can be cured. The permanent inapplicability or ineffectiveness of such a technical standard which has not been duly notified would exceed the bounds of what is necessary and appropriate as reaction to a non-notification since the violation of a duty of mere notification would turn into a prohibition to regulate the subject matter in question. The national legislation process, on the other hand, cannot be moved back to the status when the national norm was still a draft.[111] One may thus hold that the national norm is only inapplicable until the notification has been effected and the stand-still period has expired.

The considerations of the ECJ in relation to the *Directive on the Notification of Technical Standards* are not applicable to the notification of national norms and measures which implement Community law into national law[112] since their *effet utile* would be thwarted if such norms were ineffective if not notified to the Commission.[113] The reasoning of the Court, however, can be applied to the *Decision establishing a procedure for the exchange of information on national measures derogating from the principle of free movement of goods within the Community.*[114] According to this decision, the Member States must notify the Commission of all – further – measures which could lead to an impediment in the free movement of goods between the Member States, e.g. a general ban on the goods, the refusal to allow the goods to be placed on the market or the withdrawal of the goods from the market.[115]

Moreover, the ECJ rejected reversing the burden of proof at the expense of the Member States with regard to national norms and measures that have not been notified in the sense that the non-notification does not allow the Commission to assume that they have not taken the measures at all.[116] The respective Member State is therefore not convicted for not having implemented

---

111 Compare Fronia, *Annotation to the Case CIA Security*, EuZW 1996, 384.

112 Such notification obligations are standard in every act of secondary law which requires an enactment of norms by the Member States for implementation purposes. The Member States must then notify the Commission of existing pertinent legal norms, as well as the legal norms enacted for the implementation of that act.

113 Similarly ECJ in Case Braine-le-Château (fn. 43) in relation to a national permission which was to be issued on the basis of a plan which should have been notified to the Commission and which, however, was missing.

114 Decision No. 3052/95/EC of 13 December 1995 (OJ EC 1995 No. L 32, p. 1).

115 The notification obligation only applies to measures that could have a negative effect on "a particular model or type of a product" (Art. 1), thus excluding single case decisions. Also exempt are all measures which must be notified to the Community on the basis of other provisions of Community law (Article 3), in particular the *Directive on the Notification of Technical Standards*.

116 ECJ Case 96/81 "Bathing Water Directive", annotation 6 and Case 97/81 "Drinking Water Directive", annotation 6, both fn. 71.

the material provisions of Community law but for non-notification of the measures taken.

Anti-dumping law and the law on state subsidies make use of such punitive measures as allowing the administration to decide on the basis of the – not necessarily comprehensive – facts known to it if the party concerned fails to provide further information, and allowing the extension of time-limits for decisions to be taken by the authorities. Moreover, the standard of the reasoning that is to be laid down in such decision may be lowered.[117] Those sanctions are often used *vis-à-vis* companies and are part of the prohibition of *venire contra factum proprium*. The Federal Administrative Court in Germany, the *Bundesverwaltungsgericht*, argued similarly in the case of the A20 highway, which, as planned by the authorities, crossed a potential nature reservation area which might fall under the special protection of the *Flora-Fauna-Habitat Directive* which had not yet been implemented in Germany.[118] The European Community, however, has only been granted the power to impose coercive measures in singular cases, such as the penalty payment provided for in Article 228(2) EC Treaty.[119] The threat of such a penalty payment had initially proven to be particularly effective in forcing the Member States to implement European environmental law, but its use seems to have declined over recent years.[120]

4. THE GENERAL LEGAL FRAMEWORK FOR THE EXCHANGE OF INFORMATION

Even when there is a lack of explicit and specific rules on the extent and procedure to be followed for the exchange of information, the European

[117] For a more detailed analysis and respective case law and literature see Sommer, *Verwaltungskooperation* (fn. 5), 764 et seq.

[118] BVerwG, Decision of 19 May 1998, NVwZ 1998, 961 et seq. (in particular 967).

[119] See also the Communication of the Commission on the Method of calculating the penalty payments provided for pursuant to Article 171 of the EC Treaty (OJ EC 1997, No. C 63, p. 2), as well as Sach/Simm, *Kontrolle der Durchführung und der Beachtung von Gemeinschaftsrecht*, in: Rengeling, EUDUR (fn. 31), §44 annotation 75 et seq., who remark that the first cases where penalty payments had been imposed all related to environmental law.

[120] Cf. 2.8.1 of the 20th Annual report on monitoring the application of Community law (2002), COM/2003/0669 final, stating that Article 228 has continued to serve as a last resort to force Member States to comply with the judgments delivered by the ECJ, however, that "seeking improved implementation by taking Member States to the European Court of Justice is not the only, nor often the most efficient way to resolve the current problem." The Commission has brought no new cases under Article 228 EC to the Court during 2002 and only eight reasoned opinions were issued under Article 228 EC in 2002 (*ibid.*). Financial punitive measures in general are particularly effective, such as the exclusion from refunds and the forfeiture of a security as known in European agriculture law. Those measures could in particular be used with regard to information procedures that are intertwined with the funding of environmental measures. For a more detailed analysis of possible sanctions and further references see Sommer, *Verwaltungskooperation* (fn. 5), 747 et seq.

Community does not act in a field without law. The so called general principles of Community law also apply to administrative cooperation, especially the principle of proportionality, the right to be heard, the institutional autonomy of the Member States and the protection of business secrets and personal data of individuals.[121] These principles outline the legal boundaries to be respected by the Community, particularly so where the Community has wide discretionary powers at its disposal. This does not only apply to the execution and implementation of powers that already have been conferred on the Commission but also to the law-making activity of the Community itself, i.e. to information procedures *de lege ferenda*. When legal positions in play conflict in a concrete situation, they have to be weighed and balanced against each other to the best possible extent.

In the context of the *principle of proportionality*, the aspect of cost efficiency can be taken into account but only to the extent that the costs are disproportionately high in relation to the benefits to be expected.[122] The burden of proof which falls on the Member States is not easy to meet, since both costs and benefits are not easily quantified in financial terms. In cases of doubt, the European Community can evade the objection of unreasonable cost burdens by granting funds for the installation of data collection and dissemination equipment. Provided that the respective Community directive or regulation sets out uniform procedures and standards for the collection and analysis of data, the Member States are only allowed to deviate from these standards on the grounds of the costs involved[123] when the legal act explicitly allows cost efficiency to be taken into account.[124] The principle of proportionality, however, does not provide a fixed scale for the different information obligations in the sense that the least intrusive would have to be applied first before turning to a more burdensome form. The appropriateness of the duty of information and the procedure to be adopted is subject to a case by case consideration of all circumstances. Even inspections can be employed in the first instance without the necessity of issuing a prior request. If there are reasons to believe that there are irregularities and the issue is sufficiently important for the Community, it may even prescribe and subsequently execute inspections without any warning up front at all. However, under regular circumstances, the case by case consideration of all circumstances often leads to the result that the less intrusive information requests, i.e. the

---

121 For a detailed analysis and references to case law and the literature see Sommer, *Verwaltungskooperation* (fn. 5), 681 et seq.

122 ECJ Case C-426/93 (fn. 67); Case C-114/93 (Criminal proceedings against Kiefer and Thill), ECR 1997, I-3629 (paragraph 31 et seq.). See also Article 285(2) EC Treaty which had been inserted by the Treaty of Amsterdam, providing that the production of Community statistics shall not entail excessive burdens on economic operators.

123 Compare only ECJ Case C-237/90 (Commission/Germany) "German Drinking Water Regulation", ECR 1992, I-5973 (paragraph 16).

124 In this sense e.g. with regard to the monitoring of greenhouse gases and reporting Commission Decision 2004/156/EC (fn. 99), Annex I. 3.

notification and reporting duties, are the appropriate means to be applied in the first instance. Inspections depend in any case on the existence of concrete facts establishing a well founded suspicion of irregularities.

As part of the principle of legal certainty,[125] information obligations, moreover, should be sufficiently *clear and precise,*[126] a principle that has not been observed by the European Community itself very rigidly, given the enormous amount of unclear and unspecific provisions on the collection and exchange of information.

European administrative cooperation is set in a broader international context that is governed by *public international law* and the respective international bodies. Community law must be interpreted in accordance with and construed in the light of public international law as the ECJ noted in the judgments in *Safety Hi-Tech* and *Racke.*[127] International treaties that have been concluded by the European Community rank higher than European secondary law, i.e. directives and regulations and thus must be respected by secondary law and are subject to the direct effect doctrine as is all Community law.[128]

International environmental law can fill in gaps in Community law – in particular with regard to horizontal cooperation, i.e. cooperation among the Member States[129] – or inspire and ignite changes in European environmental law. International treaties can even be more specific than European law, predominantly with regard to horizontal cooperation and especially horizontal consultations. Even when there are European provisions, Member States may

125 The principle of legal certainty is part of the general principles of Community law, see only ECJ Case C-107/97 (Rombi and Arcopharma), ECR 2000, p. I-3367 (paragraph 66); Case C-354/98 (Commission/France), ECR 1999, I-4927 (paragraph 11); Case 325/85 (Ireland/Commission) "Sea fishing", ECR 1987, 5041 (paragraph 18); Case 169/80 (Zollverwaltung/Gondrand Frères), ECR 1981, 1931 (paragraph 17); Case 181/88 (Commission/Germany) "Ground Water Directive", ECR 1991, I-825 (paragraph 50 et seq.); Cases C-361/88 (paragraph 21), C-58/89 (paragraph 17) and C-59/89 (paragraph 24) (all fn. 83). Compare Schmidt-Aßmann, *Zur Europäisierung des allgemeinen Verwaltungsrechts*, in: FS Lerche, 1993, 513 (526 et seq.); Zuleeg, *Deutsches und Europäisches Verwaltungsrecht – Wechselseitige Einwirkungen*, VVDStRL 1994, 155 (170).

126 See only ECJ Case C-107/97 (Rombi and Arcopharma), *ibid.*; Case C-217/97 (Commission/Germany) "Directive 90/313/EEC", ECR 1999, I-5087 (paragraph 32); Case C-354/98, *ibid.*; Case 169/80 (Gondrand Frères), *ibid.*; Case 325/85 "Sea fishing", *ibid.* The Court uses several descriptions for this standard, see in particular Case 181/88 "Ground Water Directive", *ibid.*; Case C-361/88 "TA Luft" (fn. 83) (paragraph 21); Case C-59/89 "Air pollution – lead" (fn. 83) (paragraph 24); Case C-58/89 "Surface water" (fn. 83) (paragraph 17).

127 ECJ Case C-162/96 (A. Racke/Hauptzollamt Mainz), ECR 1998, I-3655 (paragraph 45); Case C-284/95 (Safety Hi-Tech/S.&T.), ECR 1998, I-4301 (paragraph 22) and Case C-341/95 (Bettati/Safety Hi-Tech), ECR 1998, I-4355 (paragraph 21 et seq.).

128 Article 300 para. 7 EC Treaty; ECJ Case C-416/96 (El Yassini/Secretary of State for the Home Department), ECR 1999, I-1209 (paragraph 25 et seq.); Case Racke, *ibid.*, (paragraph 31); Case C-103/94, ECR 1995, I-719 (paragraph 21 et seq.).

129 E.g. in the context of bilateral consultations relating to environmental problems which affect the territory of two or more Member States and which can be solved between the neighbouring states. See Article 8 of the Ozone Directive 2002 (fn. 26) and all legal acts cited under fn. 25.

eventually revert to the provisions for information exchange and the institutions of public international law as shown by the proceedings of Ireland against Great Britain before the International Tribunal for the Law of the Sea relating to a nuclear treatment facility at Sellafield.[130] International bodies constitute a forum for the exchange of information and help establish *epistemic communities*, i.e. communities with a common knowledge and belief in times of uncertainties about the facts.[131]

Existing networks and systems of cooperation on the international level should be borne in mind when establishing cooperation mechanisms on the European level, in particular in the case that the European Union wants to participate in these international mechanisms and intertwine its own systems with them, and thus avoid frictions and, to some extent, the duplication of work. International information procedures and institutions are numerous and are often older than the ones established by European law. Interstate cooperation on the international level is predominantly conceived as information exchange. International customary law provides, as of now, a warning obligation if there is an accident with transboundary effects, an obligation of preventive notification of potentially harmful transboundary effects arising from facilities and – not yet undisputed but maintained by some – an obligation of consultation with regard to shared natural resources.[132]

Environmental treaties contain an endless number of information obligations and procedural rules that are constantly growing at a high speed. Often, the information obligations the Member States and the European Community are subject to can only be discerned to some extent when examining both international and Community law. Both legal layers have often inspired each other. With regard to information exchange procedures, European law is not always the more progressive one. It often serves to transpose international treaties into Community law, even when the Community itself is not party to the treaty. This is particularly true when the Community wants to participate in the procedures for the international exchange of information. The Community then serves as a link between the Member States and the international bodies, bundling their efforts.

---

130 In the framework of a preliminary injunction and on the basis of customary international law and the Convention on the Law of the Sea, the International Tribunal had ordered both states to cooperate and to enter into consultations in order to exchange information on the potential consequences of the treatment facility for the Irish Sea, to monitor the risks and, if necessary, to take preventive measures (International Tribunal for the Law of the Sea, Case No. 10 of 3 December 2001, The MOX Plant Case, Ireland v. United Kingdom, in particular paragraph 82 et seq.). Great Britain had, *inter alia*, claimed that certain provisions of Community law would be applicable and that, thus, the International Tribunal for the Law of the Sea had no competence to rule on the case.

131 See *supra*, 3.4.

132 For a detailed analysis and further references see Sommer, *Verwaltungskooperation* (fn. 5), 583 et seq.

The examples are numerous and often concern the trade relations of the Member States with third countries. The *Regulation on Substances that Deplete the Ozone Layer,*[133] the *CITES Regulation,*[134] the *Regulation on Shipments of Waste*[135] and the old, as well as the new *Regulation on the Export and Import of Dangerous Chemicals*[136] with their extensive information procedures are all based on respective international treaties and are conceived to directly transpose and implement these treaties by the European Community, quasi excluding to a large extent the Member States and their administrations from direct contact with the third country counterparts and the respective international bodies.[137] In this sense, the *Regulation on the Export and Import of Dangerous Chemicals* of 2003 explicitly provides that the Commission becomes active in the framework of the international PIC procedure in the name of all national authorities of the Member States and is responsible, in particular, for the forwarding of the notifications of the Member States and of other information. The same is true for a number of information systems. After the *Decision on the Monitoring of Greenhouse Gases* was aligned with the international *Kyoto Protocol* to the *United Nations Framework Convention on Climate Change*, it became a role model for the interplay of international, European and national law.[138] In part, the

133 Regulation (EC) No. 2037/2000 (fn. 36); before Regulation No. 3093/94 (OJ EC 1994, No. L 333, p. 1) and initially Regulation 594/91 (OJ EC 1991, No. L 67, p. 1).

134 Regulation No. 338/97 of 9 December 1997 on the protection of species of wild fauna and flora by regulating trade therein (OJ EC 1997, No. L 61, p. 1, several times amended).

135 Initially Regulation (EEC) No. 259/93 of 1 February 1993 on the supervision and control of shipments of waste within, into and out of the European Community (OJ EC 1993 No. L 30, p. 1); now Regulation (EC) No. 1013/2006 of 14 June 2006 on shipments of waste (OJ EU 2006 No. L 190, p. 1). The regulations are based on the Basel Convention of 22 March 1989 on the control of transboundary movements of hazardous wastes and their disposal.

136 Regulation (EC) No. 304/2003 of 28 January 2003 concerning the export and import of dangerous chemicals (OJ EU 2003 No. L 63, p. 1). The Regulation is to transpose the Rotterdam Convention on the Prior Informed Consent Procedure for Certain Hazardous Chemicals and Pesticides in International Trade of 10 September 1998 which establishes a so called prior informed consent procedure ("PIC-procedure") for the trade with certain dangerous chemicals. See in particular Art. 5 of the Regulation. The Regulation replaces Regulation (EEC) No. 2455/92 of 23 July 1992 concerning the export and import of certain dangerous chemicals (OJ EC 1992 No. L 251, p. 13). That regulation already provided for a joint notification and information system.

137 The Regulation on the Ozone Layer and respective subsequent regulations and decisions of the European Commission implement the Montreal Protocol on the Community level (Montreal Protocol on Substances that Deplete the Ozone Layer, 16 September 1987, BGBl. II 1988, 1014 [including an English version], several times amended). The CITES-Regulation implements the Convention on International Trade in Endangered Species of Wild Fauna and Flora (CITES), Washington, 3 March 1973 (BGBl. II 1975, 773 [publication including an English version]). These are only some of the examples from a series of legal acts of the EC with a background in public international law.

138 See Decision 93/389/EEC of 24 June 1993 for a monitoring mechanism of Community CO_2 and other greenhouse gas emissions (OJ EC 1993 No. L 167, p. 31, as amended by Regulation 1882/2003, OJ EU 2003 No. L 284, p. 1). Now Decision No. 280/2004 (fn. 96). See also Decision 2002/358/EC of 25 April 2002 concerning the approval, on behalf of the European

European Community even stands proxy for the Member States with regard to their voting rights in the respective international bodies. Through the integration of public international law into Community law, those obligations can be effectively enforced by the mechanisms that are provided by the legal system of the European Community.

Finally, mention should be made of the fact that communication enhances the willingness for cooperation, so that procedures of information exchange can inspire a dynamic which reinforces itself. The call for information can also reinforce itself: the more information exists, the more questions arise and the stronger the impression that there is not enough information. Information then loses its function as a basis for decision making. It is not seldom that information gathering is initiated after the decision in essence has been made or serves as "diversion" from politically unacceptable – or not yet acceptable – material measures; information is quasi misused then as a signal and symbol for the political will and the legitimacy of decisions.[139]

Community, of the Kyoto Protocol to the United Nations Framework Convention on Climate Change and the joint fulfilment of commitments hereunder (OJ EC 2002 No. L 130, p. 1).

139 In detail Feldman/March, in: March, *Decisions and Organisations* (fn. 93), 409 et seq.

IV. EU INFLUENCE ON LAW ENFORCEMENT AND INTERNATIONAL COOPERATION IN THE FIELD OF INSIDER DEALING*

Michiel LUCHTMAN

1. INTRODUCTION

In the European Community, the practical implementation and legal enforcement of many Community matters is in the hands of the Member States. The nature and organization of this enforcement is primarily their own business. National discretion is not unlimited, however. The Court of Justice, for example, already held some time ago that EC law is to be enforced by effective, proportionate and dissuasive sanctions.[1] National discretion may also be limited through legislative intervention. A striking example is the Market Abuse Directive, which not only provides substantive rules in the field of insider dealing and market manipulation, but also lays down express requirements as to (the nature of the) responsible national authorities, their powers and their relationship with other national institutions (among which the judicial authorities), their professional duty of confidentiality and their possibilities for transnational cooperation.[2]

In this contribution, I aim to describe the influence of the Market Abuse Directive on the organization of administrative and criminal law enforcement and, particularly, how this impacts on transnational cooperation. On a national level, administrative law enforcement (financial supervision) and criminal law enforcement are often closely related. How this relationship is given shape

* With thanks to the Centre for Enforcement and European Law (CEEL) of the Utrecht School of Law and Corinne van den Berg for making the English translation possible. The author further wishes to thank Professor Sacha Prechal and Professor John Vervaele for their comments on an earlier version of this article. This contribution was published in Dutch in *SEW Tijdschrift voor Europees en economisch recht* 2006, pp. 262–274 (Dutch) and in *Utrecht Law Review* (English) Volume 2, issue 1 (June) 2006. It has not been updated since then.

1 Case 68/88, *Commission/Greece*, [1989] *ECR* 2965, subsequently repeated many times, cf. joined Cases C-387/02, C-391/02 and C-403/02, *Berlusconi a.o.*, [2005] *ECR* I-3565.

2 Directive 2003/6/EC of the European Parliament and of the Council of 28 January 2003 on insider dealing and market manipulation (market abuse), *OJ* 2003 L 96/16.

exactly, differs from one country to another. This may have an impact on transnational cooperation. Whereas in transnational cases requests for *mutual administrative assistance* are necessary for administrative law purposes, for criminal law enforcement purposes requests for *mutual assistance in criminal matters* (or *judicial assistance*) are needed. Does this distinction between mutual administrative assistance and mutual assistance in criminal matters pay due respect to differences in national law enforcement in the field of insider dealing?

There is ample reason for exploring this question, now that the European Court of Justice has recently recognized the competence of the Community (*i.e.* first pillar) to prescribe, subject to certain conditions, criminal sanctions as mandatory for violations of Community law.[3] Even more so than before, this has granted the EC the power to interfere in national law enforcement, including criminal law enforcement. What is more, it should not be ruled out that it will make use of this power in practice.[4] Of course, this will have consequences for the relationship between the administrative on the one hand and the Public Prosecution Service and the criminal courts on the other. In turn, this will have an effect on international cooperation.

I will start this contribution with an introduction on the institutional structure of the Union and the relevant provisions of the Market Abuse Directive (Section 2). The Directive includes provisions concerning both the organization of financial supervision and international cooperation. Like in many areas of Community policy, the Directive's starting point is that the practical implementation and enforcement of the rules it lays down are entrusted to the Member States. However, on some points, this Directive goes further than others in prescribing the tasks and powers of the national authorities in putting the Directive into practice. The question is how this affects national relations between administrative law enforcement and criminal law enforcement and thereby how it also affects international cooperation. In Sections 3 and 4, I will therefore discuss how two Member States, the Netherlands and Germany, have further substantiated this Community framework. In Section 5 an analysis will subsequently be given of the current possibilities for international cooperation. There I will mainly discuss the question of the extent to which the present arrangements, especially those under the Market Abuse Directive, offer scope for national discretion. In Section 6, I will briefly explore some alternatives for current interstate practice. Different solutions to the encountered problem are possible. Some will argue in favour of strict partitions between administrative and judicial assistance in order to prevent the circumvention of legal safeguards, such as the *nemo tenetur* principle; others (including the author of this

3 Case C-176/03, *Commission/Council*, [2005] *ECR* I-7879.

4 The Commission has already indicated that the possibility of mandatorily prescribed criminal law enforcement is being researched in several fields. So far, the Market Abuse Directive is not being considered in this context; COM(2005) 583 final/2.

contribution), however, oppose to such partitions. An additional issue that arises here is whether and, if so, to what extent harmonization of national laws is necessary for improving transnational cooperation. In this respect, I will also discuss the possible consequences of Case C-176/03 for the topic in hand. I will conclude with some final remarks in Section 7.

2. INTERNATIONAL AND COMMUNITY REQUIREMENTS FOR SUPERVISION AND COOPERATION

2.1. THE INSTITUTIONAL STRUCTURE OF THE EUROPEAN UNION

The European Union is structured in accordance with the well-known pillar model. It consists of three pillars, whereby the first pillar is made up of the former EC (and Euratom and the ECSC) and the third pillar concerns justice and police cooperation. The desire to retain national sovereignty in the field of criminal law appears to be the *raison d'être* of the third pillar, where decision-making is carried out in accordance with different procedures than under the first pillar.

Within the pillar structure the precise role and position of the Community in relation to national criminal law has long been controversial.[5] The Court's judgment in Case C-176/03 mentioned above gives rise to a host of new questions. These questions also concern the relationship between the criminal justice system and the administrative authorities, in this case: the supervisory authority. For example, it is doubtful whether – once the Community has made use of its criminal law powers – the Member States may still make use of administrative punitive means of sanctioning.[6] Many Member States provide for such sanctions which are sometimes applied complementarily and sometimes parallel to criminal law enforcement measures. In *Nunes & De Mattos* the Court recognized the competence of the Member States to apply criminal law means of enforcement in addition to the penalties prescribed by Community law,[7] but is this also true the other way around? How does this relate to the *ultimum remedium* character of criminal law? This question as yet remains unanswered.

---

5 See extensively on this Martin Wasmeier and Nadine Thwaites, 'The "battle of the pillars": does the European Community have the power to approximate national criminal laws?', 2004 *E.L.Rev*, no. 29, pp. 613–635.

6 Cf. among others G.J.M. Corstens, 'Criminal law in the first pillar', 2003 *European Journal of Crime, Criminal Law and Criminal Justice*, no. 1, pp. 131–144; idem, 2005 *Nederlands Juristenblad*, no. 45; Rolf Ortlep and Rob Widdershoven, 'Europa en de strafrechtelijke handhaving van milieurecht', in: Chris Backes et al. (eds.), *Lex Dura Sed Lex – opstellen over de handhaving van omgevingsrecht*, Deventer 2005.

7 Case C-186/98, *Nunes & de Matos*, [1999] *ECR* I-4883.

What does not seem controversial after the Court's judgment, however, is that issues concerning criminal law cooperation are still third pillar matters (cf. Article 34 TEU).[8] Mutual assistance in criminal matters began to develop within Europe with the (Council of Europe's) 1959 European Convention on Mutual Assistance in Criminal Matters.[9] To this Convention numerous bilateral and multilateral additions were subsequently made. This trend continued within the EU, among other things through the EU Convention on Mutual Assistance in Criminal Matters.[10] Some of these treaties also paid attention to differences in the organization of law enforcement in the various countries. Especially on the insistence of Germany, the scope of mutual assistance was extended to include what are known as *Ordnungswidrigkeiten*, *i.e.* punitive monetary sanctions that are imposed by an administrative body, but with the possibility of legal recourse to a criminal court.[11]

In addition to the development of mutual assistance in criminal matters, first through the Council of Europe and after that also in the third pillar, transnational cooperation in the field of administrative law also gradually began to receive attention within the EU. As we have seen in the introduction, this type of cooperation is known as mutual assistance in administrative matters. In the Market Abuse Directive this has been elaborated in Article 16.[12] Mutual assistance in administrative matters is therefore a first pillar affair. There are many differences between mutual assistance in criminal matters and mutual assistance in administrative matters. A common feature, however, is that they enable cooperation for criminal law and administrative law enforcement purposes respectively. Such cooperation may entail the exchange of information

8 Cf. M.J. Borgers, 'Harmonisatie van het strafrecht in de context van de Eerste Pijler', 2006 *Delikt en Delinkwent*, no. 7, pp. 76–99.

9 30 European Treaty Series.

10 Convention on Mutual Assistance in Criminal Matters between the Member States of the European Union, *OJ* 2000 C 197, and the Protocol established by the Council in accordance with Article 34 of the Treaty on European Union to the Convention on Mutual Assistance in Criminal Matters between the Member States of the European Union, *OJ* 2001 C 326.

11 Cf. Article 3(1) of the EU Convention on Mutual Assistance in Criminal Matters of 29 May 2000, *OJ* 2000 C 197.

12 Not only the Market Abuse Directive is relevant. Numerous other agreements have made the financial sector for the main part subject to European rules. See *e.g.* the Council of Europe Convention on insider trading of 20 April 1989 which also deals with mutual assistance. European Treaty Series 130, including the Protocol to this Convention, ETS 133. A special feature of this Treaty is that it also includes provisions concerning cooperation in the field of criminal law. For this contribution, however, the Treaty is less relevant, as Community agreements have priority over it (Article 16*bis*). Further, the Memorandum of Understanding which was prepared in the framework of the Committee of European Securities Regulators (CESR) which regulates cooperation between EU regulators more generally should of course be pointed out. The Memorandum can be found through www.cesr-eu.org/ (site last visited on 10 February 2006). There is also a multilateral Memorandum of Understanding of the International Organization of Securities Commissions (IOSCO): www.iosco.org/ (site last visited on 10 February 2006). However, I will focus on Article 16 of the Directive which is by far the most important provision.

upon request (but increasingly also includes spontaneous or automated data exchanges) and where necessary the collection of information by carrying out acts of investigation.[13] The distinguishing criterion between 'administrative assistance' on the one hand and 'judicial assistance' on the other is largely organic, which is to say that it is linked to the *status* of the authorities involved. If these are 'administrative' authorities, they make use of mutual assistance in administrative matters; if they are 'judicial' authorities, they use mutual assistance in criminal matters.[14] It is possible, however, that assistance in administrative matters is used to cooperate for the purpose of punitive sanctions, provided that these sanctions are imposed by administrative authorities.

In the field of transnational enforcement cooperation, two separate platforms therefore exist within the European Union framework which both deal with the same or at least with closely connected topics. The question that may be asked in this context is whether the distinction between 'administrative assistance' and 'judicial assistance', and especially the development of these instruments in separate platforms, does in fact do justice to the differences in law enforcement which may appear within the EU Member States. As will emerge below, financial supervision and criminal law enforcement are often closely interwoven at the national level. At the international level, however, they have been separated. Does the pillar structure of the Union in this way not effectively contribute towards the development in different directions of 'judicial assistance' and 'administrative assistance'? Would the opposite not make more sense, *i.e.* the mutual coordination of administrative assistance and judicial assistance? Such coordination currently hardly takes place at all.[15] It could however be a suitable tool to do more justice to the system of indirect enforcement of Community law by the Member States and the accompanying differences in the choice for either criminal or administrative sanctions. In order to be able to substantiate this further it is necessary first to discuss the question of how supervision and criminal law enforcement interfere with each other. For this reason, a brief overview will be given below of the Community requirements in these matters and of the manner in which these have been implemented in two EU Member States.

---

13 See extensively on the similarities and differences between administrative assistance and judicial assistance J. Vervaele et al. (eds), *European Cooperation between Tax, Customs and Judicial Authorities*, The Hague/London/New York 2002.

14 Vervaele et al., *supra* note 13, p. 284.

15 On the contrary, those instruments that do recognize a possible overlap between administrative assistance and judicial assistance usually provide that the rules concerning administrative assistance are without prejudice to the rules concerning judicial assistance. This mainly seems to indicate that all options should be kept open; cf. Vervaele et al., *supra* note 13, p. 264.

2.2. THE MARKET ABUSE DIRECTIVE

The Market Abuse Directive has a solid basis in Community policy.[16] It is the follow-up to Council Directive 89/592/EEC which was adopted in 1989.[17] The European Commission made the regulation of the financial sector a topic for its consideration in the context of the creation of the internal market. The European Commission's Financial Services Action Plan of May 1999 therefore set out strategic objectives to create an integrated EU capital market by April 2004 (a single EU financial services market, by open and secure retail markets, state-of-the-art prudential rules and supervision).

More so than its predecessor and more so than is usual in other areas of Community law the Market Abuse Directive provides requirements for the duties and powers of the responsible authorities. 'If the European Union is to develop integrated financial markets, there needs to be convergence (rather than divergence) in the methods of implementation and enforcement in Member States. Different sets of responsibilities and powers of national administrative authorities hinder the establishment of a fully integrated market and add to market confusion. To address this, the Directive proposes that Member States designate a single regulatory and supervisory authority [Article 11, ML] with a common minimum set of responsibilities [Article 12–15, ML]. Given the increasing number of cross-border activities, European legislation will need to ensure that regulatory and supervisory authorities work effectively together to prevent, detect, *investigate and prosecute* market abuse [italics added, ML]. For this purpose they need to be able to rely on the assistance of each other and to receive relevant information from each other in good time [Article 16, ML].'[18]

A certain degree of harmonization is therefore needed to enable effective supervision, which is in fact expressly defined as including the investigation and prosecution of market abuse. Nevertheless, the Directive does not go so far as to prescribe the type of sanctions which Member States should provide.[19] Article 14 provides that: 'Without prejudice to the right of Member States to impose criminal sanctions, Member States shall ensure, in conformity with their national law, that the appropriate administrative measures can be taken or administrative sanctions be imposed against the persons responsible where the provisions adopted in the implementation of this Directive have not been complied with.' This means that the final choice between criminal law

---

16 F.G.H. Kristen, *Misbruik van voorwetenschap naar Europees recht* (Ph.D. thesis at Tilburg University, the Netherlands), Nijmegen 2004, pp. 162 et seq.; see also Peter Nobel, *Schweizerisches Finanzmarktrecht – Einführung und Überblick*, Bern 2004, pp. 259 et seq.

17 Council Directive 89/592/EEC of 13 November 1989 coordinating regulations on insider dealing, *OJ* 1989 L 334/30.

18 COM(2001) 281 final, pp. 4–5.

19 See thereon also Kristen, *supra* note 16, pp. 205 et seq.

enforcement and administrative law enforcement is still left to the Member States. This has major consequences for cross-border cooperation.

Article 16 only lays down a duty to cooperate for the competent authorities referred to in Article 11 – *i.e. administrative* authorities. These authorities have to cooperate in the fulfilment of their duties. It would seem logical that this obligation also applies in case they wish to impose administrative sanctions which may have a punitive character as referred to in Article 6 ECHR. For the fulfilment of such requests and also of their other tasks under the Directive they have to make use of the powers referred to in Article 12. These powers also include the possibility to require existing telephone and existing data traffic records and to request the freezing and/or sequestration of assets (Article 12(2) (d) and (g)). That is remarkable. In many countries these are powers of the prosecution. For this reason, Article 12(1) provides that these powers may also be exercised in cooperation with the judicial authorities.[20] That is up to the Member States to decide.[21] Article 16(1) does however require that these powers are either directly or indirectly (*i.e.* after the involvement of the judicial authorities) exercised for the purpose of transnational cooperation.[22] In that case, cooperation takes place through multiple channels. The administrative authority that receives the request may in turn apply to the judicial authorities to collect the information and provide it to the requested authority so that the latter may provide it to the requesting authority. The whole procedure appears to be rather laborious and moreover not very transparent.

Article 16 does not regulate direct cooperation with judicial authorities. Judicial authorities are not 'competent authorities'. This means that they cannot request administrative assistance even if the violation of a provision of the Directive for which assistance is sought is dealt with administratively in the requested state.[23] However, what is permitted is that an administrative authority forwards the information to a judicial authority. Article 16(2), fourth paragraph, of the Directive expressly provides for this possibility. It states that: '*Without prejudice to the obligations to which they are subject in judicial proceedings under criminal law*, the competent authorities which receive information pursuant to

20 See thereon J.A.E. Vervaele, 'De Europese dimensie van het (economisch en financieel) strafrecht', in: Van Russen Groen et al. (eds.), *Iets bijzonders – Liber amicorum prof. jhr. Mr. M. Wladimiroff*, The Hague 2002, pp. 219–242.

21 Article 12 does not make clear whether the powers it refers to should be available for *all* the offences described in the Directive (Articles 2–5) or merely for the most serious ones. This, too, is therefore in principle left to the Member States to decide.

22 After all, Article 16(1) states that: 'Competent authorities shall cooperate with each other whenever necessary for the purpose of carrying out their duties, *making use of their powers whether set out in this Directive* [cf. Article 12(2). Italics added ML] or in national law. Competent authorities shall render assistance to competent authorities of other Member States. In particular, they shall exchange information and cooperate in investigation activities.'

23 The Council of Europe Convention, *supra* note 12, does offer this possibility.

paragraph 1 may use it only for the exercise of their functions within the scope of this Directive and in the context of administrative or judicial proceedings specifically related to the exercise of those functions [italics added, ML].' In such cases, the additional consent of the providing state is not required.

To sum up, therefore, we have seen that the Market Abuse Directive on the one hand does influence national law enforcement, but on the other hand also leaves quite a bit of room for the Member States on a number of crucial points. For this contribution it is especially relevant that: a/ information may be exchanged by supervisory authorities for punitive purposes (Article 14 in conjunction with Article 16), b/ that in this process powers may be exercised – either in cooperation with judicial authorities or not – which by their nature may be criminal procedural powers (Article 16(1) in conjunction with Article 12(2)) and c/ that information may be forwarded to the judicial authorities without prior consent if national law provides for this possibility (Article 16(2), fourth paragraph). In addition, we have also found that the Member States are (still?) free to choose between criminal law enforcement and administrative law enforcement (Article 11) and that direct contact between judicial authorities and administrative authorities is not allowed (Article 11 in conjunction with Article 16(1) following an *argumentum a contrario*).[24]

The question is whether the Directive in this way does justice to differences in the organization of law enforcement in the different Member States. For this reason it is interesting to examine how the obligations contained in the Directive have been transposed exactly. This question is dealt with below, where I will successively discuss the Netherlands and Germany.

3. THE NETHERLANDS

3.1. THE ORGANIZATION OF SUPERVISION AND INVESTIGATION

The Market Abuse Directive has recently been implemented in the Act on the Supervision of the Securities Trade 1995 [*Wet toezicht effectenverkeer* 1995 (*Wte*)].[25] If we examine this Act it is striking to note that violations of almost all provisions that are an implementation of the Directive may be enforced by both the Dutch competent authority under Article 11 of the Directive, *i.e.* the Netherlands Authority for the Financial Markets (*AFM*), and by the Public

24 Further below, I will discuss a number of (possible) explanations for this impossibility.

25 Market Abuse Act [*Wet Marktmisbruik*], *Staatsblad* 2005, 346. The Act entered into force on 1 October 2005.

Prosecution Service (*Openbaar Ministerie/OM*).[26] The organization of Dutch supervision is characterized by greatly parallel punitive powers of the Public Prosecution Service and the Netherlands Authority for the Financial Markets.[27]

The *AFM* expressly does not have any criminal procedural powers. The legislator considered that this would conflict with the Authority's special position *vis-à-vis* the market, but also *vis-à-vis* politics.[28] Criminal law enforcement is exclusively entrusted to the Public Prosecution Service which is assisted by a special investigative service that is part of the tax revenue service (*i.e.* the *FIOD-ECD*) which has special criminal procedural powers (among which the power of seizure) based on the Economic Offences Act [*Wet economische delicten/WED*].[29] The *AFM* can, however, impose punitive sanctions within the meaning of Article 6 ECHR. This is done in the shape of (among other things) administrative fines (*bestuurlijke boetes*).[30] This type of sanction may be defined as a punitive monetary sanction which is imposed by an administrative authority against which legal recourse may be had through administrative law channels. There is no recourse to the criminal courts and the guarantees of the Dutch Code of Criminal Procedure cannot be invoked. The minimum guarantees under Article 6 ECHR must, however, apply, as the sanctions involved are after all punitive.[31]

---

26 This is not to everyone's liking, by the way. Some argue in favour of transferring in particular the more complex offences to criminal law in order to prevent undermining the legal protection of the parties involved; cf. G.J.M. Corstens, 'Bestuurlijke boeten in de vierde tranche Awb', 2000 *Nederlands Juristenblad*, no. 24, pp. 1185–1190 and L.F.M. Verhey and N. Verheij, 'De macht van de marktmeesters – Markttoezicht in constitutioneel perspectief', 2005 *Handelingen NJV*, no. I, pp. 289–292. Others by contrast argue in favour of the primacy of administrative enforcement; cf. M.I. Jap-A-Joe Blagrove, *Beursfraude effectief aangepakt* (Ph.D. thesis at Maastricht University, the Netherlands), Nijmegen 2003. A.R. Hartmann, 'Strafrechtelijke handhaving van de financiële wetgeving: houden of weggeven?', 2004 *Nederlands Juristenblad*, pp. 1070–1073 goes even further than this.

27 The *AFM* is not the only financial regulator. There is also *De Nederlandsche Bank (DNB)* which is in charge of the prudential supervision of financial institutions. The *AFM* is responsible for regulating conduct. At the end of 2001 a far-reaching reform of the supervisory structure was started which eventually led to the proposal for the Financial Supervision Act [*Wet op het financieel toezicht*], *Kamerstukken II* 2005–2006, 29 708.

28 See thereon M.J.J.P. Luchtman, *Geheimhouding en verschoning in het effectenrecht*, Amsterdam 2002.

29 The Economic Offences Act applies in addition to the general rules of the Criminal Code and the Code of Criminal Procedure. The Economic Offences Act among other things extends the criminal law concept of suspicion; see Dutch Supreme Court, HR 9 March 1993, *NJ* 1993, p. 633.

30 What is known as naming and shaming is also considered a punitive sanction.

31 It is typical (and in my opinion – unfortunate) that in the Netherlands the right to remain silent under criminal procedural law as laid down in Article 29 of the Code of Criminal Procedure and the right to remain silent in the administrative fine procedure have been regulated differently; see on this, among others, G. Knigge, 'De verkalking voorbij: over de verhouding van het strafrecht tot het bestuursrecht', 2000 *RM Themis*, pp. 83–96; O.J.D.M.L. Jansen, *Het handhavingstoezicht* (Ph.D. thesis at the Universiteit van Amsterdam, the

The Netherlands thus has a two-track trajectory whereby the same offences can be dealt with by two different types of authorities which have different powers at their disposal. These authorities are increasingly cooperating. This is necessary if only to prevent problems in connection with the *ne bis in idem* principle.[32] In the past, cooperation was not always as smooth as it should have been. For a long time, the *AFM* did not have to report offences as this was thought to conflict with its sensitive position *vis-à-vis* the entities placed under its supervision. After all, the provision of sensitive financial information to third parties, including the Public Prosecution Service, might easily lead to commotion or even panic on the financial markets, if this information is not handled with utmost care. This has led to clashes between the supervisory authority and the Public Prosecution Service in the past,[33] but this now seems set to change. It no longer seems to be commonly held that the *AFM* has an absolute duty of secrecy *vis-à-vis* the Public Prosecution Service.[34] Indeed, mutual cooperation is needed now that the Netherlands has opted in favour of the collaboration model in the implementation of Article 12(2) of the Market Abuse Directive.[35] The *AFM* itself is not authorized to perform seizures or to require data traffic records. For this, it has to apply to the Public Prosecution Service, given that the powers in question are criminal procedural powers under Dutch law.

Netherlands), 1999, pp. 104–105; A.R. Hartmann, *Bewijs in het bestuursstrafrecht* (Ph.D. thesis at the University of Rotterdam, the Netherlands), Deventer 1998, pp. 87 et seq.; L. Stevens, *Het nemo-teneturbeginsel in strafzaken: van zwijgrecht naar containerbegrip* (Ph.D. thesis at Tilburg University, the Netherlands), Nijmegen 2005, pp. 128–130.

32 Cf. Article 48j of the Securities Transactions (Supervision) Act 1995, which contains what is called the *una via* provision; see on *una via* L.J.J. Rogier, *Strafsancties, administratieve sancties en het una via-beginsel* (Ph.D. thesis at the University of Rotterdam, the Netherlands), Arnhem 1992 and also A.H. Klip and H.G. van der Wilt, 'The Netherlands, Non bis in idem', 2002 *International Review of Penal Law*, pp. 1091–1137.

33 See on this Luchtman, *supra* note 28.

34 The *AFM* is *competent* to report offences or provide information (cf. Article 161 Code of Criminal Procedure). This is increasingly considered part of its tasks. That this is a competence rather than a duty may be concluded from the fact that the general criminal procedural law duty to report and cooperate under Art. 162 of the Code of Criminal Procedure does not apply to the *AFM*. The *AFM* has not been designated as such in the 'Decree of 31 March 1987 providing for the adoption of an order in council for the implementation of Article 162(4) of the Code of Criminal Procedure', as lastly amended by *Staatsblad* 2005, 690. The examining magistrate or the court may, however, oblige the *AFM* to cooperate; in that case the *AFM* might be entitled to a limited right of nondisclosure. This is connected with Case 110/84, *Hillegom/Hillenius*, [1985] *ECR* 3947. See also *Kamerstukken II* 2001–2002, 28 122, no. 2, p. 12; *Kamerstukken II*, 2003–2004, 29 708, no. 3, pp. 52–55; *Handelingen II* 2005, p. 83–4983; Luchtman, *supra* note 28, p. 140.

35 See the Dutch *traveaux préparatoires* with respect to the Act implementing the Market Abuse Directive; *Kamerstukken II*, 2004–2005, 29 827, no. 3, pp. 17–18.

3.2. NATIONAL RULES FOR CROSS-BORDER COOPERATION

What does the above imply for international cooperation? First of all, that in international dealings the *AFM* – as the requesting party – has to make use of administrative assistance (*wederzijdse administratieve bijstand*), whereas the Public Prosecution Service makes use of judicial assistance (*wederzijdse strafrechtelijke rechtshulp*). The *AFM* cannot make requests for judicial assistance, because administrative fine procedures do not qualify as 'proceedings brought by the administrative authorities in respect of acts which are punishable under the national law of the requesting or the requested Member State, or both, by virtue of being infringements of the rules of law, and where the decision may give rise to proceedings *before a court having jurisdiction in particular in criminal matters* [italics added, ML]', as referred to in Article 3(1) of the EU Convention on Mutual Assistance in Criminal Matters. The *AFM* does not have any responsibilities in the field of preliminary investigations either, which would enable it to request judicial assistance in that capacity.[36]

Where the Dutch administrative fine is concerned, therefore, a request for administrative assistance has to be made. However, neither Dutch legislation, nor the Market Abuse Directive are very clear concerning foreign variants of punitive sanctions in cases where the Netherlands is the requested party. Pursuant to Dutch law, there seems to be no bar against requests for administrative assistance by foreign authorities with punitive tasks. Of course this does raise questions as to the guaranteeing of the *nemo tenetur* principle transnationally.[37] As of what point is the person involved – when present in the Netherlands – entitled to this right? Who is entitled to it? What is the scope of such a right? To what extent can it be invoked when a request for administrative assistance, besides a punitive purpose, also serves a non-punitive purpose?[38] Dutch law, especially the rules for the implementation of the agreements concerning cooperation (Articles 45b and 29–36 of the 1995 Supervision Act),[39] is silent on this point. In my view the situation seems to be that the right to remain silent that a person would have in the Netherlands (Article 48e of the

---

36 Some countries, like for instance Switzerland, are prepared to provide judicial assistance to administrative authorities that operate at that stage and that can request the Public Prosecution Service to start a criminal investigation; cf. the Swiss Bundesgericht, Bundesgerichtentscheid/*BGE* 109 Ib 47 (with regard to the US *SEC*), *BGE* 118 Ib 457 and 121 II 153 (with regard to the French *CFB*) and Bundesgericht of 28 April 1997, no. 1A.361/1996 (with regard to the Italian *CONSOB*). The Dutch *AFM* does not in any case have these tasks.

37 On this principle under Dutch law see Stevens, *supra* note 31.

38 Cf. ECtHR in *J.B.* v. *Switzerland*, 3 May 2001, appl. no. 31827/96, Reports 2001-III.

39 The 1995 Act on the Supervision of the Securities Trade in Arts. 33–39 also includes provisions to implement international and Community obligations to cooperate. These are partly intended to implement the Investment Services Directive (Directive 93/22/EC) which has recently been replaced by Directive 2004/39/EC of 21 April 2004, *OJ* 2004 L 145/1.

1995 Act) can also be relied on when the *AFM* carries out a request for administrative assistance that serves a punitive purpose. This does not, however, answer all of the questions just raised.

Although direct contact with the foreign judicial authorities is thus not possible, there are still indirect possibilities for cooperation. It is possible that the *AFM* asks the foreign authority for its permission to forward the information to the Dutch Public Prosecution Service (Article 33(2) of the 1995 Act). In turn, the *AFM* may grant a foreign authority permission to forward the information to a foreign Public Prosecution Service. In the latter case, Article 33(3) of the 1995 Act lays down strict additional requirements which serve to prevent that the provisions concerning judicial cooperation in criminal matters are circumvented. Permission may not be given, for example, if the information in question cannot be obtained by means of mutual judicial assistance.[40] This is remarkable, as Article 16 of the Market Abuse Directive does not lay down such strict requirements. It is further remarkable because in the Dutch situation internally the importance of consultation between the Public Prosecution Service and the *AFM* is increasingly recognized. This approach apparently does not extend to the transnational level. The question is, however, whether foreign supervisory authorities that receive information from the *AFM* should pay much heed to this restriction. Above, I have stated that no permission is required for forwarding information to judicial authorities (Article 16(2) of the Directive). In other states – especially Germany – this requirement does therefore (rightly, in my view) not apply.

4. GERMANY

4.1. THE ORGANIZATION OF SUPERVISION AND INVESTIGATION

Like in the Netherlands,[41] supervision in Germany has also been radically reformed recently. Germany has opted for what is called *Allfinanzaufsicht* with one supervisory authority for the entire financial sector. This supervisory

---

40 An English translation of the 1995 Act can be found on: www.afm.nl/english.htm (site last visited on 9 February 2006). 'Section 33 (…) 3. If a foreign agency as referred to in Subsection (1) requests the person who has supplied the data or information pursuant to Subsection (1) for permission to use the said data or information for a purpose other than the one for which it was supplied, the request may be granted solely: (a) if the intended use does not conflict with Subsections (1) or (2); or (b) if the said foreign agency could obtain, in a manner other than that provided for by this Act, the data or information for that other purpose from the Netherlands in conformity with the relevant procedures; and (c) after consultation with Our Minister of Justice, if the request referred to in the opening lines relates to a criminal investigation.'

41 *Supra* note 27.

authority is the *Bundesanstalt für Finanzdienstleistungsaufsicht* or *BAFin*. Its powers have been laid down in the *Finanzdienstleistungsaufsichtsgesetz* (*FINDAG*) of 22 April 2002 and in sectoral supervision Acts, among which the federal Securities Act, the *Wertpapierhandelsgesetz* (*WpHG*).[42] This latter Act is also the implementation of the Market Abuse Directive.[43] The *BAFin* is the competent authority under the Market Abuse Directive. It does not only have executive duties, but may also perform controls and in case of violations may impose penalties. In the latter event, the relationship with criminal law becomes relevant.

As opposed to the Netherlands, Germany did not opt for parallel powers for the *BAFin* and the German Public Prosecution Service, the *Staatsanwaltschaft*. The responsibility for dealing with violations of the Directive rests upon either the *BAFin* or the Public Prosecution Service. A number of offences may be handled by the *BAFin* itself as *Ordnungswidrigkeiten* (see above).[44] Based on the *Ordnungswidrigkeitengesetz* (*OWiG*) the *BAFin* (according to Article 40 *WpHG*) may deal with violations of the Securities Act equally applying (a considerable number of) criminal procedural law powers and procedures. Based on the same Act, it also has the power to perform seizures after prior judicial authorization (Article 46 *OWiG*).[45] Unlike in the Netherlands, therefore, a procedural link exists with the law of criminal procedure, which also has consequences for international cooperation (see below).

Not all offences are dealt with by the *BAFin* itself. For the investigation and prosecution of certain offences the Public Prosecution Service is the responsible authority.[46] In that case the rules of criminal law and criminal

---

42 For the English translation see www.bafin.de.

43 This took place via the 'Gesetz zur Verbesserung des Anlegerschutzes – Anlegerschutzverbesserungsgesetz – AnSVG' of 28 Oktober 2004, published in Bundesgesetzblatt I 2004 No. 56, p. 2630. The *traveaux préparatoires* are published in Bundesrat Drucksache 341/04 of 30 April 2004.

44 Which offences these are may be found in Articles 38 and 39 *WpHG*. In Germany it is a criminal offence to acquire (*Erwerben*) or dispose of (*Veräußern*) financial instruments to which inside information relates, regardless of who committed the offence (Art. 38(10) no. 1 *WpHG*). This is different in the case of disclosing (*Weitergeben*) inside information to other persons and inducing (*Verleiten*) others on the basis of inside information to make transactions. These actions are only criminal offences when performed by primary insiders (Article 38(1) no. 2a – d *WpHG*). Only then, they fall within the competence of the Public Prosecution Service. In the case of secondary insiders the actions in question are *Ordnungswidrigkeiten*, for which the *BAFin* is competent. This distinction is to do with the lesser degree of injustice (*geringere Unrechtsgehalt*) of the latter actions; Bundesrat Drucksache 341/04, p. 78.

45 Bundesrat Drucksache 341/04, p. 57. Based on the *Ordnungswidrigkeitenrecht* investigative methods directed at telecommunications are not possible (cf. Article 12(2)(d) of the Directive). Based on Article 16b *WpHG* the *BAFin* nevertheless does have this power.

46 *Supra* note 44.

procedural law apply.[47] In such cases the role of the *BAFin* changes as well: it then has a statutory *duty* to report suspected violations (Article 4(5) *WpHG*).[48] The Public Prosecution Service in turn has a duty to start an investigation (Article 152(2) *Strafprozessordnung/StPO*). Here, therefore, there is no such thing as a 'position of trust *vis-à-vis* entities under supervision'. This has given rise to the reproach that the supervisory authority has allowed itself to become a vehicle for the prosecution. Administrative *Massenfahndung* by means of duties to inform (Article 9 *WpHG*) and report to (Article 10 *WpHG*) the *BAFin* in this way leads to the criminal law *Verwertung von Zufallsfunden*.[49] This duty to report and provide support may in fact be partly explained by the absence of special investigative services which do exist in the Netherlands. Moreover, Germany uses a rather reactive[50] concept of suspicion to mark the beginning of criminal proceedings (*Anfangsverdacht*; Article 152 *StPO*). This inherently leads to the conclusion that the role of the administrative authorities as the provider of leads to the judicial authorities becomes correspondingly more important.[51] Presumably for the same reason – although this was already the case before the adoption of the Market Abuse Directive – the *BAFin* may require that financial institutions retain existing data traffic records (Article 16b *WpHG*).

If the *BAFin* transfers a case to the Public Prosecution Service this does not necessarily mean that its own task has come to an end. It is possible that the *BAFin* carries out further investigations using its powers under the Securities Act, for example for the purpose of taking administrative measures or to carry out a foreign request for administrative assistance.[52] Parallel investigations by

---

47 To the extent that these offences overlap with offences for which the *BAFin* is responsible under the Securities Act in combination with the *Ordnungswidrigkeitengesetz*, the Public Prosecution Service may take over the prosecution of the *Ordnungswidrigkeit* by virtue of the *Prinzip der Vorrang des Strafverfahrens*; cf. Articles 35, 40–42 *OWiG*.

48 For other offences it is *competent* to report them or to disclose confidential information; see Art. 8(1) *WpHG*. The Public Prosecution Service in turn is obliged to inform the *BAFin* of certain offences; cf. Art. 40a *WpHG*.

49 See thereon *in extenso* Michael Nietsch, *Internationales Insiderrecht* (Ph.D. thesis at the University of Darmstadt, Germany), Berlin 2004; Schäfer, §16 WpHG, no. 3, in: Schäfer (ed.), *Wertpapierhandelsgesetz – Kommentar*, Stuttgart/Berlin/Köln 1999, §16 *WpHG*, no. 3; Dreyling, §16 *WpHG*, nos. 8–11, in: Assmann et al. (eds.), *Wertpapierhandelsgesetz: Kommentar*, Köln 2003; J.W. Habetha, 'Verwaltungsrechtliche Rasterfahndung mit strafrechtlichen Konsequenzen?', 1996 *Wertpapier Mitteilungen/WM*, pp. 2133–2140; Kai Müller, 'Insiderrechtliche Mitwirkungs-pflichten der Kreditinstitute im Lichte des nemo-tenetur-Grundsatzes', 2001 *Wistra*, no. 5, pp. 167–171.

50 By this I mean to indicate that the judicial authorities only become active once a reasonable suspicion has arisen that an offence has already been committed. See for the Netherlands *supra* note 29: especially for economic crimes a broader concept is used.

51 *BAFin* employees may also be involved in the investigation as experts: Art. 40a *WpHG*.

52 Article 4(5) *WpHG*; see also Bundesrat Drucksache 341/04, pp. 58–59. In the latter case, Germany is by the way free to refuse to execute the request based on Article 16(2) of the Market Abuse Directive.

the Public Prosecution Service and the *BAFin* in the same case are therefore quite possible. Here too, like in the Netherlands, this raises the question of the guaranteeing of the *nemo tenetur* principle. Persons who risk incriminating themselves are then entitled to a right of nondisclosure (*Zeugnisverweigerungsrecht*; Article 4(9) *WpHG* in conjunction with Article 383 of the German Code of Civil Procedure (*ZPO*)).

4.2. NATIONAL RULES FOR CROSS-BORDER COOPERATION

What does the above mean for international cooperation via mutual administrative assistance (*Amtshilfe*) and/or judicial assistance (*Rechtshilfe*)? This has been laid down in Article 7 *WpHG*. It provides that the *BAFin* is to cooperate with other competent authorities in the supervision (*Überwachung*) of financial instruments and markets. Again it emerges here that direct contact with the foreign justice authorities is not an option. Nevertheless, it is also true in Germany that mutual administrative assistance is quite relevant for criminal law enforcement. As we have just seen, for example, the *BAFin*, much more so than is the case in the Netherlands, operates in the preliminary stages of criminal investigations. It also makes requests for administrative assistance for the fulfilment of these tasks.

A further question is whether the *BAFin* may use administrative assistance in the investigation and prosecution of *Ordnungswidrigkeiten*. Above, we have seen that in situations like these it is in any case possible to make a request for judicial assistance.[53] Article 16 in conjunction with Article 14 of the Market Abuse Directive would, in my opinion, not prohibit this, which means that the *BAFin* in such cases could choose between administrative assistance and judicial assistance. Here, however, German law itself imposes certain limits:[54] Article 1(2) of the Mutual Judicial Assistance in Criminal Matters Act (*Gesetz über die internationale Rechtshilfe in Strafsachen/IRG*) provides that a 'criminal matter' as referred to in this Act (*strafrechtliche Angelegenheit*) can also be an *Ordnungswidrigkeit* or a comparable foreign sanction. This is commonly understood to imply that in the case of *Ordnungswidrigkeiten* the criminal law

53 *Supra* note 11.

54 One may wonder how these restrictions fit in with the declaration that Germany made to the European Convention on the Obtaining Abroad of Information and Evidence in Administrative Matters; *infra* note 70.

trajectory – *i.e.* judicial assistance – *must* be followed.[55] This could also be inferred from Article 7(6) *WpHG*.[56]

If the *BAFin* should be the requested party, the reverse is true. For administrative punitive sanctions against which appeal is possible to a court which also has jurisdiction in criminal matters, the rules concerning judicial cooperation in criminal matters are applicable. It further seems to follow from this internal German legislative system that in the execution of requests for administrative assistance only the powers of investigation under administrative law (especially Article 4 *WpHG*) may be used for the execution of the request. The powers based on the *Ordnungswidrigkeitensgesetz* are not to be used.[57] The question is whether this is compatible with Article 16(1) of the Directive where it provides that: 'Competent authorities shall cooperate with each other whenever necessary for the purpose of carrying out their duties, *making use of their powers whether set out in this Directive or in national law* [italics added, ML].' In short, when you have the powers, you have to use them. This, however, gives rise to many questions, not the least of which is the possible risk of evasion of the guarantees provided for in case of judicial assistance under criminal law, such as for example the double criminality requirement in case of certain coercive measures. It is as yet unclear how this situation is to be assessed.

The relevance of Article 16 of the Market Abuse Directive for administrative law enforcement and criminal law enforcement also becomes clear from Article 7(2) and (4) *WpHG*, which lay down the German requirements for forwarding information.[58] These are considerably more flexible than the Dutch requirements. Unlike in the Netherlands, no permission from the providing authority is required. This is fully in line with internal law enforcement. It implies recognition

---

55 Cf. Schomburg and Lagodny, p. 220, in: Albin Eser et al. (eds), *The individual as subject of international cooperation in criminal matters*, Baden-Baden 2002; G. Dannecker, 'Der Schutz der Beteiligten beim internationalen Auskunftverkehr in Steuerstrafsachen', 1990 *StVj*, pp. 124–145. One may wonder, however, whether this rule, which in itself is quite clear, is actually workable in practice. In case of suspected insider dealing it is not necessarily clear from the start whether prosecution will follow. And even where this is clear, it is moreover possible to opt for a two-track approach by imposing both a fine and a reparatory penalty (for example, halting trade). Which road should be taken in case of such cumulative goals?

56 In translation, this subsection provides that: 'The above shall be without prejudice to provisions on international assistance in criminal matters.' Concerning the lack of clarity as to the precise meaning of this, see *supra* note 15.

57 Conversely, only criminal procedural law powers could be used in the execution of requests for judicial assistance.

58 Cf. the following translation of Article 7(2) WpHG, which is relevant when Germany is the requested state (Article 7(4) applies when Germany is the requesting state): 'When communicating information, the Supervisory Authority is obliged to instruct the recipient that, *without prejudice to his prosecutorial obligations* [italics added, ML], the communicated information, including personal data, is to be used only to fulfil supervisory duties in accordance with sentence 1 and in the context of administrative and judicial proceedings relating thereto. The Supervisory Authority may allow representatives of foreign authorities within the meaning of subsection (1) sentence 1 to participate in its investigations.'

of the fact that the supervisory authority and the Public Prosecution Service are reliant upon each other. Such a lenient approach does mean, however, that a request for administrative assistance may at the same time *also* serve criminal law purposes.[59] The information may be forwarded to the judicial authorities straight away. This makes parallel investigation possible. Especially when the enforcement of the law depends upon cooperation between the Public Prosecution Service and the supervisory authority this to me appears to be a dangerous situation. There is a very real risk that the requested authority is unable to form a clear picture of what exactly it is providing assistance for. On the one hand, it is obliged to provide assistance, but on the other hand – as far as criminal law enforcement is concerned – it cannot impose any conditions as to what the information supplied may be used for (see *supra* Section 2).

5. PROBLEMS ENCOUNTERED IN COOPERATION

The above description has first of all shown that the administrative authorities and the judicial authorities rely on each other to a considerable extent. The exercise of supervision, including the exchange of information, is essential for effective law enforcement. The administrative authority (*i.e.* the supervisory authority) plays an important role in this. This is not only true for the stage of practical implementation of the law and preventive supervision, but also for the stage at which it is concluded that certain rules have been violated (repressive enforcement). Here the following possible courses of action have been distinguished:

a. the administrative authority may be obliged or competent to report violations to the Public Prosecution Service, and/or
b. the administrative authority may be charged with the further investigation of possible violations (repressive enforcement), either in the framework of criminal proceedings as an investigative service under the direction of the Public Prosecution Service[60] or as an alternative for the Public Prosecution Service in criminal proceedings,[61] or independently in a different procedure

59 The word 'also' is of the essence here. If a purely criminal law objective were at stake, then there would be a case of *détournement de pouvoir*. Supervision (*Überwachung*) as required in Article 7(1) *WpHG* would then be lacking.

60 I have not yet come across this option in financial supervision. It would not be compatible with the independent status of many regulators. It is, however, a common phenomenon in the enforcement of tax law.

61 This option does not exist either in the countries that were examined here. It has however been suggested as a possible alternative for overly extensive possibilities for administrative punitive sanctioning; cf. Corstens, and Verheij and Verhey, *supra* note 26. So far, this option has been rejected. Incorporating the regulator into the criminal procedure would also result in the applicability of criminal law control principles. Under fiscal law, however, this option

under administrative law which might possibly be directed at the imposition of a punitive sanction, and/or

c. the administrative authority is charged with the decision following the investigation (imposition of a sanction), either in the framework of a criminal investigation, or in a different procedure which might or might not be directed at the imposition of a punitive sanction.

Whichever of these options is chosen, what catches the eye every time is the close relationship between the Public Prosecution Service and the supervisory authority. What is more, the supervisory authority and the Public Prosecution Service may both operate simultaneously in one and the same investigation. Prosecution without the involvement of the supervisory authority therefore seems difficult to imagine.

And yet, this relationship is not quite extended to the transnational level, which is a second important conclusion that may be drawn from the above. National Member States are still left a considerable amount of discretion in the precise organization of their law enforcement. This has immediate consequences for international cooperation. The sanctioning of the various provisions as described in the Directive and transposed into national law offers many examples of this. For example, one might think of the national provisions transposing Article 2 of the Market Abuse Directive for which the Public Prosecution Service and the *AFM* are both responsible in the Netherlands, but for which only the Public Prosecution Service is responsible in Germany. Direct cooperation between the *AFM* and the German Public Prosecution Service is, however, not a possibility, even though this could certainly serve the underlying objectives of the Directive, namely 'to ensure the integrity of European financial markets, to establish and implement common standards against market abuse throughout Europe, and to enhance investor confidence in these markets'.[62] Contact can only be made indirectly, namely through the involvement of the Dutch Public Prosecution Service or the *BAFin*. In that case, the forwarding of information is either subject to extremely strict requirements (the Netherlands) or to almost no requirements at all.

In short, it looks as if the current distinction between administrative assistance and judicial assistance fails to do justice to the differences that exist in the structuring and organization of law enforcement within Europe which are a direct result of the discretion which the Member States have in giving shape to national law enforcement. Even the Market Abuse Directive, although it interferes in national enforcement structures more than is usual, cannot alter

---

already exists for some time, both in the Netherlands (Art. 80 of the State Taxes Act [*Algemene wet inzake rijksbelastingen/AWR*] and in Germany (Art. 386 *AO*).

62 COM(2001) 281 final, p. 2.

this to any structural degree. Would it not make sense to tackle this problem and if so, how?

In my view, the best way to solve the problem would be to completely eliminate the partitions between administrative assistance and judicial assistance. In this way, all the authorities that are responsible for guarding the objectives of the Directive – put briefly: to protect the integrity of the financial sector – would be able to approach each other directly, which would considerably increase the transparency of inter-state data traffic and thereby also its supervision.[63] In that case, the *AFM* would also be able to request data from the German Public Prosecution Service and possibly even to ask it to carry out investigations. Still, this is a highly controversial option. Opponents may point out a number of objections.

First of all it can be argued that direct contact is incompatible with the supervisory authority's position of trust *vis-à-vis* the entities placed under its supervision and its independent status.[64] Where the judicial authorities in criminal proceedings only incidentally deal with financial institutions, the supervisory authority relies on a good relationship with the institutions placed under its supervision in order to be able to fulfil its functions properly. This argument fails to convince, as the legislator actually quite often takes mutual coordination and cooperation between the judicial authorities and the administrative authorities as its starting point. It is moreover increasingly required that the supervisory authority where necessary takes corrective measures or even imposes penalties.[65] Clarity concerning the use of information would therefore appear to be more relevant for friendly relations between the supervisory authority and the regulated entities than shielding information from the judicial authorities, even in cases where abuses could sully the sector's image.[66] It is therefore only right that the 'trust argument' is slowly being abandoned, also in the Netherlands.[67] The responsibility for the integrity of the financial markets is in the hands of multiple institutions which have to rely on close cooperation. Especially in situations where the administrative authorities themselves have punitive tasks, invoking the 'position of trust' would appear to be somewhat incongruous. Cooperation would in my opinion not endanger the

---

63 This is not considering the position of the stock markets which at times also have supervisory powers.

64 Cf. A. Althaus, *Amtshilfe und Vor-Ort-Kontrolle* (Ph.D. thesis at the University of Berne) Berne 1997, pp. 119–120; R. Roth, 'Art. 38 BEHG – Amtshilfe', in: Hertig Gérard et al. (eds.), *Kommentar zum Bundesgesetz über die Börsen und den Effektenhandel* (loosleaf), Zürich 2000.

65 Article 14 of the Market Abuse Directive is in fact a perfect example of this.

66 Cf. Luchtman, *supra* note 28; M.J.J.P. Luchtman et al., *Informatie-uitwisseling in het kader van het Financieel Expertisecentrum*, Utrecht 2002.

67 This is different however for prudential supervision. The utmost discretion is required from the Dutch prudential supervisor, *De Nederlandsche Bank (DNB).*

independent status of the supervisory authority either, as long as such cooperation takes place on the basis of equality.

A second possible argument against eliminating the distinction between administrative assistance and judicial assistance could be a difference in the seriousness of the underlying offence. The idea behind this is that this distinction expresses the *ultmimum remedium* aspect of criminal law: for more serious offences a request for judicial assistance should be used, while for less serious offences and non-punitive purposes administrative assistance would be indicated. In that case the administrative methods of investigation are used. At the same time, less heavily reinforced means of legal recourse would suffice.[68] According to this line of reasoning, judicial assistance should be used for the more complex investigations where serious charges are usually levelled against the persons involved. This would offer more scope for operation, but stricter requirements would at the same time apply in respect of legal recourse. Therefore, cooperation in criminal matters should be restricted to cooperation between judicial authorities and cannot include supervisory authorities.

However, this line of reasoning ignores the fact that the current system also fails to fulfil its conditions. It presupposes consensus concerning the seriousness of the underlying facts and how worthy of punishment these are, whereas such consensus is as yet lacking in the EU Member States.[69] The above discussion of Dutch and German law alone amply illustrates this. On the contrary, the current division between administrative assistance and judicial assistance rather seems to be the result of random history and a number of parallel developments which were not coordinated. The extension of the scope of application of judicial assistance to the *Ordnungswidrigkeiten* serves as an example of this.[70] Administrative assistance and judicial assistance have developed along separate lines, especially after the Treaty of Amsterdam. Coordination between the first

---

68 Such legal protection would still have to fulfil the requirements of Article 6 ECHR, however. I will discuss this aspect later.

69 This might however be about to change, especially after the judgment in Case C-176/03, *supra* note 3, where in ground 80 the Court held that the *ultimum remedium* nature of criminal law is the prime consideration.

70 Germany attempted also to let cooperation in connection with *Ordnungswidrigkeiten* take place through administrative assistance. To this end, it made the following declaration to the 1978 Council of Europe European Convention on the Obtaining Abroad of Information and Evidence in Administrative Matters, 100 *European Treaty Series*: 'The Convention shall apply for purposes of requests addressed to the Federal Republic of Germany to any proceedings in respect of offences the punishment of which does not fall within the jurisdiction of the judicial authorities at the time of the request for assistance. In the Federal Republic of Germany such proceedings include proceedings for fines under the Administrative Offences Act (Gesetz über Ordnungswidrigkeiten) as published on 2 January 1975 (...) and last amended by Article 4 of the law of 5 October 1978 (...).'

and third pillar of the EU barely took place, even though there was ample reason for it given the coherence and overlap of the underlying subject matter.[71]

A third, much-heard argument is that the circumvention of criminal procedural law guarantees has to be prevented. In this, reference is often made to the condition of double criminality in mutual judicial assistance and the more extensive procedures for legal recourse that apply in the execution of requests for judicial assistance. For this reason, administrative assistance should be strictly separated from judicial assistance. I also doubt the tenability of this position. It is true that legal recourse against criminal law means of coercion, such as searches, is often more substantial than in investigations of an administrative law character. Administrative law demands for information for example are not always considered as acts against which separate legal recourse should be possible. However, this often becomes different in a transnational context. A number of countries, notwithstanding their domestic law, do provide for legal recourse against decisions to grant administrative assistance.[72] On the other hand, the quality of legal recourse in the case of judicial assistance should not be overestimated. The inter-state rule of non-inquiry for example causes legal recourse to be potentially less effective. In addition, the precise nature and form of individual legal protection may differ per country, which may, when these countries are involved in mutual cooperation, give rise to a situation where a person has either two options for legal recourse or none at all. This phenomenon is sometimes referred to as 'the crack in the system of international cooperation in criminal matters' (in Dutch: *systeembreuk*).[73] Furthermore, in the third pillar the abolition of national *exequatur* procedures in judicial assistance is currently favoured. Mutual recognition is the motto. The proposal for a Framework Decision concerning a European Evidence Warrant which in time is to replace mutual judicial assistance within the EU is a good example of this.[74] Grounds for refusal and the condition of double criminality will be restricted as much as

---

71 Not all of the problems noted above may be blamed on a lack of coordination between the first and the third pillar, however. Also in administrative assistance, which is unequivocally first pillar material, the implications of punitive administrative sanctioning are insufficiently recognized in transnational cooperation. This is affecting among other things the transnational protection of the *nemo tenetur* principle.

72 The Netherlands is actually a striking example of this as it expressly provides for legal protection against decisions to grant assistance in mutual administrative assistance in tax matters. Oddly, a different approach is applied in administrative assistance in financial matters.

73 A. Orie, 'De verdachte tussen wal en schip òf de systeem-breuk in de kleine rechtshulp', in: E. André de la Porte et al. (eds.), *Bij deze stand van zaken – Bundel opstellen aangeboden aan A.L. Melai*, 1983, pp. 351–361; see also A. Klip, *Criminal law in the European Union* (inaugural lecture at the University of Maastricht), 2005, p. 64; Aukje A.H. van Hoek and Michiel J.J.P. Luchtman, *The European Convention on Human Rights and Transnational Cooperation in Criminal Matters*, in this vol., pp. 473 et seq.

74 Proposal of 14 November 2003 for a Council Framework Decision on the European Evidence Warrant for obtaining objects, documents and data for use in proceedings in criminal matters, COM(2003) 688 final.

possible in the new system. This will also lower the level of legal protection in judicial assistance.[75]

It is however the fourth and last argument which will be discussed here that I consider to be the most convincing. This argument concerns what is termed the 'silver platter issue': would the elimination of the distinction not cause authorities more frequently to request the application of powers that they do not have themselves by means of a request for assistance and thereby get the requested information presented to them on a silver platter as it were? Not only might the respective powers of the cooperating authorities differ considerably per country, but the effects of this can only be reinforced when it is furthermore authorities with a different status that cooperate. Especially when – as is so often the case – the use of powers is requested that interfere with fundamental rights I consider it undesirable that the authorities themselves are able by means of mutual cooperation to expand their powers at will. This is a choice that has to be made by the legislator, not by the executive.[76]

In my view it is especially this dilemma that should be dealt with.[77] The question is whether the individual EU Member States are capable of this. It would make more sense to raise this problem to a higher, supranational level. The EU/EC – *i.e.* the first *and* the third pillar together – provide a highly suitable platform for this, especially now that the creation of a European justice area is propagated for the entire European Union (Article 2 TEU) and criminal law powers of the EC have been recognized in the first pillar. A pillar-transcending approach of transnational cooperation in the supervision and investigation of violations of the Market Abuse Directive would appear logical. It would be useful here to indicate the outlines of an alternative model, without, however, pretending to be exhaustive. This will be the subject of the next section.

6. ALTERNATIVES FOR THE CURRENT MODEL

6.1. POSSIBLE MAIN FEATURES OF A NEW SYSTEM

As has been stated above, the dilemma under discussion here is that on the one hand, major differences between the Member States may interfere with

75 See thereon Van Hoek and Luchtman, *supra* note 73.

76 For the sake of convenience, I qualify the Public Prosecution Service as part of the executive here. In some countries, however, the Public Prosecution Service is part of the judiciary.

77 It has to be said, however, that the Market Abuse Directive acknowledges this problem more than other Community legislation, given that Article 12 of the Directive defines minimum powers which the regulators – either in cooperation with the judicial authorities or not – must have. To that extent, this reduces the risk of abuses. However, my problem with this is that this approach does nothing to promote transparent cooperation. I have already touched upon this in the discussion of Article 12 in Section 2.2 above.

transnational cooperation, but that on the other hand where such cooperation is nevertheless permitted these differences may easily cause a loss of legal protection. These difficulties cannot be solved by individual states. A coordinated approach is needed, as is a certain amount of harmonization of the rules on cooperation.[78] This fact in my view compels the EU to formulate rules at European level which may deviate from the national legal order to *the extent* to which this is necessary for transnational cooperation. As this concerns matters which do not only come under the first pillar, but also under the third pillar, it would make sense to handle them in the same way and in a coordinated manner within both pillars.

What would the main features of such a system be? As I have stated, I favour a system in which the national status of an authority (*i.e.* 'judicial' or 'administrative') is not decisive for its possibilities for cooperation in a cross-border context. National differences in law enforcement are after all intrinsic to the model of indirect enforcement that has been chosen within the EU. Even more so than in the case of cooperation between authorities with similar status, it is important in the case of authorities with different status that the requested authority is able to assess for itself what exactly it is granting assistance for. Therefore, direct communication between 'administrative' and 'judicial' authorities should be made possible; the organic criterion should be abolished. This increases the transparency of the cooperation and in this way counters improper use or even abuse. Types of indirect cooperation whereby cooperation takes place via another competent authority and is difficult to supervise must be prevented. For this reason also the problem must be handled in a coordinated manner from the first and third pillar jointly.

All this is not to say that the requested authority for the execution of such requests should be given new powers or powers that deviate from the internal enforcement of law. On the contrary, the main rule should still be that the requested authority applies its own powers and procedures, also when assisting foreign countries (*locus regit actum*). For the individual, and especially for those who are not involved in the proceedings on the merits in the requesting state, this increases the accessibility and foresee-ability of government action and prevents the requested authority from handling requests that are alien to its own task. This authority should however not distinguish between *punitive administrative law* and *criminal law* procedures. After all, due to the case law of the ECtHR there is sufficient clarity concerning the interpretation of the concept

78 The precise meaning of the term 'harmonization' is still being debated. I use this term in the meaning given to it by Tadić, in: A. Klip and H. van der Wilt (eds.), *Harmonisation and harmonising measures in criminal law*, Amsterdam 2002. It does not mean unification or approximation (meaning the elimination of differences between two or more legal orders), but coordination (increasing the inner consistency of two or more legal orders), in this case by legislative intervention and supervision by the ECJ, with a view to international cooperation.

of 'punitive sanction'. If therefore for the facts under investigation a criminal procedural law power to perform searches is available in state A, this should also be applied for the purpose of punitive administrative means of sanctioning in state B. Conversely, administrative powers in state B will also have to be applied – with due observance of the *nemo tenetur* principle – following a request from a judicial authority in state A. In such cases, the obligation of professional secrecy under Article 13 and the rule of speciality under Article 16 of the Market Abuse Directive provide further guarantees against improper use.[79] They guarantee that the powers can only be used to serve the objectives for which the Market Abuse Directive was created.

These things however require the coordination and harmonization of a number of preconditions for the benefit of this cooperation. Simply being a party to the ECHR does not suffice for the purpose of such harmonization. The point is to recognize that national systems may in themselves be completely compatible with the Convention, but because of a wide margin of appreciation may differ to such an extent that cooperation may still go against the Convention or may reduce or even cancel the effect of Conventional guarantees.[80] For this reason, there will have to be agreement concerning for example the question as of what point criminal procedural powers may be used in transnational cases[81] and which authority may authorize their use or may apply them. Other questions as well, such as the question of guaranteeing the *nemo tenetur* principle,[82] the question of the use of the information supplied[83] and the question of legal

---

79 Corresponding provisions should in fact also be included in the third pillar instruments; see below.

80 *Supra* note 73.

81 Essentially, this concerns a transnationally defined concept of 'a reasonable suspicion.' In many countries the concept of a reasonable suspicion is considered an elaboration of the proportionality principle; cf. for Germany L. Schulz, *Normiertes Misstrauen: der Verdacht im Strafverfahren* (Habil. Frankfurt am Main), Frankfurt am Main 2001; J. Corts and H. Hege, 'Die Funktion des Tatverdachts im Strafverfahren, nos. 1 and 2', 1976 *JA/Juristische Arbeitsblätter: für Ausbildung und Examen*, pp. 303–308 and pp. 379–386. In the Netherlands, this is currently being discussed; cf. the proposals from the research project *Strafvordering 2001*, M.S. Groenhuijsen and G. Knigge (eds.), *Dwangmiddelen en rechtsmiddelen – Derde interimrapport onderzoeksproject Strafvordering 2001*, Deventer 2002, and the response by the Dutch Minister of Justice; *Kamerstukken II* 2003–2004, 29 271, no. 1, pp. 13 et seq.

82 Attention will also have to be paid to a transnational right to remain silent. Which persons are entitled to such a right? Do they only have this right if they are suspects or also if they are heard in a different capacity, for instance as a third party or witness? As of what point is one entitled to a right to remain silent? What is the scope of this right? Does it also apply in case a request has both punitive and non-punitive purposes?

83 Mutual agreement and clarity concerning the use of the information that has been provided are essential. Some powers for instance are so far-reaching that they are only permitted for limited purposes. Often such powers are secret by nature, which means that the person involved does not know about the measure taken. This makes the person involved into the mere 'object' of the investigation. In many countries, this has led to additional safeguards with respect to the goals for which such information may consequently be used. The question is how this principle of strict speciality is to be ensured in a transnational context.

remedies[84] should be tackled and answered at European level. Limited harmonization of national law is needed in order to tackle the problems that nowadays already exist, but even gain weight after the removal of the partitions between administrative and judicial assistance. Although the requested authority would thus in principle make use of its own powers, in given cases substitute supranational rules instead of national rules would apply. For the purpose of interpretation of these supranational rules judicial control by the European Court of Justice would seem indicated.

Again, we are not talking about the complete harmonization of national administrative and criminal procedural law as a goal in itself, but about the partial harmonization of rules that apply in cases of transnational cooperation. The underlying idea is that where on the one hand it is accepted that the practical implementation and enforcement of much of European law is carried out by the Member States, we also on the other hand need facilities which in cases of transnational cooperation are able to do justice to national differences and national autonomy, but that at the same time iron out the major differences in order to prevent a loss of transnational legal protection. I do not aim to provide complete answers to these questions. I consider it much more important that these questions are asked now and that this takes place in a coordinated fashion, whereby it is also recognized at European level that there is a considerable overlap between cooperation under the first pillar and cooperation under the third pillar.

6.2. OTHER OPTIONS

Assuming a desire to solve the problems outlined above, other options could also be defended. I will briefly mention two here. First, it could be argued that the EC should use the legislative competence in the field of criminal law which it has accepted for itself in Case C-176/03 (also) to smooth down the irregularities described above. The problem of cooperation would thereby indirectly lose

---

Similar questions may be asked in respect of the application of administrative powers of investigation which rely on the active cooperation of the person concerned. In many legal orders, such powers are permitted, as they are coupled with detailed regulations concerning the (purpose-bound and confidential) use of the information (cf. Articles 13 and 16(2) of the Market Abuse Directive). Again, the question is how this principle of strict secrecy and speciality is to be ensured in a transnational context. Attention should be paid especially to the extent to which judicial authorities are bound by such a transnational official duty of confidentiality.

84 Think of the following questions: against which acts should legal recourse be provided at the least? Should such recourse take place before or after? Should it take place in the requested or in the requesting state? What authority – for example, a court – should offer this protection? What are the rights of the persons concerned to participate in the proceedings or to appeal against decisions? What persons are entitled to legal recourse? See hereon also Van Hoek and Luchtman, *supra* note 73.

relevance, as from then on cooperation could take place through judicial channels. Faltering international cooperation could be cited as an argument in favour of (mandatory) criminal law enforcement, especially if in the near future cooperation is to take place on the basis of the European Evidence Warrant.

It is to be hoped, however, that the Community will use its newly acquired power judiciously. Intervening in the nature and organization of national law enforcement may have far-reaching consequences. After all, there is a reason that the Court applies quite strict requirements to the conditions for criminal law sanctioning: 'However, the last-mentioned finding [that, as a general rule, neither criminal law nor the rules of criminal procedure falls within the Community's competence, ML] does not prevent the Community legislature, when the application of effective, proportionate and dissuasive criminal penalties by the competent national authorities is an *essential* measure for combating *serious* environmental offences, from taking measures which relate to the criminal law of the Member States which it considers *necessary* in order to ensure that the rules which it lays down on environmental protection are *fully effective* [italics added, ML].'[85] In short, for the enforcement of the legal interest involved (in this case, the integrity of the European financial markets instead of the environment) enforcement through criminal law has to be the best possible option.[86] Only then will legislative interference be indicated. This is clearly a further elaboration of the *ultimum remedium* notion by the Court.

In its explanation to the proposed Market Abuse Directive the European Commission indicates why a certain degree of harmonization of law enforcement is preferred: 'In principle it is unacceptable in an integrated financial market for wrongful conduct to incur a heavy penalty in one country, a light one in another and no penalty in a third. However, full harmonization of penal sanctions is not provided for in the EC Treaty. Nevertheless, it is both desirable and consistent with Community law for the Directive to set a general obligation for Member States to impose and determine sanctions to be imposed for infringement of measures pursuant to the Directive in a way that is sufficient to promote compliance with its requirements.'[87] Insofar as this passage suggests that criminal law harmonization is a panacea for the problems noted, but that the EC at the time lacked the necessary power, this to me would appear to convey the wrong message. It is difficult to see why punitive administrative sanctions could not suffice here.

---

85 ECJ 13 September 2005, C-176/03, §48, *supra* note 3. It yet remains to be seen how fully the Court will review the implementation of these criteria by the European legislator; cf. Borgers, *supra* note 8.

86 This would require the existence of a certain empirical basis for that choice; cf. Corstens 2005, *supra* note 6.

87 COM(2001) 281 final, p. 5.

For this reason, criminal law enforcement which is mandatorily prescribed by the EC should be rejected, *to the extent that* such legislative intervention would be the result of a desire to promote transnational cooperation. For this purpose, such intervention would go too far, given that it also covers internal law enforcement. Moreover, it would not solve all the problems encountered. Even in the case of such a legislative operation, administrative supervision and with it administrative assistance will remain important factors. The problems outlined above will not be erased by opting in favour of criminal law enforcement: information that was provided during the supervisory stage may later prove relevant during the investigation or vice versa; the Public Prosecution Service may be in need of the expertise of the supervisory authority, etcetera. All these consequences have to be thought out before criminal law enforcement is opted for.

A second solution could be to reinforce the partitions between administrative assistance and judicial assistance.[88] By tightening the provisions concerning speciality and secrecy separate channels could be created which would also make it more difficult to circumvent legal guarantees. However, this argument also ignores the difference in law enforcement between countries. At the very least in that case all forms of administrative sanctioning, including the Dutch administrative fine, would have to be transferred to the realm of judicial assistance. But even then we would find that the administrative and the judicial authorities simply cannot do without one another. It does seem inefficient to separate punishment-orientated cooperation from other forms of cooperation at the transnational level if at the national level cooperation between judicial authorities and administrative authorities is in fact required.

7. FINAL REMARKS

Above I have discussed the growing influence of the European Union on the shape taken by national law enforcement and the consequences this has for cooperation at European level, using the Market Abuse Directive to illustrate the point. Criminal law enforcement prescribed by the EC has become possible after Case C-176/03. It cannot be ruled out that in time it will indeed be stipulated that rules provided in the Market Abuse Directive must be criminally enforced by the Member States.

---

88 Cf. Swart, p. 457, and Lagodny, p. 738, in Albin Eser et al. (eds), *supra* note 55. These authors by contrast consider the speciality principle an important guarantee; see hereon also J.J.E. Schutte, 'Administrative cooperation', in: M. Delmas-Marty (ed.), *What kind of criminal policy for Europe?*, The Hague/London/Boston 1993, pp. 191–204; J.M. Sjöcrona, 'Communautaire administratieve samenwerking bij EG-fraude: immuun voor mensenrechten', in: J.W. van der Hulst (ed.), *Administratieve bijstand in de EG*, Deventer 1995, pp. 71–88.

However, the debate which has – rightly – begun to rage concerning EC powers in the field of criminal law, threatens to elbow aside another important topic. In my view, more attention than is currently the case should be focused on the nature and manner of transnational cooperation in enforcement matters. This topic from the point of view of the creation of an integrated stock market (and also for other Community areas) would seem to me to be at least equally important. Both topics touch upon each other. Future discussions concerning the use and need for Union-wide criminal law enforcement may be influenced by the possibilities for transnational cooperation, especially in a system of indirect enforcement, in which the Member States are (for the time being?)[89] limited to operating within the confines of their own borders. Opting in favour of criminal law enforcement implies that mutual judicial assistance, and in the future possibly also the European Evidence Warrant (EEW), is gaining importance at the expense of mutual administrative assistance.

Criminal law enforcement, however, is not the miracle drug to cure all ills, especially not when it comes to international cooperation. Even in case of Union-wide criminal law enforcement mutual administrative assistance remains relevant for criminal law enforcement. After all, supervision – and, as a consequence, administrative assistance – is an indispensable part of the enforcement chain. Consequently, the problem will remain that the cooperating authorities, either directly or indirectly,[90] retain the option to choose between judicial assistance and administrative assistance. Differences in the scope of application, grounds for refusal, restriction to purpose, legal recourse, etc., in themselves may justify a choice in favour of either the one approach (*e.g.* judicial assistance) or the other (*e.g.* administrative assistance) and therefore affect the transparency of inter-state data traffic. The differences between cooperation in administrative matters and cooperation in criminal matters are even set to increase with the arrival of the European Evidence Warrant, which is based on completely different starting points than mutual administrative assistance. For this reason, coordination between the first and the third pillar is essential.

I consider it remarkable, therefore, how little attention is paid to this issue, of which I am convinced that it impedes the realization of the integrated financial market in respect of enforcement and which may – partly – be viewed as an alternative for a possible mandatory criminal law enforcement, prescribed by the EC. In my opinion, the efforts of the Union in its entirety (*i.e.* the first and the

89 Some financial Directives offer the possibility of cross-border intervention by regulators; cf. Article 57 of Council Directive 2004/39/EC of 21 April 2004 on markets in financial instruments amending Council Directives 85/611/EEC and 93/6/EEC and Directive 2000/12/EC of the European Parliament and of the Council and repealing Council Directive 93/22/EEC, *OJ* L 2004 145/1.

90 By the latter I mean the involvement of other authorities. Given the close cooperation at national level between the regulator and the Public Prosecution Service this seems an obvious solution and something that is to a certain extent even expected of these authorities.

third pillar taken together) should at this point in time primarily be focused on facilitating cooperation between the Member States, whereby the pillar structure is where necessary disregarded and whereby differences in enforcement and organization between the Member States concerned are taken into account. Transparency and limited recognition of mutual differences, but with (restrictive and coordinated) legislative intervention in both the first and the third pillar are key concepts in this. Separate platforms do not contribute to this; quite the contrary, in fact.

V. EUROPEAN VETERINARY AND FOOD LAW[*] AND THE EUROPEAN COMPOSITE ADMINISTRATION

Klaus Knipschild

1. INTRODUCTION

Veterinary and food law is one of the first law areas the European Community dealt with.[1] Even before the creation of the European Economic Community (EEC) in 1957, the veterinary administrations of the first six Member States had held discussions which laid the basis for the following work of the European Commission.[2] Today, a wide range of provisions have come into existence, which deal with nearly all forms of food products of animal origin and which cover the whole food production chain.[3]

The main objective of veterinary and food law is to protect consumers and animals against diseases resulting from animals or products of animal origin, for example food.[4] Various dangers and risks exist. Animal diseases can be

* This contribution is based on PhD research published as Klaus Knipschild, 'Lebensmittelsicherheit als Aufgabe des Veterinär- und Lebensmittelrechts', Nomos Baden-Baden 2003. A first version (in German) was published in: Eberhard Schmidt-Assmann and Bettina Schöndorf-Haubald, Der Europäische Verwaltungsverband, Mohr Siebeck. 2005, p. 87–102.

1 The history and development of European veterinary and food law is described in Knipschild, *Lebensmittelsicherheit als Aufgabe des Veterinär- und Lebensmittelrechts*, 2003, p. 116 et seq.

2 Cf. Störiko, *Deutsches Tierärzteblatt 1962*, p. 313; Brühann, *Archiv für Lebensmittelhygiene 1986*, p. 31.

3 Characteristic for this comprehensive and integrated approach are slogans like 'from stable to table', 'from the farm to the fork', 'from plough to plate' or 'from farm to table', cf. the homepage of the Directorate-General (DG) 'Health and Consumer Protection', the communication 'Consumer Health and Food Safety', COM (97) 183 final and the White Paper on Food Safety, COM (1999) 719 final; regarding the 'comprehensive and integrated approach' as a principle of European veterinary and food law see also Knipschild (fn. 1), p. 230 et seq.

4 Further objectives are the protection of humans against risks and damages resulting from animal diseases not transmittable via food, the protection against fraud, maintenance and enhancement of the quality of food, the protection of the environment against damages resulting from animals or products of animal origin and at least the protection of animal health and welfare. Cf. the 'Principles regarding the Objectives and the Organisation of the Veterinary Administration' (*Grundsätze über Aufgaben und Aufbau der Veterinärfach-*

transmitted as early as during breeding. However, the classic way of transmission is still transmission between live animals. Additional risks may result from feed and veterinary medicines. During the production and transport of food, hygiene is one of the most important issues. In any case, by-products of slaughter are processed into animal feed and this leads to certain risks for the feed and food chains.

With regard to the typical classification of German administrative law, veterinary and food law with its focus on health protection is part of the area of administration dealing with public order (*Ordnungsverwaltung*). In former times, its main objective was danger prevention. However, in our increasingly complex world the control of risks (defined as a preliminary stage of danger) becomes more important. Due to their objectives to protect the health of consumers and/or animals, the following areas of law may be identified as parts of veterinary and food law: the areas of law with regard to breeding (*Tierzuchtrecht*), animal diseases (*Tierseuchenrecht*), veterinary medicine (*Tierarzneimittelrecht*), feed (*Futtermittelrecht*), meat hygiene (*Fleischhygienerecht*), food (*Lebensmittelrecht*) and animal waste disposal (*Tierkörperbeseitigungsrecht*).[5]

The development of European veterinary and food law may be divided into roughly two phases. During the first half of the nineties of the last century, the main objective was to establish a common market (Article 2 of the Treaty establishing the European Community), and an internal market (Article 14 of the Treaty establishing the European Community). The provisions for live animals and food of animal origin have been harmonised step by step to eliminate trade barriers (e.g. import stops or numerous controls). Such barriers had been justified by the Member States with respect to the different health standards within the European Community.[6] After the internal market had been established at the beginning of the nineties, the focus changed, and various food scandals (BSE and contaminated feed) accelerated developments. The establishment of a comprehensive legal framework accentuating the objective of food safety[7] has been given greater prominence than in former times. This is also reflected in organisational decisions, for example, the

verwaltung,) issued by the 'German Working Committee of the Veterinary Civil Servants of the Federal States' (*Arbeitsgemeinschaft der leitenden Veterinärbeamten der Länder (ArgeVet)*), 1978.

5 Regarding the term *Veterinary and food law* see Knipschild (fn. 1), p. 22 et seq.

6 A good characterisation of this past situation was the slogan that after the elimination of customs duties "the customs officer was replaced by the veterinary", see Schlacht- und Viehhofzeitung 1967, p. 453. According to the Commission, the approximation of the laws of the Member States was "condition sine qua non" for the functioning of the common market (see answer to a question of the European Parliament, OJ 128, 8,8,1964, p. 2146).

7 Regarding the term *food safety* see *Knipschild* (fn. 1), p. 19 et seq.

establishment of the European Food Safety Authority (EFSA), which took up its work in 2003.[8]

In the following sections, this article will present a short overview about and a classification of the administrative actions of the Member States and the European Community so that an insight can be gained into the content of some important provisions of European Veterinary and food law. The main focus will be on provisions aiming to protect human health. Subsequently, the cooperation between the Member States and the European Community will be described and the cooperation amongst the Member States. Finally, the actions to be taken by the European Community when dangers and risks concerning the human health arise will be examined.

2. ADMINISTRATIVE ACTIONS OF THE MEMBER STATES

2.1. INTRODUCTION

Owing to the principle of indirect execution (*Prinzip des indirekten Vollzugs*), the Member States' administrations are an indispensable support for the Community in the field of European veterinary and food law. Their administrative actions are to a large extent influenced by provisions set by the European Community. These actions will be classified in the following sections. With regard to the protection of the human health, one can roughly differentiate between permits and approvals (I), veterinary checks and inspections (II) as well as the killing and disposal of animals or products (III).

2.2. PERMITS AND APPROVALS

Such actions can also be described as preventive prohibitions with reserved exceptions, a typical instrument in the field of the administration dealing with public order. In German law, permits and approvals are enacted in the form of an administrative act (*Verwaltungsakt*). Examples for such acts by the competent authorities of the Member States and which are based on European Law are the

8 See Regulation (EC) 178/2002 of the European Parliament and of the Council of 28 January 2002 laying down the general principles and requirements of food law, establishing the European Food Safety Authority and laying down procedures in matters of food safety, OJ L 31, 1.2.2002, p. 1 et seq. However, the tasks of this Authority are limited. According to Art. 23 of the aforementioned Regulation it has to provide scientific opinions and scientific and technical support for the legislation and policy of the Community. Regarding such type of Agencies see *Riedel*, in this volume, p. 157, 3.2.

approval of collection and storage centres for animal semen,[9] of assembly centres for animals and animal dealers,[10] of veterinary medicines,[11] of slaughterhouses[12] and of rendering plants (*Tierkörperbeseitigungsanstalten*).[13] Permits and approvals can therefore relate to persons, products and sites (plants, companies etc.).

9 Cf. Article 3(1) Council Directive 88/407/EEC of 14 June 1988 laying down the animal health requirements applicable to intra-Community trade in and imports of deep-frozen semen of domestic animals of the bovine species (OJ L 194, 22.7.1988, p. 10). A consolidated version is available in CELEX.

10 Cf. Article 11 and 13 Council Directive 64/432/EEC of 26 June 1964 on animal health problems affecting intra-Community trade in bovine animals and swine (OJ, English special edition: Series I Chapter 1963–1964 P. 164; consolidated version in Council Directive 97/12/EC of 17 March 1997 amending and updating Directive 64/432/EEC on health problems affecting intra-Community trade in bovine animals and swine (OJ L 109, 25.4.1997, p. 1).

11 Cf. originally Council Directive 81/851/EEC of 28 September 1981 on the approximation of the laws of the Member States relating to veterinary medicinal products (OJ L 317, 6.11.1981, p. 1) and now Directive 2001/82/EC of the European Parliament and of the Council of 6 November 2001 on the Community code relating to veterinary medicinal products (OJ L 311, 28.11.2001, p. 1). Regarding the centralised procedure with approval of the medicines by the Community see under C. Regarding the procedures in general Hinze, *Tierärztliche Umschau 1992*, p. 690 et seq. and Collatz, *Die neuen Europäischen Zulassungsverfahren für Arzneimittel*, 1996.

12 Cf. originally Article 3(1) Council Directive 64/433/EEC of 26 June 1964 on health problems affecting intra-Community trade in fresh meat (OJ English special edition: Series I Chapter 1963–1964 P. 185; a consolidated version is available in CELEX), repealed with Directive 2004/41/EC of the European Parliament and of the Council of 21 April 2004 repealing certain Directives concerning food hygiene and health conditions for the production and placing on the market of certain products of animal origin intended for human consumption and amending Council Directives 89/662/EEC and 92/118/EEC and Council Decision 95/408/EC (OJ L 157, 30.4.2004) in favour of Regulation (EC) 853/2004 of the European Parliament and of the Council of 29 April 2004 laying down specific hygiene rules for food of animal origin (OJ L 139, 30.4.2004, p. 55; corrigendum OJ L 226, 25.6.2004, p. 22), Regulation (EC) 852/2004 of the European Parliament and of the Council of 29 April 2004 on the hygiene of foodstuffs (OJ L 139, 30.4.2004, p. 1; corrigendum OJ L 226, 25.6.2004, p. 3) and Regulation (EC) 854/2004 of the European Parliament and of the Council of 29 April 2004 laying down specific rules for the organisation of official controls on products of animal origin intended for human consumption (OJ L 139, 30.4.2004, p. 206). Regulation (EC) 852/2004 deals inter alia with HACCP (Hazard Analysis on Critical Points).

13 Cf. originally Article 4 Council Directive 90/667/EEC of 27 November 1990 laying down the veterinary rules for the disposal and processing of animal waste, for its placing on the market and for the prevention of pathogens in feedstuffs of animal or fish origin and amending Directive 90/425/EEC (OJ L 363, 27.12.1990, p. 51) and now Article 10 et seq. Regulation (EC) No 1774/2002 of the European Parliament and of the Council of 3 October 2002 laying down health rules concerning animal by-products not intended for human consumption (OJ L 273, 10.10.2002, p. 1).

2.3. VETERINARY CHECKS AND INSPECTIONS

2.3.1. Introduction

Such controls are not legal acts but are merely real acts (*Realakte*). One can differentiate between controls regarding animals and products, and controls regarding sites.[14]

2.3.2. Animals and products

Veterinary checks are particularly relevant in trade, regardless of whether intra-Community trade is concerned or the trade of the Community with other states. Semen, embryos, feed, animals and food (e.g. meat) are subject to controls. In intra-Community trade, veterinary checks will be executed in principle only in the state of dispatch.[15] However, the state of destination may carry out spot checks and further checks in the event of a serious presumption of irregularity.[16] Veterinary checks on imports from third countries are carried out at border inspection posts in the Member State where the animals or products are entering the European Community for the first time.[17] If no irregularities can be found, the animals or the products can be distributed within the whole European Community without any further control. Further examples of checks and controls are the ante-mortem and post-mortem inspections of slaughter animals and the meat, respectively.[18] With regard to some animals, ante-mortem inspections have to be carried out before every slaughter, regardless of whether the meat is destined for intra-Community trade or not.

2.3.3. Site inspections

The once-only approval of plants and companies is followed up by regular inspections to be carried out by the Member States. Specifications for these

---

14 An overall control regimen is established with Regulation (EC) 882/2004 of the European Parliament and of the Council of 29 April 2004 on official controls performed to ensure the verification of compliance with feed and food law, animal health and animal welfare rules (OJ L 165, 30.4.2004, p. 1; corrigendum OJ L 191, 28.5.2004, p. 1).

15 Cf. Article 1, Article 3 and Article 4 Council Directive 90/425/EEC of 26 June 1990 concerning veterinary and zootechnical checks applicable in intra-Community trade in certain live animals and products with a view to the completion of the internal market (OJ L 224, 18.8.1990, p. 24).

16 Cf. Article 5 Council Directive 90/425 (fn. 15).

17 Cf. Article 4 Council Directive 91/496/EEC of 15 July 1991 laying down the principles governing the organisation of veterinary checks on animals entering the Community from third countries and amending Directives 89/662/EEC, 90/425/EEC and 90/675/EEC (OJ L 268, 24.9.1991, p. 65).

18 Cf. originally Article 3(1) Council Directive 64/433 (fn. 12) and now Article 5 Regulation (EC) 854/2004 (fn. 12).

inspections can be found, inter alia, in European food law.[19] The relevant provisions demand that inspections are carried out on a regular basis as well as in the event of a presumption of irregularities (ad hoc controls), as a rule without prior announcement.[20] Furthermore, the Member States have to deliver multi-annual national control plans in accordance with broad guidelines drawn up at Community level.[21] Such guidelines also stipulate that the competent authorities shall be adequately equipped with qualified personnel and the necessary technical facilities.[22]

2.4. KILLING AND DISPOSAL OF ANIMALS OR PRODUCTS

These measures are the third pillar of the administrative actions by the Member States to protect human health. They are possible consequences of a breach of the provisions of veterinary and food law, detected during checks and inspections. German law requires an administrative act prior to such killing or disposal.

Examples can be found in all areas of veterinary and food law: the killing of animals which are sick or infected or believed to be this,[23] the disposal of contaminated feed[24] and of meat originating from sick animals or of meat contaminated with unduly high residues of feed or veterinary medicines.[25]

19 See originally Council Directive 89/397/EEC of 14 June 1989 on the official control of foodstuffs (OJ L 186, 30.6.1989, p. 23) and Council Directive 93/99/EEC of 29 October 1993 on the subject of additional measures concerning the official control of foodstuff (OJ L 290, 24.11.1993, p. 14). Since 1.1.2006 Regulation (EC) No 882/2004 (fn. 14) is applicable.

20 Cf. Article 4 Council Directive 89/397 (fn. 19) and Article 3(1) and (2) Regulation (EC) 882/2004 (fn. 14).

21 The Commission yearly recommends a coordinated programme for inspections of the Member States, see Art. 14 Council Directive 89/397. Regarding these programs see Geßler, *Fleischwirtschaft 1991*, p. 886 et seq. and Heckner *Zeitschrift für Lebensmittelrecht 1993*, p. 205 (211). Regarding control plans and reports as instruments see also David, *Inspektionen im Gemeinschaftsrecht*, 2003, Chapter 1, C. II. 3.

22 Cf. originally Article 2 Council Directive 93/99 (fn. 19) and now Article 4, 6 and 51 Regulation (EC) 882/2004 (fn. 14). These stipulations are good examples of the influence of the Commission on the administrative organisation of the Member States albeit through the principle of indirect execution.

23 Cf. Council Directive 92/119/EEC of 17 December 1992 introducing general Community measures for the control of certain animal diseases and specific measures relating to swine vesicular disease (OJ L 62, 15.3.1993, p. 69).

24 See Article 8 and 13 Council Directive 95/53/EC of 25 October 1995 fixing the principles governing the organisation of official inspections in the field of animal nutrition (OJ L 265, 8.11.1995, p. 17).

25 See originally Article 5 and 7 Council Directive 64/433 (fn. 12) and now Article 5(3) together with Annex 1, Section II, Chapter V Regulation (EC) 854/2004 (fn. 12).

3. ADMINISTRATIVE ACTIONS OF THE EUROPEAN COMMUNITY

3.1. INTRODUCTION

The Member States still bear responsibility for the main part of the administrative actions. However, the Community has acquired more competences in this field since the beginning of the nineties of the last century. One can also differentiate between permits and approvals on Community level, (I) as well as between veterinary checks and inspections (II). The actions to be taken by the Community in cases of danger will be highlighted in an extra section (E).

3.2. PERMITS AND APPROVALS

In the past special attention has been given to the authorisation of certain veterinary medicines, originally stipulated in Regulation (EC) 2909/93,[26] now Regulation (EC) 726/2004.[27] The procedure is applicable to veterinary medicines produced with certain biotechnological processes as well as to veterinary medicines destined to enhance the productivity of the animals. Authorisations have to be applied for from the European Medicines Agency (EMEA), established in 1994. EMEA evaluates the requirements for authorisation and works out an opinion on the quality, safety and efficiency of the medicine. The decision on an authorisation is made by the European Commission (with participation of the Member States in the so called "management procedure" (*Verwaltungsausschußverfahren*)) or by the Council of the European Union. When an authorisation is granted, it is valid (and the medicine can be sold) throughout the Community. The refusal of an authorisation constitutes a prohibition of the placing on the market throughout the Community.

Furthermore, the Commission (with the participation of the Member States in the "regulatory procedure" (*Regelungsausschlußverfahren*)) or the Council decides on the authorisation of feed additives. According to Regulation (EC)

---

26 Council Regulation (EEC) No 2309/93 of 22 July 1993 laying down Community procedures for the authorisation and supervision of medicinal products for human and veterinary use and establishing a European Agency for the Evaluation of Medicinal Products (OJ L 214, 24.8.1993, p. 1). Cf. for this regulation the literature cited in fn. 11. Regarding the European Agency for the Evaluation of Medicinal Products see *Riedel*, in this volume, p. 157 et seq.

27 Regulation (EC) 726/2004 of the European Parliament and of the Council of 31 March 2004 laying down Community procedures for the authorisation and supervision of medicinal products for human and veterinary use and establishing a European Medicines Agency (OJ L 136, 30.4.2004, p. 1). Regarding the European Medicines Agency see *Riedel*, in this volume, p. 157 et seq. Regarding the democratic legitimisation of centralized approval procedures see Röhl, in this volume, p. 205 (220 et seq.).

1831/2003,[28] the application has to be addressed to the Commission, which decides after having received an opinion of the EFSA. The authorisation is granted by way of regulation.[29]

3.3. VETERINARY CHECKS AND INSPECTIONS

This is definitely the core of the administrative actions of the Community.[30] Controls are carried out by the Food and Veterinary Office (FVO) of the Commission, which belongs to the Directorate-General (DG) Health and Consumer Protection and has its own inspection teams.[31] The inspections are carried out in third countries[32] as well as in the Member States.

With regard to third countries, the general health standard of the livestock is evaluated as well as the legal and administrative framework in the veterinary and food area.[33] Furthermore, there are inspections of single farms and factories, which export meat to the Community, for example. Taking the inspections as a basis, the Community establishes lists of the countries and farms or factories, which may export animals and food of animal origin to the Community.[34]

---

28 Regulation (EC) 1831/2003 of the European Parliament and of the Council of 22 September 2003 on additives for use in animal nutrition (OJ L 268, 18.10.2003, p. 29).

29 Article 7 Regulation (EC) 1831/2003 (fn. 28).

30 Regarding the inspections see David (fn. 21).

31 Cf. Lugt, Enforcing European and National Food Law in the Netherlands and England, 1999, p. 33.

32 A good example for the regulation of imports into the Community was originally Council Directive 72/462/EEC of 12 December 1972 on health and veterinary inspection problems upon importation of bovine animals and swine and fresh meat from third countries (OJ L 302, 31.12.1972, p. 28). This Directive was originally applicable only to bovine animals, swine and fresh meat. After a pertinent change of its title, its scope of application was extended to meat products, sheep and goats. For meat and meat products again special regulations are now applicable, see Council Directive 2002/99/EC of 16 December 2002 laying down the animal health rules governing the production, processing, distribution and introduction of products of animal origin for human consumption (OJ L 18, 23.1.2003, p. 11). As of 2006 the Directive 72/462/EEC was repealed by Council Directive 2004/68/EC of 26 April 2004 laying down animal health rules for the importation into and transit through the Community of certain live ungulate animals, amending Directives 90/426/EEC and 92/65/EEC and repealing Directive 72/462/EEC (OJ L 139, 30.4.2004, p. 321). Regarding controls in third countries please see Article 46 Regulation (EC) 882/2004 (fn. 14). Regarding import controls see Zwingmann/Rojahn, *Tierärztliche Umschau 1994*, p. 322 (331) and Bätza, *Deutsche Tierärztliche Wochenschrift 1994*, p. 288 (290).

33 As an example see Art. 46(1) Regulation (EC) 882/2004 (fn. 14).

34 See Article 8 Council Directive 2002/99/EC (fn. 32) and Article 3 Council Directive 2004/68/EC (fn. 32). After a proposal of the Commission a Decision according to Article 249 of the Treaty establishing the European Community was adopted by the Council. See also Article 48(2a) Regulation (EC) 882/2004 (fn. 14). Regarding Decisions as instrument of the Community see Vogt, in this volume, p. 341 et seq.

The FVO furthermore ensures that the Community legislation on food safety and animal health is properly implemented and enforced.[35] To achieve this end, the FVO monitors the site inspections as well as the veterinary checks which are to be carried out by the Member States when importing animals and food from third countries or exporting to other Member States (so called "control of the control").

4. COOPERATION

Cooperation takes place amongst the Member States (so called "horizontal" Cooperation) and between the Member States and the Commission (so called "vertical" Cooperation).[36] Against the background of the decentralised execution of the European Veterinary and Food Law, the community-wide trade with animals and food results nearly inevitably in cooperation between the Member States. It is only with such cooperation that the necessary effectiveness of the administrative actions within the Community can be secured.[37]

An example of cooperation is the administrative assistance (*Amtshilfe*) to be granted by the Member States according to Directives 89/608[38] and 93/99[39] and the Regulation (EC) 882/2004. These contain detailed stipulations regarding the exchange of information amongst the Member States and between the Member States and the Commission.[40] This shows the importance of communication as the basis for all cooperation.[41] Furthermore, each Member State may instruct another Member State to check certain facts and to inform it about the results of such check.[42] It is also possible to demand from one Member State a control or an intensified control, of a single farm or production site, for example.[43]

An additional example of cooperation which is based on the exchange of information is the Rapid Alert System for Foodstuffs (RASFF) which serves the fast exchange of information on problems and risks regarding food which fails to

35 Cf. Article 45 Regulation (EC) 882/2004 (fn. 14).

36 Regarding administrative cooperation and the corresponding law see Schmidt-Aßmann, *Europarecht 1996*, p. 270 et seq. and p. 1 et seq. in this volume.

37 Cf. Schmidt-Aßmann, in: Schmidt-Aßmann/Hoffmann-Riem, *Strukturen des Europäischen Verwaltungsrechts*, 1999, p. 9.

38 Council Directive 89/608/EEC of 21 November 1989 on mutual assistance between the administrative authorities of the Member States and cooperation between the latter and the Commission to ensure the correct application of legislation on veterinary and zootechnical matters (OJ L 351, 2.12.1989, p. 34). Regarding administrative assistance in general see Wettner, in this volume, p. 313 et seq.

39 See fn. 19. This Directive is repealed by Regulation (EC) 882/2004 (fn. 14) as of 1.1.2006.

40 Regarding the originally applicable stipulations see Knipschild (fn. 1), p. 220 et seq.

41 See Schmidt-Aßmann, p. 2 et seq. in this volume.

42 See Article 4(1) and (2) Council Directive 89/608/EEC (fn. 38).

43 See Article 6 Council Directive 89/608/EEC (fn. 38).

comply with the requirements of Food Safety.[44] Such information is to be directed to the Commission from the relevant Member States by standardised form and is to be then forwarded to the other Member States by the Commission.

5. ACTIONS OF THE EUROPEAN COMMUNITY IN CASES OF DANGER

5.1. INTRODUCTION

The Community has various powers in cases of dangers or risks to human health resulting from animals or food, regardless of whether such danger has its origin within the Community or in third countries. In the following section, we will focus on dangers/risks originating within the Community. However, the rules regarding animals and food imported from third countries are comparable.

The groundwork for the power of the Community is laid in Directives 89/662[45] and 90/425[46] (so called "Veterinary Checks Directives") and in Regulation (EC) 178/2002.[47]

5.2. ACTIONS REGARDING VETERINARY CHECKS ACCORDING TO THE DIRECTIVES

The aforementioned Directives not only grant powers to the Community but also oblige and authorise the Member States to take certain actions to protect human health. However, the core element of these provisions is the obligation of the Commission to check (with the participation of representatives of the Member States) the situation in cases of danger and to decide (also with such participation) on the necessary measures to be taken.[48] The necessary measures can also be adopted by the Council.

The bans on exports imposed on the UK during the BSE-crisis and on Belgium during the so called scandal regarding contaminated feed were based

44 The system was established in 1979. Stipulations can now be found in Article 50–52 Regulation (EC) 178/2002 (fn. 8). EFSA is now also integrated in the system. See also Bach, *Zeitschrift für Lebensmittelrecht 2000*, p. 489 et seq. and Eckert, *Gemeinschaftsrechtliche Präventivmaßnahmen in Dringlichkeitsfällen*, in: Dannecker, *Lebensmittelstrafrecht und Verwaltungssanktionen in der Europäischen Union*, 1994, p. 151 et seq.

45 Council Directive 89/662/EEC of 11 December 1989 concerning veterinary checks in intra-Community trade with a view to the completion of the internal market (OJ L 395, 30.12.1989, p. 13).

46 Fn. 15.

47 Fn. 8.

48 See Article 10(4) Council Directive 90/425/EEC (fn. 15).

on these Directives.[49] A precondition for actions on the part of the Community is the occurrence of an illness or of other causes which may result in a danger to animals or to human health. According to the case law of the Court of Justice of the European Communities (ECJ),[50] only a very small likelihood of damage to humans or animals is necessary for actions to be taken by the Community. Where there is uncertainty as to the existence or the extent of risks to human health, the Community may take protective measures without having to wait until the reality and seriousness of those risks become fully apparent. The provisions, according to which the Community may enact all *necessary* measures, barely limit the powers of the Community.[51] Possible measures include bans on export or import as well as on the insertion of products on the market, obligations on the Member States to intensify and/or to carry out further controls, the intensification of inspections on the part the Community and additional notification requirements for the Member States.

The Member States can also be obliged to ban the movement of animals in their territories or to kill livestock. However, the powers of the Community are limited to the extent that the measures may only relate to animals or products of animal origin (food, for instance). Therefore, for example the Community may not demand of its Member States that they revoke licences of certain plants or production sites for access to the internal market.[52]

5.3. ACTIONS ACCORDING TO REGULATION (EC) 178/2002

The proceedings of this regulation regarding emergency measures (Article 53 et seq.) differ in various ways from the provisions of the Directives regarding veterinary checks.

First, the powers of the Commission are limited to food and feed, so that measures regarding animals, semen, embryos etc. are not possible under the regimen of this Regulation. There is explicit mention of some of the measures which the Commission may take, such as suspension of the placing on the market or of the use of the food and/or feed in question. However, the Commission is also entitled to take "*any other appropriate interim measure*". At the same time, the word "*interim*" limits the power of the Community. For instance, the disposal of food or feed is most likely not allowed since these are measures of a "*final*" character.

---

49 See Commission Decision 96/239/EC of 27 March 1996 on emergency measures to protect against bovine spongiform encephalopathy OJ L 78, 28.3.1996, p. 47 and Commission Decision 1999/363/EC of 3 June 1999 on protective measures with regards to contamination by dioxins of certain animal products intended for human or animal consumption OJ L 141, 4.6.1999, p. 24.

50 Case C-157/96, European Court reports 1998 p. I-2211 (2259 and 2261).

51 See also ECJ (fn. 50), p. 2251.

52 This does not bar such measures by the Member States according to national law.

The threshold for an intervention by the Community is a subject of discussion. According to the wording of the Regulation, it is necessary that food or feed originating in the Community or imported from a third country is *likely* to constitute a *serious risk* to human or animal health, before the Community may intervene.

The term *risk*[53] seems to indicate that the very possibility of damage to human or animal health is sufficient for such intervention. On the other hand, the risk must be *serious* and *likely* and therefore one may argue that the threshold is higher than in the Directives regarding veterinary checks. However, since the Commission may only adopt *interim* measures, it seems plausible that the same threshold is adopted in both cases.

Regulation (EC) 178/2002 deviates from the Directives regarding veterinary checks in that it entitles the Commission to provisionally adopt measures after consulting the Member State(s) concerned and only informing the other Member States. A blockade by some Member States can therefore be avoided in cases of emergency. However, the measures must be confirmed, amended, revoked or extended as soon as possible, and at most within ten working days after the adoption, in the so called "regulatory procedure" with the participation of representatives of the Member States involved.

Regulation (EC) 178/2002 furthermore entitles the Commission to set up a crisis unit in which the EFSA participates.[54] This crisis unit shall be responsible for collecting and evaluating all relevant information and identifying the available options as well as keeping the public informed.

6. CONCLUSION

In the past 50 years European veterinary and food law has not only influenced the administrations of the Member States and their actions, but almost inevitably, various relationships amongst the Member States and between the Member States and the Community have developed. It is too early to speak of a "European Veterinary and Food Administration". However, it is undeniable that the first approaches in this direction have been made, as the example of EFSA shows.

---

53 Regarding the terms *danger, risk* and *residual risk* see Knipschild (fn. 1), p. 33 et seq.

54 See Article 56 Regulation (EC) 178/2002 (fn. 8).

VI. REDUCING THE JUDICIAL DEFICIT IN MULTILEVEL ENVIRONMENTAL REGULATION: THE EXAMPLE OF PLANT PROTECTION PRODUCTS

Andrea Keessen*

Summary: This article takes the regulation of plant protection products as an example in order to evaluate the impact of the Aarhus Convention in a multilevel regulatory context and on the European composite administration in particular. The author first gives an overview of the decision-making procedures in this field and discusses two judgments by the Community courts (C-174/05 Stichting Zuid-Hollandse Milieufederatie v College voor de toelating van bestrijdingsmiddelen and Joined Cases T-236/04 and T-241/04, European Environmental Bureau, Stichting Natuur en Milieu v Commission) to demonstrate why the current judicial review procedure presents a judicial deficit. She then evaluates the reduction of the judicial deficit in this field by the implementation of the rules on judicial review of the Aarhus Convention into the European legal order.

1. INTRODUCTION

The environmental law of the EU Member States has often an international background.[1] When the EU Member States are Party to an environmental convention, they apply its rules after they have been transformed into European law by Community institutions. As a rule, the Member States are responsible

---

* Dr. Andrea M. Keessen, assistant Professor, Institute of Constitutional and Administrative Law, Utrecht University. The author wishes to thank Rob Widdershoven, Chris Backes and Marleen van Rijswick for their valuable comments. The article is a slightly revised version of the article with the same name, which appeared in *EELRev* vol. 18, 2007, pp. 26–36 and in: Andreas Follesdal, Ramses A. Wessel and Jan Wouters (eds.), Multilevel Regulation and the EU. *The Interplay between Global, European and National Normative Processes*, Martinus Nijhoff Publishers 2008, pp. 323–344.

1 See for an overview of European environmental law: Jan H. Jans, European Environmental Law, Groningen: Europa Law Publishing, 2000.

for the application and enforcement of European law. However, international and Community institutions and bodies can also take implementing measures. Yet environmental organisations depend on national courts to provide for judicial review. The national procedural rules governing these proceedings have not been designed to function in a multilevel context.[2] Moreover, as a result of the procedural differences in the EU Member States, access to court for environmental organisations is not guaranteed in all EU Member States. The Aarhus Convention on Access to Information, Public Participation in Decision Making and Access to Justice in Environmental Matters aims to redress this issue.[3] Better access to justice for environmental organisations is expected to improve the implementation of environmental law.[4] The regulation of plant protection products is used as an example in order to evaluate the impact of the Aarhus Convention in a multilevel regulatory context.[5] I will first give an overview of the decision-making procedures in this field and discuss two judgments by the Community courts to demonstrate why the current judicial review procedure presents a judicial deficit. Then I will evaluate the reduction of the judicial deficit in this field by the implementation of the rules on judicial review of the Aarhus Convention into the European legal order.[6]

---

2 A.W.H. Meij, 'Toenemende complexiteit van het Europese recht', in: Raad voor de Rechtspraak, Europa en de Nederlandse rechtspraak: de praktische gevolgen, rechtstreeks 2006 (1), p. 35. See for a more general discussion of the judicial deficit issue in relation to various types of decisions used in the European composite administration A.M. Keessen, *European Administrative Decisions. How the EU Regulates Products on the Internal Market*, Europa Law Publishing, 2009.

3 The text of the Aarhus Convention can be found on www.unece.org/env.

4 Cf. Han Somsen, 'The Private Enforcement of Member State Compliance with EC Environmental Law: an Unfulfilled Promise?', in: Han Somsen (ed), *The Yearbook of European Environmental Law* (1) Oxford: Oxford University Press, 2000, p. 311–360; Deirdre Curtin, 'The Decentralised Enforcement of Community Law Rights. Judicial Snakes and Ladders', in: Deirdre Curtin and David O'Keeffe (eds), *Constitutional Adjudication in European Community and national Law*, Dublin: Butterworth, 1992, p. 34. Nicolas de Sadeleer, Gerhard Roller and Miriam Dross (eds), *Access to Justice in Environmental Matters and the Role of NGOs; Empirical Findings and Legal Appraisal*, Groningen: Europa Law Publishing, 2005, p. 177.

5 See for another example: A.S. Mathiesen, 'Public Participation in Decision-making and Access to Justice in EC Environmental Law: the Case of Certain Plans and Programmes', 2003 EELR, p. 36–51; Jonathan Verschuuren, 'Public Participation regarding the Elaboration and Approval of Projects in the EU after the Aarhus Convention', in T.F.M.Etty and H. Somsen (eds), *The Yearbook of European Environmental Law* (4), 2005, Oxford: Oxford University Press, p. 29–48.

6 As the focus of this contribution is on the judicial deficit, the other two pillars of the Aarhus Convention, access to information and public participation, will not be discussed, even though they are of equal importance and contribute to effective judicial review. Access to justice related to denial of environmental information or public participation rights is also left out.

2. REGULATION OF PLANT PROTECTION PRODUCTS

Plant protection products are pesticides used for agricultural purposes. Their use benefits farmers as they kill weed or insects. Environmental organisations take an interest in plant protection products because they are also associated with serious risks to human health, especially children's health, and the environment. They affect people, animals and plants via their contamination of groundwater, soils, food and even the air. Rachel Carson's *Silent Spring* exposed as early as 1962 the hazards of the pesticide DDT.[7] It changed thinking about technological progress and helped setting the stage for the environmental movement and for environmental legislation regulating pesticides.

International rules and measures

The most important piece of international legislation is the 2001 Stockholm Convention on Persistent Organic Pollutants (POPs), which entered into force in 2004.[8] It aims to eliminate production, use, emissions and discharges of chemicals and pesticides exhibiting the characteristics of POPs. Both the European Union and the Member States are Parties to this Convention. Currently, the Stockholm Convention is of limited significance to them, because it targets only 12 chemicals and pesticides. It does not completely ban these POPs, e.g. it allows the use of DDT to fight malaria. Its relevance might increase in the coming years, because it contains criteria for the evaluation of chemicals and pesticides in use, it regulates their disposal and it obliges the Parties to prevent the development of new POPs. It may even introduce a POP review committee that would issue recommendations for the evaluation of chemicals and pesticides.[9]

---

7 Rachel Carson, *Silent Spring*, Boston, New York: Houghton Mifflin, 1962.

8 The text of the Stockholm Convention on Persistent Organic Pollutants (2001) can be found on www.pops.int. The Convention entered into force in May 2004. Its was preceded by the 1979 Convention on Long-Range Transboundary Air Pollution on Persistent Organic Pollutants and the Protocol on Persistent Organic Pollutants (1998) to this Convention, to which the Community is a Party as well. Other important Conventions are the Rotterdam Convention on Prior Informed Consent (1998) (preceded by a voluntary prior informed consent procedure, in effect sins 1989) and the Basel Convention on the Control of Transboundary Movements of Hazardous Wastes and their Disposal (1989). See for an overview of these three Conventions and their inter-relationship: www.pops.int/documents/background/hcwc.pdf.

9 This international review committee might act in the context of the Strategic Approach to International Chemicals Management (SAICM) within the United Nations Framework.

European rules and measures

The European Union is ahead of the international developments. It bans the POPs that the Stockholm Convention forbids from being used in plant protection products via Regulation 850/2004,[10] which also lists other active substances whose presence is forbidden in plant protection products.[11] Moreover the EU has general legislation in the field of water and waste aiming to curb pesticide pollution. What makes the EU really ahead of international developments is that it not only bans substances, but also regulates other aspects. There is European legislation regulating the marketing of pesticides[12] as well as pesticide residues on food[13] and the classification, packaging and labelling of pesticides.[14] For the time being, the regulation of the use of pesticides still belongs to the competences of the Member States. This situation will change as the Commission is developing a Community strategy and action plan on the sustainable *use* of pesticides.[15]

Within the European Union the marketing of pesticides for agricultural use is regulated by Directive 91/414/EC on the placing on the market of plant protection products.[16] This Directive harmonises the legal regimes of the

10 Regulation 850/2004 of the European Parliament and of the Council of 29 April 2004 on persistent organic pollutants and amending Directive 79/117/EEC, OJ 2004 L 158/7.

11 Council Directive of 21 December 1979 prohibiting the placing on the market and the use of plant protection products containing certain active substances, OJ 1978 L33/36, as amended.

12 Council Directive 91/414 EC of 15 July 1991 concerning the placing of plant protection products on the market, OJ 1991 L 230/1, as amended and Directive 98/8/EC of the European Parliament and of the Council, concerning the placing of biocidal products on the market, OJ 1998 L 123/1. Directive 98/8/EC was modelled on Directive 91/414/EC.

13 Directive 90/642 on the fixing of maximum levels for pesticide residues in and on certain products of plant origin, including fruit and vegetables, OJ 1990 L 350/71, frequently amended.

14 Directive 99/45 concerning the approximation of the laws, regulations and administrative provisions of the Member States relating to the classification, packaging and labelling of dangerous preparations, OJ 1999 L 200/1.

15 Communication from the Commission to the Council, the European Parliament, the European Economic and Social Committee and the Committee of the Regions, A Thematic Strategy on the Sustainable Use of Pesticides, COM (2006) 373 final, as proposed in Decision 1600/2002/EC of the European Parliament and of the Council of 22 July 2002 laying down the Sixth Environmental Action Programme, OJ 2002 L242/1, Art. 8 (c) and (d). See also: Communication from the Commission to the Council, the Parliament, the Economic an Social Committee and the Committee of the Regions on the sixth environmental action programme of the European Community, 'Environment 2010: Our future, Our choice', COM (2001) 31 final, p. 43–45.

16 Council Directive 91/414 EC. All references are to the consolidated version: CONSLEG 1991 L0414 – 01/01/2004. This Directive has been replaced by Regulation 1107/2009 of the European Parliament and of the Council of 21 October 2009 concerning the placing of plant protection products on the market, OJ 2009 L309/01. The main innovation of this Regulation is that it adds a mutual recognition procedure. It does not alter the existing procedures and the ensuing judicial deficit caused by them. Since the procedures of the Directive provide the background for a proper understanding of the cases that will be discussed later on, the author has decided not to change this part of the article.

Member States for the authorisation of plant protection products[17] by introducing common authorisation criteria in a multilevel setting.[18] Since 1992, the Commission reviews the active substances used in plant protection products,[19] while the Member States implement the outcome of this review in the authorisation for the marketing of these products. In the Community review process each applicant has to prove that an active substance can be used safely regarding human and animal health and the environment. The European Food Safety Authority ("EFSA") assists the Commission with this task. On the basis of the EFSA's advice, the Commission – assisted by the Standing Committee on the Food Chain and Animal Health – decides whether an active substance may be listed on Annex I to the Directive.[20] A positive decision is issued as a daughter directive to Directive 91/414, because it adds an active substance to the Annex. A negative decision is issued in the form of a Commission or Council decision.

The Community decisions determine the content of national decisions authorizing or rejecting plant protection products containing those active substances, because the Member States are only allowed to authorise plant protection products containing active substances that have been listed on Annex I to Directive 91/414/EC. Other Member States may recognize an authorisation issued in accordance with this multilevel procedure by issuing an identical national authorisation.[21] By contrast, a decision not to include an active substance on Annex I means that the Member States have to ban the substance as well and revoke authorisations for plant protection products containing that active substance. Even though the Directive allows the Member States to deviate from the European rules either by prohibiting plant protection products authorised by other Member States or by allowing them even if they contain banned active substances, such derogations are meant to be temporary.[22] Not all plant protection products are covered by a national authorisation issued in

---

17 In the Netherlands the Pesticides Act ('Bestrijdingsmiddelenwet'), which regulates plant protection products and biocides. See: Backes et al, *Hoofdlijnen milieubestuursrecht*, Den Haag, Boom Juridische Uitgevers, 2004, p. 252–259; E.M. Vogelezang-Stoute, *Bestrijdingsmiddelenrecht. Een rechtsvergelijking*, Deventer: Kluwer 2004.

18 Article 8 Dir. 91/414/EC.

19 In accordance with Commission Regulation 3600/92 of 11 December 1992 laying down the detailed rules for the implementation of the first stage of the programme of work referred to in Article 8(3) of Directive 91/414 OJ 1992 L 366, p. 10.

20 The review takes place in accordance with Commission Regulation 3600/92 of 11 December 1992 laying down the detailed rules for the implementation of the first stage of the programme of work referred to in Article 8(3) of Directive 91/414, OJ 1992 L 366, p. 10. The regulatory comitology procedure is followed because Article 5 and 6, 19 and 20 Council Directive 91/414/EC refer to Article 5 and 7 Council Decision 1999/468, OJ 1999 L 184/23.

21 Article 10 Dir. 91/414/EC.

22 Respectively Article 11 and Article 8(4) Dir. 91/414/EC.

accordance with the multilevel procedure of the Directive.[23] Since the Directive entered into effect without any active substances listed on the Annex I, a transition regime allows the Member States to maintain national authorisations of plant protection products until all active substances have been evaluated at Community level.[24]

3. JUDICIAL REVIEW

Getting a preliminary ruling

The European review of the active substance aldicarb resulted in Council Decision 2003/199 refusing to include aldicarb in Annex I to Council Directive 91/414/EEC. The Council ordered withdrawal of national authorisations for plant protection products containing aldicarb within 2003, but it allowed limited uses considered as essential until 30 June 2007. Two Dutch environmental organisations brought proceedings before a Dutch court against the decision by the Dutch competent authority to allow essential uses of plant protection products containing aldicarb, taken on the basis of the Council Decision. They contested the validity of Article 2 of Council Decision *vis-à-vis* Article 8(2) of the Directive. The Dutch court decided to ask a preliminary ruling.[25] The Court of Justice ("ECJ") reviewed the Council Decision marginally, out of respect for the room for discretion. It explained that Article 8(2) does not establish the period within which Member States must ensure that those authorisations are withdrawn or varied, but refers to a prescribed period, i.e. a period to be fixed in an implementing measure, which is exactly what the Council did in its Decision. Article 2(3) of the Decision sets the time limit for the withdrawal of plant protection products containing aldicarb. Moreover, it is not inconsistent that a decision sets different time limits, since the Directive does not contain a restriction in that regard. Finally, the ECJ considered whether the time limits in the Decision respect the principle of proportionality.

The ECJ first reiterated its case law on proportionality. It repeated that the principle of proportionality requires that measures adopted by Community institutions do not exceed the limits of what is appropriate and necessary in

23 C-316/04 *Stichting Zuid-Hollandse Milieufederatie v College voor de toelating van bestrijdingsmiddelen*, [2005] ECR I-9759. Cf C-125/88 *Nijman* [1989] ECR 3533.

24 According to Article 8(2) and (3) Dir. 91/414/EC, the transition period was supposed to end 12 years after notification of the Directive. It appears from the case law that the Court has accepted an extension of this period, e.g. C-443/02 *Schreiber* [2004] ECR I-7275. See for a critical review of the Dutch practise: J. Rutteman, 'De toelating van bestrijdingsmiddelen: terug naar 1975?' 2002 MenR 12, p. 312–317.

25 CBb 19 April 2005: AWB 04/300 32010; C-174/05 *Stichting Zuid-Hollandse Milieufederatie, Stichting Natuur en Milieu v College voor de toelating van bestrijdingsmiddelen, joined party: Bayer CropScience BV* [2006] ECR I-4945.

order to attain the legitimate objectives pursued by the legislation in question. When there is a choice between several appropriate measures, recourse must be had to the least onerous, and the disadvantages caused must not be disproportionate to the aims pursued. Within the context of judicial review of the application of the proportionality principle, having regard to the broad discretion enjoyed by the Council in adopting its decision, the legality of the decision can be affected only if it is manifestly inappropriate having regard to the objective which the Council seeks to pursue.[26] The ECJ argued that Directive 91/414 has the objective firstly of removing barriers to intra-Community trade in plant products and secondly of protecting human and animal health and the environment. It held that it is apparent from the preamble to the Decision that the information before the Council was not sufficient to demonstrate that under the proposed conditions of use, plant protection products containing aldicarb satisfy the requirements of Article 5 of the Directive, because of the possible impact on small birds and earthworms. However, in the absence of efficient alternatives to certain limited uses in certain Member States, it appeared necessary to allow further essential uses of those products for a limited period and under strict conditions aimed at minimising risk. The ECJ concluded from this that the Council carried out a global assessment of the advantages and drawbacks of the system to be established and that that system was not on any view manifestly inappropriate in the light of the objectives pursued.

The ECJ's preliminary ruling about the aldicarb decision demonstrates how difficult it is to challenge decisions taken in a multilevel regulation context. If the ECJ had ruled that the period of grace in the Council Decision was not proportionate, this answer would have led the national court to invalidate the national decision allowing for essential uses during a period of grace. However, since the period of grace lasted until 2007, the long duration of the proceedings diminished the relevance of the outcome. The Council Decision was taken in 1991, whereas the ECJ gave its judgment in 2006. The long duration is caused by the fact that the environmental organisations brought proceedings against the national, implementing decision. In these proceedings they questioned the validity of the Community decision, which led the national court to ask for a preliminary ruling. This detour doubles the time spent waiting for judicial review. Moreover, until the laws of the Member States will be harmonised, environmental organisations depend on the national procedural laws to be granted standing. These laws display considerable difference with regard to standing rights for environmental organisations.[27] If they may bring proceedings, they cannot request a preliminary ruling. They depend on the

26 In paragraph 28 and 29 of the judgment, the Court refers to C-265/87 *Schräder* [1989] ECR 2237, C-331/88 *Fedesa and Others* [1990] ECR I-4023, Joined Cases C-133/93, C-300/93 and C-362/93 *Fedesa and Others* [1994] ECR I-4863 and C-189/01 *Jippes and Others* [2001] ECR I-5689.

27 Nicolas de Sadeleer, Gerhard Roller and Miriam Dross (2005), p. 178 et seq.

willingness of national courts to ask questions to the ECJ about the validity of the Community measure. The national court does not need to refer if it considers the decision to be clearly valid.[28] If a national court doubts the validity of a Community measure it has to refer the case, because only the Community courts can declare a Community measure invalid,[29] whereas only the national courts can declare a national measure invalid.[30] This judgment also raises the issue of the purpose of the preliminary ruling procedure. It was devised to ensure uniformity and consistency of Community law. By contrast, the technical questions asked in this case aim to ensure compliance by Community institutions and bodies with Community law.[31] For all these reasons, the preliminary ruling does not seem the best instrument to provide for judicial review in a multilevel regulation context. Therefore, environmental organisations tried to bring proceedings against a Community decision at the European level.

Trying a direct action

In order to speed up the review of a Community decision, the European Environmental Bureau ("EEB") and a Dutch environmental organisation brought proceedings before the Court of First Instance ("CFI") against two Commission decisions concerning the non-inclusion on Annex I of atrazine and simazine (for reasons of convenience it is called the *EEB* case).[32] The environmental organisations protested against the duration of the period of grace for essential uses granted in the Commission decisions. These decisions were addressed solely to the Member States. Therefore, the environmental organisations had to pass the hurdle of direct and individual concern of Article 230(4) EC. The environmental organisations hoped to convince the CFI to relax these standing requirements, even though the ECJ had made clear in the *Greenpeace* case that it was not willing to change its case law. They hoped in vain. The CFI declared their action inadmissible, according to settled case law of the ECJ. According to the CFI, the environmental organisations are not 'individually concerned' by the Community decision, since they are not affected by reason of certain attributes peculiar to them, or by reason of a factual situation which differentiates them from all other persons and distinguishes them individually in the same way as

28 C-283/81 *Cilfit* [1982] ECR 3415. See for a critical view: Peter J. Wattel, 'Köbler, Cilfit and Welthgrove, we can't go on meeting like this', 2004 CMLRev., p. 177–190.

29 C-314/85 *Foto Frost* [1987] ECR 4199.

30 Cf. C-97/91 *Borelli*, [1992] ECR I-6313.

31 Cf. Paul Craig, 'Standing, Rights, and the Structure of Legal Argument' 2003 European Public Law, p. 503–504, who considers it a waste of resource for the ECJ to answer technical questions which do not involve any point of general importance of Community law.

32 Order of the CFI in Joined Cases T-236/04 and T-241/04, *European Environmental Bureau, Stichting Natuur en Milieu v Commission* [2005] ECR II-4945. At the same day, the CFI delivered a similar Order in T-94/04 *European Environmental Bureau (EEB) and Others v Commission*, [2005] ECR II-4919. The court took the same position in the case T-91/07 *WWF-UK v Council*, [2008] ECR II-81*, Summ.pub.

the addressee of the act would be.[33] The CFI argued that even if it were accepted that the contested provisions of the atrazine and simazine decisions have the effect of allowing certain Member States to maintain temporarily in force, for certain uses, the authorisation for plant protection products containing atrazine or simazine – active substance which, according to the applicants, harm the environment – it is clear that those provisions affect the applicants in their objective capacity as entities whose purpose it to protect the environment, in the same manner as any other person in the same situation. The CFI thus followed the judgments *UPA* and *Jégo Queré*.[34] In those cases, the ECJ declared that the Community courts do not have the competence to change the criterion of individually concerned formulated in Article 230(4) EC. Consequently, if a Commission decision impacts the environment, an environmental organisation cannot file an admissible claim, because their concern for the environment is not an individual concern.[35] Instead, it should bring proceedings in the Member State concerned. The argument that a Community decision may not be challenged before the national courts as effectively as before the Community courts did not impress the CFI, as it did not impress the ECJ in the *Greenpeace* case.[36]

The judgment in the *EEB* case demonstrates that it is not easy to persuade the Community courts to relax the standing requirements. This reluctance can be explained by the workload of the Community courts, which is estimated to increase as a result of the enlargement of the European Union and the developments in the communitarized third pillar.[37] The argument that relaxation of the standing requirements can be based on the principle of effective judicial protection[38] did not prove successful in the *EEB* case, as could have been assumed from earlier judgments. In the *Greenpeace* case,[39] the ECJ held that not allowing the applicants to bring proceedings against the Commission decision granting Spain financial assistance for the building of two power

33 The famous *Plaumann* formula, developed in: C-25/62, *Plaumann & Co v Commission*, [1963] ECR p. 95.

34 C-50/00 P *Union de Pequenos Agricultores v Council* [2002] ECR I-6677; T-173/98 *Union de Pequenos Agricultores v Council* [1999] ECR II-3357 and C-263/02 P *Jégo Queré v Commission* [2004] ECR I-3425; T-177/01 *Jégo Queré v Commission* [2003] ECR II-2365.

35 T-585/93, *Greenpeace*, [1995] ECR II-2205 and C-321/95 P *Greenpeace*, [1998] ECR I-1651.

36 *Idem.*

37 See on the challenges ahead: Bo Vesterdorf, 'The Community court system ten years from now and beyond: challenges and possibilities' 2003 E.L.Rev. (June), p. 303–323; Nikolaos Lavranos, 'The new specialised courts within the European judicial system', 2005 E.L.Rev. (April), p. 261–272; L.A. Geelhoed, 'The Expanding Jurisdiction of the Court of Justice of the EC', Coll. Asser Institute October 2004, to be published. Statistics can be found in the Annual Reports of the Court of Justice and the Court of First Instance: http://curia.europa.eu/nl/instit/presentationfr/index.html.

38 Landmark cases in this respect are: C-222/84 *Johnston* [1986] ECR 1651, C-222/86 *Heylens* [1987] ECR 4097 and C-213/89 *Factortame* [1990] ECR I-2433.

39 See note 35.

stations did not infringe this principle, because they could bring proceedings against the Spanish decision to grant a building permit. Similarly, in the *Borelli* case,[40] the ECJ stated that the applicant should bring proceedings against a national preparatory decision instead of bringing proceedings against the Community decision based on that decision, declaring that it would not grant him aid from the European Agricultural Guidance and Guarantee Fund. According to the ECJ the preparatory decision is assailable (even though under Italian law it was not), because it follows from the division of powers in the field in question between the national authorities and the Community institutions that the measure adopted by the national authority is binding on the Community decision-taking authority and therefore determines the terms of the Community decision to be adopted. In the *EEB* case, the environmental organisations found a deaf ear for the argument that the annulment of the decision in a direct action would prevent triggering a myriad of complex, lengthy and costly authorisation procedures in various Member States. The argument that a Community decision may not be challenged before the national courts as effectively as before the Community courts did not impress. Apparently, the Community courts adhere to the principle that access to court – an important element of the principle of effective judicial protection – should preferably be realised at the national level.[41]

4. THE IMPACT OF THE AARHUS CONVENTION

Both the Member States and the European Union have committed themselves to change the rules on access to court in environmental matters. They did so by creating the 1998 Convention on access to information, public participation in decision-making, and access to justice regarding environmental matters ("the Aarhus Convention") in the context of the United Nations Economic Commission for Europe. It has been signed and ratified by all EU Member States and by the EU itself.[42] It provides citizens – and environmental organizations in particular –[43] with minimum procedural rights on access to documents, public

40 C-97/91 *Oleificio Borelli* [1982] ECR 1992 I-6313.

41 Cf.: José Manuel and Corés Martín, 'Ubi Ius, Ibi Remedium? – Locus Standi of Private Applicants under Article 230(4) EC at a European Constitutional Crossroads' 11 MJ 2004 3, p. 239. See also: Eckhard Rehbinder, 'Locus Standi, Community Law and the Case for Harmonization' in: Han Somsen (ed) *Protecting the European Environment: Enforcing EC Environmental Law*, London: Blackstone Press Limited, 1996, p. 151–166. But see also: T-33/01 *Infront* WM AG v Commission [2005] ECR II-5897, para 108 and 109.

42 EU ratification by Council Decision 2005/370/EC of 17 February 2005 on the conclusion, on behalf of the EC, of the Convention on access to information, public participation in decision-making, and access to justice regarding environmental matters; deposited with the United Nations. The Aarhus Convention entered into force on 30 October 2001.

43 This can be explained by the fact that Environmental organisations played an important role in the coming into existence of the Aarhus Convention, see: Jeremy Waters, 'The Aarhus

participation in decision-making and access to justice in the field of environmental law. These procedural rights should improve the enforcement of environmental rules.[44] A real novelty is that these rights can be invoked not only before national authorities and national courts, but also before European authorities and courts. This is due to the broad definition of public authority in Article 2(2)(d) Aarhus Convention, referring specifically to the institutions of any regional economic integration organization which is a Party to the Convention, in other words, to the institutions and bodies of the EU.[45]

Access to justice at the international level

Unfortunately the Aarhus Convention addresses only in vague terms the issue of judicial review of decisions of international organizations other than the European Union. The Parties should promote the application of the principles of the Aarhus Convention in international environmental decision-making processes and within the framework of international organizations in matters relating to the environment.[46] For the regulation of plant protection products, this means that no judicial review at the international level is available against amendments of the Annex to the Stockholm Convention, e.g. the decision to broaden the use of DDT or a decision about placing new chemicals on the list after evaluation by the POP review committee of the Stockholm Convention issued by the Conference of the Parties. Judicial review will only be available against the implementation of these international decisions into Community and national decisions.

Anticipating the implementation of the Aarhus Convention at the European level

The EU signed and ratified the Aarhus Convention before finishing its implementing legislation. Since an international agreement that has been signed

Convention: A Driving Force for Environmental Democracy' JEEPL 2005, p. 2–11, in particular p. 9 and 10.

44 The Aarhus Convention focuses on procedural guarantees. This is not completely new, e.g. the Espoo Convention on Environmental Impact Assessment in a Transboundary Context (1991).

45 See for a general overview: Vera Rodenhoff, 'The Aarhus Convention and its Implications for the 'Institutions' of the European Community' 2002 RECIEL, p. 343–357. See for the (desired) impact of the Aarhus Convention on situations similar to the Greenpeace case: Femke de Lange, Beyond *Greenpeace*, Courtesy of the Aarhus Convention, in Han Somsen et al. (eds), *The Yearbook of European Environmental Law* (3), Oxford: Oxford University Press 2003, p. 227–248. Note that the Commission, in the explanatory memorandum of its proposal for the Aarhus Regulation explicitly excluded internal and judicial review of such financial decisions.

46 Article 3(7) Aarhus Convention.

and ratified forms an integral part of the Community legal order,[47] the environmental organisations could have asked the CFI to interpret Community law in accordance with international law.[48] An interpretation of direct and individual concern in conformity with the Aarhus Convention means that individuals[49] having a sufficient interest[50] may challenge the substantive and procedural legality of a decision, act or omission issued by a Community institution or body.[51] The Aarhus Convention states that what constitutes a sufficient interest must be determined in accordance with the requirements of national law and consistently with the objective of giving the public concerned wide access to justice within the scope of the Aarhus Convention. Environmental organisations, i.e. non-governmental organizations promoting environmental protection and meeting any requirements under national law, are deemed to have an interest.[52] Such an Aarhus Convention conform interpretation would have been similar to the interpretation of individual concern as proposed by Advocate General Jacobs in his Opinion in the *UPA* case.[53] He proposed that a person is to be regarded as individually concerned by a Community measure where, by reason of his particular circumstances, the measure has, or is liable to have, a substantial adverse effect on his interests. The fact that the ECJ did not follow the

47 E.g: C-459/03 *Commission v Ireland (MOX Plant)*, [2006] ECR I-4635; C-213/03, *Syndicat professionnel coordination des pêcheurs de l'Étang de Berre et de la region v Electricité de France* [2004] ECR I-7357 and C-239/03 *Commission v France (Étang de Berre)* [2004] ECR I-9325. Cf. Jan Wouters & Dries van Eeckhoutte, 'Enforcement of Customary International Law through European Community Law' in: J.M. Prinssen and A. Schrauwen (eds) *Direct Effect. Rethinking a Classic of EC Legal Doctrine*, Groningen: Europa Law Publishing, 2002, p. 193–234; K. Lenaerts and P. Van Nuffel, *Constitutional Law of the European Union*, London: Sweet & Maxwell, 1999, p. 551; Nikolaos Lavranos, *Decisions of International Organisations in the European and Domestic Legal Orders of Selected EU Member States*, Groningen: Europa Law Publishing, 2002; Piet Eeckhout, *Does Europe's Constitution stop at the Water's Edge? Law and Policy in the EU's External Relations*, Walter van Gerven Lectures (5), Groningen: Europa Law Publishing 2005.

48 See: C-84/95 *Bosphorus v Minister for Transport, Energy and Communications, Ireland and the Attorney General* [1996] ECR I-3953; T-115/94 *Opel Austria* [1997] ECR II-39; C-162/96 *Racke* [1998] ECR I-3655; C-377/02 *Van Parys* [2005] ECR I-0000; T-19/01 *Chiquita* [2005] ECR II-315; C-402/05P and C-415/05P *Kadi v Council and Commission* [2008] ECR I-6351.

49 Note that Article 9(2) Aarhus Convention uses the term members of the public concerned. This means the public affected or likely to be affected by, or having an interest in, the environmental decision-making, according to the definition given in Article 2(5) Aarhus Convention. The members of the public include legal persons.

50 Article 9(2) Aarhus Convention offers as an alternative to having a sufficient interest: maintaining the impairment of a right, where the administrative procedural law of a Party requires this as a precondition. It is ignored because this is not a precondition that follows from Article 230(4) EC.

51 Article 9(3) of the Aarhus Convention also prescribes access to justice to challenge acts and omissions by private persons. This is not implemented through Community legislation because of the subsidiarity principle (according to the explanatory memoranda). The EU Member States have to implement this part of the Convention themselves.

52 Article 9(2) and 2(5) Aarhus Convention.

53 Opinion AG Jacobs in case C-50/00 P *Union de Pequenos Agricultores v Council* [2002] ECR I-6677.

approach proposed by Advocate General Jacobs, might serve to explain why the CFI did not interpret direct and individual concern in conformity with the Aarhus Convention out of its own motion.

Yet in the *EEB* case, the CFI was confronted with an argument related to the Aarhus Convention. The environmental organisations tried to be granted access to court by referring to their specific status as environmental organisations in the light of the implementation of the Aarhus Convention in the European legal order. They argued that the CFI should grant them standing, because the Commission mentioned in the statement of reasons of its proposal for a Regulation that European environmental protection organizations which meet certain objective criteria have standing for the purposes of the fourth paragraph of Article 230 EC, and they fulfil these requirements.[54] However, the CFI responded frostily to this argument. It stated that the hierarchy of norms precludes secondary legislation from conferring standing on individuals who do not meet the requirements of Article 230(4) EC. A fortiori this rule applies to proposals for secondary legislation. Accordingly, the proposed Regulation relied on by the applicants did not release them from having to show that they are individually concerned. Moreover, even if they were acknowledged as qualified entities for the purpose of the Regulation, they had not put forward any reason why that status would lead to the conclusion that they are individually concerned by those decisions. This is impossible as long as the ECJ's interpretation of individual concern is only related to economic concern. Environmental protection is a collective concern, defended in particular by environmental organisations. Unfortunately for them, the ECJ had already showed in the *Greenpeace* case that environmental interests do not deserve a different status than economic interests.[55] Moreover, the CFI considered it irrelevant that this approach differs from the situation in some Member States, where environmental organisations have standing before the national courts to protect the environmental interest.[56] Thus, the CFI dashed the hopes of the environmental organisations that it would anticipate the implementation of the Aarhus Convention by granting them a privileged position.

---

54 Proposal for a Regulation of the European Parliament and of the Council on the application of the provisions of the Aarhus Convention on Access to Information, Public Participation in Decision-making and Access to Justice in Environmental Matters to EC institutions and bodies, COM (2003) 622 final.

55 Philippe Sands, 'Is the Court of Justice an Environmental Tribunal?' in: Han Somsen (ed), *Protecting the European Environment: Enforcing EC Environmental Law*, London: Blackstone Press Limited, 1996, p. 23–35.

56 Cf.: Michiel A. Heldeweg, René J.G.H. Seerden and Kurt Deketelaere, 'Public environmental law in Europe: a comparative search for a ius commune', EELR 2004, p. 86.

Implementing the Convention into the Aarhus Regulation

Since the ECJ stated in the *UPA* case[57] that it would take a Treaty change before it would change its interpretation of direct and individual concern, it is easy to agree with De Lange that it takes a Treaty change to implement the Aarhus rules on judicial review.[58] Unfortunately a Treaty change does not seem near after the French 'non' and the Dutch 'nee' to the Constitution in 2005.[59] But even if it were to come into effect, the Constitution would not have brought about the required Treaty change.[60] The Lisbon Treaty changes (see below in italics) the present wording of Article 230(4) EC. The new Article 263 TFEU reads: Any natural or legal person may, on grounds of lack of competence, infringement of an essential procedural requirement, infringement of this Treaty or of any rule of law relating to its application, or misuse of power, institute proceedings against a decision addressed to that person or against a decision which, although in the form of a regulation or a decision addressed to another person, is of direct and individual concern to the former *and against a regulatory act which is of direct concern to him or her and does not entail implementing measures.*[61] If it can be assumed that a regulatory act should be understood in a broad sense,[62] this facilitates the implementation of the Aarhus Convention at the European level, because it changes the requirement of individual concern. It is the requirement of individual concern that makes it so difficult for third parties to obtain access to the Community courts, particularly in environmental cases, because environment protection is a collective concern.[63]

This did not keep the Commission, the Council and the European Parliament from implementing the Aarhus Convention. In the absence of a Treaty change, they found a way to implement the Aarhus rules on judicial review in the European legal order. They took advantage of the leeway offered by Article 230(4) EC. It follows from this provision that individuals do not have to pass the direct and individual concern test if they are the addressees of a decision. Hence the Aarhus Regulation prescribes that judicial review is only open for environmental organisations that made a request for internal review of a decision.[64] Thus, they

57 C-50/00 P *Union de Pequenos Agricultores v Council* [2002] ECR I-6677.

58 Femke de Lange, 'Case Note European Court of Justice, Unión de Pequenos Agricultores v Council', RECIEL 12 (1) 2003, p. 118.

59 Respectively on 29 May and 1 June 2005.

60 Cf. Paul Craig, 'Standing, Rights, and the Structure of Legal Argument', European Public Law, 2003, p. 508.

61 R. Barents, 'The Court of Justice in the Draft Constitution', 2004 MJ 2, p. 130–134. This provision was introduced by the Constitution and was placed unaltered in the Lisbon Treaty.

62 R. Barents 2004, p. 134.

63 Femke de Lange, 2003, p. 118.

64 Article 10 Regulation 1367/2006 of the European Parliament and of the Council of 6 September 2006 on the application of the provisions of the Aarhus Convention on Access to Information, Public Participation and Access to Justice in Environmental Matters to Community Institutions and Bodies OJ 2006 L 264/13 "Aarhus Regulation").

first file a request for review before the authorities that issued the decision. Once they have obtained a review decision addressed to them, they are entitled to judicial review.[65] If the authorities do not (timely) issue a review decision, the Aarhus Regulation allows for judicial review to protest against failure to act.[66] This approach is in line with the Aarhus Convention, as it explicitly allows for internal review preceding judicial review.[67] Apart from the fact that this creates an opportunity for the authorities to reconsider their decision, it also results in a wider circle of addressees entitled to judicial review at the European level. Widdershoven argues that the implementation of the internal review construction will compel the Community courts to grant standing to environmental organisations. Once they have become addressees of a Community decision, the present framework of Article 230(4) EC allows them to bring proceedings before the Community courts.[68] That would solve an important issue of the judicial deficit for those organisations who qualify.

Although internal review may offer environmental organisations access to court without having to pass the direct and individual concern test, the Aarhus Regulation still attempts to reconcile the restrictive interpretation of the ECJ of Article 230(4) EC with the rules of the Aarhus Convention.[69] The Aarhus Regulation takes the requirement of individual concern into account by not creating an *actio popularis* against any measure that impacts the environment.[70] The Commission argued in its proposal that the establishment of a right of action for every natural and legal person is not a reasonable option because it would imply an amendment of Article 230 EC and could hence not be introduced by secondary legislation. Therefore, access to court is limited to environmental

65 Article 12(1) Aarhus Regulation. Internal review should not be confounded with public participation. In the policy areas where public participation is introduced, it takes place during the decision-making, while internal review takes place on request after a decision has been issued.

66 Article 12(2) Aarhus Regulation.

67 Article 9(2) Aarhus Convention.

68 R.J.G.M. Widdershoven, 'Rechtsbescherming in het milieurecht in Europees perspectief', 2004 MenR 9, p. 532. Contrary: Jan H. Jans, Did Baron von Munchhausen ever Visit Aarhus? Some Critical Remarks on the Proposal for a Regulation on the Application of the Provisions of the Aarhus Convention to EC Institutions and Bodies, in: Richard Macrory (ed) Reflections on 30 Years of EU Environmental Law: A High Level of Protection?, Groningen: Europa Law Publishing, 2006, p. 483, 484.

69 It was easier to make the rules on information and participation compatible with those of the Convention. Similar difficulties arise in the implementation of the rules on judicial review in the legislation directed to the Member States. The rules on information and public participation have already been implemented in respectively Directive 2003/4 and Directive 2003/35. See: Proposal for a Directive of the European Parliament and the Council on access to justice in environmental matters, COM (2003) 624 final. It presents similar rules on standing for environmental organisations as the Proposal for the Aarhus Regulation.

70 Article 4 of the proposed Directive on access to justice in environmental matters does not prescribe an *actio popularis*. Note that the proposed Directive prescribes a minimum standard.

organisations which meet a number of conditions. This is in line with Article 9(3) of the Aarhus Convention, which offers the possibility to limit standing by laying down criteria. The Aarhus Regulation also takes the requirement of direct concern into account, since it qualifies the decisions against which judicial review will be open. Thus, the implementation of the Aarhus Regulation will only result in access to the Community courts for qualified environmental organisations in relation to acts and omissions by Community institutions and bodies, which contravene environmental law.[71] The task of providing residual judicial review is still entrusted to the Member States.

Access to Court after the Aarhus Regulation

The 'individuals' that will enjoy administrative and judicial review at the European level are non-governmental organisations that meet the conditions of the Regulation. Article 12 of the Aarhus Regulation establishes four conditions to that effect. A non-governmental organisation is only entitled to make a request for internal review if:

(a) "It is an independent and non-profit-making legal person in accordance with a Member State's national law or practice;
(b) It has the primary stated objective of promoting environmental protection in the context of environmental law;
(c) It has existed for more than two years and is actively pursuing the objective referred to under (b);
(d) The subject matter in respect of which the request for internal review is made is covered by its objectives and activities"[72]

These criteria may be further defined, as the second indent of Article 12 states that the Commission may adopt the provisions which are necessary to ensure transparent and consistent application of these criteria.[73] Hence it follows from Article 10 to 12 of the Aarhus Regulation, that an environmental organisation is entitled to make a request for internal review, provided that the subject matter in respect of which a request for internal review is made is covered by its objectives and activities. Only after obtaining a review decision – unless the action is directed against a failure to decide on the request for internal review – judicial

71 Explanatory Memorandum to the Proposal for the Aarhus Regulation, p. 15, 16.

72 Article 11 of the Aarhus Regulation slightly differs from Article 12 of the proposal for the Aarhus Regulation, COM (2003) 622 final. Article 12 also demanded that a 'qualified entity' be active at Community level and that it must have its annual statement of accounts for the two preceding years certified by a registered accountant.

73 Maybe this re-introduces via the back door Article 13 of the proposed Regulation, which entitled the Commission to recognize environmental organisations. According to the proposal, only recognized environmental organisations were allowed to request internal review and subsequently bring proceedings before the Community courts.

review is possible. It is obvious that these criteria do not enable ad hoc environmental organisations to qualify. For environmental organisations like the ones that brought the proceedings discussed above, it should be easy to qualify.

Qualified environmental organisations are only entitled to internal review and hence judicial review of 'administrative acts' and 'omissions' taken by Community institutions and bodies contravening 'environmental law'. A measure qualifies as administrative act in the sense of the Aarhus Regulation, if it is a measure of individual scope under environmental law, taken by a Community institution or body, having legally binding and external effects.[74] An omission refers to the failure of a Community institution or body to adopt an administrative act, where it is legally required to do so.[75] Legally binding and external effects are known concepts to define a decision in the administrative law of the Member States. They are also familiar to the ECJ and the CFI, as they define an act which may be the subject of an action for annulment under Article 230 EC as a measure the legal effects of which are binding on and capable of affecting the interests of the applicant by bringing about a distinct change in his legal position.[76] The concept 'individual scope' is new. It is not clear what it means. It could refer to the distinction between regulations and decisions. The ECJ and the CFI used to distinguish between these measures on the basis of the abstract terminology test. They considered that a measure is of general application if it is addressed in abstract terms to undefined classes of persons and applies to objectively determined situations.[77] However, the ECJ held in the *Jégo Queré* case that even a measure of general application such as a regulation can be of direct and individual concern to some individuals and is thus in the nature of a decision in their regard.[78] Hence the distinction between decisions and acts of general application has become somewhat blurred in the European case law.[79] If the CFI and the ECJ prefer to interpret individual scope in a narrow sense, it would be a step backwards.

Whether an act or omission contravenes environmental law might be difficult to prove, but at least environmental law is broadly defined. Article 2(f) Aarhus

---

74 Article 2(g) Aarhus Regulation.

75 Article 1(h) and 10(1) Aarhus Regulation. Cf. Explanatory memorandum to the proposal for the Aarhus Regulation, p. 10.

76 C-8–11/66 *Cimenteries Cementbedrijven et al v Commission* [1967] ECR 75. See for more recent confirmations e.g.: C-66/91 *R Emerald Meats v Commission* [1991] ECR I-1143 and C-147/96 *Netherlands v Commission* [2000] ECR I-4723; T-33/01 *Infront WM AG v Commission* [2005] ECR II-0000.

77 C-789 and 790/79 Calpak SpA and Societá Emiliana Lavorazione Frutta SpA v Commission [1980] ECR 1949. See: Paul Craig and Grainne de Burca, *EU Law, Text, Cases and Materials*, third edn, Oxford: Oxford University Press, 2003, p. 493–495.

78 C-263/02 P *Jégo Queré v Commission* [2004] ECR I-3425.

79 Anthony Arnull, *The European Union and its Court of Justice*, 2nd ed., Oxford: Oxford University Press, 2006, p. 70–74.

Regulation defines environmental law as "Community legislation which, irrespective of its legal basis, contributes to the pursuit of the objectives of Community policy on the environment as set out in the Treaty: preserving, protecting and improving the quality of the environment, protecting human health, the prudent and rational utilisation of natural resources and promoting measures at international level to deal with regional or worldwide environmental problems." The definition does not add policy areas, like the proposal for the Aarhus Regulation. This is a pity, as the list of examples included chemicals and pesticides.[80] It is not necessarily disadvantageous that the list disappeared. The definition of environmental law is sufficiently broad for the regulation of plant protection products to be included. Finally, Article 10 Aarhus Regulation contains a few procedural hurdles, such as a time limit of six weeks for filing a request for internal review.

Trying a direct action again

Now it is time to consider whether the implementation of the Aarhus Convention into the European legal order will enable environmental organisations to bring direct proceedings against Community decisions concerning the regulation of plant protection products. Interestingly, in the explanatory memorandum to the proposal the Commission mentioned the relevance of the Aarhus Convention for the authorisation of products such as chemicals and pesticides. It stated that the authorisation of products such as chemicals and pesticides are as a rule taken at the level of Member States. Decisions taken at Community level – e.g. the establishment of lists of active substances or the classification of substances – are as such not aimed at as specific activities in the sense of Article 6 of the Convention.[81] Indeed product approvals are not listed in Annex I to the Convention, which lists activities that qualify for public participation in any case, e.g. decisions concerning mineral oil and gas refineries, certain chemical installations and nuclear power stations. Since Article 6 of the Convention is about public participation in the decision-making process, the Commission's point is that it does not want to introduce public participation at the European level in the decision-making procedures in product approval legislation. It wants to limit public participation at the European level to plans and programmes, mentioning its Environmental Action Programme as an example.[82] The absence

80 Article 2(1)(g) of the proposal for the Aarhus Regulation.

81 Article 9 Aarhus Regulation and Recital 9 of the Preamble to the Aarhus Regulation. In the Explanatory memorandum to the proposal for the Aarhus Regulation, p. 9, the Commission denies public participation at EU level in important decisions on the financing of projects, because the permitting procedure for the respective activity already requires public participation. This resembles to the reasoning of the Court in the *Greenpeace* case.

82 See both Recital 9 of the Preamble to the Aarhus Regulation and the Explanatory memorandum to the proposal for the Aarhus Regulation, p. 7 and 13. The example is still present in recital 9 or the Aarhus Regulation.

of participation in the decision-making process does not prejudice the availability of internal and judicial review after a decision has been issued.[83] Thus the Commission's remarks do not exclude the applicability of the Aarhus rules to product approval legislation.

Access to court under the Aarhus Regulation is only possible if the decision concerning the placing of an active substance on Annex I to Directive 91/414/EC qualifies as an administrative act in the sense of the Aarhus Regulation. That is, it should be a measure of individual scope under environmental law, taken by a Community institution or body, having legally binding and external effects. Some of these requirements are easier to fulfil than others. The Community decision whether or not to place an active substance on the Annex to the Directive is taken by the Commission or – exceptionally – the Council. Hence it is certainly a measure taken by a Community institution. Whether the regulation of plant protection products belongs to environmental law should not be difficult to decide. The proposal for the Aarhus Regulation even mentioned pesticides as an area of environmental law. The final text does not give examples, but certainly its definition of environmental law is large enough to comprise decisions in this field. However, it is not so easy to decide if the decision is 'of individual scope under environmental law'. A listing decision could be considered to have a general scope under environmental law. The ban or approval of an active substance concerns a specific substance, but it is objectively formulated and it applies to an indefinite group of persons. Hence access to the internal review procedure could be denied on this ground. That would undermine the aim of the Aarhus Convention to guarantee wide access to court. A different interpretation would emphasise the implementing nature of the decision to list or ban an active substance and consider that these Community decisions affect the environment. The Community decision to list an active substance on the Annex to Directive 91/414 or not determines whether the national authorities will grant or refuse a product authorisation for products containing that active substance. If the Community decision is considered a measure of individual scope under environmental law, it also needs to have legally binding and external effects in order to qualify. The decisions are binding on the Member States to whom they are directed, so they have both binding and external effects. Thus, it seems likely that after following the internal review procedure an environmental organisation can challenge a listing decision before the Community courts without having to pass the individual and direct concern test because it has a decision directed to it.

---

83 Although active participation in the administrative procedure is a factor that is taken into account to establish individual concern, e.g. in competition law: C-169/84 *Cofaz and Others v Commission* [1986] ECR 391; C-68/94 and C-30/95 *France and Others v Commission (Kali and Salz)* [1998] ECR I-1375; T-177/04 *Easyjet Airline v Commission* [2006] ECR II-1931.

Implementing the Aarhus Convention into the Aarhus Directive

If it turns out that it is not possible for environmental organisations to bring proceedings against a Community listing decision because its scope is too general, then at least the implementation of the Aarhus Convention into the national laws of the Member States should enable them to bring proceedings against implementing measures taken at the national level.[84] That is the appropriate level to bring proceedings against decisions, acts or omissions of national authorities or private individuals concerning plant protection products.[85] The rules of the Aarhus Convention will be implemented in the Member States via the Directive on access to court, which is still a proposal. Therefore, the European Parliament and the Council still have the opportunity to amend the proposed Directive. Moreover, as the Directive is based on Article 175 EC, it offers minimum harmonization. This means that the Member States can introduce or maintain rules that guarantee a broader access to court.[86] Therefore, this can only be a tentative description of the future national procedural rules.

Under the rules of the proposed Aarhus Directive, access to the national courts is not limited to environmental organisations. It is open for all members of the public at the national level. This does not amount to an *actio popularis.* Members of the public have access to environmental proceedings to challenge the procedural and substantive legality of administrative acts and omissions where (a) they have sufficient interest or (b) they maintain the impairment of a right, where the administrative procedural law requires this as a precondition. The Member States determine what constitutes a sufficient interest or the impairment of a right, but they have to take the privileged position of environmental organisations into account. Hence, environmental organisations have access to court without having to prove a sufficient interest or maintaining the impairment of a right, if they bring an action against a matter that is covered specifically by their statutory activities and it falls within their specific geographical area of activities.[87] It is possible to bring proceedings against decisions concerning plant protection products. These decisions clearly fall under

84 On the basis of a complaint from a Belgian environmental organisation, the Aarhus Convention Compliance Committee has warned Belgium in Communication ACCC/C/2005/11th at if the jurisprudence of the Council of State is not altered, Belgium will fail to comply with article 9, paragraphs 2 to 4, of the Convention by effectively blocking most, if not all, environmental organizations from access to justice with respect to town planning permits and area plans, as provided for in the Wallonian region.

85 Respectively Article 4 and Article 3 Proposal for a Directive of the European Parliament and the Council on access to justice in environmental matters, COM (2003) 624 final.

86 Explanatory memorandum of the Proposal for a Directive of the European Parliament and of the Council on access to justice in environmental matters, para. 3.6.

87 Article 5 Proposal for a Directive of the European Parliament and the Council on access to justice in environmental matters.

the definition of environmental law, as they are (still) explicitly mentioned in the definition of environmental law in the Directive.[88] Therefore, the implementation of the Aarhus Convention into the Aarhus Directive will safeguard access to court at the national level for concerned individuals and environmental organisations when they want to bring proceedings against plant protection product authorisations.

5. CONCLUSION

It is argued that multilevel environmental regulation presents a judicial deficit. Although implementing measures can be taken at the international, European and national level, judicial review against them is not equally distributed between these three levels. It is impossible for individuals to bring proceedings at the international level. The situation is only slightly less dramatic at the European level. Individuals have to pass the requirement of direct and individual concern to bring proceedings against decisions that are not directed to them. This proves impossible for environmental organisations due to the restrictive interpretation the Community courts give to these requirements. As the environment is a collective and not an individual concern, they never qualify. The Lisbon Treaty changed the standing requirement by introducing the phrase that a natural or legal person may institute proceedings against a regulatory act which is of direct concern to him or her and which does not entail implementing measures. It will depend on the Court's interpetation whether this provision will indeed ease the standing conditions in environmental cases. In general, environmental organisations depend on the national courts, which can – by asking for a preliminary ruling – move the case up to the European level. Unfortunately, not all Member States allow environmental organisations to bring proceedings. Moreover, the national level may not be the most appropriate level to bring proceedings for various reasons. In particular if a national decision is the pretext to challenge a Community decision, the length of proceedings and their dependence on national courts to ask for a preliminary ruling do not leave an impression of effective judicial review.

The implementation of the Aarhus Convention into the European legal order has the potential to improve judicial protection against decisions related to the environment. At the national level, the (minimum) harmonisation brought about by its implementation in a Directive and subsequently in national procedural rules should guarantee that environmental organisations can bring proceedings in all Member States against national decisions based on a Community decision. At the European level, qualified environmental organisations can obtain

[88] Article 1(g) Proposal for a Directive of the European Parliament and the Council on access to justice in environmental matters.

administrative review against decisions issued by Community institutions and bodies if the listing decisions in the field of plant protection products will be considered to be an act of individual scope under environmental law having legally binding and external effects. As administrative review will result in a decision directed to them, it seems impossible for the Community courts to refuse them standing, because the criteria of direct and individual concern only apply in relation to non-addressees. Even though these advancements will only reduce the judicial deficit at the European and national level in the area of environmental law, they are a step forwards. A growing number of direct actions related to acts or omissions in the field of environmental law may set in motion a change of the European system of judicial review applying to all fields of Community law.

VII. THE EUROPEAN AVIATION SAFETY AGENCY AND THE INDEPENDENT AGENCIES OF THE EC – A SYSTEMATIC ANALYSIS*

Daniel Riedel

1. INTRODUCTION

Today, the European Community can look back on a history of more than four decades. Starting in the 1950s with a primarily economic objective, the course of integration has gained substantial influence not only in purely commercial policy areas but also in the spheres that form the traditional *domaine réservé* of national sovereignty. Accordingly, the character of community administration itself has changed. For a long time, decentralised enforcement of Community law dominated over a strictly limited direct enforcement by the European Commission. Evolving from this, the European administration has increasingly transformed – speaking in the words of Nils Bohr – into a complex "Kern-Schalen-Modell"[1] (nucleus-orbital model) of administrative co-operation. In this process, a unique part has been played by the independent agencies of the EC. Up to now, 23 independent agencies have been established all over the territories of the Member States, from Warsaw to Lisbon. Despite the fact that these agencies form an institutional category of their own, their organisational structure, their objectives and the extent of powers conferred on them can substantially differ from case to case.[2]

---

* This contribution is based on the author's doctoral thesis "Die Gemeinschaftszulassung für Luftfahrtgerät – Europäisches Verwalten durch Agenturen am Beispiel der EASA", Berlin 2006. An earlier version of this contribution has been published in: Eberhard Schmidt-Aßmann and Bettina Schöndorf-Haubold, Der Europäische Verwaltungsverbund, Mohr Siebeck 2005, p. 103–125.

1 *Schmidt-Aßmann*, Strukturen Europäischer Verwaltung und die Rolle des Europäischen Verwaltungsrechts, in: Blankenagel/Pernice/Schulze-Fielitz (eds.): Liber Amicorum für Peter Häberle, Tübingen 2004, pp. 395 (396).

2 For an outline of the existing independent agencies see *Fischer-Appelt*, Agenturen der Europäischen Gemeinschaft, Berlin 1999, pp. 46–77; *Berger*, Vertraglich nicht vorgesehene

One of the most recent additions has been that of the European Aviation Safety Agency (EASA)[3] based in Cologne. EASA is primarily responsible for the certification of products in the field of aircraft technology, but its competence far exceeds that remit. Conceived as a "specialised expert body",[4] it is entitled to collect and bring in its expertise in all areas connected with aviation safety.[5] Not least due to these expertise objectives, EASA has taken a special position among the other agencies of the EC. It is the objective of this article to examine the newly-created EASA in comparison with the other existing independent agencies of the EC using a unique systematic approach of classification. To this end, a review of the organisational profile and the powers delegated to EASA will be presented first (2). After that, a new typology of the existing European agencies will be developed (3). In a third and final step, the question on the positioning of EASA within this typology will be addressed (4).

2. OBJECTIVES, COMPETENCIES AND ORGANISATIONAL STRUCTURE OF EASA

2.1. INTRODUCTION

Calls for the creation of a single European organisation responsible for aviation safety, modelled on the Federal Aviation Authority (FAA)[6] in the United States, are nothing new in the European Union.[7] For long time, it seemed preferable to establish a centralised European Aviation Safety Authority as an international organisation based on a mixed agreement between the European Union and its Member States – and also open to other European countries.[8] What was finally

Einrichtungen des Gemeinschaftsrechts mit eigener Rechtspersönlichkeit, Baden-Baden 1999, pp. 32–57; *E. Chiti*, Le agenzie europee, Milan 2002.

3 Established by Regulation (EC) No. 1592/2002 of 15 July 2002 on common rules in the field of civil aviation and establishing a European Aviation Safety Agency, OJ L 240/1, 7.9.2002 ("Basic Regulation").

4 11th Whereas of the Basic Regulation (fn. 3).

5 See Proposal for a Regulation on establishing common rules in the field of civil aviation and creating a European Aviation Safety Agency of 27 September 2000 (COM(2000) 595 final), p. 6.

6 For the tasks of the FAA see in detail *Bermann*, Regulatory Cooperation with counterpart agencies abroad, Law & Policy in International Business 24 (1993), pp. 669 (674–684).

7 For example: the European Parliament called for the establishment of a European Civil Aviation Authority as early as 1991 (see Legislative Resolution embodying the opinion of the European Parliament on the Commission proposal for a Council directive on the harmonisation of technical requirements and procedures applicable to civil aircraft, OJ C 267/154, 14.10.1991).

8 See Recommendation of the Commission on a negotiating mandate for the creation of a European Civil Aviation Organisation of 10 December 1996 (SEK(96) 2152 final).

accepted, however, was a proposal for the establishment of an internal EC body acting according to Community law.[9]

2.2. THE INTERNAL STRUCTURE OF THE EASA

Having the same legal characteristics as the other independent agencies,[10] EASA has been endowed with legal personality under the auspices of the EC.[11] It has not been provided for in the Community Treaties, but has rather been set up on the sole basis of secondary legislation passed by the Commission and the Parliament. Therefore, it is a part of the so called "tertiäre Organisationsstruktur"[12] (tertiary structure) of the Community (term introduced by M. Hilf). The Agency is administered by the Management Board responsible for overall political decisions[13] with the Executive Director being the manager of its administrative staff.[14] One of its main features is hence its dualistic management structure,[15] which is also typical of the other independent agencies in the EC.

The organisational feature specific for EASA, however, is the Agency's Board of Appeal, which is to provide for an "appropriate appeal mechanism".[16]Any natural or legal person directly and individually affected can bring an action against any decision of the Agency.[17] The decisions of the Board of Appeal are in turn subject to the jurisdiction of the Court of Justice and the Court of First Instance.[18]

2.3. THE AGENCY'S CERTIFICATION TASKS – THE CORE ACTIVITY OF EASA

According to the intention of its founding fathers, the certification of aeronautical products, parts, and appliances designed, manufactured, maintained or used by

---

9 For the origins of the Basic Regulation see in detail *Stiehl*, in: Frohnmeyer/Berry, EG-Verkehrsrecht, No. 111, paras 155–186.

10 See for example the phenotypic definition of *Kreher*, Agencies in the European Community, JEPP 4 (1997), pp. 225 (227).

11 Article 19(1) of the Basic Regulation (fn. 3).

12 For this term see *Hilf*, Die Organisationsstruktur der Europäischen Gemeinschaften, New York 1982, especially p. 109.

13 This encompasses for example the appointment of the leading officials of the Agency (Art. 30 of the Basic Regulation (fn. 3)), the adoption of the Agency's annual programme of work (Art. 24(2) lit. c of the Basic Regulation (fn. 3)), and the draft estimates (Article 48(5) of the Basic Regulation (fn. 3)).

14 Stated explicitly in Article 29(1) S. 1 of the Basic Regulation (fn. 3).

15 *Fischer-Appelt*, Agenturen (fn. 2) p. 221.

16 See the 15th Whereas of the Basic Regulation (fn. 3).

17 Articles 35–36 of the Basic Regulation (fn. 3).

18 Article 41 of the Basic Regulation (fn. 3).

persons under the regulatory oversight of the Member States shall be the "core activity"[19] of EASA. Due to extensive international guidelines issued by the International Civil Aviation Organisation, the certification of new aeronautical products had been effected in a two-stage procedure even before the EASA Regulation came into force.[20] Under the laws of almost every Member State of the EC, after the type certification procedure of a new product has been completed,[21] every single copy of a sample had been subjected to a separate airworthiness certification procedure before it was released for circulation in the market.[22]

The conformity of the prototype with the applicable airworthiness and environmental standards was approved as part of the type certification-process. The subsequent individual airworthiness certificate was to secure the conformity of the single product to the approved type design. This two-stage procedure has now been transferred to the new EASA system; only the competent authority has changed: While the issue of the single airworthiness certificate still lies within the competence of the airworthiness authorities of the Member States,[23] it is now EASA that is solely authorised to release the design certifications valid in all Member States of the European Community.[24]

The certification competence of EASA also implies its powers of surveillance over the applicants for a European type certificate. For these purposes EASA has been authorised to inspect and to audit the applicant's production halls as well as those of their contractors in order to ensure their compliance with the relevant procedural and organisational standards.[25] Up to now, such extensive powers of surveillance in respect of the Member States have only been conferred on the European Commission and its officers, but never before vested in an independent agency. The Basic Regulation No. 1592/2002 is therefore the first attempt ever to empower an independent agency to conduct formal inspections within the territories of the Member States.[26]

---

19 Explicitly stated in the Proposal of the Commission for the Basic Regulation (fn. 5), p. 15.

20 See §2 of the German Luftverkehrsgesetz. For the existing German system of airworthiness certification see in summary *Baumann*, Private Luftfahrtverwaltung, Cologne 2002, pp. 257–262.

21 §§1 ff. of the German Luftverkehrszulassungsordnung.

22 §§6 ff. of the Luftverkehrszulassungsordnung.

23 In the case of Germany, the competent authority was the Luftfahrtbundesamt based in Brunswick.

24 Article 15(1) of the Basic Regulation (fn. 3).

25 The powers transferred to the Agency's auditors and inspectors are thereby on a par with the powers transferred in other fields of European administrative law (see Art. 46 of the Basic Regulation (fn. 3)).

26 For details see *David*, Inspektionen im Europäischen Verwaltungsrecht, Berlin 2003, pp. 30–116; (see also *David* in this vol., p. 363 et seq.).

2.4. THE AUTONOMOUS RULE-MAKING ACTIVITIES OF EASA

Another task of the Agency, to some extent related to its certification assignments, is its capacity to issue Certification Specifications (CS).[27] This collective term includes different sorts of technical regulations developed by EASA to be used in the certification process. On the one hand, it encompasses the so-called airworthiness codes that provide for detailed technical standards for several products and product categories.[28] On the other hand, Basic Regulation No. 1592/2002 allows the Agency to develop acceptable means of compliance, which form procedural guidelines for the applicant on how to verify the conformity of his products with the Agency's airworthiness codes.[29]

The Certification Specifications form the basis of the Agency's own certification procedures, i.e. the issue of type certificates. They are also applicable to the procedures still carried out by the competent authorities of the Member States, in particular, all those related to issuing airworthiness certificates.[30]

All Certification Specifications are formally non-binding.[31] However, this does not mean that they have no legal effect.[32] Besides their purely factual relevance as a source of stability and accountability in the certification process, the Certification Specifications issued by the Agency can also produce an indirect legally "self-binding effect"[33] for the Agency as the author of the applicable regulation.

2.5. THE FORMULATION OF OPINIONS

Apart from issuing detailed rules of an administrative character, EASA is also supposed to participate in the EC legislative process. First of all, the Agency is

---

27 See Article 14(2) of the Basic Regulation (fn. 3).

28 For example CS-APU (Decision No. 2003/5/RM of the Executive Director of the Agency of 17/10/2003 for auxiliary power units).

29 See Decision No. 2003/1/RM of the Executive Director of the Agency of 17/10/2003 on acceptable means of compliance and guidance material for the airworthiness and environmental certification of aircraft and related products, parts and appliances.

30 Likewise *Groß*, Exekutive Vollzugsprogrammierung durch tertiäres Gemeinschaftsrecht?, Die öffentliche Verwaltung 2004, pp. 20 (22) presuming that the Certification Specifications of the Agency are exclusively applicable on the national airworthiness authorities. As Article 15(1) lit. a of the Basic Regulation (fn. 3) shows, the Certification Specifications are also to be used in the certification activities of the Agency itself.

31 See Proposal of the Commission for the Basic Regulation (fn. 5), p. 7. Likewise the predominant views in literature (for example *Groß*, DÖV (fn. 30), p. 23; *Giemulla/van Schyndel*, Die Joint Aviation Requirements (JAR) und deren Überleitung in die Vorschriften der EU und der Agentur für Flugsicherheit (EASA), VdL-Nachrichten, No. 3/2003, p. 14).

32 Noteworthy in respect of possible indirect legal effects of formally non-binding Community acts, for example ECJ, Case C-322/88 *Grimaldi* (1989) E.C.R. 4407, para 18.

33 *Senden*, Soft Law in European Community Law, Oxford 2004, p. 404.

involved in the preparation of secondary legislation according to Articles 251–252 of the EC Treaty. In this regard, Basic Regulation No. 1592/2002 provides for the participation of the Agency in the decision-making process whenever the legislator plans to amend the Basic Regulation itself.[34] To this end, the Agency is empowered to produce drafts for the projected amendment, which are then communicated to the Commission as opinions of the Agency. These opinions form the basis of the Commission's proposal which is to be introduced in the formal legislative procedure. Due to the Commission's exclusive right to initiate legislation in Community matters,[35] the opinions of the Agency do not exert any binding effect on the Commission, neither regarding the Commission's choice whether to initiate the legislative process or not, nor regarding the contents of a proposed legislative act.

Of a somewhat different character, however, is the participation of the Agency in the process of implementation of Basic Regulation No. 1592/2002 by the Commission, in accordance with Article 211, fourth indent, of the EC Treaty.[36] "In order to assist the Commission",[37] the Agency is empowered to prepare drafts for implementing rules and to submit these drafts to the Commission. As opposed to the participation in the legislative process, these Agency opinions do have at least a procedural binding effect on the Commission. As far as "technical rules" and rules relating to "operational aspects" are concerned, the Commission may not deviate from the content of the Agency's drafts without first having consulted with the Agency.[38]

2.6. THE ROLE OF THE AGENCY IN MONITORING THE UNIFORM APPLICATION OF COMMUNITY RULES

According to Article 211, first indent, of the EC Treaty, the Commission ensures compliance with the provisions of the Community Treaties and the measures taken by the institutions. Hence, the Commission is also referred to as the "Guardian of the Treaties".[39] In order to fulfil this task, the Commission needs proper mechanisms to gain information on the application of the Community rules by the Member States. Besides other instruments, such as special

---

34 See Article 14(1) of the Basic Regulation (fn. 3).

35 *Lenaerts/van Nuffel*, Constitutional Law of the European Union, 2nd edition, London 2005, para 10–059.

36 For the implementing powers of the Commission in particular see *Riedel*, Die Durchführungsrechtsetzung nach Art. 211, 4. Sp EG, Europarecht 41 (2006), pp. 512; *Möllers*, Die Durchführung des Gemeinschaftsrechts, Europarecht 37 (2002), p. 483; see also *Möllers* in Schmidt-Aßmann/Schöndorf-Haubold (eds.), *Der Europäische Verwaltungsverbund* (2005), p. 293 et seq.

37 Article 14(1) of the Basic Regulation (fn. 3).

38 The Basic Regulation uses in this regard the term "prior coordination" (Article 12(2) lit. b of the Basic Regulation (fn. 3)). A term so far unknown in European administrative law.

39 *Lenaerts/van Nuffel*, Constitutional Law (fn. 35), para 10–57.

notification duties of the Member States or the Commission's rights to requests information,[40] European administrative law provides in many cases for different forms of inspections to be carried out in the Member States. A rather recent development in Community law has been the delegation of such inspection tasks to independent agencies of the EC. In fact, EASA is the second independent agency endowed with powers to inspect national public authorities.[41] Pursuant to Article 16 of the Basic Regulation, it has been authorised to conduct standardisation inspections in order to monitor the application of the Regulation by national aviation authorities.[42] In order to furnish the Commission with the necessary information on possible shortcomings, the Agency is to submit reports to the Commission on the outcome of such inspections. These reports can then serve as a basis for infringement proceedings[43] according to Article 226 of the EC Treaty.[44] In this context, it must be pointed out that the formal decision whether to initiate such proceedings or not must, according to the competence order of the Treatise, remain within the exclusive competence of the Commission[45] and hence this decision cannot be transferred to an independent agency such as EASA.

2.7. FURTHER COMPETENCIES

Apart from the four main tasks mentioned above, Basic Regulation No. 1592/2002 contains provisions for various other activities of EASA. The Agency is for example empowered to formulate opinions on all matters covered by the Basic Regulation[46] and to develop and finance its own research.[47] EASA is also intended to play a leading role in the future information network to consist of national authorities and the Commission.[48] Further activities of EASA are connected to its competence in the sphere of international relations. In this context the Agency will, in particular, be authorised to co-operate and to conclude working arrangements with third countries and international actors.[49]

---

40 In general to these instruments *Sommer*, Verwaltungskooperation am Beispiel administrativer Informationsverfahren im Europäischen Umweltrecht, New York 2003, pp. 102–155; (Also *Sommer* in this vol., p. 55 et seq.).

41 For the first example ever see Art. 3 of the Regulation (EC) No. 1406/2002 of the European Parliament and of the Council of 27 June 2002 establishing a European Maritime Safety Agency, OJ L 208/1, 5.8.2002 ("Maritime Safety Agency-Regulation"). In detail see 3.4.

42 Article 16 of the Basic Regulation (fn. 3).

43 See for example *Schermers/Waelbroeck*, Juridical Protection in the European Union, 6th Edition, The Hague 2001.

44 Proposal of the Commission for the Basic Regulation (fn. 5), p. 7.

45 See also *David*, Inspektionen (fn. 26), p. 191.

46 Article 12(2) lit. a of the Basic Regulation (fn. 3).

47 Article 17 of the Basic Regulation (fn. 3).

48 Article 11 of the Basic Regulation (fn. 3).

49 Article 18(2) of the Basic Regulation (fn. 3).

3. TYPES OF INDEPENDENT EUROPEAN AGENCIES

3.1. INTRODUCTION

It will be clear, even at first glance, that the concept of regulation by independent agencies is of major significance as far as the administration of the internal market is concerned. With a total of approximately 3,000 permanent and temporary posts,[50] the role of the independent agencies of the EC is no longer limited to exceptional cases. In fact, the emergence of a unique European agency model[51] can be considered perhaps even as an "explosion of the agency model".[52] In spite of the heterogeneity[53] already mentioned, it seems possible to reduce the existing agencies to a small number of basic categories.[54] To this end, I will chose four agencies in the following section, each standing as an example for one archetype of an independent European agency. These four archetypes differ – above all – in their respective field of activity, from which a particular profile in terms of organisational setting and competence can be derived.

3.2. THE EUROPEAN MEDICINES AGENCY – SCIENTIFIC EXPERTISE IN SUPRANATIONAL AUTHORISATION PROCEDURES

3.2.1. Introduction

First of all the European legislator has established independent agencies within the field of the Community procedures for the authorisation of newly developed products. This type of independent agencies encompasses the European Food Safety Authority[55] based in Parma and the European Medicines Agency[56]

50 See the 2006 General Budget of the European Union.

51 See for example already *Bangemann*, Arzneimittel und europäischer Binnenmarkt, in: *Schwarze* (ed.), Unverfälschter Wettbewerb für Arzneimittel im europäischen Binnenmarkt, Baden-Baden 1998, p. 83 (85).

52 *E. Chiti*, The emergence of a community administration: The case of European agencies, CMLR 37 (2000), p. 309 (311).

53 The diversity of existing European agencies may result from the fact that the foundation of new agencies is often due to special necessities of the political sector involved. See for example *Dehousse*, Regulating by networks in the European Community, JEPP 4 (1997), p. 246 (255).

54 For the method of reconstructing a "typus", its problems and value see *Larenz*, Methodenlehre der Rechtswissenschaft, 6th Edition, Berlin et al. 1991, pp. 461–472.

55 Established by Regulation (EC) No. 178/2002 of the European Parliament and the Council of 28 January 2002 laying down the general principles and requirements of food law, establishing the European Food Safety Authority and laying down procedures in matters of food safety, OJ 31/1, 1.2.2002 ("Food Safety Authority-Regulation"). See also *Knipschild* in this vol., p. 123 et seq.

56 Established by Council Regulation (EEC) No. 2309/93 of 22 July 1993 laying down Community procedures for the authorisation and supervision of medicinal products for human and veterinary use and establishing a European Agency for the Evaluation of

based in London. The latter will serve here as an example for this first agency type.

3.2.2. *The Medicines Agency's field of activity*

The Medicines Agency's field of activity basically consists of participating in the European authorisation procedures for medicinal products. The "chief task"[57] of the Agency thereby is to provide the Community institutions with scientific opinions on the marketability of a new medicinal product for which authorisation[58] has been applied. Within the so-called centralised authorisation procedure, the Agency is always and immediately concerned with the evaluation of an application for a European authorisation. Within the decentralised procedure, however, a scientific opinion from the Agency is only necessary if the Member States have failed to reach unanimity on a certain application in a special *inter partes* procedure.[59] Neither within the centralised nor the decentralised procedure is the Agency entrusted with the final authorisation decision. The final decision as to whether a medicinal product may be authorised or not rests exclusively with the Commission, assisted by a regulatory committee.[60] The opinion of the Agency in this respect is not binding on the Commission. However, the Commission must give a reason whenever it intends to differ from the views of the Agency as expressed in the latter's scientific opinion.[61] Therefore, as a matter of fact, the opinions of the Agency are of crucial importance within the European authorisation procedures. This stems not least from the superior expertise of the Agency in the field of the evaluation of medicinal products.[62]

3.2.3. *Scientific Committees as a specific organisational feature*

This special expertise is mainly the result of a specific organisational feature of the Agency: its Scientific Committees. To date, four such committees[63] have been

Medicinal Products, OJ L 214/1, 24.8.1993. Replaced by Regulation (EC) No. 726/2004 of the European Parliament and of the Council of 31 March 2004 laying down Community procedures for the authorisation and supervision of medicinal products for human and veterinary use and establishing a European Medicines Agency, OJ L 136/1, 30.4.2004 ("Medicines Agency Regulation").

57 19th Whereas of the Medicines Agency Regulation (fn. 56).

58 See Article 57(1) lit. a of the Medicines Agency Regulation (fn. 56).

59 For a detailed description of the centralised and the decentralised authorisation procedure see *Wagner*, Europäisches Zulassungssystem für Arzneimittel und Parallelhandel, Stuttgart 2000, pp. 194–198 and 241–252.

60 Article 10(2) of the Medicines Agency Regulation (fn. 56).

61 Article 10(1) of the Medicines Agency Regulation (fn. 56).

62 See also *Blattner*, Europäisches Produktzulassungsverfahren, Baden-Baden 2003, pp. 152–154.

63 These are according to Art. 56(1) lit a-d of the Medicines Agency-Regulation (fn. 56) the Committee for Medicinal Products for Human Use, the Committee for Medicinal Products

established under the auspices of the Medicines Agency, each composed of experts delegated by the competent national authorities.[64] Inside the Agency, it is their task to prepare the Agency's scientific opinions.[65] In fact, these Scientific Committees pre-dated the Agency.[66] They were originally established as committees for the co-ordination of national decisions in the field of medicinal security.[67] However, their votes did not have any legally binding force on the Member States participating in the committee process.[68]

By transferring these committees into European agencies, their character has evolved in two ways. On the one hand, the informal pre-existing committee structure has been consolidated in both procedural and organisational respects. Although the procedural provisions of the European authorisation procedure for medicinal products are sometimes referred to as being "lacunose"[69] or disjointed, the organisational evolution of the committee structure is evident. Acting under the auspices of the Medicines Agency they can rely on a rich infrastructure, including a permanent Secretariat[70] and a network of accredited experts.[71] On the other hand, the Medicines Agency's Basic Regulation now strengthens the position of the committees as purely scientific bodies.[72] The expertise and independent role of the committee members is highlighted in various provisions of the Agency's Basic Regulation. For example, no member of a scientific committee may have interests in the pharmaceutical industry which could affect his impartiality.[73] Also the Member States must refrain from giving committee members and experts any instructions that are incompatible with their tasks.[74] Furthermore, the committee members ought not to be chosen for purely political considerations, but rather on the basis of their scientific expertise.[75] Within the regimes of the authorisation procedure for medicinal products, the scientific stage of the procedure is also organisationally separated from the final political decision making. Risk assessment is allocated to the Scientific Committees of the

for Veterinary Use, the Committee on Orphan Medicinal Products, and the Committee on Herbal Medicinal Products.

64 See Article 61(1) of the Medicines Agency Regulation (fn. 56).

65 Article 57(1) lit. a of the Medicines Agency Regulation (fn. 56).

66 See for example the Second Council Directive (EEC) No. 75/319 of 20 May 1975 on the approximation of provisions laid down by Law, Regulation or Administrative Action relating to proprietary medicinal products, OJ L 147/13, 9.6.1975.

67 See *Collatz*, Die neuen europäischen Zulassungsverfahren für Arzneimittel, Aulendorf 1996, p. 42.

68 *Kwizda*, Zulassungsverfahren für Humanarzneimittel in der Europäischen Union, Vienna 1998, p. 22.

69 See *E. Chiti* (fn. 52), p. 335.

70 Article 56(1) lit. e of the Medicines Agency Regulation (fn. 56).

71 See Article 62(2) of the Medicines Agency Regulation (fn. 56).

72 Explicitly stated in the 24th Whereas of the Medicines Agency Regulation (fn. 56).

73 Article 63(2) of the Medicines Agency Regulation (fn. 56).

74 Article 61(6) of the Medicines Agency Regulation (fn. 56).

75 Article 61(1) of the Medicines Agency Regulation (fn. 56).

Agency by their scientific opinions, while risk management is the domain of the Commission, which decides by accepting or declining an application on the basis of risk analysis.[76] This organisational dichotomy was entirely unknown in the pre-existing committee structure. By incorporating the Scientific Committees into the European Medicines Agency, the status of these committees has changed significantly from that of a body representing and deliberating the Member State's interests to an independent body of purely scientific expertise.[77]

3.2.4. Conclusions

The main characteristic of the European Medicines Agency is thus its role within the European authorisation procedures in the field of pharmaceutical products. It stands as an example for a first type of independent agencies of the EC, providing an independent and scientific expertise within the Community's procedures for the authorisation of new products. The creation of such expertise bodies first and foremost facilitates the use of scientific and technical experts who are not part of the normal bureaucratic structure of the Community institutions,[78] especially of the Commission with its limited number of employees. Opting for the creation of a European agency is therefore advantageous insofar as it consolidates and institutionalises the proliferate European committee structure, increasingly criticised as intransparent.[79] By establishing such European agencies the EC has succeeded in keeping scientific expertise distant from the political sphere of the Commission,[80] while at the same time the experts primarily recruited from the Member States are committed to acting for the benefit of the supranational entity.[81]

---

76 Stated for the European Food Safety Agency by *Casper*, Zur Vergemeinschaftung von Verwaltungsverfahren am Beispiel von Gentechnik- und reformierten Lebensmittelrecht, DVBl. 2002, p. 1437 (1440).

77 See also *E. Chiti* (fn. 2), p. 177 differentiating between "collegi reali" and "collegi virtuali".

78 *Vos*, Reforming the European Commission: What role to play for the EU agencies?, CMLR 37 (2000), p. 1113 (1119); further *Craig/de Búrca*, The evolution of EU law, Oxford et al. 1999, p. 45.

79 See *Harlow*, Accountability in the European Union, Oxford 2002, p. 68.

80 *Geradin/Petit*, The development of agencies at EU and national levels, Jean Monnet Program Working Paper 1/4, New York 2004, p. 36. For the legitimation of European Agencies by their distance from political influence see also *Uerpmann*, Mittelbare Gemeinschaftsverwaltung durch gemeinschaftsgeschaffene juristische Personen des öffentlichen Rechts, AöR 125 (2000), p. 551 (565–566).

81 See *E. Chiti* (fn. 2), p. 178; especially from the perspective of political science *Majone*, Theories of regulation, in: *Majone* (ed.), Regulating Europe, London 1996, p. 28 (41–42).

3.3. THE OFFICE FOR HARMONISATION IN THE INTERNAL MARKET – AN INDEPENDENT COMMUNITY ADMINISTRATION FOR INDUSTRIAL PROPERTY RIGHTS

3.3.1. Introduction

Another main field of activity for independent European agencies concerns the administration of industrial property rights. This second "typus" of agencies encompasses the Community Plant Variety Office[82] and – first and foremost – the Office for Harmonisation in the Internal Market (Trade Marks and Designs)[83] based in Alicante.

3.3.2. The Office's field of activity

The discussion on the creation of a uniform legal framework for the administration of trade marks started in the early days of the European Economic Community.[84] However, the establishment of such a uniform framework took place only in 1994 with the introduction of Regulation No. 40/94 on the Community trade mark. Before that regulation entered into force, the trade mark regimes of the Member States had been largely limited to their respective territories. According to the Regulation, the new Community trade mark regime explicitly does not replace the existing national trade marks.[85] It has rather been based on the coexistence of national and Community trade marks.[86] The choice between the possible frameworks is left to the individual applicant.[87]

---

82 Established by Council Regulation (EC) No. 2100/94 of 27 July 1994 on Community plant variety rights, OJ L 227/1, 1.9.1994.

83 Established by Council Regulation (EC) No. 40/94 of 20 December 1993 on the Community trade mark, OJ L 11/1, 14.1.1994 ("Community trade mark Regulation"). Extended by Council Regulation (EC) No. 6/2002 of 12 December 2001 on Community designs, OJ L 3/1, 5.1.2002.

84 For an example see *v.d. Groeben*, Rechtsangleichung auf dem Gebiet des gewerblichen Rechtsschutzes im Rahmen der Europäischen Wirtschaftsgemeinschaft, GRURInt 1959, p. 629.

85 See the 5th Whereas of the Community trade mark Regulation (fn. 83). The remaining trade mark regimes of the Member States were though subject to vast substantial harmonisation efforts by the EC (see for example the First Council Directive (EEC) No. 89/104 of 21 December 1988 to approximate the laws of the Member States relating to trade marks, OJ L 40/1, 11.2.1989).

86 *v. Kapff*, in: *Ekey/Klippel* (eds.), Heidelberger Kommentar zum Markenrecht, Heidelberg 2003, Art. 1 GMV, para 45.

87 The Community trade mark is therefore a case of a facultative harmonisation. For the different strategies of harmonisation within the EC see in general *v. Danwitz*, in: *Dauses* (ed.), Handbuch des EU-Wirtschaftsrechts, Munich 2004, Vol. 1 B II, para 83.

The Community trade mark regime is administered entirely by the Office for Harmonisation.[88] Accordingly widespread is the competence allocated to the Office by its Basic Regulation. What is of particular interest is its capacity to adopt legally binding decisions addressing the individual applicants and directly affecting their position within the respective markets.[89]

3.3.3. Procedural and organisational autonomy as a specific feature

The most prominent characteristic of the Office can therefore be seen in its high level of autonomy. Autonomy has been conferred on the Office in procedural and organisational respects. In terms of the Community trade mark procedures, the Office can adopt any decisions without co-operating with the Commission or other Community institutions, as well as without the national trade mark administrations. Insofar as the Community trade mark Regulation still provides for such co-operation, the Member States only act with the assistance of the Office.[90] The regular national trade mark procedures remain mainly unaffected by the Community trade mark regime and vice versa.[91] The same applies to the organisational aspects. Here, the Office is to a very high degree separated from the Commission. Although its Basic Regulation provides for an explicit review of legality by the Commission over the decisions of the Office, this review is restricted to those acts "in respect of which Community law does not provide or any review of legality by another body".[92] With this restriction, the major part of the Office's decisions is in fact excluded from any direct supervision by the Commission. Decisions in trade mark matters in particular are subject to a special proceeding before the Office's own Board of Appeal and to the jurisdiction of the Court of Justice.[93] This may in the first place be due to technical and practical reasons, especially to an attempt to reduce the workload of the Court of

88 For details of the Community trade mark-procedures see *Ingerl*, Die Gemeinschaftsmarke, Stuttgart et al. 1996, pp. 125–143.

89 For example Art. 40 of the Community trade mark Regulation (fn. 83).

90 For an example see the application for the registration of a Community trade mark. The application can be submitted both to the Office itself or to a competent office of the Member States. If the applicant chooses to submit his application to an office of a Member State, the national authority is restricted to refer the application to the Office for Harmonisation without a further examination (Art. 25 of the Community trade mark Regulation (fn. 83)). Also see the possibility of the Office to search the Member State's registers of trade marks in Art. 39(2) of the Community trade mark Regulation (fn. 83).

91 In reverse, the Office for Harmonisation itself is only partially concerned in the national trade mark procedures. See for example the rules for submission, publication and transmission of a request for conversion of a Community trade mark (Art. 109 of the Community trade mark Regulation (fn. 83)). The relationship between the Office for Harmonisation and the Member State's offices can therefore be deemed to be one of "reciprocal auxiliarity" (*E. Chiti* (fn. 52), p. 320).

92 Article 118(1) of the Community trade mark Regulation (fn. 83).

93 In detail see *v. Mühlendahl/Ohlgart*, Die Gemeinschaftsmarke, Bern et al. 1998, §31 para 16.

Justice.[94] At the same time, this feature marks the Office's significant degree of organisational independence in relation to the Commission. The Office's autonomy plays a role also in other contexts: the Community Plant Variety Office and the Office for Harmonisation are the only agencies of the EC directed by a President who is appointed not by the Commission and the Administrative Board of the respective agency, but solely by the Administrative Board acting in co-operation with the Council of the EC.[95]

3.3.4. Conclusions

These characteristics define the Office for Harmonisation as an Internal Market player that stands model for a second type of independent agencies of the EC, designed as widely independent regarding technical matters as well as sufficiently autonomous in regard to legal, administrative and financial issues.[96] Its field of activity encompasses the entire range of procedures and actions necessary for the administration of the Community trade mark, without involving any other Community bodies, especially the Commission, in its day to day working routine. The Office for Harmonisation is therefore part of the administrative sphere of the Commission to a lesser degree than other independent agencies of the EC. Rather, it stands independently alongside the Commission[97] – an autonomy also characteristic for many of the Member States' administrations of industrial property rights.[98]

3.4. THE EUROPEAN MARITIME SAFETY AGENCY – CO-ORDINATION AND SUPERVISION OF THE NATIONAL ENFORCEMENT OF COMMUNITY RULES

3.4.1. Introduction

The third type of independent European agencies is formed by agencies that have in common a special co-ordination function within the enforcement of Community law by the Member States. Alongside their co-ordination function,[99] some of the more recent agencies of this type have also taken part in the formal Community supervision process. An early prototype has certainly been the

94 See *Dammann*, Die Beschwerdekammern der europäischen Agenturen, Frankfurt 2004, p. 21.

95 Article 120 of the Community trade mark Regulation (fn. 83).

96 11th Whereas of the Community trade mark Regulation (fn. 83).

97 Likewise before also Hilf (fn. 12), p. 162: "freies und weitgehend selbständiges Glied der Gemeinschaft".

98 For relevant examples see the working document of the Commission – "Community trade mark" (III/D/1294/79-DE) of October 1976, published in GRURInt 1980, p. 33 (42).

99 *Uerpmann* (fn. 80), p. 562.

European Environment Agency.[100] For a better understanding, especially of the supervision function of this type of agencies, the focus here will lie on the European Maritime Safety Agency. With regard to coordination and monitoring of EC law enforcement by the Member States, the Agency fulfils the following two major tasks.

3.4.2. The Maritime Safety Agency and the administration of networks

The first major task is that this Agency plays an important role in the administration of networks within the EC. The notion of a network is used in different contexts, though. On one hand, the Agency is entitled to develop and to operate a vessel traffic monitoring and information system.[101] This information system and network will make it possible to effectively monitor the traffic and any incidents and accidents at sea, thus facilitating an immediate response from the competent authorities of the Member States to any unsafe condition.[102] Within this information network, the Agency will act as a "clearing house".[103] All in all, the system aims at effectuating the enforcement of existing Community rules for maritime safety by the Member States.[104] A positive effect on the enforcement of these Community rules is therefore achieved by interlacing the competent authorities of the Member States into a co-operative information process[105] to be carried out by the Community.[106]

But the notion of administration via networks also has a second dimension that exceeds the "purely impersonal exchange of data"[107]: the second major task – that of the administration via "networks of public authorities".[108] Such

[100] Established by Council Regulation (EEC) No. 1210/90 of 7 May 1990 on the establishment of the European Environment Agency and the European Environment Information and Observation Network, OJ L 120/1, 11.5.1990. For details see *Epiney*, Umweltrecht in der Europäischen Union, 2nd Edition, Cologne 2005, pp. 47–51.

[101] Article 2 sub d of the Maritime Safety Agency-Regulation (fn. 41).

[102] For the monitoring system see the Directive (EC) No. 2002/59 of the Council of 27 June 2002 establishing a Community vessel traffic monitoring and information system, OJ L 208/10, 5.8.2002.

[103] *Sommer* (fn. 40), p. 211.

[104] For these existing Community rules see for example Council Directive (EEC) No. 93/75 of 13 September 1993 concerning minimum requirements for vessels bound for or leaving Community ports and carrying dangerous or polluting goods, OJ L 247/19, 5.10.1993.

[105] See *v. Bogdandy* Information und Kommunikation in der Europäischen Union, in: *Hoffmann-Riem/Schmidt-Aßmann* (eds.), Verwaltungsrecht in der Informationsgesellschaft, Baden-Baden 2000, p. 133 (177).

[106] This positive effect of information networks is also recognised by *Ladeur*, Die Europäische Umweltagentur und die Perspektiven eines europäischen Netzwerks der Umweltverwaltungen, NuR 1997, p. 8 (10). See also *Fischer-Appelt* (fn. 2), p. 548.

[107] See *v. Bogdandy* (fn. 105), p. 176.

[108] This term was first mentioned in the 15th Whereas of Council Regulation (EC) No. 1/2003 of 16 December 2002 on the implementation of the rules on competition laid down in Articles 81 and 82 of the Treaty, OJ L 1/1, 4.1.2003. For the network concept in general see *Schuppert*, Verwaltungswissenschaft, Baden-Baden 2000, pp. 384–400.

networks of public authorities also appear within the sphere covered by the Basic Regulation establishing the Maritime Safety Agency. By way of example, we can mention the competence of the Agency to organise training activities for Member States' officials and to offer technical assistance related to the enforcement of the regulation.[109] It is mainly these activities that are aimed at, in particular, establishing a permanent personal and functional co-operation between the Member States and the Community, enabling the Community itself to intervene and to steer the Member State's conduct.[110] Rather than by means of formal supervision instruments, this is primarily achieved by creating dynamic adherent effects[111] between the Community level and the Member States.[112]

3.4.3. The competence of the Maritime Safety Agency to carry out inspections

The competence of the Maritime Safety Agency is, however, not restricted to informal, legally non-binding activities. In fact it has also been delegated the formal power to carry out inspections within the territories of the Member States.[113] These inspections are aimed at ensuring the proper enforcement of the European system for "port State control",[114] which constitutes a harmonised set of rules for the supervision and control of maritime traffic by the Member States. As mentioned above, up to now such extensive powers of surveillance in relation to Member State authorities have been conferred only on the Commission.[115] The establishment of the Maritime Safety Agency has therefore been a major step forward in the enhancement of the Community's institutional system.[116] Effectuating the enforcement of Community law by means of independent European agencies that carry out formal inspections has therefore become a new strategic element in European Community law.

---

109 See 4th Whereas of the Maritime Safety Agency-Regulation (fn. 41).

110 *Fischer-Appelt* (fn. 2), p. 548.

111 See *Ladeur* (fn. 106), p. 13.

112 This network concept is, however, most visible in other independent agencies of this third typus. See for example Article 9(1) of Regulation (EC) No. 881/2004 of the European Parliament and of the Council of 29 April 2004 establishing a European railway agency, OJ L 164/1, 30.4.2004 ("Railway Agency Regulation"); Art. 3 lit. c Regulation (EC) No. 460/2004 of the European Parliament and of the Council of 10 March 2004 establishing the European Network and Information Security Agency. OJ L 77/1, 13.3.2004 ("Information Security Agency Regulation").

113 Article 2 lit. b i) of the Maritime Safety Agency-Regulation (fn. 41).

114 See Council Directive (EC) No. 95/21 of 19 June 1995 concerning the enforcement, in respect of shipping using Community ports and sailing in the waters under the jurisdiction of the Member States, OJ L 157/1, 7.7.1995.

115 In detail see again *David* (fn. 26), pp. 30–116.

116 For example, also the Commission recognises the agencies carrying out inspection functions as a type of agencies of its own (See Communication from the Commission – The operating framework for the European Regulatory Agencies of 11.12.2002 (COM(2002) 718 final), p. 4).

3.4.4. Conclusions

All in all, the European Maritime Safety Agency stands model for the third group of independent European agencies, mainly dedicated to improving the enforcement of Community law in the Member States' legal systems.[117] The rise of this type of agencies is first and foremost due to a change of perspective starting in the latter half of the 1980s. Since then, the focus of the European institutions has changed significantly from reaching Community goals by means of Community legislation to dealing with issues related to the national enforcement of such legislation.[118] On the one hand, a serious lack of enforcement of Community law by the Member States was discovered, especially in the sector of environmental law.[119] On the other hand, however, all parties agreed that to overcome these difficulties neither a substantial enlargement of direct enforcement of Community law nor an increase in the Commission's personnel would serve as acceptable solutions.[120] Hence, creating independent European agencies served as a compromise between a continuous increase of Community policies and the Member States' fear of losing their national influence[121] – or in the words of E. Chiti: "an instrument to confer centralised competencies to decentralised Community institutions".[122] With regard to the delegation of formal inspection powers, the agency model indeed seems favourable, for the national authorities which do not find themselves standing up against a nameless Community institution, but have the possibility to exert influence through participation in the management board of the agency in question.[123] The European agencies are therefore an example of a "co-operative and balanced hierarchy" (kooperativ abgefederte Hierarchie)[124], in line with Community law.

---

117 This aim is expressed in the whereas of the respective basic regulations that consistently refer to the pre-existing harmonisation guidelines in the policy sector involved. For example see 4th Whereas of the Maritime Safety Agency Regulation (fn. 41); 2nd Whereas of the Railway Agency Regulation (fn. 112); 6th–9th Whereas of the Information Security Agency Regulation (fn. 112).

118 Likewise *v. Borries*, Die Verwaltungskompetenzen der Europäischen Gemeinschaft, in: *Due/Lutter/Schwarze* (eds.), Festschrift für Ulrich Everling, Vol. 1, Baden-Baden 1995, p. 127 (130); *Magiera*, Die Durchsetzung des Gemeinschaftsrechts im europäischen Integrationsprozeß, DÖV 1998, p. 173 (174); *Snyder*, The Effectiveness of European Community Law, MLR 56 (1993), 19.

119 Representative for the large number of publications in this matter *Albin*, Die Vollzugskontrolle des europäischen Umweltrechts, Berlin 1999, pp. 73–84.

120 See *Dehousse*, (fn. 53), p. 254; *Fischer-Appelt* (fn. 2), p. 546; *E. Chiti* (fn. 2), pp. 54–55.

121 *M.P. Chiti*, in: *M.P. Chiti/Greco*, Trattato di diritto amministrativo europeo, Milan 1997, p. 186.

122 *E. Chiti* (fn. 2), p. 64: 'strumento di devolutione di compiti centrali ad uffici comunitari decentrati'.

123 *Uerpmann* (fn. 80), p. 563.

124 *Schmidt-Aßmann*, Europäische Verwaltung zwischen Kooperation und Hierarchie, in: *Cremer* (ed.), Festschrift für Helmut Steinberger, Berlin et al. 2002, p. 1375 (1388), see also *Schmidt-Aßmann* in this vol., p. 1 et seq.

3.5. THE EUROPEAN MONITORING CENTRE FOR DRUGS AND DRUG ADDICTION – AN INFORMATION AGENCY SUPPORTING MEMBER STATE'S POLICIES

It is a well-known fact that the competencies of the European Community differ depending on the policy sector involved. Especially those sectors in which the EC has only supporting competencies, such as the social and the employment policies,[125] represent a major field of action for the existing European agencies. For the purpose of this survey, the European Monitoring Centre for Drugs and Drug Addiction,[126] based in Lisbon, has been chosen. According to its Basic Regulation, the powers of the Centre are limited to collecting and analysing data existing at national and Community level, improving the methods for data comparison and the dissemination of such data.[127] Like most of the other agencies of this type, the Centre is also empowered to operate an information network,[128] connecting national information systems and the information systems of other European or non-European actors.[129] With respect to its powers, Article 1(4) of the Centre's Basic Regulation underlines that the "Centre may not take any measure which in any way goes beyond the sphere of information and the processing thereof".[130] Although the primary importance of this provision is to delimit the tasks of the Centre against those of the European Police Office (EUROPOL), it also reflects the restricted competencies of the Community in the domain of social policy.

With its respective set of competencies, this fourth type of European agencies corresponds closely to the category of "information function agencies"[131] elaborated by A. Kreher. Due to the limited range of powers conferred on the Community by the Member States in the fields of social and employment policy, these agencies basically depend on collecting and distributing information as their cardinal means of action.[132] Their competencies are thus consistently

---

125 See *Constantinesco*, Das Recht der Europäischen Gemeinschaften, Vol. 1, Baden-Baden 1977, p. 256: *flankierende Politiken*.

126 Established by Council Regulation (EEC) No. 302/93 of 8 February 1993 on the establishment of a European Monitoring Centre for Drugs and Drug Addiction, OJ L 36/1, 12.2.1993 ("Monitoring Centre-Regulation").

127 See Article 2 of the Monitoring Centre-Regulation (fn. 126).

128 For the information networks of the other agencies of this type see for example Article 4 of the Council Regulation (EC) No. 1035/97 of 2 June 1997 establishing a European Monitoring Centre on Racism and Xenophobia, OJ L 151/1, 10.6.1997; Article 5 of the Regulation (EC) No. 851/2004 of the European Parliament and of the Council of 21 April 2004 establishing a European Centre for disease prevention and control, OJ L 142/1, 30.4.2004.

129 Article 5(1) of the Monitoring Centre Regulation (fn. 126): European Information Network on Drugs and Drug Addiction (Reitox).

130 Article 1(4) of the Monitoring Centre Regulation (fn. 126).

131 *Kreher* (fn. 10), p. 236.

132 *Schmidt-Aßmann*, Zur Europäisierung des allgemeinen Verwaltungsrechts, in: *Badura/Scholz* (eds.), Festschrift für Peter Lerche, Munich 1993, p. 513 (522): "Steuerungsfaktor Information".

restricted to activities without formal legally binding effects.[133] To see this primarily as a deficiency, however, would be to neglect the fact that supplying the respective policy actors with high-quality information is of great importance particularly in these sectors of "indirect regulation".[134] Most agencies of this informational type were established in a short period of time starting in the 1990s[135] – a period in which the Community was endowed with special powers in the field of social policy for the first time by the Single European Act.[136] At the same time the social dimension of the internal market was discovered.[137]

3.6. THE TRANSLATION CENTRE FOR THE BODIES OF THE EUROPEAN UNION – AN ADDITIONAL TECHNICAL UNIT OF THE COMMUNITY

The four types described above already encompass the major part of the existing European agencies. However, a few agencies remain unconsidered. One of them, for example, is the Translation Centre for the Bodies of the European Union.[138] Its main objective is to provide the various bodies of the European Union, as well as other decentralised agencies and EUROPOL, with any necessary translation services.[139] The Centre is therefore endowed with mostly apolitical and additional administrative tasks. Primarily, it is an additional technical resource for the Community's administrative actors. This also has a number of organisational consequences. First and foremost, a stronger connection of the Centre to the supranational entities is ensured in its Basic Regulation. For example, the management board of the Centre comprises two members instead of one designated by the Commission, and additional members delegated by the bodies for which the Centre provides translation services.[140] All in all, the fifth agency type can therefore be described as a "subcontractor for special technical Community tasks".[141]

---

133 *Fischer-Appelt* (fn. 2), p. 548.

134 Likewise *Majone*, The new European agencies: regulation by information, JEPP 4 (1997), p. 262 (264–265). See also *Schmidt-Aßmann*, Einleitende Problemskizze, in: *Schmidt-Aßmann/Hoffmann-Riem* (eds.), Strukturen des Europäischen Verwaltungsrechts, Baden-Baden 1999, p. 9 (16).

135 *Fischer-Appelt* (fn. 2), p. 548: "Gründungswelle der 90er Jahre".

136 See *Ketelsen*, in: *Röttinger/Weyringer* (eds.), Handbuch der europäischen Integration, Vienna 1991, p. 770.

137 See for example the Commission Working Paper on the Social Dimension of the Internal Market of 14 September 1988 (SEK(88) 1148 final).

138 Established by Council Regulation (EC) No. 2965/94 of 28 November 1994 setting up a Translation Centre for bodies of the European Union, OJ L 314/1, 7.12.1994 ("Translation Centre Regulation").

139 Article 2 of the Translation Centre Regulation (fn. 138).

140 Article 4 of the Translation Centre Regulation (fn. 138).

141 *Fischer-Appelt* (fn. 2), p. 47: "Subkontrahent von speziellen technischen Gemeinschaftsaufgaben".

4. EASA – A STEP TOWARDS A GENUINE COMMUNITY ADMINISTRATION

4.1. INTRODUCTION

Despite the unavoidable uncertainty inherent to the typological method, it has been shown that the bulk of the existing independent European agencies can in fact be reduced to five main categories. In the following section, the question on the positioning of EASA within the framework of the existing agencies will be answered. To that end, it will be necessary to take a closer look at two features of EASA: the autonomy of the Agency in the field of authorisation procedures and – more generally – the overall tasks and objectives of the Agency.

4.2. THE AUTONOMY OF EASA IN THE FIELD OF AUTHORISATION PROCEDURES

As mentioned above, in the Commission's proposal for the Basic Regulation of EASA, the certification of aeronautical products, parts and appliances has been seen as the core activity of the Agency. The degree of EASA's independence and autonomy in the certification process corresponds without any doubt to the autonomy of the Community administration for industrial property rights enjoyed by the Office for Harmonisation in the Internal Market and the Plant Variety Office. Like EASA, these Offices are empowered to carry out the entire process from the application to the final decision in complete procedural autonomy from the Member States or other Community institutions. But important similarities can also be found in respect of the organisational setting of EASA and the two Community Offices named above. Just like EASA, the Harmonisation Office and the Plant Variety Office also have special Boards of Appeal to provide the "necessary remedies"[142] against the decisions of the agencies. But the administration of industrial property rights and the authorisation of new aeronautical products differ in a substantial way: the nature and the legal effect of the final decisions of the agencies involved. The type certification process carried out by EASA results in a legally binding decision of the Agency that directly determines the access of the applicant's product to the market. The type certificate issued by EASA is therefore a strict and binding unilateral decision on the technical safety of a new product. In comparison, the decisions of the Office for Harmonisation and the Plant Variety Office are of a significantly different character.[143] Although the decisions of these Offices also have a direct effect on the position of the applicant within the market, they do not constitute a precondition for market access. In addition to this significant

142 15th Whereas of the Basic Regulation (fn. 3).

143 For these significant differences see also *E. Chiti* (fn. 52), p. 314.

difference, the coexistence of the Community trade mark regime and national trade marks offers various possibilities for an applicant to register an industrial property right, while the type certification of EASA is the only possibility for an applicant to obtain the authorisation necessary for a product. All in all, the decisions of EASA have a far stronger legal impact on the position of the private applicant than the decisions of the Offices of the EC.

With its special legal features, the type certification issued by EASA is more comparable with the European authorisation for medical products and, hence, with the field of activity of the European Medicines Agency. However, the most striking difference between EASA and the Medicine Agency lies within the specific tasks conferred on the two agencies by the Community legislator. While the Medicines Agency is limited to formulating opinions on private applications, EASA is also empowered to issue the final authorisation decision itself. Or, to put it in a different way, while the Medicines Agency is confined to the risk assessment process, EASA combines risk assessment and risk management within its competence.[144] The concept of EASA is therefore clearly a novelty in European administrative law. For the first time, a final decision in a European authorisation procedure is not reserved for the Commission as one of the institutions of the Community set up in Article 7 of the EC Treaty, but conferred on an independent European agency. Thus, EASA and its Basic Regulation have been another step towards conferring binding executive decisions of major political importance on independent agencies.

4.3. EASA AS THE COMMUNITY'S SPECIALISED EXPERT BODY IN AVIATION SAFETY

The analysis of the Agency's tasks and competencies (see section 2) has already shown that the field of activity of EASA encompasses not only the execution of the type certification process, but it is meant to play a crucial role in all matters related to aviation safety. By contrast, nearly all of the other agencies described above are characterised by their special administrative tasks within their respective policy sectors. To confine EASA only to a limited administrative task would be misleading.

At the same time, the creation of EASA coincides with a new period in which the EC pushes forward the establishment of independent agencies. Starting in the year 2002, this new period of activity culminated in six proposals from the Commission for the establishment of new agencies in 2003.[145] Like EASA, most

144 This also has consequences in relation to the organisational setting of EASA. Unlike the Medicines Agency, EASA does not have a distinct scientific committee structure, but rather a hierarchic administrative staff, accountable to the Executive Director of EASA (See Article 29(2) lit. g of the Basic Regulation (fn. 3)).

145 See for details *Geradin/Petit* (fn. 80), p. 38.

of these newly established or newly proposed agencies are characterised by their widespread tasks and activities within their respective policy sectors. For example, the proposed European Chemicals Agency will be also empowered with extensive tasks in the field of chemical safety. These tasks encompass issuing opinions for the safety of single chemicals within a new European registration procedure, administering an information network related to dangerous chemicals as well as providing technical support for the Commission.[146] The recent crisis of the Commission[147] and the subsequent process launched to overcome[148] this crisis and to reform the Commission[149] have been regarded as major catalysts for this development. A crucial point of this reform has been the Commission's approach to "refocus (...) on its core tasks"[150] and – connected to this – the strategy to transfer the day-to-day business to independent European agencies.[151] Establishing new European agencies within the various policy sectors of the Community has hence served as a means to advance the Community's resources for "technical evaluations of very high quality"[152] and has been closely related to the described concept on the reformation of the European Commission.[153] In conclusion, EASA can be described as the first step towards a "third generation" of European agencies.[154] While the older agencies of the EC used to be established for special and strictly limited tasks in given policy sectors, these new agencies of the third generation tend increasingly towards a more general set of tasks, including participation in nearly all Community functions within the respective sector.

---

146 See Article 4–6, 52 and 73 of the Commission's proposal for the European Parliament and Council regulation concerning the Registration, Evaluation, Authorisation and Restriction of Chemicals (REACH) and establishing a European Chemicals Agency (COM (2003) 644/15final).

147 For the BSE crisis see especially the Court of Auditors' Special report No. 19/98 concerning the Community financing of certain measures taken as a result of the BSE crisis, OJ 1998 C 383/1, 9.12.1998. See also *Wägenbauer*, Vertrauenskrise um Rinderseuche BSE, EuZW 2000, p. 738; in detail also *Lafond*, The creation of the European Food Authority, Paris 2001, pp. 4–6.

148 First steps have been taken. See for example White Paper – Reforming the Commission of 5 April 2000 (COM(2000) 200 final), the White Paper on European governance of 25 July 2001 (KOM(2001) 428final), the Communication from the Commission on the collection and use of expertise by the Commission of 11 December 2002 (COM(2002) 713 final) and the Communication from the Commission on the operating framework for the European Regulatory Agencies (fn. 116).

149 In general to the crisis of the Commission see *Mehde*, Verwaltungsreformen in der Europäischen Kommission, ZeuS 2001, p. 403.

150 White Paper on European governance (fn. 148), p. 9.

151 For this function of independent agencies see for example *Craig/De Búrca* (fn. 78), p. 45.

152 Communication from the Commission on the operative framework for the European Regulatory Agencies (fn. 116), p. 5.

153 See for example the 60th Whereas of the Food Safety Authority-Regulation (fn. 55) that explicitly refers to "recent food safety incidents"; see also *Caspar*, Zur Vergemeinschaftung von Verwaltungsverfahren am Beispiel von Gentechnik- und reformiertem Lebensmittelrecht, DVBl. 2002, p. 1437.

154 For the notion of agencies of the first and second generation see *Fischer-Appelt* (fn. 2), p. 46.

VIII. CROSS-BORDER COOPERATION OF THE POLICE AND CUSTOMS AUTHORITIES*

Lothar Harings

1. INTRODUCTION

The relationship between Member States and the European Community in security matters was for a long time one of cooperation in the field of cross-border cooperation of the police, probably due to views on sovereignty, or generally the intervening authority removed borders. There was a tense relationship between formal independence (sovereignty) on the one hand and their factual global integration on the other.[1] As European integration progressed came the realisation that the existing economic and political complexities would have to be accompanied by a reinforced cooperation of police, customs and justice authorities. During the long period of informal cooperation and personal contacts, the acting bodies let the matter rest, and an international treaty on the subject was lacking, but at the end of the twentieth century legislation was introduced for this matter.[2]

2. MODES OF CROSS-BORDER COOPERATION

2.1. INTRODUCTION

Successive modes of cross-border cooperation, for example the Schengen Agreement, the Europol Treaty as well as the Naples II Agreement will be

* The contribution is based on a dissertation by the author entitled *Grenzüberschreitende Zusammenarbeit der Polizei- und Zollverwaltungen und Rechtsschutz in Deutschland*, Duncker & Humblot, Berlin 1998 and on his grenzüberschreitende Zusammenarbeit der Polizei- und Zollverwaltungen, in Eberhard Schmidt-Assman and Bettina Schöndorf-Haubold (eds.), Der Europäische Verwaltungsverbund, Mohr Siebeck, Tübingen 2005, pp. 127–152; the author wishes to thank Jethro Schiansky, Graf von Westphalen, Brussels, for his assistance.

1 Schermers/Blokker, International Institutional Law, §3.

2 Cf. Harings, *Grenzüberschreitende Zusammenarbeit der Polizei- u. Zollverwaltungen und Rechtsschutz in Deutschland*, 1998, 46ff, 63ff and 113.

illustrated, but first the basic international law position will be outlined for a better understanding.

2.2. INITIAL SITUATION IN INTERNATIONAL LAW AND PARALLELS IN NATIONAL LAW

The authority of national officers is, in principle, limited to their respective national territories. Acts of state on foreign territory are only admissible with the consent of the state concerned. These are distinguishable from acts of state with effect outside the territory of the state, which are undertaken on home territory, whose effects, however, range beyond it, and directly concern persons or objects on foreign sovereign territory.[3] Such acts of state are admissible according to international law. In so far as the powers of intervention are connected with the presence of officers on foreign territory, these powers of intervention must, on the one hand, be according to international law in the relationship between the states, and on the other according to national law in relation to citizens: in particular, the responsibility for the action taken by the responsible national body is to be defined with regard to liability and matters of legal protection.

These questions are not alien to the federal system of the Federal Republic of Germany. They are identifiable on a national level in a similar way as the relationship of the state police to each other. The local jurisdiction of the state police does not, in principle, reach beyond the area of the respective federal states. An extension of the localised jurisdiction to another state can only be achieved by law or by treaty. If police officers of one state are active in that area, as a result of a treaty with the agreement of the public authority responsible for another state, the applicable measures are those of the public authority responsible for this state.[4] Although this attribution is approved in principle, the consequences drawn from this are themselves contested between states. The legal questions of cross-border policing require legal control all the more in the relationship between different states.

3 See as this way of differentiating Schlochauer, *Die extraterritoriale Wirkung von Hoheitsakten nach dem öffentlichen Recht der Bundesrepublik Deutschland und nach internationalem Recht*, 1962, 10; Siegrist, *Hoheitsakte auf fremdem Staatsgebiet*, 1987, 2 with further references.

4 Cf. §78 sec. 2 BWPolG, Article 11 sec. 4 &. 5 BayPOG, §7 sec. 2 &. 3 BbgPOG, §81 sec. 2 &. 3 BremPolG, §30 a sec. 2 HbgSOG, §102 sec. 2 &. 3 HSOG, §9 sec. 2 SOG M-V, §103 sec. 2 & 3 NdsSOG, §9 sec. 2 & 3 POG NRW, §86 sec. 2 & 3 RhpfPOG, §88 sec. 2 &. 3 SPolG, §77 sec. 2 &. 3 SächsPolG, §91 sec. 2 &. 3 SOG LSA, §170 sec. 2 LVwG SH, §11 sec. 2–4 ThürPOG; Cf. Also the Agreement between the Federal States of the Federal Republic of Germany on the extended competence of the States' police in criminal proceedings from 8.11.1991, printed in: GVBl. NW 1992, p. 58.

2.3. THE SCHENGEN AGREEMENT

The decisive step towards juridification of the cross-border cooperation of policing took place parallel with the abolition of internal borders in Europe. The idea of an abolition of internal borders for the realisation of free movement had already been discussed in 1974 at the summit of state and government leaders in Paris. It was not until ten years later that, with the accession of the Benelux countries, an initiative was launched by Chancellor Kohl and President Mitterand in the first Schengen Agreement on the facilitated and gradual phasing-out of border controls.[5] This Agreement set the aim of achieving the abolition of border controls, if possible by 1990. Concrete, binding provisions and regulations for the realisation of this aim were ultimately formulated in the Schengen Convention of 19 June 1990.[6] The Schengen Convention came into effect on 1 September 1993. In a general statement of the 1993 Schengen Convention, the contracting States established that the Convention should only actually come into effect if the compensation measures for the abolition of border controls had been implemented, in particular that the Schengen Information System (SIS) was operational. The enactment of the Schengen Implementation Agreement was effected for the five founding states as well as for Portugal and Spain on 26 March 1995. Since then, Italy, Portugal, Spain, Greece, Austria and the Scandinavian states have acceded. Further states, the eastern European in particular, were given associate status. Ireland and Great Britain, who did not sign the Agreement, only took on certain parts of the Schengen acquis.[7]

With the Treaty of Amsterdam, the so-called Schengen acquis, i.e. the Convention, the Agreement, and all the provisions assumed on the basis of this legal instrument,[8] were adopted in section IV of the Treaty of the European Community and section VI of the Maastricht Treaty and was thereby included within the framework of the EU.[9] Primary legal regulations on cross-border cooperation expand the scope of the Schengen acquis.

The core item of the compensatory measures to set off the removal of checks at internal borders is the composition of the Schengen Information System (SIS) as a general tracing system of the Schengen countries. This system has a national component, which is managed by each Schengen Member State, and a technical

---

5 GMBl. 1996, p. 79; on that, Harings, *Grenzüberschreitende Zusammenarbeit* (fn. 2), 63 et seq.

6 BGBl. 1993 II, p. 1010.

7 After the collectivisation they are also not bound by Schengen; *Jour-Schröder/Wasmeier*, in: Von der Groeben/Schwarze (eds.), *Maastricht Treaty-/Treaty of the European Community*, 6. Edition, 2004, Vorb. Article 29–42 Maastricht Treaty, margin no. 37.

8 The Schengen acquis was determined by a European Council decision on 20.5.1999 (OJ 1999 No. L 176, p. 1).

9 See Protocol No. 2 in the Contract for the establishment of the European Community for the inclusion of the Schengen acquis in the framework of the European Union. (1997); only Jour-Schröder/Wasmeier, in: v.d.Groeben/Schwarze, EU-/EC-contract (fn. 7), Vorb. Article 29–42 EUV. 35 et seq.

support unit in Strasbourg. Constant comparison of data of the national systems with the central computer ensures the validity of the data in all Member States.[10] Further compensation measures are the strengthened cooperation of border police (cross-border observation and pursuits) as well as improvements in the sphere of legal aid and extradition.

2.3.1. Cross-border police cooperation according to the Schengen Convention

Article 39 et seq. of the Schengen Convention provide for both improved information exchange between the police authorities as well as, to a limited extent, cross-border operational measures.

Overview

Without a corresponding international contractual basis, cooperation between the authorities of different states occurs on the principle of international legal aid and the law relating to administrative assistance.[11]

Letters rogatory are in principle to place the foreign ministries of the participating states on the diplomatic path, i.e. via the appropriate specialist government agency, and finally on the official channels to the participating agencies. This involves considerable organisational resources and time, and this frequently impedes cooperation in practice.

In contrast, Article 39 Schengen Convention provides for an improvement of police communication in the areas of preventative combat and the reconnaissance of criminal activity.[12] The central sites that are entrusted with cross-border cooperation with the police are in the mid point of the exchange of information, but Article 39 allows direct contact between the police departments concerned in cases of emergency. Article 39(1) Schengen Convention contains an extensive obligation of administrative assistance on the police to one another as long as

---

10 Also in detail Harings, *Grenzüberschreitende Zusammenarbeit* (fn. 2), 71 et seq., 81 et seq., as well as Scheller, JZ 1992, 904 et seq. The system will be extended by a direct bi- or multilateral information exchange in the context of the so-called SIRENE-Netzes; see also the SIRENE-Handbuch (OJ 2003 No. C 38, p. 1) as well as Reg (EC) No. 378/2004 from 19.2.2004 on proceedings for is alteration (OJ 2004 No. L 64, p. 5). See also the decision of the Commission from 22.09.2006 on amending the Sirene Manual (OJ 2006, No L 317, p. 1–40). As the original Schengen Information System is for technical reasons not able to include the accession states, it has been replaced by a new system, the SIS II. Reg. (EC) No 1987/2006 of the European Parliament and of the Council of 20 December 2006 on the establishment, operator and use of the second generation Schengen Information System (SIS II) (OJ 2006, No L 381, p. 4–23).

11 For Community law mutual administrative assistance see Wettner, The General Law of Procedure of EC Mutual Administrative Assistance, in this volume, p. 313 et seq.

12 On information exchange as 'basic form of cooperation of the police' Hecker, EuR 2001, 824 (834 et seq.).

this is permissible in accordance with national law.[13] The authority of the national police authorities in relation to the citizens concerned is not extended by Article 39 Schengen Convention.[14] According to Article 46 Schengen Convention, the police departments can disclose information to each other without prior request (so-called spontaneous information) that could be of importance to prevent criminal activity or protect public safety and order. According to information from central units concerned with information exchange much use is made of this.

The centre of section III, subsection 1 Schengen Convention under the heading of 'Police cooperation' however contains Articles 40 and 41 Schengen Convention concerning cross-border observation and pursuit. Under certain conditions, the officers of a contractual party are granted the right to continue observation that began within the home country and the prosecution of an offender suspected of a fresh offence on the sovereign territory of a neighbour state. This is an altogether new quality of cross-border cooperation,[15] permitted by the agreement of foreign sovereign parties and the exercise of their sovereign function on their own national territory.

Cross-border observation

The Schengen Convention does not define what is to be understood by the term 'observation'; it supposes this term is well known. In Germany, one understands it predominantly as the orderly observation of persons, groups, or objects to gain information for police activity.[16] In international parlance, there is no standardised definition. *Joubert/Bevers*[17] use the short expression, 'watching without being watched' but do not stress that this can be used as the generally valid characterisation. Indeed observation often takes place without the knowledge of the persons under observation, and yet the secrecy of the measure is not a feature. Rather open observation can be carried out, with the aim of unsettling the relevant parties or to induce a particular conduct. An observation can take place for the purpose of prevention of threats to public safety and in the context of a preliminary proceeding. It is then supported by various legal bases.[18]

---

13 This is welcomed by Krüger, *Kriminalistik 1994*, 773 et seq., and Wolter, *Kriminalistik 1995*, 172 (173), as a decisive novelty of Art. 39 Schengen Convention; Criticised by Busch, *Grenzenlose Polizei? Neue Grenzen und polizeiliche Zusammenarbeit in Europa*, 1995, 322 et seq.

14 Cf. Joubert/Bevers, *Schengen investigated – a comparative interpretation of the Schengen provisions on international police-cooperation in the light of the European convention on human rights*, 1996, 448.

15 O'Keeffe, *Yearbook of European Law 1991*, 185 (202): 'pursuit (Nacheile, d. Verf.) as an infringement of the basic conceptions of sovereignty'; Cf. also Martínez Soria, in: Baldus/Soiné, *Rechtsprobleme der internationalen polizeilichen Zusammenarbeit*, 1999, 59 et seq.

16 Cf. verification of Harings, *Grenzüberschreitende Zusammenarbeit* (fn. 2), 73.

17 Schengen investigated, 127 et seq., 133, on international parlance and terms.

18 Cf. Harings, *Grenzüberschreitende Zusammenarbeit* (fn. 2), 73, mwN. On a discussion of the punitive process-related basis of intervention.

Legitimacy of the border crossing

According to Article 40(1) of the Schengen Convention, officers of a contracting party, who in the context of preliminary proceedings are following a person in their country, who is suspected of an extraditable offence, are authorised to continue the observation on the sovereign territory of another contracting party if this is in line with an appropriate letters rogatory. The request must be directed to the authorities identified in Article 40(5) of the Schengen Convention, who are either authorised to decide themselves or convey it to the appropriate place. The Federal Criminal Police Office was specified as the German authority in respect of Article 40(1 and 2) of the Schengen Convention does not have its own decision-making authority. It must forward the application to the appropriate public prosecution service. According to No. 1 letter c) of the Federation – state prorogation dated 1 July 1993,[19] the Federal Government transferred its authority to the provincial government in whose territory the border crossing should take place. The provincial governments made use of their authority of further transferral according to No. 3 of the prorogation.[20] As a result of this chain of transfer, the public prosecution service is responsible in the territory in which the border crossing is to be expected. Their agreement to allow observation applies to the whole federal territory.[21] Details of the cooperation between the contracting states may be bilateral agreements arranged in accordance with Article 39(4), Article 40(6) and Article 41(10) of the Schengen Convention. Article 5(2) of the German-Luxemburg Agreement[22] provides that the licensing authority is the acting senior public prosecutor responsible for cross-border observation.

No obligation on the contracting states to submit detailed letters rogatory and to accord agreement to cross-border observation exists under the Schengen Convention. However, embedding into the law of legal assistance (Article 40(1) presumes letters rogatory to be the rule) applies for Article 1 of the European Legal Assistance Convention dated the 20 April 1959[23], which obliges the contracting states to afford legal assistance to one another 'as far as possible'. However, this obligation is not enforceable. In practice, the contracting states examine the letters thoroughly rather than leniently. On the basis of reciprocity, similar conduct may be expected in opposing requests. Agreement to allow

19 German Federal Gazette 1993, p. 6383.

20 Cf. for Baden-Württemberg for example the '*gemeinsame Verwaltungsvorschrift des Justiz- und Innenministeriums Baden-Württemberg über die Ausübung der Befugnisse im Rechtshilfeverkehr mit dem Ausland in strafrechtlichen Angelegenheiten*' from 9 December 1994, GABl. 1994, 835.

21 Cf. No. 1 lit c) of the prorogation of jurisdiction.

22 BGBl. 1996 II, p. 1203.

23 BGBl. 1996 II, p. 1386; 1976 II, p. 1799; 1982 I, p. 2021, as well as the ancillary protocol on this in BGBl. 1990 II, p. 124; 1991 II, p. 909.

observation may be connected with conditions according to Article 40(1) of the Schengen Convention: in particular, temporary or special limitations may be imposed.

In urgent cases crossing the border does not require the prior approval of the neighbouring state, if during the observation, notice is given to the appropriate authority and subsequently letters rogatory are promptly filed. They must also contain the reasons for the urgency. In every case the observation must be regulated, if the other contracting party demands it or if an appropriate agreement does not happen within five hours after the border crossing.[24] The range of offences of which the observed person is suspected is again limited in urgent cases. Not all extraditable offences but only those serious offences[25] specified in Article 40(7) of the Schengen Convention justify crossing the border.

Modalities of cross-border observation

According to Article 40(3) of the Schengen Convention, the admissibility of cross-border observation is dependant on compliance with certain conditions. Firstly, the observing officers are bound by the conditions of Article 40 of the Schengen Convention, and by the law of the contracting party on whose territory the observation takes place. As such observations are generally carried out by officers of mobile task forces, these must be familiar with the main features of the law of the neighbouring state. In every case, the observing officers must follow any directions of locally competent authorities. They are prohibited from entry into private homes and land not publicly accessible according to Article 40(3e) of the Schengen Convention. Furthermore, they are not entitled to hold or arrest the person under observation. They may carry their service weapons with them, subject to objection by the requested contractual party in prior letters rogatory; the use of them is only permitted in self-defence. Officers must always show that they are acting in their official capacity.

Cross-border pursuit

A more sophisticated rule than observation applies to cross-border pursuit under Article 41 of the Schengen Convention. The basic requirement of pursuit is that a person is caught in the perpetration of an offence and is subsequently pursued. Offences that authorise pursuit are, according to Article 41(4) of the Schengen Convention either all extraditable offences or particular catalogued acts that

---

24 Cf. Article 40 sec. 2 Schengen Convention.

25 Also included are. murder, manslaughter, rape, aggravated theft, robbery, extortion, kidnapping and hostage taking, unlawful dealings with narcotics as well as weapon and explosive offences.

correspond in general to those in Article 40(7) of the Schengen Convention. Pursuit is also permissible for the pursuit of a person on remand or a person serving a custodial sentence. A continuation of the pursuit on the territory of the other contracting state can occur without this state's authorisation, if these authorities are not able to be informed in time or are not in a position to take over the pursuit. The pursuing officers must contact the competent authority of that area no later than when they cross the border. The pursuit is to be regulated on the demand of the contractual party on whose territory it takes place.

The authority of the pursuing officers and the special boundaries of the right of pursuit are not laid down specifically in the Schengen Convention but, similar to offences warranting pursuit, they are inferred in the declarations of the contracting parties.[26] Here, Germany has followed the laws of its neighbouring states, to the widest possible extent. It has allowed pursuit without spatial or temporal limitations for all extraditable offences for which a custodial sentence/ detention order can be demanded/imposed. In contrast, German officers have no detention right in France, or only during the first 30 minutes after the border crossing in Belgium. Luxemburg like Holland allows a right of arrest but imposes a spatial limitation on the pursuit to an area of 10 km along the border.

The pursuing officers are bound, in the same way as the observing officers, by the appropriate provisions of the Schengen Convention as well as the law of the contracting party whose territory they have entered. Entry of residences and land not publicly accessible is forbidden. The pursuing officers must be clearly recognisable as officers and be in a position to prove their official function. They may carry their service weapons with them, but their use is only permissible for self-defence. Further intervention measures are in general limited to the self-defence of the officers.

The legal status of officers operating across-borders, and legal basis for acts of intervention

Article 42 of the Schengen Convention states that officers operating on the territory of another contracting party shall, according to Article 40 and 41 of the Schengen Convention, be regarded as officers of that party with respect to offences committed by them or to which they fall victim. The limitation of the equal footing of 'offences' is striking in this provision. Entirely equal treatment of foreign officers with domestic officers was thus not intended but they should be granted the same protection that the legal system of the country of residence affords its own officers. In return, in respect of their criminal law responsibilities, they have the same as those of officers on whose territory they are operating. The

26 The statements of the 5 founding states are printed in the German Federal Gazette from the 23.11.1990, attachment No. 217 a, p. 26 et seq; a comparison can be found in Bonnefoi, *Europe et Sécurité Intérieure, TREVI – Union Européenne – Schengen*, 1995, 123, 125.

provision relates to the offence committed by the officer of the appropriate legal system. It concerns the personal legal status of officers who are bound in respect of their relationship to the legal system of the country of residence.

Burdensome measures in respect of citizens provided for in Articles 40 and 41 of the Schengen Convention find their legal basis directly from the Statute requiring assent from the German Federal Statute on the Schengen Convention. This transforms the international agreement into domestic law.[27] Articles 40 and 41 of the Schengen Convention can be transformed in such a way that they themselves establish requirements of legality for the act of the foreign officers. Further national implementation acts are no longer necessary. The authority of the foreign officers is limited to continuation of an investigative measure in accordance with Articles 40 and 41 in the area of prosecution. The Federation, following legislation competence also in accordance with Article 32 of the German Constitutional law has the competence for termination of the international law agreement. In contrast, provisions pertaining to state law in the police laws[28] that explicitly allow operations of foreign police officers due to international law agreements only have a declaratory character in this respect: they require treaty based provisions on preventive action of foreign officers.

2.3.2. The Schengen Information System (SIS)

The Schengen Information System stores data concerning persons and data identified in Articles 94 et seq. of the Schengen Convention. Contracting states may submit reports with the aim of arresting a person for extradition (Article 95 Schengen Convention), for denial of entry of third country nationals (Article 96) as well as, noteworthy in the context of this article, for hidden registration or targeted controls (Article 99).[29]

An announcement in the SIS according to Article 95 Schengen Convention corresponds in accordance with Article 64 Schengen Convention to an application for provisional arrest according to Article 16 of the European Extradition agreement dated 13 December 1957.[30] Announcements, according to Articles 96 to 99 of the Schengen Convention, correspond to letters rogatory in the sense of the European Convention on mutual assistance in criminal matters.[31] The requesting national authority enters the data of the person being

---

27 Cf. for Austria also the Federal law on international police cooperation (Polizei Kooperationsgesetz-Pol KG), Federal Law Gazette I. No. 104/1997.

28 E.g. §§78 sec. 4 BwPolG, 102 sec. 3 HSOG, 103 sec. 3 NdsSOG, 86 sec. 3 RhpfPolG, 77 sec. 4 SächsPolG, 91 sec. 3 SOG LSA, 170 sec. 1 LVwG SH.

29 On further proposal categories cf. Art. 97 and 98 Schengen Convention.

30 BGBl. 1964 II, p. 1369; 1976 II, p. 1778; 1982 I, p. 2071; also consider the second ancillary protocol, BGBl. 1990 II, p. 118; 1991 I, p. 874, as well as the European Convention on the Suppression of Terrorism from 27 January 1977, BGBl. 1978 II, p. 321, 907.

31 Cf. *Scheller*, JZ 1992, 904.

sought into their national alert system. These are transferred from the national central office (in Germany the Federal Criminal Police office[32]) to the host system of the SIS in Strasburg. By way of a data comparison with the other national information systems, the data of the person searched is acquired by all contracting states.[33] The advantage of this automated data transfer in contrast to conventional Interpol tracing does not simply lie in the speed of data transfer but also in the legal effects connected with the submission. Whereas in the context of the Interpol manhunt there is often no response to the application, or weeks could go by before the manhunt is initiated in the state to which the application has been made, the submission in SIS contains 'behavioural guidelines' according to which foreign police officers conduct the requested measures.[34] Should a submission meet objections from another contracting state, it has the possibility under Article 94(4) of the Schengen Convention of indicating it in the national portfolio with the consequence that it will not be implemented there.[35]

2.4. THE EUROPOL CONVENTION

The Member States of the European Union aspire to greater cooperation in information exchange on the basis of Article 29 Maastricht Treaty with the establishment of the European police force (Europol). The convention[36] was signed on 26 July 1995. It contains the legal basis for the operation of the European police department Europol. Europol was founded by the Member States of the EU as an independent establishment when it was granted the status of a legal entity. The department is an international organisation, which acts autonomously in respect of Member States and their citizens, and exercises

32 Competence of the Federal Criminal Police office comes from Art. 108 Schengen Convention in connection with Art. 6 No. a of the Convention applying the Agreement dated 19 June 1990 concerning the gradual reduction of controls on common borders, BGBl. 1993 II, p. 1011.

33 For operation of the SIS and the data protection standard, Gusy/Gimbal, in: Baldus/Soiné, *Rechtsprobleme* (fn. 15), 124 et seq.; see also the Council Framework Decision 2006/960/JHA of 18 December 2006 on simplifying the exchange of information and intelligence between law enforcement authorities of the Member States of the European Union (OJ 2006, No. L 386, p. 89–100).

34 Cf. also Scheller, *Ermächtigungsgrundlagen für die internationale Rechts- und Amtshilfe zur Verbrechensbekämpfung – Konkretisierung des Gesetzesvorbehalts, 1997,* 35; Busch, *Grenzenlose Polizei*, 346: 'Rechtshilfeautomatismus'; Sturm, *Kriminalistik 1997, 99 (102): ein Trefferfall 'zwinge' zu abkommenskonformen Reaktionen*; Weichert, CR 1990, 62 (64): the submission generates a non-revisable effect of the facts for compulsory measures; likewise *Würz, Das Schengener Durchführungsübereinkommen, 1997,* margin No. 175.

35 Further details on that in Harings, *Grenzüberschreitende Zusammenarbeit* (fn. 2), 82 et seq.

36 Council Act dated 26th July 1995 drawing up the Convention of the establishment of a European police force (Europol Convention), OJ 1995 No. C 316, p. 1.

sovereign rights; it is not merely a joint organ or element of intergovernmental cooperation[37] but rather an organ entrusted with independant powers.[38]

Europol liaises with a single national unit in every Member State.[39] The task of these units, according to Article 4(4) of the Europol convention is to transfer information to Europol (also on their own initiative) as well as ensure the legitimacy of the information exchange with Europol. Furthermore the national unit delegates a minimum of one liaison officer to Europol who supports the information exchange to his national centre and observes the interests of Europol. The national centre in Germany is the Federal Criminal Police Office in accordance with Article 2(1) of the Europol Convention.[40] In contrast to the Schengen Information System, the supporting system of Europol is not a tracing system but an investigation system. According to the provisions of the Convention, Europol does not yet have executive power meaning that by deployment of its own officers it can carry out investigations in the Member States.[41] However, Article 30(2) of the Maastricht Treaty, inserted in the Treaty of Amsterdam, allows an extension of Europol's powers for operative functions.[42] The first signs are appearing of the future participation of Europol in common investigation teams and groups.[43]

2.5. COOPERATION OF CUSTOMS AUTHORITIES

As with cross-border cooperation in policing, international customs cooperation must differentiate between activities of the customs authorities in tax and duties issues (§208 AO) and their activities in the context of criminal prosecution (§§385, 404 AO). The basis for cross-border criminal prosecution of the customs authorities is the same as before the European Convention on mutual assistance in criminal matters and as domestic law the Act on international mutual

37 But Zieschang, ZRP 1996, 427.

38 In this Europol differs from independent administrative units within the EC (e.g. office for harmonisation of the internal market ('Trademarks and designs'), OJ 1994 No. L 11, p. 1 or the Community Plant Variety Office, OJ 1994 No. L 227, p. 1), whose legal personality is also awarded and who the citizens immediately confront sovereignty; the subject of attribution of their activities is however the European Community that also exercises legal control over the Commission. On agencies see, Riedel, in this volume, p. 157 et seq.

39 According to the altered Article 4 Sec. 2 & sec. 1 p. 2, in the future the Member States can also permit direct contact between the national responsible authorities and Europol; see Article 1 subsection. 3 a of the amendment log from 27.11.2003 (OJ 2004 No. C 2, p. 1).

40 Convention applying the Agreement dated 26th July 1995 due to Art. K.3 of the Convention of the establishment of a European police force (Europol-Convention), BGBl. 1997 II, p. 2150.

41 On the public discussion in relation to this Harings, *Grenzüberschreitende Zusammenarbeit* (Fn. 2), 119.

42 Also Milke, *Europol und Eurojust, 2003*, 5 et seq.; Jour-Schröder, in: v.d.Groeben/Schwarze, *Maastricht Treaty-/Treaty of the European Community* (Fn. 7), Article 30 EU margin No. 55 et seq.

43 See par. 2.6.

assistance in criminal matters (IRG). Newer and extended provisions are built on these rules, for example Article 40 and Article 92 et seq. of the Schengen Convention. The Schengen Convention regulates not only cooperation in *policing* but also establishes the officers of the customs investigation authority, as ancillary officers of the Public Prosecution Service in the area of unauthorised dealings with narcotics and of unauthorised trade with weapons, the possibility of cross-border observation and pursuit.[44] With regard to, customs authorities are also entitled to demand access to data saved in the Schengen Information System (SIS), according to Article 101(1) of the Schengen Convention.

International tracing measures establish to the customs authorities in addition to the Convention on the use of information technology for customs purposes (ZIS) on the 26 July 1995[45], enact, in the context of the third pillar of the European Union, as well as Regulation (EC) No. 515/97 of the Council dated the 13 March 1997 'over the reciprocal administrative assistance between administrative authorities of the Member States and the cooperation of these authorities with the Commission with regard to the correct application of customs and agricultural regulation' (EC Regulation on Administrative Assistance).[46] The Convention has not yet come into effect due to Article K.3 of the Maastricht Treaty concerning reciprocal administrative assistance and cooperation of the customs authorities (Naples II Convention).[47] This Convention will replace the so-called Naples I Convention from the year 1967[48] when it comes into effect. In addition to rules of administrative assistance with and without request, provisions for cross-border observation and pursuit, it contains hidden investigation and controlled supply.

Measures of the customs authorities *with effect abroad* are, according to underlying understanding especially proposals of the customs authorities in the Information Systems (SIS, ZIS). However, alongside this, from the area of conventional cooperation, letters rogatory and information for cross checks, for foreign centres are to be observed. These can also be relevant for constitutional rights and trigger a necessity for legal protection. All tracing measures must be distinguished from measures with (only) effect abroad that necessitate a personal border crossing of the acting officer, so that the act of intervention takes place on foreign territory. Also worthy of mention here are, based on the Schengen

44 Cf. Article 40 Sec. 4 and Article 41 Sec. 7 Schengen Convention.

45 OJ 1995 No. C 316, p. 33.

46 OJ 1997 No. L 82, p. 1. See on administrative assistance F. Wettner, The General Law of Procedure of EC Mutual Administrative Assistance, in this volume, p. 313 et seq.

47 OJ 1998 No. C 24, p. 1, enacted by the Council on 18.12.1997; see also the approved explanatory report of the Council on the Naples II Convention (OJ 1998 No. C 189, p. 1); further Jour-Schröder, in: v.d.Groeben/Schwarze, *Maastricht Treaty-/Treaty of the European Community* (fn. 7), Article 30 EU margin No. 10 et seqq. Cooperation of the customs authorities shall in the future also be further extended; Cf. the Council resolution of 2.10.2003 concerning a strategy for cooperation in customs matters (OJ 2003 No. C 247, p. 1).

48 BGBl. 1969 II, p. 65; 1970 II, p. 987.

Convention or the Naples II Convention, cross-border observation and pursuit as well as the carrying out of controlled consignments and undercover investigations abroad.

2.6. JOINT INVESTIGATION GROUPS IN THE CONTEXT OF THE EUROPEAN CONVENTION ON MUTUAL ASSISTANCE IN CRIMINAL MATTERS AND OF EUROPOL

An intensification of the cooperation between the police and customs authorities would enable common investigation groups to develop in the future.[49] According to Article 1 of the framework decision for common investigation groups[50] and according to Article 13 of the not yet effective European Convention on mutual assistance in criminal matters of 29 May 2000[51], the responsible authorities from two or more Member States may form a common investigation group for a particular reason and for a limited time period for the implementation of criminal law investigations in one or more of the Member States who are participating in the group and the group will be supervised by a representative of the concerned country and will operate according to the legal provisions of this Member State. According to these rules, the Europol Convention should be extended by a new Article 3a that should allow Europol to participate in the joint investigation group.[52] In addition, Article 24 of the Naples II Convention[53] provides for the formation of 'special common investigation teams' for cooperation between customs administration departments.

---

49 Also Felgenhauer, in: *Wolter/W.-R. Schenke/Rieß/Zöller (Hrsg.), Datenübermittlungen und Vorermittlungen, 2003, 75 (88* et seq*q.); Hackner/Lagodny/Schomburg/Wolf, Internationale Rechtshilfe in Strafsachen, 2003*, margin No. 210 et seq.

50 Framework resolution of the Council from 13.6.2002 concerning joint investigation groups (OJ 2002 No. L 162, p. 1). The decision should also effect a faster implementation of Art. 13 European Convention on mutual assistance in criminal matters 2000; cf. Felgenhauer, in: Wolter et al, *Datenübermittlungen* (fn. 49), 75 (89).

51 Convention according to Article 34 of the Maastricht Treaty established by the Council on legal aid in criminal cases between Member States and the European Union (OJ 2000 No. C 197, p. 1); see also the approved explanatory report of the Council (OJ 2000 No. C 379, p. 7); also Huber, in: Wolter et al., *Datenübermittlungen* (fn. 49), 135 (142).

52 Article 1(2) of the protocol on the amendment of the establishment of a European Police Force and the protocol on the privileges and immunities of Europol, the members of the judiciary, the assistant executives and the civil servants of Europol from 28.11.2002 (OJ 2002 No. C 312, p. 1). The protocol has not however yet come into effect. Cf. also Milke, *Europol und Eurojust* (fn. 42), 60 et seq.

53 See fn. 47.

3. STRUCTURE AND MODES OF ACTION FOR CROSS-BORDER COOPERATION

3.1. INTRODUCTION: MODELS OF ADMINISTRATIVE CORPORATION

The fundamental option for the structure of cooperation is either pure cooperation between states or the establishment of a new international organisation or institution. The creation of Europol implies that an independent international organisation has been created, one with a legal personality. The newly established central authority will add vertical cooperation with Member States' authorities, while there is already horizontal cooperation between their authorities.[54]

Differences in responsibility result from this structural divergence. The international organisation bears responsibility alongside the states that remain responsible for their acts.

3.2. INSTITUTIONALISED INFORMATION EXCHANGE

The exchange of information as "the basis of every administrative cooperation" is the central feature of cross-border cooperation of police and customs authorities.[55] In contrast to the selective cooperation in traditional equity and legal assistance law, the informational cooperation in the Convention described here is a lasting one and consequently independent informational cooperation structures develop. Since there is some institutional solidification, networking develops. The institutionalisation of the cooperation takes place at the highest level in the Council.[56] This institutionalisation ranges from the appointment of central offices in the Member States and contact and coordination centres on a regional level to the lower administration levels.

Cooperation between Member States is separate from formal records of the State concerned in the course of close collaboration. Letters rogatory are not a precondition for triggering the exchange of information, rather it is the substantive concern (*materielle Betroffenheit*) of another State. The best example is the extensive increase of the possibility of issuing voluntary disclosures to other states (Section III of the Naples II Convention). According to Article 46 of

54 On the structures of cooperation of the police and the interlocking of institutions Hecker, *EuR 2001*, 824 (esp. 836 et seq.).

55 Schmidt-Aßmann, EuR 1996, 270 (290); J. Sommer, Information Cooperation Procedures – with European Environmental Law serving as an illustration, in this volume, p. 55 et seq.

56 Cf. Article K.3 Sec. 1 Treaty on European Union old version: 'In the areas of Article K.1 Member States instruct and consult each other in the Council in order to coordinate their approach. They justify cooperation between their competent administrative offices for this.'

the Schengen Convention, every contractual party can transfer information without a prior request from another contractual party that could be of significance to *them* for combating or the prevention of a criminal act or averting danger.[57]

A refinement of the consultation mechanism is associated with the increase of the exchange of information and informational interdependence. In cases in which the interests of the state, from which information originates, are affected by the informational activity of the executive branch of another state, this state must participate in the adjudication proceedings of the executive branch concerned. In such cases, different levels of involvement are to be decided which range from a requirement of consent to a simple notification. Furthermore, there are special consultation proceedings that are not exhausted in the declaration of intent but rather require the close consultation of the states involved.[58]

4. LEGAL PROTECTION AGAINST MEASURES IN THE CONTEXT OF CROSS-BORDER COOPERATION

4.1. INTRODUCTION

According to Article 19(4) of the Constitution (Grundgesetz), legal protection must be assured if somebody alleges to have had his rights violated by public violence. Article 6 of the European Convention Human Rights (ECHR) contains a similar guarantee that is applicable to all Member States of the Council of Europe as well as to states and organs of the European Union under Article 6(2) 2 of the Maastricht Treaty.[59] Shifting authority to foreign responsible bodies may not lower the standard of legal protection significantly. In its Maastricht judgement[60] the Federal Constitutional Court clarified that it provided for, "legal protection by Constitution in Germany, in so far as not only in respect of German government bodies".[61] An interpretation of Article 19(4) in conformity with international law must observe the immunity of foreign states, if not, the

57 Article 7 of the European Agreement on Legal Aid in Criminal law Enforcement from 2000 (not yet in force) (fn. 51) provides spontaneous disclosure in the field of responsibility of the receiving authorities.

58 Also in detail, Harings, *Grenzüberschreitende Zusammenarbeit* (fn. 2), 137 et seq., 143.

59 Cf. also now Article II-107 of the EU-Draft Constitution, version CIG 87/04 from 6.8.2004.

60 Federal Constitutional Court 89, 155 (174 et seq.).

61 Cf. also Schmidt-Aßmann, in: Schoch/Schmidt-Aßmann/Pietzner (eds.), VwGO, Lsbl. Stand 2003, preamble, Margin No. 9: 'The limitation of Article 19 Sec. 4 GG the past belongs to the German public force.'

operations of foreign officers in Germany would be accountable to German sovereignty.[62]

4.2. ACCOUNTABILITY TO GERMAN SOVEREIGNTY

Accountability to German sovereignty would be acceptable if cross-border investigations by foreign officers on German territory would be a case of *international law organ loan*. There are a few arguments in favour of this. Long term observations would then, in practice, only be pursued across borders by officers of the state of origin if it was not possible for officers of the host state to take over the observation. The foreign officers therefore 'substitute' the officers of the host state. Furthermore, according to Article 40(3a) of the Schengen Convention, the foreign bodies that are responsible are subject to the legal system of the host state and the instructions of the responsible authorities. Any losses caused by the observing officers on the territory of the host state are, according to Article 43 of the Schengen Convention, compensated as if their own officers had operated.

However, the officers operate on the territory of the host state in the *performance of their own affairs,* not in the interest of the host state. The cooperation also exceeds the scope of legal assistance. It is characteristic that the requested state performs duties made by the requesting state. By its agreement to the cross-border operations of foreign officers, the state of residence allows them to perform their own duties. The officers do not act in the name of the host state, but simply with its consent. In cases of spontaneous observation, the officers act completely independently until contact with the competent authority has been established. Indeed, they are acting under the legal system of the state of residence, in that they are carrying out their assignment with sole responsibility within borders which have been removed. Article 42 of the Schengen Convention only equates the observing officers with the officers of the host country in respect of their *personal* legal status and not in respect of their full official capacity. This corresponds to the fact that the powers of the foreign officers are limited in comparison to those of the host state's own officers.

In addition, accountability of the operations of foreign officers according to national law is not possible throughout the country. Indeed some police laws of the German federal states (§§102 sec. 3 HSOG, 103 sec. 2 NdsSOG, 86 sec. 3 RhpfPOG, 91 sec. 3 sentence 2 SOG LSA, 170 sec. 2 LVwG SH) include provisions

---

62 On legal protection with regard to the cross-border cooperation of the police in Europe, also Gleß, Jura 2000, 400 et seq.; Baldus, *Transnationales Polizeirecht, 2001*, 347 et seq.; on questions of legal protection especially in connection with administrative assistance J. Hofmann, Legal Protection and Liability in the European Composite Administration, in this volume, p. 447 et seq.; and his *Rechtsschutz und Haftung im Europäischen Verwaltungsverbund,* PhD thesis, Berlin, 2004.

for attributing responsibility. However, these are not available in most Federal States, in a similar situation as that of the customs authority.[63] Consequently, the German state can only be held responsible for the operation of responsible foreign agents on German territory if some form of attributing responsibility already exists or if the German authorities actually exercise their authority to issue instructions.

In the case of the joint investigation groups, this attribution may occur more easily, as in each case they only operate under the supervision of an officer of the country in which the investigation takes place, so that primary legal protection could also be sought before their courts.[64]

4.3. RENOUNCEMENT OF IMMUNITY

Jurisdiction is given to German courts in cross-border operations of foreign officers if the country committing the officers has renounced its immunity in respect of this operation. If such a waiver does not explicitly exist, it could however have been expressed by inference.[65] An indication for this would be the stipulation in Article 40(3a) of the Schengen Convention. The provision comprises two components, which deserve a mention in connection with this; one is the relationship with the law of the host state and the other is the obligation to follow the instructions of the locally competent authorities. In the agreement of domestic law in an international law or a civil law contract of a country, there is in principle no provision on the submission under the concerned system of legal protection. All that is provided for is the substantive law which has to be applied on the contract and the operation, respectively. In its decision on the supplementary treaty of the NATO Statute on Troops (NTS), the Federal Constitutional Court found that reference to material German law did not mean submission to the sovereignty of the Federal Republic of Germany as regards to procedural law.[66] In the same way as under Article II NTS ("a troop and its civilian entourage, its members as well as their dependants, to pay regard to the law of the host country…"), a mere material connection with German law is accepted.[67] A general waiver of the immunity of armed forces is not expressed therein.

---

63 On legal protection in connection with international customs investigation Harings, in: Baldus/Soiné, *Rechtsprobleme* (fn. 15), 167 et seq.

64 On secondary law liability see under par. 4.4.3. According to Article 2 of the protocol for the alteration of the Europol Convention and the protocol on privileges and immunity for Europol (fn. 52) Europol civil servants will not be granted immunity for activities in the context of joint investigation groups.

65 Also Harings, *Grenzüberschreitende Zusammenarbeit* (fn. 2), 245.

66 German Federal Constitutional Court 77, 170 (207 et seq.).

67 VGH Kassel NJW 1989, 470 (473); O. Lepsius, *Deutsches Recht auf NATO-Truppenübungsplätzen, 1995*, 52 et seq.; Kraatz, *DÖV 1990*, 382 (383); weakening Randelzhofer/Harndt, NJW 1989, 425 (429) and Raap, ArchVR 29 (1991), 53 (77 et seq.).

Another situation could, however, arise out of the submission to the authority of the locally competent German authority. In any case, therein lies an explicit waiver of state immunity in respect of the sovereignty of the German Executive, in this case the locally competent authorities. Initially, this provision does not involve the jurisdiction of the German courts. A waiver in this respect also cannot be inferred from the fact that the locally competent German authority on their part is subject to German jurisdiction. According to international law, in view of the principle of state immunity, there is a significant difference whether a claim is itself directed against a foreign state or whether the Federal Republic of Germany should be judged against a foreign state with regard to a measure. From the view of the state concerned, it is also less drastic to be subject to instructions of the Executive as having to accept legal review of the Acts of state. As a result Article 40(3a) does not warrant the jurisdiction of German courts over foreign sovereign Acts of state on German territory in the context of cross-border observation.[68]

4.4. LEGAL PROTECTION IN GERMANY

The degree of foreign contact in cases of cross-border investigation can vary. If the length of stay on the foreign territory is limited to a few hours without incident, then foreign contact is slight anyway. On the other hand, a repeated observation or an observation lasting several days in the other country can have its own focus. The greater the significance for the foreign country, the greater the attention has to be paid to the concept of legal protection before the courts of the host country. The following can act as an illustration of legal protection in Germany.

4.4.1. Legal protection before the courts where Germany is the country of origin

First there will be examination of the 'normal case' of cross-border observation, which is arranged in Germany and begins after the border has been crossed with the agreement of the French authorities in France. Legal protection in Germany is not excluded by foreign contact.

Three possible purposes of the offensive of the German authority need to be considered:

- *authorisation* of the observation by the public prosecutor;
- appointment of *letters rogatory* by the public prosecutor;
- actual *carrying out* of the observation by police authorities.

68 Also Martínez Soria, in: Baldus/Soiné, *Rechtsprobleme* (fn. 15), 59 et seq.

The authorisation of the observation by the public prosecutor cannot be independently challenged before a court because as an *internal official act* it cannot affect the interest of the person concerned.[69] It cannot be compared with the regulatory character concerned and external effect displayed, but just with the measures of the dependant authority. In the same way, the German letters rogatory cannot be challenged as it does not directly interfere with the law of the country concerned, in respect of the subsequent observation. The actual interference by the observation in France in fact precedes an *autonomous decision* of the French authorities on the assenting to the requested legal assistance. Consequently, the purpose of the intrusive act remains the actual carrying out of the observation in Germany and France. Since this is the case, it may be argued that the conditions for an observation are not given according to the code of penal procedure (StPO) or the observation in Germany violates other domestic law. It is problematic whether there can be criticism of violations of German law in France against provisions of the Schengen Convention or against French law to which the officers are bound according to Article 40(3a) of the Schengen Convention. It is no longer possible to regulate according to the argument that German public law may only be applied on German territory.[70] The area of application of German law is, in fact, to be determined from two perspectives. From the perspective of public international law, it must be asked whether the application of national law for facts outside the own sovereign territory is permitted according to international law, whilst the national law establishes its own area of application within international law boundaries. Public international law only makes minor requirements. It basically gives the countries freedom to include foreign facts in the area of applicability of the national law as long as there is a certain relation to the home country.[71]

If public international law does not oppose a validity of German law abroad, it is not apparent why German officers should no longer be subject to the law of their home country. Fundamental rights also bind German officers in their operations abroad.[72] Similarly, officers are subject to their national public services law and the corresponding provisions which define and limit their actions *vis-à-vis* the citizens. The distinctive feature of the international law provisions on the powers of the officials concerned of the Schengen Convention

69 Cf. Federal Administrative Court Germany NJW 1997, 2534, decision v. 29.4.1997 (1 C 2.95), and Administrative Court Mannheim DVBl. 1995, 367, for the structure of the assignment of a hidden observer.

70 Also Ehlers, in: Schoch/Schmidt-Aßmann/Pietzner, VwGO (fn. 62), margin No. 68 before §40.

71 Seidl-Hohenveldern, *Völkerrecht*, margin No. 1366.

72 Cf. only Stern, *Staatsrecht*, Bd. III/1, 1230 et seq.; Isensee, HbStR V §115 margin No. 90; German Federal Constitutional Court 6, 290 (295) and OVG Münster NVwZ-RR 1997, 174, support a binding fundamental law in cases in which the effects of State activity enter into foreign territory; see in respect of activity in the foreign territory also the decision of the Higher Administrative Court Münster DVBl. 1983, 37.

lies in the fact that these provisions are not constitutive to independent performance of measures on foreign sovereign territory but rather regulate the *continuation* of an action which started on their own territory. In the same way, the border crossing does not cause any suspension of the law of the country of origin but it subjects the action of the officers to an additional legal system, that of the host state.

According to conventional opinion in law, public international law alone is *state orientated* so that individuals can derive no or only indirect rights from it. This opinion should now be seen as outdated.[73] It is widely accepted that direct international law rights and obligations can also be claimed by the individual. In this way, the right to sue is explicitly granted, according to Article 111 Schengen Convention, to every individual citizen and as well as the right to appeal to the court responsible in every contracting state. On the other hand, certain Regulations in the Schengen Convention only aim at the protection of national sovereignty of contracting states. The limitations of cross-border investigative operations are in principle assigned to this area. They neither establish individual legal positions, nor do they make a declaration of legal protection. They limit the surrender of sovereignty due to authorisation of sovereign activity on foreign territory. As a result, it may be assumed that Articles 40 et seq. of the Schengen Convention only serve the protection of sovereignty of the particular host state and do not confer individual rights in international law. However it cannot be concluded that this Convention includes no third-party effect whatsoever in favour of the citizen concerned but rather that the international law state orientation does not exclude an individually protective effect in domestic law from the outset. In any case, a citizen can invoke the general rules of international law, which are an integral part of federal law according to Article 25 German Constitution (GG). The contracts for the cooperation of security services are not included in this; they are, however, binding domestically through the Statute requiring assent of the Federal Council (*Zustimmungsgesetz*) and can thereby be contested by the person concerned by a measure which can be asserted where his rights are violated. A person concerned with an interfering administrative act should be able to count on adherence to all the determining norms of the act of the officers.[74] However, all such provisions are excluded that only concern the relationship of the participating states with one another. In this way, it cannot be successfully contested that the letters rogatory were not submitted in the correct manner. The person concerned can however support the illegality of a measure directed against him by a violation of Article 40(3f) that prohibits the officer from arresting or detaining the person under observation. This provision, like

73 Jennings/Watts, *Oppenheim's International Law*, 848; in detail Harings, *Grenzüberschreitende Zusammenarbeit* (fn. 2), 278 et seq.

74 Also German Federal Administrative Court NVwZ 1993, 884 (885); Kopp, VwGO, §42 margin No. 47 et seq., 79 et seq.; Wahl/Schütz, in: Schoch/Schmidt-Aßmann/Pietzner, VwGO (Fn. 62), §42 margin No. 45 et seq., 70.

Article 40(3b) of the Schengen Convention, also limits the power of the officers in respect of the citizen.

This conclusion does not negate the fact that the Federal Constitutional Court decided in 1994 that the adverse international law use of an agent provocateur did not constitute an obstruction to proceedings in a criminal procedure.[75] In fact, in its consideration of a decision of the US Supreme Court, the Federal Constitutional Court states that, even with the existence of a capture contrary to international law, the termination of criminal proceedings would not normally made available according to international law. This decision concerns the existence of an obstruction to proceedings, or rather of an exclusion of improperly obtained evidence in the criminal procedure. In addition, if the Federal Constitutional Court ultimately rejects this consequence, there can be no doubt that the lawfulness of acts of interference of public force is to be judged otherwise. In criminal proceedings, not every breach of proceedings leads to an exclusion of improperly obtained evidence and only rarely and in exceptional cases is a termination of proceedings considered. On the other hand, on the first level of legal protection the illegality of the act under attack is itself to be assessed and not only in respect of the requirements of international law aspects.

If one considers, as here, the provisions that regulate the continuation of investigative measures instituted from the home country, as independent provisions standards of authority, then limitations to this authority must also be referred to for an assessment as to the legality of the acts. If the act of a foreign officer is therefore subject to the domestic legal system, then the act must also be measured against this. If an officer violates the foreign law declared as applicable he thereby goes beyond his *authority* in respect of the citizen concerned. This is subject to the controls of the appropriate court. Accordingly, the competent German court must judge the legality of the acts of German officers against the provisions of foreign law on the scale of the foreign law.[76] In such a case, the foreign law can be effective in a power-limiting, not a power-widening capacity, as the acting officer remains bound by the law of his own country and acts and may not carry out acts that violate this.

4.4.2. Primary legal protection before the courts of the country of residence

Legal protection before the courts of the country of residence may certainly be considered if a citizen of this state is affected by measures of foreign officers; this protection is not however limited to this. The reason for demanding legal protection could also be that individual legal protection has been developed in specific measures in Germany, and a foreign citizen, might expect an

[75] German Federal Constitutional Court NJW 1995, 651.

[76] Different §17 Sec. 4 PolKG for legal protection in Austria.

improvement in his legal position (forum shopping) by referring his case to a German court.

Legal protection from measures of foreign officers in Germany only exists if their act is attributable to a German authority. Such a standard of attribution does not exist in all police laws (see above para. 4.2), making a consistent conclusion impossible. Even if a corresponding attribution standard was valid, the legal protection position would remain unclear. Legal protection with regard to the observation could be found within the context of §§23 ff. EGGVG[77] but the Higher Regional Court of Stuttgart[78] decided:

> *"The decision of a court of the region Rheinland-Pfalz in proceedings according to §§23 et. seqq. EGGVG would however not be binding for a legal authority of the Baden-Württemberg region as in these proceedings just as little as is proceedings according to §§109 ff. Penal law [...] whose additional cargo is stipulated."*

If one follows this interpretation, a court judgement that prohibits observations in Rheinland-Pfalz could not prevent them from being resumed in Hessen after transgression of the region's border. Observations cannot be affected in the federal states that that do not stipulate an attribution of the acts of foreign officers. Legal protection must be sought against the authorised locally competent authorities here.

4.4.3. Secondary legal protection before the courts of the country of residence

According to Article 43(2) of the Schengen Convention, the host country is obliged to compensate damage caused by foreign officers in their intervention, to the extent it would have been compensated if the host country's officers had acted. Similar rules are also stipulated for the acts of collective investigative groups.[79]

Legal basis in material law

The provisions of the Convention do not represent the direct roots of liability in relation to the citizen concerned. In Germany, the appropriate /pertinent provisions are §839 German Civil Code (BGB) in conjunction with Article 34 Federal Constitutional law (GG) as well as the corresponding provisions of the Police Acts. A breach of foreign law of the country of origin of the officer cannot

---

77 EGGVG: Einführungsgesetz für Gerichtsverfassungsgesetz, which is the act to introduce the act on the organisation of courts into the German legal system.

78 NStZ 1997, 103 (104).

79 See Article 3 of the framework agreement on joint investigation groups (fn. 50); Article 16 European Agreement on Legal Aid from 2000 (fn. 51); Art. 39a Europol Convention of the amendment protocol from 28.11.2002 (fn. 52).

be contested before the German courts. The Federal Republic of Germany bears no responsibility whatsoever for adherence to this law by foreign officers on its sovereign territory.

Procedural questions

According to Article 34 sentence 3 Federal Constitutional law (GG) and §40 sec. 2 sentence 1 VwGO, the ordinary courts are responsible for deciding on claims concerning official liability. According to the case law of the Federal Court of Justice, the opponent of an official liability case is in principle the employment body, i.e. the body that entrusted the office to the public officer on whose exercise he acted incorrectly.[80] In the context of cooperation between police authorities, the problems of attributing responsibility start as early as at the point of deployment of officers from other federal states. In cases of the causation of damage by Bavarian police officers on the territory of the federal state of Hessen, the Higher Regional Court of Frankfurt am Main[81] dismissed the obligation of Hessen to pay these damages, although §102 sec. 2 HSOG attributes the measures of Bavarian police to the federal state of Hessen. Its grounds, it stated, were that the perception of executive policing functions for the federal state of Hessen do not, according to §102 HSOG, lead to regarding the Region as the continued employers of the foreign officers. The court wishes to make only one exception, and that is in the case that the breach of official duty would have been brought about by the precise instruction of Hessen's authorities. The opinion of the Higher Regional Court at Frankfurt has been rightly criticised in literature.[82] The attribution standard of §102 sec. 2 HSOG supersedes the general considerations for person presenting an opposing claim in the context of Article 34 Federal Constitutional law (GG).

4.5. SUMMARY AND OUTLOOK

The legal protection position which has been outlined with regard to cooperation of the police in Europe is not satisfactory.[83] International law principles, such as the principle of state immunity, conflict with coherent and effective legal protection. Such a legal protection model could provide that appeal can be made in the home country against a foreign sovereign act with cross-border effect. In addition, both countries must forgo their immunity and submit to the

80 Cf. only BGHZ 99, 326 (330); BGH VersR 1991, 1135 (1136).

81 NVwZ-RR 1995, 553 (554).

82 See Rachor, in: Lisken/Denninger, *Handbuch des Polizeirechts*, 2nd Edition. 1996, Section L margin No. 39; cf. also Würtenberger/Heckmann/Riggert, *Polizeirecht in Baden-Württemberg*, 2nd Edition l. 1994, margin No. 160.

83 Or arguably Martínez Soria, in: Baldus/Soiné, *Rechtsprobleme* (fn. 15), 59 (63, there fn. 64).

jurisdiction of the neighbouring state. For sovereign acts on foreign territory, according to Articles 40, 41 of the Schengen Convention, a foregoing of immunity to that effect is not far off, as the provisions already stipulate a subservience to the law of the state of residence in a material respect and in a formal respect in relation to the instructions of the executive. The acknowledgement and also the jurisdiction of the respective state of residence could close the existing legal protection loopholes. In the same way, a joint provision concerning the responsibility of the responsible national authorities[84] with regard to the operations of foreign officers would be suitable to ensure effective legal protection in cases of cross-border operations. This would be a real symbol of an integrative "area of freedom, of security and of justice" which the European Union strives for according to Articles 2 and 4 of the Maastricht Treaty.

[84] Cf. §17 Sec. 2 and 3 PolKG for Austria; also Drobesch, in: Baldus/Soiné, *Rechtsprobleme* (fn. 15), 206 et seq.

IX. CONFORMITY ASSESSMENT IN EUROPEAN PRODUCT SAFETY LAW*

Hans Christian Röhl

Administration in the European Union still primarily means administration by Member State administrative authorities with their different structures, which are marked by their own law traditions, organizations and culture. For reasons of subsidiarity, the EC institutions only have enforcement competences in exceptional cases. This constitutes a serious problem for the enforcement of European law, because enforcement essentially determines whether the intention of the legislation is actually put into practice and because the harmonization of Member State administrative structures is still a distant prospect for legal and political reasons. In view of this, it is not astonishing that the EU has created a genuinely European administrative structure at the core of the European integration process, the free movement of goods. This is supported, above all, by private entities, which ultimately and bindingly decide on market access for products in their function as "Notified Bodies". The state administrations are only a point of reference, which guarantees the private bodies' orientation towards the common good.

1. PRODUCT SAFETY LAW ACCORDING TO THE NEW APPROACH AND GLOBAL APPROACH

1.1. BASIS: THE REALIZATION OF THE FREE MOVEMENT OF GOODS

The system of product safety law on the basis of the "New Approach"[1] and the Global Approach"[2] serves as a harmonization measure for the realization of the

* This article is a further development of the thoughts presented in my publication: "Akkreditierung und Zertifizierung im Produktsicherheitsrecht, Heidelberg 2000".

1 See the Council Resolution from 7.5.1985 on a New Approach to technical harmonization and standards, OJ 1985 No. C 136, p. 1.

2 A Global Approach to Certification and Testing, COM (89) 209 final – SYN 208 from 24.7.1989, OJ 1989, No. C 267, p. 3; see Council Resolution from 21.12.1989 on a Global Approach to Conformity Assessment, OJ 1990, No. C 10, p. 1.

free movement of goods stipulated in Article 34 TFEU. Just on the basis of Article 28 TEC, the free movement of goods cannot be realized, as long as reasons of public interest according to Article 36 TFEU or mandatory requirements on the basis of the European Court of Justice's case-law in *Cassis* justify a regulation by each Member State.[3] For these reasons, every Member State could determine the level of protection for product safety itself and unilaterally decide on the administrative structure for its enforcement.[4] The primary legislation basis of Article 34 TFEU solely requires the Member States to regard foreign regulations and administrative structures as equivalent[5], when such equivalency in fact exists.[6] For this reason, in the area of product safety one cannot manage without a harmonization of the level of protection both with regard to legal standards as well as administrative structures.[7]

1.2. BASIC PRINCIPLES OF THE NEW APPROACH AND GLOBAL APPROACH

The directives of product safety law[8] solve the harmonization problem on the basis of the New Approach and Global Approach by differing according to three separate regulatory areas with the integration of private actors[9]: *legislation* specifies the requirements for products in abstract terms, *market access* regulates the admission to the European market for the individual product and *market surveillance* reacts to dangers emanating from products, which are already on the market.

- With the launch of the New Approach[10] as a legislative strategy, the Community legislator turned away from the previously envisioned detailed harmonization which had been realized in the area of motor vehicles

3 ECJ, Judgement of 28.1.1986, Case 188/84 *Wood processing machines,* [1986] ECR 419 (at Para. 15–22).

4 *Götz*, in: idem/Selmer/Wolfrum (Eds.), Lib. Am. Jaenicke, 1998, 763 (766).

5 On equivalency clauses *v. Borries/Petschke*, DVBl. 1996, 1343 et seq.

6 ECJ, Judgement of 17.12.1982, Case 272/80 *Biologische Producten,* [1980] ECR 3277 (at Para. 13–15); Judgement of 28.11.1986 Case 188/84 *Wood processing machines,* [1986] ECR 419 (at Para. 15–17).

7 For clarification see *Steindorff*, in: Festschrift für W. Lorenz, 1991, 561 (569–571).

8 The following presentation foregoes detailed differences, which exist in certain product segments, e.g. due to their international orientation [Directive on marine equipment (96/98/EC)] or their technical or regulatory peculiarities [Directive 89/106/EEC (Construction products); Directive 96/48/EC (Interoperability of the European high-speed railway system)], without having any effect on the actual principle. For details, see e.g. *Röhl*, Akkreditierung und Zertifizierung im Produktsicherheitsrecht, 2000, 4 et seq.

9 Applied to the example of the machine directive *Scheel*, Privater Sachverstand im Verwaltungsvollzug des europäischen Rechts, 1999, 55 et seq.

10 See e.g. *Bruha*, ZaöRV 46 (1986), 1 et seq.; *Falke*, JBStVwW 3 (1989), 217 et seq.; *Joerges*, JBUTR 1994, 141 et seq.; *Marburger/Enders*, JBUTR 1994, 333 (359–367); *Di Fabio*,

legislation, e.g. On the level of *legislation*, the EU refrained from regulating all product safety requirements in legal acts. Instead, the New Approach directives limit themselves to laying down "essential requirements".[11] The products must satisfy those in order to be put on the market. More detailed requirements are contained in "harmonized" technical standards, which are drawn up by the European standardization organizations by means of special procedures. Unlike the essential requirements of the directives, these standards are not binding, although a product is assumed to conform to a directive when it meets the harmonized standards.[12]

- The focus of the following considerations will be the second modification introduced by the New Approach[13] and the Global Approach: the restructuring of *market access*. The entire market access regime in the Member States – to the extent that the products are affected by the directives – has been subject to a largely uniform system in a remarkably consistent manner. To all these products the rule applies that they only may be put on the market when their *conformity* with the requirements of a certain directive – not with the harmonized standards![14] – is *certified* and this conformity is confirmed by affixing the *CE marking*.[15] When the CE marking is affixed the respective product is subject to the free movement clause, is marketable EC-wide and additional authorization procedures or systematic controls by a Member State are not permitted.[16] This also includes indirect restrictions.[17]
  In a large share of cases the manufacturer is already able to certify such conformity with the directives him/herself and affix the CE marking. For products with a higher potential of danger, he/she must consult a "Notified

Produktharmonisierung durch Normung und Selbstüberwachung, 1996, 6 et seq.; *Marburger*, in: Festschrift für Feldhaus, 1999, 387 (390–396).

11 E.g. Article 3 Directive 1999/5/EC (Radio and telecommunications terminal equipment); Article 3 in conjunction with Annex I Directive 93/42/EEC (Medical devices).

12 Qualified as in violation of the EC Treaty e.g. by *Breulmann*, Normung und Rechtsangleichung in der Europäischen Wirtschaftsgemeinschaft, 1993, 175 et seq.; *Rönck*, Technische Normen als Gestaltungsmittel des Europäischen Gemeinschaftsrechts, 1995, 170 et seq.; *Schulte*, in: Rengeling (Ed.), Handbuch zum europäischen und deutschen Umweltrecht (EUDUR), Vol. 1, 2nd Edition 2003, §17 margin number 104–120; critique also in *Klindt*, EuZW 1998, 426. A convincing statement against this qualification in *Di Fabio*, Produktharmonisierung (fn. 10), 6 et seq.; in particular *v. Danwitz*, in: Rengeling (Ed.), Umweltnormung, 1998, 187 (205 et seq.); in addition *Marburger*, in: Festschrift für Feldhaus (fn. 10), 387 (395).

13 Council Resolution on a New Approach (fn. 1) under Annex II 1 B V, p. 5 et seq.

14 Hence, matters concerning conformity assessment procedures must be clearly separated from problems of European standardization; another view in *Di Fabio*, Produktharmonisierung (fn. 10), 24 et seq. and 126. In any case, abiding by the standards does lead to a presumption of conformity with the directives, and the conformity assessment procedure can additionally be simplified.

15 E.g. Article 11, 17 Directive 93/42/EEC (Medical devices), correspondingly §6 para. 1 Medical Devices Law; *Di Fabio*, Produktharmonisierung (fn. 10), 59 et seq.

16 See Article 4 Para. 1 Directive 93/42/EEC (Medical devices).

17 ECJ, Judgement of 25.3.1999, Case C-112/97 *COM/Italy*, [1999] ECR I-1821 (at para. 43–45).

Body" for this purpose, which assesses the conformity of the product with the requirements of the respective directive. Without its participation the product cannot be put on the market.

- The Member State administrations only come in contact with the products during the third phase of the market access regime established by the product safety directives, i.e. during *market surveillance*.[18] The authorities of the Member States monitor the market for products which do not comply with the requirements of the directives or are not correctly marked with the CE marking. Accordingly, they take the necessary measures, which can lead to a ban on the product. Highly differentiated cooperation mechanisms are provided for during these surveillance activities[19], which range from informal cooperation[20], institutionalized cooperation in committees under the auspices of the Commission as well as formal mechanisms for information exchange[21] to a formalized decision-making procedure, the safeguard clause procedure.[22]

These regulatory spheres are by principle separated from one another. They are linked together by means of feedback mechanisms: for example, the product documentation, which has to be drawn up for market access, is an important point of reference for the market surveillance authorities. Close cooperation between them and the Notified Bodies is required, too.[23] The most important

18 E.g. Article 8 para. 1 Directive 93/42/EEC (Medical devices); §25 et seq. Medical devices law; §§8 et seq. For the MPG see below fn. 54, for the GPSG below fn. 39.

19 Explicit general provisions on cooperation among the Member States can only be found in Article 17 Directive 97/23/EC (Pressure equipment) as well as Recital 29, Article 20 Directive 98/79/EC (In-vitro diagnostics).

20 E.g. in the Product Safety Enforcement Forum for Europe, a voluntary federation of market surveillance authorities.

21 The general product safety information system RAPEX based on Article 12 para. 3 in conjunction with Annex II of the Directive 2001/95/EC on General product safety; for medical devices the observation and registration system based on Art. 10 Directive 93/42/EEC and Article 11 Directive 98/79/EC, see §29 Medical Devices Law, as well as the regulatory data bank, Article 14a Directive 93/42/EEC in the version from Directive 98/79/EC.

22 The foundations are Article 95 para. 10, also Art. 174 Para. 2 Sub-paragraph. 2 TEC and the Council Decision on a New Approach (fn. 1), Annex II 1 B V, p. 6 et seq. A safeguard clause procedure is provided for in all directives on product safety, e.g. Art. 8 Directive 93/42/EEC (Medical devices); Article 9 Directive 1999/5/EC (Telecommunication terminal equipment). See ECJ, Judgement of 5.10.1977, Case 5/77 *Tedeschi*, [1977] ECR 1555 (at Para. 35 et seq.); Judgement from 2.12.1980, Case 815/79 *Cremonini*, [1980] ECR 3583 (at Para. 10–12).
The lack of effectiveness of the safeguard clause procedure, in particular its long duration, is currently a continual point of criticism, see e.g. Communication from the *European Commission*, Enhancing the Implementation of the New Approach Directives, COM(2003) 240 final version from 5/7/2003, 2.5.4, p. 21 et seq. During the revision of the New Approach, a revision of the safeguard clause procedure is also planned, see the Proposal for a Decision of the European Parliament and of the Council on a common framework for the marketing of products from 14.2.2006, COM(2007) 53 final, Article 35 et seq., Recital 8.

23 *European Commission*, Guide to the Implementation of Directives Based on New Approach and Global Approach, 2000, No. 6.3, p. 76 [the so-called "Blue Guide", in the following Guide ('blue')].

and at the same time most significant feedback mechanism for understanding the system of the directives based on the New Approach is the safeguard clause procedure: accordingly, a product ban declared by a Member State in the course of market surveillance must be reported to the Commission. It only comes to bear when it is confirmed by the Commission according to a "Community control procedure" (Article 114 para. 10 TFEU) with the participation of all Member States and as a rule the manufacturer. In this case the other Member States are obligated to take corresponding measures.[24] If a deficiency in a technical standard is determined, its presumptive effect[25] can be revoked as the Commission and Member States eliminate the standard from the published list. If the product danger is attributed to deficiencies in the Notified Body, the Member State must examine its recognition.[26]

1.3. CONFORMITY ASSESSMENT PROCEDURES BASED ON THE GLOBAL APPROACH

The conformity assessment procedures serve to test and certify that the products subject to the directives meet the requirements of the respectively applicable directive. The conformity assessment procedures, which generally cover both the product design phase as well as the production phase, basically follow the scheme as determined by the Council in its Modules Decision[27] based on the Communication from the Commission "A global approach to certification and testing".[28] Which of the various procedures from this scheme are used for certain products is specified in the respective directives. These generally offer the manufacturers a selection between different procedures.[29] The applied procedure and thus the intensity of testing is determined with regard to the danger potential of the product type; it can still depend on whether harmonized standards can be applied to the assessment of the respective product.

Having these conformity assessment procedures conducted by the manufacturer or the Notified Body and the affixing of the CE marking is a

24 Council Resolution on a New Approach (fn. 1), Annex II B VII 3, p. 7.

25 Which precludes another decision by a Member State, ECJ, Judgement of 25.3.1999, Case C-112/97 *Cremonini*, [1999] ECR I-1821 (at para. 36–39).

26 On the implementation problems see below p. 228 et seq.

27 Council Decision of 22 July 1993 concerning the modules for the various phases of the conformity assessment procedures and the rules for the affixing and use of the CE conformity marking, which are intended to be used in the technical harmonization directives (93/465/EEC) – Modules Decision, OJ 1993, No. L 220, p. 23 (replaces Council Decision 90/683/EEC, OJ 1990, No. L 380, p. 13).

28 Above fn. 2.

29 E.g. Article 11 para. 1–3 Directive 93/42/EEC (Medical devices).

necessary prerequisite[30] for access to the European market[31], and failure to do so is an administrative offence in German law. Notified Bodies with various tasks are incorporated into the conformity assessment procedures as third parties.[32] As a rule, these are private bodies designated by the Member States for this purpose and notified to the Commission. They certify products by issuing certificates of conformity and hence grant them access to the market.[33] Procedures requiring the intervention of a Notified Body are supervised product testing (Module Aa), EC-type examination (Module B), assessment and surveillance of quality assurance systems (Modules D, E and H), examination of the design dossier (Module H in particular cases[34]) and even verification of individual products in the production or the design and production phase (Modules F and G). The Notified Bodies can carry out their certification activities throughout Europe, every manufacturer may consult the Notified Body of his/her choice in every Member State[35], and the certificates are valid in all of Europe. If the intervention of the Notified Body is prescribed by law, the procedure can only be carried out by one single body.[36] The tests and surveillance measures required for this are ultimately also carried out outside the EC, if the production facilities of a manufacturer are located there.[37]

---

30 E.g. Article 11, 17 Directive 93/42/EEC (Medical devices); another view in *Peine*, Gesetz über technische Arbeitsmittel (Gerätesicherheitsgesetz), 3rd edition 2002, §9 margin number 18 et seq.

31 E.g. §§40 et seq. MPG; §5 Machine ordinance [Neunte Verordnung zum Geräte- und Produktsicherheitsgesetz (Maschinenverordnung) – 9. GPSGV] in conjunction with §19 GPSG.

32 Only the pressure equipment directives provide for manufacturer or user inspectorates for some inspections, Article 14 Directive 97/23/EC (Pressure equipment), Article 9 Directive 1999/36/EC (Transportable pressure equipment). For justification for this self-surveillance see *Becker*, in: Festschrift für O. Wlotzke, 1996, 445 (460 et seq.).

33 One special case is the European approval of materials according to Article 11 Directive 97/23/EC (Pressure equipment), which is issued by a body especially notified for this purpose. This does not only involve conformity assessment of a product, but also a (provisional) substitute for a technical standard: for materials which comply with the authorizations, a presumption of conformity with the essential requirements applies (Article 11 para. 4 Directive 97/23/EC). Due to this particular significance, the Notified Body must consult the European Commission and Member States before the issue of the authorization and take potential opinion statements into consideration. The issued authorization is published in the Official Journal. After a harmonized standard for the type of materials has been issued, the European approval for pressure equipment must be revoked, Article 11 para. 5 Directive 97/23/EC.

34 E.g. Annex II No. 4 Directive 93/42/EEC (Medical devices).

35 E.g. Article 11 para. 9 Directive 93/42/EEC (Medical devices).

36 E.g. Annex II No. 3.1. tir. 3 Directive 93/42/EEC (Medical devices). A corresponding clause for all modules including quality systems is provided for during the revision of the New Approach, see the Proposal for a Decision on a common framework for the marketing of products (fn. 22), Annex I, e.g. Module B No. 3.1. tir 2, passim.

37 In explicit terms e.g. Annex C No. 5 Directive 96/98/EC (Marine equipment): "A notified body is entitled to perform conformity-assessment procedures for any economic operator established within or outwith the Community. A notified body may perform conformity-

1.4. IMPLEMENTATION IN GERMANY

Based on the requirements of the respective directives the detailed structure and sequence of conformity assessment procedures in German law result from a complex combination of EC directives, national laws and ordinance provisions. These requirements are generally obligatory for putting a product on the market. The largest product sector falls in the scope of the Equipment and Product Safety Law (under 1), significant product segments fall under the Medical Devices Law (under 2).[38]

1.4.1. Equipment and Product Safety Law

The requirements of a large number of directives, which fall under the Equipment and Product Safety Law (*Geräte- und Produktsicherheitsgesetz* – GPSG)[39], have been implemented into German law by means of special Ordinances.[40] The requirements for placing products on the market result from these ordinances, which primarily refer to the demands of the directives.

Hence, an EC-wide uniform approval system based on the directives has emerged for a broad array of products. Not only was the already heterogeneous German system for placing products on the market harmonized, but this harmonization also spanned the entire European market. This innovative power becomes evident when one realizes that a two-digit number of product segments now are subject to a uniform system of market access within the scope of the GPSG alone. Unlike in other EC Member States, state authorization procedures or obligatory tests by third parties were previously only prescribed by law for certain products in Germany, in particular for equipment requiring authorization according to §24 *Gewerbeordnung* such as lifts and pressure equipment.[41]

---

assessment procedures in any Member State or State outwith the Community using either its home-based means or the personnel of its branch office abroad."

38 The product sectors of the directives implemented by means of other laws will not be considered here for reasons of space.

39 Gesetz über technische Arbeitsmittel und Verbraucherprodukte (Geräte- und Produktsicherheitsgesetz) – GPSG/Law on Technical Equipment and Consumer Products (Equipment and Product Safety Law). This law consolidates the old Gerätesicherheitsgesetz (GSG)/Equipment Safely Law and the Produktsicherheitsgesetz (ProdSG)/Product Safety Law, without providing for fundamental modifications for the concerned area; see *Klindt*, NJW 2004, 465.

40 E.g. Directive 2006/95/EC (Low-voltage directive); Directive 88/378/EEC (Safety of toys); Directive 87/404/EEC (Simple pressure vessels); Directive 90/396/EEC (Appliances burning gaseous fuels); Directive 89/686/EEC (Personal protective equipment); Directive 2006/42/EC (Machines); Directive 94/25/EC (Recreational craft); Directive 94/9/EC (Equipment and protective systems intended for use in potentially explosive atmospheres); Directive 95/16/EC (Lifts).

41 *Eckstein*, in: Hansen (Ed.), Zertifizierung und Akkreditierung von Produkten und Leistungen der Wirtschaft, 1993, 99 (104). See the (German) Lifts Ordinance (Aufzugsverordnung – AufzV) from 1980 and the Pressure Gas Ordinance (Druckgasverordnung) from

However, the main part of the inspection was left up to private bodies here, in particular the *Technische Überwachungsvereine – TÜV* (Technical Inspection Associations). For most product areas, on the other hand, an approval was not yet necessary, and the compliance with the safety requirements defined above all in DIN standards was left up to private self-regulation (e.g. machines[42], toys), and partially supported by the establishment of a voluntary safety mark by the state (the "GS mark", see the current §7 GPSG). Effective self-regulation existed (and exists) above all for electro-technical products[43], which were subject to a voluntary inspection by the VDE Inspection and Certification Institute on the basis of the VDE standards.[44] This voluntary certification system also constitutes an integral part of a (private) European mutual recognition procedure.[45] Altogether though, the regulatory situation in the EC Member States was marked by a high degree of heterogeneity. Above all, third-party inspections were frequently bindingly prescribed by law in other states.[46]

Now for the majority of the products affected by the GPSG and its Ordinances, in particular for most machines[47], an internal control of production by the manufacturer with technical documentation according to Module A suffices.[48]

1968. According to the 1980s version of the Lifts Ordinance individual construction parts for elevators could only be tested by Technical Inspection Associations (Technische Überwachungsvereine – TÜV) designated in §17 of the Ordinance. As a result of Directive 84/528/EEC (Lifting and mechanical handling appliances) and 84/529/EEC (Electrically operated lifts) and their implementation in §17 para. 3 of the version of the Lifts Ordinance (Aufzugsverordnung) valid as of 1988, the construction parts tests by other testing bodies within the EC had the same effect. To this extent, a preliminary model to the Notified Bodies resulting from the Global Approach can be found in these lifts directives as well as in the Directive 76/767/EEC (Pressure vessels). The latter was implemented by §9 para. 5 of the Pressure Vessels Ordinance (Druckbehälterverordnung) from 1980, according to which construction type inspections by notified bodies from all Member States of the EC could replace the inspections by German bodies.

42 See *Eckstein*, in: Hansen, Zertifizierung und Akkreditierung (fn. 41), 99 et seq.

43 See *Dreger*, in: Hansen, Zertifizierung und Akkreditierung (fn. 41), 109 et seq.

44 This is supported by a presumptive effect (*Vermutungswirkung*) in §1 para. 1 Zweite Durchführungsverordnung zum EnWG (Energiewirtschaftsgesetz)/2nd Enforcement Ordinance for the EnWG, Bundesgesetzblatt /Federal Law Journal I 1987, 146.

45 *Dreger*, in: Hansen, Zertifizierung und Akkreditierung (fn. 41), 114 et seq.

46 *Eckstein*, in: Hansen, Zertifizierung und Akkreditierung (fn. 41), 99 (104); *Dreger*, *ibid.* 109 (112).

47 §3 para. 1 No. 2 of the 9th GPSGV (Fn. 31) in conjunction with Article 12 para. 2, para. 3 lit. a) Directive 2006/42/EC (Machines).

48 Electrical operational equipment in low-voltage areas, according to §3 Para. 1 Erste Verordnung zum Geräte- und Produktsicherheitsgesetz (Verordnung über das Inverkehrbringen elektrischer Betriebsmittel zur Verwendung innerhalb bestimmter Spannungsgrenzen) – 1. GPSGV; Toy, when the manufacturer respects harmonized standards, §3 Para. 1 Zweite Verordnung zum Geräte- und Produktsicherheitsgesetz (Verordnung über die Sicherheit von Spielzeug) – 2. GPSGV; simple personal protective equipment, §3 Achte Verordnung zum Geräte- und Produktsicherheitsgesetz (Verordnung über das Inverkehrbringen von persönlichen Schutzausrüstungen) – 8. GPSGV. See *Klindt*, EWS 2000, 298 et seq.; critique in *Marburger/Enders*, JBUTR 1994, 333 (367 et seq.); *Marburger*, in: Festschrift für Feldhaus (Fn. 10), 387 (395).

The participation of the bodies authorized according to §11 para. 1 GPSG is required for more high-risk products, e.g. for more hazardous machines.[49] As a rule, a product is subject to conformity assessment both in the product design phase as well as the production phase.[50] The modules accordingly refer to the product design phase, the product manufacturing phase or both and can be combined with one another so that entire conformity assessment procedures can be brought together. In certain cases a document inspection procedure may suffice, when harmonized standards exist and are respected.[51]

1.4.2. Medical devices law

The systematic market access regime for medical devices, which comprises all products, is also a new phenomenon: according to the previous legal situation, only implantable and several especially listed medical devices were subject to the requirement of an official authorization.[52] All other medical devices were not subject to an authorization, but the manufacturer could subject them to a voluntary GS inspection. Now a conformity assessment procedure is compulsory every time before a medical device[53] is placed on the market, §6 para. 1 Medical Devices Law – MPG.[54] To meet this objective, medical devices are divided into different classes.[55] Based on this classification, Article 11 of the directive determines which of the conformity assessment procedures described in Annexes II-VI is required.[56] The bodies who operate in this framework are notified to the

49 Which are listed in Annex IV of the Directive 98/37/EC. This also holds e.g. for simple pressure equipment, §3 Para. 3 Sechste Verordnung zum Geräte- und Produktsicherheitsgesetz (Verordnung über das Inverkehrbringen von einfachen Druckbehältern) – 6. GPSGV; Appliances burning gaseous fuels (Art. 8 Para. 1 Directive 90/396/EEC and §3 Para. 1 Siebte Verordnung zum Geräte- und Produktsicherheitsgesetz [Gasverbrauchseinrichtungs-verordnung] – 7. GPSGV), Safety construction parts for lifts (Art. 8 Para. 2 Directive 95/16/EC) and (as a rule) personal protective equipment, §6 of the 8th GPSGV (fn. 48).

50 Council Decision 93/465/EEC, Appendix A I. c).

51 E.g. for simple pressure equipment in accordance with §3 para. 3 2nd sentence 6th GPSGV (fn. 49) in conjunction with Annex II No. 3 Directive 84/404/EEC.

52 §5 of the earlier MedGV (Verordnung über die Sicherheit medizinisch-technischer Geräte – Medizingeräteverordnung [Ordinance on the safety of medical-technical equipment – Medical equipment ordinance] – from 1/14/1985, Bundesgesetzblatt/Federal Law Journal I 93). Once again here the main focus of the inspection was the assessment by a (private) testing body, §5 para. 2 of the Ordinance.

53 See the directives on Active implantable medical devices and Medical devices (90/385/EEC and 93/42/EEC). The directive on In-vitro diagnostics (98/79/EC) is equivalent to the system of the first two directives.

54 Medizinproduktegesetz – MPG. See *Schlund*, ArztR 1995, 235 et seq.; *Meyer-Lüerßen/Will*, PharmaRecht 1995, 34 et seq.; *Deutsch/Spickhoff*, Medizinrecht, 5th edition 2003, margin numbers 1196 et seq., 1213 et seq.

55 According to the criteria of Annex IX of the Directive 93/42/EEC (Medical devices).

56 Class I: Internal production control of the manufacturer, coupled with drawing up documentation (Module A), Article 11 para. 5 Directive 93/42/EEC in conjunction with Annex VII.

EC Commission in accordance with §15 para. 1 Medical Devices Law after an accreditation procedure is carried out.

2. CONFORMITY ASSESSMENT BY NOTIFIED BODIES AS A EUROPEAN ADMINISTRATIVE ACTIVITY

The harmonizing effects of European product safety law are already remarkable at the national level with regard to the historically grown diversity of the replaced technical safety law. However, the term "deregulation" would be the wrong label for the result. The essential requirements for products which now exist in the form of legal provisions are as a rule significantly more precise than the previous provisions.[57] Above all, the result is an increase in the procedural obligations for the manufacturers on the whole: in each case they are required to draw up product documentation, and products which were authorization-free according to previous laws are more frequently subject to a testing procedure than before. These authorization procedures are de-nationalized. Nevertheless, categorizing this as self-regulation would not do justice to the peculiarity of this construction[58]: according to mandatory laws, the authorization procedures are carried out by third-parties, primarily private bodies, who owe their legal status

---

Class IIa: EC declaration of conformity, coupled with a unit verification of the products or the assessment of a quality system, Article 11 para. 2 Directive in conjunction with Annex IV, V or VI (corresponds to Module A, coupled with D, E or F).

Class IIb: full quality assurance system (Annex II, corresponds with Module H) or the EC type-examination, coupled with a unit verification of the products or the assessment of a quality assurance system (Annex III, coupled with Annex IV, V or VI, coincides with Module B, coupled with F, D or E), Article 11 para. 3 Directive.

Class III: full quality assurance (Annex II, corresponds with Module H, supplemented with an EC design-examination certificate) or EC type-examination, coupled with a unit verification of the products or the assessment of a quality assurance system (Annex III, coupled with Annex IV or V, corresponds with Module B, coupled with F or D), Article 11 para. 1 Directive.

57 *V. Danwitz*, in: Rengeling (Ed.), Umweltnormung (fn. 12), 187 (204). See Annex I of the Directive 93/42/EEC (Medical devices) and in comparison to this §3 para. 1 of the earlier MedGV (fn. 52): "Medical-technical devices may only be put on the market or exhibited for commercial purposes or independently by an enterprise, when they comply with the provisions of this Ordinance, the acknowledged rules of technology as well as the work safety and accident prevention provisions. It must be ensured that patients, employees or third-parties are protected against dangers to their lives and health when using the devices for the intended purposes to the extent that the intended type of use allows. One may deviate from the acknowledged rules of technology as well as the work safety and accident prevention provisions, as long as the same level of safety is guaranteed by other means."

58 However, see e.g. *Di Fabio*, Produktharmonisierung (fn. 10), 64; *Schmidt-Preuß*, VVDStRL 56 (1997), 160 (173 fn. 38); *Seidel*, Privater Sachverstand und staatliche Garantenstellung im Verwaltungsrecht, 2000, 269 et seq.

and structure to EC legal provisions, and not the mere self-organization among private entities.

The Notified Bodies are the administrative core of the European product approval laws presented here. As an independent structure for enforcing European norms, they are a new phenomenon which is not easy to classify according to the conventional categories of public law. A precise analysis of their legal status, which is founded in EU law and shaped by national law shows that they assume unilateral decision-making powers in the public interest (see below I). This authority, which spans across the entire Community area, results from an allocation of competences by the Community legislator (see below II). To this extent, Notified Bodies assume European administrative tasks and thus are core elements of a new European administrative structure.

2.1. UNILATERAL DECISION-MAKING POWERS OF THE NOTIFIED BODIES

This classification as "administrative" structure requires justification, as the Notified Bodies are generally private entities, which operate on the basis of a contractual relationship with the manufacturer of the product.[59] Accordingly, it is sometimes assumed that they take on tasks during the certification activities which lie within the scope of responsibility of the manufacturer.[60] An analysis of the legal relationship between the manufacturer and Notified Bodies as well as the legal consequences of the conformity assessment procedure shows, however, that the Notified Bodies are granted unilateral decision-making powers, which cannot be understood as an expression of private self-regulation:

The manufacturer indeed has a free selection among the available Notified Bodies, including those abroad. Nevertheless, one cannot speak of a "responsibility" of the manufacturer.[61] The manufacturer cannot avoid mandating a Notified Body: Third-party conformity assessment bodies must be consulted during the procedure for market access by virtue of law. The respectively addressed body is then the only body to ultimately and bindingly decide on market authorization.[62] In cases of rejection, the binding effects also span to the decision on conformity with the directive upon which the certificate

59 §16 para. 3 MPG therefore states that the manufacturer coordinates with the Notified Body how the conformity assessment procedure is to be carried out; according to §3 para. 2 MPV the manufacturer mandates a Notified Body of his/her choice.

60 *J. Hofmann*, Rechtsschutz und Haftung im Europäischen Verwaltungsverbund, 2004, 42, in particular fn. 108; *Schmidt-Aßmann*, Das Allgemeine Verwaltungsrecht als Ordnungsidee, 2nd edition 2004, Chap. 3 margin number 57. A similar view also in *Peine*, Gerätesicherheitsgesetz (fn. 30), §9 margin number 21; in agreement with him *Schmidt-Preuß* (fn. 58), VVDStRL 56 (1997), 160 (167, fn. 18).

61 However, see *Seidel*, Privater Sachverstand (fn. 58), 270.

62 E.g. Annex II No. 3.1. tir. 3 Directive 93/42/EEC (Medical devices).

of conformity is based: other bodies would no longer be able to grant market authorization.

Furthermore, EC law does not allow Member States' market surveillance authorities to conduct a systematic control of the products once they have been placed on the market.[63] Measures restricting the marketability are only permissible in special cases of suspicion. The market surveillance authorities can then indeed deny the conformity with the directives and ban the sale of the product. However, this is only temporary until a safeguard clause procedure has been completed.[64]

The Notified Body is additionally authorized to *unilaterally revoke* its certificate of conformity. In medical devices law this authorization is conferred by law, §18 MPG. In other product areas this authorization is indeed only based on the contractual agreement with the manufacturer, but the Notified Bodies are as a rule forced to use such a contractual clause due to EC law[65], national law or by virtue of the guidelines of the accreditation bodies or the designating ministries. Consequently it is generally impossible for a manufacturer to conclude a contract on conformity assessment, which does not contain such a clause. Due to this, the position of the manufacturer does not differ from a situation in which such a revocation possibility was directly granted by law.[66] These unilateral decision-making authorities comprise the authority of the Notified Bodies to pay unannounced visits to the operational facilities of the manufacturer during quality control, which is required by EC law and substantiated by the mandate for certification.[67]

Altogether, it appears that the Notified Bodies selected by the manufacturer "enforce" European law on the basis of unilateral authority. To this extent, conformity assessment clearly goes beyond self-surveillance or third-party surveillance.[68] For this reason, it differs from the activities of a financial auditor,

---

63 Accordingly §8 para. 2 No. 2 GPSG for example only provides for a random check; the further wording of §26 para. 2 MPG: "to an appropriate extent/in angemessenem Umfang" is not unproblematic.

64 See above Section 1.2 in fn. 22. To this extent, this residual authority of the Member State administrations differs little from the competences of the competent authorities of the home Member States according to Directive 2006/48/EC relating to the taking up and pursuit of the business of credit institutions.

65 Now more explicitly in Article 16 para. 6 Directive 93/42/EEC (Medical devices) and Article 15 para. 6 Directive 98/79/EC (In-vitro diagnostics).

66 *Hiltl*, PharmaRecht 1997, 408 (411).

67 See e.g. Annex VI No. 4.3. and 4.4. Directive 93/42/EEC (Medical devices); a legal authorization does not exist. The right to conduct such inspections is also required by German law though, see §15 para. 2 MPG.

68 See *Peine*, Gerätesicherheitsgesetz (fn. 30), §9 margin number 21; *Di Fabio*, VVDStRL 56 (1997), 235 (244); *Schmidt-Preuß*, VVDStRL 56 (1997), 160 (167, here fn. 18); *Seidel*, Privater Sachverstand (fn. 58), 270 et seq.; *K. Weber*, Europäische Einwirkungen auf die Aufgabenerfüllung von Ordnungsbehörden, 2003, 202.

for example.[69] These unilateral decision-making and surveillance powers of the Notified Bodies, which are essentially based on legal mandate, not on the approval of the manufacturer, are aimed against third parties. They are thus of sovereign (*hoheitlich*) character despite being vested in private law.[70]

2.2. ESTABLISHMENT OF THE NOTIFIED BODIES' COMPETENCES IN EUROPEAN LAW

From a purely national perspective there would be some reasons to categorize the Notified Bodies as being vested with public authority (*Beliehene).*[71] In view of the Europe-wide activities of the Notified Bodies and the Europe-wide regulatory impact of their certificates, the legal regime that governs the relationships to the manufacturer cannot be national public law though, as it would be the case with a *Beleihung.*[72] A specific European law does not exist. Therefore the legal relationships must be governed within the framework of private contract laws existing in all Member States. Notwithstanding this applicability of private law between Notified Body and manufacturer, no conclusion has been drawn yet in constitutional law, European law and international law, because these layers of law must autonomously categorize the respective arrangement.

A look at the international activities of the Notified Bodies is useful here: according to the applicable provisions, the manufacturer can turn to a Notified

---

69 An auditor must indeed also be consulted (§§316 et seq. HGB), but not consulting him/her (§316 para. 1 2nd sentence HGB) or the denial of the seal of confirmation (§322 HGB) only has civil law consequences in internal societal relations; see, on the other hand, the classification in *Seidel*, Privater Sachverstand (fn. 58), 270. Incidentally, an understanding of the Notified Bodies as private bodies would raise new issues with regard to anti-trust law: The Notified Bodies are urged by European law to regularly coordinate their approaches with one another. Such coordinated behaviour among private entities would be questionable in terms of anti-trust laws; this is only permissible, because the Notified Bodies operate as part of a European executive structure.

70 The term "sovereign" activity is to be understood here as a *unilateral decision-making authority* granted by a government or the EU, not as *official* action of a public authority (*behördliches Handeln*).

71 In German administrative law, the term "Beleihung" signifies the act of vesting a private entity with public authority; the entity is called "Beliehener". Such a classification is supposed by *Scheel*, DVBl. 1999, 442 (446 et seq.); *idem*, Privater Sachverstand (fn. 9), 97 et seq., for the GPSG; *Kadelbach*, Allgemeines Verwaltungsrecht unter europäischem Einfluß, 1999, 329 et seq. See also BVerwG, NVwZ-RR 1991, 330 et seq., for the inspection of a mining test track by a notified (but not yet according to the Global Approach) testing body. A similar situation applies to Dutch law, *G. Evers*, Tilburg Foreign Law Review 2003, 342 (355).

72 Contrary to *Kadelbach*, Allgemeines Verwaltungsrecht (fn. 71), 331, one would have to assume the same for the relationship between the environmental verifier and the audited firm according to the Eco-Audit-/EMAS Regulation because the verifier may also operate across Europe, Article 4 para. 5 Regulation 761/2001 (EMAS).

Body of his/her choice, including one from another EC Member State.[73] The certificates of this body are legally effective in Germany as well. This is a Community-wide execution of decision-making powers by the Notified Bodies, as can also be observed elsewhere with the phenomenon of the transnational administrative act.[74] The decisions of the Member States or their designating authorities to recognize a conformity assessment body for EC law purposes also apply to the entire EC and constitute transnational administrative acts. Such execution of regulatory powers by foreign bodies as part of the German legal system ("*Verschränkung*")[75] must stay within the constitutional limits of Article 23 and 24 GG (*Grundgesetz*).

This phenomenon of decisions effective in the entire EC is only imprecisely defined with the term "recognition".[76] Member States are obliged to accept decisions from other Member States as immediately *legally relevant*[77], we are facing a case of Community-wide regulatory powers.[78] Certificates of the Notified Bodies or transnational administrative acts such as the designation of the Notified Bodies obtain validity directly in the legal system of the other Member States without the intervention of a special recognition act. They apply by virtue of the directive together with the national law that implements it ("genuine transnationality"[79]); the directives establish a "European system of repartition of competences".[80] The constitutional law foundations for the Community-wide decisions by the administrations and Notified Bodies can thus be found in Article 23 para. 1 GG (*Grundgesetz*).

---

73 §15 para. 3 MPG and §2 para. 15 No. 2 GPSG make the foreign bodies equivalent to the German bodies.

74 As far as public authorities or private entities vested with public authority (*Beliehene*) have been notified, German lawmakers have designed the certificates as transnational administrative acts anyway.

75 According to BVerfGE 73, 339 (374), see *Cremer*, ZaöRV 60 (2000), 103 (131 et seq.).

76 According to *Götz*, in: idem et al., Lib. Am. Jaenicke (fn. 4), 763 (763 et seq., 777 et seq.), who also adheres to a uniform designation; also *Beyer*, Rechtsnormanerkennung im Binnenmarkt, 1998, 25 et seq. Another view in e.g. *Happe*, Grenzüberschreitende Wirkung von nationalen Verwaltungsakten, 1987, passim; *Bleckmann*, JZ 1985, 1072 (in particular 1074 et seq.); *idem*, NVwZ 1986, 1 et seq.; *v. Danwitz*, Verwaltungsrechtliches System und europäische Integration, 1996, 407 et seq., in particular 414; *Schwarze*, in: *idem*, Verwaltungsrecht unter europäischem Einfluß, 1996, 123 (135 et seq.); *Hatje*, Die gemeinschaftsrechtliche Steuerung der Wirtschaftsverwaltung, 1998, 433 et seq.

77 *Götz*, in: idem et al., Lib. Am. Jaenicke (fn. 4), 763 (778 et seq.); see also *Steindorff*, in: Festschrift für W. Lorenz (fn. 7), 561 (566).

78 *E. Klein*, in: Starck (Ed.) Rechtsvereinheitlichung durch Gesetze, 1992, 117 (140 et seq.); *Neßler*, Europäisches Richtlinienrecht wandelt deutsches Verwaltungsrecht, 1992, 79; *Schlag*, Grenzüberschreitende Verwaltungsbefugnisse im EG-Binnenmarkt, 1998, 172; *Royla*, Grenzüberschreitende Finanzmarktaufsicht in der EG, 2000, 58 et seq.

79 *Schmidt-Aßmann*, EuR 31 (1996), 270 (301).

80 *Götz*, in: idem et al., Lib. Am. Jaenicke (fn. 4), 763 (779, 787 et seq.); see *Seidel*, in: Magiera (Ed.), Entwicklungsperspektiven der Europäischen Gemeinschaft, 1985, 169 (182).

The decisive basis for the transnational impact of the decisions is still the directive[81], which in turn is based on the lawmaking power conferred to the EU.[82] By virtue of this power, the EU transfers authority to the administrative system of the democratically organized Member States and the ensemble of the Notified Bodies. Community law creates a system of European administrative competences, as the Community *allocates* competences to the Member States and Notified Bodies to be executed[83], but does not *delegate* its authority to the Member States. According to the EC Treaty, this distribution of administrative authority is – except for several special assignments of tasks such as Article 105 or Article 118 TFEU – the task of the Community legislator[84], which must respect the general guidelines of primary legislation, and above all the principle of subsidiarity.

A consequence of the classification as *allocation* of competences, not as delegation, is that the measures allocated to the Member State administrations remain those of the national legal systems.[85] Therefore they are basically subject to national procedural and liability law. Above all, this classification offers the proper perspective for the legal analysis of such an allocation of competence: it concerns standards for the establishment of European administrative structures. Contrary to the general perception[86], the TEU does not provide the Community legislator any precise guidelines on the type of administrative structures, to whom it must transfer administrative powers[87], in contrast to the German Constitution, which stipulates the state or federal administrative system as a rule in Article 83 GG et seq. Such a dynamic distribution of administrative powers by simple legislation is basically unknown in the German constitution.[88] On the other hand, in the EC Treaty there may be a priority in favour of the Member States' administrative structures, but is not explicitly specified that they or the EC's own administration must be used.

---

81 *Ehlers*, Die Europäisierung des Verwaltungsprozeßrechts, 1999, 11.

82 Likewise, the Federal Law is the foundation for the transregional impact of administrative acts of the German *Länder*, see *Isensee*, HStR IV, §98 margin number 35; for a partially critical standpoint *Lerche*, in: Maunz-Dürig, GG Kommentar, Article 83 margin number 50.

83 For this distinction see *Rengeling*, Rechtsgrundsätze beim Verwaltungsvollzug des Europäischen Gemeinschaftsrechts, 1977, 30 et seq.

84 *H.P. Ipsen*, Europäisches Gemeinschaftsrecht, 1972, §9 margin number 26; see also *Jarass*, AöR 121 (1996), 173 (181–183).

85 *Schmidt-Aßmann*, DVBl. 1993, 924 (935 et seq.).

86 E.g. *Pühs*, Der Vollzug von Gemeinschaftsrecht, 1997, 73 et seq.; *Streinz*, HStR VII, §182, margin number 1 et seq.; *V. Danwitz*, Verwaltungsrechtliches System (fn. 76), 486, describes the Member State executive responsibilities as "the opposite principle in constitutional law to the imperative of uniform applicability of EC law".

87 *Di Fabio*, Produktharmonisierung (fn. 10), 89.

88 Article 87 para. 3 1st sentence GG to a great extent unrestrictedly permits the transfer of administrative powers to the federal level by means of a simple federal law. For clearly more restrictive view see *Britz*, DVBl. 1998, 1167 et seq.

2.3. NEW STRUCTURES OF THE EUROPEAN ADMINISTRATIVE SYSTEM

The transfer of unilateral decision-making authority by the European lawmaker to the ensemble of the Notified Bodies supplements the hitherto existing administrative organization with new structures.[89] Administrative organization law is not obligated to treat these new structures concurrently to national administrative structures.[90] The answers to questions concerning procedural requirements, sufficient legal protection against measures by Notified Bodies, state liability and the applicability of fundamental rights can therefore turn out to be rather different from those concerning national administrative bodies[91], as long as the asymmetrical relationship between the Notified Body and manufacturer created by the unilateral decision-making authority is sufficiently taken into account. Appropriate consequences are drawn, for example, by the new version of the MPG, which calls for the principle of proportionality for unilateral measures towards the manufacturer, §18, and stipulates hearing requirements.

3. DEMOCRATIC LEGITIMACY AND COMMUNITY-WIDE DECISION-MAKING COMPETENCES

3.1. DEMOCRATIC LEGITIMACY

The EC Treaty allows for the allocation of Community-wide decision-making powers to the Member State level. However, the selected arrangements must be compatible with the principles of the EC Treaty, as they were assured by Article 23 para. 1 GG (*Grundgesetz*). The main focus of the following considerations is the principle of democracy (Article 6 para. 1 TEU, Article 23 para. 1 GG): This principle is addressed when the enforcement of European law by other Member States is called a "risk"[92] and "danger"[93] with regard to the Community-wide impact of decisions. The administrative enforcement is described as a "process of realization with a variety of consequences and above all a strong source of different results in the application of law".[94] This summarizes the problem of administrative legitimacy in the EC.

---

89 *Schmidt-Aßmann*, Ordnungsidee (fn. 60), Chapter 3 margin number 57.

90 *Röhl*, Akkreditierung (fn. 8), 97.

91 In detail *Röhl*, Akkreditierung (fn. 8), 79 et seq.

92 *Götz*, in: idem et al., Lib. Am. Jaenicke (fn. 4), 763 (783 et seq.).

93 *Hatje*, Gemeinschaftsrechtliche Steuerung (fn. 76), 42 et seq.

94 *Wahl/D. Groß*, DVBl. 1998, 2 (3); see in general *Di Fabio*, VVDStRL 56 (1997), 235 (266); *Hatje*, Gemeinschaftsrechtliche Steuerung (fn. 76), 111–114; for a detailed overview of

Administrative legitimacy for Community-wide decisions cannot be created following a legitimization model[95] which has been developed with view to the traditional ministerial organization of administration. This would require the closest possible link between the administrative agents and the head of the respective authorities. For Community-wide administrative activities this would accordingly have to be the European Commission. This kind of centralization drawing on the legitimacy of the EC institutions, as can be observed for certain authorization procedures in medicine law[96], must be regarded as an exception due to the obligations for decentralization and subsidiarity.[97] Cooperation between all national administrations would come under consideration, as is the case with the authorization of medicinal products or the approval of genetically modified organisms.

Such a legitimization model drawing on the head of the administrations of the EC or the Member States is abandoned, when decisions with a Community-wide impact based on EC law can be made without the participation of the other Member States or the Commission. Up to now, such a regulatory model can be found above all for the authorization of services, and more seldom during product approvals, for example the authorizations for the provision of banking or insurance services, transactions in securities[98] or the licensing of railway undertakings[99] or air carriers[100], as well as the authorization as an environmental verifier.[101] In particular, the designation or recognition of Notified Bodies has a transnational impact. The conventional understanding of creating administrative legitimacy by participation of all Member States, who are affected by the decision or by the institutions of the EC[102] cannot be found here. The fact that Community lawmakers no longer view this as necessary may have to do with the low political significance of the decisions, and therefore a lesser need for mechanisms and procedures which support administrative legitimacy: the legal provisions upon which the Member States' decisions are based are harmonized by Community

individual executive models now *Sydow*, Verwaltungskooperation in der Europäischen Union, 2004, 117 et seq.

95 Explicitly in *Jestaedt*, Demokratieprinzip und Kondominialverwaltung, 1993, 302 et seq.; *Axer*, Normsetzung der Exekutive in der Sozialverwaltung, 2000, 296.

96 Article 4 et seq. Regulation 726/2004/EC for certain high-tech or higher-tech medicinal products.

97 *V. Danwitz,* Verwaltungsrechtliches System (fn. 76), 410 et seq.; *Kadelbach*, Allgemeines Verwaltungsrecht (fn. 71), 110 et seq.; *Götz*, in: idem et al., Lib. Am. Jaenicke (fn. 4), 763 (783, 785).

98 See *Ehlers*, Europäisierung (fn. 81), 10.

99 According to Article 1 para. 3 Directive 95/18/EC.

100 Regulation 2407/92/EEC.

101 Article 4 Regulation 761/2001/EC.

102 The decision on the authorization of Notified Bodies can be examined by the European Commission, when the harmonized standards on accreditation and certification are not taken into account.

law[103]; moreover, the later conduct of the entrepreneur can still be monitored after an authorization for service activities.[104] However, in the case of a product approval the control via the manufacturer is terminated once the product is placed on the market.

3.2. LEGITIMACY PROBLEMS OF MEMBER STATE ADMINISTRATIONS

The resulting decentralized administrative model is reminiscent of federal structures.[105] The decisions remain legal acts of another Member State. According to the conventional concept of legitimacy, it would be precarious to accept them.[106] An European administrative legitimacy, which replaces the administrative legitimacy derived from the Member States, can only justify such an exercise of sovereign power, if it permissibly follows other principles than the conventional concept of administrative legitimacy. Therefore, it must be possible to replace the instruments of administrative legitimization: instructions, control and a consistent "chain of appointments", by other, structural mechanisms, which equally ensure that tasks are fulfilled in a functional manner and in conformity with the common good.

Such a concept of structural legitimacy would not fulfil the requirement of democratic legitimacy by means of a hierarchical link to the central level, rather by providing structures for administrative units, which are oriented towards the common good and which are "entrusted" with the execution of the competences transferred by the EC. The principle of *trust* addressed here could prove to be, under certain conditions, more suitable than the hierarchy principle as a foundation for the construction of administrative legitimacy in decentralized decision situations. This can already be found in Article IV Sec. 1 of the US Constitution.[107] And for EC law as well, the mutual trust in the administrative authorities of the Member States is cited as a crucial requirement for the

103 See *Neßler*, Europäisches Richtlinienrecht (fn. 78), 30; *Schmidt-Aßmann*, DVBl. 1993, 924 (936).

104 Consequently, the focus of these directives is also on the control of the conduct of the entrepreneur. For example, according to Article 4 para. 5 Regulation 2407/92/EEC the continual monitoring by the authorizing Member State can be examined by the Commission upon request of another Member State.

105 Which would not have to be equated with the structures of federal states; see the use of the term for the arrangements between the Union and Member States in *v. Bogdandy*, Supranationaler Föderalismus als Wirklichkeit und Idee einer neuen Herrschaftsform, 1999, 61 et seq.

106 *Schmidt-Aßmann*, DVBl. 1993, 924 (936).

107 "Full faith and credit shall be given in each state to the public acts, records, and judicial proceedings of every other state." Taken as a reference in *Seidel*, in: Magiera, Entwicklungsperspektiven (fn. 80), 169 (182); *Beyer*, Rechtsnormanerkennung (fn. 76), 26.

establishment and proper functioning of Community-wide administrative structures.[108]

To this end, structures would have to be created which – as called for in Article 10 TEC according to the ECJ – align the Member State administrations within the decentralized decision-making system of the EC with the interest of the Community, when they operate as the trustees for the fulfilment of their EC-law obligations.[109] By these means the allocation of cross-border administrative powers was made possible, without a hierarchical reference being necessary, e.g. by means of permanent decisional authority for the Commission.[110] Only under such conditions can the EC and its Member States assume when transferring decision-making powers that the consulted administrative units guarantee the execution of European law consistently with the common good.

Trust in the administrative structures of the respective Member States as a legally relevant element which justifies such a transfer of decision-making powers in view of the principle of democracy cannot be prescribed[111], rather must be created by concrete mechanisms: in the national context continual practice leads to familiarity with certain structures, with an administration's competence and its resources.[112] Such common experience is lacking at the European level. In the European context Member States as well as citizens do not put trust in the assessments that certain administrative bodies reach only because these bodies are components of the respective national administrative organization.[113] The organizational affiliation to the administration substantiates under certain conditions even the suspicion of a tendency to favour national interests.[114] The

108 *Seidel*, in: Magiera, Entwicklungsperspektiven (fn. 80), 169 (181); *Bleckmann*, JZ 1985, 1071 (1074); *Happe*, Grenzüberschreitende Wirkung (fn. 76), 111; *Troberg*, in: Groeben/Thiesing/Ehlermann (Eds.), Kommentar zum EU-/EG-Vertrag, Art. 57 margin number 6; *Streinz*, WiVerw 1996, 129 (146); *Majone*, Mutual Trust – Credible Commitments and the Evolution of Rules for a Single European Market (EUI Working Paper), Badia Fiesolana 1995; *Beyer*, Rechtsnormanerkennung (fn. 76) 26, 53; *Oppermann*, Europarecht, 2nd Edition 1999, margin number 1299, 1590, 1613, 1620; *v. Bogdandy/Arndt*, EWS 2000, 1 (1 et seq.).

109 See *Weatherill*, in: Micklitz/Roethe/Weatherill (Eds.), Federalism and Responsibility, 1994, 153 (193 et seq.).

110 In contrast e.g. *Pühs*, Vollzug (fn. 86), 293 et seq.

111 *Majone*, Mutual Trust (fn. 108), 15.

112 Typical the appeal to "time-tested facilities with a long security technology tradition", e.g. in *Becker*, in: Festschrift für O. Wlotzke (fn. 32), 445 (460). On the boundaries of the exportability of German notions of security with regard to machines, see ECJ, Judgement of 28.1.1986, Case 188/84 *Wood processing machines*, [1986] ECR 419 (at para. 15–22).

113 "The idea underlying the new approach is that it is desirable to limit direct involvement by the public administrations to that which is absolutely necessary to ensure compliance with the essential requirements […].This principle is fully consistent with the fact that the authorities are still required to be responsible for surveillance of the market and of the use of the products." *European Commission*, Global Approach, OJ 1989, COM (89) 209 final, OJ No. C 267, p. 3 (23).

114 See *Majone*, Mutual Trust (fn. 108), 19.

establishment of Community-wide administrative powers cannot simply leave it at a simple recognition model.[115] Trust-creating mechanisms must instead guarantee that the existing decision-making structures promote the common good. Thus, compliance with the structural requirements must be *institutionally guaranteed* and externally checkable.[116] A first step includes trust-promoting techniques such as accompaniment rights for officials from other Member States of the EC during inspections. These should contribute to generating the necessary trust in the controls conducted by other Member States in order to facilitate the mutual recognition of decisions.[117] However, it cannot be left at this. Actors must also commit to drawing up concepts for surveillance activities, carrying out measures to promote transparency, as well as setting up control measures[118], which focus on the implementation of the structural requirements, i.e. neutrality requirements, procedural rules for information quality and role competence. A more advanced concept for trust-promoting measures relies on the establishment of secondary structures. These institutionalize mistrust, so that trust can be drawn from their performance. Such secondary structures do not determine the decisions and actions in terms of content, rather guarantee the adherence to the organizational and procedural rules.[119] By these means they guarantee compliance with the structural prerequisites for legitimacy.

3.3. THE CONCEPT OF LEGITIMACY APPLIED TO THE NOTIFIED BODIES

With the system of the Notified Bodies, the EC has selected a solution which operates without Member State administrations and thus establishes a genuinely European administrative structure. This stands to reason because neither a cooperative administrative solution nor a decentralized administrative model that builds on Member State administrations are suitable alternatives: For product authorizations as a mass business, the efforts dedicated to such a cooperative administrative solution would be too great. In any case, it is

115 According to the approach of *v. Danwitz*, Verwaltungsrechtliches System (fn. 76), 407 et seq., 484 et seq.

116 See also the accreditation of paying agencies within the framework of the clearance of accounts of the European Agricultural Guarantee Fund (EAGF) and of the European Agricultural Fund for Rural Development (EAFRD) according to Regulation 885/2006/EC (laying down detailed regulations for Regulation 1290/2005/EC) which is similar to the system of accreditation and certification presented here.

117 See *Schlag*, Verwaltungsbefugnisse (fn. 78), 14.

118 For these structural requirements as elements of European environmental law, see *Schmidt-Aßmann/Ladenburger*, Umweltverfahrensrecht, EUDUR I (fn. 12), §18 margin number 3 in fn. 23, margin number 4 et seq., 20 and 28. For more on transparency mechanisms, see *Hatje*, Gemeinschaftsrechtliche Steuerung (fn. 76), 120 et seq.

119 See *Shapiro*, American Journal of Sociology 93 (1987), 623 (636 et seq.).

uncertain whether the individual Member States have sufficiently developed administrative capacities. From the perspective of the EC, the intervention of private, profit-oriented units has the effect of a detachment from national interests and thus de-politicization, in particular because procedures and organizations of these bodies are framed by European norms. Operational requirements for private bodies with secondary structures for their surveillance can be enforced more easily, because they do not have to touch existing Member State administrative structures.[120] The establishment of such a new administrative structure is full of preconditions, though. Currently, substantial shortcomings can still be observed, which will be elaborated on in the following.

4. IMPLEMENTATION AND FURTHER DEVELOPMENT OF THE NEW APPROACH AND THE GLOBAL APPROACH

4.1. GUIDELINES FOR THE NOTIFIED BODIES AND THEIR IMPLEMENTATION

The Global Approach establishes a new administrative structure to administer market access. The basis of this structure is the Notified Bodies, which are, as a rule, private agencies, and in any case need not be Member State or European administrative agencies.[121] For this reason the Notified Bodies do not inherently possess the qualities commonly associated with official administrations, i.e. neutrality, expertise, and the capacity to balance interests. As a decentralized administrative structure, the ensemble of Notified Bodies also requires a mechanism, which guarantees the uniform interpretation and application of the standards they work with. Therefore, Community law and the regulations of the Member States must first formulate and enforce the requirements for the Notified Bodies.

Guidelines in terms of content have in part already been formulated: the basis is the general requirements for the bodies to be notified, which the Global Approach and the Council Decision 93/465/EEC provide for.[122] However, only

---

120 For the so far low intensity of the impact of Community law on Member State administrative organizations see *Hatje*, Gemeinschaftsrechtliche Steuerung (fn. 76), 113, and *Kahl*, DV 29 (1996), 341 et seq., who emphasizes the indirect means of influence. By contrast, the assessment by *v. Danwitz*, Verwaltungsrechtliches System (fn. 76), 194 et seq., in particular 201.

121 The notification of public authorities is not ruled out, but both the exclusive as well as competitive notification can lead to legal problems, see *Röhl*, Akkreditierung (fn. 8), 68 et seq. Another factor is the requirement to sufficiently separate Notified Bodies from the market surveillance authorities, *European Commission*, Guide ('blue'), (fn. 23), 44.

122 Above fn. 27.

the criteria for the designation of bodies stipulated by the sectoral directives are ultimately binding. As material requirements for designation, the directives all list similar competence criteria[123], which indeed differ upon more detailed analysis[124], without there always being an evident reason.

The decisive problem is however not the lacking or different substantial criteria for the designation, rather the fact that procedures and organizations for the selection, designation and continual surveillance of Notified Bodies, which are at the discretion of the Member States, are only insufficiently established.[125] This is motivated by a conscious political decision to place emphasis on the principle of mutual recognition and thus leave the designation and notification of the bodies up to national authorities to the greatest possible extent, i.e. also with regard to organization and procedure.[126]

4.1.1. Requirements for the designation

After all, the institute of accreditation plays a certain role in this context. Accreditation is defined as a "third-party attestation related to a conformity assessment body conveying formal demonstration of its competence to carry out specific conformity assessment tasks".[127] The assessment whether certain bodies have the sufficient expertise and independence for conformity assessment procedures takes place here on the basis of accreditation standards, which are drawn up at the European and international level by means of standardization committees.[128] Such an accreditation is carried out by an accreditation body. In

---

123 Summary in *European Commission*, Guide ('blue'), (fn. 23), 40.

124 *Ensthaler u.a.*, Akkreditierung von Prüf- und Zertifizierungsstellen (KAN-Bericht 30), 2003, 15, 56 et seq., 66 passim; Communication from the *European Commission*, Enhancing the Implementation of the New Approach Directives, COM(2003) 240 final version p. 10 (under 2.2.3).

125 *Ensthaler u.a.*, Akkreditierung (fn. 124), 19, 66, 70 passim.; as a problem in *Scheel*, Privater Sachverstand (fn. 9), 168 et seq.; for the Dutch situation *G. Evers* (fn. 71), TFLR 2003, 342 (356 et seq.).

126 Communication COM(2003) 240 final version (fn. 124), 9 (under 2.2.3).

127 Section 5.6. DIN EN ISO/IEC 17000 Conformity assessment – Vocabulary and general principles.

128 Among the most significant standards are ISO/IEC 17000:2004 Conformity assessment – Vocabulary and general principles; ISO/IEC 17011:2004 Conformity assessment – General requirements for accreditation bodies accrediting conformity assessment bodies; this standard replaces the previous European standards DIN EN 45003:1995 Accreditation systems for calibration and inspection laboratories and DIN EN 45010:1998 General Requirements for the assessment and accreditation of certification bodies; ISO/IEC 17020:1998 General criteria for the operation of various types of bodies performing inspection; ISO/IEC 17024:2003 Conformity assessment – General requirements for bodies operating certification of persons; ISO/IEC 17025:1999 General requirements for the competence of testing and calibration laboratories; DIN EN 45011: General requirements for bodies operating product certification systems (identical to ISO Guide 65:1996, General requirements for bodies operating product certification systems; standard under review); ISO/IEC 17021 Conformity assessment – Requirements for bodies providing auditing and

Europe these bodies typically are associated with the state, albeit in very different forms. The situation is most complex in Germany, where up to now a large number of originally sectorally separated accreditation bodies are active under the auspices of the Deutscher Akkreditierungsrat – DAR *(German Accreditation Council).*[129]

According to the Modules Decision[130] an accreditation based on the series EN 45000 substantiates a presumption of conformity with the requirements of the directives for the Notified Bodies. Similarly, albeit inexplicitly, presumptions are contained in the directives, which also refer to this series of standards.[131] Due to this, numerous Member States – with all their differences upon detailed analysis – fall back on the results of an accreditation procedure during the designation of the bodies. Altogether though, the designation and notification procedures in the Member States demonstrate a high degree of variation.[132] The Member States still have little reliable information on the designation systems of the other Member States.[133] Hence the primary basis for mutual trust in the Notified Bodies, their organizational and procedural basis, is still underdeveloped in the individual Member States.

4.1.2. Continual surveillance

Besides the non-uniform rules on the designation and notification, another shortcoming is that guidelines for continual surveillance do not exist yet. The directives indeed stipulate that the Member States must withdraw the notification, when its requirements are no longer met.[134] However, the directives do not say how to create an informational basis for such a decision. The continual and effective monitoring of the Notified Bodies is not guaranteed.[135] The

---

certification of management systems (supersedes and replaces ISO/IEC Guide 62:1996 and will thus replace DIN EN 45012:1998 which was identical to this).

129 The complex German accreditation system is currently being restructured. The first step was to establish an Accreditation Council, which primarily is supposed to support the external representation of the German accreditation system. More on the need for reform in the German accreditation system *Röhl/Schreiber*, Konformitätsbewertung in Deutschland, 2006, 161 et seq., 184 et seq. (available online at URL: www.ub.uni-konstanz.de/kops/volltexte/2006/1933/ – 31.1.2007).

130 Above fn. 27, Annex I A.m).

131 E.g. Art. 16 Directive 93/42/EEC (Medical devices); Article 12 para. 2 Directive 97/23/EC (Pressure equipment).

132 Communication COM(2003) 240 final version (fn. 124), p. 9 (under 2.2.3); *Ensthaler u.a.*, Akkreditierung (fn. 124), 13.

133 See the statement of the *European Commission*, Communication COM(2003) 240 final version (fn. 124), 9 (under 2.2.3). See also *Röhl/Schreiber*, Konformitätsbewertung in Deutschland (fn. 129), p. 65 et seq., as well as the description of the accreditation systems of different European states in the Annex (starting p. 243).

134 E.g. Article 12 Para. 3 Directive 97/23/EC (Pressure equipment), similar Article 16 para. 3 Directive 93/42/EEC (Medical devices).

135 *Ensthaler u.a.*, Akkreditierung (fn. 124), 73.

Commission's guidelines indeed define surveillance as an obligation of the Member States[136], but there are no binding provisions for this. At least an accreditation, which is used in many cases, leads to continual monitoring requirements.[137] However, an accreditation is not yet mandatory at the moment, and it is currently not entirely transparent in which cases an accreditation procedure is conducted and thus continual controls guaranteed.

4.1.3. Actual procedure and structure: no experiences

The consequence of leaving the selection modes, the designation and monitoring to the Member States is that the system of the Notified Bodies as a whole is rather complicated. The Commission makes efforts to increase the general level of information by means of measures such as mutual visits or workshops. However, this is deficient: the Notified Bodies approve products for the entire Community territory and thus for every Member State. Therefore, it does not suffice that it is only possible to tediously gather knowledge on the different notification systems in numerous Member States. Uniform and transparently inspected notification and surveillance procedures must be established.

4.2. THE ROLE OF MARKET SURVEILLANCE WITHIN THE FRAMEWORK OF THE NEW APPROACH

The restructuring of product approval regimes by the New Approach also entails long-term changes with regard to the tasks of the Member State authorities. The instrument of preventive control has been taken away from them, they are restricted to post-market control for the prevention of hazards. In order to assume these prevention tasks, the separation of the Notified Bodies which are granting market access and the market surveillance authorities proves to be a critical point. Formerly lawmakers were able to react to typically or potentially hazardous situations with the instrument of approval, thus the official authorization of a product: The person who is in charge of a potential source of danger, i.e. he/she who has a product, is forced to produce information on this potential source of danger and then share the information with the authority. The manufacturer, who has something to gain, i.e. market access, provides the information in this situation on his/her own incentive. Thus, the approval requirement solves, in particular, the information problem of determining which products are placed on the market in what condition. Without this information,

---

136 *European Commission*, Guide ('blue'), (fn. 121), 42.

137 Communication COM(2003) 240 final version (Fn. 124), p. 12 (under 2.2.5). The ISO Accreditation Standards stipulate such requirements, see e.g. ISO/IEC 17011:2004 Conformity assessment – General requirements for accreditation bodies accrediting conformity assessment bodies, 7.11 Reassessment and Surveillance.

best product safety provisions would serve no purpose, because their enforcement would be unsuccessful.

It is this very *information problem* that market surveillance through Member State authorities is faced with, because no systematic information on the products on the market is available and it is much more difficult to watch over a product during the entire product life-span than to inspect it during a market access procedure. It is indeed the task of the Member States to take all necessary measures so that products are only marketed and operated with when they either pose no hazard[138] or comply with the demands of the directive.[139] However, the required information for fulfilling this task is lacking, when no concrete data on sources of danger exist.

The heterogeneity of the products covered by the directives proves to be an additional problem here. For example, market surveillance with regard to malfunctions which are also noticeable to the public, e.g. in toys, might also build on information from the public. The possibility to pay unannounced visits to the production facilities may provide sufficient information. However, in particular in the case of more complicated products, sources of danger cannot be determined without inspection. If these inspections may only be conducted after concrete indications for hazards, i.e. if investigatory measures without concrete reasons are not permitted, the chances for effective market surveillance are greatly diminished, in particular for products with a high potential of danger.

The abolishment of the authorization requirement and the ban on preventive controls has additionally led to a resource problem: above all, public institutions do not have sufficient financial resources to establish their own inspection capacities for hazardous products, and due to this the required knowledge on dealing with hazardous products can no longer be produced within state organizations. In Germany's federal structure an additional coordination problem comes to bear due to the fragmentation of responsibilities, which makes the European coordination measures required for effective market surveillance more difficult to reach.

4.3. FURTHER DEVELOPMENT

The described structural deficits have been recognized at the European level. Based on a Communication of the Commission[140] the Council has taken on the task of enhancing product safety law in a resolution.[141] In particular the deficient guidelines for the Notified Bodies have been described as a problem. One

138 E.g. Article 4 para. 1 Directive 2006/42 EC (Machines).

139 E.g. Article 2 Directive 93/42/EEC (Medical devices).

140 Communication COM(2003) 240 final version (fn. 124).

141 Council Resolution from 10.11.2003 on the Communication of the European Commission "Enhancing the Implementation of the New Approach Directives", OJ 2003 No. C 282, p. 3.

potential enhancement would be to draw up a horizontal legal act, which stipulates uniform structural guidelines for the system of conformity assessment for all product areas.[142] Such an enhancement could simultaneously serve to satisfy the demands for democratic foundations for the conformity assessment structure outlined under C.

5. SUMMARY

The "administration of the Community area" as an issue in European administrative law has taken on a broader perspective thanks to the new administrative structure established on the basis of the directives based on the New Approach: while it was previously assumed that exclusively the Member States and Community institutions must be treated as administrative structures, it now appears that the EC has additional enforcement structures. The analysis of their shortcomings and advantages can equally contribute to a deeper understanding of the other executive concepts. At the same time, practical experience shows that the establishment of such executive structures is a demanding task. There is a pressing need for such developments to be accompanied by attentive evaluation by scholars of administrative law.

142 Council Resolution (fn. 141), under c). Meanwhile the European Commission has pushed ahead with the preparations for horizontal legal acts, which deal in particular with quality assurance in conformity assessment and the reinforcement of market surveillance. The Commission has presented a Proposal for a Regulation on setting out the requirements for accreditation and market surveillance relating to the marketing of products from 14.2.2006, COM(2007) 37 final, and a Proposal for a Decision on a common framework for the marketing of products from 14.2.2006, COM(2007) 53 final.

X. TRANSNATIONAL WATER MANAGEMENT

Ellen HEY and Marleen VAN RIJSWICK*

1. INTRODUCTION

One of the developments in European environmental law that concerns the Water Framework Directive (WFD) and its implementation into the laws of the Member States of the European Community.[1] With most rivers in Europe covering the territory of several states, the river basin approach, which is central to the WFD, has turned water law in Europe into transnational law, at least in terms of substance if not institutionally. Implementation of the WFD raises many questions, one of which will be the focus of discussion in this contribution: the relationship between the WFD and international treaties. Questions about the relationship between the WFD and international treaties arise, because the WFD requires that Member States cooperate both among themselves and with non-member states in order to implement the Directive. International treaties are often used as a way of realising such cooperation also among Member States. We suggest that Member States use treaties for this purpose because European law does not provide them with a legal instrument that they can use to implement their mutual cooperation obligations under European law. This topic is particularly important for the Netherlands since all the river basins located on Dutch territory are transboundary.

---

* Authors are, respectively, Professor of Public International Law at the Erasmus University Rotterdam and Professor of European and Dutch Water Law at the Centre for Environmental Law and Policy/NILOS at Utrecht University. This contribution is based on a report of the Advisory Committee on Water Management Legislation, titled '*Samenwerking over de grenzen*', The Hague 2004, research on this chapter was concluded in early 2006. Both authors are members of this committee. This contribution and its conclusions, however, reflect the views of its authors and not necessarily those of the Commission or its individual members. For updates see Ellen Hey, *Multi-Dimensional Public Governance Arrangements for the Protection of the Transboundary Aquatic Environment in the European Union, International Organizations Law Review*, vol. 6 [2009], pp. 191–223.

1 Directive 2000/60/EC, OJ L 327, 22-12-2000 and Decision no. 2455/2201/EC, OJ L 331, 15-12-2001.

The underlying reasoning behind the WFD's obligations to cooperate is that in transboundary river basins cooperation is essential for attaining the environmental objectives specified in the WFD. Cooperation is of special significance for downstream areas of a river basin, since downstream Member States are to a significant degree dependent on the measures taken by upstream states for their own compliance with the environmental objectives formulated in the WFD. This is particularly relevant because the WFD holds each Member State individually responsible for fulfilling the environmental objectives and other obligations that it specifies. In other words, a Member State cannot, at least not in legal terms, hide behind the veil of ineffective cooperation if it is brought before the Court of Justice of the European Communities (European Court of Justice) for non-compliance with its obligations under the WFD.[2]

The relationship between the WFD and international treaties has a number of facets. Its characteristics depend both on the nature of the international treaty in question and the role which the WFD allocates to various forms of international cooperation. Clarity about the relationship between the WFD and international treaties is important when negotiations are taking place on the implementation of the WFD, within the context of international treaties or within treaties which the WFD seeks to implement. The principal question in this contribution thus focuses on the nature of the legal relationship between the WFD and international treaties.

In this context, particular attention will be paid not only to treaties which are directed at the management of specific rivers or river basins but also to treaties of a more general nature that relate to, for example, the protection of the marine environment, like the OSPAR Convention, and to the protection of fresh water in general, like the Helsinki Convention.

In the course of our analyses we will consider a number of subsidiary questions, since no simple answer can be given to the main question considered. These subsidiary questions are as follows.

- What are the legal consequences of the river basin approach, i.e. the central aspect of the WFD determining cooperation between Member States and cooperation between Member States and non-member states?
- What forms of international cooperation can be discerned on the basis of the WFD and what role do treaties play in that respect?
- What is the nature of the legal relationship between the WFD and the various types of treaties linked to the Directive?
- What law – international law or European law – applies to the interpretation and application of treaties drawn up in order to implement the WFD, and

2 See A. Keessen, J. van Kempen and H. van Rijswick, *Transnational River Basin Management in Europe*, Utrecht Law Review, vol. 4 [2008], Issue 3, pp. 35–56.

which court or courts – international or European – have jurisdiction to rule on disputes concerning such treaties?

This contribution will consider each of these questions consecutively and will close with concluding remarks in which we will suggest that consideration should be given to developing an instrument in European law through which Member States can shape their mutual obligations to cooperate under European law. In the context of European water law such an instrument might take the form of a European water authority.

2. THE WFD AND THE RIVER BASIN APPROACH

2.1. THE AIMS AND CONTENT OF THE WFD

The aim of the WFD is to establish an integrated and coherent water policy within the European Community by protecting and improving all waters within the Community, including surface waters, groundwater, transitional waters and coastal waters. This aim is to be attained by managing water systems in their entirety, and individual river basins in particular. Given that river basins often extend over several states, European water management and law will have to have a strong transboundary dimension with transnational cooperation playing an important role. Since the approach chosen is based on river basins, including the protection of surface waters as well as groundwater, the protection of the soil and ground also fall within the scope of the Directive.

A second important feature of the WFD is that it is strongly purpose oriented, in the sense that achieving the environmental objectives set out in Article 4 of the Directive takes priority. The ultimate environmental objective is to achieve a 'good status' for all European waters by 2015. The legally vague concept of 'good status' is defined further in the Annexes to the Directive. A distinction is made between the good status of groundwater and surface waters. Good status consists of a chemical component, i.e. the good chemical status of respectively groundwater and surface waters, and an ecological component that only applies to surface waters. Protected areas are listed separately in the environmental objectives. Protected areas are not areas, which are designated on the basis of the WFD, but they must be designated according to other Community regulations such as, for example the Habitat Directive.[3] The WFD requires that these areas be listed in a register and stipulates that the most stringent protection regime is applicable to them.

The legal standing of this 'good status' is that of an environmental quality standard. The elaboration of the good status must be laid down as quality

[3] OJ 1992 L206/7.

standards in statutory provisions. These quality standards are not new in water law: many quality standards have already been determined on the basis of older directives, both for waters with a particular function (drinking water, bathing water, fishing waters and shellfish waters[4]) and for specific substances.[5] It may be deduced from case law of the European Court of Justice that quality standards must be regarded as an *obligation of result* with which Member States have to comply under all circumstances, and, if this is not attainable by means of legal measures such as permits, then additional (actual) measures must be taken.[6] In a judgement by the European Court of Justice in which it ruled against Luxembourg because it had not complied with the obligations of the WFD, the Court established, on the one hand, that Member States are free in choosing the type of instruments that they adopt to implement the Directive – integrated water laws not being required – but the Court determined, on the other hand, that the obligations in Article 7(2) and the environmental objectives of Article 4 of the Directive must be viewed as obligations of result.[7] In view of the fact that environmental quality standards have been in existence in European water law and European law in general for a longer period of time, it is astonishing that it is this aspect of the WFD, in particular, which has caused so much discussions when implementing these obligations in the national laws of the Member States.[8]

The chemical quality standards, as mentioned, have been part of European water law for awhile. The WFD, however, refers only to standards for priority substances, and a Directive on such substances should have been ready by the end of 2006. Work on this Directive, however, is still ongoing. Some of the environmental quality standards are new; to some extent they already exist, for example in the form of the former grey-list of substances (List II) in Directive 76/464/EEC. They are new in so far as they refer to ecological standards. The very fact that the protection level may in no case be lower than that under existing regulations implies that all existing environmental quality standards continue to be applicable under the WFD.

---

4 Based on the Council Directive of 16 June 1975 concerning the required quality of surface water intended for the production of drinking water in the Member States, OJ 1975 L194/34, amended by Directive 79/869; Council Directive of 8 December 1975 concerning the quality of bathing water, OJ 1976 L31/1, Council Directive of 18 July 1978 concerning the quality of fresh water that requires protection or improvement in order to make it suitable so that fish can live in it, OJ 1978 L222 and Council Directive of 30 October 1979 concerning the required quality of shellfish water, OF 1979 L281/47.

5 Based on Directive 76/464/EEC.

6 ECJ 18 June 2002, C-60/01; ECJ 8 March 2001, Case C-266/99; ECJ 14 July 1993, Case C-56/90; ECJ 12 February 1998, Case C-92/96; ECJ 25 November 1992, Case C-337/89; ECJ 14 November 2002, Case C-316/00. With regard to water directives, the case law often concerns directives that also have the protection of public health as an objective.

7 ECJ 30 November 2006, Case C-32/05, Commission v Luxembourg, consideration 75.

8 See A.M. Keessen, J.J.H. van Kempen, M. van Rijswick, J. Robbe and Ch.W. Backes, *European River Basin Districts: Are they all swimming in the same Implementation Pool?*, Journal of Environmental Law, Advanced Access published March 11, 2010.

The standard of a 'good status' for all waters in 2015 applies to those waters which Member States have not designated as artificial or heavily modified. A slightly less stringent protection regime is imposed for the latter waters; they have to comply with a good chemical status, but need have no more than a 'good ecological potential' as far as their ecological status is concerned. The WFD also contains a number of possibilities for setting less stringent objectives or for postponing the deadline by which the objectives have to be achieved, albeit under strict conditions.

The *instruments* with which the environmental objectives must be realised are integrated river basin management plans (preferably for the entire river basin) on the one hand and programmes of measures setting out the steps which Member States intend to take to achieve these aims, on the other. These measures should also include at least those that need to be taken on the basis of a number of existing directives.[9] Here again there will have to be intensive transnational cooperation because of the existence of transboundary river basins.

The WFD also contains the obligation to recover the costs of 'water services' in accordance with the principle of the polluter pays, and it also devotes a great deal of attention to *public participation*.

While source-oriented policies also figure in the WFD (Article 10), its focus, as set out above, is on effected-oriented policies, environmental standards in particular. It is this latter element which will be used to determine whether the requirements of the WFD have been met. The crucial question in this context is whether a Member State for its waters has met the 'good status', specified in the WFD.

2.2. THE RIVER BASIN APPROACH

Member States are obliged to identify individual river basins lying within their national territory and designate river basin districts in order to realise the objectives of the Directive (Article 3(1)). A river basin district is described as 'the area of land and sea, made up of one or more neighbouring river basins with their associated groundwater and coastal waters…' (Article 2(15)). In this context, coastal waters are the 'surface waters on the landward side of a line, every point of which is at a distance of one nautical mile on the seaward side from the nearest point of the baseline from which the breadth of the territorial waters is measured, extending where appropriate up to the outer limit of transitional waters' (Article 2(7)). Transitional water is 'a body of surface water in the vicinity of a river

9 Article 10 WFD and part A of Annex VI; it concerns in any case the measures in the Bathing Water Directive, the Wild Birds Directive, the Drinking Water Directive (80/778), the Seveso Directive, the EIA Directive, the Sewage Sludge Directive, the Urban Waste Water Directive, the Plant Protection Products Directive, the Nitrate Directive, the Habitats Directive and the IPPC Directive.

mouth, which is partly saline in character as a result of its proximity to coastal waters, but which is substantially influenced by freshwater flows' (Article 2(6)).

River basin districts therefore consist of an entirety of associated waters, including surface waters, groundwater and coastal waters, and can extend up to a kilometre from the baseline into the marine area or to where the marine waters are substantially influenced by freshwater flows. Smaller river basins may be combined into one larger river basin district. Groundwater that does not entirely follow a particular river basin will be assigned to the closest or most appropriate river basin district, and coastal waters will also be allocated to the closest or the most appropriate river basin district or districts (Article 3(1)).

For each river basin district, Member States are responsible for making 'appropriate administrative arrangements, including the identification of the proper competent authorities', which are responsible for implementing the WFD (Article 3(2)). Member States may identify existing organisations as competent authorities (Article 3(6)). Such authorities had to be identified by 22 December 2003 and the relevant information communicated to the Commission by 22 June 2004. Member States are to draw up a river basin management plan for each river basin district (Article 13(1)). River basin management plans should be published by 2009 and will be reviewed and updated no later than 2015; six-yearly reviews are required after this date (Article 13(6) and (7)).

The river basin approach also applies to transboundary river basins and it is the origin of the obligations to cooperate which the WFD imposes on the Member State. This is particularly important for the Netherlands since the four river basins located on Dutch territory – the Meuse, Rhine, Schelde and Ems – extend beyond the borders of the Netherlands.

3. TYPES OF INTERNATIONAL COOPERATION IN THE WFD AND THE ROLE OF INTERNATIONAL TREATIES

3.1. INTRODUCTION

There are several types of references to international cooperation and also to international treaties in the WFD. The first distinction to be made is between the international treaties which the WFD aims to implement (Article 1 and preambule) and treaties that seek to implement the obligations to cooperate contained in the WFD (Article 3). In the latter case, a second distinction needs to be made, that of cooperation between Member States (Article 3(3) and (4)) and cooperation between one or more Member States and non-member states (Article 3(5)). These two obligations ensue from the river basin approach. This section outlines the roles played by international cooperation and treaties in the implementation of the WFD.

3.2. TREATIES WHICH THE WFD AIMS TO IMPLEMENT

One of the aims of the WFD is to achieve 'the objectives of relevant international agreements, including those which aim to prevent and eliminate pollution of the marine environment by Community action' regarding priority hazardous substances (Article 1 in conjunction with Article 16(3)). The aim of this action is to 'ultimately achieve concentrations in the marine environment which are near background values for naturally occurring substances and close to zero for man-made synthetic substances' (Article 1). Relevant international agreements include those treaties referred to in the preamble to the WFD.

The WFD's preamble refers to international treaties which contain obligations to protect the marine environment and to which the Community and a number of Member States are party: specific mention is made of the Convention for the Protection of the Marine Environment of the Baltic Sea Area,[10] the Convention for the Protection of the Marine Environment of the North-East Atlantic (OSPAR Convention)[11] and the Convention for the Protection of the Mediterranean Sea from Pollution (Barcelona Convention)[12] and its Protocol for the Protection of the Mediterranean Sea from Pollution from Land-Based Sources (Athens Protocol).[13] The WFD aims to 'assist' the Community and the Member States in fulfilling their obligations arising from these treaties.

The OSPAR Convention is particularly important for the Netherlands since it covers the protection of the marine environment in the north-eastern part of the Atlantic Ocean, including the North Sea. One of its aims is to reduce and eliminate pollution of the marine environment from land-based sources. As a result, parties to the OSPAR Convention have adopted decisions and recommendations regarding the discharge of polluting substances into surface waters and on priority substances. The OSPAR Convention thus links up with the source oriented aspects of the WSD.

In addition, the preamble of the WFD refers to 'Community obligations within the scope of water protection and management, and more precisely the Convention of the United Nations Economic Commission for Europe on the Protection and Use of Transboundary Watercourses and International Lakes (Helsinki Convention),[14] and later agreements on the application of this

[10] 9 April 1992, OJ L 73, 16–3–1994, p. 20.
[11] 22 September 1992, OJ L 104, 3–4–1998, p. 2.
[12] 16 April 1976, OJ L 240, 19–9–1977, p. 3.
[13] 17 May 1980, OJ L 76, 12–3–1983, p. 3.
[14] 7 March 1992, OJ L 186, 5–8–1992, p. 42.

convention.' The WFD states that it 'will contribute to the implementation of Community obligations' as they arise from such treaties (section 35, preamble).

Both the Community and Member States, including the Netherlands, have become parties to the Helsinki Convention. The Helsinki Convention is a so-called framework convention which sets out the contours for international cooperation in the field of water management and is further elaborated on by way of protocols. The Protocol on Water and Health is an example of one such protocol: parties undertake to take steps to improve water quality with the intention of protecting public health and the environment. This protocol has not been ratified by the Community and has been ratified by some Member States, but not by the Netherlands. The protocol entered into force in August 2005.[15]

3.3. COOPERATION OBLIGATIONS IN THE WFD

Article 3 of the WFD makes no reference to specific international treaties, but formulates two different obligations to cooperate.[16] Firstly, the obligation of Member States to cooperate in the management of river basins located within the territory of more than one Member State (Article 3(3) and (4)). Secondly, the obligation of one or more Member States to endeavour to cooperate with non-member states in the management of river basins extending beyond the boundaries of the Community (Article 3(5)).

Article 3(3) establishes that 'Member States shall ensure that a river basin covering the territory of more than one Member State is assigned to an international river basin district'. Each Member State also has the obligation to ensure 'appropriate administrative arrangements, including the identification of the appropriate competent authority, for the application of the rules of this Directive within the portion of any international river basin district lying within its territory' (Article 3(3)). Member States are also obliged to ensure that implementation of the measures to be taken under the WFD is coordinated for the whole of the river basin district (Article 3(4)), and may, for this purpose, 'use existing structures stemming from international agreements' (Article 3(4)).

Examples of international river treaties to which The Netherlands and other Member States are parties and which serve to implement Article 3(3) and (4) are the Meuse Convention,[17] the Convention on the Protection of the Schelde

15 See website of the UN Economic Commission for Europe: www.unece.org/env/water.

16 See also H.F.M.W. van Rijswick, J.J.H. van Kempen and H.K. Gilissen, *The need for international and regional transboundary cooperation in European river basin management as a result of new approaches in EC water law*, ERA Forum (2010) 11, pp. 129–157.

17 The Meus Convention which was adopted on 3 December 2002 in Ghent (Treaty Series. 2003, 75) has not yet come into effect, so the Convention for the Protection of the Meus of 26 April 1994 is still in effect (Treaty Series 1994, 149). This convention will be replaced by the 2002 Meus Convention when it enters into force.

(Schelde Convention),[18] and the Convention concerning the Protection of the Rhine (Rhine Convention).[19] Bilateral harmonisation with Flanders takes place within the framework of the Netherlands-Flemish Integral Water Consultation (NVIWO) and four transboundary river basin committees set up in 1994. Bilateral cooperation with the Walloon region of Belgium takes place within the Netherlands-Walloon water consultation. With Germany there is bilateral agreement within the framework of the German-Dutch Transboundary Water Commission (PGC)[20] and the Steering Group and Coordination Group for the Ems. In addition, the Trilateral Wadden Sea Forum between Denmark, Germany and the Netherlands also is relevant to the implementation of the WFD.[21]

Article 3(5) deals with the cooperation between Member States and non-member states in relation to river basins extending outside the Community. In this case, it is laid down that Member State or States involved must aim for suitable coordination with the non-member states concerned 'with the aim of achieving the objectives of this Directive throughout the river basin district', imposing on Member States the obligation to ensure that the provisions of this Directive are applied within their territories.

The Rhine Convention is an example of an international river treaty to which the Netherlands is a party and which partly serves to implement Article 3(5) WFD. Under this treaty, Belgium, Germany, Luxembourg and the Netherlands (Member States) work together with Switzerland (non-member state). The European Community also is a party to the Rhine Convention.

River basin management plans should preferably also be drawn up for transboundary river basins. For river basins encompassing more than one Member State, the Member States involved need to draw up coordinated programmes of measures with the aim of achieving a single river basin management plan. If this aim cannot be achieved, individual Member States must as a minimum develop separate plans for that part of the river basin district falling within their territory (Article 13(2)). For river basin districts extending beyond the boundaries of the Community, Member States are to endeavour to develop one single river basin management plan. If this is not possible, then they must produce a plan that at least covers the part of the river basin district lying within their territory (Article 13(3)).

---

18 Convention for the Protection of the Scheldt of 26 April 1994 (Treaty Series 1994, 150).

19 Convention for the Protection of the Rhine of 12 April 1999 (Treaty Series 1999, 139).

20 The German-Dutch Transboundary Water Commission (PGC) was established under Article 64 of the Convention between the Kingdom of the Netherlands and the Federal Republic of Germany with regard to the joint border, the transboundary waters, landownership close to the border, transboundary traffic by land and inland waterways and other topics related to the border, 1960 (Treaty Series 1960, 68).

21 See also: J. Verschuuren, Towards a trilateral Convention on the Waddensea, The relations between International Treaties and EC-Directives and the Westerschelde case, in: Lambers et al, Trilateral or European protection of the Waddensea?, The Hague, 2003.

The obligations to cooperate which are imposed on the Member States under Article 3 can be summarised as follows:

- *For transboundary river basins or the part of the transboundary river basin located within the Community:* the obligation to reach coordinated implementation on the basis of the environmental objectives set out in the WFD and the required measures (obligation of result), preferably in a river basin management plan (obligation of conduct).
- *For those river basins extending beyond the Community:* the obligation to endeavour to achieve appropriate cooperation with non-member states in order to fulfil the objectives of the Directive for the entire river basin (obligation of conduct), preferably in a river basin management plan (obligation of conduct).

3.4. FURTHER DIFFERENTIATION

The international treaties discussed above can be divided into three types of agreements:

- Treaties, the so called *inter se* agreements, which are concluded by a restricted number of Member States amongst themselves for the implementation of Article 3(3) and (4).
- Treaties, the so called *inter se cum tertis* agreements, which are concluded by one or more Member States with a non-member state for the implementation of Article 3(5). Note that the term *inter se cum tertis* is not completely accurate when only one Member State is involved.[22]
- Treaties concluded by all or a number of Member States and non-member states and to which the Community is a party – the so-called mixed agreements.

These mixed agreements include those treaties referred to in the preamble and Article 1 of the WFD. Treaties that implement Article 3(5), like the Rhine Convention, however, also qualify as mixed agreements, since the Community and several Member States are parties to them.

3.5. THE WFD AND TREATIES

The treaties referred to in Article 1 and the preamble to the WFD serve as part of the international legal framework within which the Member States and the

22 For more information, see de Witte 2000 and 2002.

Community are to shape their water policy. They contain the minimum obligations which the water policy and law of the Member States and the Community must fulfil under international law. Such treaties do not restrict the competence of the Member States or the Community to adopt more stringent environmental standards for activities in their territories or within their jurisdiction.

For the sake of completeness, it should be remarked here that the latter does not apply to ships flying a foreign flag which are present in the territorial sea, including the coastal waters beyond the baseline to which the WFD applies. The coastal state, and also the Community, in this case may not impose standards as to design, construction, crew and equipment of the ship which are more stringent than the applicable international norms.[23]

In addition, the WFD requires Member States to work together on transboundary river basins within the boundaries of the Community, and it also obliges the Member States to seek cooperation with non-member states for river basins extending beyond the boundaries of the Community. As already mentioned above, the first aspect involves an obligation of result so that there is coordinated implementation of environmental objectives and programmes of measures for each river basin district. Linked to this is an obligation of conduct to devise a single river basin management plan. It aims to attain coordinated implementation of the objectives of the Directive, preferably in a single river basin management plan.

When the question of whether a Member State has fulfilled its obligations under Article 3(3), (4) and (5) of the WFD arises, these obligations as elaborated in the river basin approach contained in the Directive will be the primary touchstone. It should be noted that Article 3 of the WFD does not impose an obligation on Member States to enter into international treaties with regard to river basins which are partially outside their territories, but it goes without saying that such treaties and the activities undertaken under their auspices play a part when an assessment is made as to whether a Member State has fulfilled its cooperation obligations under Article 3 of the WFD. The fact that a treaty has or has not been entered into in itself, however, does not determine the answer to the question whether a Member State has fulfilled its cooperation obligations under Article 3. The answer to this question will be determined on the basis of the substantive results of any cooperation engaged in (for the obligations of result) and on the basis of the efforts made to achieve cooperation (for the obligations of conduct). In the case of the Netherlands, for example, it is to be expected that the results of the various forms of international cooperation mentioned above,

23 Article 21(3) UN Convention on the Law of the Sea. For further information, see Advisory Committee for Water Management Legislation, *Waarborgen voor een samenhangend beleid voor de Noordzee*, April 2003.

including treaties, will determine whether the Netherlands has fulfilled its obligations under Article 3(3), (4) and (5) of the WFD.

4. THE VARIED NATURE OF THE RELATIONSHIP BETWEEN THE WFD AND TREATIES

4.1. INTRODUCTION

The question concerning the relationship between the WFD and international treaties arises for a number of related reasons. Firstly, European law does not offer Member States a legal instrument on the basis of which they can shape cooperation for purposes of implementing European law. This is one of the reasons why Member States have turned to international law, and treaties in particular. Secondly, some treaties play several roles in relation to the WFD, and this can lead to a lack of clarity during negotiations. Thirdly, the division of competences between the Member States and the Community is often unclear, including the competence of Member States to take more stringent environmental measures. These factors result in a complex situation in which many of the water related international treaties contain rules and standards that give rise to obligations under both European and international law. The three complicating factors will be addressed in this section.

4.2. COOPERATION BY WAY OF TREATY

Although the WFD obliges the Member States to cooperate with regard to the management of river basins encompassing the territory of several Member States, European law has no general legal instrument to regulate this kind of cooperation. As already mentioned in the introduction, a Member State is not only responsible for fulfilling the cooperation obligations, but also for fulfilling the underlying key obligations of the Directive, i.e. achieving a good status for its waters as determined by the environmental objectives elaborated in the WFD. These underlying environmental objectives, in fact, often only can be achieved through transnational cooperation, which includes cooperating in the development of international river basin management plans and programmes of measures for the entire river basin. Member States have turned to an international legal instrument – the treaty – as a means of implementing these obligations under Article 3(3) and (4).

This has resulted in the remarkable situation that, on the one hand, European law governs the WFD when it comes to, for example, its adoption and implementation whereas, on the other, instruments intended to implement the

WFD, when it comes to their adoption and implementation, are subject to a combination of international law and national law of the individual Member States. This situation seems to suggest, quod non, that Member States enjoy a greater freedom of action, associated with international law, with regard to these implementing instruments than they do with respect to the WFD itself. The origin of this confusing situation is related to the characteristics of the European legal system on the one hand and the characteristics of the international legal system on the other. Firstly, European law comes into existence through decision-making procedures which do not require the consent of each individual Member State. Secondly, due to the primacy of European law, national legislation which conflicts with European law can and must be declared inoperative by the European courts, including national courts as well as the European Court of Justice and the Court of First Instance. This contrasts with international law which, in principle, only legally binds a state if that state has consented to the rule or treaty in question. Moreover, national courts often are not entitled to directly apply international law. In the Netherlands for example, Dutch courts may only declare Dutch laws inoperative in those cases where the law in question conflicts with a self-executing provision of an international treaty or other written source of international law (art. 94 Dutch Constitution [*Grondwet*]).[24]

The freedom which international law offers states, however, is not compatible with the European legal system and thus not available to Member States when they are implementing the WFD or other European law instruments. This situation entails that if Member States conclude *inter se* agreements to shape their mutual cooperation, European law prevails over those agreements, which raises the question to what extent international law still applies to these type of treaties. The WFD gingerly avoids this problem since it does not require Member States to conclude international treaties for purposes of implementing the cooperation obligations in of Article 3(3) and (4). Instead, it focuses on the obligation of result to attain specified environmental quality objectives, by devising coordinated programmes of measures, and the obligation of conduct to seek develop river basin management plans for the whole of the river basin. Member States may choose to attain these ends by a variety of means, including the conclusion of international treaties.

The above implies that, although a treaty could be one of the most immediately apparent instruments to implement these obligations, the Member States will not able to avail themselves of the freedom which the treaty instrument might offer in the implementation of the cooperation obligations under Article

24 The role of national courts in applying international law depends on the national legal order of states and differs from Member State to Member State of the European Union. In some states, like the United Kingdom, for instance, national courts may not review national legislation against treaties, even if it concerns a self-executing treaty provision. In such cases, international law must first be transposed into national legislation before the international law can have effect in the national legal order.

3(3) and (4) of the WFD: at least, insofar as exercising this freedom would conflict with the obligations of the Member States pursuant to the WFD. This means that the Member States are at all times required to implement the obligations as laid down in the WFD, even when they have opted for a treaty as a means of meeting those obligations.

A similar reasoning is applicable, by analogy, to treaties concluded for the implementation of Article 3(5) of the WFD. In this case, the WFD takes as its point of departure the obligation of conduct imposed on the Member States to achieve implementation of the WFD for the entire river basin, preferably through a river basin management plan. In this case a treaty is the instrument *par excellence* to give legal substance to the international cooperation required, international law being applicable to the relationship between non-member states on the one hand and Member States and the Community on the other hand. Certainly, other instruments are available – consider, for instance, Ministerial Declarations – but these types of instruments generally are not legally binding. Also in this case, however, the WFD places the obligation of conduct, instead of the type of instrument used to achieve it, centre stage.

4.3. THE MULTIPLE ROLES OF SOME TREATIES

In practice, the relationship between the WFD and the international treaties mentioned above is not unequivocal. The WFD serves, on the one hand, to implement international obligations arising out of treaties by which the Member States and the Community are bound, while – on the other – Member States may use existing treaties to comply with their obligations arising out of the WFD. The particular problem which then crops up is the fact that in some cases the very same treaty fulfils these two roles, a problem that concerns mixed treaties, in particular. Treaties like the OSPAR Convention provide a relevant example: it regulates pollution of the marine environment from land-based sources, among other things, and serves as a framework within which rules concerning priority substances can be determined. Such rules, which also apply to industries which discharge upstream in rivers, are implemented by the Member States and the Community through the framework of the WFD, including the cooperation between the Member States on the basis of Article 3. The Member States and the Community, however, also can use the OSPAR Convention to support implementation of the WFD in cooperation with non-member states by agreeing on rules or standards on, for example, discharges, with these non-member states. Like the OSPAR Convention, the Helsinki Convention can also fulfil this double role.

Mixed treaties which relate to a specific river, like the Rhine Convention, can also be affected by this problem. A treaty like the Rhine Convention, for example, also can fulfil several roles in relation to the WFD. Firstly, the Member States may use such a treaty to implement their mutual cooperation obligation under

Article 3(3) and (4) of the WFD. Secondly, the Member States can use this type of treaty to implement the cooperation obligation with non-member states defined in Article 3(5) of the WFD, in which the Community and the Member States are both involved because of their joint competences. Thirdly, agreements on ecological objectives or priority substances, for example, can be made with non-member states within the framework of a treaty like the Rhine Convention. The Community and the Member States are bound to such agreements by the operation of international law and the WFD forms the framework, in conjunction with the national legislation of the Member States, within which the Community and the Member States implement such agreements.

The multifaceted relationship between treaties and the WFD may result in confusion as to what is being negotiated when such treaties are being developed. Moreover, it raises questions as to the role that international law plays in *inter se* agreements. While the WFD seeks to avoid these questions by focusing on obligations of result and conduct, the lack of a European legal instrument that Member States can use to implement their mutual obligations to cooperate remains problematic. Developing such an instrument in European law would go some way towards addressing the confusing relationship between treaties and the WFD and would structure the development of transnational law within the European Union.

4.4. SHARED COMPETENCE AND MORE STRINGENT MEASURES

Another complicating factor related to the fact that the Member States and the Community share competences in the field of water policy is that Article 176 EC gives the Member States the competence to adopt and enforce more stringent environmental protection measures, also within the framework of international treaties. This competence may be exercised subject to a number of conditions. It only concerns environmental measures based on Article 175 EC (and not, for instance, Articles 95, 133 or 37 EC), because a so-called minimum harmonisation is involved. In addition, these more stringent measures may not conflict with other – more general – provisions of European law, such as the free movement of goods and the rules on competition. A number of elements play a role in this context.

Firstly, the European Commission prefers to start negotiations with non-member states on mixed agreements or on measures to be agreed within the framework of such an agreement, only after measures on the topic of negotiation have been agreed within the Community. This approach is prevalent especially where measures are at stake, which in their application, are not restricted to a certain area, such as measures regarding priority substances, and possibly also measures for controlling groundwater pollution.[25] Such Community measures then apply uniformly across the whole of the Community. The adoption of more stringent measures within a mixed agreement conflicts with the desire of the Commission to maintain uniformity within the Community, irrespective of the competence allocates to Member States under Article 176 EC.

Secondly, if more stringent measures are adopted by a Member State, by the Member States amongst themselves, or by one or more Member States together with non-member states, these measures need to conform to European law, insofar as they affect the Member States. In such a case the European Commission must be informed of the measure and will test the compatibility of the measure with European law under article 176 EC as well as other provisions of the EC Treaty. The dispute between the Netherlands and the European Commission concerning a prohibition on the use of chlorinated paraffins adopted by the Netherlands pursuant to a decision adopted within the framework of the OSPAR Convention, of which the European Commission was informed of under Article 95(4) EC, is illustrative of the problems that may arise.[26] In this case the Commission maintains that it is entitled to be informed and must approve also national measures related to uses not mentioned in Directive 2002/45/EC,[27] the Netherlands disputes this view. Only the European Court of Justice can provide certainty as to the compatibility of the measure with European law, and in all such cases it is the primacy of European law within the Community that is at stake.

A third complicating factor arises when the European Court of Justices declares that a more stringent measure which has been agreed on within the context of an international treaty is in conflict with European law. In this case, the Member States violate international law if they fail to implement the measure, and they violate European law if they implement it. Where an *inter se* treaty is concerned, this problem is of a more limited nature since all the parties to such a treaty are bound by European law and they would have to either withdraw or amend the measure adopted. The situation is more complex when a mixed treaty is involved because, if the Member States (and the Community for that matter) fail to implement their obligation under the treaty, they would be violating international law with regard to the non-member states. The significance of this problem, however, should not be overestimated. Firstly, the Community is party or can be a party to these mixed treaties which have some connection to the WFD and is represented by the European Commission. It could then be surmised that the Commission will refrain from agreeing to measures which would not be in accordance with European law, since the Community itself would be bound

25 The situation is different in the case of specific ecological objectives, which are agreed on for particular areas and are therefore restricted to an area and cannot, by definition, be equally applicable for all Member States.

26 See Case C-103/04, pending before the European Court of Justice.

27 OJ 2002 L 177/21.

by these measures. Secondly, the principal of loyalty to the Community (Article 10 EC) obliges the Member States to cooperate with the Commission, even if the Community is not a party to the treaty in question.

5. APPLICABLE LAW AND COMPETENT COURTS

5.1. INTRODUCTION

As was illustrated above, a complicating factor in the relationship between the WFD and the treaties that serve to implement this directive is that these treaties involve obligations under international and under European law. *Inter se* and mixed treaties are both treaties under international law in terms of their legal structure, which implies that they are subject to international law with regard to their entry into force, their interpretation and their application. Secondly, both types of treaties are related to European law, which suggests that European law is also applicable, in so far as Member States and the Community are concerned. Moreover within the Community, European law would take precedence over international law (the principle of the primacy of European law).

5.2. THE CASE LAW OF THE EUROPEAN COURT OF JUSTICE

Established case law of the European Court of Justice illustrates that the court regards treaties that have a link with European law as part of the European legal system and it interprets and applies them accordingly. An analysis of the case law of the European Court of Justice gives rise to the following conclusions concerning the relationship between European law and international treaties.

1. European law takes precedence within the legal order of the Community. This entails that *inter se* agreements and decisions taken within the framework of such treaties should be compatible with European law.[28] In other words, the internationally applicable legal rule that treaties entered into at a later date take precedence over treaties entered into at an earlier date[29] does not apply within the relationship between European law and *inter se* agreements.

28 Case C-3/91, *Exporteur SA v/ Lor SA et Confiserie du Tech* [1992] ECR I-5529, par. 8 (For more information see de Witte 2000 and 2002).

29 Article. 30, Vienna Convention on the Law of Treaties.

2. Treaties concluded by Member States with non-member states must also be compatible with European law.[30] The only exceptions to this rule are the treaties entered into by a Member State with non-member states before the former became a member of the Community.[31]
3. Treaties to which the Community is a party, including mixed treaties, form an integral part of the legal order of the Community.[32]
4. Treaties which form part of the legal order of the Community include those treaties which relate to policy areas where the Community is competent, but to which the Community cannot become a party in view of the provisions of the treaty in question.[33]
5. A treaty to which the Community is not a party and which concerns a policy area in which the Community has not or has not yet exercised its competences is not part of the legal order of the Community.[34]
6. Decisions which have come into effect within the context of international treaties which are part of the legal order of the Community are an integral part of the legal order of the Community[35] because of the 'direct link' which they have with the treaty in question; non-legally binding decisions, such as recommendations, adopted within such a treaty will also be considered by the European Court of Justice.[36]
7. The European Court of Justice will also establish whether a provision of a treaty is directly applicable, that is self-executing. The Court applies the following criterion. A provision must be regarded as directly applicable 'when, regard being had to its wording and to the purpose and the nature of the agreement, the provision contains a clear and precise obligation which is not subject, in its implementation or effects, to the adoption of any subsequent measure.'[37] Relevant in this context is the judgement in which the European Court of Justice determined that Article 6(3) of the Athens Protocol to the

---

30 The so-called Open Skies cases: Case C-467/98, *Commission v. Denmark*, [2002] ECR I-9591; Case-468/98 *Commission v. Sweden*, [2002] ECR I-9597; C-469/98, *Commission v. Finland*, [2002] ECR I-9627; Case C-471/98, *Commission v. Belgium, [2002]* ECR I-9681; Case C-472/98, *Commission v. Luxembourg*, [2002] ECR I-9741; Case C-475/98, *Commission v. Austria, [2002]* ECR I-9797; Case C-476/98, *Commission v. Germany*, [2002] ECR I-9855; Case C-466/98, *Commission v. Great Britain and Northern Ireland* [2002] ECR I-9427 (for a discussion see Holdgaard).

31 Article 307 EC.

32 Case 181/73 *Haegeman v. Belgium*, [1974] ECR 499, par. 4–6 and Case 12/86 *Demirel v. Stadt Schwabisch Gmund*, [1987] ECR 3719, paras. 6–12 (for a discussion of recent case law, see Koutrakos).

33 Opinion 2/91, [1993] ECR I-1061 paras. 5–6.

34 Case C-379/92, *Peralta* [1994] ECR I-3453.

35 Case 30/80 *Greece v Commission* [1989] ECR 3711 and Case c 192/89 *Sevince* [1990] ECR I-3461.

36 Case C-188/91, *Shell*, [1993] ECR I-363.

37 Para. 39, Case C-213/03, 15 July 2004 in which previous case law was referred to, particularly the judgments in Demiral, para. 14 and Wählergruppe Gemeinsam, C-171/01, I-4301, para. 54.

Barcelona Convention and Article 6(1) of the revised Protocol are self-executing.[38] The relevant provisions stipulate that permits are required for the discharge of certain priority substances into the Mediterranean Sea. The Court regarded itself competent to interpret these provisions and established that the lack of implementation legislation at Community level did not release the Member States from their obligation to implement the relevant provisions of the Protocol.

5.3. THE WFD, TREATIES AND DISPUTES

If the European Court of Justice has to adjudicate a dispute concerning a treaty that is somehow linked with the WFD,[39] the Court will include the treaty and the decisions, even if not legally binding, taken on the basis of this treaty, in its considerations. Due to the primacy of European law, a situation could develop in which the European Court of Justice deems that an internationally adopted measure is in conflict with European law. That situation, as suggested above, however is unlikely to materialize with great frequency. Much more likely is the situation where the European Court of Justice will be providing a judicial means of enforcing internationally agreed rules and standards, whether legally binding under international law or not, within the European Union.

Problematic is the situation in which Member States submit their mutual disputes concerning a treaty that is related to European law to an international court or to an arbitral tribunal. The problem that arises concerns the fact that, due to the relationship between the treaty and European law, in interpreting the treaty in question the court or tribunal may have to interpret European law. If this where to be the case, the obligation imposed on Member States by virtue of Article 292 EC is at issue. This provision imposes the obligation on Member States to submit disputes concerning the interpretation and application of European law to the European courts.[40] This situation actually emerged in the dispute between Ireland and the United Kingdom in the so called *MOX Plant* case, which was submitted to an international arbitral tribunal.[41] The arbitral

38 Case C 123/03, 15 July 2004.

39 Compare with the case of *Peralta* (note 32) when the Court judged that there was insufficient connection between the Marpol Convention of 2 November 1973 (with Protocols and Annexes and Appendices (Treaty Series 1975, 147) and with the Protocol to that Convention of 17 February 1978 with Annex and Appendix (Treaty Series 1978, 188)), and the European legal order, because the Community was neither competent with regard to the pollution from shipping activities nor was it party to this convention.

40 In the Protocol of Signature agreed on under the Rhine Convention, there is the explicit stipulation that disputes which do not involve non-member states should be resolved in accordance with art. 292 EC [219 old].

41 Permanent Court of Arbitration, press release, 14 November 2003, available at www.pca-cpa.org.

tribunal suspended the case until the European Court of Justice had ruled on the case.[42] Now that the judgement of the European Court of Justice has been delivered, it must be concluded that it has exclusive jurisdiction in relation to disputes between Member States that arise from the a mixed-agreement such as United Nations Convention on the Law of the Sea, to the extent that such an agreement is part of the 'Community Legal Order'.[43]

In view of the course of events during this arbitration, it seems that there must always be a proper examination of whether European law might be at issue in a particular dispute among Member States. Whenever this might the case, such a dispute is not to be submitted to a court or tribunal other than the European courts. Article 10 EC loyalty to the Community requires this approach.

The situation is different when a dispute occurs between one or more Member States and/or the Community and a non-member state. This kind of dispute can only be submitted to an international court or an arbitral tribunal, since non-member states may not appear before the European courts, and international law applies to legal relationships between one or more non-member states and one or more Member States and/or the Community.

6. FINAL REMARKS

The multi-facetted relationships that exist between international and European legal instruments might be characterized as giving rise to a situation of multi-level governance. We however, suggest that this situation is unduly complex because European law does not provide Member States with a legal instrument that they can use to implement their mutual obligations to cooperate under European law. Member States as a result have recourse to international law, and to treaties in particular, to implement European law. Even though the European Court of Justice has managed to bring a considerable amount of clarity into the matter, this situation remains problematic because the discretion that states have in international law is not available to Member States under European law. Establishing a European law instrument for cooperation among Member States of course would only serve to clarify matters with respect to the issues now treated in inter se agreements. We suggest that it is with respect to these agreements where the role of international law within Community law is most problematic. In all other situations treaties, and mixed-agreements in particular,

---

42 These proceedings relate to proceedings of the European Commission against the United Kingdom, concerning the nuclear systems which are a feature of the MOX Plant. The discussion concerned the inadequate access allowed to Community inspectors, as a result of which inspection of certain storage facilities for nuclear waste was not possible.

43 ECJ EC Case C-459/03.

would still be required, as it is the way in which cooperative relationships between Member States and the Community, on the one hand, and non-member states, on the other hand, can be given legal significance.

The cooperation obligations imposed on Member States under Article 3(3) and (4), as those under of Article 3(5), of the WFD owe their immediate origin to the river basin approach which is the central feature of the WFD. Taking that approach one step further one might argue that the WFD should have provided for the establishment of European transnational water authorities, for example but not necessarily in the form of transnational water boards, under European law. Such a transnational instrument would have facilitated the implementation of the obligations to cooperate as contained especially in article 3(3) and (4) of the WFD, and would have prevented Member States from having recourse to international law to implement these obligations. Logically, it also would be this transnational authority which would appear before the Court of Justice when the obligations set out in the WFD (and in particular those related to the environmental quality objectives) are not met, for example because insufficient measures have been taken within a particular river basin.

We realize that the political climate in Europe might at present not be ready for such a step, with Member States preferring, when possible, to avail themselves of the discretion that international offers. However, we suggest that thinking along these lines may be required if European water law is to become a stable and sustainable system of law, a system in which the substantive and institutional aspects are in balance. International law, we add, would be an undesirable way of establishing such transnational agencies within the European Community, amongst others, due to the immunities that such institutions are likely to be entitled to under international law.

In developing transnational water law within the European Community, international treaties among Member States should ideally play a very limited, if any, role. However, given the fact that European law does not offer Member States a legal instrument which they can use to implement their obligations to cooperate, which are based on that same European law, including the WFD, Member States will continue to conclude such treaties, at least, in the near future.

BIBLIOGRAPHY

'*Pragmatische Implementatie Europese Kaderrichtlijn Water in Nederland*', Policy Document of the Secretary of State for Transport and Water for the Lower House, April 2004. Proceedings of the Lower House 2003–2004, 28808, no. 12.

Bohne, E., (ed.) *Tagungsband "Ansätze zur Kodification des Umweltrechts in der Europäschen Union: Die Wasserrahmenrichtlinie und ihre Umsetzung in nationales recht*, Schriftenreihe der Hochschule Speyer, Volume 169, Duncker & Humblot, Berlin, 2005.

De Villeneuve, C.H.V., "*Grenswaterlopen en de stroomgebiedbenadering*," A. Driesprong, M.V. van Ginkel, H.G. Heegstra and W.H.M.A. Pluimakers (red.), *Lex aquarum, Liber amicorum, Opstellen over waterstaat, waterstaatswetgeving en wetgeving opgedragen aan mr. J.H.A. Teulings*, Dutch Ministry of Transport and Water Management, 2000, pp. 73–83.

De Witte, B., "*Internationale verdragen tussen de lidstaten van de Europese Unie*," Preliminary advice Nederlandse Vereniging voor Internationaal Recht (NVIR), *Medelingen van de NVIR*, no. 123, 2002, T.M.C. Asser Press, pp. 79–131.

De Witte, B., "*Old-fashioned Flexibility: International Agreements between Member States of the European Union*," G. de Búrca and J. Scott (red.), *Constitutional Change in the European Union: From Uniformity to Flexibility*, 2000, pp. 31–58.

Dieperink, C., *Tussen zout en zalm, Lessen uit de ontwikkeling van het regime inzake de Rijnvervuiling*, dissertation, Amsterdam 1997.

Dieperink, C. and P. Glasbergen, *Het beheer van onze internationale rivieren: lessen uit de ontwikkeling van de Rijn-, Maas- en Scheldecommissies*, in: A. van Hall, T.G. Drupsteen and H.J.M. Havekes (ed.), De staat van water, Lelystad, Vermande 1999.

Grimeaud, D., *Reforming EU Water Law, Towards Sustainability*, European Environmental Law Review, March 2001.

Grimeaud, D., *The EC Water Framework Directive – An Instrument for Integrating Water Policy*, RECIEL 13 (1), 2004.

Hey, E., "*Multi-Dimensional Public Governance Arrangements for the Protection of the Transboundary Aquatic Environment in the European Union: The Changing Interplay between European and Public International Law*", 6 *International Organizations Law Review* 2009, pp. 191–223.

Hey, E., "*The European Community's Courts and International Environmental Agreements*," 7 *Review of European Community & International Environmental Law* 1998, pp. 4–10.

Holdgaard, R., "*The European Community's Implied External Competence after the Open Skies Cases*," 8 *European Foreign Affairs Review* 2003, pp. 365–394.

Journal for European Environmental & Planning Law (JEEPL3/2004), which is largely devoted to the implementation of the Water Framework Directive in various Member States.

Keessen, A., van Kempen, J. and van Rijswick, H., *Transnational River Basin Management in Europe*, 4 *Utrecht Law Review* 2008, Issue 3, pp. 35–56.

Keessen, A., van Kempen, J., van Rijswick, H., Robbe, J. and Backes, Ch., *European River Basin Districts: Are they all swimming in the same Implementation Pool? Journal of Environmental Law*, Advanced Access published March 11, 2010.

Koutrakos, P., "*The Interpretation of Mixed Agreements under the Preliminary Reference Procedure*," 7 *European Foreign Affairs Review* 2002, pp. 25–52.

Maes, F., & L. Lavrysen (eds.), *Integraal waterbeleid in Vlaanderen en Nederland*, Die Keure, Bruges, 2003.

Neuray, J., (ed.), *La directive 2000/60/CE du 23 octobre 2000 établissant un cadre pour une politique communautaire dans le domaine de léau, Droit européen, Droit interne – Droit compare*, Bruyant, Brussels, 2005.

Van Rijswick, H., van Kempen, J. and Gilissen, H., *The need for international and regional transboundary cooperation in European river basin management as a result of new approaches in EC water law*, ERA Forum (2010) 11, pp. 129-157.
Van Rijswick, H., (ed.), *The Water framework Directive, Implementation into German and Dutch Law*, CELP/NILOS, Utrecht, 2003.
Van Rijswick, H., A.A. Freriks, C.W. Backes and R.J.G.M. Widdershoven, *EG-Recht en de Praktijk van het Waterbeheer*, STOWA, 2003.
Von Keitz / Schmalholz (ed.) *Handbuch der EU-Wasserrahmenrichtlinie*, ESV, 2002.

XI. PUBLIC ACCESS TO DOCUMENTS IN THE EUROPEAN COMPOSITE ADMINISTRATION

Ton DUIJKERSLOOT

1. INTRODUCTION

Public access to documents is an interesting subject with regard to questions concerning the mixed or shared governmental structure that is characteristic for the EC legal order. Both at the European level and at the national level regulatory systems concerning disclosure of documents which are in the possession of the authorities have been developed. Whereas those national systems have a longer history, the European system has just recently been designed. The functioning of these two regulatory systems concerning access to documents in the composite EC legal order raises various questions. What is the degree of openness on both these levels? Does it make any difference whether a citizen makes a request for documents to the national (e.g. Dutch) authorities or to the EC authorities? Do national powers with regard to giving access leak away to the European level? On the other hand, how is dealt with securing the European powers with regard to giving access? How has been taken care of the protection of both European and national interests in this field?

The purpose of this study is to enquire into the problems and questions just pointed out. The central question will be how in the system of access rules developed on EC level on the hand, and the national (Dutch) system of access rules on the other hand, the interests of Member States and EU are safeguarded when Community authorities are confronted with a request for access to documents which originate from a Member State and vice versa. In section 2 the importance of access to documents in the 'state based on the rule of law' ('Rechtsstaat') will be addressed. Section 3 elaborates in general on the different rules and regulations with regard to the subject of access to documents in the EU and in the Netherlands. In section 4 we will examine the provisions in Community law that have the aim of safeguarding the interests of Community and Member States with regard to access to documents, especially those in Regulation 1049/2001. In section 5 we will analyse the case law of European courts (the Court of First Instance and the Court of Justice) relating to the provisions which serve the safeguarding of the interests of the Member States: Article 4(4) and 4(5) of Regulation 1049/2001. In section 6 we deal with the case law of Dutch courts relating to the provisions which serve the safeguarding of the interests of the Community: Article 5 of Regulation 1049/2001. Finally, in section 7 we will analyze the implications of this case law as far as the before mentioned balancing of interests is concerned.

2. THE IMPORTANCE OF ACCESS TO DOCUMENTS IN THE 'STATE BASED ON THE RULE OF LAW' ('*RECHTSSTAAT*')

It is – or should be – more or less common knowledge that in a state which is based on the rule of law ('Rechtsstaat') it is of the utmost importance that citizens are aware of what their government is up to. Government policy should be laid down in general rules and decisions which are made public before they enter into force. In totalitarian states the absence of this fundamental knowledge paves the way for arbitrariness and abuse of power.

A citizen has to play a fundamental role in this 'Rechtsstaat'. In 'Openbaarheid van bestuur', Hofman and Van Schagen describe a true citizen as the person who plays autonomously, judiciously and loyally, the double role of governing and being governed. Citizenship presupposes being engaged in the government of the state in which he lives and engagement presupposes, in its turn, knowledge of that government.[1] In short, the transparency of public administration is one of the fundamental pillars upon which the proper functioning of the 'Rechtsstaat' is based.

In 'The right to information: a fundamental right', Verhoeven indicates in more detail three reasons why openness in government can be regarded as important.[2] First, transparency in government facilitates control of the actions and inactions of public authorities. It is based on the premise that power corrupts. From an individual point of view, control requires access to information concerning one's own position *vis-à-vis* the government in order to be able to defend oneself against potential abuses. From the perspective of the citizen or the public as a whole, control is essentially about preventing abuses by those we have chosen to govern us. The Committee of Ministers of the Council of Europe also stresses this aspect with regard to the more specific subject of access to

---

1 See A. Hofman and J.A. van Schagen, Openbaarheid van bestuur, Ars Aequi cahiers, Nijmegen 2003, p. 11–12.

2 A. Verhoeven, The right to information: a fundamental right?, Lecture at EIPA (Maastricht), May 29th, 2000, www.eipa.nl/Publications/Summaries/1997_2000/WorkingPapers/Conference Proceedings/Amaryll.

documents in its Recommendation (2002) 2 on access to official documents.[3] It considers that wide access to official documents helps to maintain their integrity by avoiding the risk of corruption.

A second rationale behind openness, according to Verhoeven, is the desire to increase the rationality, deliberateness and effectiveness of the decision-making process and thus public confidence therein. In short, accountable governors, i.e. governors that can be required to explain their actions to the public, reach better and more rational decisions in a more efficient manner. On the other hand, governing 'in the sunshine' not only brings about the benefits thus mentioned, but too much stress on accountability might also lead to attitudes of legalism and risk aversion (which favours the maintenance of the *status quo*). This does not mean, however, that openness and effectiveness are opposites. Effectiveness could go very well with openness. The Committee of Ministers in its above-mentioned Recommendation explicitly states that wide access to documents fosters the efficiency and effectiveness of administrations.

The third rationale mentioned by Verhoeven links openness more explicitly with citizenship as active participation in political affairs. It considers transparency as an essential condition for the process of will-formation that is crucial in a democratic society. In its Recommendation the Council of Ministers also points in a more implicit manner at this argument. It considers the importance in a pluralistic, democratic society of the transparency of public administration and of the ready availability of issues of public interest. It also underlines that wide access to official documents allows the public to have an adequate view of, and to form a critical opinion on, the state of the society in which they live and on the authorities that govern them, whilst encouraging informed participation which contributes to affirming the legitimacy of administrations as public services and to strengthening the public's confidence in public authorities.

All these reasons make it clear that the transparency of public government in a democratic 'Rechtsstaat' is of the utmost importance. It is useful, however, to note that the transparency of public government comprises several different aspects. One could well distinguish the following three elements.[4] In the first place, there is the element that governmental decisions with a general character are public, i.e. are adequately proclaimed. Secondly, citizens should have access to the decision-making process in the representative organs, in other words the assembly of these organs should be accessible. Thirdly, citizens should as a result of certain information contained in documents be able to form an opinion about the decision-making or acting of their government. This last element is especially

3 Adopted by the Committee of Ministers on 21 February 2002, http://cm.coe.int/stat/E/Public/2002/adopted_texts/recommendations/2002r2.htm.

4 See Hofman and Van Schagen, loc. cit.

concerned with the aspect of access to documents. It is this aspect of the transparency of the public administration which this study shall focus upon.

Here it is already noteworthy that the just mentioned rationales behind openness are also enshrined in the EC regulation with regard to the specific aspect of public access to documents, Regulation 1049/2001.[5] In recital two it says that openness enables citizens to participate more closely in the decision-making process and guarantees that the administration enjoys greater legitimacy and is more effective and more accountable to the citizen in a democratic system. Openness contributes to strengthening the principles of democracy and respect for fundamental rights as laid down in Article 6 of the EU Treaty and in the Charter of Fundamental Rights of the European Union.

3. RULES ON ACCESS TO DOCUMENTS AT THE LEVEL OF THE EU AND THE NETHERLANDS: THE LEGAL FRAMEWORK

3.1. INTRODUCTORY REMARKS

Access to documents has traditionally been the subject of regulation on the level of the nation state. The extent of the right to access and the possible exceptions which the government may invoke so as not to give access to certain documents has lain at the heart of this regulatory activity. That does not mean that the nation state level is the only regulatory platform. As has been mentioned already, also at the level of the EU access to documents has been the subject of regulation. But before this EU activity took place this subject was already dealt with within the framework of other international organizations.

At the level of the *United Nations*, for instance, article 19 of the Universal Declaration of Human Rights declares: "Everyone has the right to freedom of opinion and expression; this right includes freedom to hold opinions without interference and to seek, receive and impart information and ideas through any media and regardless of frontiers". The United Nations Human Rights Commission has affirmed in a resolution entitled 'promotion of the right to democracy', amongst other things that the rights of democratic governance include, *inter alia*, 'the right to freedom to seek, receive and impart information through any media' (this might, but not necessarily does, include a right of access to public documents) and 'transparent and accountable government institutions.'

At the level of the *Council of Europe*, as mentioned earlier, the Committee of Ministers has issued Recommendation (2002)2 to the Member States on access

5 OJ 2001, L145/43.

to official documents. In this Recommendation it stresses the importance in a pluralistic, democratic society of the transparency of public administration and of ready availability on issues of public interest. It underlines that wide access to official documents, on a basis of equality and in accordance with clear rules, is necessary to achieve important aims in a society. In this recommendation the Committee recommends that Member States should guarantee the right of everyone to have access, on request, to official documents held by public authorities.

The right of access to documents could also be regarded as guaranteed in Article 10 of the *European Convention on Human Rights*. One has to say, however, that to date the question whether the freedom of expression set out in Article 10 ECHR actually includes a right of access to public documents is a fairly hotly debated one. Whilst many advocate in favour of the recognition of such a right, there are reasons to be reluctant concerning the matter. In cases concerning restrictions on freedom of the press the ECtHR has on a number of occasions recognised that the public has a right to receive information as a corollary to the specific function of journalists, which is to impart information and ideas on matters of public interest.[6] In the famous Leander case the ECtHR considered, however, that freedom to receive information, referred to in Article 10(2) of the Convention, "basically prohibits a government from restricting a person from receiving information that others wish or may be willing to impart to him". This Leander case is frequently cited as an indication that access to public documents is not a human right.[7] In the also famous Guerra case the ECtHR added that the freedom protected in article 10 cannot be construed as imposing on a State positive obligations to collect and disseminate information of its own motion.[8]

When talking about *the EU* activities on this point, the right of access to documents has gone through an interesting development.[9] First in a declaration added to the Maastricht Treaty in 1992, the importance of a right of access to documents was stressed, particularly in order to enforce the democratic character of the Community institutions and to enhance the confidence of the public in their operation. Subsequently, the Council and Commission framed a Code of Conduct concerning access to their documents. This Code laid down the principles which those institutions had to implement in order to ensure access to the documents held by them. It stated the general principle that the public should have the widest possible access to documents held by them but provided also for exceptions which they could rely on to refuse the right of access. This Code of

6 See, among others, the Observer and Guardian v. the United Kingdom, judgment of 26 November 1991, Series A no. 216, p. 30, section 59 (b), and the Thorgeir Thorgeirson v. Iceland judgment of 25 June 1992, Series A no. 239, p. 27, section 63.

7 ECtHR 26 March 1987, Series A, no. 116.

8 ECtHR 19 February 1998, Reports of Judgments and Decisions 1998-I, section 57.

9 See f.i. K. Lenearts, In the Union we trust: trust-enhancing principles of community law, CMLRev. 2004, p. 318–323.

Conduct was implemented by two Decisions, Council Decision 9/731 and Commission Decision 94/90.

Then, it was the Court of Justice and the Court of First Instance that in various judgments related to this Code and these Decisions paved the way for the acceptance of access to documents as a general principle of Community law.[10]

Since 1 May 1999, the date on which the Treaty of Amsterdam came into force, the EC Treaty contains an article 255 which enshrines the principle of public access to European Parliament, Council and Commission documents. According to article 255 any citizen of the Union, and any natural or legal person residing or having its registered office in a Member State, shall have the right of access to European Parliament, Council and Commission documents, subject to the principles and the conditions to be defined in accordance with paragraphs 2 and 3. Paragraph 2 then prescribes that general principles and limits on grounds of public or private interest governing this right shall be determined by the Council, acting in accordance with the procedure referred to in Article 251 within two years of the entry into force of the Treaty of Amsterdam. According to paragraph 3 each institution referred to in paragraph 1 shall elaborate in its own Rules of Procedure specific provisions regarding access to its documents. The implementation of Article 255 paragraphs 1 and 2 has taken place with the enactment of the above-mentioned important Regulation 1049/2001 on public access to European Parliament, Council and Commission documents.[11] Also the Charter of Fundamental Rights of the European Union contains an article concerning the right of access. Article 42 contains the right for any citizen of the Union, and any natural or legal person residing or having its registered office in a Member State, to have access to European Parliament, Council and Commission documents. Because of the non-binding character of this Charter, the judicial status of this right of access is limited.

3.2. REGULATION 1049/2001: AN OVERVIEW

As far as Regulation 1049/2001 is concerned, in the recitals we can read that, in principle, all documents of the institutions should be accessible to the public. According to article 2 any citizen of the Union, and any natural or legal person residing or having its registered office in a Member State, has a right of access to the documents of the institutions, subject to the principles, conditions and limits defined in this Regulation. The 'authorship rule' – which meant that requests to, for instance, the Commission for documents originating from another

[10] See Lenearts, loc. cit. and also H. Kranenborg, De Eurowob in de hand, de EU transparant?, SEW 2002, p. 447–456.

[11] See M.E. de Leeuw, The Regulation on the Public Access to European Parliament, Council and Commission Documents in the European Union: Are Citizens Better Off?, E.L. Rev. 2003, p. 324–348.

institution, a third party, a Member State etc. should be directed towards the original drafter of those documents, and which was upheld under inter alia the former Commission Decision 94/90 – was changed so that it now corresponds with the Dutch Act on public access to government information, the Wet openbaarheid van bestuur (Wob): according to Article 2(3), Regulation 1049/2001 applies to *all* documents *held* by an institution, that is to say, documents drawn up or *received* by it and in its *possession*, in all areas of EU activity.

The applicant is not obliged, as is the case under the Dutch Wob, to state the reasons for the application (Article 6). Unlike the Dutch Act, Regulation 1049/2001 contains a 'document system'. This means that a citizen looking for information has to describe the document which contains this information. This could of course turn out to be quite difficult. In order to facilitate this duty, Community institutions have to keep a register of documents. Access to the register should be provided in electronic form.

Certain public and private interests can be protected by governmental authorities by way of exceptions. Like the Dutch Wob some of these exceptions in Regulation 1049/2001 have an absolute character, others are of a relative nature. According to Article 4(1) the institutions shall refuse access to a document where disclosure would undermine the protection of: (a) the public interest as regards public security, defence and military matters, international relations, and the financial, monetary or economic policy of the Community or a Member State or (b) privacy and the integrity of the individual, in particular in accordance with Community legislation regarding the protection of personal data (absolute exceptions). Article 4(2) contains the relative exceptions to the right to access. It stipulates that the institutions shall refuse access to a document where disclosure would undermine the protection of: the commercial interests of a natural or legal person, including intellectual property, court proceedings and legal advice, the purpose of inspections, investigations and audits, unless there is an overriding public interest in disclosure.

Also a few other exceptions to the right to access should be noticed. According to Article 4(3) access to a document, drawn up by an institution for internal use or received by an institution, which relates to a matter where the decision has not been taken by the institution, shall be refused if disclosure of the document would seriously undermine the institution's decision-making process, unless there is an overriding public interest in disclosure. Access to a document containing opinions for internal use as part of deliberations and preliminary consultations within the institution concerned shall be refused even after the decision has been taken if the disclosure of the document would seriously undermine the institution's decision-making process, unless there is an overriding public interest in disclosure. Article 4(4) and 4(5) and Article 5 are especially of importance in the type of situations where a citizen seeks access to national documents held by Community institutions or vice versa. We will deal with them separately in para. 4. A special regime is created in Article 9 for 'sensitive documents'. Sensitive documents are, in the wording of Article 9(1), documents originating from the institutions or the agencies established by them, from Member States, third countries or International Organisations, classified as 'TRÈS SECRET/TOP SECRET', 'SECRET' or 'CONFIDENTIEL' in accordance with the rules of the institution concerned, which protect the essential interests of the EU or of one or more of its Member States in the areas covered by Article 4(1)(a), notably public security, defence and military matters. These documents will not be automatically recorded in a register and they will only be released with the consent of the originator. Access to these documents is thus not excluded, but will be quite limited: although the provision of access, as is the case with 'normal' documents, will be judged with a view to the exceptions of especially Article 4, the interests pointed out in Article 4(1) shall in many cases turn out to be a barrier. Under the Dutch Wob a special regime for sensitive documents is lacking.

3.3. THE DUTCH ACT ON PUBLIC ACCESS TO DOCUMENTS: WET OPENBAARHEID VAN BESTUUR (WOB)

Notwithstanding the important developments on different international levels, one has to stress that, traditionally, it was at the level of the nation state that the recognition and regulation of the right of access to documents took place. In the various Member States of the European Union this recognition and regulation has been implemented in different ways. In some Member States, this right is guaranteed in the Constitution. In others, this right has (only) been provided for in legislative acts. An interesting overview can be found in a Commission study with regard to Member States' national legislation concerning access to documents.[12]

The Dutch Wob holds that anyone can make a request to an administrative authority for access to information laid down in documents concerning an administrative matter, which means a matter concerning the policy of an administrative authority, including the preparation and implementation thereof. One is not obliged to indicate the interest in having this information. Moreover, information which is made public to one citizen is supposed to be made public in general.[13] Also – contrary to Regulation 1049/2001 – one is not obliged to indicate the specific document that should contain the information.

Articles 10 and 11 contain justifications for denying a request. Especially article 10 is of importance here. In this article various legitimate grounds for the

12 See http://europa.eu.int/comm/secretariat_general/sgc/acc_doc/index_fr.htm.
13 Council of State, 25 April 2000, JB 2000/142.

government to deny access are mentioned. Certain interests are of such importance that they in themselves justify a denial of access (absolute exceptions). They are in an absolute manner deemed to be of more importance than the interest of access. This is the case with: a. the interest of not damaging the unity of the Crown, b. the interest of not damaging the security of the state, c. the interest of confidential information relating to companies or manufacturing statistics, and d. personal data within the meaning of paragraph 2 of the Personal Data Protection Act, unless access to these data does not manifestly infringe privacy. According to the second indent access may also be denied in cases where the interest of giving access is outweighed by certain other interests (relative exceptions): a. relations between the Netherlands and other states and international organizations, b. the economic and financial interests of the Dutch state, other public bodies or some administrative organs, c. the investigation and prosecution of criminal offences, d. inspection and supervision by administrative organs, e. respect for privacy, f. the interest of the addressee in obtaining knowledge of the information first, and g. the prohibition of disproportionately benefiting or prejudicing third parties which are concerned with the matter. With regard to the provision of access to information with regard to environmental matters the third and second indent provide for some specific exceptions. Article 11 contains an exception for information held in documents drafted for the purpose of internal deliberations. Information in these documents, which is concerned with personal policy views, will not be made possible.

4. SAFEGUARDING THE INTERESTS OF THE COMMUNITY AND THE MEMBER STATES: PROVISIONS IN REGULATION 1049/2001

From what we have encountered in the paragraphs above we can establish that access to documents has been part of regulatory activity on different governmental levels in different ways. When we compare Regulation 1049/2001 with the Dutch Wob as far as the level of openness is concerned we might draw the conclusion that these level differ: many exceptions which have an absolute character in Regulation 1049/2001 have a relative character in the Dutch Wob. This concerns e.g. the protection of international relations, the protection of the financial, monetary or economic policy of the Community or a Member State and the protection of privacy of the individual. On the other hand, the protection of the commercial interests of a natural or legal person, including intellectual property, is a relative exception in Regulation 1049/2001, whereas it has an absolute character in the Dutch Wob, as far as it concerns company data which are presented to the authorities with a confidential character. Finally, some interests are just an exception according to one of the two regulations, e.g. the protection of the unity of the Crow under the Dutch Wob and the protection of court proceedings and legal advice under Regulation 1049/2001.

Of course, case law of both the European and the Dutch courts is of importance when we want to evaluate those exceptions. The Turco case e.g. makes clear that the overriding public interest, under Article 4(2) of Regulation No 1049/2001, capable of justifying the disclosure of a document which undermines the protection of legal advice must, as a rule, be distinct from the principles of openness, of democracy and of greater participation of citizens in the decision-making process, principles which are implemented by the provisions of that regulation as a whole. If that is not the case, it is, at the very least, incumbent on the applicant to show that, having regard to the specific facts of the case, the invocation of those same principles is so pressing that it overrides the need to protect the document in question. This judgment leads to an important restriction compared to the Dutch Wob. According to this Wob the interest of openness is something which indeed should be balanced with the interest which a relative exception is protecting. A (tentative) general conclusion might thus be that the level of openness under the Dutch Wob is higher than it is under Regulation 1049/2001.

These different levels of openness have far reaching consequences. On the hand, when it concerns documents which are both in the possession of national (Dutch) authorities and EC institutions, a European citizen might direct its request for access to the authority acting under the most open regulatory system. On the other hand, Member States and European institutions might be confronted with the situation that a certain document which could be kept secret under their own regulatory system might be given access to under another system.

Regulation 1049/2001 provides for concepts and rules that are intended to mitigate those risks. Recital 10 stipulates that in order to bring about greater openness in the work of the institutions, access to documents should be granted by the European Parliament, the Council and the Commission not only to documents drawn up by the institutions, but also to documents received by them. In this context, it is recalled that Declaration No 35 attached to the Final Act of the Treaty of Amsterdam provides that a Member State may request the Commission or the Council not to communicate to third parties a document originating from that State without its prior agreement. Recital 15 holds that, even though it is neither the object nor the effect of this Regulation to amend national legislation on access to documents, it is nevertheless clear that, by virtue of the principle of loyal cooperation which governs relations between the institutions and the Member States, Member States should take care not to hamper the proper application of this Regulation and should respect the security rules of the institutions. Those general considerations have been implemented in the important Articles 4(4), 4(5) and 5 of Regulation 1049/2001.

According to Article 4(4) with regard to third-party documents, the institution shall consult the third party with a view to assessing whether an exception in paragraph 1 or 2 is applicable, unless it is clear that the document shall or shall not be disclosed. With regard to documents originating from a Member State, in accordance with Article 4(5) this Member State may request the institution not to disclose that document without its prior agreement. Article 5 prescribes that 'where a Member State receives a request for a document in its possession, originating from an institution, unless it is clear that the document shall or shall not be disclosed, the Member State shall consult with the institution concerned in order to take a decision that does not jeopardize the attainment of the objectives of this Regulation. The Member State may instead refer the request to the institution.'

With regard to the latter situation – a Member State is requested to give access to a Community document –one might add the following. For this conflict situation, generally speaking, two extreme positions or solutions could be discerned. On the one hand, one could defend the stance that, because of the principle of supremacy, European law takes precedence over national law and that if a national authority or court is to decide on requests for access to the documents of European Union institutions (such as Council or Commission documents), it has to set aside its own national laws and abide by the EU rules on access. On the other hand, one could argue that European access rules can in no circumstance detract from national rules. The level of access accorded by any and all of the Member States should be considered as 'acquired' and that, since access rights bear on citizenship, the EU rules can only have a supplementary function (in other words, the effect of the EU rules can only be more access, not less). The first position gives EU law an unconditional precedence, the second inverts the hierarchy and places national law at the absolute top. Of course one could also think of solutions which are less extreme. One could think of a 'solution' whereby a potential conflict between EU and national access laws is settled by way of mutual concertation, taking account of the duty of loyalty to which the EU institutions and the Member States are mutually bound (Article 10 EC). National authorities should not disclose documents of EU provenance if the EU shows an overriding interest in seeing confidentiality upheld. It is this last solution which more or less seems to be included in Article 5 of Regulation 1049/2001.

Case law of both European and Dutch courts has shed some light on how those Articles 4 and 5 of Regulation 1049/2001 should be interpreted. This case law will be analyzed in the next two paragraphs.

5. CASE LAW OF EUROPEAN COURTS RELATING TO ARTICLE 4(4) AND 4(5) REGULATION 1049/2001

As mentioned before, in Article 4 of Regulation 1049/2001 a special position is created for Member States as 'third parties'. In the case of normal third-party documents, an institution has to consult this third party with a view to assessing whether an exception in paragraph 1 or 2 is applicable, unless it is clear that the document shall or shall not be disclosed (Article 4(4)). With regard to documents originating from a Member State Article 4(5) stipulates that this Member State may request the institution not to disclose the document without its 'prior agreement'.

Prior agreement could be interpreted as giving Member States a right of veto with respect to giving access to their documents which are in the possession of an EU institution. This would ensure that their national access systems remain intact. On the other hand, one could argue that the decision on a request for access was directed to the European institution, so it has to be this institution that takes the decision, thereby assessing, for instance, whether one of the absolute or relative exceptions had to be applied. By giving Member States a veto this decision process could be circumvented and the right of access could be limited. In a few judgments the Court of First Instance (CFI) has dealt with this subject and concluded that article 4, paragraph five, attributed to the Member States a right to veto The CFI started its veto-line with its judgment in the Messina case in 2003.[14] Although this judgment was concerned with an untypical exercise of a Member State's 'veto right', because of the fact that the veto was issued after the Commission had already taken the decision not to provide access to the requested information, it already made clear that the CFI had interpreted article 4(5) of Regulation 1049/2001 in a sense that 'without prior agreement' means 'right to veto'. In the more recently decided Tierschutz I case this becomes even clearer.[15] Because of its importance, and especially because the Court of Justice itself recently quashed this Tierschutz I judgment of the CFI (Tierschutz II, see below), we pay specific attention to this case.

5.1. THE TIERSCHUTZ I JUDGMENT OF THE CFI

IFAW Internationaler Tierschutz-Fonds GmbH (TF), a non-governmental organisation active in the field of protecting animal welfare and nature

[14] Court of First Instance 17 September 2003, case T-76/02. Annotated by M.E. de Leeuw in CMLRev. 2004, p. 261–280.

[15] Court of First Instance 30 November 2004, case T-168/02, AB 2005/245 with annotation by A.P.W. Duijkersloot.

conservation, exchanged correspondence with the Commission with a view to being granted access to certain documents. These documents related to a project concerning the Mühlenberger Loch site which consisted of the enlargement of the Daimler Chrysler Aerospace Airbus GmbH factory and the reclamation of part of the estuary for a runway extension. The correspondence was exchanged in accordance with the rules on access to documents laid down in Commission Decision 94/90 on public access to Commission documents which was then in force. In the course of that correspondence, the Commission communicated certain documents to TF. Then TF requested access to a series of additional documents pursuant to Regulation 1049/2001, including documents originating from the German authorities. The Commission informed the applicant that, because of Article 4(5) of Regulation 1049/2001, the Commission was obliged to receive an agreement from the German authorities before disclosing any documents received from them. TF replied that it did not accept that interpretation of Article 4(5) of the Regulation. It stated that the German authorities may request the Commission not to disclose a document originating in that Member State without its prior agreement, but the final decision concerning disclosure remains with the Commission and must be based upon one of the exceptions (Article 4) where there is no overriding public interest in the disclosure.

Then the Federal Republic of Germany asked the Commission not to disclose the requested correspondence. Consequently the Commission informed TF that the documents originating from the German authorities could not be made available to it. Before the CFI TF submitted, in essence, that whilst the Member State from which a document originates may request the institution in possession of that document not to disclose it under Article 4(5) of the Regulation, it does not have a right of veto with respect to such disclosure, as the final decision is a matter for the institution.

The CFI, as we could expect from the Messina case, was clear on this point: the argument by TF was based on a misinterpretation of the provisions of the Regulation and could not be upheld. The reasoning by the CFI started by considering that the right of access to documents of the institutions provided for in Article 2 of the Regulation covers all documents held by the European Parliament, the Council and the Commission, that is to say, documents drawn up or received by them and in their possession within the meaning of Article 2(3). Accordingly, the institutions may be required, in appropriate cases, to make available documents originating from third parties, including, in particular, the Member States, in accordance with the definition of 'third party' in Article 3(b) of the Regulation. Then the CFI stressed the changing of the authorship rule, the rule under which the request had to be sent directly to the author and an institution was not authorised to disclose documents originating from a wide category of third parties, including the Member States, and the person requesting access was obliged, where necessary, to make his request directly to the third party in question.

Consequently the CFI explained the regime of Article 4(4) concerning 'normal' third party documents. Article 4(4) of the Regulation places the institutions under an obligation to consult the third party concerned with a view to assessing whether an exception in Article 4(1) or (2) is applicable, unless it is clear that the document should or should not be disclosed. The CFI considered that it follows that the institutions are under no obligation to consult the third party concerned if it is clearly apparent whether the document should or should not be disclosed. In all other cases, the institutions must consult the relevant third party. Accordingly, in cases where there could be doubt as to the duty to disclose or not to disclose documents, consulting the third party is, as a general rule, a precondition for determining whether the exceptions to the right of access provided for in Article 4(1) and (2) of the Regulation are applicable in the case of third-party documents. However, the Commission's duty to consult third parties under Article 4(4) of the Regulation does not affect its power to decide whether one of the exceptions provided for in Article 4(1) and (2) of the Regulation is applicable.

The CFI then, citing the Messina case, pointed out that the regime concerning Member State documents is a different one. It added that Article 4(5) of the Regulation places the Member States in a different position from that of other parties and lays down a *lex specialis* to govern their position. Under that provision, the Member State has the power to request an institution not to disclose a document originating from it without its 'prior agreement'. The obligation imposed on the institution to obtain the Member State's prior agreement, which is clearly laid down in Article 4(5) of the Regulation, would risk becoming a dead letter if the Commission were able to decide to disclose that document despite an explicit request not to do so from the Member State concerned. Thus, contrary to what TF had argued, a request made by a Member State under Article 4(5) does in the words of the CGI, 'constitute an instruction to the institution not to disclose the document in question'. This instruction can hardly be called anything other than a 'right to veto'.

Then the Court addressed a few other interesting questions. Do Member States have to state their reasons for vetoing access to certain information? Do these reasons have to be justified by one of the exceptions under national or Community access law? Without giving reasons, the answer of the CFI to the first question was in the negative. This means that a Member State can simply request the withholding of access. Whether this secrecy is justified in some public interest is irrelevant. From an openness point of view, this is not very satisfactory. This is even less so because another question – whether there is a duty for the Commission to examine whether the non-disclosure of the document in question is justified in, for example, the public interest, in a case when a Member State uses its veto right – is also answered in the negative. This means that Member States can very easily and without any scrutiny on the European level block the access to documents originating from them and which are currently in the hands of a European institution. For a citizen the only way to obtain access to this information is to make a request to the national authorities under national law.

This last point makes clear that, on the one hand, the reasoning of the CFI resulting in a veto right on the part of the Member States is on the one hand understandable. It pays respect to the political declaration that Member States' access regulations should not be touched upon or undermined by Regulation 1049/2001. On the other hand, from a openness point of view, the judgment is unsatisfactory. The main goal of Regulation 1049/2001 is maximum access. This could imply that restrictions to the right to access should be interpreted strictly. One could not say that the CFI is doing just that. There were points of reference for a more liberal approach. From the text of Article 4(5) one should not per se conclude the existence of a veto right, because it uses the word 'request'. A comparison with Article 9(3), which has to do with sensitive documents makes this even more clear: this article bluntly contains a right to veto, because these documents will be released 'only with the consent of the originator'. Also the structure of article 4 does not point in a veto direction, because of the fact that Article 4(1), (2) and (3) contain the material exceptions to the right of access, whereas Article 4(4) and further, contain procedural prescriptions. Interpreting Article 4(5) as comprising a veto right would lead to the conclusion that this indent would become a separate material exception. Thirdly, the consequence of the right to veto is in fact that the authorship rule, which was explicitly omitted from Regulation 1049/2001, would in fact be restored. So, there were some arguments contrary to a right to veto, but the CFI paid more attention to the rationale behind Article 4(5): leaving national access systems untouched.

5.2. THE TIERSCHUTZ II JUDGMENT OF THE COURT OF JUSTICE

As already announced before, recently the Court of Justice itself in Tierschutz II has dealt with all these observations and set aside the Tierschutz judgment of the CFI.[16]

Firstly, the Court considered that, where a Member State has made use of the option given to it by Article 4(5) of Regulation 1049/2001 to request that a specific document originating from that State should not be disclosed without its prior agreement, disclosure of that document by the institution requires the prior

16 Court of Justice 18 december 2007, case C-64/05P, AB 2008/111 with annotation of J.A. van Schagen.

agreement of that Member State to be obtained. Since an agreement is legally different from a mere opinion, the very wording of Article 4(5) of Regulation 1049/2001 precludes an interpretation to the effect that the provision merely confers on a Member State making use of the possibility given by that provision the right to be consulted by the institution before the institution decides, possibly despite the opposition of the Member State in question, to allow access to the document concerned. The fact that Article 4(5) of Regulation 1049/2001 uses the words 'may request' simply emphasizes that that provision gives the Member State an option, and only the actual exercise of that option in a particular case has the consequence of making the prior agreement of the Member State a necessary condition of the future disclosure of the document in question.

Secondly, with regard to the veto-issue, the Court held that it is clear from recital 10 in the preamble to, and Article 2(3) of, Regulation 1049/2001 that all documents held by the institutions are within the scope of the Regulation, including those originating from the Member States, so that access to such documents is in principle governed by the provisions of the Regulation, including those which lay down substantive exceptions to the right of access. Thus the exceptions set out in Article 4(1) to (3) of the Regulation must be interpreted and applied strictly. Those exceptions delimit the exercise of the power conferred by Article 4(5) on the Member State concerned, the latter being given in that respect nothing more than a power to take part in the Community decision. Seen in that way, the prior agreement of the Member State referred to in Article 4(5) resembles not a discretionary right of veto but a form of assent confirming that none of the grounds of exception under Article 4(1) to (3) is present. It follows that Article 4(5) of Regulation 1049/2001 cannot be interpreted as conferring on the Member State a general and unconditional right of veto, so that it could in a discretionary manner oppose the disclosure of documents originating from it and held by an institution, with the effect that access to such documents would cease to be governed by the provisions of that Regulation and would depend only on the provisions of national law.

Thirdly, this assent should be motivated. The Court considers that a Member State which, at the conclusion of the dialogue with a Community institution concerning the possible application of the exceptions laid down in Article 4(1) to (3) of Regulation 1049/2001, objects to disclosure of the document in question is obliged to state reasons for that objection with reference to those exceptions. The institution cannot accept a Member State's objection to disclosure of a document originating from that State if the objection gives no reasons at all or if the reasons are not put forward in terms of the exceptions listed in Article 4(1) to (3) of Regulation 1049/2001. Where, despite an express request by the institution to the Member State to that effect, the State still fails to provide the institution with such reasons, the institution must, if for its part it considers that none of those exceptions applies, give access to the document that has been asked for.

In essence, this Tierschutz II judgment makes very clear that concerning the Court Article 4(5) of Regulation 1049/2001 has a much more limited meaning than the CFI was suggesting.

6. CASE LAW OF DUTCH COURTS RELATING TO ARTICLE 5 REGULATION 1049/2001

How do national courts tend to deal with the situation in which access to a Community document that is (also) in the hands of a national authority is requested for from that national authority? In recent years the (highest) Dutch courts have delivered a few judgments that can shed some light on the manner in which they resolve this problem. Most of these judgments do not concern the application of Regulation 1049/2001 though. Some of the cases concern specific European regulations that contain rules on access or secrecy. Others deal with the former internal rules of the Council and Commission on access (the Codes of Conduct). Recently the Council of State has given two judgments about the interpretation of art. 5 of Regulation 1049/2001 though.[17] With this Eurowob I and Eurowob II case we will deal in the second and third part of this section. Firstly, we discuss briefly the earlier Dutch case law.

6.1. FROM METTEN AND BEYOND

The famous Metten case concerned the request made by the Member of the European Parliament Alman Metten to the Minister of Finance for access to documents that contained minutes of meetings of the Council.[18] According to the Council of State the request for access could be dismissed because of the duty to uphold secrecy that was inserted in the Council's Rules of Procedure. Even though these Rules of Procedure had no direct effect, in the view of the Council of State the principle of the supremacy of Community law implied that this part of Community law prevailed over national rules on access. More recently in the Denkavit case the Council of State has taken another view.[19] Denkavit contained a request for access to a report drafted by the Commission, which dealt with the Dutch treatment of the swine fever epidemic. The Dutch authorities denied access to this report. The Council of State applied Dutch law (the Wob) and ruled that because of Article 10(2) sub a of this Act – which provides for an exception to access to documents because of the protection of international relations – this

17 Council of State 23 November 2005 (Eurowob I), JB 2006/28 and 9 April 2008 (Eurowob II), JB 2008/124.

18 Council of State 7 July 1995, AB 1997/117.

19 Council of State 7 July 2000, JB 2000/244.

denial was justified. The granting of access would burden relations between the Netherlands and the Commission in such a way that this outweighed the interest of providing access to the requested report. This judgment was based on the fact that the Commission itself attached great value to the secrecy of the report. A clear indication of this attitude was the fact that the Commission itself had rejected the request for access to this document based on its Code of Conduct.

The difference between both judgments is clear. In Metten Community 'access law' was applied, in Denkavit national 'access law'. In practice, though, the result is quite the same. When it is clear that a Community institution is reluctant to provide information, there is not much room for the national authorities under national law (Article 10 paragraph 2 sub. of the Wob) to come autonomously to another decision.

Also in a few other cases Dutch courts delivered judgments with regard to specific EU regulations on the subject of access to documents. These concerned the Loek Fafié case[20] – in which the Council of State considered that, in view of the provisions in the Community Regulation 1468/81, the State Secretary could already take the position that access to the requested documents should be denied, without paying attention to the exceptions to the right of access under national (Dutch) law – the Scholze case[21] – in which the Council of State concluded that a provision of the Code of Conduct of the Customs Code Committee was not applicable, so Dutch law had to be applied – and the *ECHR Rules of Procedure case*[22] – in which the Council of State considered that, when taking notice of the text and the history of the Dutch Wob and also according to the settled case law of the Council, special access rules and international rules posed by treaties which are operative in the Netherlands prevail over the Wob when they have an exhaustive character and, according to the Council, this was the case with Article 33 (old) ECHR, in connection with Article 2 European Agreement and Rule 17 para. 2 Rules of Procedure of the ECHR.

6.2. THE EUROWOB I CASE

As said before, recently the Council of State has given two judgments on the meaning of Article 5 of Regulation 1049/2001. The first one, the Eurowob I case, was about the refusal by the Ministry of VROM of giving access to documents containing the reaction of the European Commission on the report by the Dutch authorities of a decision and an agreement concerning a concession which might be regarded as aid granted by states in the meaning of Article 87 EC Treaty. The Ministry based its refusal – like in the Denkavit case – on Article 10(2)(a) Wob:

20 Council of State 17 July 2002, JB 2002/249.
21 Council of State 18 December 2002, AB 2003/89.
22 Council of State 9 April 2003, JB 2003/142.

access may be denied when the interest of giving access is outweighed by the interest of the relations between the Netherlands and other states and international organizations. The Council of State held that the Dutch administrative authorities have to take into account the provisions of the Eurowob which are directly applicable, like article 5 Eurowob (see before) which contains the duty to consult the European institution concerned before giving access to a document originating from that institution. Taken into consideration the opinion of the Commission – that contained a comprehensive exposition of arguments why the documents should not be revealed according to Article 4(2) Regulation 1049/2001 (the purpose of inspections, investigations and audits, especially concerning state aid) – the Dutch Ministry was correct in its opinion that the disclosure of the documents did not outweigh the interest of the relation between the Netherlands and the Commission, so the refusal was justified.

This judgment seems, in line with the Denkavit case, to imply that, with regard to documents originating from the Council, the Commission and the European Parliament that fall within the scope of the Eurowob, a negative opinion of such an institution when it is consulted about the possibility of disclosing a certain document by the Dutch authorities, does not leave much discretion for an independent judgment made by these authorities.

6.3. THE EUROWOB II CASE

The Eurowob II judgment of the Council of State deals with the way Dutch authorities have to apply the consultation requirement of Article 5 Regulation 1049/2001, especially the question when this duty to consult exists.

The authorities of the municipality of Middelburg had refused the lawyers office AKD access to certain documents that related to a complaint about the public tender of the building of a new city hall which had been investigated by the European Commission. The authorities had not consulted the European Commission about the decision to give access. They were of the opinion that this was not necessary, because the disclosure of the documents could be refused under national Dutch law, especially according to Article 10(2) a, b and g and article 11 Wob. According to the Middelburg authorities this made it clear that, with a view to the text of Article 5 Regulation 1049/2001, the disclosure could be refused.

The Council of State considers that the question whether renouncing the duty to consult was allowed, had to be assessed in the context of the aim and purpose of Regulation 1049/2001 combined with Article 10 of the EC Treaty, the principle of loyal cooperation. According to Article 1 of Regulation 1049/2001 the purpose of Regulation 1049/2001 was to ensure the widest possible access to documents. Consideration 15 stated that, even though it is neither the object nor the effect of this Regulation to amend national legislation on access to documents, it is nevertheless clear that, by virtue of the principle of loyal cooperation which governs relations between the institutions and the Member States, Member States should take care not to hamper the proper application of this Regulation and should respect the security rules of the institutions.

This consideration 15 combined with Article 10 EC Treaty implies according to the Council of State that Article 5 of Regulation should be interpreted as follows: in a situation that national law leaves discretion to national authorities about the disclosure of a document and it is not clear in advance whether Article 4 of Regulation 1049/2001 compels to the refusal of the disclosure, national authorities should only take a decision to refuse access after consulting the relevant Community institution. Because of the fact that in this case the exceptions of Article 10(2) a, b and g and article 11 Wob did leave discretion to the authorities, the Council of State decided that the decision of the Middelburg authorities was not prepared with the necessary precision, which meant a violation of Article 3:2 of the General Administrative Law Act (GALA).

7. EVALUATION: BALANCING OF INTERESTS

The case law of European and Dutch court dealt with in section 5 and 6 about the interpretation of Article 4(5) and 5 of Regulation 1049/2001 makes clear that those provisions assure the influence of European institutions on the disclosure of their documents by national authorities. They also make clear that national authorities have a say in the disclosure of their documents by European institutions. In an general sense, those provisions make sure that Community and national interests with respect to openness are safeguarded in a certain way. Some more specific observations have to be made though.

Although it seems attractive to interpret Article 4(5) and Article 5 of Regulation 1049/2001 in a more or less balanced way, the Court in Tierschutz II denies this kind of reasoning. It holds that it is not possible to accept the argument that Article 4(5) of Regulation 1049/2001 should be interpreted by reference to Article 5 of the Regulation, in order to ensure a balance between the treatment given to documents originating from the institutions in the possession of the Member States and that given to documents originating from the Member States in the possession of the institutions. According to the Court that is shown by the simple fact that the Community legislature expressed itself in very different terms with respect to those two classes of documents, by laying down in the first paragraph of Article 5 of Regulation 1049/2001 merely an obligation on the Member States to 'consult' the institutions when access is sought to a document originating from them, while Article 4(5) is talking about 'prior agreement'. To put it simply, this would mean that the influence of Member States on a Community decision is greater than vice versa. In the Eurowob I judgment, like in Denkavit, we have seen that the Dutch Council of State attributes quite a great importance to the opinion of the Community institution though: a motivated negative opinion of the institution might or even should lead to the refusal of the disclosure. In other words, the Council seems to accept a more or less decisive role of the Community institution in the decision-making process. Vice versa, in Tierschutz II, the Court makes clear that the motivated negative opinion of a Member State, based on the applicability of one of the exceptions in Regulation 1049/2001, has to result in the non-disclosure of the documents by the Community institution as well.[23]

This last point raises the interesting question which arguments Community institutions and national authorities may put forward when expressing their views and opinions about the disclosure of certain documents. Should these arguments be founded in Community law or national law? With regard to the opinion of a Community institution about the disclosure of its documents by national authorities it seems to be clear, also from the Eurowob I judgment of the Council of State, that the arguments can be based on the applicability of one of the exceptions of Regulation 1049/2001. Vice versa, Tierschutz II at first sight seems to make clear that the arguments of the Member States about the disclosure of its documents by Community institutions should not be based on their own national law but on Regulation 1049/2001. The Member States should (only) indicate whether the Member State is of the opinion that one the exceptions of this Regulation to be applicable.[24]

This raises the question whether there is room for Member States to rely on national interests. Off course, there is the possibility to put forward those national interests in terms of the exceptions of Regulation 1049/2001. But, as we have dealt with in section 3, those exceptions differ at least partly from e.g. the exceptions in the Dutch Wob. One quite ambiguous consideration in Tierschutz II seems to open up at least a slight possibility for Member States to rely on national interests and national law. In consideration 84 the Court holds that 'there is nothing to exclude the possibility that compliance with certain rules of national law protecting a public or private interest, opposing disclosure of a document and relied on by the Member State for that purpose, could be regarded as an interest deserving of protection on the basis of the exceptions laid down by that regulation'. This might imply that a Member State might base its opinion on national interests and national law – e.g. exceptions in the Dutch Wob – which eventually might force the European institution to refuse the disclosure of the documents. The European institution could then base its decision – like the Dutch authorities have done in Eurowob I using Article 10(2) Wob – on the exception of the protection of international relations, this time as protected under Article 4(2) of Regulation 1049/2001.

---

23 Tierschutz II, cons. 90.

24 Tierschutz II, esp. cons. 67 and 76.

Whether this consideration 84 should be interpreted in such a way that is leaves room for Member States to base their opinion on national interests and national law, which eventually should lead to the non-disclosure of the document by the Community institution is questionable though. The Court, also in this consideration 84, is referring to the exceptions laid down in Regulation 1049/2001. This might indicate that those national interests and national law arguments should be put forward and should be assessed in terms of Regulation 1049/2001 accordingly. The exception of the protection of international relations in Article 4(2) Regulation 1049/2001 is, unlike its complement in Dutch law Article 10(2) Wob, very probably not aiming at the protection of the relations between the EU and its Member States, but of the relations between the EU and third parties, like non-Member States and international organizations. This implies that this exception in Article 4(2) can not serve as a ground for refusal. New case law of the Court of Justice could clear up this point.

Finally, a remark should be made about the important subject of judicial protection. This interest is of great importance for Community citizens. Off course, the Community decision to refuse the disclosure of a national document can be challenged before a European court (Article 230 EC). The same holds for a national decision refusing access to a Community document. According to the Dutch Wob such a decision is an applicable decision.

The question remains what kind of judicial protection exists as far as the opinion of the Community institution or Member State is concerned. The opinion of the Community institution is not an applicable decision. It has to be dealt with before the national (Dutch) court as part of the appeal against the decision of the national authorities to refuse access. In this procedure arguments can be put forward concerning the validity of the opinion, e.g. the lack of motivation. This eventually might lead the national (Dutch) court to the conclusion that the decision of the national authorities to refuse access, based on the opinion of the institution and Article 10(2) Wob (the protection of international relations), can not be justified.

The opinion of the Member State towards the European institution is not applicable as well, one might argue. Therefore the Court in Tierschutz II expressly holds that the institution is itself obliged to give reasons for a decision to refuse a request for access to a document. Such an obligation means that the institution must, in its decision, not merely record the fact that the Member State concerned has objected to disclosure of the document asked for, but also set out the reasons relied on by that Member State to show that one of the exceptions to the right of access in Article 4(1) to (3) of Regulation 1049/2001 applies. That information will allow the person who has asked for the document to understand the origin and grounds of the refusal of his request and the competent court to exercise, if need be, its power of review. Problems might develop when consideration 84 in Tierschutz II really implies that Member States can found their negative opinion purely on national interests and national law. In such a case those national arguments can hardly be assessed by European institutions, including European courts. In this sense they are binding. From the well known Borelli-case, it is clear that effective judicial protection means that a binding opinion of a Member State has to be subject to judicial protection.[25] If this is not the case at the European level, this has to be the case at the national level. This should imply that this binding opinion of a Member State, based on national interests and national law, has to be open to judicial protection of a national court. According to Dutch law such an opinion should have to be qualified as a 'decision' (Article 1:3 GALA). This raises various difficult questions with regard to the legal basis for such an advice, the legal effect of such an advice and so on. In the end the answer according to Dutch law might very well be positive in a way that the binding opinion of the Dutch authorities, based on national interests and national law, is applicable. From a Borelli point of view it should be. On the other hand, these considerations and complications concerning national law and national judicial protection might serve as an indication that the Court in its ambiguous consideration 84 in Tierschutz II simply meant that national interests and arguments should be put forward and 'translated' in terms of the exceptions in Article 4 Regulation 1049/2001. Case law of the Court of Justice could also clear up this point in the future.

25 Court of Justice 3 december 1992, case C-97/91.

B. ACTS AND PROCEDURES

XII. EUROPEAN COMPOSITE ADMINISTRATION: THE TRANSNATIONAL ADMINISTRATIVE ACT

Matthias Ruffert*

1. INTRODUCTION

The basic function of the institutions of the General Administrative Law lies in regulating and arranging the variety of administrative organisations, administrative procedures and administrative actions as well as the administrative legal relations, and through this provide reliability and legal security.[1] Ever since the administrative law doctrine of 19th century constitutionalism,[2] the structuring of administrative law has advanced by pulling rules, principles and institutions from specific areas into the general administrative law area. Transboundary administrative procedures were mainly omitted from recent systematisation processes because of the emphasis on state territorial sovereignty, which has only recently started to decrease.[3] International Administrative Law, which used to have only a part on the borderline in the general picture of administrative law scholarship seems hardly recognisable as

* Translated version of the writer's speech in defence of his *Habilitation* in front of *Habilitationskollegium* (colleagues) and the council of scholars of the Faculty of Law (*Fachbereitsrat des Fachbereichs Rechtswissenschaft*) at the University of Trier on 13 December 2000. Translation not by the author.

1 Krause, *Rechtsformen des Verwaltungshandelns* [Legal Forms in Administrative Actions], 1974, 14; Ossenbühl, JuS 1979, 681 (682); Schmidt-Aßmann, *Das allgemeine Verwaltungsrecht als Ordnungsidee* [General Administrative Law as Ordering Idea], 1998, 1/2.

2 See also Stolleis, *Geschichte des öffentlichen Rechts in Deutschland* [History of public law in Germany], Vol. 2, 1992, 394 ff.

3 That this tendency can be traced back until Otto Mayer is proven by Bülck, in: *Festschrift für Kraus* [Festschrift for Kraus], 1964, 29 (55 ff.); see Mayer, *Deutsches Verwaltungsrecht* [German Administrative Law], Vol. 2, 1. Edition, 1896, 457. The annex (there p. 435 ff.) "Internationales bundesstaatliches Verwaltungsrecht" [International federal administrative law] can no longer be found in the following editions.

part of administrative legal disciplines,[4] in so far its transitory nature has not been explicitly argued.[5]

Procedures of transboundary administrative cooperation, as they increase and concentrate cumulatively on newer developments and the way in which they complete supranational administrative procedures appearing within the scope of the Europeanisation, in particular, are being included into their international and European legal assumptions to a greater degree, indeed, but there are as yet few scientific definitions of this phenomenon.[6] This applies in particular to the integration of transboundary forms of action of the administration in German administrative law. The term transnational administrative act was introduced at the beginning of the 1990s.[7] In addition, other transnational administrative processes or – more generally – administrative procedures are being recognised to an increasing degree.[8] Specifically, the transnational administrative act is extensively understood as a novel legal institute,[9] which requires conceptional clarification.[10]

This clarification has to take the specific functions of the form of action administrative act[11] into account. After the reduction in the judicial protective function of the administrative act because of the form of action becoming independent of legal process introduced by the general clause of §40(1) Phrase 1 VwGO[12], the act depends especially on its legal securing and stabilising functions and through this on continuance, fact and determinative effect.[13] However, those

4 The article of Hoffmann, in: von Münch (ed.), *Besonderes Verwaltungsrecht* [Special Administrative Law], 7. Auflage, 1985, 14th chapter no longer appears in the following editions of the benchmark. Other textbooks do not include a detailed chapter about International Administrative Law. Cf. Wolff/Bachof/Stober, *Verwaltungsrecht I,* [Administrative Law] 11. e 1999 Edition, §1 mn. 23; §21 mn. 12; §27 mn. 16.

5 Achterberg, *Allgemeines Verwaltungsrecht* [General Administative Law], 2. 1986 Edition, §1 mn. 97. Further estimations in Grof, in: Mellinghoff/Trute (eds.), *Die Leistungsfähigkeit des Rechts*, 1988, 303 (306 with fn. 9). *Cf.* for a more detailed occupation with International Administrative Law, Delbrück, in: Jeserich/Pohl/von Unruh (eds.), *Deutsche Verwaltungsgeschichte V* [German Administrative History V], 1987, 386 (403).

6 Cf. Papier/Olschewski, DVBl 1976, 475 (476), as well as Pühs, *Der Vollzug von Gemeinschaftsrecht*, 1997, 215. Sceptically regarding generalisations Götz, in: *Liber Amicorum Jaenicke*, 1998, 763 (785 f.).

7 For the first time by Schmidt-Aßmann, DVBl 1993, 924 (935).

8 Schröder, in: *Festschrift für Ritter 1997*, 957 (958 and 960). *Cf.* also Pitschas, in: Schmidt-Aßmann/Hoffmann-Riem (eds.), *Strukturen des Europäischen Verwaltungsrechts*, 1999, 123 (130): "transnational communication" (the original in italic).

9 See Nessler, NVwZ 1995, 863.

10 Schmidt-Aßmann, EuR 1996, 270 (301); Stelkens, in: Stelkens/Bonk/Sachs, VwVfG, 5. 1998 Edition, §35 marginal number (= mn.) 256. Different in Wahl/Groß, DVBl 1998, 2 (prefix):"… dogmatically already introduced figure of the so called 'transnational administrative act'… "sceptically/questioning Becker, DVBl 2001, 855 (prefix).

11 About this, see Schoch, in: Hoffmann-Riem/Schmidt-Aßmann (eds.), *Innovation und Flexibilität des Verwaltungshandelns*, 1994, 199 (201 f.); Stelkens (fn. 10), §35, mn. 24 ff.

12 See only Stelkens (fn. 10), §35, mn. 33 f.

13 Schmidt-Aßmann, EuR 1996, 270 (299).

effects are – especially in the transboundary context – not unproblematic, since they could also become a burden for the citizens.[14]

Under these premises, the following article approaches the legal institute of the transnational administrative act as a supranational legal institute of German administrative law, in two steps. First, the manifestations of the transnational administrative act are listed and ordered in order to reach a conceptual clarification (below 2.2). Two parts will be omitted, the special development of which excessively complicates an inclusion in an observation aiming at generalisation, namely the International Social Law[15] and the International Tax Law.[16] A second step deals with the particular conditions for constitutional and administrative effectiveness of transnational administrative acts (below 3.). The article closes with a short summary on the meaning of the administrative act as an action form for interstate administrative cooperation (4.).

2. TERM AND FORMS OF APPEARANCE OF THE TRANSNATIONAL ADMINISTRATIVE ACT

Multiple circumstances complicate the conceptual coverage of the transnational administrative act. Therefore, the international law doctrine has focused on the examination of *extraterritorial* effects on sovereignty acts with good reasons.[17] This orientation is based on a specific examination objective: it is about the states' authority to regulate facts beyond their sovereign area *without* the approval of other concerned states and to the international legal borders to this authority, as they have become relevant, especially in economic international legal conflicts.[18] However, here the consensual, cooperative globalisation of the Public Law is in question. Extraterritoriality and transnationality are not characteristics of administrative acts, which are contradictory to each other, but characteristics of transboundary sovereign actions, which come to the fore from a specific perspective.[19]

In addition, International Law literature generally deals with sovereign acts and not only with administrative acts in particular. This becomes obvious in the International Legal concept of *jurisdiction*.[20] At this point, a basic difficulty becomes obvious: the administrative act as an institute of German administrative law has been provided with specific characteristics and legal effects. Already its

---

14 *Cf.* also Schmidt-Aßmann, DVBl 1993, 924 (936).

15 Eichenhofer, *Sozialrecht*, 3. 2000 Edition, mn. 74 ff. with further references (especially mn. 82 ff.).

16 For a summary Tipke/Lang, *Steuerrecht*, 16. Edition 1998, §2 mn. 30 ff.

17 Basically, Meng, *Extraterritoriale Jurisdiktion im öffentlichen Wirtschaftsrecht*, 1994, 73 ff.; Schlochauer, *Die extraterritoriale Wirkung von Hoheitsakten*, 1962, 10 ff.

18 See Meng (fn. 17), 299 ff.

19 Similarly, Rauser, *Die Übertragung von Hoheitsrechten auf ausländische Staaten*, 1991, 138.

20 Meng (fn. 17), 1 ff.; Schwarze, *Die Jurisdiktionsabgrenzung im Völkerrecht*, 1994.

probably closest foreign relative, the French *acte administratif*, is conceptually by no means identical with it, since it also includes normative acts and contracts, for instance.[21] While transnational administrative acts, which are issued by German authorities, can also be judged regarding their effect abroad according to the traditional regulations of the German administrative law, the inclusion of foreign, transboundary administrative actions into the German administrative law structure meets difficulties because these actions cannot be qualified as transnational *administrative acts* just like that.[22] However, this basic problem cannot be overcome by regarding the possible forms of appearance of transnational administrative acts.

Eventually, the present discussion concerning the transnational administrative act is, according to the place of its "discovery", concentrated on specific appearances in European Community law.[23] Accordingly, it is defined as a decision, which is effective within the entire Community,[24] but which is brought into connection with the benchmarks of secondary Community law.[25] If transnational administrative acts, on the one hand, often appear in the Community law, there are, on the other hand, quite a few traditional forms of appearance, which are based upon international law, as well as newer developments, which exceed the narrow scope of EU and EC. Logically, the meaning of the transnational administrative act as reaching beyond European law is recognised, whereas it is defined, albeit superficially referred to rules of European law regulations, as especially distinguished fact of the transboundary effect of foreign sovereignty acts[26] or as administrative act, the effects are not

21 Chapus, *Droit administratif général*, Tome 1, 13ème ed. 1999, mn. 651 ff.

22 *Cf.* Happe, *Die grenzüberschreitende Wirkung von nationalen Verwaltungsakten*, 1987, 17; Biscottini, *L'efficacité des actes administratifs étrangers*, RdC 104 (1961-III), 635 (639); Stelkens, in: Stelkens/Bonk/Sachs (eds.), VwVfG, 6. Auflage 2001, §35 mn 255. Indicated by Röhl, *Akkreditierung und Zertifizierung im Produktsicherheitsrecht*, 2000, 27 in fn. 23 at the end – Hoffmann (fn. 4), 868, includes such actions of foreign authorities in terms of the administrative act, which are in accordance with the term of the German administrative act; similarly König, *Die Anerkennung ausländischer Verwaltungsakte*, 1965, 9. *Cf.* also Schwarze (fn. 20), 20 f. about the international, legal, motivated necessity of the orientation on the national law.

23 See especially Nessler, *Europäisches Richtlinienrecht wandelt deutsches Verwaltungsrecht*, 1994, 2. *Cf.* also Ehlers, *Die Europäisierung des Verwaltungsprozessrechts*, 1999, 9 f.; Hufen, in: Schmidt-Aßmann/Hoffmann-Riem (eds.) (fn. 8), 99 (109). Denying, Kadelbach, *Allgemeines Verwaltungsrecht unter Europäischem Einfluss*, 1999, 328.

24 Becker, DVBl 2001, 855 (856); *Nessler* (fn. 23), 5; Schoch, in: Schmidt-Aßmann/Hoffmann-Riem (eds.) (fn. 8), 279 (308).

25 Burgi, *Verwaltungsprozeß und Europarecht*, 1996, 55 f.; *Ehlers*, in: Erichsen (ed.), *Allgemeines Verwaltungsrecht*, 11. Edition 1998, §3 mn 64; Erichsen, *id.*, §12 mn 10; Ossenbühl, *id.*, §8 mn. 16; Götz, in: *Liber Amicorum Jaenicke*, 763 (778); Röhl (fn. 22), 27; Stelkens (fn. 10), §35 mn. 255 (who besides also mentions International Law Treaties); Schmidt-Aßmann (fn. 1), 7/50; Schwarze, in: *id.* (ed.), *Das Verwaltungsrecht unter Europäischem Einfluss – Zur Konvergenz der mitgliedstaatlichen Verwaltungsrechtsverordnungen in der Europäischen Union*, 1996, 123 (135 f.); Vedder, *EuR Beiheft I*, 75 (89 f.).

26 Schmidt-Aßmann, *DVBl 1993*, 924 (935).

limited to the federal territory of the issuing authority.[27] The term in its breadth is used at first as a working definition, in order to be specified in more detail on the basis of the following appraisal.[28]

2.1. THE TYPOLOGY OF TRANSNATIONAL ADMINISTRATIVE ACTS

2.1.1. Effect-related transnationality

The first form of appearance of the transnational administrative act is the administrative act, the transnationality of which is arranged by virtue of its legal effects. Concerning the allocation of the types of the transnational administrative act, this administrative act requires the least discussion; sometimes the descriptions of the transnational administrative act are limited even explicitly to this type of administrative act, which is enacted in a state with regard to the addressee resident there, and which develops a legal effect beyond the borders of this state.

Already the traditional examples concretely illustrate the transnationality by virtue of a legal effect. By virtue of customary international law, the legitimacy of the conferment of the citizenship acts in accordance with the law of the conferring state and can only be subject to a revision by international authorities and not by other states.[29] Therefore, customary international law classifies the transnational effect of the conferment act. Even more illustrative is the example of driving licences.[30] The Vienna Convention on Road Traffic obliges the treaty parties to accept the issued driver's licences.[31] According to Art. 4 of the German Regulation on the International Motor Vehicle Traffic[32], consequentially, not only the person owning an international driver's licence or a driver's licence according to EU law is allowed to drive a vehicle in Germany, but every person not living in Germany with a valid foreign driver's licence.[33] Applying this example, the regulation model for the effect-related transnationality of administrative acts is the combination of an International Law acceptance obligation combined with a German legal norm to the execution of acceptance.

27 Fastenrath, *Die Verwaltung 31* (1998), 277 (301); similarly Nessler (fn. 23), 27.

28 *Cf.* also the "graduated scale" by Rauser (fn. 19), 138 ff. extending beyond the transnational administrative acts.

29 Hoffmann (fn. 4), 869; Meng (fn. 17), 95; Verdross/Simma, *Universelles Völkerrecht*, 3. Edition 1984, §§1192 and 1199. Critically Parry, *ZaöRV* 19 (1958), 337.

30 This and the following examples are current and classic at the same time, *cf.* already König (fn. 22), 16 f.

31 Article 41 with Annex 7 of the Convention of 08.11.1968.

32 Of 12.11.1934 (RGBl. 1935 I p. 1137), last changed on 18.08.1998 (BGBl. I p. 2214). About the entire affair Hentschel, *Straßenverkehrsrecht*, 36.Edition 2001, §31 FeV mn. 16.

33 For the motor vehicle licence see §32 a (1a) StVZO and on this Stelkens (fn. 10), §35 mn. 255.

Thereby, the term of the acceptance in this relation is rather confusing,[34] since it lacks acts of acceptance of the *administration* in the individual case, which could be differentiated from a foreign "basic act".[35] The effect-related transnationality is part of a certain automatism.[36]

The EC's harmonised internal market law is also the main application area of the transnational administrative act which follows this regulation pattern by virtue of its legal effect.[37] Within the internal market law, the area of free movement of goods and the product safety does not occupy – as one might think at first sight – the centre stage. Here, the transnational administrative act is already a "phase-out model". "New conception" and "global concept" have replaced official sanctions as far as possible by a graded model of conformity appraisal in the sphere of the "labelled institutions".[38] An exception is represented by the motor vehicle sector – type licensing.[39] Here, the official permission for a vehicle type is given on the basis of regulations, which have been harmonised in detail, in a Member State and accepted in another Member State, by virtue of implementation law.[40] A community wide product approval is also given for novel food products, but direct administrative procedures of Member States and the Community are geared to each other.[41] After all, the regulation in Art. 250 of

---

34 In addition it has to be delimited from the International Law term of acceptance, see König (fn. 22), 25. Sure enough the concept of acceptance is less problematic, if one considers already the simple application and allowance of foreign law, respectively foreign administrative acts by internal authorities, being an act of acceptance.

35 Schmidt-Aßmann, in: *Festschrift für Bernhardt*, 1995, 1283 (1303) and similarly Röhl (fn. 22), 29 f., as well as by Bar, *Internationales Privatrecht I*, 1987, mn. 253. Differently Götz, in: *Liber Amicorum Jaenicke*, 763 (779), under the accentuation of the Member State execution competence and the text of various directives, as well as Royla, *Grenzüberschreitende Finanzmarktaufsicht in der EG 2000*, 55 ff. and on the affair also König (fn. 22), 27. About the differentiation between norm acceptance and the acceptance of administrative actions Beyer, *Rechtsnormanerkennung im Binnenmarkt*, 1998, 26 f.; about the authority reference of the acceptance already Käte Weiß, *Die Anerkennung ausländischer Verwaltungsakte*, Dissertation Göttingen 1932, 45.

36 Schlag, *Grenzüberschreitende Verwaltungsbefugnisse im EG-Binnenmarkt*, 1998, 49 with fn. 127.

37 Sceptically however, Engel, *Die Verwaltung 25* (1992), 437 (452). In the synopsis Pernice/Kadelbach, DVBl 1996, 1100 (1109 f.).

38 Röhl (fn. 22), 3 ff.

39 Röhl (fn. 22), 21.

40 Article 7 of Council Directive 70/156/EEC of 6 February 1970 on the approximation of the laws of the Member States relating to the type-approval of motor vehicles and their trailers, OJ L 42, 23.2.1970, 1 in the version of Council Directive No. 92/53/EEC of 18 June 1992 amending Directive 70/156/EEC on the approximation of the laws of the Member States relating to the type-approval of motor vehicles and their trailers, OJ L 225, 10.8.1992, 1, implemented in Germany by §8 EG TypVO (BGBl. 1994 I, p. 3755).

41 About the procedure of the "Novel Food" Regulation (EC) No. 258/97 of the European Parliament and of the Council of 27 January 1997 concerning novel foods and novel food ingredients, OJ L 43, 14.2.1997, p. 1, Wahl/Groß, DVBl 1998, 2 (5 ff.). In detail, *Groß, Die Produktzulassung von Novel Food*, 2000.

the Community Customs Code[42] belongs thematically to the free movement of goods, whereby administrative acts of the Member State customs authorities – as decisions legally defined in Article 4 No. 5 of the Community Customs Code[43] – are binding for the other Member States.

Accreditation decisions in the area of the freedom of establishment and services are transnational administrative acts particularly.[44] Within this scope again, the acceptance of professional qualifying examinations on material legal harmonised basis is especially illustrative. For healthcare professions, for example, there is an obligation for the acceptance of equivalent diplomas.[45] With directive 89/48/EEC[46] a general acceptance obligation for higher education diplomas has finally been added on a notedly thin harmonisation basis.[47] A special regulation exists for lawyers; here the registration in a register is intended to be a national authority decision.[48]

---

42 Council Regulation (EEC) No 2913/92 of 12 October 1992 establishing the Community Customs Code, OJ L 302, 19 October 1992, 1, in the version of Regulation (EC) No 82/97 of the European Parliament and of the Council of 19 December 1996 amending Regulation (EEC) No 2913/92 establishing a Community Customs Code, OJ L 17, 21.1.1997, 1.

43 Definition: "any official act by the customs authorities pertaining to customs rules giving a ruling on a particular case, such act having legal effects on one or more specific or identifiable persons…", thereto Witte, in: *id.*, *Zollkodex*, 2. Edition 1998, Art. 4 mn. 2 "Entscheidung"; Kadelbach (fn. 23), 326.

44 Sometimes also the broadcasting state principle according to the Council Directive 89/552/EEC of 3 October 1989 on the coordination of certain provisions laid down by law, Regulation or Administrative Action in Member States concerning the pursuit of television broadcasting activities, OJ L 298, 17 October 1989, p. 23; amended by Directive 97/36/EC of the European Parliament and of the Council of 30 June 1997 amending Council Directive 89/552/EEC on the coordination of certain provisions laid down by law, regulation or administrative action in Member States concerning the pursuit of television broadcasting activities, OJ L 202, 30. 7.1997, p. 60 is brought in connection with the transnational administrative act (e.g. by Stelkens (fn. 10), §35 mn. 255, fn. 1392). This is erroneous insofar as the directive does not necessarily require an approval of television shows.

45 See the debate concerning the individual directives Stumpf, in: Dauses (ed.), *Handbuch des EU-Wirtschaftsrechts, Loseblatt, Stand: Dezember 1997*, chapter E II mn. 40 ff. *Cf.* there mn. 56 ff. also for the legal situation for craft professions.

46 Council Directive 89/48/EEC of 21 December 1988 on a general system for the recognition of higher-education diplomas awarded on completion of professional education and training of at least three years' duration, OJ L 19, 24.1.1989, p. 16 (supplemented by Council Directive 92/51/EEC of 18 June 1992 on a second general system for the recognition of professional education and training to supplement Directive 89/48/EEC, OJ L 209, 24 July 1992, p. 25). *Cf.* in addition the (standardised) Directive 1999/42/EC of the European Parliament and of the Council of 7 June 1999 establishing a mechanism for the recognition of qualifications in respect of the professional activities covered by the Directives on liberalisation and transitional measures and supplementing the general systems for the recognition of qualifications, OJ L 201, 31 July 1999, p. 77.

47 Cf. Götz, in: *Liber Amicorum Jaenicke*, 763 (781 f.).

48 Article 3 of Directive 98/5/EC of the European Parliament and of the Council of 16 February 1998 to facilitate practice of the profession of lawyer on a permanent basis in a Member State other than that in which the qualification was obtained, OJ L 77, 16 February 1998, 36.

Additionally, according to the relevant directives, as well as the mandatory official accreditation of banking establishments ("European Passport")[49] as that of direct and life insurance establishments apply to the entire Community.[50] Similar regulations exist for investment funds and bond services,[51] whereby in all mentioned cases material administrative regulations about the premises of the acceptance of such establishments exist.[52] For banks and insurance companies, the transnationality also expands to include surveillance measures, since for the bank, or insurance surveillance, the state of origin remains responsible according to the principle of state of origin control.[53] Individual case decisions of the responsible authority abroad, being addressed to the bank or insurance resident there, can, with their legal effect, also concern the branches of these companies in the Federal Republic of Germany.[54]

---

49 Now Article 18 f of the Directive 2000/12/EC of the European Parliament and of the Council of 20 March 2000 relating to the taking up and pursuit of the business of credit institutions, OJ L 126, 26.05.2000, p. 1 (in the version of Directive 2000/28/EC of the European Parliament and of the Council of 18 September 2000 amending Directive 2000/12/EC relating to the taking up and pursuit of the business of credit institutions, OJ L 275, 27 October 2000, p. 37), reaching back to Article 18(1) Second Council Directive 89/646/EEC of 15 December 1989 on the coordination of laws, regulations and administrative provisions relating to the taking up and pursuit of the business of credit institutions and amending Directive 77/780/EEC, OJ L 386, 30 December 1989, p. 1, on this Hübner, in: Dauses (ed.) (fn. 45), Chapter E. IV. mn. 11; Schlag (fn. 36), 46; Hellenthal, *Das Bankenaufsichtsrecht in der Europäischen Gemeinschaft*, 1992, 50 ff.

50 Article 5 of the First Council Directive 73/239/EEC of 24 July 1973 on the coordination of laws, regulations and administrative provisions relating to the taking-up and pursuit of the business of direct insurance other than life assurance, OJ L 228, 16 August 1973, p. 3, in the version of Article 7 of the Council Directive 92/49/EEC of 18 June 1992 on the coordination of laws, regulations and administrative provisions relating to direct insurance other than life assurance and amending Directives 73/239/EEC and 88/357/EEC (third non-life insurance Directive), OJ L 228, 11.8.1992, p. 1; Article 7(1) of the First Council Directive 79/267/EEC of 5 March 1979 on the coordination of laws, regulations and administrative provisions relating to the taking up and pursuit of the business of direct life assurance, OJ L 63, 13.3.1979, 1 in the version of Article 4 of the Council Directive 92/96/EEC of 10 November 1992 on the coordination of laws, regulations and administrative provisions relating to direct life assurance and amending Directives 79/267/EEC and 90/619/EEC (third life assurance Directive), OJ L 360, 9.12.1992, p. 1. On this, Hübner (fn. 49), Chapter E. IV. mn. 75.

51 Article 14(1) oft he Council Directive 93/22/EEC of 10 May 1993 on investment services in the securities field, OJ L 141, 11 June 1993, p. 27; Article 4 Subparagraph 2 of the Council Directive 85/611/EEC of 20 December 1985 on the coordination of laws, regulations and administrative provisions relating to undertakings for collective investment in transferable securities (UCITS), OJ L 375, 31 December 1985, p. 3. In detail – also about amendments proposed– G. P. Calliess, *EWS 2000*, 432.

52 Erichsen (fn. 25), §3 mn. 10 with fn. 41; about bank and insurance law, Hübner (fn. 49), mn. 7 ff. and 61 ff.

53 Banks: Article 26(1) of the credit institution directive (fn. 49); insurances: Article 13 of the direct and Article 15 of the life insurance directives (fn. 50). *Cf.* Royla (fn. 35), 41 ff.

54 According to Article 1 No. 3 of the credit institutions directive (fn. 49) branches are places of business which form a legally dependent, i.e. not capable of holding rights, part of a credit institution.

Setting aside the special regulation of the professional accreditation for lawyers, the transnational effect appears in the cases referred to because of the Community's legal requirement set out in the relevant directive, combined with the German legal implementation act. Accordingly, one can speak about genuine transnationality[55] to this extent. The German legal implementation act (*Umsetzungsrechtsakt*) in question should not be stressed too much, since its meaning is heavily relativised[56] by the detailed legal requirements of the directive as well as the possibility of direct effect and interpretation in accordance with the directive.[57] Apart from the genuine transnationality, the transnationality is affected by the requirement of additional acceptation acts by the target state of the service or the branch.[58] A German administrative act facilitating the transnationality of decisions of a foreign authority becomes subject to judicial protection as well as to the continuance, factual and declaring effect.[59] However, the transnationality persists within the scope of the binding pre effects of foreign decisions, which can be distinct in various ways, depending on whether they concern the foreign administrative act as a whole or determinations of single facts in terms of the caveat of additional Member State examination.[60] In individual cases, this examination caveat can allow the decision in such a measure to be shifted completely to the German authority and that the term transnationality can no longer be applied – not even in very wide terms. Such possibilities of examination by Member States also exist because of the caveats in Articles 30, 39(3), 46, 55 in connection with Articles 46 and 58 of the EC Treaty as well as because of the immanent limits of the fundamental freedoms,[61] so that the principle of acceptance does not lead to a creation of transnational administrative acts in primary law.[62]

For the effect-related transnationality of administrative acts, there are advancements which reach beyond the law of the single European market. The

55 Schmidt-Aßmann, EuR 1996, 270 (301).

56 In this direction as well Röhl (fn. 22), 29 f. Different in emphasis, Fastenrath, *Die Verwaltung 31* (1998), 277 (303); explicitly differing Stelkens (fn. 22), §35 mn. 255a, as well as Becker, DVBl 2001, 855 (862), to whom "…European legal regulations merely are impulse or catalyst…" for the administrative laws of the according Member States are.

57 On this, Ruffert, in: Calliess/*id.* (eds.), *EUV/EGV*, 1999, Article 249 EGV mn. 69 ff. and 106 ff.

58 About this gradation, Schmidt-Aßmann, *EuR* 1996, 270 (301).

59 Cf. Fastenrath, *Die Verwaltung 31* (1998), 277 (303), as well as Meng (fn. 17), 92 f., the latter referring to all acts of acceptance.

60 About the individual stages of intensity Neßler (fn. 23), 24 ff.

61 Basically, Hoffmann, *Die Grundfreiheiten des EG-Vertrages als koordinationsrechtliche und gleichheitsrechtliche Abwehrrechte* 2000, 56 ff.

62 Instructive Götz, in: *Liber Amicorum Jaenicke*, 763 (764 ff.), as well as Marburger/Enders, in: *Jahrbuch des Umwelt- und Technikrechts 1994* (UTR 27), 333 (336 ff.), with reference to the ECJ's jurisdiction each time. About the principle of acceptance in primary law, also Bleckmann, JZ 1985, 1072 (1075 ff.), about the administrative legal implications beyond transnational administrative acts, von Danwitz, *Verwaltungsrechtliches System und Europäische Integration*, 1996, 407 ff.

uniform visa according to Article 10 of the Schengen Agreement[63] still belongs to European law and applies in the entire Community except for the UK and the Republic of Ireland.[64] Beyond the Community level, the stadium of genuine transnationality has not been reached, but it is not excluded for the future. According to Article 4 of the Agreement on the Application of Sanitary and Phytosanitary Measures,[65] which has been concluded within the scope of the WTO, the WTO-members have to recognise the measures of other members, if the protection level, which is regarded as appropriate by the importing member, is objectively reached. This examination caveat destroys so far the unlimited transnationality of sanitary and phytosanitary measures abroad. In the WTO requirements for product safety, developments are moving more towards a differentiated administrative regime of the conformity evaluations.[66]

Numerous indications for this approach to the term of the transnational administrative act can be deduced from the analysis of administrative acts, the transnationality of which is communicated by their legal effects. Transnational administrative acts have to be aimed at being able to be effective beyond the territory of the state of residence of the issuing authority. This requirement is fulfilled in an especially demonstrative way, if it is only those legal effects, which quasi cross the boarder. Thereby, it becomes obvious that not every German administrative act with a foreign reference is a transnational administrative act.[67] The official decisions directed at a foreign citizen, but also the banishment out of the federal territory, do not belong to it. They are enacted by International Law in conformity with the exercise of territorial sovereignty.[68] Foreign authorities are not bound by their legal effects. The transnational effects also have to appear specifically as legal effects, not only as factual results as in the case of the approval of environmentally relevant facilities close to borders. Accordingly, in this situation, the transboundary protection of subjective-public rights does not depend on a transboundary effect of the approval, for which there is no legal basis.[69] This leads to the consequence that foreign parties concerned have the administrative legal right of action as well as keep their *foreign* civil law

63 According to Art. 1 of the Protocol (No 2) of the Schengen acquis within the EU's scope, the Schengen Agreement is part of the Union law since the coming into effect of the Amsterdam Treaty; cf. Brechmann, in: Calliess/Ruffert (fn. 56), Art. 61 EGV mn. 10.

64 Harings, *Grenzüberschreitende Zusammenarbeit der Polizei- und Zollverwaltungen und Rechtsschutz in Deutschland*, 1998, 152.

65 OJ L 336, 23.12.1994, 40.

66 See the regulations of the Agreement on Technical Barriers to Trade (TBT-Agreement), OJ L 336, 23.12.1994, 86, printed at Hilf/Schorkopf (fn. 65), mn. 6, as well as at Tietje (fn. 65), mn. 5.

67 Cf. Meng (fn. 17), 76f., and Schlochauer (fn. 17), 11, related to the exterritoriality.

68 Cf.Gloria, in: Ipsen, *Völkerrecht*, 4. Auflage 1999, §23 mn. 4.

69 BVerwGE 75, 285 (286); Brandt, DVBl 1995, 779 (783 f.); Kloepfer, *DVBl 1984*, 245 (248) on the one hand, as well as *id.*, *Umweltrecht*, 2. Auflage 1998, §9 mn. 120, on the other hand; Rauschning, *ArchVR 25* (1987), 312 (314 f.); Weber, *DVBl 1987*, 377 (378). Differentiating Rausner (fn. 19), 139.

claims because of the preclusion effect of §14 Phrase 1 BImSchG (German Law on Federal Immission Control) (where required with §7 (6) AtomG (German Atomic Energy Act)).[70]

Additionally, the issuance by an institution of the public administration also belongs to the characteristics of transnational administrative acts, according to the traditional administrative act term, as well as the individual case reference. The administrative structures of EC Product Safety law, in particular, demonstrate that there is no implicitness in the former. Forms of action beyond the one-sided, public legal orders by authorities are rightly not included in the term.

In addition, the individual case reference of the transnational administrative act results from the typical regulation subject, by virtue of legal effect. The examination of the individual operation of a single person or – in border areas – of a single product, is always in question. Insofar it is harmless, that in legal systems, other than the German, partly also normative acts (*Normativakte*) are considered to be administrative acts.

Finally it has to be mentioned that the transnationality of administrative acts requires a minimum level of confidence in the material legal regulations of other legal systems. This confidence is usually created by international or community legal harmonisation,[71] in the individual case also by procedural links with the supranational levels.[72]

2.1.2. Adressee-related transnationality

For the second form of decision in transnational administrative acts, the transnational character results from the fact that the issuing authority and the addressee of the administrative act are located in different states. Such "correspondence administrative acts" go deeper into the area of territorial sovereignty than those whose transnationality results from their effect, since according to the traditional rules the mere service of official acts abroad is already regarded as illegitimate. The decisive factor is determined by the basis on which the states admit the intrusion by transnational actions in their territory.

Not only the harmonisation of material legal benchmarks, but the mandatory transboundary authority participation, in particular, builds this basis in an especially demonstrative case of the application of addressee-related transnationality. The permission for the shipment of waste according to

---

70 BVerwGE 75, 285 (287 f.); on this Bothe, *UPR 1987*, 170 (171); Beyerlin, *EuGRZ 1987*, 119 (121). Critically about this aspect Wolfrum, *DVBl 1984*, 493 (500 f.). However, the execution of foreign civil law judgements will fail because of the *ordre public*: BVerwGE 75, 285 (287) under reference to BVerfGE 72, 66 (78 f.).

71 Explicitly, *Götz*, in: *Liber Amicorum Jaenicke*, 763 (780); also see Hoffmann-Riem, in: Schmidt-Aßmann/id. (eds.) (fn. 8), 317 (358); Klein, in: Starck (ed.), *Rechtsvereinheitlichung durch Gesetze*, 1992, 117 (140); Schlag (fn. 36), 50, as well already Weiß (fn. 35), 5.

72 As it is the case in the "Novel-Food" Regulation, see above fn. 41.

Regulation (EEC) 259/93[73] is given by the responsible authority of the country of destination with regard to the applicant in the shipping country (Art. 4(2), 5 of the Regulation). However, prior to this permission the participation of the shipping country is required and, if necessary, that of one or more transit states. The receiving state, being responsible for the issuance is bound by the objections and obligations of those other states, and includes them – if it comes to a positive decision in consideration of them – in terms of a "kind of concentration effect" in the shipment approval.[74] The transnational administrative act as the result of a uniform administrative procedure,[75] is an exceptional phenomenon of the highly integrated Community law system, which has yet not appeared outside this legal system. This can be shown by the example of the transfrontier shipment of waste. According to the international Basel Convention, nevertheless, coordination between the states concerned is necessary. However, the approval is given on the basis of the acceptance of the shipping state by the state receiving, so that an addressee-related transnational legal effect does not develop.[76] In turn, transnational procedural participations are also provided for in other parts of the EC law, as in Article 7 of the Council Directive 85/337/EEC of 27 June 1985 on the assessment of the effects on the environment of certain public and private projects[77] and Article 17(2) of the Council Directive 96/61/EC of 24 September 1996 concerning integrated pollution prevention and control.[78]

---

73 Council Regulation (EEC) No 259/93 of 1 February 1993 on the supervision and control of shipments of waste within, into and out of the European Community, OJ L 30, 6 February 1993, 1, in the version of Council Regulation (EC) No. 120/97 of 20 January 1997 amending Regulation (EC) No 259/93 on the supervision and control of shipments of waste within, into and out of the European Community, OJ L 22, 24 January 1997, 14 and 1999/816/EC: Commission Decision of 24 November 1999 adapting, pursuant to Articles 16(1) and 42(3), Annexes II, III, IV and V to Council Regulation (EEC) No 259/93 on the supervision and control of shipments of waste within, into and out of the European Community (notified under document number C(1999) 3880) (Text with EEA relevance), OJ L 316, 10.12.1999, 45.

74 Schröder, in *Festschrift Ritter*, 1997, 957 (958).

75 Schröder, *id.*, 957 (960 and 964); Engels, *Grenzüberschreitende Abfallverbringung nach EG-Recht*, 1999, 120 ff.; Krieger, in: Rengeling (ed.), *Handbuch zum europäischen und deutschen Umweltrecht*, Band 2, 1998, §75 mn. 37.

76 Article 6(1) and (2) of the Basel Convention of 22 March 1989 on the Control of Transboundary Movements of Hazardous Wastes and their Disposal, German version in: BGBl. II 1994, 2704; on this Beyerlin, *Umweltvölkerrecht*, 2000, mn. 436; Karsten, *Europarechtliche und völkerrechtliche Aspekte der grenzüberchreitenden Abfallentsorgung*, 1997, 203 f. Similar Art. 6 of the – not yet effective – Bamako Convention on the Ban of the Transport into Africa and the Control of Transboundary Movement and Management of Hazardous Wastes Within Africa of 29 January 1991, I.L.M. 30 (1991), 773.

77 Council Directive 85/337/EEC of 27 June 1985 on the assessment of the effects of certain public and private projects on the environment, OJ L 175, 5 July 1985, 40, in the version of Council Directive 97/11/EC of 3 March 1997 amending Directive 85/337/EEC on the assessment of the effects of certain public and private projects on the environment, OJ L 73, 14 March 1997, 5; also see §4 a BauGB (= the German Statutory Code on Construction and Building) and §16 ROG (= German Regional Planning Act), which do not trace back to Community law obligations (for §4 a BauGB, Schrödter, in: *id.*, BauGB, 6. Auflage 1998, §4a mn. 3).

78 Council Directive 96/61/EC of 24 September 1996 concerning integrated pollution prevention and control, OJ L 257, 10 October 1996, 26.

However, there is another kind of addressee-referred transnational administrative act which reaches beyond Community law. At the same time, administrative decisions within the scope of transboundary regional municipal cooperation are a sort of form of action with a certain tradition, and they are historically antecedents of the European integration by EC and EU.[79] Institutions of municipal and regional transboundary cooperation can also be founded by foreign law.[80] As an example of such transboundary administrative management,[81] the transboundary regional administration union according to Article 11 of the Karlsruhe Agreement may be mentioned, which was signed by Germany, France, Luxembourg and Switzerland in 1996.[82] This administrative union is subject to the law of the state of its domicile (Article 11(1) phrase 2).[83] Individual case decisions[84] which are binding in Germany, therefore, can also be made by foreign law, since this domicile is not in Germany. They are then transnational administrative acts. Unlike the waste shipment case, they are certainly not the result of uniform transnational administrative procedures. The transboundary participation of German authorities in the transboundary cooperation is, however, decisive for the acceptance of their transnational effect.

In general, an examination of the addressee-related form of decision confirms the findings made so far concerning the term of transnational administrative act. This does not only apply to the characteristics of the official authorship and the provision in individual cases (*Einzelfallregelung*), which both are not challenged by the inclusion of the addressee related form of appearance, but also for the necessity of a basis justifying the transnationality, here by a procedural coordination of the participating administrations. Also the concept of transnationality as phenomenon of transboundary legal effects of administrative acts is upheld. Administrative acts directed at legal subjects abroad, or directed at legal subjects in Germany in the regulation areas described are not just sovereign acts on foreign state territory, as the issue of a visa by a foreign embassy or the signing of a certificate of appointment by an administration official on a state visit, for example:[85] they are directed more towards transboundary consequences.

---

79 Beyerlin, *Rechtsprobleme der lokalen grenzüberschreitenden Zusammenarbeit*, 1988, 43 ff.; *id.*, ArchVR 27 (1989), 286 (289 ff.); furthermore, Witmer, *Grenznachbarliche Zusammenarbeit*, 1979.

80 Beck, *Die Übertragung von Hoheitsrechten auf kommunale grenznachbarliche Einrichtungen*, 1995, 32 and 140 ff.; Schröder, *ThürVBl 1998*, 97 (98).

81 Term: Schröder, *ThürVBl 1998*, 97.

82 BGBl. 1997 II, 1159. At a glance, Heberlein, *BayVBL 1997*, 737. Further comparable conventions at Halmes, *DÖV 1996*, 933 f.

83 *Cf.* on this Heberlein, *DVBl 1999*, 1244 (1247).

84 See Article 8(4) and *e contrario* Article 9(2) of the Agreement as well as the delimitation by Article 4(3): no regulation and police authorisation.

85 Cf. Schlochauer (fn. 17), 11.

2.1.3. *Authority-related transnationality*

The concept of sovereign acts on foreign state territory, which is borrowed from international law,[86] has probably added to the fact that a last category is predominantly not counted as one of the forms of appearance of the transnational administrative act.[87] In addition, the situation in which a foreign authority itself crosses the state border in order to issue an administrative act abroad, even in the rather rare cases so far, in which authorities of other states are granted the competence for crossing the frontier crossing still belongs to the marginal phenomenon. However, this does not justify leaving the authority-related transnationality out of the considerations. Indeed, the administrative act itself does not cross – figuratively speaking – the border, but is "transported" by the issuing authority abroad. However, the legal effects are identical. Whether the authority abroad issues an administrative act which is effective in Germany or addresses this act to an addressee in Germany or crosses the borders itself in order to issue an administrative act there – the precisely chosen and agreed modus cannot only depend on factual logics but also on coincidences, so that a falling apart of the legal effects would be inadvisable.

Often, the already rare authorisations concerning the execution of sovereign tasks by physically crossing the frontier have to be located fundamentally outside administrative law. The usual transboundary police authorisations of pursuit, observation and undercover investigation[88], according to Article 39 ff. of the Schengen Agreement refer only to the activities as part of criminal investigations. However, in this context, transnational *administrative acts* are possible but it is not possible to speak of transnational administrative acts in the criminal procedural area merely because of the quality of some basic right interventions which are similar to administrative acts – proved by §§23 ff. EGGVG (= German introduction law of the Constitution of the Courts).[89] The administrative decisions within the scope of the Schengen Information System should be linked to a border crossing of the decision making agency in the rarest cases.[90] However, the bilateral police law agreement between Switzerland and Germany covers the competences of pursuit, transboundary observation and undercover investigation also for pre-emptive police measures[91] and thereby enables the issuance of

86 Cf. Siegrist, *Hoheitsakte auf fremdem Staatsgebiet*, 1987.

87 Cf. Harings (fn. 64), 153 f.; see however the link at Ehlers (fn. 23), 8 f.

88 Cremer, *ZaöRV 60 (2000)*, 103 (106 ff.).

89 Criminal procedural "measures" in terms of Art. 23(1) EGGVG (also see (2) of the provision) are related to the administrative acts but are not identical: Böttcher, in: Rieß (ed.), Löwe-Rosenberg, *Großkommentar StPO*, 10. Lieferung 1999, §23 EGGVG mn. 43 f.

90 See Article 102 ff. of the Schengen Agreement.

91 *Cf.* Article 15, 16(1) No. 2 and (7) as well as 18(1) of the Treaty between the Swiss Confederation and the Federal Republic of Germany concerning transboundary police and judicial Cooperation (Swiss-German Police Treaty) of 27 April 1999 (not ratified yet by the Federal Republic of Germany), BT-Drucksache 14/5735 of 30 March 2001. On this, Cremer, *ZaöRV 60*

transnational administrative acts of specific individual case arrangements in the terms mentioned. Similar restrictions apply to the related authorisations of the common border check agencies, although their importance is decreasing.[92]

Doubts concerning the transnationality of these administrative acts may arise as a consequence of individual regulations in the police laws of the *Länder* (German States). It has been determined in §86(3) 2nd clause in connection with (2) POG RP (Police Law of Rhineland-Palatine) that public servants of foreign police authorities who are carrying out activities in Rhineland-Palatine in accordance with international law provisions have the same authority/powers as the Rhineland-Palatine police. Several German states have comparable regulations for the activity of foreign police men. These regulations follow the example of §52(2) MEPolG (Draft of a Uniform Police law), which, however, only refers to the activities of police officials from one German states in another.[93] However, state law provisions can neither create nor expand authority for foreign police officers. Under §86(3) 2nd clause POG RP, Belgian, Luxembourg or French police officials are not converted into Rhineland-Palantine nationals and their decisions are not converted into decisions of the state of Rhineland-Palatine, but this clause completes the international law based powers of foreign police by a limitation under the constitution.[94] Without a basis in international law, such state law provisions would be void. Consequently, in addition to the provisions of the Schengen Agreement,[95] the bilateral Police Treaties[96] bind the police in their transboundary activities with regard to the legal system of the state on whose territory they are active.

A further example of possible authority-related transnationality leads back to the harmonised law for domestic markets. Within the scope of the bank and insurance supervision by the state of origin, the supervising authority can also

---

(2000), 103 (107, 108 and 110 f.). The Treaty between the Federal Republic of Germany and the Czech Republic concerning the Cooperation of Police Authorities and Border Patrol Authorities in the Border Areas (BR-Drucksache 579/01 of 17 August 2001), signed 19 September 2000 (ratification approved by the Bundeskabinett on 20 June 2001), indeed also concerns the preemptive police actions (preamble, Article 1 and 4), but pursuit (Article 8) is only acceptable under very restricted circumstances. The transboundary exercise of execution authorisations is not acceptable (Article 11(1) phrase 1).

92 Cf. E. Kirchhof, *Die gemeinsamen Grenzabfertigungsstellen der Bundesrepublik Deutschland mit Nachbarstaaten*, 1986, 66 ff. and 86 ff.

93 §78(4) PolG BW; Article 11(5) phrase (2) BayPOG; §102 (3) phrase 2 HessSOG; §9 SOG MV; §103(2) Phrase 2 NdsGefAG, §88(4) SaarlPOlG; §77(4) SächsPolG; §91(3) Phrase 2 SOG LSA; §170 LVwG SH. Therefore, no according regulation exists in Brandenburg, Bremen, Berlin, Hamburg, North Rhine Westphalia and Thuringia.

94 On this term also Cremer, *ZaöRV* 60 (2000), 103 (116 ff.).

95 Article. 40(3a) and 41(5a). On this, Matínez Soria, *VerwArch 89* (1998), 400 (415 f.).

96 Article 15(4) Phrase 2 in connection with Article 14(3) No. 1, Article 16(4) Nr. 1 of the Swiss-German Police Treaty (regarding preemptive-police authorisations); Article 8(2a) of the German-Czech Police Treaty.

examine branches abroad on-site or have them examined.[97] The German inspectors abroad, or the foreign inspector in Germany are also authorised to impose sanctions except that of direct force (*unmittelbarer Zwang*).[98] However, transnational administrative acts are hard to imagine here at the moment, since in practice similar dispositions are issued against the company to which the branch belongs, because these branches are not capable of holding rights themselves.[99] However, once the transboundary economic administrative law inspection has been permitted, it seems that other constructions will not be excluded in the future. Furthermore, with regard to the contact with territorial sovereignty, it may not be underestimated that the supply of information abroad can pave the way for internal administrative acts.[100]

2.2. INTERMEDIATE RESULT: THE CHARACTERISTICS OF THE TRANSNATIONAL ADMINISTRATIVE ACT

Like the usual administrative act of German administrative law, the characteristic form of the transnational administrative act can also be found by an abstraction of single occurrences in special regulation areas. The transnational administrative act can be defined as an official individual case decision, which is directed at the creation of a legal effect abroad, by either having the legal effect occurring abroad, the addressee being beyond the state border, or by having the authority cross that frontier physically. The transnationality of this legal form requires a procedural or material basis.

Transnational administrative acts of foreign authorities are not administrative acts in Germany in terms of §35 VwVfG (= German Administrative Procedural Law Act) or the states' administrative procedural regulations, since those can, according to §1 VwVfG and the appropriate states' administrative procedural regulations, only be applied to the administrative activity of German authorities. The transnational administrative act is not codified in §35 VwVfG, but is a form of action, created out of the synopsis of transboundary administrative

97 Bank: Article 29(1) of the Credit Institute Directive (fn. 49), respectively, Article 24(1) of the Directive on investment services in the securities field (fn. 51), implemented in Germany by §24 a KWG (= banking law) for German banks with branches abroad and §53 b KWG for foreign banks with branches in Germany (the provisions correspond: Braun, in: Boos/Fischer/Schulte-Mattler (eds.), *Kreditwesengesetz*, 2000, §24 a mn. 6); *cf.* on this: Gramlich, in: R. Schmidt (ed.), *Öffentliches Wirtschaftsrecht*, BT 1, 1995, §5 mn. 42 f; Schlag (fn. 36), 56 ff.; *Versicherungen*: Article 14 Direct Insurance Directive, respectively, Art. 16 Life Insurance Directive (fn. 50), in Germany implemented by §110 a (3) Phrase 2 VAG (= Law on Insurance Supervision).

98 Royla (fn. 35), 103; Schlag (fn. 36), 61 ff.

99 See above, fn. 54. In the result also Stelkens (fn. 10), §35 mn. 257, who thinks however, that at this point "many things are not clear, yet". Critically from a practical point of view, Kurth, WM 2000, 1521 (1529).

100 Groß, JZ 1994, 596 (599).

procedures, of transboundary administrative management. Only German authorities can issue administrative acts according to §35 VwVfG,[101] which is however, not a statement about a possible corresponding application of provisions and principles of the German administrative law on such administrative acts, which are enacted abroad with the objective of an effect in Germany.

2.3. THE SUPRAREGIONAL ADMINISTRATIVE ACT IN FEDERAL STATES

The problem of the regulation of transboundary individual cases also occurs within the Federal Republic of Germany.[102] This does not apply only to the alternative of supraregionality by virtue of the addressee relation because of local administrative competence which has expanded over the federation. Known phenomena also include a supraregionality by virtue of legal effect by the crossing of state borders by state authorities. While the crossing of state borders by the police is covered by corresponding state law regulations according to the Draft for a uniform Police Law,[103] it lacks a general simple sub-constitutional or even constitutional acceptance provision for effect-related supraregional administrative acts, and this is remarkable insofar as there is a convincing historical role model[104] in Article IV of the American Constitution of 1787, which provides all single state legal actions in the entire area of the USA with "full faith and credit".[105]

For the problem of the supraregional effect of administrative acts of state authorities, solutions have been found, which have been at least practically convincing, if also not always satisfactory, whereby the independent category of a "supraregional administrative act", which receives its binding effect for other state authorities by its very supraregionality, has been rightly rejected as circular.[106] For the execution of federal laws by the states, it has been argued with some persuasiveness, using the argument that a federal state required even legal

101 Nessler (fn. 23), 28 with fn. 109.

102 This parallel is also made by Becker, DVBl 2001, 855 (863).

103 Critical about these regulations regarding the knowledge of the police officers and the problems of judicial protection, Drews/Wacke/Vogel/Martens, *Gefahrenabwehr*, 9. Edition 1986, §73 3 b β (115 f.).

104 Also Switzerland and Austria have no comparable provision for administrative acts; Article 61 BV old version/ Article 122(3) BV 1999 at least regulates the acceptance of cantonal civil judgments throughout Switzerland.

105 "Section 1. Full faith and Credit shall be given in each State to the public Acts, Records and judicial Proceedings of every other State. And the Congress may by general laws prescribe the Manner in which such Arts, Records and Proceedings shall be proved, and the Effects thereof."

106 Lerche, in: Maunz/Dürig (eds.), *GG*, Article. 83 (Stand: 1983), mn. 49; Isensee, in: *HStR IV*, §98 mn. 35. The term has been formed by Wolff/Bachof, *Verwaltungsrecht I*, 9. Auflage 1974, §50 IV a. In older literature (reference at Lerche, id., fn. 179) it also covered an administrative

execution. This is no longer in question in the administrative practise, and is supported by the power of validity of the federal laws being connected to their federation-wide execution.[107] However, in the wide area of execution of *Länder* laws by the *Länder* themselves, things basically remain at the territorial limitation of federal state (*Gliedstaat*) administrative powers, and this also regards the legal effects of the execution of these powers.[108] This is an unsatisfactory conclusion in the light of the narrow relations in the Federal Republic of Germany, and is remedied by the agreements between the states and other forms of cooperation in the course of cooperative federalism.[109] In addition, the Constitution contains special constitutional guarantees in which, from the perspective of those whose rights are infringed, the recourse to administrative assistance in accordance with Article 35 of the German Constitution[110] or a specific obligation to ensure the general interest[111] which is difficult to infer from the Constitution seems less convincing than the argument that the repudiation might be an intervention based on basic rights which are indigent in a justification.[112] This – for the area of the public service – can possibly be combined with the guarantee included in Article 33(2) GG. In the light of the attempts at well constructed cooperative solutions already mentioned, there have been so far no subsequent administrative legal problems of the continuance, factual and determining effect.[113]

3. THE EFFICIENCY OF TRANSNATIONAL ADMINISTRATIVE ACTS IN GERMAN ADMINISTRATIVE LAW

3.1. THE INTRASTATE EFFECTS OF TRANSNATIONAL ADMINISTRATIVE ACTS

However, in these effects lies the core of the difficulty concerning transnational administrative acts. The issuance of a transnational administrative act by a

act, for which an administrative competence of the Federation by virtue of the affair should have existed.

107 Seibert, *Die Bindungswirkung von Verwaltungsakten*, 1989, 274 f.; Henneke, in: Knack (ed.), *VwVfG*, 6. Auflage 1998, §35 mn. 3; Lerche (fn. 106), Article. 83 mn. 50.

108 BVerfGE 11, 6 (19); on this Lerche (fn. 106), Article. 83 mn. 49 sub bb).

109 Seibert (fn. 107), 278. Main example: Acceptance of certificates; *cf. Püttner/Rux*, in: Achterberg/Püttner/Würtenberger (eds.), *Besonderes Verwaltungsrecht I*, 2. Edition 2000, §14 mn. 148.

110 BVerwGE 22, 299 (307); von Mangoldt/Klein, *GG*, Band II, 1966, Article. 35 annotation IV; Seibert (fn. 107), 286 f.; Maunz, in: *id.*/Dürig (eds.) (fn. 106), Article. 35 (Stand: 1973) mn. 7.

111 Bleckmann, *NVwZ* 1986, 1 (4); Seibert (fn. 107), 287.

112 Bleckmann, NVwZ 1986, 1 (4); Seibert (fn. 107), 287.

113 See however the federally valid acceptance of private suppliers by a state media agency ByVGH, NVwZ-RR, 552 (553 f.); on this Stelkens (fn. 10), §35 mn. 256 with further references.

foreign authority can have binding effects for the subsequent decision-making of German authorities.[114] The factual effect embodied in the existence and regulation content of the transnational administrative act[115] may have effects beyond the obligations of authorities and beyond the narrower range of administrative law and demand attention also in judicial procedures, – not only in administrative procedures, but also in civil or criminal cases.[116] A transnationally effective approval prevents by virtue of its legalising effect – as subcategory of the factual effect[117] – the access of the regulatory and criminal prosecution authorities which could restrict the activity as well as the recourse of the approval's addressee in civil law, since their legal effects reach beyond the application area of the national laws.[118] A comparable obligation usually amounts to principally consistent factual determinations, if such a determining effect[119] represents the exception here, as in interstate law. The usage of the transnational administrative act as executory title[120] is also basically possible, especially in the case of transboundary authorisations in the field of supervision and danger prevention.

The importance of the described effects is especially significant if the material legal situation and the procedural requirements on the one hand, and the actual provision, on the other hand, become separated. This raises the question concerning the continuance of unlawful transnational administrative acts.

3.2. THE EVALUATION OF THE LAWFULNESS OF TRANSNATIONAL ADMINISTRATIVE ACTS

Transnational administrative acts are not issued by supranational institutions, but by state authorities. Besides the practically rare situation of complete harmonisation, they are made on the basis of national law. If the lawfulness of transnational administrative acts is only evaluated by the law of the issuing state, or is its lawfulness influenced by the law of the state, where its legal effects expand? Are legal mistakes according to the benchmarks of German

114 Cf. Erichsen (fn. 25), §13 mn. 4.

115 About the factual effect of transnational administrative acts, Happe (fn. 22), 66; Neßler (fn. 23), 120. About the factual effect of administrative acts in general, Erichsen (fn. 25), §13 mn. 4; Henneke (fn. 107), Vor §35 mn. 6.1.2; differentiating, Sachs, in: Stelkens/Bonk/*id.* (fn. 10), §44 mn. 132 and 145 ff.

116 *Cf.* only Schröder, VVDStRL 50 (1991), 196 (221 f.); Schoch, in: Hoffmann-Riem/Schmidt-Aßmann (eds.) (fn. 11), 199 (238 ff.).

117 Erichsen (fn. 25), §13 mn. 4, fn. 18; Fluck, *VerwArch 79* (1988), 406 (408 ff.); Schoch, in: Hoffmann-Riem/Schmidt-Aßmann (eds.) (fn. 11), 199 (238).

118 Against, Fastenrath, *Die Verwaltung 31* (1998), 277 (303), this would also have to apply to the civil law preclusional effect.

119 About the determining effect of administrative acts, Erichsen (fn. 25), §13 mn. 4; Sachs (fn. 115), §44 mn. 152.

120 About the title function oft he administrative act in general, Löwer, *JuS* 1980, 805 (806).

administrative law important for the evaluation of foreign administrative acts in Germany?

German International Administrative Law, which has to be the recourse for the question of the applicable law, remains in a basic dogmatic-theoretic controversy.[121] The first main movement, founded by *Karl Neumeyer*, tries to discover the *border norms*, one-sided collision norms, hidden in the material regulations of the administrative law, which describe the meaning of national German administrative law.[122] The opposite school of thought, which is specially linked to the work of *Klaus Vogel*, denies the existence and necessity of such border norms. The function of the International Administrative Law diverged from that of the Private International Law, since as a consequence of the territory principle, the norms of international administrative law were basically only directed at a state's own authorities, so that the typical question in the Private International Law concerning the choice of the applicable legal system rarely appeared. Therefore, a legal classification of the applicability of foreign law did not belong to the factual norms; the territory principle would not conflict with such an application.[123]

This basically legal conflict on dogma, which concerns both the basic understanding of International Administrative Law and conflict of laws in general, needs to be recognised at this point, but need not be solved, however. Both basic concepts lead to the same result in evaluating the transnational administrative acts, even though they do not use the term of transnational administrative act.[124] By using the category of the "acceptance", both establish that foreign administrative law is applicable to the administrative act which has to be evaluated and that the result of the interpretation and application of the respective provisions has to be accepted by the German authorities.[125] As already indicated, the term acceptance is erroneous, since an additional examination, which is prior to the legal effects of the administrative act, contradicts the concept of transnationality. The intention is rather that the administrative act made abroad is not further examined in Germany, since the German legal system accepts it, by virtue of the higher authority. Only the foreign law is important for

---

121 See the demonstrations at Beyerlin (fn. 79), 399 ff.; Meng (fn. 17), 191 ff.; and Rausner (fn. 19), 124 ff.

122 Neumeyer, *Internationales Verwaltungsrecht*, Vierter Band, Allgemeiner Tei l, 1936, 105 f., 115 ff. Following, Hoffmann (fn. 4), 859; König (fn. 22), 11; Wolff/Bachof/Stober (fn. 4).

123 Vogel, *Der räumliche Anwendungsbereich der Verwaltungsrechtsnormen*, 1965, 298 ff.; *id.*, in: Bernhardt (ed.), Encyclopedia of Public International Law I, 1992, 22 (24 f.). Subsequent to Vogel, Sonnenberger, in: MünchKomm, BGB, Band 10, 3. Auflage 1998, Einl. IPR, mn. 356; von Bar (fn. 35), mn. 250. Sceptically also Matscher, in: *Festschrift für Beitzke*, 1979, 641.

124 Cf. Rauser (fn. 19), 125.

125 Kopp, *DVBl 1967*, 469 (470 f.); Neumeyer (fn. 122), 295 ff. (306, 310); Steindorff, in: Strupp/ Schlochauer (eds.), *Wörterbuch des Völkerrechts*, Band III, 1962, 581 (582); Vogel (fn. 123), 333 ff.; Weiß (fn. 35), 49. In detail about the category of the acceptance Happe (fn. 22), 63 ff.; Meng (fn. 17), 90 ff.

the evaluation of the lawfulness and indeed in a way an examination on its benchmark no longer needs to be executed in Germany.[126] This also applies to the execution of foreign transnational administrative acts in administrative assistance.[127]

This rule can be based upon the basis of state immunity in international law only very restrictively, since it withdraws institutions of other states acting sovereignly from the German force (*Zwangsgewalt*), but does not forbid the legal evaluation of sovereign acts which are effective in Germany.[128] There is no international law *act of state*-doctrine.[129] Rather, the international or Community law basis which is subject to the respective transnational administrative acts is more important. The transboundary effect of administrative action would be questioned, if there was a general caveat of the compatability with the law of the state, where the decision was to become effective.[130]

There could be an exception to the described rule for void transnational administrative acts.[131] This would include such administrative acts which are the object of a serious and obvious mistake,[132] according to the rules of the German administrative procedural law as well as the jurisdiction of the ECJ. At first sight, the lack of transnationality of void administrative acts seems to be inescapable. Void administrative acts are effectless, they show no legal effects and more than ever no transnational legal effects. However, when examined more closely, the transboundary continuance, factual and determining effect would have to become effective in the described terms, if the assumed voidness results from a violation of legal provisions, including responsibility provisions.[133] On the requirement basis, the voidance is only different from the unlawfulness to the

126 Following Neßler (fn. 23), 30 (on the other hand p. 31 above: no transnational effects of unlawful administrative acts), v. Danwitz, in: Schmidt-Aßmann/Hoffmann-Riem (eds.) (fn. 8), 171 (187 f.); Erichsen (fn. 25), mn. 10 with fn. 39; Stelkens (fn. 10), §35 mn. 256.

127 Groß, JZ 1994, 596 (604); Schlag (fn. 36), 233 ff.

128 Harings (fn. 64), 245 f. Basically, ICJ, France *v* Turkey (Lotus case), PCIJ Reports, Ser. A, No. 10, sub. III. – Different than here, Becker, DVBl 2001, 855 (857). About the question, if the acceptilating state by a part renunciation concerning its sovereignty can even be the defendant, Schlag (fn. 36), 222.

129 Meng, in: Bernhardt (ed.), *Encyclopedia of Public International Law IV*, 2000, 50 (52). About the *act of state*- doctrine of the American law, Folz, *Die Geltungskraft fremder Hoheitsäußerungen*, 1975.

130 Erichsen (fn. 25), mn. 10, fn. 39.

131 Explicitly, Neßler (fn. 23), 31, fn. 120; *id.*, NVwZ 1995, 863 (865, fn. 32); Engels (fn. 75), 123; Hatje, *Die gemeinschaftsrechtliche Steuerung der Wirtschaftsverwaltung* 1998, 212; Klett/Kaminski/Konzak, *WiVerw 1995*, 40 (54); Schröder, in: *Festschrift Ritter* 1997, 957 (965), as well already König (fn. 22), 54; Witte (fn. 43), Art. 250 mn. 4; also Sachs (fn. 115), §44 mn. 10 at the end; as well Happe (fn. 22), 66, in terms of a minimal examination according to the law of the issuing state.

132 ECJ, European Court reports 1987, 1005, mn. 9 (Consorzio cooperative d'abruzzo *v* Commission); European Court reports 1994, I-2555, mn. 49 (Commission *v* BASF). More detailed W. Cremer, in: Calliess/Ruffert (fn. 56), Art. 230 EGV mn. 8.

133 Different opinion in Götz, in: *Liber Amicorum Jaenicke*, 763 (786).

extent that there is a different degree, but not a different kind of violation of a provision. This – usually handled under the topic "mutual recognition" (*Anerkennung*) – concept of the transnational effect of administrative acts, however, prohibits in general a further examination of the lawfulness by authorities of the state, in which the legal effects of the administrative act become effective.[134] This also applies for minor as well as for more serious mistakes. A different evaluation is only possible in narrow, exceptional cases because of actual reasons of void administrative acts. Removing non-exercisable or immoral administrative acts – as far as they would actually appear in transboundary administrative procedures[135] – from the concept of transnationality can be justified by the assumption of according general legal principles, which are binding for the administrations on both sides of the frontier. Facing the practical irrelevance of those cases of voidance, one should not waste too much energy on the dogmatic and comparative difficulties of the reasons of such legal principles. However, the supranational formulation of the voidance benchmarks would be possible,[136] or, as in the case of import approvals applicable throughout the Community in applying the Convention on International Trade in Endangered Species of Wild Fauna and Flora, the abrogation in accordance with the issuing authority.[137]

Finally, the reference to foreign law, which is to be applied by foreign authorities exclusively also leads to a move of the judicial protection abroad.[138] There are no legal remedies for appeal under German administrative procedural law for transnational administrative acts, which develop legal effects in Germany. This can lead to practical difficulties with the addressee and authority-related transnationality, in particular. Exceptions can become meaningful and necessary for sensitive areas concerning constitutional rights, in which citizens, who usually do not have sufficient resources for prosecution abroad, are usually the addressees of aggravating administrative acts (*belastende Verwaltungsakte*).[139]

---

134 Other opinion *König* (fn. 22), 85.

135 At *Weiß* (fn. 35), 60, the problem of acceptance of immoral administrative acts without any sample cases, is mentioned.

136 *Cf. Schröder*, in: Festschrift Ritter, 957 (966). Even if the ECJ in the procedure according to Art. 226 of the EC Treaty has determined the unlawfulness of an administrative act under Community law, the mentioned result should stay the same, since the determining judgement is only effective *inter partes*, according to Art. 228(1) of the EC Treaty. Here, one is only provided the resort by a tabling according to Art. 234 of the EC Treaty (about this question *Vedder*, EuR Beiheft I/1995, 75 (90)).

137 *Cf.* the corrigendum of Article 11(2a) of the Council Regulation (EC) No 338/97 of 9 December 1996 on the protection of species of wild fauna and flora by regulating trade therein, OJ L 298, 1.11.1997, 70 (thereto: Gellermann, in: Rengeling (fn. 75), §79 mn. 63); about the problems linked to the previous regulation see the unpublished disclosed decision of the OVG NW of 19.1.1001, at Vedder, *EuR Beiheft I*/1995, 75 (90, fn. 131).

138 Cremer, *ZaöRV 60* (2000), 103 (136); Ehlers (fn. 23), 11 f.; Fastenrath, *Die Verwaltung 31* (1998), 277 (302). In detail about the problems of judicial protection regarding Article 19(4) GG, Harings (fn. 64), 336 ff.; Rauser (fn. 19), 305 ff.

139 Harings (fn. 64), 341.

However, they have to be explicitly negotiated between the countries concerned, such as the special regulation in the Schengen Agreement and the Swiss-German Police Treaty on the degree of liability.[140] Exceptionally, in these cases, it is the state in which the foreign police officers are active, which is liable for damages caused by the officers and can seek recourse from the state which employs them. For an explicit exceptional rule for primary legal protection in terms of an fictitious administrative act,[141] a basis in international law beyond the provision in some of the German states[142] already mentioned would be required, because the obstacle of the state immunity would have to be overcome in any case at this point. However, the administrative acts which are actually issued by the foreign authorities would remain transnational in terms of the definition formulated here, but would however be subject to the interest of the judicial protection of a diversified legal system.

3.3. THE BASIS OF THE EFFECTIVENESS OF UNLAWFUL TRANSNATIONAL ADMINISTRATIVE ACTS

Already the continuance of unlawful administrative acts according to German law is categorised as a situation creating a constitutional problem, whereby the discussion can be made even more extreme, by referring to the historical origin of the continuance of late constitutionalism[143] in the doctrine of administrative law. The tension evoked by constitutional considerations will inevitably become stronger, as the continuance in Germany can be neither relativised by a possibility of appeal nor by the corrective of the voidance by extensive unlawfulness, by the benchmarks of German administrative law. Also the effect of retraction and avoidance, which breaches the continuance, depends on the possibilities of foreign administrative law and the activity of the authorities there.[144]

In the *Rechtsstaat* of the constitution a legal basis[145] is required for the authorisation of the administration to make regulations which are binding in individual cases and the effectivity of which does not depend principally on their lawfulness. For administrative acts of German authorities this basis[146] is represented by §43(2) VwVfG (if necessary in connection with the administrative

---

140 Article 43(2) of the Schengen Agreement, Art. 32(3) of the German-Swiss Police Treaty (cf. Cremer, *ZaöRV 60* (2000), 103 (117)), Article 13(3) of the German-Czech Police Treaty.

141 Such as fiction is not unknown in German administrative law: Jachmann, *Die Fiktion im öffentlichen Recht*, 1998, 234 ff.

142 Different opinion, Harings (fn. 64), 255 ff.

143 Especially striking Schmidt-De Caluwe, *Der Verwaltungsakt in der Lehre Otto Mayers*, 1999, 14 ff; similarly Becker, *DVBL 2001*, 855 (858).

144 *Cf.* also Neßler (fn. 23), 77 f.

145 Schmidt–De Caluwe (fn. 143), 306 f.

146 Schmidt–De Caluwe, *VerwArch 90* (1999), 49 (64).

procedural laws of the states) with its enumeration of circumstances annulling the effectivity of administrative acts.[147] This section, §43(2) VwVfG, does not directly apply to transnational administrative acts, since the regulation only refers to administrative acts according to Part III of the VwVfG which is only applicable for actions of German authorities.[148] Not only argues the basic notion in public law according to which objections are raised against the creation by analogy of burdens to be imposed on citizens in the public law against an analogous application for transnational administrative acts. §43(2) VwVfG is also part of a regulatory system which cannot be breached by individual analogies. Withdrawal, revocation and other reasons for abrogation, especially the abrogation in administrative procedures, are executed by a foreign authority following foreign law in a transnational administrative act. However, those possibilities of abrogation build the basis of a consequent command in §43(2) VwVfG, so that its analogous application can be rejected.

The basis of the continuance of the transnational administrative act is rather more the particular special provision, which is also subject to its transnationality, no matter whether its nature is one of international or Community law. The international cooperation extends the allocation of competences between the authorities beyond the frontiers[149] and covers the regulation system of the administrative procedural law. The act of assessment of the particular international law treaty or the directly applicable Community law, or the provisions for its implementation, allocate less significance to Title III of the VwVfG as special provisions in the background and at the same time provide a legal basis sufficient for the constitutional caveat of the law.[150]

From this it follows first that there must be the development of the assurance of conformity of transnational administrative acts with the material law on the level of fundamental international law or the supranational law making. The clearer the harmonised regulations at supra state level are and the greater their relationship to the facts, the smaller will be the probability of the development of unlawful transnational administrative acts.[151] Harmonised, special procedural regulations – if necessary by the introduction of transnational authority participation – remove the requirements for the lawfulness of transnational administrative acts from general national procedural law.

---

147 Schmidt–De Caluwe, *VerwArch 90* (1999), 49 (64).

148 Different opinion – denying the existence of a dogmatic category of the transnational administrative act – Becker, *DVBl 2001*, 855 (859).

149 Different opinion, explicitly Becker, *DVBl 2001*, 855 (859).

150 Insofar in agreement, Becker, *DVBl 2001*, 855 (860), who on the other hand, gives greater emphasis, regarding the opinion represented here, to the (Member State of) origin of the legal validity command for administrative acts.

151 General administrative legal principles in terms of a *ius commune* can be added to this: Schröder, *ThürVBl* 1998, 97 (100).

3.4. THE CONSTITUTIONAL CONFORMITY OF TRANSNATIONAL ADMINISTRATIVE ACTS

Furthermore, the conclusion of an appropriate International Law Treaty or the inclusion in supranational lawmaking establishes the International Law conformity of the transnational administrative acts, which are based on it.[152] Considering the long-range interstate effect of transnational administrative acts, and their continuance based upon the concept of transnationality also in case of unlawfulness, coverage in the constitution is required. Transnational administrative acts in the Federal Republic of Germany cannot become effective beyond constitutional sovereignty (*jenseits konstituierter Hoheitsgewalt).* Even though, according to the constitution, created sovereignty (*verfasste Hoheitsgewalt*) as a result of the supranational inclusion of Germany cannot be regarded as state power alone,[153] the direct access of foreign authorities to legal users and subjects[154] in the Federal Republic is considered almost unanimously as illegitimate. Since Article 24(1) GG would only explicitly allow such a conferment of sovereign rights in terms of this provision for "cross-national institutions", the constitution excluded the breach of the German sovereignty in favour of foreign states.[155] If this were to be applied consequently, this interpretation of Art. 24(1) GG would lead to the illegitimacy of transnational administrative acts in Germany.[156] This conclusion requires a differentiating examination, not only because of the factual diversification and amendment, which Article 24(1) GG has experienced through constitutional amendments in the 1990s.

At first, the preferential special norm is Article 24(1a) GG referring to institutions in neighbouring states. Since such institutions – as already mentioned – can also be established as legal persons of the foreign Public Law, which issue the transnational administrative acts according to that foreign legal system, one cannot speak of a blocking effect against the sovereign access of

---

152 König (fn. 22), 65. International Law does not have any general acceptance obligation: Geck, in: Strupp/Schlochauer (fn. 125), 55 (56); Meng (fn. 129), 349; Papier/Olschewski, *DVBl 1976*, 475 (476); Schlochauer (fn. 17), 62 (related to dispossession); Vogel (fn. 123), 335.

153 Hobe, *Der offene Verwaltungsstaat zwischen Souveränität und Interdependenz*, 1998, 380 ff., as well as already basically Vogel, *Die Verfassungsentscheidung des Grundgesetzes für eine internationale Zusammenarbeit*, 1964.

154 As the typical definition for the conferment of sovereign rights, *cf.* only Randelzhofer, in: Maunz/Dürig (eds.) (fn. 106), Article 24(1) (Stand: 1992) n. 30; Baldus, *Die Verwaltung 32* (1999), 481 (489).

155 Becker, *DVBl 2001*, 855 (857); Jarass, in: *id.*/Pieroth, *GG*, 5. Auflage 2000, Art. 24 mn. 7; Mosler, in: *HStR VII*, §175 mn. 38 at the end; Pernice, in: Dreier (ed.), *GG*, Band II, 1998, Art. 24 mn. 24; Rojahn, in: von Münch/Kunig (eds.), *GG*, Band II, 5. Auflage 2001, Art. 24 mn. 18; Streinz in: Sachs (ed.), *GG*, 2. Auflage 1999, Art. 24 mn. 19.

156 As already – referring to an example from tax law – Papier/Olschewski, *DVBl 1976*, 475 (477 ff.).

foreign institutions in terms of Article 24(1a) GG.[157] The "compensation" for this "loss of sovereignty" lies in the participation of German authorities in the institution of a neighbouring state or more general, the cooperation with neighbouring states, on whose part the institution appears. This participation also establishes sufficient level of legitimisation of the institution, in so far as a sufficient determination of the purpose of the cooperation and the institution's tasks is reached with the conclusion of the cooperation.[158]

The legal situation is more difficult with regard to transnational administrative acts legally founded on a union and community basis. Indeed, with Article 23(1) phrase 2, there exists a special provision to Article 24(1) GG, as well, and the wording of this special norm differs in so far from the formulation of Article 24(1) GG, as the Union is not explicitly mentioned as the subject for the allocation of conferring sovereignty. The "hereto" (*hierzu*) in Article 23(1) Phrase 2 GG refers to the realisation of the European Union, mentioned in Phrase 1, which can also necessitate a closer integration of Member State administrative structures.[159] Such an understanding of Article 23(1) Phrase 2 GG, however, seems to conflict with the conventional concept of the execution of Community law, which differs between direct Community and direct Member State execution[160] Meanwhile, in the literature, there is the awareness that the primary legal guidelines for the execution of Community law are not opposed to the secondary legal guidelines for the development of cooperative administrative structures.[161] Their legitimacy is judged by the interpretation of the appropriate competence norm of TEU and ECT. For the mostly relevant harmonisation competences in Article 95 and 47(2) of the EC Treaty, this can be assumed, since the principle of mutual acceptance, which is reflected in the action level of the transnational administrative act, is already inherent in the fundamental freedoms, and certainly in the legal adjustment.[162]

Beyond the European cooperation and cooperation between neighbouring states, at first sight, Article 24(1) GG actually seems to exclude the transboundary,

---

157 Bauer/Hartwig, *NWVBl 1994*, 41 (48); Beck (fn. 80), 104 and 138 ff.; Halmes, *DÖV 1996*, 933, 941 f.); Jarass (fn. 154), Art. 24 mn. 16; Schwarze, in: *Festschrift für Benda*, 1995, 311 (331). Different opinion Baldus, *Die Verwaltung 32* (1999), 481 (502, fn. 96); Beyerlin, *ZaöRV* 54 (1994), 586 (606); Grotefels, *DVBl 1994*, 785 (787); Rennert, in: *Festschrift für Böckenförde*, 1995, 199 (217); Rojahn (fn. 154), Art. 24 mn. 83, Stein, *VVDStRL 53* (1994), 26 (43 f.); Streinz (fn. 154), Art. 24 mn. 44.

158 Beck (fn. 80), 162 f. About the legitimisation see also below at fn. 180.

159 As here, Classen, in: von Mangoldt/Klein/Strack (eds.), *GG*, Band II, 4. Auflage 2000, Art. 23 mn. 13.

160 Unlike all the others, Rengeling, *Rechtsgrundsätze beim Verwaltungsvollzug des Europäischen Gemeinschaftsrechts*, 1977, 9 ff.; *id.*, VVDStRL 53 (1994), 202 (205 f. with further references in fn. 7).

161 Groß, *JZ 1994*, 596 (600); Röhl (fn. 22), 30 ff.; Royla (fn. 35), 87; Schlag (fn. 36), 178 ff.

162 Completing the Internal Market: White Paper from the Commission to the European Council,
COM(85) 310 final, mn. 77, as well as Röhl (fn. 22), 37 f.; Happe (fn. 22), 155 ff.

continuing transnational administrative acts which generate administrative cooperation. As a matter of fact, this has been recently explicitly confirmed, for transboundary police activities,[163] in particular. The existing practice is justified by a reference to the tradition prior to the constitution,[164] or declared as in conformity with the constitution with regard to the contestable argument that if the Federal Republic of Germany could transfer parts of its territory to a foreign state, it could also confer sovereign rights.[165] For transboundary police activities, one can argue with more convincing power, that this would not be about the opening of the German legal system to foreign (individual case) regulations, but rather more about the mere acceptance of foreign sovereignty at the borders of the German state territory,[166] an argument which, however, can only conditionally be convincing once it comes to the issuance of real transnational administrative acts.[167] The latter also applies to the assumption that German sovereignty is not withdrawn during the transboundary authority cooperation, so that Article 24(1) GG would not be applicable,[168] since the conferment of sovereign rights in terms of this provision is especially understood as not being a cession procedure. Eventually, it is also not sufficient to turn for recourse to the constitutional principle of the open statehood (*Verfassungsprinzip der offenen Staatlichkeit*), which could not reach a breach of blocking effects (*Sperrwirkungen*) positively codified in the constitution by itself.[169]

The key to the constitutional conformity of transnational administrative acts lies in the interpretation of the term "interstate institutions" in Article 24(1) GG. The inclusion of other states or of integrated legal persons of one state, at first sight, appears as an impossible way of interpretation. Consequently, the term is only referred to in such international structures which have sufficient organisational structure to exercise supranational sovereign rights.[170] Taking a closer look, this perspective proves to be a narrower one. The new International Law has institutionalised forms of cooperation ahead of the supranationality or even of the cooperative consolidation with an international organisation.[171] It therefore strongly advocates for subsuming such forms of cooperation under the

---

163 Baldus, *Die Verwaltung 32* (1999), 481 (502); Gramm, *DVBl 1999*, 1237.

164 Baldus, *Die Verwaltung 32* (1999), 481 (503); Gramm, *DVBl 1999*, 1237 (1238); Kirchhof (fn. 92), 59. Similarly Fastenrath, *Die Verwaltung 31* (1998), 277 (304 f.).

165 Rauser (fn. 19), 251 ff.; following him Neßler (fn. 23), 79 ff. On the other hand, as here Classen (fn. 158), Article 24 mn. 65.

166 Cremer, *ZaöRV* 60 (2000), 103 (133 f.).

167 Indicated by Cremer, *ZaöRV 60* (2000), 103 (134, fn. 158).

168 This is the centre of the argumentation at Hecker, *AöR 127* (2000), appearing especially sub IV 1b, bb, and (about the inapplicability of Article 23, 24 GG) in detail sub V.

169 Gramm, *DVBl 1999*, 1237 (1238). Basically about this principle, Vogel (fn. 152).

170 Streinz (fn. 154), Art. 24 mn. 19.

171 On this Churchill/Ulfstein, *American Journal of International Law 94* (2000), 623 (as example of international environmental law), as well as Ruffert, ArchVR 38 (2000), 129 (141 ff. with further references).

constitutional term of the transnational institutions.[172] If the Federal Republic of Germany joins such a cooperation, it is in many cases integrated in such organisational structures, if it is by participation in transboundary active or consulting bodies or if it is because – in some measure on a lowest level of the institutionalisation – the particular authorisations for actions of the participating states are balanced by reciprocal guarantees.[173] From this point of view, Article 24(1) GG does not prevent the conferment of sovereign rights on international organisations, the authorisations of actions for which are not yet compressed by the supranationality – this could at least be argued for the WTO – for example, in police cooperation. Within this scope, transnational administrative acts could find their constitutional basis. After all, according to the jurisdiction of the Bundesverfassungsgericht (the German Constitutional Court) such an interpretation of the wording of Article 24(1) GG is not excluded. In the Kehler-Haften case (1953), it did not grant the quality of an interstate institution to a corporation according to German public law, but this case was about the establishment of the responsibility of the state Baden and not about the preventing a transboundary cooperation.[174] In the Pershing-case, the Court arguments, regarding military authorisations of the President of the United States, that in this case, Article 24(1) GG cannot be applied *directly*.[175]

That Article 24(1) GG should enable the inclusion of Germany into such cooperative networks also becomes obvious regarding the purpose of Article 24(1) GG. In this provision, the constitution enables the opening of German statehood to the outside (*die Öffnung deutscher Staatlichkeit nach aussen*) and prevents at the same time its dissolution into another state.[176] Steps in this direction would be illegitimate; as counter model for the cooperation forms, which are assumed as being inadmissible here, the cession of sovereign authorisations in the computerised tax administration to an Asian state because of financial reasons, could, in terms of an *argumentum ad absurdum* be brought up.

Also the historical interpretation supports the point of view supported here. Article 24(1) GG – which has not been disputed in the parliamentary council (*Parlamentarischen Rat*) under the point of view examined here[177] – is located in the historical context of the history of an international singular development of interstate organisations, namely the foundation of the United Nations, the

172 Going even further Classen (fn. 158), mn. 66. *Cf.* also Niedobitek (fn. 122), 438 f.: *The entirety of the contracting states as interstate institutions.*

173 The lacking inclusion of German authorities in the decision structures of the interstate institutions is the decisive point so far therefore, to exclude states from this: Tomuschat, in: *Bonner Kommentar zum GG*, Article 24 (Stand: 1981) mn. 44.

174 BVerfGE 2, 347 (377 f.).

175 BVerfGE 68, 1 (91).

176 Clearly, Randelzhofer (fn. 153), Art. 24 mn. 53.

177 About the history, see Menzel, *Bonner Kommentar zum GG*, Article 24 (Stand: 1981).

European Council as well as the institutions of Bretton Woods. A cooperation of the states with transnational administrative authorities, as it can be seen today, was beyond the imaginable. In addition, the circumstances of the time of the occupation did not serve as a motivation for the drafters of the constitution to include a provision concerning the conferment of sovereign rights to other states in the constitution.

With this new orientation in the interpretation of Article 24(1) GG as well as the realisation of the regulation content of Article 23(1) Phrase 2 and 24(1a) GG, which has attracted less attention, at the same time, there is no longer a need for concern arising from other constitutional principles.[178] This applies primarily to the legal guarantee of judicial protection in Article 19(4) Phrase 1 GG, which is an obstacle to the practical concordance put into perspective to that effect by the constitutional decision for an international cooperation, which is expressed in the determinations of Article 24(1) GG old version mentioned in the following, that the chosen construction for the conferment of sovereign rights has to satisfy the minimal requirements of the rule of law.[179] This can also be effected by the grant of judicial protection abroad.[180] In conclusion, the problem of the democratic legitimisation of cooperative administrative structures, from which transnational administrative acts arise, lies outside the doctrine of forms of action discussed here. To this extent, the indication that the administrative organisational perspective also has to come from Article 23(1) phrase 2, 24(1) and (1a) should be enough. It is sufficient, if the respective conferment act ensures a sufficient level of legitimisation[181] in consideration of the supranational structures.[182] Apart from the personal legitimisation by the participation of German officials, content-factual legitimisation through harmonised legal basics and institutional legitimisation by the transboundary participation of authorities, attempts have to be increased to base the legitimisation on reciprocity and mutual confidence also,[183] which is not possible at this point.

---

178 In addition, in a next step, material limits for the conferment would have to be formulated, and could go beyond Article 79(3) GG and a basic legal core existence and include basic principles legally anchored as to constitution in the administrative law; see beyond Article 23, 24 GG, *Hecker*, AöR 127 (2002), forthcoming, sub IV.

179 See BVerfGE 58, 1 (41) with indication of the constitutional decision investigated by Vogel (fn. 152), as well as BVerfGE 63, 343 (378); Beyerlin (fn. 79), 252; Rauser (fn. 19), 305 ff.

180 Instructively VGH BW, NVwZ 2001, 338 (339). – Sceptically (against the opinions mentioned in fn. 178), Huber, in: von Mangoldt/Klein/Strack (eds.) (fn. 158). Article 19(4) mn. 527; Harings (fn. 64), 225 ff. expands despite the prevailing opinion (see only Schmidt-Aßmann, in: Maunz/Dürig (ed.) (fn. 106), Art. 19 Paragraph 4 (Stand: 1985) mn. 47) the guarantee of Article 19(4) GG to the judicial protection against foreign authorities. The newer jurisdiction of the BVerfG in the Maastricht case (BVerfGE 89, 155 (175)) can remain out of consideration here, since it is not only challengeable in its constitutional dogmatic premises (explicitly and correct, Schulze-Fielitz, in: Dreier (ed.), *GG*, Band I, 1996, Article 19(4) mn. 38), but only refers to supranational institutions, as well and not to other states.

181 Abou the concept of the level of legitimation, BVerfGE 83, 60 (72); 93, 37 (67).

182 Instructively, Schmidt-Aßmann, *AöR 116*, (1991), 329 (340).

183 Röhl (fn. 22), 44 ff. Still too narrow, Schmidt-Aßmann, *AöR 116* (1991), 329 (341).

4. THE MEANING OF THE LEGAL FORM OF THE ADMINISTRATIVE ACT FOR INTERSTATE ADMINISTRATIVE COOPERATION

Legally binding individual case decisions are essential, as forms of action of the permanently growing international administrative cooperation.[184] Even if the frontiers lose their meaning for the administration's activity and thereby a de-territorialisation[185] of the administrative actions and the law can be observed, this does not lead however at the same time to a dissolution of the traditional forms of action. With regard to German administrative law, the transnational administrative act is not identical with the form of action codified in Title III of administrative procedural law. However, as type of a decision on individual cases issued by an authority, being directed at a legal effect outside the country and being legally binding, it can be determined in three different ways. The transnationality of the administrative act is either, effect, addressee or authority related. The concept of transnationality also establishes the special continuance and factual effect of the transnational administrative act, whereby the basis of the transboundary administrative cooperation in International or Community law has to carry the transnationality for continuance building also for unlawful, and even for void administrative acts. In the thus ensuing problems concerning judicial protection, it shows, that the legal system of the transnational administrative acts can handle factually reasoned and constitutionally necessary modifications without the existence of the newly created legal form's characteristics being threatened.

In addition the constitutional problems, linked to the institution of the transnational administrative act, can be dealt with, if the interpretation of Article 23(1) phrase 2, 24(1), 24(1a) GG is directed at the newer developments of the law of administrative cooperation. At the same time, it becomes obvious that transnational administrative acts appear in all areas of the Public Law and that they cannot be understood without reference to the International and Community law fundamentals, sometimes also to the Private International Law, the constitutional limits and special fields of the law. This comprehensive variety may tie up with what the American expert on international law *Philipp C. Jessup* intended with the concept of *transnational law*, in 1956.[186] In this way, one could also face the concept of transboundary administrative cooperation, despite the concerns with regard to the acceptance of an outdated term of the "nation". In summary, the transnational administrative act in German administrative law represents in itself a form of action according to the guidelines of International and the Community law, the effects of which can be seen in constitutional law, especially.

---

184 Historical overview already at Menzel, *DÖV 1969*,1; broad now Niedobitek (fn. 122), 7 ff.

185 Fastenrath, *Die Verwaltung 31* (1998), 277 (299); Klein, in: Starck (ed.) (fn. 71), 117 (141); Schmidt-Aßmann, *DVBl 1993*, 924 (936).

186 Jessup, *Transnational Law*, 1956, 2.

XIII. THE GENERAL LAW OF PROCEDURE OF EC MUTUAL ADMINISTRATIVE ASSISTANCE*

Florian WETTNER**

1. INTRODUCTION: EC MUTUAL ADMINISTRATIVE ASSISTANCE

Community legislation has been paying attention to cross-border mutual administrative assistance between Member State authorities (horizontal mutual administrative assistance) and between these and Community authorities (vertical mutual administrative assistance) for the proper implementation of Community law – here the so-called EC mutual administrative assistance – for a long time. However, unlike German law or international law, Community law does not provide for any general rules,[1] for example, by way of a general regulation on mutual administrative assistance;[2] rather, the Community has adopted numerous provisions for mutual administrative assistance in individual areas of administration.[3] The issue of mutual administrative assistance has

* This contribution is based on the author's thesis *'Die Amtshilfe im Europäischen Verwaltungsrecht'*, Mohr Siebeck, 2005. A first version is published (in German) in: Eberhard Schmidt-Aßmann and Bettina Schöndorf-Haubold (ed.), Der Europäische Verwaltungsverbund, Mohr Siebeck, Tübingen 2005, p. 181–212. The author expresses his gratitude to Hildegard Rosenzweig for her essential support as regards the translation of the German version of the article into English.

** The author works as a lawyer in the Frankfurt office of the law firm Gleiss Lutz.

1 With respect to German law, cf. Sec. 4 et seq. Administrative Procedures Act (*Verwaltungsverfahrensgesetz, VwVfG*); with respect to international law, European Convention of 24 November 1977 on the Service Abroad of Documents Relating to Administrative Matters; European Convention of 15 March 1978 on the Obtaining Abroad of Information and Evidence in Administrative Matters.

2 Cf. Meier, EuR 1989, 237 (248), who considered such regulation to be necessary even at the time of introduction of the Single Market in 1993; cf. also Becker, DVBl. 2001, 855 (864) for the creation of general laws on cross-border administrative cooperation in the legal systems of the Member States.

3 With respect to mutual administrative assistance in the areas of European customs administration, tax administration, agricultural administration, competition supervision administration, social administration, food and veterinary administration, and financial

gained further importance by the introduction of the Single Market as of 31 December 1992 and the related abolition of border controls, which required increased administrative cooperation in many areas in order to ensure the proper implementation of Community law. Since the late 1980s, prior to and later during the course of the introduction of the Single Market, new rules for EC mutual administrative assistance were established, or existing rules were developed. Today, sophisticated Community rules concerning mutual administrative assistance exist mainly in the areas of tax and customs administration,[4] social administration,[5] and the administration of competition supervision.[6]

Despite increasing legal regulation in this respect, there is as yet no consistent administrative law governing EC mutual administrative assistance.[7] The rules under EC secondary law sometimes contain considerable divergences with regard to the understanding of the term 'mutual administrative assistance' and its requirements and limitations. In the interest of legal certainty and unambiguity, however, the mutual administrative assistance that has been established in specific areas should be developed into an overall legal concept that follows general rules of administrative law.[8] That general administrative law of EC mutual administrative assistance comprises, apart from organisational

markets supervision administration, cf. Wettner, *Die Amtshilfe im Europäischen Verwaltungsrecht*, 2005, 45 et seq.; with respect to informational mutual administrative assistance in the European environmental administration, cf. Sommer, *Verwaltungskooperation am Beispiel administrativer Informationsverfahren im europäischen Umweltrecht*, 2003, passim.

4 Directive No. 77/799/EEC of 19 December 1977 concerning mutual assistance by the competent authorities of the Member States in the field of direct taxation, OJ EC 1977 No. L 336, 15 et seq.; Directive No. 76/308/EEC of 15 March 1976 on mutual assistance for the recovery of claims resulting from operations forming part of the system of financing the European Agricultural Guidance and Guarantee Fund, and of agricultural levies and customs duties, OJ EC 1976 No. L 73, 18 et seq.; Regulation No. 1798/2003/EC of 7 October 2003 on administrative cooperation in the field of value added tax, OJ EU 2003 No. L 264, 1 et seq.; Regulation No. 515/97/EC of 13 March 1997 on mutual assistance between the administrative authorities of the Member States and cooperation between the latter and the Commission to ensure the correct application of the law on customs and agricultural matters, OJ EC 1997 No. L 82, 1 et seq.

5 Art. 76 et seq. of Regulation No. 883/2004/EC of 29 April 2004 for the Coordination of Social Security Systems, OJ EU 2004 No. L 166, 1 et seq. (applies from the date of an implementation regulation entering into force); at present still Art. 84 et seq. of Regulation No. 1408/71/EEC of 14 June 1971 in relation to the application of the social security systems to employees and their families, OJ EC 1971 No. L 149, 2 et seq.; supplemented by provisions of Regulation No. 574/72/EEC which was adopted for its implementation, OJ EC 1972 No. L 74, 1 et seq.

6 Art. 11 et seq., 20(5) and (6), 22 of Regulation No. 1/2003/EC of 16 December 2002 on implementation of the rules on competition laid down in Articles 81 and 82 of the Treaty, OJ EC 2003 No. L 1, 1 et seq.

7 Also, the assessment of v. Bogdandy/Arndt, EWS 2000, 1 (1).

8 In this respect, Wettner, *Amtshilfe* (fn. 3).

aspects[9] and issues of legal protection and liability,[10] the *law governing the procedure of mutual administrative assistance* between the authorities involved, on the one hand, and their relationship with private persons, on the other hand. The latter shall be the subject matter of this paper. At first, this requires a general understanding of the structural characteristics of mutual administrative assistance, an understanding which is not limited to specific areas, (2). Following this, an overview will be provided of the types of the law determining the process of EC mutual administrative assistance (3). Finally, there is a description of the individual general rules of procedure, i.e. the procedural standards (4).

2. STRUCTURAL CHARACTERISTICS OF EC MUTUAL ADMINISTRATIVE ASSISTANCE

2.1. INTRODUCTION

Mutual administrative assistance has structural characteristics which distinguish it from other forms of cooperation and which cause or require that specific procedural rules governing mutual administrative assistance apply.[11] The structure of mutual administrative assistance is basically determined by the characteristics of the act of mutual administrative assistance, which are hereinafter cursorily described (2.2), by the characteristics of the administrative proceedings that are assisted by such an act (main proceedings) (2.3), and finally by the procedure taking place between the parties to the mutual administrative assistance, namely of providing and claiming the assistance (2.4).

2.2. ACT OF MUTUAL ADMINISTRATIVE ASSISTANCE

The most frequent acts of mutual administrative assistance result from the divergence occasionally occurring between the administrative task to be performed and the administrative powers being available for that purpose. In the *horizontal* relationship between administrative authorities of Member States, such divergence follows from the principle of territory under international law,

9 In respect of the organisational aspects of direct or indirect dealings between authorities and the networks as infrastructure of mutual administrative assistance, cf. Wettner, *Amtshilfe* (fn. 3), 277 et seq. Generally with respect to the European law of administrative organisation, which has so far been given little attention, cf. Franchini, *Rivista trimestrale di diritto pubblico* 2002, 651 et seq.

10 In this respect, cf. J. Hofmann, *Rechtsschutz und Haftung im europäischen Verwaltungsverbund*, 2004.

11 For details on the difference between the structural characteristics of mutual administrative assistance and alternative forms of cooperation, Wettner, *Amtshilfe* (fn. 3), 120 et seq.

which also applies between the Member States of the Community, according to which it is not permitted for a state to act in a sovereign manner on the territory of another state without permission to do so under international law; in the *vertical* relationship, such divergence follows from the allocation of competences between the Community and Member States by the EC Treaty. Taking this into account, it is possible to identify three typical acts which cross over the borders of states or competences which the competent authority may perform for the authority to be assisted by way of mutual administrative assistance. The *determination of the facts that are of relevance to the decision*, which must be made first in the context of administrative proceedings, defines the important area of mutual administrative assistance by way of establishing and forwarding information (assistance by information).[12] The administrative decision made on that basis must then be made effective, which may under certain conditions require the *service* of such an administrative decision (assistance by service). And finally, the *compulsory enforcement* of administrative decisions made by Member States or the Community may be required under certain conditions (assistance by enforcement).[13] However, the concept of EC mutual administrative assistance is not limited to these supporting acts; rather, any real or legal acts may be considered as mutual administrative assistance within the scope of the following definition.

The aforementioned acts of mutual administrative assistance are mere *supplementary contributions* to foreign administrative proceedings. No assistance by way of mutual administrative assistance is deemed to exist, if the entire task of a foreign authority is performed on its behalf, by the authority rendering the assistance assuming the other authority's position as a whole.[14] This may occur on the basis of a so-called inter-administrative delegation (*zwischenbehördliche Delegation*).[15]

Further, a differentiation has to be made between the mutual administrative assistance and assisting acts that are assigned to the assisting authority as *tasks of its own*.[16] Assisting acts are deemed to be an authority's 'own task', if the relevant act is specifically defined as a task to assist certain other authorities, i.e.

12 In respect of determination of facts by *inspections*, David, *Inspektionen im Europäischen Verwaltungsrecht*, 2003.

13 Four situations of assistance by enforcement can be identified: (1.) enforcement of Community monetary claims (Article 256 EC Treaty); (2.) enforcement of national monetary claims, which is regulated only in specific areas (e.g. by Directive 76/308); (3.) enforcement of Community non-monetary claims, in particular in terms of enforcement of the Commission's right to inspections (e.g. according to Article 20(5)(6) Regulation 1/2003); (4) enforcement of national non-monetary claims (e.g. right to inspections by national authorities in the area of financial markets supervision).

14 Cf. Loebenstein, *International Mutual Assistance in Administrative Matters*, Österreichische Zeitschrift für öffentliches Recht, Supplementum 2, 1972, 15.

15 In respect of delegation under Community law, Wettner, *Amtshilfe* (fn. 3), 134 et seq.

16 For German law explicitly stated in Sec. 7 (2) No. 2 VwVfG.

if it is not only generally included in those functions of the authority which it is authorised to perform in order to fulfil its other tasks. An example is the activity of so-called information agencies of the Community which collect and process information and make it available to other authorities, such as the rendering of scientific advice to Member State authorities responsible for the inspection of foodstuffs by the European Food Safety Authority (EFSA).[17] The differentiation between assistance as part of the performance of an authority's own tasks on the one hand and mutual administrative assistance by measures not belonging to the authority's original own tasks is required by law. The assignment to an authority of an own task of assistance confers on that authority not only a right to perform such a task, but creates an obligation to do so which is basically unconditional. Certain objections which the assisting authority may raise against its obligation to render assistance are, therefore, not suited for distancing itself from that obligation to fulfil a task of its own.[18]

A further structural characteristic of mutual administrative assistance is that the supporting authority, although functionally being incorporated into foreign administrative proceedings, is *not subject to the directions* of the supported authority when performing the assistance. The supported authority determines the act of mutual administrative assistance only by way of its request and is merely entitled to make suggestions and express wishes regarding the actual performance of the assistance. The acts of mutual administrative assistance are, therefore, not deemed to be acts of the supported authority, but are performed by the supporting authority *in its own name*. This distinguishes mutual administrative assistance from forms of administrative cooperation that also exist under Community law, under which the assisting act is attributed to the supported authority.[19] This is the inter-administrative mandate (*zwischenbehördliches Mandat*), in particular, under which the supporting authority acts 'on behalf and for the account' of the supported authority.[20]

---

17 One of the EFSA's tasks is to supply the Member States with the best possible scientific opinions in all cases submitted to it and on any issue which comes within the scope of its tasks (Article 23 lit. a Regulation 178/2002). As the EFSA prepares the opinions solely for the specific assistance for national authorities, and not also for purposes of its own, it does not render mutual administrative assistance, but performs a task of its own.

18 In respect of the German law of national mutual administrative assistance explicitly, Schlink, *Die Amtshilfe*, 1982, 202. To the possible objections see below 4.

19 In this respect, Wettner, *Amtshilfe* (fn. 3), 147 et seq.; in respect of corresponding questions of liability and legal protection, J. Hofmann, *Rechtsschutz und Haftung* (fn. 10).

20 The inter-administrative mandate plays only a marginal role in Community law; very few examples can be found. For example, according to the wording of Article 22(1) Regulation 1/2003, a competition supervisory authority conducts inspections in the sovereign territory of its Member State 'on behalf and for account' of the competition supervisory authority of another Member State. However, despite this wording implying an inter-administrative mandate, the act is not attributed to the supporting authority, but the inspection is conducted by way of mutual administrative assistance. Therefore, the term 'on behalf' in this context is merely an expression denoting that the inspection is conducted for the purposes of another authority.

2.3. MAIN ADMINISTRATIVE PROCEEDINGS, IN PARTICULAR, DIFFERENTIATION BETWEEN MUTUAL ADMINISTRATIVE ASSISTANCE AND SUPPORT IN SUPERVISORY RELATIONSHIPS

The subject matter of the main proceedings to be supported by EC mutual administrative assistance is the implementation of EC law.[21] This distinguishes mutual administrative assistance under Community law from classical cross-border mutual administrative assistance under international law as a result of the subsequent application of General Principles of Community Law.[22] The implementation of EC law comprises both its application and enforcement *vis-à-vis private persons* and *vis-à-vis the Member States, and the supervision of its implementation by the Member States*. In the first case, a differentiation must be made between mutual assistance in administrative matters on the one hand and *mutual assistance in criminal matters* on the other, which shall not be further discussed in this paper.[23] In the second case, there is the question whether a differentiation must be made between mutual administrative assistance on the one hand and *support in supervisory relationships* on the other. The latter takes place, for example, when in areas of indirect implementation where the Commission does not perform independent administrative proceedings against private persons, the Commission requests the Member States to carry out inspections at its request in order to procure information for the Commission to enable it to assess the implementation by the Member State.[24] The aforementioned cooperation has so far not been qualified unambiguously, either by the legal terminology of Community law or by legal literature.[25]

---

21 Also, the assessment of Meier, EuR 1989, 237 (240).

22 In this respect, see below 3.2.

23 In respect of the differentiation, more explicitly Wettner, *Amtshilfe* (fn. 3), 165 et seq. Comprehensively in respect of the transitions of mutual assistance in administrative matters and judicial assistance in criminal matters in accordance with Community law provisions, Vervaele/Klip (ed.), *European Cooperation between Tax, Customs and Judicial Authorities*, 2002; in respect of the legal situation in competition law, O. Jansen in: Dannecker/id. (ed.), *Competition Law Sanctioning in the European Union*, 2004, 257 et seq.

24 E.g. Article 18(3) in conjunction with Article 7 Regulation 515/97. Generally the demand for Member State inspections by the Commission in areas of indirect implementation, where the Commission does not itself implement Community law and in this respect the collected information does not serve the purposes of administrative proceedings conducted by the Commission itself, must be deemed to have a supervisory function, cf. David, *Inspektionen* (fn. 12), 132.

25 Against a qualification of supervisory support as mutual administrative assistance, cf. Huber, in: *FS für Brohm*, 2002, 127 (135); Sommer, *Verwaltungskooperation* (fn. 3), 460 et seq. In favour of such qualification, explicitly Meier, EuR 1982, 154 (157, 161); see also Vervaele/Klip, in: id., *European Cooperation* (fn. 23), 25, who conclude from the Commission's supervisory function that the Commission is a suitable partner in relations of mutual administrative assistance.

A dogmatically reasonable approach to a differentiation between mutual administrative assistance and the support in supervisory relationships could follow from the finding that mutual administrative assistance occurs in a *relationship of equality*. The equality becomes apparent by a right of examination and refusal which the requested authority has regarding the requested act of mutual assistance. Although there is a basic obligation to render the requested assistance, which is determined either by EC secondary law or by the principle of loyal cooperation, this applies only within specific limitations concerning mutual administrative assistance.[26] The requested authority is entitled to examine whether these limitations have been observed and, as the case may be, to refuse to render the assistance. The request for mutual administrative assistance does not therefore automatically result in such assistance being provided.[27] Consequently, due to a lack of regulatory effect, the request for mutual administrative assistance does not constitute either a binding administrative act of a national authority (*Verwaltungsakt*) or a decision by a Community authority (*Entscheidung*).[28]

If the described right to examination and refusal does not exist, a *request* for mutual administrative assistance obtains the quality of a supra- or transnational *order*, and the support rendered thereupon is no longer mutual administrative assistance in a relationship of equality, but support in a supervisory *relationship of super- and subordination*. Such order is in any event inherent in the request for assistance by a *decision* of the Commission directed at the Member States, such as occurs within the scope of supervision of state aids.[29] However, it cannot be finally and clearly determined whether an *ordinary supervisory request* of the Commission also generates a liability which is stronger than the obligation to render mutual administrative assistance, which would justify a differentiation between these two acts of assistance. On the one hand, rules of EC secondary law suggest that supervisory acts of assistance should be included in the concept of EC mutual administrative assistance, because and to the extent that no indications of a diverging binding effect can be inferred from these rules.[30] On

26 In this respect, see below 4.2.

27 For mutual assistance in criminal matters, explicitly BVerfGE 67, 9 (23 et seq).

28 Cf. also the assessment of David, *Inspektionen* (fn. 12), 346, which determines this to be the case uniformly for Commission requests for Member State inspections both in the area of direct implementation and in supervisory constellations.

29 In the context of assessing new state aids, the Commission is entitled, pursuant to Art. 10(3) Regulation 659/1999, to request information from a Member State by way of a 'decision'. This is a decision as referred to in Article 249(4) EC Treaty.

30 For example, inspections by Member States in competition law at the request of the Commission – which serve the purposes of administrative proceedings conducted by the Commission – are, according to the wording of the relevant secondary law, subject to the same conditions as, for example, in agricultural law, where they are intended to support the assessment of the Member States' implementation of EC law by the Commission; cf. Article 22(2) sub-section (1) Regulation 1/2003 on the one hand and Article 6(1) sentence 3 Regulation 2729/2000 on the other hand.

the other hand, it is hardly imaginable that certain unwritten reasons for refusal under the law of mutual administrative assistance, such as a disproportionately large expense connected with the mutual administrative assistance or the risk that the authority's own tasks may be endangered,[31] may also be stated as reasons for refusal of a request for assistance in supervisory matters. However, the latter objection must be viewed from a relative perspective, because on the one hand the principle of proportionality must also be observed in supervisory matters,[32] on the other hand, it may only be used cautiously in the law governing mutual administrative assistance.[33]

Ultimately, it is only possible to determine a slight difference, if any at all, between acts of assistance for supervisory proceedings and such acts of assistance which serve administrative proceedings directed at private persons. This finding may justify the opinion that Member States' acts of assistance to the Commission that serve to supervise the respective Member State should also be regarded as mutual administrative assistance rendered to the Commission.

2.4. PROCEDURE OF RENDERING AND USING MUTUAL ADMINISTRATIVE ASSISTANCE

As regards the procedure of rendering and using administrative assistance, a differentiation may be made between *three* possible types of procedure by which the mutual administrative assistance is to be defined:

The main component of acts of EC mutual administrative assistance is the classical assistance rendered upon *request*.

Besides that, increasing importance is being attached to *spontaneous mutual administrative assistance*,[34] which mainly takes the form of the spontaneous forwarding of information, as an expression of the common responsibility of all authorities involved in the proper implementation of Community law. The spontaneous assistance by providing information occurs when the interested party cannot file a request because it does not know the facts, i.e. it has no clue/ foundation on which it could base a request for assistance. Contrary to different opinions, the spontaneous act of assistance does not deviate from the classical mutual administrative assistance rendered upon request to such an extent that it would appear to be justified to distinguish it from the concept of mutual administrative assistance.[35]

---

31 See below 4.2.4.

32 Cf. David, *Inspektionen* (fn. 13), 239.

33 See below 4.2.1 (introduction).

34 E.g., Title II Regulation 515/97: 'spontaneous assistance'; Article 8 Regulation 2729/2000: 'unsolicited assistance'.

35 Both the spontaneous mutual administrative assistance and the assistance upon request can serve to initiate administrative proceedings, since a request for assistance is not limited to

In contrast, the granting of *online access* to databases of another authority, which is possible in EDP-based information systems,[36] and which may, for example, be admitted in the VAT information exchange system (VIES),[37] no longer constitutes mutual administrative assistance. In this case, a traditional characteristic of cooperation, i.e. the communication between the parties involved, no longer exists and it has been replaced by a unilaterally initiated flow of information. This procedural particularity poses further threats to the legal protection of those persons to whom the data relate that are available online. While the classical forwarding of data is preceded by a decision of will by the forwarding authority and that authority continues to be able to examine the intended use and the data protection and confidentiality to be observed by the receiving authority etc., this is solely in the hands of the receiving authority in the case of a unilateral direct retrieval of data. Consequently, special precautionary measures regarding data protection and data safety as well as responsibility and liability become necessary in the latter case, and these go beyond the measures that are provided for in the law of mutual administrative assistance.

3. TYPES OF THE LAW GOVERNING EC MUTUAL ADMINISTRATIVE ASSISTANCE

3.1. INTRODUCTION

As regards the question what types of law govern mutual administrative assistance, a differentiation must be made between the act of mutual administrative assistance (‘*Amtshilfehandlung*’, I.) and the service of mutual administrative assistance (“*Amtshilfeleistung*”, II.).[38] The *act of mutual administrative assistance* is the administrative measure taken by the assisting authority in order to be able to provide the assistance. The scope of the obligation to provide mutual administrative assistance, i.e. the act of assistance *vis-à-vis* the

ongoing proceedings but can be filed in order to assess whether proceedings should be started. Furthermore, in both cases the assisted authority is liable for incorrect information and the administrative decision based hereon.

36 Such an *information system* is characterised by the linking of databases in which information is kept available for the purpose of being used by other authorities, in this respect Sommer, *Verwaltungskooperation* (fn. 3), 210.

37 Article 23, 24 Regulation 1798/2003: Other authorities must be able to ‘obtain directly and without delay, or have direct access to’ the information. However, where the information stored in such a system is *transmitted* in a traditional manner by the authority operating the respective database, there is no difference from other mutual administrative assistance as regards procedural law.

38 In respect of that differentiation in German law of mutual administrative assistance, E. Schnapp, DVBl. 1987, 561 (562).

authority receiving assistance subject to the specific requirements and limitations of the law of mutual administrative assistance, constitutes the *service of mutual administrative assistance.*

3.2. ACT OF MUTUAL ADMINISTRATIVE ASSISTANCE

Both the law of the supporting authority and – because the act of assistance is a complementary contribution to proceedings of another authority – the law of that supported authority can be taken into consideration as the law governing the act of mutual administrative assistance.

In the current Community law concerning mutual administrative assistance, the act of mutual administrative assistance is predominantly fully determined by the *supporting authority's own law.*[39] This means that both the *competences to act* and the *formal and procedural rules* are subject to that law which the supporting authority has to apply including that outside a procedure of providing mutual administrative assistance.[40] In cross-border cooperation under international law, the competence to act by virtue of the respective country's own *national* rules of competences is considered to be an essential requirement for mutual administrative assistance, because the performance of the act of assistance according to rules of competence of a foreign legal system constitutes a case of the so-called organ loan (*Organleihe)*[41] According to the concept of cross-border *Organleihe,* an authority is not only functionally but organisationally incorporated into foreign administrative proceedings to the extent that it renders its assistance under the foreign law and this includes the rules of competences of this foreign law.[42] However, in the Community legal system as a multi-level system, an *allocation of competences by Community law* to the national assisting authority can take place without a change of the regulated cooperation,[43] as has

39 E.g. 'in accordance with national law': Article 22(1) Regulation 1/2003; Article 5(1) Directive 76/308. A reference to the law of the requested national authority can also be inferred from the wording that the requested national authority shall act in such a manner 'as though acting on its own account or at the request of another authority in its own Member State': Article 5(4) Regulation 1798/2003; Article 4(2) and Article 9(1) Regulation 515/97. Pursuant to Article 7 Regulation 515/97, an authority shall 'as far as possible' keep a special watch on certain persons, places, etc. at the request of another authority, which comprises, in addition to its factual means, also the legal possibilities available under its law.

40 Cf. for national mutual administrative assistance in Germany Sec. 7(1) VwVfG.

41 Bünten, *Staatsgewalt und Gemeinschaftshoheit bei der innerstaatlichen Durchsetzung des Rechts der Europäischen Gemeinschaften durch die Mitgliedstaaten,* 1977, 181 et seq.

42 By the full application of foreign law by the assisting authority the *Organleihe* can be distinguished from the *inter-administrative mandate,* see above 2.2 (at the end).

43 Unlike the case where national procedural law is supplemented and modified by General Principles of Community Law; in respect of the application of those principles, see 3.3.

been the case in the law of competition.[44] Even if – as is the case in the competition law, for example – the powers are the same as those which the supported Community authority has in the exercise of its own duties[45], this is not conditional – unlike classical cross-border cooperation – on the existence of *Organleihe*.[46] It is an *allocation of competences by Community law* which does not prejudice the legal construction of the regulated assistance.[47]

Besides that full application of the assisting authority's own law – irrespective of whether that law is originally of national law or Community law provenance – the international law concerning cross-border administrative and judicial assistance contains regulations according to which the requested authority has to apply the mere *formal and procedural law of the agency receiving the assistance*. In this respect, the observance of special procedural requests by the agency receiving the assistance is customary in the international law governing mutual assistance by service.[48] Corresponding general provisions are also contained in Article 4 of the EU Convention on Mutual Assistance in Criminal Matters 2000[49] and Article 9(6) of the Naples II Convention[50] in the Third Pillar of the EU. In these cases, the supporting authority does not act on the basis of foreign rules of competence, but merely exercises competences existing under its own law by applying the formal and procedural rules of the supported authority.[51] The purpose of such rules is to ensure the validity of the measure in the main proceedings of the supported authority, in particular, to ensure the utilisability of information investigated by the supporting authority in those proceedings. With the current status of integration, the national laws of procedure have not yet been synchronised, even within the scope of the Community, in such a manner that the cross-border utilisability of information is basically ensured.

44 Pursuant to Article 20(5) Regulation 1/2003, officials of the national competition authority shall assist the Commission in its inspections at the request of the Commission or at the authority's own request and 'to this end, they shall enjoy the powers specified in paragraph 2.' This is an innovation compared to the predecessor provision of Article 14(5) Regulation 17/62, according to which the assisting officials' powers were subject to national law.

45 Article 20(2) Regulation 1/2003: powers assigned to officials of the Commission for the purpose of conducting inspections of its own.

46 Compare in that sense, however, Bünten, *Staatsgewalt und Gemeinschaftshoheit* (fn. 41), 181 et seq.

47 Also in the example of competition law, the acts of assistance performed by national authorities remain national acts and are not attributed to the Commission, respectively the Community.

48 See only Article 6(1) lit. b European Convention of 24 November 1977 on the Service Abroad of Documents Relating to Administrative Matters.

49 Council Act of 29 May 2000 establishing in accordance with Article 34 of the Treaty on European Union the Convention on Mutual Assistance in Criminal Matters between the Member States and the European Union, OJ EC 2000 No. C 197, 1 et seq.

50 Council Act of 18 December 1997 drawing up, on the basis of Article K.3 of the Treaty on European Union, the Convention on mutual assistance and cooperation between customs administrations, OJ 1998 No. C 24, 1 et seq.

51 Therefore these cases are not based on the legal concept of *Organleihe*.

Remarkably, however, Community law does not provide for regulations in this respect. However, in the interest of effective implementation of Community law, which is intended by the instrument of EC mutual administrative assistance, compliance with the procedural law of the supported authority appears to be desirable and should be implemented by future Community law.[52]

3.3. SERVICE OF MUTUAL ADMINISTRATIVE ASSISTANCE

The service of mutual administrative assistance is governed by three types of law. Basic provisions regarding the requirements and limitations of the obligation to provide mutual administrative assistance are determined by *EC secondary law* mainly in the form of directives and regulations. In certain areas of administration, the secondary law allows for *agreements* between the Member States, respectively their authorities, and with the Commission to specify in detail the technical-administrative modalities of mutual administrative assistance (e.g. the language to be used in mutual administrative assistance dealings, special cost reimbursement, etc.):[53] these agreements take the form either of binding international-law treaties between the Member States or, predominantly, of informal non-binding (administrative) agreements.[54] It is not possible to derive general procedural standards from those agreements, which are mainly entered into bilaterally, and therefore they do not require to be discussed in further detail in this paper; however, in a growing European administrative territory their greater flexibility gives them advantages over a central implementing legislation of the Commission. Future EC secondary law concerning mutual administrative assistance, and, in particular, a general regulation on mutual administrative assistance, should therefore leave the technical-administrative execution of mutual administrative assistance to be governed increasingly by such agreements.

---

52 In this respect, see also 4.3.2.

53 In the area of *customs administration*, Article 47 Regulation 515/97 represents a kind of general clause for regulating the modalities of mutual administrative assistance by agreement between the Member States. In *tax administration*, Article 38 Regulation 1798/2003 provides, for example, that the 'requesting and requested authority' – i.e. the respective ministries of finance – may agree on the language to be used in the request for mutual administrative assistance. In *social administration*, too, the 'agreement' is known as a common form of regulating the specific modalities of mutual administrative assistance; for example, the details of assistance by enforcement may be regulated by means of 'agreements between Member States', Article 92(2) Regulation 1408/71 in conjunction with Article 116(1) Regulation 574/72. Also in the *financial markets supervision administration*, non-binding administrative agreements to perform mutual administrative assistance – known as memoranda of understanding – are common, although not explicitly provided for in the Community legal acts.

54 In respect of legal qualification, see Wettner, Amtshilfe (fn. 3), 213 et seq.

Finally, the *General Principles of Community Law*, which the European Court of Justice establishes and specifies from the common constitutional traditions of the Member States and their obligations under international law,[55] are of fundamental importance for obtaining general procedural standards, and these will be presented in detail below. These unwritten principles apply with the same priority as EC treaty law[56] and supplement the rules of EC secondary law concerning mutual administrative assistance. Apart from Community authorities, national authorities, too – both those providing and those receiving mutual administrative assistance – are bound by the General Principles of Community Law, because of and to the extent they implement Community law.[57] The European Court of Justice expressly found, in the case of Member State assistance by enforcing Commission inspections in the legal case of *Höchst*, that the authorities providing mutual administrative assistance are in fact bound by these Principles[58] and confirmed this finding in the legal case of *Roquette*.[59] This fits in with the category of the authorities being bound by the General Principles when implementing Community law. This is because mutual administrative assistance is a supplementary contribution to main proceedings conducted for the purpose of implementation of Community law, either directly or indirectly, and as such must also be considered to be an implementing measure.

4. PROCEDURAL STANDARDS OF EC MUTUAL ADMINISTRATIVE ASSISTANCE

4.1. INTRODUCTION

Under the term of procedural 'standards' of mutual administrative assistance, an outline will be given below of the general legal rules following from the legal sources referred to above, according to which the authorities involved cooperate in the relationship with one another (inter-administrative procedural standards, 4.2 below) and which determine the legal position of private persons in such cooperation (procedural standards protecting private persons, 4.3 below).[60]

---

55 Tridimas, *The General Principles of EC Law*, 1999, 3.

56 Tridimas, General Principles (fn. 55), 32 et seq.

57 In respect of extensive reference to the court practice of the European Court of Justice regarding the Member States' obligation to observe the General Principles of Community Law in the 'implementation of Community law', Ranacher, *ZÖR 2003*, 21 et seq.

58 ECJ, Joined Cases 46/87 and 227/88 (Höchst), Reports of Cases 1989, I-2859 et seq. (para. 33 in conjunction with para. 19).

59 ECJ, Case C-94/00 (Roquette), Reports of Cases 2002, I-9011 et seq.

60 In this respect, cf. Schmidt-Aßmann, EuR 1996, 279 (295), who implemented the more general term 'Kooperationsstandards' (standards of cooperation).

4.2. INTER-ADMINISTRATIVE PROCEDURAL STANDARDS

4.2.1. Introduction

As presented above, a structural characteristic of mutual administrative assistance is that the basic obligation to render mutual administrative assistance, which follows from legal rules of secondary law or from the principle of loyal cooperation,[61] is bound by certain limitations; the obliged authority is entitled to examine whether such limitations have been observed and to refuse to provide the mutual administrative assistance, as the case may be.[62] Apart from formal rules of procedure regarding the form and language to be used, time limits to be observed, and cost allocation between the administrative authorities involved, there are also substantive rules of procedure, which shall be presented below and which determine those limitations and the respective rights of refusal of the requested authority. The general scope of the mutual administrative assistance owed follows from the so-called rule of equivalence in mutual administrative assistance (4.2.2) and from the procedural law of the requested authority which is modified, as the case may be, by the principle of effectiveness (4.2.3). Further important objections can be inferred from the general principle of (inter-administrative) proportionality (4.2.4). Finally, the general obligation to render mutual administrative assistance may sometimes be subject to reservations which are due to the sovereignty of the Member States (4.2.5).

It must be noted that these possibilities of refusing to provide mutual administrative assistance which are available to the requested authorities are mitigated by cooperation both in terms of substantive law and procedural law. As regards substantive law, a cautious form and handling of the possibilities of refusal is explicitly requested by proposed European Constitution of 29 October 2004, which determines under the section title of 'Administrative Cooperation' in Article III-285 (1) the 'effective implementation of Union law by the Member States [...] as a matter of common interest'; that common interest which is followed by using mutual administrative assistance takes priority over own (national) interests of the partners of mutual administrative assistance. Apart from this substantive guideline, there is a general procedural obligation on the part of the partners in mutual administrative assistance, which can be derived from Article 10 of the EC Treaty, to endeavour to reach agreement and to consult with one another regarding the requested mutual administrative assistance.[63]

---

61 In respect of an unwritten obligation to render mutual administrative assistance derived from Article 10 EC Treaty, see Wettner, *Amtshilfe* (fn. 3), 234 et seq.

62 See above 2.3.

63 In respect of a corresponding obligation regarding the Member States' assistance by enforcement, ECJ, Case C-94/00 (Roquette), Reports of Cases 2002, I-9011 (para. 90 et seq.).

4.2.2. Rule of equivalence in administrative assistance as a special form of the general principle of non-discrimination

According to the so-called rule of equivalence in mutual administrative assistance,[64] the assisting authority must act in such a manner 'as though acting on its own account or at the request of another authority in its own Member State'[65] or 'as though implementing its own legislation'.[66] This has the effect of a legal requirement of equal treatment and means, at first, that the measures to be executed as cross-border mutual administrative assistance for authorities of the Community or of other Member States must not be subject to more unfavourable legal rules than the performance of own tasks or mutual administrative assistance provided solely within a Member State; secondly, it means that the legal possibilities which are available must be exhausted. In addition, a standard of diligence is established for the act of mutual administrative assistance, for example with regard to the intensity of inquiries or the personal efforts of the persons acting. The rule of equivalence in mutual administrative assistance can be regarded as a special form of the principle of non-discrimination and is, therefore, no indication of the intensity of the administrative cooperation in a fully harmonised area,[67] but the expression of a general procedural principle which also applies without being explicitly laid down in secondary law.

4.2.3. Limitation of legal impossibility and effect of the effectiveness principle

As a consequence of the circumstance that the act of mutual administrative assistance is generally performed in accordance with the law of the requested authority, all requirements of the applicable law must be satisfied, otherwise the requested authority is entitled to refuse to render the assistance because of *legal impossibility.*[68] While it can be left at this limitation in international cross-border mutual administrative assistance, in the Community legal system the ability to invoke national law by the national assisting authority may be restricted by the principle of effectiveness. Accordingly, the application of national provisions must not act as a practical impediment to the legal consequences provided for by Community law – here, the obligation to render assistance – and these national provisions must be disregarded to the extent that this is necessary according to the criteria of effectiveness and equivalence.[69] Although the restriction on the

64 In respect of the rule of equivalence as a formal principle of the Community law of administrative cooperation, Schmidt-Aßmann, EuR 1996, 270 (297).

65 Article 5(4) Regulation 1798/2003.

66 Article 76(4) Regulation 883/2004.

67 See, however, v. Bogdandy/Arndt, EWS 2000, 1 (2).

68 This means that all requirements of the respective legal bases must be satisfied and no other legal restrictions must apply.

69 Cf. ECJ, Case 205–215/82 (Deutsche Milchkontor/Deutschland), Reports of Cases 1983, I-2633 (para. 22). In the *Höchst* judgment, ECJ, Joined Cases 46/87 and 227/88 (Höchst),

limitation of legal impossibility established by the principle of effectiveness must be determined on an individual case basis, it can be expected, as a rule, that, in the case of mutual administrative assistance which shall be performed in any event solely 'in accordance with national law', the national law will prevail.[70]

4.2.4. Limitations following from the principle of inter-administrative proportionality

Important limitations on the obligation to render mutual administrative assistance can be inferred from the General Principle of inter-administrative proportionality,[71] which the Commission defined to be a material cornerstone of a Community law of administrative cooperation.[72] The principle of proportionality requires that the purpose pursued – the efficient implementation of the respective Community law in the main proceedings – and the means employed for that purpose – the administrative expense connected with the mutual administrative assistance – are in a reasonable proportion. The relation between purpose and means in mutual administrative assistance which is so defined must be created on the basis of the criteria of suitability, mainly, however, on the basis of the criteria of necessity and reasonableness. Accordingly, the following three forms of the principle of proportionality under the law of mutual administrative assistance can be determined:

First, it follows from the criterion of necessity, according to which the least burdensome of several equally suited means must be chosen,[73] that the mutual administrative assistance must be limited to that 'which is absolutely necessary in the relevant case'.[74] A milder means excluding the necessity of mutual administrative assistance is the exhaustion of an authority's own possibilities of

---

Reports of Cases 1989, I-2859 (para. 5) the ECJ found with regard to Member States' assistance by enforcement concerning inspections of the Commission that the assisting national authorities must act in accordance with national procedural rules designed to ensure respect for undertakings' rights, but that the Member States are required to ensure that the Commission's action is effective, while respecting the general principles of Community law.

70 In view of the fact that national authorities, when implementing Community law, act in accordance with their law in any event due to the absence of other Community provisions, the explicit reference to national law by secondary legal acts must be understood to the effect that national law is also generally binding in those of its parts which conflict with the obligation to give mutual administrative assistance. Occasionally, there are even express provisions according to which the relevant secondary legal act does not impose an obligation to perform assistance, if the laws or administrative practices of the requested Member State do not authorise the authority to perform such act for its own purposes, e.g. Article 40(2) Regulation 1798/2003; Article 8(1) Directive 77/799.

71 Contrary to German law, the principle of proportionality does not only apply to protect individual (fundamental) rights, but also sovereign interests.

72 COM (1994) 29 final, 5.

73 ECJ, Case C-101/98 (Union Deutsche Lebensmittelwerke), Reports of Cases 1999, I-8841 (para. 30).

74 COM (1994) 29 final, 5.

action, which the authority requesting mutual administrative assistance has. Therefore, it is also without express rules of secondary law that it can safely be assumed that *cross-border mutual administrative assistance is* basically *subsidiary to an authority's own possibilities of action*, if the latter are equally suitable.[75]

Furthermore, it follows from the aspect of reasonableness, according to which there must be a balanced proportion between the advantages of a measure in view of the purpose pursued and the disadvantages connected with such purpose at the same time, that a general right to refuse mutual administrative assistance exists, if a *disproportionately large administrative expense* would be connected with the assistance.[76] Such expense must be assessed in terms of expenditure of personnel, time and financial means,[77] whereby the Commission has specifically emphasised the cost aspect as the central aspect of reasonableness of administrative cooperation.[78]

Finally, it follows as a special form of the right of refusal, if there is a disproportionately large administrative expense, that the requested authority is entitled to refuse to render mutual administrative assistance if the performance of its own tasks would be seriously jeopardised thereby, i.e. that therefore *the performance of the authority's own tasks has priority.* Beyond the explicit provision of such limitation only in tax law,[79] such a rule is a general standard due to the structure of EC mutual administrative assistance.[80] As mutual administrative assistance is the exceptional use of an authority's powers for the tasks of a foreign authority and the latter is under a general obligation to perform the tasks assigned to it by means of its own, it is reasonable to assume that the performance of an authority's own tasks takes priority over assistance in tasks of a foreign authority.

---

75 In this respect, the purpose of *administrative efficiency*, which is occasionally pursued by mutual administrative assistance, can be fulfilled, so that an authority may use the mutual assistance of another authority despite its ability to act on its own, if this appears to be more efficient. This corresponds to the previous practice (prior to the application of Regulation 1/2003) of the Commission in competition law, to request Member State competition authorities to perform inspections only if those authorities had already been dealing with the case.

76 Such right of refusal as a general standard is confirmed by a corresponding principle of German law, as expressed by Sec. 5(3) No. 2 VwVfG.

77 Cf. Söhn, in: Hübschmann/Hepp/Spitaler (ed.), *Kommentar zur AO/FGO*, §117 AO margin no. 306 in conjunction with §112 AO margin no. 37.

78 COM (1994) 29 final, 5: 'The cooperation should also secure a counter-value for the costs incurred, by ensuring that the benefit is in a reasonable proportion to the employed resources.'

79 However, only in the German implementing rule of Sec. 3(2) No. 4 EG-Amtshilfegesetz.

80 This, too, is confirmed by a corresponding general principle of German law governing mutual administrative assistance, see Sec. 5(3) No. 3 VwVfG.

4.2.5. *Limitations by state sovereignty*

Finally, the provision of mutual administrative assistance is sometimes subject to reservations that are rooted in the sovereignty of the Member States: the reservations of reciprocity known in the international law concerning mutual administrative and judicial assistance and the reservations of *ordre public*.

Reciprocity

Reservations of so-called reciprocity under secondary law, according to which the requested authority is entitled to refuse mutual administrative assistance if the requesting authority itself would not be able to render such assistance in the opposite case, can only be found in tax law.[81] According to this, the requesting authority must be able to perform the requested act in 'the same manner and quality'.[82] Unlike the international law concerning mutual administrative assistance,[83] an unwritten reservation of reciprocity does not exist under Community law. To the extent that rules for mutual administrative assistance are established in secondary law without such a reservation, this follows from the sole consideration that such a reservation, as a rule of general international law, is overridden by conflicting Community law. Furthermore, the *exclusively national* interest of reciprocity, namely to render the mutual administrative assistance in order to obtain it in the same way in the opposite situation, is fully overridden by the common European interest in the proper execution of Community law.[84]

Ordre public in the sense of fundamental state interests

In some legal acts of the Community, provisions can be found which are known from the international law concerning assistance, according to which the administrative authorities of Member States are released from the obligation to render *horizontal* mutual administrative assistance, 'where that would be likely to be injurious to public policy or other fundamental interests, in particular with regard to data protection, of the Member State in which they are based'.[85] The

---

81 Article 40(3) sentence 1 Regulation 1798/2003; Art. 8(3) Directive 77/799.

82 Cf. Söhn, in: Hübschmann/Hepp/Spitaler, AO/FGO (fn. 77), §117 AO margin no. 173 a.

83 Specifically in respect of mutual administrative assistance, Söhn, in: Hübschmann/Hepp/ Spitaler, *AO/FGO* (fn. 77), §117 AO margin no. 172 et seq. Generally in respect of reciprocity as a principle of general international law governing any international interaction, Verdross/ Simma, *Universelles Völkerrecht*, 1984, §64; Simma, in: Bernhardt (ed.), *Encyclopedia of Public International Law*, 2000, entry 'Reciprocity', 29 (29 et seq.).

84 In respect of Community interest, see above 4.2.1.

85 Article 48(1) of Regulation 515/97; congruent Article 13(1) Directive 89/608; Article 8(2) Directive 77/779; Article 40(4) Regulation 1798/2003; Article 4(3) c Directive 76/308.

national basic values[86] which form that so-called *ordre public* comprise, in addition to fundamental principles of constitutional law and in particular the national fundamental rights,[87] further material interests of the *state*.[88] The latter include interests of the internal and external national security[89] as well as other material interests of various types.[90]

The understanding of the term *ordre public*, which is originally a purely national understanding, must be 'Europeanised' in the context of Community law. This means that the European Court of Justice is entitled to review the national interpretation and to define uniform limitations for invoking reservations in substantive law; it stated these explicitly in the *Krombach* judgment in respect of the *ordre public* reservation of the European Convention on Jurisdiction and the Enforcement of Judgments in Civil and Commercial Matters (Brussels Convention).[91] This follows firstly from the competence of the European Court of Justice to interpret Community law terms according to Article 234 of the EC Treaty, and secondly from the intention of the Community acts regulating mutual administrative assistance, namely to facilitate and strengthen the cooperation between administrative authorities; the stipulated aim of optimum cooperation between national authorities concerning the execution of Community law could be challenged, if the *ordre public* reservation was to be understood as a mere reference to the respective national evaluations.[92]

While an *ordre public* reservation applies to mutual administrative and judicial assistance under international law also without an explicit provision, namely as a general principle,[93] this must be denied, however, under Community

86 Seidl-Hohenveldern, in: Bernhardt (ed.), *Encyclopedia of Public International Law*, volume 3, headword 'ordre public', 1997.

87 See below 4.3.3.

88 Loebenstein, *International Mutual Assistance* (fn. 14), 57.

89 For the protection of material security interests, Article 296(1) an EC Treaty already grants Member States a right of refusal to provide information.

90 For example, as a special form of an *ordre public* reservation, Article 14 Directive 76/308 provides that the recovery of monetary claims may be refused, if this would create serious economic or social difficulties in the Member State in which the authority pursuing the recovery is situated. In this respect, the jeopardising of jobs as a result of an insolvency or the unfavourable change of regional economic structures are taken into consideration, see Beermann, in: Hübschmann/Hepp/Spitaler (ed.), *Kommentar zur AO/FGO*, §250 AO margin no. 155.

91 ECJ, Case C-7/98 (Krombach), Reports of Cases 2000, I-1935 (para. 22 et seq.); confirmed in ECJ, Case C-38/98 (Renault/Maxicar), Reports of Cases 2000, I-2973 (para. 57 et seq.).

92 In respect of the *ordre public* of Art. 27 No. 1 European Civil Jurisdiction Convention cf. AG Alber, opinion in the case C-38/98 (Renault/Maxicar), Reports of Cases 2000, I-2973 (para. 58); Völker, *Zur Dogmatik des ordre public*, 1998, 292 et seq., 300 et seq.

93 Disputed; pro Loebenstein, *International Mutual Assistance* (fn. 14), 57. With regard to *ordre public* in the sense of material fundamental rights, this follows in any event from the binding effect of national fundamental rights that continues to exist in international legal relations, see below 4.3.3.

law,[94] because the Member States have submitted themselves to the *ordre public* established by the EC Treaty.[95] On account of that common basis and the resulting obligations of the Member States to cooperate loyally *vis-à-vis* one another and *vis-à-vis* the Community, the relevant reservation under international law is no longer applicable.[96]

4.3. PROCEDURAL STANDARDS PROTECTING PRIVATE PERSONS

4.3.1. Introduction

Mutual administrative assistance is a means of cooperation which has developed in the general interest, and of which private persons are not entitled to claim the use.[97] However, mutual administrative assistance can definitely not be interpreted as a purely internal action of an authority, but touches upon legal positions, or fundamental rights of private persons, in a variety of manners.[98] Consequently, the legal position of private persons in dealings of EC mutual administrative assistance is characterised by rights against the use of mutual administrative assistance, or by rights for the mutual administrative assistance to be disciplined by the rule of law. However, Community law traditionally tends 'to make the functionality of the Community and of its law into the paramount formula of interpretation'[99] and to subordinate the interests of the private person to that. If one disregards data and secret protection, which is an issue consistently taken into account in legal acts of administrative cooperation,[100] that finding can also be confirmed in the secondary Community law concerning mutual administrative assistance. However, here, too – just as in the inter-administrative relationship – it is possible to show uniform procedural guidelines on account of

94 In respect of the reasons for denying a reservation in the sense of guarantees of material fundamental rights, see below 4.3.3. As here, in respect of the general question whether the Member States, for reasons of *ordre public*, are allowed to dispense with obligations of the EC Treaty, Schneider, *Die öffentliche Ordnung als Schranke der Grundfreiheiten des EG-Vertrages*, 1998, 53 et seq.

95 H.P. Ipsen, *Europäisches Gemeinschaftsrecht*, 1972, §26 margin no. 13.

96 In respect of the corresponding argumentation for the legal situation in the Federal State, cf. Kopp/Kopp, BayVBl. 1994, 229 (231 et seq.).

97 Wettner, *Amtshilfe*, (fn. 3), 307 et seq.

98 Of the range of typical acts of mutual administrative assistance, not only acts of enforcement and investigation may constitute interferences with fundamental rights, but the inter-administrative cross-border transmission of personal and company-related data and of business secrets also interferes with the fundamental right of data protection under Community law, respectively the fundamental right of property; explicitly Wettner, *Amtshilfe* (fn. 3), 311 et seq.

99 Schmidt-Aßmann, DVBl. 1993, 924 (931).

100 However, the rules are characterised by remarkable inconsistency. Explicitly Wettner, *Amtshilfe* (fn. 3), 356 et seq.

the application of General Principles of Community Law. For example, the General Principles of the rule of law and of proportionality place restrictions on the unhindered performance of mutual administrative assistance. Hereinafter, the application of Community rights of defence as well as the exclusions of information improperly obtained in the context of informational mutual administrative assistance (4.3.2) and the reservation of *ordre public* in the sense of material fundamental rights (4.3.3) shall be shown.

4.3.2. Application of Community rights of defence and the exclusion of information improperly obtained

As both the act of mutual administrative assistance and the decision to be taken or enforced with its help in the main proceedings may interfere with legal positions of private persons, the compliance with the rights of defence of such private persons on the one hand and with the corresponding exclusion of information improperly obtained in case of non-compliance with the required rights of defence on the other hand is of substantial importance.

Application of Community rights of defence

The provisions of secondary law concerning mutual administrative assistance do not provide for any rules with regard to the rights of defence to be observed in the mutual administrative assistance procedure. However, the European Court of Justice has developed these rights as General Principles of Community Law which shall apply as primary law.[101] With regard to their application in mutual administrative assistance procedures, it must, however, be taken into account that they were developed for administrative proceedings which may lead to the imposition of penalties, whereas the measures taken as part of mutual administrative assistance will often merely be *preparatory procedural acts* in connection with the main proceedings of the supported authority. The European Court of Justice makes a differentiation in this respect. On the one hand, there are procedural rights, such as the right to legal representation and the privileged nature of correspondence between lawyer and client, which must in any event be complied with even in the preliminary proceedings.[102] On the other hand, other rights, such as the right to be heard, basically relate only to the contentious proceedings which follow the delivery of the statement of objections. The underlying reason for that court practice is that it is sufficient for the affected person's legal protection if he is able to submit his objections against the

[101] An overview is provided by Arnold, EuR 1995, *Beiheft 1*, 7 (14 et seq.); Lenaerts/Vanhamme, CML Rev. 1997, 531 et seq.; Dannecker, ZStW 1999, 256 et seq.; Pernice/Kadelbach, DVBl. 1996, 1100 (1103).

[102] ECJ, Joined Cases 46/87 and 227/88 (Höchst), Reports of Cases 1989, I-2919 (para. 16).

preparatory measure in the main proceedings in which any detriments can be corrected, as the case may be, for example by non-utilisation of the evidence obtained.[103] An important exception from that principle is made, however, if the preparatory measure is connected with *irreparable burdens* which can no longer be removed in the main proceedings.[104] To the extent that measures to be taken as part of the mutual administrative assistance procedure create such irreparable burdens, the rights of defence under Community law must, therefore, be observed as General Principles of Law when taking such measures.[105]

Application of Community exclusion of information improperly obtained

The utilisability of information obtained by way of mutual administrative assistance in the main proceedings is generally determined by the law of the authority receiving the assistance and conducting the main proceedings.[106] The national rules concerning the utilisation of evidence thus applicable in national main proceedings may, however, be supplemented by two types of Community exclusion of evidence improperly obtained. Firstly, the rules of secondary Community law concerning mutual administrative assistance may take into consideration that the collection of information and the utilisation of such information are performed in different national sovereignties and that, therefore, the rights of defence to be observed may possibly differ substantially.[107] For example, more recent regulations in the supervision of competition and tax administration provide for an exclusion of evidence in the case that the supporting authority fails to observe the *national* rights of defence provided for under the national rules of the receiving authority.[108] Secondly, the logical

103 Cf. Schwarze, *Europäisches Verwaltungsrecht*, Volume 2, 1988, 1282.

104 ECJ, Joined Cases 46/87 and 227/88 (Höchst), Reports of Cases 1989, I-2919 (para. 15).

105 In respect of the right to be heard regarding inspections, David, *Inspektionen* (fn. 12), 306 et seq.

106 The application of *national* rules of utilisation of the authority rendering mutual assistance in proceedings of authorities of other Member States or the Community is generally not conceivable, because the latter authorities are not obliged by the national law of a Member State or another Member State.

107 The divergence of national procedural rights and rights of defence is increased, if information that was collected and transmitted by way of mutual administrative assistance by means of administrative procedural law can be used, at the recipient or generally in the receiving Member State, for sanctioning proceedings of a criminal-law nature, i.e. *transprocedurally*; in this respect, there is the additional problem of the divergence of the procedural rights and rights of defence between the individual types of proceedings. See Widdershoven, in: Vervaele (ed.), *Transnational Enforcement of the Financial Interests of the European Union*, 1999, 131 (141); 'a 'transprocedural' use of information'.

108 Article 12(3) Regulation 1/2003 permits the utilisation of exchanged information for the purpose of imposing sanctions on *natural* persons only subject to the condition that 'the law of the transmitting authority foresees sanctions of a similar kind in relation to an infringement of Article 81 or Article 82 of the Treaty' or that 'the information has been collected in a way which respects the *same level of protection of the rights of defence of natural*

consequence of the fact that the Member States are bound by Community rights of defence as General Principles of Community Law is the general application of exclusions of evidence improperly obtained in Member State proceedings, if such exclusions follow from the violation of these rights of defence.[109] The European Court of Justice has confirmed this in the *Steffensen* case. The fact that the information to be utilised was collected and transmitted by a Community authority or an authority of another Member State, i.e. that the utilisation of the evidence was preceded by an act of vertical or horizontal mutual administrative assistance, does nothing to alter this legal situation.

In the first-mentioned provision of exclusion of evidence in case of non-observance of national rights of defence, there is evidence, at least, of a certain tendency – which is desirable – to observe the legal protection of private persons. However, it would be more in line with the purpose of effective execution if an obligation was imposed on the assisting authority, when performing the act of assistance, which obliges it to observe the procedural requirements of the law of the authority receiving the assistance also with regard to the rights of defence of private persons, in order to avoid problems concerning utilisation from the outset.[110] Ultimately, however, the expectations regarding legal protection can only be fulfilled in the long term, if the unwritten rights of defence already applying as General Principles of Community Law, and the exclusion of evidence improperly obtained which can be derived from them, are laid down as secondary Community law.[111]

4.3.3. *Ordre public in the sense of national fundamental rights*

As presented above, the provisions of secondary law concerning horizontal mutual administrative assistance sometimes contain so-called *ordre public* reservations.[112] According to these reservations, the mutual administrative assistance may be refused for the protection of the affected private persons,[113] if the main proceedings to be supported conflict with the national basic values, respectively with the substance of the *fundamental rights* of the requested

---

persons as provided for under the national rules of the receiving authority' (italics by the author).

109 Also Widdershoven, in: Vervaele, *Transnational Enforcement* (fn. 107), 131 (148); also H.C. Röhl, ZaöRV 60 (2000), 331 (361).

110 See above 3.2 at the end.

111 Also, Widdershoven, in: Vervaele, *Transnational Enforcement* (fn. 107), 131 (149).

112 See above 4.2.5.

113 In contrast, however, in favour of a purely state-protecting character of the *ordre public* reservation, Brenner, FR 1989, 236 (238); Harings, *Grenzüberschreitende Zusammenarbeit der Polizei- und Zollverwaltungen und Rechtsschutz in Deutschland*, 1998, 223. As here in respect of international agreements on judicial assistance, Hackner/Lagodny/Schomburg/Wolf, *Internationale Rechtshilfe in Strafsachen*, 2003, margin no. 50; Rieser, ÖJZ 1988, 713 (716).

state.[114] From that aspect of protection, the *ordre public* under the law of mutual administrative assistance has recently become an issue once more in international dealings of mutual assistance outside the Community law.[115]

It is for one thing the purpose of the proceedings to be supported (*substantive ordre public*), and secondly the form of such proceedings (*procedural ordre public*), which are to be assessed according to fundamental national rights. While it is probably no longer possible, on account of the concurrence in the Member States of the basic concepts of substantive law, to find a case of application within the Community that is of practical relevance to the substantive *ordre public*, the latter – i.e. the procedural *ordre public* – is definitely of practical importance. For example, a protection of *company-related data* that is less stringent in the recipient state than in the transmitting state comes into consideration,[116] or a level of *rights of defence* that is less stringent in the assisted state than in the state providing the assistance.[117] The national determination of the guarantees of fundamental rights constituting the *ordre public* must be 'Europeanised' within the Community, as presented above with regard to the determination of fundamental national interests. In the *Krombach* decision the European Court of Justice stipulated that, in order to be able to invoke fundamental national rights, there must be corresponding fundamental rights in the Community legal

114 R. Hofmann, *Grundrechte und grenzüberschreitende Sachverhalte*, 1994, 332; Vogel, *Doppelbesteuerungsabkommen, Kommentar*, 3rd ed., 1996, Art. 26 margin no. 112; Papier/Olschewski, DVBl. 1976, 475 (478); Schomburg/Lagodny, *Kommentar zum Gesetz über die internationale Rechtshilfe in Strafsachen*, 3rd ed., 1998, §73 IRG margin no. 7.

115 BVerfG JZ 2003, 956 et seq.: Prevention of the service of an American statement of claim in Germany. Explicitly v. Danwitz, DÖV 2004, 501 et seq.

116 Due to the harmonisation of the national rights of data protection by the Data Protection Directive (Directive 95/46) and the introduction of a corresponding standard for the Community authorities by the Data Protection Regulation (Regulation 45/2001), there is no longer any scope of application in respect of *personal data*. Although there are still differences in specific details in this regard, the fundamental concepts of data protection law are now uniformly codified throughout the Community. However, this is not the case for *company-related data*, respectively business secrets. Such data and secrets are protected by the fundamental rights of the Community, and to that extent such protection is theoretically uniform (Wettner, Amtshilfe (fn. 3), 315 et seq.); however, the protective provisions of the ordinary laws have so far not been harmonised to correspond with Community law, so that divergences may exist in the national protective provisions which are of relevance to the fundamental rights.

117 An example is provided by the ECJ, Case C-7/98 (Krombach), Reports of Cases 2000, I-1935 et seq., for an *ordre public* reservation regarding mutual assistance by enforcement: The French Cour d'assises had ordered Mr Krombach to pay damages based on personal injury without previously having heard Mr Krombach, represented by his lawyers. In that specific case, this was permissible under French law. The German Federal Court of Justice (*BGH*) submitted the question to the ECJ whether the enforcement of the judgment in Germany could be refused on the basis of the European Civil Jurisdiction Convention due to a violation of the right to be heard and thus a violation of the German *ordre public* pursuant to Article 27(1) European Civil Jurisdiction Convention.

system.[118] Any national understanding of fundamental rights which goes beyond that cannot entitle a state to refuse to render mutual administrative assistance.

A reservation of *ordre public* understood in this sense could follow as a general standard of mutual administrative assistance from the fact that the assisting authority is bound by national law to the national fundamental rights. According to the German dogma concerning fundamental rights, fundamental rights are applied in international dealings of mutual administrative assistance in their function as protective rights (*Schutzrechte*).[119] They are aimed at averting an expected interference with fundamental rights in the foreign proceedings from the outset, because and to the extent that the affected person does not enjoy a corresponding protection in those proceedings on account of the foreign legal system being applicable; such interference is averted by the refusal to grant the requested mutual administrative assistance. However, that protection is no longer required with the status of integration that has since been achieved. The German Constitutional Court (*Bundesverfassungsgericht*), in a judgment concerning the enforcement of Austrian titles related to taxes, assumed on the basis of the German-Austrian agreement on legal assistance that a reservation of *ordre public* is only necessary where a minimum of legal protection 'appears not to be *generally* guaranteed'.[120] This correlates conspicuously with the statements of the court concerning the protection of fundamental rights against Community law applicable on German sovereign territory, namely that the *Bundesverfassungsgericht* does not exercise its competence of examination, if and as long as the protection of fundamental rights is *generally* guaranteed at Community level.[121] In this case, such a waiver of the application of German fundamental rights, which is apparently always permitted if and to the extent

118 ECJ, Case C-7/98 (Krombach), Reports of Cases 2000, I-1935 (para. 38 et seq.): 'With regard to the right to be defended, to which the question submitted to the Court refers, this occupies a prominent position in the organisation and conduct of a fair trial and is one of the fundamental rights deriving from the constitutional traditions common to the Member States. More specifically still, the European Court of Human Rights has on several occasions ruled in cases relating to criminal proceedings that, although not absolute, the right of every person charged with an offence to be effectively defended by a lawyer, if need be one appointed by the court, is one of the fundamental elements in a fair trial and an accused person does not forfeit entitlement to such right simply because he is not present at the hearing [...]. *It follows from that case-law* that a national court of a Contracting State is *entitled* to hold that refusal to hear the defence of an accused person who is not present at the hearing constitutes a manifest breach of a fundamental right' (italics by the author).

119 In respect of that effect of national fundamental rights in cross-border mutual administrative assistance, explicitly Schemmer, *Der ordre public-Vorbehalt unter der Geltung des Grundgesetzes*, 1995, 130 et seq.; Ruegenberg, *Das nationale und internationale Steuergeheimnis im Schnittpunkt von Besteuerungs- und Strafverfahren*, 2001, 340. At least according to the German dogma regarding fundamental rights, the application of an *ordre public* reservation under the law governing mutual administrative assistance is not bound by explicit provisions.

120 BVerfGE 63, 343 (378).

121 BVerfGE 102, 147 (161, 164 et seq.).

that a corresponding protection of fundamental rights is *generally* guaranteed, will have to be assumed for all forms of mutual administrative assistance, including those forms outside assistance by enforcement measures. Due to the fact that, within the scope of Community law, the Community as well as the national authorities are bound by the fundamental rights of the Community as General Principles of Community Law,[122] a *generally* guaranteed minimum of legal protection must be assumed to be available at the supported authority. Examination of the foreign proceedings by the standard of national fundamental rights is generally not an option from a German point of view.[123] The fact that the legal protection is nevertheless not guaranteed *in an individual case*, because a state may disregard the Community fundamental rights, is not too harmful insofar as that infringement can be asserted before the competent courts of that state and it is therefore no longer required for the national assisting authority to assume the position of a 'guardian'.

As such a reservation of national fundamental rights is also not required by Community law, *ordre public* reservations of secondary law exceed that which would be required according to general rules and therefore appear to be an anomaly. Consequently, there is then, in any event, no unwritten reservation of *ordre public* in the sense of the substance of national fundamental rights as a general principle of Community law concerning mutual administrative assistance.

5. CONCLUSION

The divergence of regulations concerning mutual administrative assistance in the various areas of European administration often appears to be due to coincidences in the history of their origins rather than due to distinctive features of the respective subject matter. By applying the General Principles of Community Law, in particular, it is possible to develop general procedural rules which are not limited to specific areas. That general Community procedural law of mutual administrative assistance has a greater affinity with the national law concerning mutual administrative assistance than with the respective international law.[124] For in many places it reflects the weakening of the sovereignty of Member States which still continues to exist in the legal system of the Community; for example, reservations of reciprocity or of *ordre public*

122 See above 3.3.

123 In respect of the enforcement of Community titles in accordance with Article 256 EC Treaty, also Pernice, RIW 1986, 353 (356); differently Brenner, DVBl. 1999, 877 (884).

124 In respect of comparisons of the Community law regarding mutual administrative assistance with federal state models and international law models regarding mutual administrative assistance, more explicitly Wettner, *Amtshilfe* (fn. 3), passim and in summary p. 198 et seq. and p. 303 et seq.

generally applying in dealings of mutual administrative assistance under international law can still only be found in exceptional cases in Community law. Furthermore, a general obligation of administrative authorities to render mutual administrative assistance, which ensues from the principle of loyal cooperation, exists in the common interest of effective implementation of Community law. This formation of a unity, in terms of procedural law, of the European administrations when implementing Community law[125] would be matched by the codification of the law concerning mutual administrative assistance in a general legal act of the Community, as considered at the beginning of this paper. Impulses directed at the formation of such unity can be expected from the European Constitution, which pays specific attention to administrative cooperation for the purpose of implementing Union law.[126]

125 In respect of the formation of an organisational unity by the increasing direct contact between the competent authorities and by the establishment of network structures, Wettner, *Amtshilfe* (fn. 3), 277 et seq.

126 See above 4.2.1.

XIV. THE DECISION AS A MEANS OF NORMATIVE LAWMAKING*

Matthias VOGT

1. INTRODUCTION

The European Community as a "Community of law"[1] is founded and based upon the law. It strives to attain its goals as expressed in Article 2 et seq. of the EC Treaty through legal rules and procedures. In the course of this, European institutions make use of the legal instruments predominantly[2] named in Article 249 EC. If, therefore, the European legal system, similar to German administrative law, is based on a principle of action,[3] a thorough analysis of the modes of action and instruments underlying this structure is of the utmost importance. The historical development of a scholarly analysis of European lawmaking shows that Regulations and Directives are the two legal instruments that have attracted most authors' attention throughout the last decades.[4] The decision within the meaning of Article 249(4) EC has so far been broadly neglected.[5] This article will

---

* This contribution is based on the author's dissertation with the title "Die Entscheidung als Handlungsform des Europäischen Gemeinschaftsrechts", Mohr Siebeck, 2005. A first version (German) is published in: Eberhard Schmidt-Aßmann and Bettina Schöndorf-Haubold, "Der Europäische Verwaltungsverbund", Mohr Siebeck, Tubingen, 2005, p. 213–236.

1 The definition of the EC as a Community based on the law (*Rechtsgemeinschaft)* was first introduced by Hallstein, *Die Europäische Gemeinschaft*, 5th ed., 1979, pp. 51 et seq.; the term's development and its substance are described by *Zuleeg*, NJW 1994, pp. 545 et seq. For an introduction on the rule of law in the EU see v. Bogdandy, in: v. Bogdandy (ed.), *Europäisches Verfassungsrecht*, 2003, 149, at pp. 165 et seq.

2 The catalogue in Article 249 EC does not contain all European legal instruments; see Schroeder, in Streinz (ed.), EUV/EGV, 2003, Article 249, at notes 2, 10, 26 et seq.

3 This has already been noted by v. Danwitz, *Verwaltungsrechtliches System und Europäische Integration*, 1996, p. 168.

4 A short survey of the historical development is given by J. Bast, in: v. Bogdandy, *Europäisches Verfassungsrecht* (cited above fn. 1), 479, at pp. 481 et seq.

5 Early commentators have focused on the decision established by the ECCS, which, however, has a structure completely different from today's decision. This will be explained later at B.I. The conclusion that the decision has been paid little attention is also shared by Bockey, *Die Entscheidung der Europäischen Gemeinschaften*, 1998, p. 16. However, Bockey's explanation that the "Decision is an act with exclusively individual concern and does not have a normative character" is insufficient to grasp its true nature, as will be shown later.

explain the decision's impact and its flexibility as a means of normative lawmaking. In order to do so, the first part will provide a short introduction on the traditional concept of the decision as an equivalent to the national administrative act of individual concern (2.). In contrast to this argument, an analysis of its actual use in European lawmaking will be able to demonstrate that the decision is a most complex and flexible legal instrument (3.).

2. THE COMMON PERCEPTION OF THE DECISION AS A EUROPEAN ADMINISTRATIVE ACT

2.1. LEGACY OF THE INDIVIDUAL DECISION ACCORDING TO THE PARIS TREATY ESTABLISHING THE ECSC

The Treaty Establishing the European Coal and Steel Community of April 18, 1951 already acknowledged legal acts named "decisions". Article 14(2) defined them as instruments "binding in their entirety". Moreover, Article 15(2) and (3), with a view to the notification of legal acts, differentiated between decisions of an individual character and other measures,[6] thus introducing the separation of an individual decision from a general one.[7] However, the Treaty did not define the concept of these distinctive legal acts, leaving that task to the European judicature and legal scholars.[8] Once it had been decided when a Community act should be a legally binding decision in the first place,[9] a number of Treaty provisions led to a debate on how to distinguish individual from general decisions. While, formally speaking, a legal act seemed to be of general character when it was published in the official journal,[10] the provision of Article 33(2) suggested a more material approach in asking for the individual concern of a measure.[11] Thus, Attorney General *Lagrange* in Case 8/55[12] stated that a measure,

---

6 Here, according to Article 15(3) ECSC, individual notice was replaced by publication.

7 Jerusalem, *Das Recht der Montanunion*, 1954, p. 29 et seq. This differentiation had impacts on the question of enforcement of the ECSC Decisions; see Osterheld, *Die Vollstreckung von Entscheidungen*, 1954, pp. 24 et seq.

8 For an early definition in literature see Wiesner, *Der Widerruf individueller Entscheidungen*, 1966, at pp. 12 et seq.

9 The Court of Justice in cases 23/63, 24/63 and 52/63 *Usines Émile Henricot v High Authority* [1963] E.C.R. 467, at 483 et seq. has used a purely material approach and opposed the High Authority's efforts to formally define its legal acts in their headings; see Article 1 of Decision No 22/60 of 07/09/1960 concerning the implementation of Article 15 of the Treaty, [1960] OJ B61/1248 et seq.

10 This is the conclusion drawn from Article 15(3) ECSC by Conrad, *Formen der Vollziehung*, 1968, p. 156. Against such a formal differentiation already Fuss [1964] NJW 945, at p. 949, where he notes that an individual notice is merely a consequence of individual concern, not a legal characteristic.

11 Cases 7/54 and 9/54 *Groupement des industries siderurgiques* [1955] E.C.R. 55 at [87] *et seq.*

12 Case 8/55 *Fédération Charbonniere de Belgique* [1955] E.C.R. 245 *et seq.*

which is not normative in nature and which is designed to deal with a specific case, shall be an individual decision with regard to those individuals that are directly affected by the measure in its entirety.[13] However, this definition was of a limited value when it came to decisions addressed to Member States, as the requirement of individual concern was not applicable to them according to Article 33(2). This resulted in yet another differentiation: according to some authors, general decisions should not only be separated from individual decisions within the meaning of Article 33(2), but also from a third and broader category of the so-called "single decisions", including both individual decisions and non-normative state-addressed measures.[14] As this concept merely introduced another term but could not help to clarify the substance of the duality between individual and general legal acts, it did not have a lasting influence in European legal scholarship.[15] The crucial point remained that the dividing line had to be drawn along the criterion of individual concern.[16] Thus, it is not surprising that, from the beginning of legal analysis, scholars saw the individual decision as an equivalent to the German *Verwaltungsakt*, the Dutch *beschikking* or the French *acte individuel*.[17] General decisions, on the other hand, were defined as a European variant of the *Rechtsverordnung* known in German public law, a normative legal act issued not by a Parliament, but by the executive branch of a government.[18]

2.2. CONCEPT OF THE EC DECISION AS EQUIVALENT TO THE INDIVIDUAL ECSC DECISION

This starting-point of a scholarly analysis of European lawmaking had its impact on the conception of the legal acts described in Article 249 EC. While general

13 Case 8/55 *Fédération Charbonniere de Belgique* [1955] E.C.R. 245, at [296].

14 A state-addressed Decision was considered to be a single, not a general decision where the measure was designed to deal with a specific situation *vis-à-vis* a Member State or a number of Member States; Conrad, cited above fn. 10, p. 156.

15 See only Ipsen, *Europäisches Gemeinschaftsrecht*, 1972, par. 21 notes 2 and 12.

16 It was, however, unclear, which criteria should be chosen to identify a decision of individual concern. Börner, *Die Entscheidungen der Hohen Behörde*, 1965, p. 117 et seq. only wanted to take into account the number of situations covered, irrespective of the persons concerned, thus treating the German acts called *"Allgemeinverfügung"* as general Decisions. On the other hand, Fuss, [1964] NJW 945, pp. 950 et seq. wanted to ask whether the number of addressees was already specified when the measure in question was adopted.

17 See Wiesner, cited above fn. 8, pp. 12 et seq. This comparison was generally accepted; see Grabitz, in: Grabitz/Hilf (ed.), *Das Recht der Europäischen Union*, January 2004, Article 189, note 67.

18 See Wiesner, cited above fn. 8, p. 12. Jerusalem, cited above fn. 7, p. 29, on the other hand, regards all decisions, recommendations and opinions of the High Authority as administrative acts, so that in German public law terminology the general decisions and recommendations would be so-called *"Allgemeinverfügungen"*.

decisions were seen to be replaced by Regulations,[19] individual decisions seemed to have evolved into the decision within the meaning of Article 189(4) EEC[20] and Article 249(4) EC.[21]

Thus, it did not come as a surprise, when German scholars strived to describe the decision as an instrument specifically designed to deal with individual cases (*Einzelfallentscheidung)*[22], to be separated from normative acts.[23] Most commentators chose to discuss the decision, its character and its typical functions on a very abstract level, adopting a legal concept well-known from the German *Verwaltungsakt.*[24] This approach, however, lacked a thorough analysis of the actual use of the legal instrument within the lawmaking process of the European institutions. As was arguably shown by *H.C. Röhl*, this development was strongly supported by the European Court of Justice and the way it defined the autonomous term of "decision" within the meaning of Article 230(4) EC, where it had to be designed specifically for the needs of judicial protection.[25] This tendency also became prevalent in English literature[26] and has so far never been

19 Rabe, *Das Verordnungsrecht der Europäischen Wirtschaftsgemeinschaft*, 1963, pp. 65 et seq. explicitly notes that it is not justified to define the nature of both legal acts differently, once as an executive regulation (*Verordnung*), once as formal law. See also Daig, in: Groeben/Boeckh/Thiesing, *Kommentar zum EWG-Vertrag*, 2nd ed. 1974, Article 189 note III.2.A.

20 Conrad, cited above fn. 10, pp. 155 et seq.

21 Biervert, in: Schwarze, *EU-Kommentar*, Article 249 note 4. Also P. Stelkens/U. Stelkens, in: Stelkens/Bonk/Sachs, VwVfG, 6th ed. 2001, par. 35 note 252: "Inzwischen herrscht Einigkeit darüber, daß die Einzelfallentscheidung mit der Entscheidung i.S.d. Article 249 Abs. 4 EGV und die allgemeine Entscheidung mit der Verordnung i.S.d. Article 249 Abs. 2 EGV gleichzusetzen ist."("Meanwhile, it has become common knowledge that the individual Decision equals the Decision according to Article 249(4) EC and that the general Decision equals the Regulation according to Article 249(2) EC.").

22 That is the term used by Schweitzer, in: FS für Klein, 1994, 85, p. 98, who derives the individual character of the decisions directly from the alleged wording of Article 249(4) EC: "Die Einzelfallentscheidungen gemäß Artikel 189 IV EGV sind in allen ihren Teilen für diejenigen verbindlich, die sie bezeichnen." ("The individual decisions according to Article 189(4) EC are binding in their entirety upon those to whom they are addressed.").

23 See, for example, Bülow [1963] AWD, p. 244: "Die Grenze zwischen Verordnung und Entscheidung dürfte nach dem EWG-Recht dort zu ziehen sein, wo sich auch nach deutschem Recht Rechtsetzung und Verwaltungsakt voneinander unterscheiden" ("The dividing line between Regulation and Decision will have to be drawn where according to German law legislative acts and administrative acts differ.").

24 See Thierfelder, *Die Entscheidung im EWG-Vertrag*, 1968. See also P. Stelkens/U. Stelkens, in: Stelkens/Bonk/Sachs, cited above fn. 21, par. 35 notes 250 b et seq.; especially in note 250 d: "Dies rechtfertigt, die Entscheidung nach Artikel 249 Abs. 4 EG ihrer Funktion nach mit dem VA des §35 VwVfG zu vergleichen." ("Thus, it is justified to compare the function of the Decision according to Article 249(4) EC with the administrative act of par. 35 VwVfG.").

25 H.C. Röhl [2000] ZaöRV 331; see also his The voidable Decision according to Article 230(4) of the Treaty establishing the European Community as a Form of Legal Protection, in this vol., 439 *et seq.*

26 See insofar Lauwaars, *Lawfulness and legal force of Community Decisions*, 1973, p. 50, who explicitly refuses to differentiate between decisions addressed to states and decisions addressed to private individuals and who concludes: 'The legal act itself is analogous with the administrative act known in national law.'

seriously questioned. As a consequence, most commentators, when discussing the concept of the decision, limited the scope of their analysis to legal acts addressed to private individuals,[27] a representative of the decision that, of all the instruments in European law, clearly shows most characteristics familiar from the administrative acts of national public laws.[28]

2.3. A CRITICISM OF THE COMMON VIEW

This understanding of the decision as an instrument designed to deal with individual cases, however, can only reflect a small part of the actual role the decision plays within the complex lawmaking procedures of European institutions. With its characteristic combination of strictly binding effects and limited personal applicability, the decision is clearly the most suitable instrument to deal with specific issues *vis-à-vis* private individuals or enterprises. This function of the decision can, for example, be found where the Commission grants an exemption from competition laws or allows the marketing of a new medicinal product.

Where they are addressed to Member States, however, decisions can operate in various ways, fulfilling very different functions. Here, the nature of the decision is far more complex than most commentators choose to assume and cannot be appropriately described according to the common perception of a European administrative act. This is true even where decisions are dealing with individual cases in relation to a state. In some areas of law, especially in state aid control, Member States are in a subordinate position similar to that of a private individual.[29] In these circumstances, decisions are an indicator of a partial

---

27 This can clearly be seen in Junker, *Der Verwaltungsakt im deutschen und französischen Recht und die Entscheidung im Recht der Europäischen Gemeinschaft*, 1990, where the title already expresses the view that the decision should be seen in one line with national administrative acts, which are limited to dealing with individual cases. See also Bockey, cited above fn. 5. Similarly, Brenner, *Der Gestaltungsauftrag der Verwaltung in der Europäischen Union*, 1996, p. 138 concludes that the decision can be called the administrative act of Community law. Bleckmann [1993] DÖV 837, pp. 844 et seq. also sees the decision in line with the notion of an administrative act, which in all national legal frameworks is linked with certain rules regarding procedure, judicial protection and substantive rules.

28 See Schweitzer, *Europäisches Verwaltungsrecht*, 1991, p. 37. For a detailed analysis of the decision as a European administrative act see Vogt, *Die Entscheidung als Handlungsform des Europäischen Gemeinschaftsrechts*, 2005, pp. 60 et seq.

29 Similarly Mager [2001] EuR 661, p. 669. Where private individuals are involved in such supervisory relationships, their private interests appear to be mostly in line with the interests of the Member States, both being confronted with a contradictory Community interest. This is the reason why the protection of confidence known in national laws is not applicable to the same degree in Community law, where state aid has to be repaid following a Commission decision declaring it incompatible with Community law. For details see Attorney General *Jacobs* in case C-24/95 Alcan II [1997] E.C.R. I-1591, at [26]; see also Berrisch [1997] EuR 155, p. 161; Fastenrath [1998] DV 277, pp. 293 et seq.

hierarchy established between the Commission as the most important administrative body at European level and the Member States.[30] Such acts might therefore be defined as a kind of a special, state-addressed administrative act. Elsewhere, Member States play the role of the EC administration's equal partner so that private individuals perceive both levels of government as one administrative body. The decision can, for example, be part of a multi-stage administrative procedure, authorising or instructing a national authority to issue an administrative decision towards a private entity. It seems obvious that such decisions have little in common with an administrative act but are specifically designed to serve as a coordinating instrument as part of the European Composite Administration (*Verwaltungsverbund*). Their legal nature can neither be grasped by using the German concept of an intra-administrative instruction (*Weisung*)[31] nor by a comparison with national multi-stage administrative acts.[32]

This article, however, does not concern itself with such types of individual decisions and the different ways in which they operate in European administrative law. Its aim is to give an impression of the most overlooked of the decision's various functions beyond a purely administrative nature. This is the one it performs, in co-operation with Regulations and Directives, as a means of normative lawmaking within a framework that could be described as a "legislative-administrative composite network" (*legislativ-administrativen Verbund*).

---

30 See also Hatje, *Die gemeinschaftsrechtliche Steuerung der Wirtschaftsverwaltung*, 1998, pp. 167 et seq., who sees a tendency towards a factual hierarchy, which is, however, limited to the agricultural area and to a hierarchy among administrative bodies, thus not taking into account supervisory relationships between EC institutions and national lawmakers. For a French analysis of the situation see Cartou, Communautés européenne, 10th ed. 1991, p. 135; for an English perspective see Gil Ibáñez, *The Administrative Supervision and Enforcement of EC Law: Powers, Procedures and Limits*, 1999, p. 306: "[…] from a legal point of view we can speak of a quasi-hierarchical relation between the Commission and national administrations considered individually […]".

31 For an analysis speaking of instructive powers (*Weisungsbefugnissen*) of the Commission vis-à-vis national authorities see Graf Vitzthum/Schenek, in: Graf Vitzthum (ed.), *Europäische und Internationale Wirtschaftsordnung aus der Sicht der Bundesrepublik Deutschland*, 1994, 47, at p. 82.

32 See Caspar [2002] DVBl. 1437 et seq.; Lienhard [2002] NuR 13, at pp. 15 et seq. Kadelbach, *Allgemeines Verwaltungsrecht unter europäischem Einfluß*, 1999, p. 336 already noted that the authorisation of genetically modified organisms could be defined as a multi-stage administrative act (*mehrstufiger Verwaltungsakt)* according to the terminology of general administrative law.

3. ANALYSIS OF THE DECISION'S FUNCTION IN A EUROPEAN "LEGISLATIVE-ADMINISTRATIVE COMPOSITE NETWORK" (LEGISLATIV-ADMINISTRATIVER VERBUND)

3.1. INTRODUCTION

An analysis of the decision as a means of action in EC law cannot make any valid statements without taking a closer look at such legal acts, which – in relation to both private parties and Member States – have so little in common with individual cases that one can only speak of a general and abstract guidance. In order to bring the large number of such decisions in an orderly structure, the following paragraphs will differentiate between these acts according to their legal basis. A first part will deal with decisions based directly on the Treaty (3.2.), while a second part will discuss those instruments that are based on secondary legislation, i.e. Regulations and Directives (3.3.).

3.2. SOFT LAW GUIDING THE MEMBER STATES DIRECTLY BASED ON THE TREATY

3.2.1. Introduction

The first type of normative guidance through decisions is represented by such measures that are already envisaged in primary legislation. Here, we are not talking about so-called derived legal acts, based on Regulations or Directives.[33] Moreover, the decisions in question – unlike those the Commission issues according to Article 86 EC – are not concerned with resolving an individual case or a specific dispute *vis-à-vis* a Member State. Generally speaking, such decisions based on primary law can be found where the Treaty itself authorises an institution not only to issue Directives or Regulations, but in a non-specific way speaks about "measures" to be taken or "decisions" to be adopted.[34] General statements on the legal character and typical features of normative decisions based on the Treaty are difficult to make due to the diversity of this type of legal

[33] For a legal analysis of these so-called derived legal acts (*habilitierte Rechtsakte*) see v. Bogdandy/Bast/Arndt [2002] ZaöRV 77, at p. 93. The term means the same as the term implementing measure. Unlike the latter, however, it has the advantage that it does not necessarily imply a strictly hierarchical relationship between the basic legal act and the implementing measure, which does not exist.

[34] Above all, this may be the general harmonising power of Article 95(1) EC, but also various substantial powers such as Article 37 EC in common agricultural law, Article 157 EC in the common industrial policy, Article 175 EC in the environmental area or Article 285 EC in statistical matters.

acts and the political contexts they relate to. Nevertheless, a number of essential and recurrent characteristics can be described.

3.2.2. Cooperative guidance by means of programmatic benchmarking

With a view to the formal quality of the acts, the first thing to be noted is that all relevant decisions were enacted exclusively by the legislature, i.e. as a cooperation between the Parliament and the Council. In most cases, the applicable procedure is the one of co-decision outlined in Article 251 EC. The subject matter of normative decisions based on the Treaty is usually to establish a political or administrative programme over a number of years, sometimes called "action plan",[35] "action programme",[36] "guidelines"[37] or just "programme".[38] Thereby, these decisions define medium- and long-term goals for a certain policy area and try to outline the way in which these goals are to be put into practice. Responsibility for taking the legal and factual steps necessary to achieve a policy goal falls primarily on the EC institutions themselves. Thus, despite the fact that they are formally addressed to the Member States, these decisions set out a number of tasks for the Commission, the one institution equipped with the necessary administrative capacities. For example, the Commission is asked and authorised to take the steps necessary and relevant to achieve a defined political goal,[39] to provide regular reports on the state of affairs[40] and to function as a coordinating authority in order to bring together various activities on national and European levels.[41] In some cases, however, tasks like the co-ordination of a

---

35 See, for example, Decision No 276/1999/EC of the European Parliament and of the Council of 25 January 1999 adopting a multi-annual Community action plan on promoting safer use of the Internet by combating illegal and harmful content on global networks ("action plan internet"), OJ L 33 of 6 February 1999, p. 1.

36 See, for example, Decision No 253/2003/EC of the European Parliament and of the Council of 11 February 2003 adopting an action programme for customs in the Community ("customs 2007"), OJ L 36 of 12 February 2003, p. 1.

37 See, for example, Decision No. 1719/1999/EC of the European Parliament and of the Council of 12 July 1999 on a series of guidelines, including the identification of projects of common interest, for trans-European networks for the electronic interchange of data between administrations ("IDA"), OJ L 203 of 3 August 1999, p. 1.

38 See, for example, Decision No. 1230/2003/EC of the European Parliament and of the Council of 26 June 2003 adopting a multiannual programme for action in the field of energy: "Intelligent Energy – Europe" (2003–2006), OJ L 176 of 15 July 2003, p. 29.

39 Article 12 of Decision No. 253/2003/EC ("customs 2007"), cited above fn. 36; Article 2 lit. c) and Article 10 of Decision No. 96/411/EC of the Council of 25 June 1996 on improving Community agricultural statistics ("agricultural statistics"), OJ L 162 of 1 July 1996, p. 14.

40 Article 19(3) of Decision "customs 2007", cited above fn. 36; Article 4 of Decision No. 2367/2002/EC of the European Parliament and of the Council of 16 December 2002 on the Community statistical programme 2003 to 2007 ("statistical programme"), OJ L 358 of 31 December 2002, p. 1; Article 11 of Decision "agricultural statistics", cited above fn. 39.

41 Article 5(5), Article 11(1) of Decision "customs 2007", cited above fn. 36; Article 3 of Decision "agricultural statistics", cited above fn. 39.

programme may be conferred on institutions established outside the framework of the Treaty.[42]

On the other hand, European administration heavily depends on national authorities and resources.[43] Normative programmatic decisions cannot be put into action by European institutions alone. Therefore, Member States are usually assigned their own tasks and responsibilities in the realisation process of the programme. They are, for example, instructed to work together in the establishment of a communication and information exchange network,[44] to arrange a set of data or statistics,[45] or simply to carry out all measures which they consider appropriate to achieve common goals.[46]

Irrespective of the details of the allocation of the various responsibilities among different authorities, it can be noted that all the decisions are characterised by a highly co-operative approach. The Commission, for its part, is asked to fulfil its responsibilities in co-operation or after consultation with national authorities.[47] In this context, the term partnership is frequently used;[48] sometimes the duties are just defined as common duties.[49] This procedural co-operative approach with a view to specific tasks is often accompanied by a

---

42 In the area of Community statistics, this may be the Community institution Eurostat. See paragraph 11 of the reasons given for Decision "statistical programme", cited above fn. 40.

43 For this aspect, that in any case requires national execution of Community law for practical reasons, see Schroeder, *Das Gemeinschaftsrechtssystem*, 2002, p. 389.

44 Article 5 of Decision "customs 2007", cited above fn. 36.

45 This can be seen in paragraph 9 of the reasons given for the "statistical programme" decision, cited above fn. 40, even though the decision itself does not require any action from the Member States, but merely describes the goals that are to be achieved as part of the programme (Article 2).

46 Article 6(6) of Decision No 1229/2003/EC of the European Parliament and of the Council of 26 June 2003 laying down a series of guidelines for trans-European energy networks and repealing Decision No 1254/96/EC ("guidelines trans-European networks"), OJ L 176 of 15 July 2003, p. 11; Article 5(1) of Decision No. 1152/2003/EC of the European Parliament and of the Council of 16 June 2003 on computerising the movement and surveillance of excisable products ("computerising"), OJ L 162 of 1 July 2003, p. 5: "Member States shall ensure that they complete, by the date specified in the management plans mentioned in Article 4(2), the initial and routine tasks allocated to them".

47 See Article 5(5) of Decision "customs 2007", cited above fn. 36. Article 9(1), on the other hand, asks the participating countries to fulfil their tasks "in cooperation with the Commission". Paragraph 10 of the reasons given for the "statistical programme" Decision, cited above fn. 40, asks for a coordinated and coherent cooperation between Eurostat and the national authorities.

48 See, for example, paragraph 4 of the reasons given for the "customs 2007" Decision, cited above fn. 36, as well as in its Articles 3(2), 5(2), 8, 10(1) and 12. The term of an administrative partnership is also used in German administrative law. Here it does not, however, describe co-operation between different public authorities, but between the state and private individuals, for example in policing and environmental law or in the area of state aids; see *Pitschas* [2004] DÖV 231, at pp. 237 et seq.

49 Paragraph 18 of the reasons given for the "IDA" Decision, cited above fn. 37.

second type of co-operation on an institutional level, which becomes apparent in committees with representatives from Member States.[50]

3.2.3. Decisions as soft law lacking concrete and imperative orders

Normative decisions based on the Treaty are always addressed to all the Member States in their entirety. According to the concept laid down in Article 249(4) EC, they are consequently only binding on Member States. If one adopts the common perception of a binding legal act, the decisions in question should thus be viewed as either conferring rights upon Member States or imposing specific duties on them.[51] In contrast to individual state-addressed decisions, however, the normative acts under scrutiny do not comply with this traditional understanding of what constitutes a binding act, which has obviously been derived from administrative acts known in national laws.[52] Decisions are special in two aspects. Firstly, as already mentioned, on a substantive level they do not only address Member States, but also – and above all – the Commission as the EC institution mainly responsible for and capable of the realisation of the political programmes developed by Parliament and Council. It is the Commission that is instructed to take all steps necessary for reaching the goals put forward, either alone or in co-operation with the Member States. But even where the latter are also being awarded responsibility in accordance with the formal nature of the decision, neither the decision itself nor its reasons state any specific measures that the national authorities should take. In contrast to the very concrete and detailed instructions given in the so-called "state-addressed administrative acts"

---

50 In most cases, this will be a management committee according to Article 4 of the Comitology Decision 1999/468/EC, which has recently been amended by Decision No 2006/512/EC. See Article 6 of Decision No. 2256/2003/EC of the European Parliament and of the Council of 17 November 2003 adopting a multi-annual programme (2003–2005) for the monitoring of the Europe 2005 action plan, dissemination of good practices and the improvement of network and information security ("MODINIS"), OJ L 336 of 23 December 2003, p. 1; Article 4(2) and Article 7 of Decision "computerising", cited above fn. 46; Article 8 of Decision "IDA", cited above fn. 37; Article 8 of Decision "Intelligent Energy – Europe", cited above fn. 38; less frequently the committees will be regulatory committees; Article 10 of "guidelines trans-European networks" Decision, cited above fn. 46; Article 5 of "action plan internet" Decision, cited above fn. 35.

51 For this view see Bockey, cited above fn. 5, at p. 39; Hetmeier, in: Lenz/Borchardt (ed.), EUV/EGV, 3rd ed. 2003, Article 249 note 16. See also Kraußer, *Das Prinzip begrenzter Ermächtigung im Gemeinschaftsrecht als Strukturprinzip des EWG-Vertrages*, 1991, 87: "Verbindlichkeit bedeutet dabei die unmittelbare Begründung von Rechten und Pflichten der Adressaten aus dem Akt selbst heraus." ("An act being legally binding in this context means that the respective legal act on its own directly creates rights and duties of its addressees.").

52 This parallel is not explicitly mentioned, but can implicitly be drawn from the clear wording in *Bockey*, cited above fn. 5), pp. 31 and 39, where the definition of the Decision is derived from Article 4 No. 5 of the customs codex. This comparison is, however, more confusing than helpful, as the definition of Article 4 of the customs codex is exclusively related to measures of national authorities and can thus not be used to develop a concept of the Decision of Article 249(4) EC.

or inter-administrative decisions within multi-stage procedures, these legal acts do not say anything about the way in which or the means by which political goals should be realised. Instead, normative decisions based on primary legislation show a specifically purposive and target-oriented, open structure (*Finalstruktur)*. They lack clear and definite rules or orders, but merely provide a general target, which requires further administrative measures or even needs to be filled out by later legislation.[53] In this "targeting approach" (*Zielverbindlichkeit*[54]) these decisions show a high degree of similarity with the basic concept laid down for Directives in Article 249(3) EC. Other than Directives, however, decisions do not aim at a far-reaching harmonisation of national laws. They do not require Member States to achieve a specified objective or result,[55] i.e. a unified legal situation, within a certain time-limit.[56] Thus, despite the first impression given by the wording of Article 249 EC, it is not a characteristic trait of decisions to necessarily issue the most intense imperative orders.[57] On the contrary, when compared with Directives, normative decisions based on primary legislation show a specifically limited degree of legally binding effects (*abgeschwächter Verbindlichkeitsgrad*).

3.3. NORMATIVE GUIDANCE (*STEUERUNG*) BASED ON SECONDARY LEGISLATION

3.3.1. The decision as the Commission's instrument of implementation

Where normative decisions are not based on the Treaty itself, they function as a kind of implementary legislation within the meaning of Article 202(3) and Article 211(4) EC. In this context, the term "implementation" is used in a narrow

---

53 Surprisingly, it is the decision with its alleged concrete-individual character, which shows the unique target-oriented, open structure that is an overall characteristic of Community law. For an overview of this rather soft guidance of administrative action also see Schoch [2004] DVBl. 69, at pp. 72 et seq.

54 This term is taken from Schliesky [2003] DVBl. 631, at p. 637.

55 The German version of the Treaty uses the term "Ziel", meaning "tasks" or "goals" to be achieved. However, to avoid confusion with general tasks laid down in Article 3 EC, it is widely accepted that in Article 249(3) one should speak of a result to be achieved by a Directive; see Biervert, in: Schwarze, *EU-Kommentar*, Article 249 note 25; Grabitz, in: Grabitz/Hilf, cited above fn. 17, Article 189 note 57; Hilf [1993] EuR 1, at p. 4; for an earlier analysis see Ipsen, in: *FS für Ophüls*, 1965, 67, at p. 73.

56 For this two-stage regulatory approach of Directives see, for example, Grabitz, in: Grabitz/Hilf, cited above fn. 17, Article 189 notes 51 and 57.

57 This is expressly stated by Ruffert, in: Calliess/Ruffert (ed.), EUV/EGV, 2nd ed. 2002, Article 249 note 117: "Anders als Richtlinien sind staatengerichtete Entscheidungen nicht nur hinsichtlich des Ziels, sondern insgesamt verbindlich und ermöglichen so eine intensivere Verpflichtung der Mitgliedstaaten." ("Other than Directives, state-addressed decisions are binding in their entirety and thus impose a more stringent obligation on the Member States.").

sense, not in line with the wider terminology of the Treaty, or at least not in line with the interpretation given to it by the European Court of Justice.[58] The Treaty, when demarcating the rights and duties of the institutions, talks about the Council conferring on the Commission, in the acts which the Council adopts, powers for the implementation of the rules which the Council lays down.[59] The Commission, in contrast, is obliged to exercise the powers conferred on it by the Council for the implementation of the rules laid down by the latter.[60] Thus, the term "implementation" comprises all legal measures taken by the Commission not on the basis of the Treaty itself, but on the basis of secondary law enacted by the European legislator, i.e. Council and Parliament. It serves as a general term for the execution and concretization of Regulations and Directives both in the form of normative legal acts and of individual measures.[61] Here, however, following *Ch. Möllers,*[62] only normative concretization of secondary law as a kind of executive lawmaking by the Commission shall be called implementation. It represents an intermediate step within a gradual concretisation of European law, starting with the Treaty, followed by secondary legislation and implementation, finally to be executed in individual cases by administrative acts.[63]

In general, literature only takes into account Regulations and – less frequently – Directives as typical instruments for normative implementation.[64] The decision is usually not even mentioned in this context. An analysis of the daily practice of lawmaking, however, shows that the state-addressed variant of the decision is an

58 Case 16/88 *Commission v Council* [1989] E.C.R. 3457, at [11].

59 Article 202(3) EC.

60 Article 211(3) 4 EC.

61 Schroeder [2004] AöR 3, p. 9; *idem*, cited above fn. 43, p. 387; Adam, *Die Mitteilungen der Kommission: Verwaltungsvorschriften des Europäischen Gemeinschaftsrechts?*, 1999, p. 5. For a thorough analysis of this general term of implementation, comprising both the execution through individual acts and the implementation through normative acts, see Riedel [2006] EuR 512, at pp. 517 et seq.; see also Rengeling [1974] EuR 216, at pp. 217 et seq. and Kadelbach, cited above fn. 32, pp. 17 et seq.; all citing Zuleeg, *Das Recht der Europäischen Gemeinschaften im innerstaatlichen Bereich*, 1969, pp. 47 et seq. From English literature see Lenaerts/van Nuffel, *Constitutional Law of the European Union*, 1999, note 11–047. For a criticism of the actual use of such a broad definition of the term implementation see *v.* Bogdandy/Bast/Arndt [2002] ZaöRV 77, at p. 93.

62 Möllers [2002] EuR 483. With regard to the EC's limited powers he asks for a clear delineation of a predominantly normative implementation on the one hand, and an execution in individual cases on the other hand, which should be left to national authorities (pp. 496 et seq.).

63 For an analysis of this multi-step procedure see Möllers [2002] EuR 483, at pp. 496 and 514 et seq. This is essentially what the Draft Treaty for a European Constitution suggests in Articles I-33 et seq.; see also Maurer [2003] integration 440, at p. 442.

64 Möllers [2002] EuR 483, at p. 496: "Das Gemeinschaftsrecht kennt sowohl Durchführungsrichtlinien als auch Durchführungsverordnungen." ("Community law knows both implementing Directives and implementing Regulations.").

instrument perfectly suitable for more closely defining the Member States' duties resulting from Regulations or Directives.[65]

3.3.2. *Types of "implementing decisions"*

The decision as an administrative guideline

The abstract and general decisions equipped with normative effects are exclusively addressed to Member States. Here, they award responsibility primarily to national public authorities.[66] Above all, decisions based on Regulations, due to the general and direct applicability of the latter, in most cases have the aim of guiding national administrations in the application of the underlying Regulations.[67] But even decisions based on Directives frequently merely ask for administrative application rather than for normative implementation by national lawmakers.[68] The way in which these measures influence the legal frameworks of the Member States varies broadly: insofar as they are addressed to all Member States, as they usually are,[69] they may be described as a detailed harmonisation of the application of law in some cases. And yet in others, they may be more appropriately described as purely technical guidelines for administrative procedures. To give an example of the latter, i.e. for the regulation of technical details of legal implementation, a decision might oblige national authorities to use a specific official form.[70] Such decisions are intended to simplify uniform administrative procedures throughout the Community. Their impact is directed at the internal organisation of authorities

65 It shall not be left unmentioned that in some cases Decisions might also be used to change a Regulation. This usually occurs where provisions of a Regulation have to be quickly brought in line with new technical, scientific or merely factual developments; see e.g. Decision No. 2004/232/EG of the Commission of 3 March 2004 amending Regulation (EC) No. 2037/2000 of the European Parliament and of the Council with regard to the use of halon 2402, OJ L 71 of 10 March 2004, p. 28.

66 The Member State remains addressee, and EC institutions are not allowed to adress their decisions directly to the Member States' agencies, organs and officials.

67 See, for example, Commission Decision No. 2001/681/EC of 7 September 2001 on guidance for the implementation of Regulation (EC) No. 761/2001 of the European Parliament and of the Council allowing voluntary participation by organisations in a Community eco-management and audit scheme (EMAS), OJ L 247 of 17 September 2001, p. 24.

68 See, for example, Council Decision No 88/408/EEC of 15 June 1988 on the levels of the fees to be charged for health inspections and controls of fresh meat pursuant to Directive 85/73/EEC, OJ L 194 of 22 July 1988, p. 24; repealed by Council Directive No 93/118/EEC of 22 December 1993 amending Directive 85/73/EEC on the financing of health inspections and controls of fresh meat and poultry meat, OJ L 340 of 31 December 1993, p. 15.

69 The few exceptions of normative Decisions addressed to individual states can be found, for example, where the Commission allows a Member State to depart form requirements laid down in a Directive.

70 See, for example, Commission Decision No 2003/803/EC of 26 November 2003 establishing a model passport for the intra-Community movements of dogs, cats and ferrets, OJ L 312 of 27 November 2003, p. 1.

that are responsible according to national laws. In this, they show some similarity to internal administrative guidelines (*Dienstvorschriften*) known in German public law.[71] As mentioned above, implementing decisions can also be used to give detailed guidance to national authorities in the application and interpretation of substantive provisions of Community law.[72] This variant of concretisation has usually already been foreseen in the secondary legislative act. Its objective is not only to harmonise technical details of application, but to fill out broad and general clauses of Regulations and Directives in an abstract and general way. Thus, when comparing them to national phenomena, one might speak of concretising administrative guidelines, or *normkonkretisierenden Verwaltungsvorschriften* as they are called in German administrative law.[73]

Despite these functional similarities, however, the term of administrative guidelines or *Verwaltungsvorschriften* should be used with care. The characteristics and dogmatic difficulties attached to it in German public law are rooted in the classical differentiation between internal and external administrative law. It focuses, above all, around the question of external effects of administrative guidelines, i.e. whether they are binding on subjects outside the administrative hierarchy.[74] Insofar, normative decisions are fundamentally different from administrative guidelines in two ways. Firstly, EC institutions and Member States, although they can be described as forming a composite administration, must not be regarded as hierarchically subordinated bodies within a single state-like entity. Secondly, as the decisions under consideration are addressed to the Member States as such, they are not only binding on public administrative authorities, but have to be applied by national courts as well.[75] Even if one decides to follow a more recent tendency in German law that wants to free administrative guidelines from their purely internal effects to establish them as another form of executive lawmaking,[76] one important difference still

71 In this context, the differences and dogmatic variances to be outlined in the following are equally applicable. For an outline of the essential characteristics of so-called "Organisations- und Dienstvorschriften" (organisational and internal guidelines) see Maurer, *Allgemeines Verwaltungsrecht*, 13th ed. 2000, par. 24 note 8.

72 This is, among others, true fort he guideline Decision based on the EMAS Regulation, cited above fn. 67, which points out to national authorities what parts of an undertaking are to be registered as participating organisation, how the procedure of evaluation has to be carried out in detail, in which intervals environmental information has to be updated, and how the EMAS certificate may be used by participating organisations.

73 For a similar perception of state-addressed Decisions as binding interpretation guidelines see Rengeling [1974] EuR 216, at p. 234.

74 See Rogmann, *Die Bindungswirkung von Verwaltungsvorschriften*, 1998.

75 According to the traditional view in German public law, administrative guidelines do not have such binding force *vis-à-vis* the courts; see Maurer, cited above fn. 71, par. 24 note 17.

76 In that view, administrative guidelines are to be treated as a third type of executive law in addition to Satzungen, i.e. laws issued by self-governing bodies, and *Rechtsverordnungen*, a kind of general legislation issued by the top of the executive branch on a ministerial level. See v. Bogdandy, *Gubernative Rechtsetzung*, 2000, pp. 449 et seq. Similarly *Wahl*, in: *FG 50 Jahre Bundesverwaltungsgericht*, 2003, pp. 571 et seq. and Schmidt-Aßmann, *Das Allgemeine*

remains: administrative guidelines are characterised by an inherent limitation of legally binding effects. It allows their addressees to question the appropriateness of the provisions contained in them on a case-by-case basic. Therefore, if necessary, an authority might have good reasons not to apply a guideline under certain circumstances.[77] Such a flexible approach in the application of decisions, however, is not compatible with the strict bindingness provided for in Article 249(4) EC.

Decisions as instructions to national legislation

Beyond their function as a kind of administrative guideline, however, state-addressed decisions can also be directed at national legislators and require a specific action from them. This is usually the case where decisions concretise or alter[78] the provisions of Directives, as these are conceptually designed to initiate a two-stage legislative procedure. Similarly, Regulations might sometimes have a general and broad wording so that, just like Directives, in some parts they depend on further normative implementation through national legislators. This is often the case where the substantive provisions of a Regulation and their application within the Member States require an elaborate organisational and institutional framework to be established on the national level.[79] In these circumstances, a decision based on such a Regulation can be used to describe the national legislative measures to be taken in some more detail.

3.3.3. The decisions' impact and their direct applicability

This article cannot possibly discuss the multitude of legal implications emanating from the decision's nature as a normative act.[80] One of the most pressing questions, however, shall be considered in some more detail: the problem of

---

Verwaltungsrecht als Ordnungsidee, 2nd ed. 2005, chapter 6 par. 88, who see administrative guidelines as a third category of lawmaking by the state.

77 For an outline of this specific regulatory mode of administrative guidelines see v. Bogdandy, cited above fn. 76, at pp. 467 et seq.; Schmidt-Aßmann, cited above fn. 76, chapter 6 par. 90.

78 Above all, the Commission is authorised to modify or supplement Directives, where these Directives harmonise security, hygiene or health standards and where they are considered to represent the most recent scientific standards. In these circumstances, it might be affordable to bring the relevant provisions in line with modern developments in natural sciences or to deal with emergencies; see Knipschild, *Lebensmittelsicherheit als Aufgabe des Veterinär- und Lebensmittelrechts*, 2003, at pp. 197 et seq.

79 The most prominent example is the EMAS-Regulation, cited above fn. 67. For an analysis of such "hermaphrodite" legal acts between Regulation and Directive see Kahl [1996] DV 341, at pp. 347 et seq. with further examples in fn. 37; Stober, in: J. Ipsen (ed.), *Verfassungsrecht im Wandel*, 1995, 639, at pp. 644 et seq.; Emmerich, in: *FS für Ritter*, 1997, 839, at p. 842.

80 It can, for example, be shown that the traditional interpretation of Article 241 EC, according to which Decisions cannot be regarded as "Regulations" within the meaning of that provision, is not consistent with the Decision's true nature; Vogt [2006] 31 E.L.Rev. 364, at pp. 372 et seq. Other issues that have to be considered are publication and procedural requirements, judicial

direct applicability.[81] In dealing with that issue, one should take an incremental approach. Firstly, because it is formally addressed to the Member States, a decision can clearly be legally binding only on the states themselves according to the concept laid down in Article 249(4) EC. Thus, a legal obligation can only be established in the bilateral relationship between the Community and the Member States.[82] This fact, however, does not oppose the notion of a direct applicability of state-addressed decisions with encumbering effects for private individuals. It has been mentioned above that a decision addressed to a Member State does not necessarily rely on a national implementing measure, unless it specifically requires such implementation. At this point, one has to take into consideration the case-law of the European Court of Justice, where it held that the decision's unlimited obligatory powers have to be respected and adhered to by all national authorities.[83] Therefore, administrative bodies can and must enforce the decisions' substantive and procedural provisions *vis-à-vis* their citizens. In the case of a state aid that was found to be in violation of Community law, it is an individual Commission decision that forces the relevant national authorities to retrieve the moneys already distributed. In that case, the authorities might have to rely on a provision within their national legal framework that allows them to do so in the form of an administrative act. However, if no such provision exists in national law, this does not change the state's obligation to reclaim the aid.[84]

---

protection or legal certainty; for a discussion of these entire issues see Vogt, cited supra fn. 28.

81 For a discussion of this issue see Greaves, [1996] E.L.Rev. 3, at pp. 12 and 16; Scherzberg, in: Siedentopf (ed.), *Europäische Integration und nationalstaatliche Verwaltung*, 1991, 17, at p. 37. J. Bast, in: v. Bogdandy, cited above fn. 1, 479, at p. 532 considers a state-addressed decision to be a sufficient basis for state action detrimental to the individual. However, the case-law this view appears to be based upon is not very helpful in this context. The cited decision in Case C-192/94 *El Corte Inglés v Cristina Blázquez Rivero* [1996] E.C.R. I-1281, at [17] states that the Community has the power to enact obligations on individuals with immediate effect only where it is empowered to adopt regulations or decisions. However, this passage when talking about decisions only talks about such acts that are formally addressed to private individuals. In any case, the Court does not explicitly mention a possible, direct negative effect of state-addressed decisions.

82 This is correctly noted by Greaves [1996] E.L.Rev. 3, at p. 12. Therefore, one should not talk about a "direct negative effect" of Decisions, if the term "direct effect" is meant to express the enactment of obligations on individuals with immediate effect.

83 Case 249/85 *Albako* [1987] E.C.R. 2345, at [17].

84 See the judgment of the Berlin-Brandenburg Supreme Administrative Court, *OVG BerlinBrandeburg* [2006] NVwZ 104, where it was held that authorities might retrieve an aid via an administrative act, even if there is no express legal basis for such state action. The decision has been rightly criticised by commentators for contravening general principles of the rule of law; see Uwer/Wodarz [2006] DÖV 989, at pp. 995 et seq.; *Arhold* [2006] EuZW 94, pp. 95 et seq. The case clearly shows the difficulties connected with the decision's obligatory powers: An individual Commission decision can hardly be recognised as a legal basis within the meaning of the German concept of *Gesetzesvorbehalt*, which is part of the rule of law. However, it has to be appropriately and effectively applied and executed irrespective of the problems stemming from national constitutional law.

Similarly, a normative decision can instruct administrative bodies throughout the Community on how to act under certain circumstances, which are described in the decision in an abstract and general manner. The inner-state differentiation between legislation on the one hand and executive powers on the other is of utmost importance in the understanding of Directives and Regulations, and the distinctive concepts of lawmaking they represent. When it comes to the decision, this distinction loses much of its structuring powers.[85]

This finding of a far-reaching direct applicability does not, however, answer the question whether normative decisions, in the context of the rule of law,[86] can be a sufficient legal basis for an intervention by the public authorities in the sphere of private activities.[87] The same problem can arise with regard to Directives, where, however, the issue is less acute due to the indirect nature of the lawmaking process characteristically attached to them.[88] The decision as a specific instrument of lawmaking, with the features ascribed to it by Article 249(4) EC, does not itself give an answer to the question. Its simple objective is to issue instructions that are strictly binding on any national authority responsible for carrying out these instructions according to the respective national laws. It leaves it to the Member States to make arrangements for the legal framework that might be necessary for the implementation of the decision's substantive provisions pursuant to their constitutional or administrative legal requirements. In any case, the decision's strictly binding nature cannot be questioned by arguing that national constitutional laws do not allow state interference with the private sphere on the basis of a provision which is only binding on the state itself, but not on individuals.[89] Instead of interpreting the legal acts known in Community law in a way that is not reconcilable with their true nature and the way in which they function in order to bring them in line with national

85 Thus, it cannot be agreed with Thierfelder, cited above fn. 24, at p. 142 et seq., who wants to limit the Decision's function to a pure instruction for lawmaking action.

86 It is recognised in Community law that "any intervention by the public authorities in the sphere of private activities of any person, whether natural or legal, must have a legal basis and be justified on the grounds laid down by law"; Cases 46/87 and 227/88 *Höchst v Commission* [1989] E.C.R. 2859, at [19]. However, its content is still not very clear due to the specialties of Community law both regarding the definition of "law" and the institutional framework; see Hilf/Classen, in: FS für Selmer, 2004, at p. 71.

87 This seems to be supported by J. Bast, in: v. Bogdandy, cited above fn. 1, 479, at p. 532. More explicitly Weber, *Rechtsfragen der Durchführung des Gemeinschaftsrechts in der Bundesrepublik*, 1988, at pp. 19 et seq. See also Sachs, in: Stelkens/Bonk/Sachs, cited above fn. 21, par. 44 note 91, who considers every valid Community legal act as a sufficient basis with regard to the rule of law, excluding only Directives.

88 For an analysis of the difficulties arising from directly applicable Directives in the context of the rule of law, see Schmidt-Aßmann, in: FS für Stern, 1997, 745, at pp. 754 et seq.

89 This is, however, argued by Royla/Lackhoff [1998] DVBl. 1116, at p. 1119, who strive to limit the direct negative effect of Directives, arguing that a Directive cannot be sufficient as a legal basis for an intervention by the public authorities in the sphere of private activities of any person. This argument seems to be ill-founded, as can be seen in the recent Case C-201/02 *Delena Wells* [2004] E.C.R I-723, at [56] et seq.

constitutional laws, it appears now that legal scholars will have to rethink the national dogma of the rule of law, taking into account the findings drawn from a scholarly analysis of Community legal instruments.[90] In effect, where national laws require a generally binding legislative act to give effect to the decision's provisions, Member States will have to create such a legal basis or to make use of an existing one. For example, under German constitutional law as it stands to date, it may be doubted whether the decision alone, with its limited personally binding effects, will be a sufficient basis for an interference with individual rights of private entities. As state-addressed decisions themselves cannot create any obligations for individuals whatsoever, the first legal act creating such obligations would be the national administrative act which applies them.[91] Put in other words, the decision may order German authorities to act in a specific way, but it cannot authorise them to do so *vis-à-vis* its citizens. In such a case it appears that German law will either have to accept normative decisions as a form of *Gesetz* (law) within the concept of *Gesetzesvorbehalt* (i.e. the prerequisite of a legal basis for an intervention by the state in the private sphere), or this concept will have to be superseded according to the supremacy of EC law. Thus, to avoid any doubts and reduce potential conflicts with national constitutional laws, EC institutions should be careful when issuing state-addressed decisions and should rather make use of the Regulation as their legal instrument of choice when they want to impose obligations on Member States that might be detrimental to the states' citizens.[92]

On the other hand, the decision's direct applicability cannot be restricted in line with the rules that have been developed for Directives. In the case of the latter, the rule of limited direct effects on the private sphere must be seen in the context of the Directive's legislative nature. Its aim is to initiate a two-step legislative procedure and to be transposed into national laws. Consequently, Member States should not be able to profit from a failure to act accordingly as this would mean that they are being rewarded for a breach of Community law.[93] Thus, the limited scope of a Directive's direct applicability is a logical

---

90 For an example in this respect with regard to the Directive see Triantafyllou, *Vom Vertrags- zum Gesetzesvorbehalt*, 1996, at pp. 86 et seq.

91 At this point, the usual perception must be called into question, according to which any written legal act of Community law that is directly applicable (i.e. that need not be transposed into national law) may be regarded as a law within the meaning of the rule of law; see Sachs, in: Sachs (ed.), GG, 3rd ed. 2003, Article 20 note 107; *Jarass*, in: Jarass/Pieroth, GG, 7th ed. 2004, Article 20 note 38. It should rather be said that the legal act in question itself must be able to directly create obligations for private individuals, which a state-addressed Decision cannot do.

92 That duty of EC institutions not to make use of state-addressed Decisions excessively could be derived from the general obligation to cooperate included in Article 10 EC.

93 Case 148/78 *Ratti* [1979] E.C.R. 1629. at [20] et seq.; Case 152/84 *Marshall* [1986] E.C.R. 723, at [46] et seq.; for a summary see *Götz*, [1992] NJW 1849, at pp. 1855 et seq. The English term of 'community estoppel' clearly gives expression to this underlying rationale; see Schermers/ Waelbroeck, *Judicial Protection in the EU*, 6th ed. 2001, pars 366 et seq. For a critical view on

consequence of its proportionately limited binding effects that, of necessity, only require a normative transformation.[94] In the case of many decisions, however, such a neglect of implementing duties by the Member States is not relevant in the outset, as they merely ask for application, not for implementation.[95] It is true that the rules on positive (i.e., in favour of private individuals) direct effects of state-addressed decisions, as they were developed in the so-called *Leberpfennig* judicature,[96] were later to become a basis for the long line of case-law on Directives' direct applicability. However, with a view to the state-addressed decision itself and the legal regime applicable to it, these judgments can only be regarded as a starting point, not as an ultimate conclusion of scholarly analysis.

4. CONCLUSION: THE DECISION AS THE MOST FLEXIBLE EUROPEAN LEGAL ACT

In multiform interaction with Directives and Regulations the decision, as demonstrated, plays an important role within a complex legal framework which has been described as a legislative-administrative composite network (*legislativ-administrativer Verbund*) in this article. Within this context, it is often difficult to find a clearly recognisable dividing line between the decision of Article 249(4) EC and the two other normative legal instruments known in Community law.

Vis-à-vis the generally applicable Regulation,[97] it appears that the decision, always being directed at a specified number of addressees, is of limited legal

the usefulness of the comparison with the principal of estoppel see Kadelbach, cited above fn. 32, at pp. 75 et seq.

94 For this connection between the subjective direct applicability of a legal act and the existence of a corresponding obligation see also J. Bast, in: v. Bogdandy, cited above fn. 1, 479, at p. 530. Therefore, unlike a Decision, for a Directive to become directly applicable to the detriment of private parties, a triangular constellation is needed, where one private individual invokes provisions of that Directive that are beneficial to him, but that at the same time have adverse repercussions on the rights of third parties; see Case C-201/02 *Delena Wells* [2004] E.C.R I-723, at [56] et seq. This judgment can be seen as carrying forward the rules already developed in Case C-431/92 *Commission v Germany* [1995] E.C.R. I-2189 combining them with the principles laid down in Case C-443/98 *Unilever Italia* [2000] E.C.R. I-7535, at [45] et seq.

95 For a similar analysis see Mager [2001] EuR 661, at pp. 679 et seq. For a different view see Erichsen/Frenz [1995] Jura 422, p. 423, who recognise a direct applicability of Decisions only in line with the principles developed for Directives.

96 Case 9/70 Franz Grad [1970] E.C.R. 825, at [5] et seq. For a detailed analysis see Grabitz [1971] EuR 1 et seq.

97 Its general applicability converges the Regulation with the classical Act of Parliament known in national laws; see *Biervert*, in: Schwarze (ed.), EU-Kommentar, Article 249, note 18; see also *Grabitz*, in: Grabitz/Hilf, cited above fn. 17, Article 189, note 43 (substantially equal to an Act of Parliament); affirmative with regard to the normative quality also *Ruffert*, in: Calliess/Ruffert, cited above fn. 57, Article 249, note 38. But even with regard to the Regulation, one must be careful not to ignore the peculiarities of European legal instruments; see *Schroeder*, in: Streinz, cited above fn. 2, Article 249, note 1 and *Grams*, Zur Gesetzgebung der Europäischen Union, 1998, at p. 73.

effect in two respects. Where it is addressed at private individuals, its binding force is limited in a personal way. Where it is addressed to a Member State, the decision's impacts are additionally limited in territorial terms.[98] However, the decision is largely converging with the classical legislative instrument of the Regulation where it is addressed not only to a single, but to all Member States, and thus loses its territorially restricted effects. As far as it is addressed to the Member States as such, as is the case with a majority of abstract and general decisions, it becomes applicable within the entire Community territory. Even in this case, the decision keeps its inherent limitation regarding its personal scope. However, the impact of this limitation is minimised by the fact that state-addressed decisions are binding on all public bodies including the national courts. Just like Regulations and unlike Directives, decisions do not rely on national transformation to become fully effective, unless they expressly ask for it.[99]

The equalising effect of Community legal instruments appears to go even further if one considers decisions in comparison with Directives. In any case, the distinction made in Article 249(3) EC, according to which Directives are only binding "as to the result to be achieved" while decisions are "binding in their entirety", is not appropriate for delineating a specific normative character of Directives.[100] On the other hand, the alleged restriction of the decision to concrete and individual cases[101] is of equally little usefulness. In this context, it may be true that the subject matter covered by most decisions is more limited and concrete than the substance of the Regulations and Directives they are based on. This is, however, merely a relative distinction. It is intrinsically connected to these decisions' specific purpose as implementing measures, defining the scope of their underlying legal acts more precisely. It is not a distinction attributed to

---

98 For an analysis of this potential limitation in a territorial and a personal respect see already *J. Bast*, in: v. Bogdandy, cited above fn. 1, 479, at p. 530.

99 *Biervert*, in: Schwarze (ed.), EU-Kommentar, Article 249, note 35. A different view was still taken by *Thierfelder*, cited above fn. 24, at pp. 142 et seq. However, one should not mistake this functional convergence as meaning that Decisions and Regulations also have the same legal effects. They merely confirm what has been assumed by other authors before, i.e. that the Decision is to be regarded as a legal act directly applicable by national administrative authorities and courts; see *Ress*, in: Gedächtnisschrift Arens, 1993, 351, at p. 353. It is important to note that the fundamental difference which remains is the fact that only the Regulation has the power to simultaneously bind both the state and private citizens in one legal act.

100 That becomes apparent when one realises the difficulties of differentiating between the "result", "form" and "method" of a Directive; see *Bleckmann*, Europarecht, 6th ed. 1997, at paragraphs 422 et seq. Moreover, it can be noted that Directives increasingly tend to be very detailed legal acts, leaving Member States hardly any or no implementing discretion; see *Scherzberg*, in: Siedentopf, cited above fn. 81, 17, at pp. 27 et seq.; *Grams*, cited above fn. 97, at p. 88.

101 See, above all, *Mager* [2001] EuR 661, at pp. 672 et seq. According to this concept, the Directive is a means of normative legal harmonisation, whereas the state-addressed Decision is merely a means of concrete harmonisation in individual cases.

the nature of the decision as such. The decision is not structurally limited to act as a concrete instructive measure harmonising administrative action on the narrowest factual level,[102] but it can also be used to harmonise the abstract legal foundations of such an administrative action.

The most prominent specific characteristic feature of the decision in comparison to the Directive appears to be its legal flexibility as to the possible interaction with national law: The decision can, on the one hand, issue an order to national legislative authorities, just like the Directive. On the other hand, it is binding on all parts of a Member State and thus may ask for mere application (as distinguished from implementation), be it in the form of national administrative rules, administrative acts or simple action. When it comes to the decision, the strict differentiation between legislative action and administrative execution becomes less important, as it may be addressed to any national authority, which will have to adhere to the decision's substance with the instruments available to it.[103]

These findings have far-reaching impacts on the assessment of the legal framework accorded to the decision.

Article 254 EC requires Regulations and Directives addressed to all Member States to be published in the Official Journal, whereas decisions must only be notified to their addressees, unless they were adopted in accordance with the procedure referred to in Article 251. It must be questioned whether this differentiation is an appropriate one to address the impacts of state-addressed decisions[104] outlined above.

As a conclusion, it can be summarised that the decision is by no means limited to act as a purely administrative instrument dealing with individual cases.[105] On the contrary, it can be stated that a legal analysis of the decision and the variety of functions it fulfils becomes most complex when it takes into account the realm of normative lawmaking. Here, the decision can come very close to the Directive as an instrument relying on implementation through national legislators.[106] Where it does not require transposition into national laws, but gives instructions directly to the administrative or judicial bodies responsible according to the national legal framework, it can, however, be very similar to the Regulation as well. The scholarly analysis of the concept of decisions as an

---

102 This limited effect to merely harmonise the factual administrative action is what *Mager* [2001] EuR 661, at p. 673 regards to be the specific trait of the Decision in contrast to the Directive.

103 This ultimately results in fundamental differences of the direct applicability of state-addressed Decisions on the one hand and Directives on the other; see above at fn. 93 et seq.

104 For a detailed analysis of this specific issue see Vogt, cited above fn. 28, at pp. 215 et seq.

105 Thus, the remark of *OVG Berlin-Brandenburg* [1999] NuR 283, at p. 285, according to which it must be questioned whether a Decision is *prima facie* able to have an abstract and general substance, is more than misleading.

106 Sparwasser/Engel/Voßkuhle, *Umweltrecht*, 5th ed. 2003, paragraph 1, note 128 consider this two-stage legislative variant to be the only possibility where Decisions can act in a "quasi-legislative" way.

instrument of Community lawmaking should no longer ignore these findings. The legal and dogmatic issues connected to them are complex and must be considered carefully.

XV. INSPECTIONS AS AN INSTRUMENT OF CONTROL OF IMPLEMENTATION IN THE EUROPEAN COMPOSITE ADMINISTRATION*

Antje David

1. INTRODUCTION

The efficiency and credibility of the Community and of the Member States not only depends on the quality of the creation of laws, but also on the efficiency of its law enforcement.[1]

---

* The article is based on the dissertation of the authoress carrying the title "Inspections in the European administrative law", Duncker & Humblot, Berlin 2003. An earlier version was published (in German) as Antje David, Inspektionen als Instrument der Vollzugskontrolle im Europäischen Verwaltungsverbund, in: Eberhard Schmidt-Aßmann and Bettina Schöndorf-Haubold (eds.), Der Europäische Verwaltungsverbund, Mohr Siebeck, Tübingen 2005, p. 237–264.

1 Majone, *Mutual Trust, Credible Commitments and the Evolution of Rules for a Single European Market*, EUI Working Paper RSC No. 95/1, p. 24; similarly Pühs, *Der Vollzug von Gemeinschaftsrecht – Formen und Grenzen eines effektiven Gemeinschaftsrechtsvollzug und Überlegungen zu seiner Effektuierung*, 1997, 46: "Dieser Zielsetzung liegt die Einsicht zugrunde, dass die Gemeinschaft langfristig nur bestehen kann, wenn es ihr gelingt, glaubhaft zu machen, dass sie die ihr übertragenen Kompetenzen und Aufgaben tatsächlich wirksam ausübt bzw. erfüllen kann" (= This ambition underlies the perception that the Community can only be of long duration, if it manages to make it credible that it can actually exercise and fulfil its vested competences and tasks). V. Bogandy, in: Hoffmann-Riem/Schmidt-Aßmann (eds.), *Verwaltungsrecht in der Informationsgesellschaft*, 2000, 133, 139 mentions the "legitimation by effort". The requirement of efficiency is also underlined by Scharpf, *Regieren in Europa*, 1999, 30; about the execution problems in EC law, also Swart, in: Harding/Swart, *Enforcing European Community Rules*, 1996, 1 ff. Generally about the implementation deficit in EC law Jans/de Lange/Prechal/Widdershoven, *Inleiding tot het Europees bestuursrecht*, 1999, 223 f. In detail about the meaning of law enforcement for the European integration Magiera, DÖV 1998, 173 ff.; cf. also Majone, 8 ff.: "The implementation deficit has become so serious over the years that the Member States now realise that non-compliance threatens the credibility of their collective decisions." Also Schmidt-Aßmann, in: id./Hoffmann-Riem (eds.), *Strukturen des Europäsichen Verwaltungsrechts*, 1999, 9, 12 emphasises the care for an efficient and regular application of the EC provisions as an important task of the administration of the Union area.

Inspections can be defined as a process of the investigation of the facts by on-site screening of authorities. They represent a manifestation of the functional collaboration of the European administrations and are aimed at effectuating the execution of European administrative law. In German public law, they are known as official controlling instruments, and include rights to enter premises and the authorisation of on-site inspections. As measures for the acquisition of official information, they represent a part of the larger instrument for surveillance available to the administrative authorities in order to monitor that the compliance of provisions is subject to public law.[2] In EC law, inspections are used in order to supervise economic operators or Member State administrations on the spot. On the European level, inspections fulfil a dual function: micro-administratively, they are an expression of direct controls with regard to EU citizens. And on a mid-level they also provide an overview and create trust concerning the administrations of independent Member States.

The Member States have to cooperate with the Commission and the other Member States in different ways during the implementation of the inspections. The inspections usually involve various additional duties regarding the exchange of information. The results of the inspections can become part of the decisions of other administrative units and appear in different forms of institutional consolidations. Compared to German law, EC law inspections have become a much more complex institute due to the expansion of functions and the amendment of elements of horizontal and vertical cooperation. The core elements of administrative cooperation – informational, procedural and institutional cooperation[3] – can be found clustered in the legal institute of the inspection

2. FUNCTIONAL CLASSIFICATION

Provisions concerning inspections can be found in nearly all the areas of European administrative law. For example, one needs only to look at agricultural law, economic law (e.g. competition law and bank supervision), food law, environmental law as well as the law concerning the fight against fraud.[4]

2 As examples only cf. §22 (1) Nr. 3 BtMG, §64 (4) Nr. 1 AMG, §45 BBiG, §22b (1) Nr. 1 FIHG, §14 (3) Nr. 3 KrWG, §13 1st sentence GSG, §44 (1) 2nd sentence KWG, §25 2nd sentence BSeuchG, §93 (1) BNotO, §44 (1) 4th sentence AWG, §45 (1) Nr. 2 PostG, §19 (2) 1st sentence AtomG, §41 (1) 2nd sentence LMG.

3 Cf. in more detail Schmidt-Aßmann, *Das allgemeine Verwaltungsrecht als Ordnungsidee*, 2nd edition 2004, 384, 7/11; *id.*, EuR 1996, 270 ff. 274.

4 A detailed presentation on the basis of the reference areas mentioned by David, *Inspektionen im Europäischen Verwaltungsrecht*, 2003, 30 ff.

Inspections represent an instrument of the investigation of the facts and circumstances between government supervision and economic supervision.[5]

- Within the scope of the *direct controls*, Member State or Commission departments fulfil their supervisory function directly with regard to citizens of the Union. The purpose of the inspection is the examination of the economic operators regarding behaviour accepted by the Community. This can be considered to be an "economic supervision".
- The second approach focuses on administrative enforcement by the Member State. Commission inspections on the spot should ascertain that the Member States satisfy the administrative tasks assigned by EC law (*Execution control* in the form of enforcement control). If the task of the national administration is based on the compliance with provisions by the economic participants, it is a so-called *control of control*. With due care, this can be called "governmental supervision" or "Composite administrative supervision" (*Verbundaufsicht*).

Often, both characteristics exist side by side in the relevant legal acts.[6] The regulation mechanism of such a combined and tiered control regime can be illustrated by the example of the European Law of agricultural financing. Article 8 of the Council Regulation 1258/1999 (EAGGF) represents the central provision for the enforcement duties of the Member States within the scope of the measures financed by the European Agricultural Guidance and Guarantee Fund

5 About the terms and the dichotomy of government supervision and economic supervision Kahl, *Die Staatsaufsicht*, 2000, 362 ff.: Wirtschaftsaufsicht als "die staatliche Aufsicht über alle Wirtschaftssubjekte, also Hersteller, Anbieter oder Verteiler von Gütern oder Dienstleistungen, welche die selbstverantwortliche Teilnahme am Wirtschaftsverkehr mit den dafür geltenden Rechtsregeln in Einklang halten soll" (362) ('Economic supervision as the governmental supervision over all participants in the economy, i.e. producers, suppliers or distributors of goods or services who should maintain their responsible participation in commercial intercourse in accordance with the applicable legal rules'). Staatsaufsicht iwS. als "Sammelbegriff für alle Aufsichtsvorgänge innerhalb des Staates im weiten Sinne. Als solcher vereint er die Bereiche der völker- und gemeinschaftsrechtlichen Aufsicht, der Bundesaufsicht, der Behördenaufsicht, der Dienstaufsicht sowie der Verwaltungsaufsicht unter einem Dach" (364) (Governmental supervision in the broader sense, as 'collective term for all supervision processes within the state in the broader sense. As such it combines the area of international and community legal supervision, federal supervision, official supervision, regular supervision and the administrative supervision, altogether'). cf. also Schmidt-Aßmann, in: id./Hoffmann-Riem (eds.), *Verwaltungskontrolle*, 2001, pp. 9, 13 and 33 (Inspections as a link of economical supervision and administrative controls); about the issue economical supervision see also Ehlers, *Ziele der Wirtschaftsaufsicht*, 1997; Bullinger, VVDStRL 22 (1965), 264 ff. (respectively in the German context), as well as Brenner, *Der Gesamtauftrag der Verwaltung in der Europäischen Union*, 1996, 281 ff. and Lühmann, DVBl. 1999, 752 ff. (in the Union).

6 Called First line and Second line Control by Vervaele, in: id. (ed.), Compliance and Enforcement of Community Law, 1999, 361, 364.

(EAGGF).[7] According to this article, the Member States "shall, in accordance with national provisions laid down by law, regulation or administrative action, take the measures necessary to satisfy themselves that transactions financed by the Fund are actually carried out and executed correctly, prevent and deal with irregularities, recover sums lost as a result of irregularities or negligence".

According to Article 8(3) of the Council Regulation 1258/1999 (EAGGF), the Council, acting by a qualified majority on a proposal from the Commission, shall lay down general rules for the application of this Article. On this basis, the broad provision of Article 8(1) is supplemented by manifold detailed community stipulations concerning the way in which the guarantee concerning the independent implementation of the measures being financed by the funds has to take place. Various Community rules include provisions about the inspection of accounts, minimum rates, criteria for the sampling, analysis methods and general, controlling criteria justified by the risk of fraud.[8] The controls which have to be made by the Member State authorities include independent administrative controls, such as the inspection of applications for the accuracy of the calculations and probability (*Plausibilität*), substantial controls and inspections in the enterprises.[9]

Independent controlling competences for commission officials are established by Article 9 of the Council Regulation 1258/1999. The Member States provide the Commission with all the information necessary for the functioning of the Fund and take all measures appropriate to facilitate possible controls – *including on-site inspections* – the implementation of which appears to be functional within the scope of the community financing. The authorised representatives appointed by the Commission to carry out inspections on the spot have access to the books and all other documents and "check whether administrative practices are in accordance with Community rules, whether the requisite supporting documents exist and tally with the transaction financed by the Fund, the conditions under which transactions financed by the Fund are carried out and checked".

This provision represents the basis for the Commission's inspections. The Commission then implements the inspections on its own initiative with the national authorities, which have to grant access to all the relevant documents to the Community inspectors. But this provision also allows inspections at the favoured economic operators, especially inspections of the accounts and

---

7 Council Regulation (EC) No 1258/1999 of 17 May 1999 on the financing of the common agricultural policy, Official Journal L 160, p. 103. Except for some smaller editorial amendments, Article 8 and 9 of the new Regulation accord literally with Article 8 and 9 of the previous Regulation No 729/70 (EAGGF), so that concerning the controlling provisions, no amendments have arisen.

8 *Cf.* the examples by Mögele, *Die Behandlung fehlerhafter Ausgaben im Finazierungssystem der gemeinsamen Agrarpolitik*, 1997, 108 f.; *id.*, in: Dauses (ed.), *Handbuch des EU-Wirtschaftsrechts (HbEUWiR)*, Lsbl. Stand Mai 2004, G, marginal number (= mn.) 144.

9 Cf. Mögele, in: Dauses, HbEUWiR (fn. 8), G, mn. 172 ff., 191.

operations flows.[10] However, the controls of the market participants have only a supplementary character,[11] since the main controlling object is the administrative enforcement by the national administrative authorities and not the behaviour of the economic operators. The Commission uses its controlling powers for the implementation of system inspections in particular, by referring to the effectiveness of the controlling provisions and systems of the Member States. Special investigations are implemented specifically in the case of considerable lack of execution.[12]

Therefore, the Community law allocates the responsibility for the enforcement of preferably effective controls by the national execution institutions to the Member States on the first level. In addition, the Commission is still authorised to use independent implementation of controls. Only the combined action of the provisions involved ensure the effective execution of Community Law. The dualism of European administrative law with its two reference objects – the Member State and the Union citizen – is therefore also reflected in the different forms of control. In both functional cohesions, the inspections are incorporated in a complex system of administrative cooperation. Cooperation elements can be found in manifold forms with the direct controls as well as within the scope of the model of the control of control.[13]

The functional cohesions observed can be seen in the different *forms of participation* in particular. The Commission's officials can *participate* in many ways within the scope of execution controls, which the Member States' officials enforce on the spot at the economic operators. This is then a matter of *accompanying control*, such as in agricultural law[14], fisheries law[15] and food law, in particular.[16] In all of the cases, the authority of the Commission's officials is derived from Member States' officials, though obviously limited to some extent. Besides that, there are also provisions which provide the Commission with the

---

10 Cf. the illustration by Mögele, *Fehlerhafte Ausgaben* (fn. 8), 112 ff.

11 ECJ, case C-366/88 (France *v* Commission), European Court reports 1990, I-3595, mn. 20; ECJ, case C-55/91 (Italy *v* Commission), European Court reports 1993, I-4858, mn. 31.

12 Mögele, in: Dauses, HbEUWiR (fn. 8), G, mn. 238.

13 An overview of administrative cooperation during control of compliance with Community law is provided by Jans/de Lange/Widdershoven, *Europees bestuursrecht* (fn. 1), 245 ff.

14 Article 40(2) lit. a) of the Council Regulation (EC) No 2200/96 of 28 October 1996 on the common organisation of the market in fruit and vegetables, OJ L 297, 21 November 1996, p. 1; cf. also Article 6(3) of the Council Regulation (EEC) No 2048/89 of 19 June 1989 laying down general rules on controls in the wine sector, OJ L 202, 14 July 1989, p. 32.

15 Council Regulation (EEC) No 2847/93 of 12 October 1993 establishing a control system applicable to the common fisheries policy, OJ L 261, 20 October 1993, p. 1 (essentially amended by the Council Regulations (EC) No 686/97 of 14 April 1997 amending (EEC) Regulation No 2847/93 of 12 October 1993 establishing a control system applicable to the common fisheries policy, OJ L 102, 19 April 1997, p. 1 and (EC) No 2846/98, OJ L 358, 31 December 1998, p. 5.

16 Article 5(2) of the Council Directive 93/99/EEC of 29 October 1993 on the subject of additional measures concerning the official control of foodstuffs, OJ L 290, 24 November 1993, p. 14.

possibility of *requesting* the Member State to implement an inspection. Such enforcements on request represent an alternative to autonomous commission controls. They are often standardised in one and the same legal act. Inspections at the Commission's request can take place in the areas where the Commission carries out an inspection itself[17], as well as where the execution is allocated to the Member States.[18] Also, officials of the Commission can participate in cases of inspections on request.[19] However, their competences remain those of an accompanying nature.

If the Commission's officials undertake their independent controls in the Member States, officials of the Member State concerned can participate.[20] This

17 As, fore example, in the Regulation No 17 First Regulation implementing Articles 85 and 86 of the Treaty, OJ 13, 21.2.1962, p. 204: The Commission does not only have the authority to implement the autonomous controls itself, but it can request the competent authorities of the Member States to undertake the investigations (Article 13 of the Regulation No 17). Correspondingly, even partly further-reaching authorities can be found in the following Council Regulation (EC) No 1/2003 of 16 December 2002 on the implementation of the rules on competition laid down in Articles 81 ad 82 of the Treaty, OJ L 1, 4 January 2003, p. 1. This similarly applies to the cross-section area of anti-fraud. Besides the implementation of independent controls on the spot, the Commission also can request the Member States to implement Article 6(1) of the Council Regulation (EEC) No. 595/91 of 4 March 1991 concerning irregularities and the recovery of sums wrongly paid in connection with the financing of the common agricultural policy and the organisation of an information system in this field and repealing Regulation (EEC) No. 283/72, OJ L 67, 14 March 1991, p. 11. Article 18(3) of the Council Regulation (EC) No. 515/97 of 13 March 1997 on mutual assistance between the administrative authorities of the Member States and cooperation between the latter and the Commission to ensure the correct application of the law on customs and agricultural matters, OJ L 82, 22 March 1997, p. 1. In competition law as well as in anti-fraud law the Commission can participate in those inspections.

18 Main reference area is the law of agricultural financing. At the request of the Commission and in concert with the Member States concerned, the responsible Member State officials undertake their inspections or investigations (Article 9(2)(4) of Regulation (EC) No. 1258/1999 (fn. 7); Article 18(3) of Regulation (EC) No 515/97 (fn. 17). For the Structural Funds, cf. Article 38(2)(3) of the Council Regulation (EC) No. 1260/1999 of 21 June 1999 laying down general provisions on the Structural Funds, OJ L161, 26 June 1999, p. 1. Article 6 of Regulation (EEC) No. 2048/89 (fn. 14) and Article 18(4) of the Council Regulation (EC) No. 515/97 (fn. 17); Article 30(2) of Regulation (EEC) No. 2847/93 (fn. 15).

19 Article 9(2)(4) of Regulation (EC) No. 1258/1999 (fn. 7); Article 18(4) of Regulation (EC) No. 515/97 (fn. 17).

20 Article 9(2)(3) of Regulation (EC) No. 1258/1999 (EAGGF, fn. 7); Article 11 of the Commission Regulation (EEC) No. 3887/92 of 23 December 1992 laying down detailed rules for applying the integrated administration and control system for certain Community aid schemes, OJ L 391, 31 December 1998, p. 36; relevant amendments of the implementation regulation by the Commission Regulation (EC) No 1678/98 of 29 July 1998 amending Regulation (EEC) No 3887/92 laying down detailed rules for applying the integrated administration and control system for certain Community aid schemes, OJ L 212, 30 July 1998, p. 23; Article 14(5) of the Regulation No. 17 (fn. 17): Officials of the competent authority of the Member State in whose territory the investigation is to be made may, at the request of such authority or of the Commission, assist the officials of the Commission in carrying out their duties; Article 38(2)(2) of the Council Regulation (EC) No 1260/1999 (fn. 18), Article 4(1) of the Council Regulation (EURATOM, EC) No 2185/96 of 11 November 1996 concerning on-the-spot checks and inspections carried out by the Commission in order to protect the European

opportunity to participate offers advantages for both sides. The Commission's officials always have a contact agency they can consult if questions arise. And the Member State administrations are given the opportunity to follow the activity of the Commission's inspectors on their territory. The rights to accompany of the Member States serve primarily to create transparency. Under certain circumstances, the opportunity to participate can become a duty to participate. This is particularly true if the Commission depends on the support of the responsible Member State authorities.

Opportunities for participation are particularly noticeable with regard to *horizontal* participant constellations, i.e. the cooperation of administrative officials of different Member States during the implementation of on-site inspections, as part of horizontal administrative assistance efforts.[21] If a Member State requests another to execute certain inspections, its own officials can often join the investigations. However, this participation requires the approval of the requested Member State.[22] In this context it should be emphasised that the direction lies with the officials of the Member State requested. The officials of the requesting Member State have no independent inspection rights on the territory of the requested Member State.[23] These opportunities to participate fulfil the function of the creation of trust. However, they transcend the usual standards of the traditional law of mutual administrative assistance, i.e. the execution of the requests by the requested authority without personal opportunities to participate of the requesting authority.[24] By the on-site contacts, the officials of the requesting authority can indicate details which are of special interest for their

Communities' financial interests against fraud and other irregularities, OJ L 292, 15 November 1996, p. 2.

21 Especially as in agricultural, fisheries and food law.

22 Cf., e.g. Articles 7, 9, 19 of Regulation (EC) No. 515/97 (fn. 17); Article 7(2) and (4) of Regulation (EEC) No. 2048/89 (fn. 14).

23 Cf. e.g. the wording of Article 7(4) (3) of Regulation (EC) No 2729/2000 (fn. 14):" The officials of the body appealed to shall remain in charge of the control operations at all times." Also see Article 9(2) (2) of Regulation (EC) No 515/97 (fn. 17).

24 This principle still applies to some of the examined reference areas. Even though Council Directive 89/608/EEC of 21 November 1989 (on mutual assistance between the administrative authorities and the Member States and cooperation between the latter and the Commission to ensure the correct application of legislation on veterinary and zootechnical matters, OJ L 351, 2 December 1989, p. 34) still leans on the provisions of the Council Regulation on EC Mutual Assistance (fn. 17), on its basis, applications of the requesting authority concerning the supervision of certain enterprises, depots or means of transportation by the requested authority, are permissible (cf. Article 6 and 8(2) lit. b) Directive No. 89/608). However, no opportunity to participate for the requesting authority is standardised. Also according to the Council Regulation on Fisheries Control inspections on request are possible, but in this context, no rights to participate are standardised (Article 34(2)(2) of Regulation No. 2847/93, fn. 15). However, the Member States can implement among themselves, on their own initiative, surveillance, control and supervision of the fisheries activities (Article 34 b (2) of Regulation No. 2847/93). Supposedly, the common programmes also provide common inspections.

request, and gain an insight into the administrative practice of other Member States at the same time.

The horizontal cooperation attains a new quality with the inspections in the law of banking supervision. The provisions of the European law of banking supervision are based on a concept of stronger exteriorisation. The EC law allocates the Member State community-wide supervision tasks. The banking supervision of a Member State is responsible for the surveillance of all business activities of the banks located in its territory (so-called country of origin control).[25]

This surveillance applies independently of the fact which particular Member State the bank provides its services in. In this case, the activities of branches of German banks in other EC countries are also subject to supervision by the German banking supervision. Accordingly, the inspection authorisations are also characterised by a stronger dissolution of boundaries. Officials of the country of origin can verify supervisory legally relevant data in the branches on the spot. The authority to investigate transnationally is generally provided for and is not bound by the permission of the host country. Prior notice is the only requirement.[26] Therefore, the regulation encompasses more then the mere opportunity to make a request of the banking supervision of the host Member State. The support of a host Member State must be requested only if the exercise of direct force is necessary. The exercise of sovereign rights by supervision officials of the Member State in another Member State represents a new level of cooperation. These forms of transnational cooperation express the Europeanisation of the supervisory responsibilities in a special way. Multiple administrations work together in order to accomplish *one* task, namely economic supervision functioning on a Community-wide basis.

3. LEGAL FRAMEWORK

On the level of *legislative procedure*, the Treaty establishing the European Community provides a broad reservoir of competences concerning the introduction of inspection provisions and their procedural and institutional definition. In the light of the final orientation of the authorisation bases, procedural and organisational provisions, which serve the accomplishment of material provision aims, can be justified as harmonisation of the Member State administrative systems as well as administrative competences for the Community Besides the individual legal bases, Article 308 of the EC Treaty and Article 284 of

25 Article 26(1) of the Directive 2000/12/EC of the European Parliament and the Council of 20 March 2000 relating to the taking up and pursuit of the business of credit institutions, OJ L 126, 26 May 2000, p. 1.

26 Article 29(1) of Directive No. 2000/12 (fn. 25).

the EC Treaty provide transregional authorisation bases for the information and review competences of the Commission. Also the allocation of inspection authorisations to dependent or independent authorities and agencies on an EC level[27] or the Member States' obligation to arrange special administrative points, which have to carry out powers to inspect,[28] is basically in accordance with the primary legal provisions of the EC Treaty.

The initial point on the *execution level* is the characterisation of the inspection relations as multipolar and tiered legal relations. There are horizontal and vertical processing legal relations between the administrative bodies involved in the inter-administrative relations (see 3.1., 3.2.) as well as in the relations with the outside world with regard to the control of economic operators subordinate to these authorities (see 3.3.). The cooperation of the administration points which has already been illustrated is characteristic of the legal relations in inter-administrative relations. Only recently has there been realisation of the significance of the creation of fixed cooperation provisions for an effective and constitutional administration of the Community area. The principle of sincere cooperation (*Grundsatz der loyalen Zusammenarbeit*), which is manifested in Article 10 of the EC Treaty, is the overarching basic principle, to which the cooperation – be it horizontal or vertical – has to orient. Further connecting factors for the creation of administrative cooperation standards are the basic principles of Community law.

3.1. INSPECTIONS IN VERTICAL INTER-ADMINISTRATIVE RELATIONS: SUPERVISION STRUCTURES IN THE EUROPEAN COMPOSITE ADMINISTRATION

Inspections serve as a control on the execution of Community law and through this help achieve even execution of and compliance with it. According to the ideal of a *national* ministerial administration with its classical centralistic organisation, hierarchic structures, in particular, provide an even legal execution:

27 The European Anti-Fraud Office (OLAF) is an example of an institution being linked to the Commission but independent and with very far-reaching authorities to inspect, cf. more detailed David, *Inspektionen* (fn. 4), 183 ff. An agency with its own legal personality is the European Environment Agency, which is at the moment not yet entrusted with inspection tasks. However, this is under discussion in the context of the request for an environment inspectorate on the European level, cf. more detailed David, l.c., 192 ff.; about the agencies cf. Riedel, in this volume, p. 157 et seq.

28 A classic example is the control points for the olive oil and tobacco market organisations. In both sectors, an EC regulation has dictated to the Member States that they install special administrative independent control points. The officials of these control points are responsible, under an activity programme, for the implementation of the inspection tasks within the scope of the olive oil and tobacco market organisations; this programme has to be drawn up in advance by the Member States; cf. more detailed David, *Inspektionen* (fn. 4), 38 f.

supervising and directing authorisations of the leading authorities align all subcategories or parts of the system so that the law can be applied rationally and uniformly.[29] The different authorisations of particular supervision authorities, as elements of the supervision, need to be differentiated: authorisations to investigate the facts and circumstances of the case represent the supervising whereas the possibility of imposing instructions or other correctional measures represents the correcting element of the supervision.[30] With reference to the differentiation between observation (*Beobachtung*) and correction (*Berichtigung*), the on-site inspections by the Commission at the administrations of the Member States represent the observational element of supervision in the EC. Without independent authorisations to investigate the facts of the case, no supervision can be exercised.[31] In this case, the inspections represent an important instrument. Through the on-site visit, the Commission's officials can form a visible picture of the execution activities of the Member States.

This implies that the Commission's authorisations to inspect represent investigating authorisations, which should ensure the realisation of its function as guardian of Community law (Article 211 of the EC Treaty). The object of control can either be the Member States or the economic operators. However, the position of the Member States cannot be compared to that of the economic operators. The relationship between the economic operators and the inspector is of a subordinate-legal nature. The administration agencies of the Member State can at least enforce their inspections by administrative force and they can also provide supporting functions for the Commission's inspectors. In *inter-administrative relations*, i.e. with regard to the Member State administrations, such a subordinate relationship is lacking. With regard to the Member State administrations, the Commission's officials have no possibility of enforcing their inspection rights by order and force. They depend more on the voluntary cooperation of the Member States. However, the inspections offer – at least indirectly – an effective supervisory instrument, which is characteristic of the Community's own combination of "soft supervisory instruments" and cooperation.

In their function as execution controllers, the Commission's officials perform inspections at the Member States' administrations: they are authorised to access

---

29 Cf. broadly Dreier, *Hierarchische Verwaltung im demokratischen Staat*, 1991; Kahl, *Staatsaufsicht* (fn. 5) with the attempt at 'de-hierarchysised redetermination'.

30 This differentiation can be found for national law (e.g. Lerche, in Maunz/Düring, GG, Article 84, mn. 162 – following Triepel, also Maurer, *Allgemeines Verwaltungsrecht*, 13th edition 2000, §23, mn. 19 ff.) as well as for international law (e.g. Hahn, in: Strupp-Schlochauer, Band I, 69; Conrad, *Formen der Vollziehung*, 1968, 178). It is also adopted for EC law, cf. Pühs, *Vollzug* (fn. 1), 133.

31 Van Rijn, in: *Festschrift für Schermers*, 409 detects accurately: "Supervision can only be properly exercised if the supervision organ has the necessary powers to investigate into the matter. Investigatory and supervisory powers are intrinsically linked. Therefore, I will assume them both under the notion 'supervision'."

records and make copies of them.[32] In addition, they can demand explanations and information. They can often accompany the control officials from the Member State on their on-site work.[33] At the same time, the administrative points of the Member States as the "object" of the Commission's controls have to tolerate and give active support during the inspection visits of the Commission's officials. Within the scope of the economic operators' own on-site controls by their inspectors, the Commission's officials must be included to a wide extent: in particular, at the request of the Commission's officials, the inspectors have to take samples and make them available to the officials.[34] If the Commission's officials are entitled to their own authorisation of direct control at the economic operators, the Member State administrations are obliged to provide support and aid during the execution. They have to overcome any opposition by using coercive measures. Legal acts also determine to some extent that the officials can implement their independent inspections at the Commission's request and transfer the information received to it.[35]

In vertical relations the principle of sincere cooperation (*Grundsatz der loyalen Zusammenarbeit*), i.e. the requirement to respect mutual legitimate interests (*Rücksichtnahmegebot*) demands the Commission to take into consideration the concerns of the Member States temporally and locally in its control activities and planning. Concerning the frequency and the intensity of the control activities, the Commission has to supervise all Member States equally and can only deviate from it in substantiated cases. This can be expressed to the outside world, e.g. by the creation of control concepts and plans. The *principle of proportionality* (*Verhältnismäßigkeitsprinzip*) requires that there is a proportional relationship between the burden on the Member State where the inspections are performed and the Commission's interest concerning the determination of lacks of enforcement in individual cases. In the light of the common responsibility of the Member State administrations and the Commission for the administration of the Community area, the Member States have only very few opportunities of refusing their cooperation and support, for example by the claim of *rights to deny data* under the narrow requirements of Article 296 of the EC Treaty.

In flexible systems *supervision as a means to create unity* is also necessary. However, supervision in the European composite administration cannot be

---

32 As, e.g. Article 6(4) of Regulation No 595/91 (fn. 17); Article 6(2) in connection with Article 4 of the Commission Regulation (EC) No. 2729/2000 of 14 December 2000 laying down detailed implementing rules on controls in the wine sector, OJ L 316, 15 December 2000, p. 16.

33 "Accompanying controls", as, e.g. in agricultural law (Article 40(2) lit. a), Regulation No. 2200/96 (fn. 14), Article 6(3) of Regulation No 2048/89 (fn. 14); fisheries law (Article 29(2) of Regulation No. 2847/93 (fn. 15)); food law (Article 5(2) of Directive No 93/99/EEC (fn. 16)).

34 E.g. according to Article 15 of Regulation No. 2729/2000 (fn. 32).

35 An alternative to the autonomous Commission's controls, e.g. according to Article 6(1) of Regulation No 595/97 (fn. 17), Article 18(3) of Regulation No 515/97 (fn. 17) or a kind of supervisory measure in the direct execution, e.g. according to Article 9(2) of Regulation No. 1258/1999 (fn. 8), Article 38(2) of Regulation No 1260/1999 (fn. 18), Article 30(2) of Regulation No 2847/93 (fn. 15); more detailed, *David*, Inspektionen (fn. 4), 129 ff.

created a priori by a mere concept of hierarchic supervision. It is composed more by a mix of hierarchic and cooperative elements,[36] which can be illustrated by the inspections. The cooperative design of the inspections with its tendency to the system controls, which is abstract from the single case, with the opportunity to participate and mutual support, may not belie the fact that the law of the Commission about the directed on-site representation provides stronger opportunities to interfere than the instruments of federal supervision, known from German law.[37]

The inspections also have a supervisory effect even without the opportunity of correction by the Commission itself,[38] following the inspection. There is already the possibility that the visit of the Commission's officers to view the supervising and executing activities of the Member States on-site will raise the pressure on the Member States to execute properly. They themselves will then strive to perform their control tasks properly and to correct the defects within the control system.[39] In addition, the inspections serve as an instrument to determine the facts of the case if an infringement procedure has to be initiated. The close connection with this possible procedure already awards the inspections a kind of "threatening potential".

Other elements alongside inspections in vertical relations illustrate a *combination of hierarchy and cooperation.* The obligation of the Member States to create independent control agencies and the opportunity of the Commission to influence their activity (programmes) are not qualified needlessly as "quasi-supervising interventions" into the administrative structure of the Member States.[40] The obligation which is often imposed on the Member States of creating control plans and inspection reports has to fulfil rationalising and instructional functions for the Member State itself, on the one hand but, at the same time, these plans and reports are a means of justification with regard to the Commission. Therefore, they can also be categorised as a special form of creating

---

36 Schmidt-Aßmann, in: *FS für Steinberger*, 2002, 1375, 1389, characterises the European administration as a "cooperatively suspended hierarchy"; *id.*, in this Volume, 1 (14 ff.).

37 Also Pühs, *Vollzug* (fn. 1), 328, who emphasises the Commission's "extended resources in order to ascertain data", which represents however, no superior supervising authority with directing functions, but "merely" an institution of the legal supervision in the interest of a uniform administrative execution.

38 Especially emphasised by Pühs, *Vollzug* (fn. 1), 323: "Doch ergibt ein genauer Blick auf die tatsächlichen Kompetenzen der Bediensteten, dass keinesfalls feststellbar ist, dass die Kommission hier eine gleichsam "berichtigende" Aufsichtsgewalt wahrnimmt." (= However, a closer look at the actual competences of the officials reveals that it is not detectible under any circumstances that the Commission acquires a quasi "correcting" supervision power).

39 Also van Rijn, in: Vervaele (ed.), *Administration Law and Enforcement of Community Law*, 1994, 143, 157. The clearing of control effects by exercising supervising functions is also emphasised by Kadelbach, in: Schmidt-Aßmann/Hoffmann-Riem, *Verwaltungskontrolle* (fn. 5), 205, 227.

40 As Götz, *EuR* 1986, 29, 34, who refers to the regulations as "in every aspect unusual"; critically v. Danwitz, *Verwaltungsrechtliches System und Europäische Integration*, 1996, 202 f.

hierarchic relations.[41] The reports also serve as self-disciplinary actions and create *transparency* for all participants. This also applies for the opposite existing information and reporting duties of the Commission. Transparency and mutual information about forms and standards of execution replace the traditional steering means of the hierarchy. Information and communication between the Commission and the Member Sate administrations create conscious acceptance and so ensure the existence of a Community which has to waive the traditional means of the directive.

3.2. INSPECTIONS IN HORIZONTAL INTER-ADMINISTRATIVE RELATIONS: CONFIDENCE-BUILDING IN THE NETWORK OF EUROPEAN COMPOSITE ADMINISTRATION

An examination of the *legal relations in horizontal relations* can be used as a basis to illustrate the adjustment process, to which an instrument known from German administrative law of economic supervision within the scope of Europeanisation is exposed. The possibilities of transnational inspections or participation in them, the creation and enforcement of bi-lateral or multi-lateral inspection programmes and the manifold provisions on information exchange are an expression of a *common responsibility* of the Member States for the administration of the Community area. The economic supervision is no longer a task which every Member State has to fulfil by itself: rather it has become a common economic supervision in the European federation.

In horizontal relations there is still very little differentiation of the standards on which the cooperation must be based. Besides the (negative) *prohibition of discriminating control practices* which follow from the principle of the free movement of goods, however, some general positive standards of the cooperation can be discerned. From the principle of sincere cooperation (*Grundsatz der loyalen Zusammenarbeit*), the ECJ has deducted a duty to inform about changes in control practices.[42] Furthermore, a *duty to substantiate information, inspection and other requests for administrative assistance*, their *answer or enforcement without iniquitous delay* as well as a *procedural principle of equivalence* should be seen as general standard in the meantime.[43]

The *sovereignty* left to the Member States, in particular, delimits the transnational control activities. These limits cannot also be easily overridden by principles which have a contrary effect, such as the principle of sincere cooperation. The inspection activities of a Member State on the territory of

41 Hatje, *Die gemeinschaftsrechtliche Steuerung der Wirtschaftsverwaltung*, 1998, 155.

42 ECJ, case 47/82, European Court reports 1983, 1013, mn. 36.

43 A detailed derivation by David, *Inspektionen* (fn. 4), 269 ff.

another Member State are basically forbidden apart from permission for specific cases. Exceptions only exist, if they have been constituted by secondary law, as in the banking supervision law, for instance. Even the mere observational participation in its different designs usually requires the prior approval of the affected Member State.[44] In this connection, the principle of Community loyalty becomes effective, by basically chartering the approval and admitting rejections only in justified exceptional cases. In either case, there are still development possibilities in this area. The requirement of approval should be abolished by-and-by. It does not conform to a European administrative area (anymore), in which the supervising authorities have to fulfil a common responsibility.

Another factor which can limit horizontal cooperation is the *principle of proportionality*, the effects of which depend on the specific configuration of the case and – also with a particularly strong orientation to particular cases – the *proviso of the ordre public*. The latter should only be relevant in rare and exceptional cases.[45]

Even though the legal system can still and must be further expanded, the cooperation of the Member States during their supervision activities is now important for the creation of the *trust in functioning administrative structures* which function throughout the Community. This mutual trust as such can only partly be established by legal acts. The creation of confidence rather has to be supported by trust-creating techniques.[46] The opportunity to gain an insight into the way on-site execution takes place in other Member States creates greater trust and raises the willingness to recognise the supervision by other Member States, to waive additional own controls as well as a willingness to execute properly in their own country.[47]

---

44 Cf., e.g., Article 9(2) of Regulation No 515/97 (fn. 17), Article 7(4) of Regulation No. 2729/2000 (fn. 32); first erosion of the requirement for agreement, e.g. in the veterinary law. There, the Commission's officials can let themselves be accompanied by inspection officials from a third Member State as observers. The Member State in which the inspection should take place, only has a singular refusal left. To a certain extent as a compensation, the accompanying officials have to be put on a list in advance, which is listed by the Commission, Article 4(1) of the Commission Decision No. 98/139 of 4 February 1998 laying down certain detailed rules concerning on-the-spot checks carried out in the veterinary field by Commission experts in the Member States, OJ L 38, 12 February 1998, p. 10; more detailed, David, *Inspektionen* (fn. 4), 267 ff.

45 A detailed derivation by David, *Inspektionen* (fn. 4), 269 ff.

46 Essentially Majone, *Mutual Trust* (fn. 1), 9 ff.: "Without concrete measure to increase the level of mutual trust, therefore the obligation of Community loyalty (…) remains dead letter and cannot serve as a basis for a system of effective enforcement." Therefore, information and communication are the efforts, by which the demand for transnational effect of the administrative execution is effectively "earned", cf. Schoch, in: Schmidt-Aßmann/Hoffmann-Riem, *Strukturen* (fn. 1), 279, 308 f.; Wahl/Groß, DVBl. 1998, 2, 3. Referring to the factor of mutual trust of the Member States in a functioning food supervision, Streinz, WiVerw 1993, 1, 57 f.

47 The characterisation of the control harmonisation as foundation of trust creation and the principle of mutual recognition also by Falke, in: Hill/Hof (eds.), *Wirkungsforschung zum*

The development of trust in the national administrative authorities is a legitimising factor which is not to be underestimated in a European administrative area, characterised by transnational networking, in which the traditional, merely national, structures lose their legitimising power and a genuine European legitimising structure is still in the initial phase. New structures, which allow for the particularities of Europe-wide administrative activity, exist side-by-side with the classical instruments to constitute administrative legitimisation.[48]

3.3. LEGAL RELATIONS WITH THE ECONOMIC OPERATORS

The differentiated mechanisms of participation and information exchange with trust-building and control-crossing ambitions previously described cover a broad area within the different inspection provisions. The cooperation between the Member States and the Commission should serve the goal of effective execution, which is the constant target. The heavy significance of this principle of effectiveness is characteristic for the final structure of European administrative law. It thereby rises up from the Member States' administrative laws. While the Member States' administrative laws are bound by the interest concerning the functionality of state action and the protection of freedom of the people at the same time, the "specific purpose rationality" of Community law tends to "make the functionality of the Community and its law into the outstanding interpretation topos".[49] The more intensely the legal positions of the economic

Recht II – Verwaltung als Adressat und Akteur, 2000, 265, 266.

48 Detailed about trust as an element of administrative legitimation in a decentralised European Union, Röhl, *Akkreditierung und Zertifizierung im Produktsicherheitsrecht*, 2000, 44 ff. Also see Magiera, DÖV 1998, 173, 183: "Entscheidend für den neuen kooperativen Kontrollmechanismus und seine Wirksamkeit spricht, dass eine verbesserte Zusammenarbeit zwischen den Verwaltungen der Mitgliedstaaten untereinander und mit der Kommission geeignet ist, das gegenseitige Verständnis und Vertrauen zu fördern. (...) Eine wesentliche Voraussetzung dafür ist, das Gemeinschaftsrecht nicht als eine fremde, sondern als Teil der eigenen Rechtsordnung zu erkennen, deren Durchsetzung im gemeinsamen und zugleich im eigenen Interesse liegt." (= Decisive in favour of the new cooperative control mechanism and its effectiveness is, that an improved cooperation between the administrations of the Member States among each other and the Commission is qualified for an improvement of the mutual understanding and trust. (...) An essential requirement for this is, to recognise the Community law not as a strange but as a part of a proper legal order, whose implementation is not only in the common interest but also in the own interest.)The factor trust as important requirement for a functioning European administration is also emphasised by Majone, *Mutual Trust* (fn. 1); Happe, *Die grenzüberschreitende Wirkung von nationalen Verwaltungsakten*, 1987, 111; v. Bogdandy/Arndt, EWS 2000, 1.

49 Schmidt-Aßmann, DVBl. 1993, 924, 931; Schoch, JZ 1995, 109, 117; cf. Also Hegels, *EG-Eigenverwaltungsrecht und Gemeinschaftsverwaltungsrecht*, 2001, 159 ff.; qualifying, Classen, DV 31 (1998), 307, 318 f.

operator are effected by execution provisions and activities, the more strongly questions will come up concerning the possibilities of their constitutional limitation and bonding. The argument of the function cannot be applied without limit. The ideas of effectiveness can only be realised in legally bound forms.[50]

During the inspections, numerous measures may interfere in legally protected interests which are protected by fundamental rights. This applies to the specific controls on-site as well as to sanctions which may be relevant and which can be linked to the detection of violations. In comparison there seem to be, at first sight, relatively few provisions which are dedicated to the limitation of the possibilities for cooperation and which guarantee the rights of those subject to the controls. Therefore, some critics say this should be considered as a deficit.[51] The question of whether this is actually the case will be examined in the following section. Thereby, one has to refer to those measures in connection with the inspections, which can interfere in individual legally protected interests protected by fundamental rights.

The single inspection powers on-site – be it by the Commission's officers or by the Member States' officials – form the basis of direct interference in the rights of those subject to the controls. The most important inspection powers are the following:

- Right to access commercial premises
- Right of search
- Right of access to records and documents
- Request for information on-site
- Sampling
- Confiscation of items or documents as well as sealing of rooms
- Imposition of administrative fines and the implementation of direct force in order to enforce the inspection authorisations.

---

50 Scheuing, in: Hoffmann-Riem/Schmidt-Aßmann (eds.), *Innovation und Flexibilität des Verwaltungshandelns*, 1994, 289, 351; Pernice/Kadelbach, DVBl. 1996, 1100, 1113. Also indicating the difficulties of the development of constitutional principles within the scope of the final structure of the European Community law, Rengeling, VVDStRL 53 (1994), 202, 222 ff.

51 Cf, for the example of the Regulations No. 515/97 (fn. 17) and No. 2185/96 (fn. 20) Widdershoven, in: Vervaele (ed.), *Transnational Enforcement of the Financial Interests of the European Union*, 1999, 131, 138 ff:; also Vervaele, in: id., *Compliance of Enforcement* (fn. 6), 361, 381: "(…) but also at this point we have to underline the fact that the necessary rules concerning legal protection (privacy, principles of due law) are rather soft and under-developed"; Berg, *Implementing and Enforcing European Fisheries Law*, 1999, 292: "Still, it is often questionable whether in striving towards more effective enforcement, principles of law are sufficiently guaranteed and individual rights adequately protected. In striving for the general observance of Community law, in particular in the fields of enforcement of common policies such as agriculture and fisheries the near total subordination of individual interests to the objectives of market regulation becomes clear" and Dannecker, ZStW 108 (1996), 577, 606 ff. (from a criminal law perspective). Critically about the offensive application of the demand of uniform legal application, also Danwitz, *Verwaltungsrechtliches System* (fn. 40), 118 ff.; qualifying, Wittkopp, *Sachverhaltsermittlung im Gemeinschaftsverwaltungsrecht*, 1999, 242.

By the inspection activity on-site, sovereignty is performed directly with regard to the economic operator. On the basis of the inspection results, subsequent drastic sanction decisions can be made. Because of these reasons, the constitutional limitation of the inspection actions and therewith the compliance with the procedural and defence laws are of high importance.

3.3.1. Procedural and defence rights

In the individual *national* legal systems the procedural and defence rights of the people are protected by differentiated systems. *Community law* does not include an all-encompassing normative provision of the rights to which people are entitled. Several procedural and defence rights are explicitly codified in material law.[52] In addition, general legal principles have been established by the case-law of the ECJ, which builds the framework of procedural and defence rights[53] and applies them in the direct as well as in the indirect execution of Community law.

In the inspection clauses of European administrative law, procedural and defence rights are standardised rather rudimentarily, or not at all explicitly. While the Community legal acts, e.g. normally include a clause establishing that the Commission has to inform the *Member State* concerned in advance about the implementation planned,[54] there are no such provisions about the date and manner of the prior announcement as well as clauses concerning a notice of the allegations and a duty to justify with regard to the economic operator concerned in most of the respective inspections, or legal acts. Partly, the inspections explicitly provide for the enforcement of unannounced checks.[55] This could be justified, regarding the attainability of the particular purpose of the control, e.g. in anti-fraud law or food law. However, this does not discharge the responsible agencies from the obligation of informing the party concerned about the content

52 Those isolated area-based procedural provisions, which are additionally mentioned in the discussion about the general principles, are certified as having "a strong ad-hoc quality" by Vervaele, in: id., *Transnational Enforcement* (fn. 51), 53, 88.

53 An overview is provided, e.g. by Pernice/Kadelbach, DVBl. 1996, 1100, 1103 and Arnold, EuR 1995, Beiheft 1, 7 ff.; see also Lenaerts, EuR 1997, 17, 26 ff.; Classen, DV 31 (1998), 307, 310 ff.; Harding, *European Community Investigations and Sanctions*, 1993, 41 ff.; Jans/de Lange/ Prechal/Widdershoven, *Europees bestuursrecht* (fn. 1), 208 ff.; referring to the investigation activity of the Commission as an EC competition authority, Schwarze, in: id. (ed.), *Der Gemeinsame Markt – Bestand und Zukunft in wirtschaftlicher Perspektive*, 1987, 159 ff. and Dannecker, ZStW 111 (1999), 256, 269 ff.

54 Cf. only Article 14(2) of Regulation No 17 (fn. 17), Article 4 of Regulation No 2185/96 (fn. 20), Article 9(2) of Regulation No 1258/99 (fn. 8), Article 5(2) of Directive No 93/99 (fn. 16), Article 3 of Decision No 98/129 (fn. 44).

55 E.g., Article 17 of the Commission Regulation No. 2419/2001 of 11 December 2001 laying down detailed rules for applying the integrated administration and control system for certain Community aid schemes established by Council Regulation EEC No 3508/92, OJ L 327, 12 December 2001, p. 11; Article 29(2) lit. a) of Regulation No. 2847/93 (fn. 5), Article 4(4) of the Council Directive No 89/397/EEC of 14 June 1989 on the official control of foodstuffs, OJ L 186, 30 June 1989, p. 23.

and the purpose of the planned inspection directly before the implementation of the inspection at the latest. The ECJ has characterised the compliance with the requirements as essential for the guarantee of the rights of defence of the companies concerned.[56] The scope of the obligation to state the reasons on which decisions ordering investigations are based could not be restricted on the basis of considerations concerning the effectiveness of the investigation. Although the Commission was not required to communicate all the information at its disposal concerning the presumed infringements to the addressee concerning a decision ordering an investigation, nor required to make a precise legal analysis of those infringements, it must nonetheless clearly indicate the presumed facts which it intends to investigate. The cited decision of the ECJ concerns investigations according to Article 14 of Regulation No. 1/2003 on the implementation of the rules on competition laid down in Articles 81 and 82 of the Treaty which in the meantime has replaced Regulation No. 17. Accordingly, the investigation by the Commission determines subject, purpose and date of the investigation and indicates possible arbitrary measures as well as the law to bring an action before the ECJ. Regulation No 2185/96 does not contain a comparable provision. However, before the Commission's officials make use of their authorisation, they have to submit a written authorisation showing their identity and position, together with a document indicating a subject matter and purpose of the on-site check or inspection.[57] The (partly) independent inspections in the agricultural and veterinary law lack provisions about the justification of the investigation measures. However, the written investigation assignment is in general the appropriate instrument to inform the party subject to the control about the content, purpose and complexity of the planned investigation measure.[58]

The standardisation of the duty of information, as well as the duty to enable access to the floors of the operation, to offices and to the records and the removal of samples to the authority control officials can lead to a disclosure of personal data, and business and office secrets. An *absolute* protection of secrets, in terms of investigation prohibitions, does not exist in the legal acts analysed. It would also only be imaginable, where the disclosure would be impermissible because of a legally protected interest which has greater rank above the interest of state information. The rights of the party being obliged to give information are given greater protection by the differentiated provisions of a *relative* protection of secrets.[59] The data, the company and business secrets have to be disclosed to the

56 ECJ, joined cases 46/87, 227/88 (Hoechst/Commission), European Court reports 1989, 2859, 2919, mn. 41.

57 Article 6(1) of Regulation No 2185/96 (fn. 20); about Ulrich, *Kontrollen der EG-Kommission bei Wirtschaftsbeteiligten zum Schutz der finanziellen Interessen der Gemeinschaft*, 1999, 203; Kuhl/Spitzer, EuZW 1998, 37, 42.

58 More detailed David, *Inspektionen* (fn. 4), 303 ff.

59 Cf. about the differentiation between absolute and relative secret protection, W. Berg, *GewArch 1996*, 177, 179; also see Engel/Freier, EWS 1992, 361, 365 (referring to the complexity

responsible authorities. They are allowed to use those secrets with due consideration for the *principle of appropriation*, the *equivalence principle* as well as the other requirements established by the *national law*, to which it is referred to in individual cases.

General Legal Principles of Community Law[60] compensate to some extent for the overall lack of explicit procedural provisions in the secondary legal provisions in order to protect the economic operations subject to the control. Thus, those General Legal Principles have been primarily established by the ECJ for the *right to self administration*. However, they have also developed an effect for the *execution activities of the Member States* and therefore can serve as a *minimum standard*. This does not prevent the Member States from exceeding this minimum standard in their national procedural law. A higher protection in the individual case under national procedural law should not be taken away too hastily due to considerations of effectiveness and the application of priority.

Altogether, the minimum standard derived from the General Legal Principles of the Community Law provides a sufficient level of protection. However, it is unfortunate for the economic participants in the Member States that the rights they are entitled to do not result directly from the legal acts which underlie an inspection. In order to achieve more legal clarity and transparency, it would be preferable to include those rights at least in the most important inspection acts.

3.3.2. Individual judicial protection

As already described, the inspection and the actions connected to it (especially the inspection order or search but also the transmission of the attained information) affect the legal position of the particular party subject to the controls. German constitutional law as well as European Community law requires an effective judicial protection against actions of public authorities. The judicial protection system in European administrative law is based on the assumption of a model of separation. The separation of the tasks and the authorisations between the Member States and the Community in the execution of Community law also extends to the areas of liability and judicial protection. State courts provide protection against executive actions of the authorities of this State but judicial protection has to be sought at the ECJ and the CFI against acts of European public powers.

During the enforcement of inspections however, the system of cooperation is often complicated, as already shown. If inspections are implemented on request or together with other authorities, problems can occur concerning the allocation

---

of the obligation to give out information according to Regulation No. 17).

60 This does not only apply to the justification and secret protection provisions being discussed here, but also to further rights of defence such as the right to be heard, the right of protection from self-incrimination as well as the right to consult a lawyer and the legal professional privilege, in detail thereto, David, *Inspektionen* (fn. 4), 306 ff.

of responsibility. It is questionable whether there can be sufficient definition of individual judicial protection levels in combinations where responsibility is allocated in various ways. This applies especially if the actions of the administrative actors at different levels are organised hierarchically. In the light of increasing horizontal and vertical cooperation between the authorities themselves, it has to be considered whether these forms of administrative cooperation should not be followed by judicial cooperation.[61]

The following applies to judicial protection against *mixed inspections in horizontal or vertical cooperation*. Those inspectors, who participate only in an accompanying, or supervisory capacity in the control on the spot lack the proper authority to interfere with the economic operators who are checked. Therefore, they cannot take measures with regulatory effect which would offer the concerned party the possibility to seek judicial protection. Accordingly, any judicial protection – including preliminary – has to be sought according to the national provisions against national authorities, if these are leading authorities, and against the Community, if autonomous control by the Commission is concerned.[62]

The aspect of the legal protection raises questions concerning real "*common controls*", according to Article 4 Subparagraph (2) of Regulation No. 2185/96 (Control Regulation), for instance. These common controls are an independent form of control in addition to the Commission's controls, in which the member state control officials "only" participate in an accompanying role. Here, the question arises of whether judicial protection during the common controls should be provided by the CFI as well as by the national courts. It is certain that national participation in the common control has to be given greater significance than mere participation – if not, this additional possibility would not have been

61 See extensively about these questions concerning judicial protection in the European composite administration J. Hofmann, *Rechtsschutz und Haftung im Europäischen Verwaltungsverbund*, 2004, 215 ff., and his contribution in this volume, p. 447 et seq.; Priebe, ZLR 1990, pp. 266 and 286 also points at the danger of problematic allocation of individual acts to control officials and urges on the fact that control should not be improved and made more effective at the price of a reduced judicial protection or an uncertain liability for malpractice. The thoughts of Vervaele in his *Transnational Enforcement* (see fn. 51), pp. 53, and 89 ("integrated legal protection must be strived for") turn in the same direction and Widdershoven also, in: Vervaele, *Transnational Enforcement* (see fn. 51), pp. 131 and 143 ff. Also Harings, *Grenzüberschreitende Zusammenarbeit der Polizei- und Zollverwaltungen und Rechtsschutz in Deutschland*, 1998, p. 225 (pro transnational cooperation in police administration and customs officials); *id.*, EuR Beiheft 2/1998, pp. 81 and 96 ff.; *id.*, in this volume, p. 181 et seq.; Burgi, *Verwaltungsprozeß und Europearecht*, 1996, 56 (pro transnational administrative action) and Schmidt-Aßmann, JZ 1994, pp. 832 and 833 (with further examples for the different forms of "administrative interlocking" in administrative execution) emphasises the necessity of developments of an adequate system of transnational judicial protection; about "counter-rotating structural principles" followed by the "cooperative execution" and the common judicial system, also Klepper, *Vollzugskompetenzen der Europäischen Gemeinschaft aus abgeleitetem Recht*, 2001, 173 ff.

62 On this, see also Hofmann, *Rechtsschutz und Haftung* (fn. 61), 226 f.

added.[63] As a particularity of the common inspections, the Treaty text merely determines that the inspectors in the individual states are requested to countersign the report being made by the Commission's inspectors after a common inspection.[64] The other provisions do not differentiate whether an inspection is implemented as a common check or not. According to Articles 4 and 6, in particular, the preparation and implementation of a check on-the-spot, under the supervision and responsibility of the Commission, is carried out in close cooperation with the Member States. Due to a lack of explicit differentiation, this also applies to the common controls, implying that the common controls are also Community controls. As a consequence, judicial protection against these community controls can only be sought in the European courts. The definition of common control with the counter-signature on the control reports by the control inspectors of the Member States therefore only serves as better preparation of the sanctions and other following measures, which have to be made exclusively by the Member States.

In connection with the questions concerning judicial protection, it becomes obvious how problematic it is if Member States carry out *parallel proper procedures*, in addition to the Commission's control.[65] If the Member States, where the Commission implements autonomous controls at the economic operators, do not confine themselves to their accompanying role, the party being subject to the control always faces two authorities with autonomous control authorisations and may have to bring two lawsuits. This no longer has anything to do with procedural clarity or economy.

The implementation of inspections on request and the management of execution assistance (*Vollzugshilfe*) in horizontal and vertical respects are further cooperation constellations which are typical of administrative cooperation. They cause problems on points of judicial protection. Here too, the different levels of judicial protection must be differentiated. Inspections on request or the performance of execution assistance (*Vollzugshilfe*) in horizontal (e.g. banking supervision) and vertical respect (e.g. anti trust law) are performed by the requested Member State on its own responsibility and are not instigated by directives of the requesting Member State or the Commission. Through this, the independent intervention of the Member States has its own individual character, since the intervention is not completely determined by the requesting party but is only determined by the implementing authority concerning the content and the implementation.[66]

---

63 Also Ulrich, *Kontrollen* (fn. 57), 187.

64 Article 8(3) of Regulation No 2185/96 (fn. 20).

65 Cf. this practice of the Member States the Commission Staff Working Document on the application of Regulation No. 2185/96 SEC (2000), 844.

66 Rengeling/Middeke/Gellermann, *Rechtsschutz in der Europäischen Union*, 1994, mn. 149; Kadelbach, *Allgemeines Verwaltungsrecht unter europäischem Einfluss*, 1999, p. 339 ff. wants to permit legal protection against the request for administrative assistance as long as the

In the Hoechst case,[67] referring to the inspections of the Commission according to the anti-trust Regulation No. 17, the ECJ has differentiated the judicial protection levels as follows. The *investigation decision* of the Commission can only be examined on the European level, i.e. primarily by the CFI concerning its legitimacy. The CFI examines whether this measure appears arbitrary or disproportionate. The *national court*, on the other hand, is responsible for the control of the *enforcement* of this measure by direct force. It can declare the authenticity of the inspection decision and examine whether the intended coercive measure is arbitrary or – in relation to the subject of the investigation – disproportionate. The consideration regarding the subject and the legitimacy, which are the Commission's motive for ordering the investigation, however, are not subject to the judgement of the national court.[68] They are only subject to the legitimacy control of the ECJ (or the CFI).[69]

The allocation of responsibilities can be generalised to that effect that the basic act – i.e. in this case the investigation decision – as an act of the Commission is only subject to the control of the European judicial protection institutions. The power to carry out execution measures in the form of direct coercion, on the other hand, is allocated to the national authorities. Therefore, it is the national courts that enforce the check on legitimacy.[70] If they find the investigation decision illegal within the scope of the investigation of the execution act, they have to provoke an ECJ decision by way of preliminary ruling.

To promote the effectiveness of administrative and execution assistance in *horizontal relations* one could argue that also in these relations the assessment by the requesting authority has to be considered as being binding for the requested authority as well as for a court being in charge of the control of the execution assistance acts, as long as the necessity of execution assistance acts as

administrative assistance action is determined by the request for administrative assistance without the assisting authority having its own right to refuse. About the administrative assistance see Wettner, in this Volume, 313 ff. Further about the constellations of the liability concurrence in the administrative bond Hofmann, *Rechtsschutz und Haftung* (fn. 61), 330 ff.

67 ECJ, joined case 46/87 and 227/88 (Hoechst), European Court reports 1989, 2919 ff.

68 ECJ, *ibid.* The ECJ has linked its Hoechst case with a new case on 22.20.2002 (case C-94/00 Roquette Frères, EuZW 2003, 14 ff. with further comments by Feddersen): It was about the complexity of the investigation competence of a national (here French) court, which according to national law was responsible for the approval of investigation in corporations, if there was the suspicion concerning a violation against competition regulations. According to this ruling, the national court has to make sure essentially that serious evidence is available which is sufficient to support the suspicion in regard to a violation against competition regulations and to control the proportionality of the coercive measures measured on the subject of the investigation. In order to enable the national court to enforce its task, the Commission has to brief it about the main characteristics of the claimed violation. However, the national court cannot demand the transmission of the information and evidence in the records of the Commission on which their suspicion is based.

69 In detail about the allocation of the responsibility in judicial protection in the Hoechst case cf. Lenz/Mölls, WuW 1991, 771, 790 f.

70 Kamburoglou/Pirrwitz, RIW 1990, 263, 266 ff.

such is effected.[71] Therefore, the control by the courts of the Member State requesting administrative assistance is limited to examining the legitimacy of these administrative assistance actions. The legitimacy of the underlying request for the enforcement of inspections or the effort of execution aid, on the other hand, is not subject to the control of the courts of the requesting Member State.

The principle of separation (*Trennungsprinzip)* reaches its limits in those cases when judicial protection is not only sought against the inspection measures themselves, but also – and this would be the case more often – against those measures which the administration made according to the information it has received during the inspection (e.g., reclaiming finances, imposing obligations on firms, but also the inclusion in community information systems such as being listed as unreliable economic operator on the so-called Black List[72]). The party concerned will argue that malpractice during the enforcement of the controls lead to the illegality of the ensuing measure.

The power to impose a sanction on violations of EC law is usually allocated to the Member States.[73] Therefore, judicial protection against those sanction measures has to be sought at the courts of the Member State in question. In order to make the decision about the sanction measures, the Member States' administrations can use the results of the Commission's or other Member States' inspections as a basis. The divergence of the authorisation of the determination of the circumstances and of the sanctions has to be considered in a coherent judicial protection system. In detail, questions arise concerning the *appreciation of evidence* by the Member State courts, or the permissible *investigation complexity* concerning the binding nature of the results of the inspections on other administrative parties; these can only be indicated here. Some areas of Community law lack all provisions concerning the value of evidence and the inspection reports of the Commission or other responsible authorisations of other Member States, in particular.[74] Due to several individual provisions in other areas, the evidence material which has been collected by the Commission's

71 Also, Hatje, *Gemeinschaftsrechtliche Steuerung* (fn. 41), 137; in detail Schlag, *Grenzüberschreitende Verwaltungsbefugnisse im EG-Binnenmarkt*, 1998, 227 ff., especially 233 ff.; Groß, JZ 1994, 596, 604.

72 Especially about questions concerning judicial protection in connection with the acceptance in the so-called Black List cf. Krüger, ZfZ 1999, 74, 81 ff.

73 This is also emphasised by Priebe, ZLR 1990, 266, 270. About the (little) sanction competences of the Commission towards private parties, cf. Lenaerts, EuR 1997, 17, 18 ff.; shortly also Bleckmann, *Europarecht*, 6th edition, 1997, mn. 258.

74 This applies to fisheries law, e.g., cf. see the criticism by Berg, *European Fisheries Law* (fn. 51), 286 and Vervaele, in: id., *Transnational Enforcement* (fn. 51), 53, 88. Priebe, ZLR 1990, 266, 277, on the other hand, considers the recognition of an equal evidence value for the establishment of foreign and proper inspectors as natural – it should not be taken for granted by any court of the Community that it would differentiate the value of evidence of an authority detection only by the "origin" of the controlling officer; about transnational questions concerning the evidence effect also Jans/de Lange/Prechal/Widdershoven, Europees bestuursrecht (fn. 1), 252 ff.

officials or other Member States (usually, control reports, but also other information or notifications could be considered), has the same evidential value as the reports of the national officials.[75] Therefore, one step forward has been made towards a complete lack of evidence rules. However, in the long term it will not be sufficient if the EC provisions only refer to the national provisions on evidence. They can be completely different,[76] as in some countries the signature of the party affected on the inspection report is necessary and in others it is not. These differences can lead to inspection reports not being used uniformly as evidence. Therefore, the aim should be to replace the references in national law by uniform provisions on evidence at Community level in the future.

In the light of the cooperation procedures described, a consistent system of individual judicial protection must not persevere undifferentiated with the separation dogma.[77]

4. CONCLUSION

Behind the different definitions of the inspection, the aim of serving the inter-administrative building of confidence becomes clear. The inspections label the administration in the composite administration as a complex of hierarchic and cooperative elements. In *vertical relations*, the inspections can fairly be characterised as instruments of cooperative supervision. In *horizontal relations*, the aspect of trust building must be especially emphasised. However, those characteristics do not stand isolated next to each other. The supervision structures, which become obvious in the administrative inspection relationship, show *control interlacings* which serve the building of or trust especially. The success of a project depends essentially on the fact that the participants stick to their own created rules. The allocation of supervision authorisations to a central control authority supports confidence that each Member State will actually fulfil its administrative obligations. The opportunities for official experts from other Member States to participate in the Commission's inspections not only serve the inclusion of external expert knowledge, but also increase trust. On the contrary,

---

75 Article 8(3) of Regulation No. 2185/96 (fn. 20), on this Kuhl/Spitzer, *EuZW* 1998, 37, 41; Article 12, 16 of Regulation No 515/97 (fn. 17), also see Article 17 of Regulation No. 2729/2000 (fn. 32 "The findings of the specific officials of the Commission or the officials of a competent body of a Member State in the course of application of this Title may be invoked by the competent bodies of the other Member States or by the Commission. In such cases, they shall have no less value because of the fact that they do not come from the Member State in question."; about the appreciation of evidence in transnational circumstances in general, Hatje, *Gemeinschaftsrechtliche Steuerung* (fn. 41), 215 f.

76 This is also emphasised by Vervaele, in: id., *Transnational Enforcement* (fn. 51), 53, 83.

77 For the further development Schmidt-Aßmann, JZ 1994, 832, 839, does not only propose clear allocations according to the particular cooperation contribution, but also forms of judicial protection concentration.

the described mechanisms do not only work as trust- building, but also include control elements: each request for cooperation contributions is a new "test case" for the functionality of a horizontally networked administrative system.[78] Administrative cooperation is the expression of a common responsibility for the effective execution of Community law. As much as flexibility is asked for, a certain juridification of the inter-administrative cooperation standard has already been made and is able to improve further.

With the common responsibility for the administration of the Community area, there is a corresponding common responsibility for compliance with constitutional principles with regard to those who embody this Community area, the people of the Union. The extension and the development of an individual (judicial) protection system, which is in line with the administrative cooperation which is part of the European composite administration remains an urgent task of the application of law and legal scholarship.

---

78 The effect of control networks in increasing trust is analysed by Schmidt-Aßmann, in: *Festschrift für Steinberger* (fn. 36), 1375 (1396 f.); *id.* in this volume, p. 1 et seq.; cf. also *id.*, in: Schmidt-Aßmann/Hoffmann-Riem, *Verwaltungskontrolle* (fn. 5), p. 9 and 32 ff.

XVI. EC GRANT MANAGEMENT AS A CHALLENGE FOR EUROPEAN ADMINISTRATIVE LAW*

Wolfgang Schenk

1. INTRODUCTION

European grant management makes use of the allocation of various European grants (2). The budget regulation reform of 2002 gave the law of Community grant management a comprehensive legal framework which, for the first time, also included substantial system guidelines for the general European administrative law (3).

2. COMMUNITY GRANTS

The general budget of the European Communities[1] provides appropriations for grants in various areas of common policy. These funds can be divided into three large categories of expenditure.

The expenditure within the Common Agricultural Policy and the policy aiming at economic and social cohesion (Cohesion Policy) are still given first priority. Each year over three quarters of the appropriations at the Community's disposal are spent on these two policy areas. This is significant due to the nature of the Common Market, which inevitably involves this expenditure. With respect to agriculture, this is expressed in Article 32 of the EC Treaty. The bulk of agricultural expenditure is still linked to the considerable differences concerning agriculture between, but also within, the Member States. The expenditure which is planned to reach the cohesion target (Article 158 of the EC Treaty) is also

* This essay (in German) was first published in 'Eberhard Schmidt-Aßmann and Bettina Schöndorf-Haubold, Der Europäische Verwaltungsverbund, Mohr Siebeck 2005, p. 265–291. It is based upon the authors PhD research, which has been published as Wolfgang Schenk, Strukturen und Rechtsfragen der gemeinschaftlichen Leistungsverwaltung, Mohr Siebeck, Tübingen 2006.

1 Compare the 'General Budget of the European Union for the financial year 2004', adapted according to the enlargement, OJ 2004 No. C 105, 2 volumes.

meant to contribute, in particular, to mitigating the disadvantages related to the Common Market as well as to allowing for making use of the opportunities it offers. In addition to this, the budget also serves to finance activities largely in the areas of research and development, education, cultural affairs and the environment. As the Community lacks more far-reaching legislative competence, grants within these internal policy areas are often the sole instruments for framing and controlling which are available to the Community.[2] Lastly, the Community also plays an important role in the area of the funding of activities in third countries. Not only does this funding concern development cooperation, but it also concerns such activities as reconstruction in the former Yugoslav countries as well as actions to assist countries in their preparations for a possible future membership in the Community (pre-accession assistance).

The Community grants often do not cover the overall costs of an activity. The prospect of Community funding is meant rather to encourage the appropriation of private and public funds in the respective Member States and third countries. In this way, these countries also contribute to the realisation of the objective which is connected with the Community grant and increase the effectiveness of the use of Community funds. This public co-financing, in the area of the cohesion policy in particular, also reflects a mutual responsibility of the Community and the Member State for specific objectives in the common interest.

3. RULES ON THE ALLOCATION OF COMMUNITY GRANTS: COMMUNITY GRANT MANAGEMENT LAW

3.1. INTRODUCTION

The allocation of these grants[3] imposes high demands on European administrative law and the European administration. Two of these aspects will be illustrated in the following section. On the one hand, the nature of grants requires extensive operations of analysing, planning, evaluating and selecting before they are actually awarded to a beneficiary. The expenditure on agriculture

[2] Explicit in particular in recital 13, Decision No. 1230/2003/EC of the European Parliament and of the Council of 26 June 2003 adopting a multi annual programme for action in the field of energy: 'Intelligent Energy for Europe' Programme (2003–2006) (OJ 2003 No. L 176, p. 29): 'Since many Community measures on energy efficiency [...] are not binding on the Member States, there is a need for specific promotion programmes at Community level to create the conditions for moving towards sustainable energy systems.'

[3] As regards European administrative law as grant management *Schmidt-Aßmann*, in: Cremer et al. (eds.), FS für Steinberger, 2002, 1375 (1378).

is the only exception where the beneficiary and the amount of grants are prefixed in detail due to the provision laid down in secondary law.

Moreover, the public co-financing and the allocation of competence between the Community and the Member States regarding the administrative implementation involve the responsibility of the administrations of Member States and third countries for the award of grants financed by Community funds, implying, therefore, that these countries also have to manage Community funds. Although they are bound to adhere to the Community legal provisions, it is at the same time in their interest that as many funds as possible are used within their territory.[4] This conflicting relationship can only be resolved in favour of legitimate administrative behaviour.

So far, these demands have not been met to the full extent. A number of administrative irregularities[5] within the allocation of Community grants which have been revealed are responsible for the Commission's resignation in 1999 to a considerable extent and for the ensuing process of the 'Reform of the Commission'[6] which had a great effect on the term of the subsequent Commission. The reform included basic models for the allocation of Community grants (3.2.). Furthermore, the organisation and procedure of the allocation have been changed at Community level (3.3.). Although the reform did not include the mechanisms which are required if the decision on the funding of a specific action is to be reached at Member State level, these are still significant (3.4.). Of particular importance for the further development of the Community grant management was the enactment of a new budget regulation.[7] This already indicates that Community grant management is significantly influenced by the relation of administrative and budgetary implementation, which is quite complicated even at Community level. This relation will play a key role in the course of the following explanations.

---

4 In this context compare the continuous political discussion about the role of Member States as net contributors or recipients.

5 *Committee of Independent Experts,* First Report on Allegations regarding Fraud, Mismanagement and Nepotism in the European Commission, 15 March 1999 (www.europarl.eu.int/experts/report1_de.htm; as of: 24 January 2004).

6 In this context see in particular *Commission*, Reforming the Commission – White Paper COM (2000) 200 final/2 (2 volumes); most recently *id.*, Communication from the Commission – Completing the Reform Mandate: Progress Report and Measures to be implemented in 2004. COM (2004) 93 final.

7 Council Regulation (EC, Euratom) No. 1605/2002 of 25 June 2002 on the Financial Regulation applicable to the general budget of the European Communities (OJ L 248/1 p. 1; hereinafter: FR 2002).

3.2. BASIC MODELS FOR THE ALLOCATION OF COMMUNITY GRANTS

3.2.1. Introduction

In accordance with the first paragraph of Article 53 of the new Financial Regulation, the budget is implemented by the Commission by shared or decentralised management or by joint management with international organisations. The standards attached[8] and the rules for the implementation of the budget regulation[9] explain and describe these basic models in detail.[10]

In fact, these models imply only few fundamental innovations. Predominantly, they systematise the administrative structures which have developed in the area of specific legislation for more than three decades. But special attention should be paid to the standards, as they represent the first attempt in the area of European administrative law to legally include at least the essentials of different administration models detached from special areas of expenditure for the purpose of Article 249(2) of the EC Treaty and thus form a binding legal instrument.[11]

3.2.2. Presentation of the different models[12]

Centralised management of funds

When Community grants are allocated at Community level, the funds are managed centrally; on this centralised basis, the funds can be managed either directly or indirectly.

In the case of *direct centralised management*, the Commission itself awards the grants.[13] Due to the division of powers within the Commission, it is usually the Directors-General who are responsible for the funding decisions and the legal commitment to the beneficiaries.[14] Grants generated for the promotion of research and technical development, in particular, are managed centrally and

---

8 Article 53 para. 2–57 FR 2002.

9 Articles 35–43 Commission Regulation (EC, Euratom) No. 2342/2002 of 23 December 2002 laying down detailed rules for the implementation of Council Regulation (EC, Euratom) No. 1605/2002 on the Financial Regulation applicable to the general budget of the European Communities (OJ L 357 of 31 December 2002, p. 1; hereinafter: RfI FR 2002).

10 See below 3.2.2.

11 Cf. Craig, ELRev 2003, 840 (841): '*The new Financial Regulation now provides a legal framework for the structure of Community administration*'. However, in principle this statement is to be restricted to European grant management.

12 See also Craig, ELRev 2003, 840 (841 ff.).

13 Article 53 2. 1st alternative FR 2002.

14 Cf. Reichenbach/von Witzleben, *Verwaltungsmodernisierung in der EU-Kommission*, in: Siedentopf (eds.), *Der Europäische Verwaltungsraum*, 2004, 39 (41).

directly.[15] At present, the legal basis for this promotion is the decision concerning the sixth framework programme of the European Community for research, technological development and demonstration activities[16] and the specific programmes for the purpose of its implementation[17] (compare Article 166 of the EC Treaty).

In the case of *indirect centralised management*, however, the Commission delegates the management tasks as well as the financial management to legally independent bodies[18] such as executive, Community or so-called national agencies.

The *executive agency*,[19] which is governed by Community law, is a type of body that has been established in the course of the reform for the specific purpose of Community grant management. Executive agencies are set up by means of a decision by the Commission. The 'Intelligent Energy Executive Agency' is the first institution of its kind.[20] It is responsible for the implementation of certain tasks in the context of the Community funding within the scope of the programme 'Intelligent energy – Europe'.[21]

Although *Community agencies*[22] are legal persons governed by Community law, they differ from executive agencies in that they are established by means of a regulation which is, depending on the legal basis, promulgated exclusively by the Council or together with the Parliament. Community agencies can be classified in different categories.[23] At present the Salonika-based European Agency for Reconstruction[24] is the only Community agency to perform grant managerial tasks on a considerable scale. It is responsible for the most important aid

15 With regard to the mechanism of centralised direct management see below 3.3.

16 Decision No. 1513/2002/EC of the European Parliament and of the Council of 27 June 2002 concerning the sixth framework programme of the European Community for research, technological development and demonstration activities, contributing to the creation of the European Research Area and to innovation (2002 to 2006).

17 Council Decision of 30 September 2002, adopting a specific programme for research, technological development and demonstration: 'Integrating and strengthening the European Research Area' (2002–2006) (2002/834/EC OJ 2002 No. L 294, p. 1) and the 'structuring the European Research Area' (2002–2006) (2002/835/EC OJ 2002 No. L 294, p. 44) as well as a specific programme (Euratom) for research and training on nuclear energy (2002 to 2006) (2002/837/Euratom OJ 2002 No. L 294, 29 October 2002, p. 74).

18 Article 53 2. 2nd alternative, Art. 54 2., 3., Article 56 FR 2002.

19 Article 55 FR 2002. With regard to the executive agencies see below B.II.2 in more detail.

20 Commission Decision of 23 December 2003 setting up an executive agency, the 'Intelligent Energy Executive Agency', to manage Community action in the field of energy in application of Council Regulation (EC) No. 58/2003 (OJ EU 2004 No. L 5, p. 85).

21 Decision No. 1230/2003/EC (fn. 2).

22 With regard to this term Schmidt-Aßmann, in: Blankenagel et al. (eds.), FS für Häberle, 2004, 395 (401).

23 See *Commission,* Communication from the Commission: The operating framework for the European Regulatory Agencies, COM (2002) 718 final.

24 Council Regulation (EC) No. 2667/2000 on the European Agency for Reconstruction (OJ 2000 No. L 306, p. 7).

programmes[25] for the former Yugoslavia countries and maintains operational centres in Pristina, Belgrade, Podgorica and Skjope for this purpose. Its mission makes the European Agency for Reconstruction currently an alien element among the Community agencies. This is the reason – more than any other – that it can best be classified in the category of 'additional management resource of the Community'.

Finally, the allocation of Community grants involving *national agencies* represents a model where the Commission includes public bodies belonging to the different Member States, or bodies governed by private law – provided that they fulfil certain requirements in terms of organisation and financial management.[26] This model is currently applied in the award of Erasmus mobility grants for students on the basis of the Socrates programme, for example.[27] The Member States appoint a Socrates/Erasmus National Agency, which allocates benefits to eligible universities for the purpose of mobility grants. Public or private universities which have arranged an arrangement with a partner university concerning the required places for exchange students are eligible and they receive a so-called Erasmus University Charta by the Commission. Due to arrangements with the Commission, it is the national agency (the DAAD in Germany) which allocates the overall subsidies. The universities, for their part, award the individual scholarships and in doing so act as Community management authorities. Basically, this complicated administrative structure, which is characterised by contractual relations, consists of what is called 'management by networks of national agencies'[28] by the Commission. However, this network is formed primarily between the Commission and the respective

25 On the basis of Council Regulation (EC) No. 2666/2000 on assistance for Albania, Bosnia and Herzegovina, Croatia, the Federal Republic of Yugoslavia and the Former Yugoslav Republic of Macedonia (OJ 2000 No. L 306, p. 1). For lack of specific primary law authorisation this Council Regulation as well as Council Regulation (EC) No. 2667/2000 (fn. 24) are based on Art. 308 of the EC Treaty. This seems to be problematic as the reconstruction aid hardly contributes to achieve one of the Community's objectives 'in the course of the operation of the common market'. Thus the politically desired action of the Community lacks legal certainty.

26 See in particular Craig, ELRev 2003, 840 (852).

27 Decision No. 253/2000/EC of the European Parliament and of the Council of 24 January 2000 establishing the second phase of the Community action programme in the field of education 'Socrates' (OJ 2000 No. L 28, p. 1).

28 Cf. *Commission*, Communication from the Commission – Management of Community programmes by networks of national agencies COM (2001) 648 final. The concept of a network administration does not only exist in the European grant management law: in accordance with the fundamental reform of the antitrust procedure law set up by Council Regulation (EC) No. 1/2003 (of 16 December 2002 on the implementation of the rules on competition laid down in Articles 81 and 82 of the EC Treaty [OJ 2003 No. L 1, p. 1]), the Commission and the competition authorities of the Member States should 'form together a network of public authorities applying the Community competition rules in close cooperation', so recital 15; with regard to this see in particular *Commission*, Commission Notice on cooperation within the Network of Competition Authorities, OJ 2004 No. C 101, p. 43; Schweda, *Wirtschaft und Wettbewerb* 2004, 1133 ff.; Böge, *Europäisches Wirtschafts-*

national agencies but only on a small scale between the national agencies themselves. For this reason, it may be more accurate to depict this administrative structure by describing it as 'star administration'.

Shared management of funds

As for the shared management of funds, the Member State as such is responsible for the tasks in the context of the allocation of Community grants.[29] The national level on which they are performed depends on the respective national division of powers. Principally, the Commission has no firm control over certain institutions in the Member States. This represents the fundamental difference with the indirect centralised management involving national agencies. Most grants in the context of the Common agricultural and cohesion policy[30] are awarded on the basis of shared management. As the Financial Regulation refers solely to these two areas, it assumes that this administration model cannot be applied beyond them.

Decentralised and joint management

When funds are managed on a decentralised basis, third countries perform tasks relating to the allocation of Community grants, whereas international organisations fulfil this role with regard to joint management.[31] At present, decentralised management can be found in the context of grants for the purpose of bringing acceding countries closer to the EU.

3.2.3. The overarching meaning of Article 274(1)(1) of the EC Treaty

In compliance with the first paragraph of Article 53 of the Financial Regulation, the budget is implemented by the Commission according to the models mentioned above. This leads to Article 274(1)(1) of the EC Treaty: the Commission implements the budget drawn up jointly by the Council and the Parliament[32] pursuant to Article 272 of the EC Treaty on its own responsibility. The central role played by Article 274(1)(1) of the EC Treaty in the area of Community management of grants will be elaborated on in the following sections.

---

und Steuerrecht 2003, 441 ff.; id./Scheidgen, *Europäisches Wirtschafts- und Steuerrecht 2002*, 201 ff.

29 Cf. Article 53 3 FR 2002.

30 See below 3.4.

31 Article 53 4. – para. 6 or Article 53 7. FR 2002.

32 Cf. Streinz, *Europarecht*, 6th ed. 2003, marginal number (= mn.) 586 ff.

Article 274(1)(1) of the EC Treaty as a provision defining powers

Article 274(1)(1) of the EC Treaty is particularly important with regard to the configuration of the European law of grant management. Apart from union competence of the Community, this regulation includes an institutional competence of the Commission and defines the Commission's autonomy in implementing the Community budget.[33] As far as the comitology decision is concerned,[34] the Commission, in particular, cannot be bound to procedures beyond the hearings procedure for measures relating to the budgetary implementation.[35]

However, for the awarding of Community grants, no special competence of administrative implementation of the Community and the Commission follows from Article 274(1)(1) of the EC-Treaty. In a fundamental judgement, the Court of Justice decided accordingly.[36] The criticism on this judgement expressed in various literature on this subject[37] fails to be convincing. The Commission's competence only refers to the implementation of the budget according to the principles of sound financial management. It does not, however, refer to administrative adoption of the legal acts regulating the basis of Community grants (so-called basic legislative acts). For this reason, the Court of Justice rightfully decided that 'the Commission's power to implement the budget is not such as to modify the division of powers resulting from the various provisions of the Treaty which authorize the Council and the Commission to adopt generally applicable or individual measures within specific areas, and from the institutional provisions of the third indent of Article 202 and Article 211'.[38]

In the first instance, the Community budget implementation consists of financially finalising the decisions on Community expenditure reached as part

---

[33] ECJ, case 93/85 – Commission *v* United Kingdom, [1986] ECR 4011 (mn. 21); *Magiera*, in: Grabitz/Hilf (eds.), Recht der Europäischen Union, Altband II, Art. 205 TEC (EL 7) mn. 1; *Niedobitek*, in: Streinz (eds.), EU/EC Treaty, 2003, Art. 274 TEC mn. 2.

[34] Council Decision of 28 June 1999 laying down the procedures for the exercise of implementing powers conferred on the Commission (1999/468/EC) (OJ 1999 No. L 184, p. 23; hereinafter Comitology decision); in this regard compare Lenaerts/Verhoeven, [2000] CMLR 645 ff.; Mensching, EuZW 2000, 268 ff.; in regard to comitology procedures Schmidt-Aßmann, in: FS für Steinberger (fn. 3), 1375 (1393 ff.).

[35] *Magiera*, in: Grabitz/Hilf, EU/EC Treaty (fn. 33), Art. 205 EC Treaty (EL 7) mn. 1.

[36] ECJ, case 16/88 – Commission *v* Council, [1989] ECR 3457; in this regard see Forman, [1990] CMLR 872 ff.

[37] See in particular Bieber, in: von der Groeben/Schwarze (eds.), EU/EC Treaty, 6th Edition 2004, Art. 274 TEC mn. 15 f. See also Magiera, in: Grabitz/Hilf, EU/EC Treaty (fn. 33), Art. 205 TEC (EL 7) paragraph 1; Niedobitek, in: Streinz, EU/EC Treaty (fn. 33), Art. 274 TEC mn. 10; Schoo, in: Schwarze (eds.), EU Commentary, 2000, Art. 274 TEC mn. 10 f.

[38] ECJ, case 16/88 – Commission *v* Council, [1989] ECR 3457 (mn. 16): Court of Auditors opinion No. 2/2001 on a proposal for a Council regulation for the Financial Regulation applicable to the general budget of the European Communities, OJ 2001 No. C 162, p. 1 (44 f.). In regard to the concept of implementation for the purposes of Article 202, Article 211 TEC see *Möllers*, EuR 2002, 483 ff.

of the administrative process. Correspondingly, the administrative and budgetary implementation are necessarily related. Still, according to the conception of primary law, a specific measure does not pertain to the administrative and budgetary implementation at the same time.[39] So Article 274(1)(1) of the EC Treaty is not opposed to the administrative and financial management on the part of third parties, the Member States in particular. Article 274(1)(1) of the EC Treaty rather assumes the latter administration model. However, Member States do not implement the budget within the meaning of Article 274(1)(1) of the EC Treaty when they manage Community funds.[40] The general budget is only[41] to be implemented by the Commission. The Commission's competence is exclusive under Article 274(1)(1) of the EC Treaty and cannot be delegated to the Member States – not even for the purpose of implementation only. This also follows from Article 274(1)(1) of the Treaty which refers to the Member States' use of funds but not to the implementation. Moreover, the result is that the European Parliament only gives discharge to the Commission in respect of the budget implementation as regards the last phase of the budget procedure, and not, however, to Member States or even other third parties.[42]

Attribution of responsibility according to Article 274(1)(1) of the EC Treaty

In accordance with Article 274(1)(1) of the EC Treaty, the Commission implements the budget 'on its own responsibility'. Consequently, each grant funded by the Community budget has to be attributable to the Commission in such a way that it can be held accountable by the Parliament as discharge authority for this specific expenditure. In this respect, Article 274(1)(1) also has a significant organisational and procedural dimension.

Within the areas where the Commission decides on concrete funding on its own account, it can usually assume this responsibility without any problems. When taking this decision, the Commission can take care of compliance with the relevant legal and particularly normative[43] regulations directly.

However, more problems are caused when responsibilities are assumed in areas where individual grant decisions are made by third parties, particularly due to the absence of Community competence with respect to administrative implementation on the part of the Member States, or where the responsibilities

39 However, this does not indicate that such double assigning is not provided for by secondary law.

40 See *Committee of Independent Experts*, Second report on Reform of the Commission, 10 September 1999 (www.europarl.eu.int/experts/default_de.htm; as of: 24 January 2004) I.3.1.6: 'It is the Commission which implements the budget on its own responsibility, a responsibility not shared with the other Institutions or the Member States.'

41 The only exception is the position of the other independent institutions relating to the implementation of their sections in accordance with Article 274 2. TEC.

42 See Niedobitek, in: Streinz, EU/EC Treaty (fn. 33), Article 276 TEC mn. 6.

43 Other legal requirements can be a particular result of the comitology procedure; cf. ECJ, case 16/88 – Commission *v* Council [1989] ECR 3457.

are otherwise vested in a third party due to delegation. For these areas Article 274(1)(1) of the EC Treaty calls for a certain legal instrument available to the Commission which has to allow the Commission the opportunity to verify the legality of the expenditure that the third party intends or already has implemented at the expense of the Community budget and, if required, to exclude the expenditure from Community funding. The Commission then has either to refuse the funding to the third parties or has to be able to claim back Community funds that have already been made available to third parties for the purpose of financial management.[44] In the case that the third party manages the budgetary funds on the basis of Community secondary law, Community law has to arrange the relationship between the Commission and the third party accordingly. If the Commission delegates the management of Community budgetary funds to third parties on its own account,[45] it is bound to reserve the appropriate legal options concerning the delegation as defined in Article 274(1)(1) of the EC Treaty. When there is no such instrument at the Commission's disposal, the management of budgetary funds by third parties contravenes Article 274(1)(1) of the EC Treaty. In that case, the violation is indirect as the Council in the capacity of sole Community legislator arranged the secondary law inadequately and also restricted the discharge competence of the European parliament in an inadmissible way, so that the Commission cannot be held accountable for its incompatibility with primary law. The Commission can be held fully responsible, however, when the legal instrument was available but was not used consistently because of the Commission's wish to make concessions to Member States, for example, and thereby Community law was ignored.[46]

Differentiation between budget implementation and funds management

In this context, a certain phrasing in the new Financial Regulation on the basic models for the purpose of awarding Community grants seems problematic. It is not the budget implementation by the Commission that is performed in accordance with the stated principles.[47] In addition, the Commission does not delegate tasks relating to the budget implementation to third parties.[48] Third

44 This conception of Article 274(1)(1) TEC also forms the basis of Article 53 5. FR 2002; also compare *Committee of Independent Experts*, Second report (fn. 40), I.3.1.6.: 'Community legislation [...] must respect this Treaty provision by giving the Commission the powers to exercise this responsibility and to fulfil its obligation of accountability to the discharge authority.'

45 Such a transfer decision is not yet an implementation of the budget; in such a case it is only the payment of real and effective contributions for the purpose of further financial management which belongs to the budget implementation.

46 Concisely expressed *Committee of Independent Experts*, Second report (fn. 40), I.3.1.7: 'The realisation of the 'acquis communautaire' in this field should not be limited to legal texts.'

47 See however Article 53 1. FR 2002.

48 See however Article 53 3., 4., Article 54 2. FR 2002. With regard to an apparent exception relating to executive agencies, see below.

parties can, as stated above, manage Community funds but they never implement the budget. The intention to dispel concerns regarding their competence is likely to be the reason for the phrasing. The Financial Regulation is based on Article 279(1)(a) of the EC Treaty which, by its wording, only legitimates implementing the budget 'specifying in particular the procedure to be adopted for establishing and implementing the budget'. In contrast, regulations concerning the general administrative (organisational) law are not stated explicitly.[49]

3.3. CENTRALISED MANAGEMENT OF FUNDS

3.3.1. Introduction

With respect to the area of centralised management this article will examine two aspects in detail. First, it will introduce the general provisions for the procedure of direct centralised management as well as the financing agreements concluded in this context (3.3.2), and second, the executive agency as a new organisational form of the Community shall be examined in greater detail (3.3.3).

3.3.2. General provisions for the procedure and the financing Agreements

In order to implement an expenditure, the implementation of the budget requires a budgetary commitment, a validation, an authorisation and a payment.[50] The budgetary commitment is included by primary law in Article 248(2)(3). It is the operation reserving the appropriation necessary, in order to cover subsequent payments to honour a legal commitment. Thus, it represents the precondition for the Community to enter a legal commitment.[51] As regards the direct centralised budgetary commitment, the Community makes legal commitments to the beneficiary of a Community grant.

The granting procedure

For the first time, the new Financial Regulation provides general regulations for the grant procedure which precedes the legal commitment.[52] Particular importance is attached to the procedure's transparency and equal treatment of

49 See also below.

50 Article 75 1. FR 2002.

51 Article 76 1 subparagraph 1 FR 2002. When the budgetary commitment becomes binding, a commitment appropriation is used as regards differentiated appropriations; as for non-differentiated appropriations, the commitment is the first paragraph of the budgetary implementation. On the system of differentiated and non-differentiated appropriations as well as the commitment and payment appropriations Article 7 1. FR 2002.

52 Article 108 ff. FR 2002, Article 160 ff. RfI FR 2002.

the potential beneficiaries[53] of grants and avoidance of any conflicts of interest of persons involved in the Commission's procurement procedure. The award procedure will be briefly described in the following section.

For the generally multi-annual support programmes, an annual plan has to be adopted which is subject to the requirements of publication.[54] Such a plan comprises the programme's priorities and objectives as well as a provisional division of the funds provided by the budget. The adoption of the annual plan, a decision which is political to a greater degree, is reserved for the College of Commissioners. The adoption belongs to the normative implementation of the basic legislative act.[55] This is why the Commission, as a rule, decides by the procedure of comitology.[56] The basic legislative act is to provide the management procedure in accordance with the criteria of the comitology decision,[57] which are still non-binding.[58]

The annual plan forms the basis for the first phase of the award procedure, the call for proposals. This call is to be published at least on the internet and in the Official Journal of the EU in order to reach the broad circle of potential proposers and it must include, in particular, the criteria by which the proposals will be evaluated in the selection and award process. On the one hand, the indication of these criteria is to set the costly and time-consuming production of the proposals more precisely and target-oriented in a context, and on the other, it serves as basis for understanding the reasons for the subsequent selection decision.

A first assessment of the proposals is made by a committee consisting of Commission officials which can be supported by authorised experts. The selection decision is made in the light of this judgement. It comprises a list of beneficiaries with the amounts determined for them and has to be based on the selection and award criteria. According to jurisdiction, such decisions are contestable as defined in the fourth paragraph of Article 230 of the EC Treaty.[59] They are legally binding[60] in so far as the exclusion of a proposal from the list

---

53 Article 109 1. FR 2002; *Commission*, Proposal for a Council Regulation (EC, ECSC, Euratom) on the financial regulation applicable to the general budget of the European Communities, COM (2000) 461 final, p. 24.

54 *E.g.* 'Commission Decision of 25 February 2004 adopting the work plan for 2004 for the implementation of the programme of Community action in the field of public health (2003 to 2008), including the annual work programme for grants (2004/192/EC)' (OJ 2004 No. L 60, p. 58).

55 On the definition of basic act see above 3.2.3.

56 Cf. recital 6 of the decision No. 2004/192/EC (fn. 54).

57 Article 2 (a)alt. of the comitology decision (fn. 34).

58 ECJ, case C-378/00 – COM *v* Parliament and Council, [2003] ECR I-937 (mn. 43 ff.); Lenaerts/Verhoeven, [2000] CMLR 645 (666).

59 ECJ, case C-48/96 P – Windpark Groothusen, [1998] ECR I-2873 (mn. 25 f.).

60 On the condition of the decision within the meaning of Article 230 4. TEC *Röhl*, ZaöRV 2000, 331 (341 ff.).

represents its ultimate rejection.[61] This selection decision is also usually made in a procedure of comitology. The appropriate procedure is to be defined in the respective basic act.

The award procedure ends with written statements to the proposers disclosing the decisions on the proposals. Notifications of rejections include relevant reasons so that the person concerned receives precise information on the content and the reasons of the decision.[62] In this way, the statement measures up to the requirements that have to be met for the start of the period for filing the action defined in Article 230(5) of the EC Treaty.

Financing agreements

A written financing agreement, that is a contract between the Community and the beneficiary of the grant, is required as a form of action for entering the legal commitment in the context of the direct centralised management of funds. This implies that adoption in the list does not yet qualify the proposer for receiving Community grants. So the notification to the selected proposer is only a call for entering into contract negotiations with the Commission. The room for negotiation is, however, limited. The Commission has to take several binding provisions of the Financial Regulation into account and, furthermore, the action to be funded is predefined to a large extent by the proposal in the award procedure.

The financing agreements have to provide, in particular, a check on the beneficiaries and, where applicable, on the contractor for the Commission's and Court of Auditor's authorisation with a view to the monitoring the correct use of the Community funds by the beneficiary. By means of the latter provisions, these financing agreements could even influence the form of contracts that are concluded as part of the context of implementing the action funded by the Community. The unilateral rights of redress,[63] however, which are conferred on the Commission in the case of an assumed violation of the obligations on the part of the beneficiary, provided for in the legislation and the financing agreement, are no longer in line with the contractual context of the relationship between the Commission and the beneficiary. In such cases, the Commission can suspend, reduce or cancel the financial aid after the beneficiary has been given the opportunity to comment. This leads to a privileged position for the Commission and it gives the beneficiary an own responsibility to start possible proceedings. Effective financial management is, in fact, desirable, but since such matters are likely to be clarified by the courts anyway, the standardisation of rights to refuse grants or claims to repayment, pertinent to the contractual

61 Cf. ECJ, case C-48/96 P – Windpark Groothusen, [1998] ECR I-2873 (mn. 19).
62 ECJ, case C-48/96 P – Windpark Groothusen, [1998] ECR I-2873 (mn. 25).
63 J.-P. Schneider, VVDStRL 2005.

framework, would have been sufficient. But above all, it would not have evoked such an alien element within the contractual relations.

The Community's authority to conclude contracts is provided for in primary law in Article 238 and in Article 288(1) of the EC Treaty. Contracts closed by the Community can be governed by public or private law.[64] As the financing agreements – in contrast to the award of contracts by the Community[65] – are concluded directly for the purpose of implementing a Community policy provided for in primary law,[66] it seems reasonable to classify them under public-sector contracts of the Community. The fact that the contracts include additional references to the private law of a Member State, is also not initially contrary. German law, for example in §62(2) of the Administrative Procedures Law (VwVfG), explicitly demands the additional application of private law to contracts governed by public law. In the Commission's opinion, however, such financing agreements are governed exclusively by private law.[67]

The role of the authorising officer

From now on, only one person is required to be responsible for the budgetary commitment, the implementation of the award procedure and, in particular, for the selection decision and the legal commitment. This person, the 'responsible authorising officer'[68] is usually the corresponding Director-General and thus a highest-ranking officer. He is fully responsible to the College of Commissioners for awarding a grant. This is supposed to create a climate where officers cannot evade their responsibility[69] and which is intended to improve the administrative culture in the Commission considerably.[70] The former allocation of powers to

64 So far, the administrative contracts of the Community represent an area which has received little attention in the scientific world; see, however, Bleckmann, DVBl. 1981, 889 ff.; Grunwald, EuR 1984, 227 ff. The following consideration is by no means intended to anticipate an extensive examination.

65 Article 88 ff. FR 2002, Article 116 ff. RfI FR 2002; these rules are geared to the conditions for the award of contracts/procurement by the Member States. On the adherent 'parallelisation' Schmidt-Aßmann, *Das allgemeine Verwaltungsrecht als Ordnungsidee*, 2nd ed. 2004, Chapter 7 mn. 16.

66 Karpenstein, in: Grabitz/Hilf (Eds.), *Das Recht der Europäischen Union*, Lsbl., Volume II, Article 238 TEC (EL 16) mn. 17. Ultimately, on the basis of this criterion classified as contract governed by public law see also Pfeiffer, *Die Forschungs- und Technologiepolitik der Europäischen Gemeinschaften als Referenzgebiet für das europäische Verwaltungsrecht*, 2003, 206 ff.

67 Cf. the report on its presentation in *CFI*, case T-85/01 – Commission v SNUA mn. 21 ff.

68 The powers of authorisation concern the authorisation to adopt specific legal acts regarding the budget implementation. The Financial Regulation also allocates the responsibility for administrative tasks to the authority officer.

69 *Commission*, EU reform part I (fn. 6), in particular at pages 8, 24. In detail and with a presentation of the previous legal situation Craig ELRev 2003, 840 (845 ff.). See also the extensive research by Harlow, *Accountability in the European Union*, 2002.

70 Priebe, DV 2000, 379 ff.; Mehde, ZEuS 2001, 403 ff.; *id.*, [2003] CMLR 423 ff.

various persons within the Commission resulted in a system in which the different persons involved were less likely to feel responsible.

Codification of a general law of grant management

The codification of a general law of grant management in a regulation is appreciated, and it can help to increase the transparency of the procedures and prevent irregularities. Still, it seems arguable whether Article 279(1)(1)(a) of the EC Treaty can form the legal basis for these regulations concerning the administrative implementation. The European Community's authorisation to pass general regulations for the purpose of direct implementation can, indeed, be considered to be a fact. However, the only contractual legal basis for this is Article 308 of the EC Treaty.[71] Due to the necessary overlapping of administrative and budgetary implementation, the Financial Regulation has virtually set itself up as an instrument for managing the mentioned provisions. In this respect, it could be assumed that the first paragraph of Article 279 of the EC Treaty also comprises the passing of a general law of grant management for the direct implementation by virtue of factual connection.

3.3.3. Establishment of a new type of organisation: The executive agencies

The establishment of the executive agency has to be classified under the framework of the Commission's externalisation policy.[72] The term externalisation refers to the Commission's delegation of certain tasks to other institutions.[73] In fact, this does not represent something new[74] but now the externalisation is to be implemented coherently and manageably[75] instead of being without a proper concept and resulting in a completely intransparent division of tasks between the Community and third parties involved in the management. One reason for the externalisation is the lack of staff which has been much bemoaned by the Commission. Apparently, the number of staff has not increased in proportion to the increase in the number of tasks of which the Commission has now been put in charge.[76] Another reason is that the Commission often lacks the necessary

---

71 Schwarze, *Europäisches Verwaltungsrecht*, vol. I, 1988, 47; Kahl, NVwZ 1996, 865 (869).

72 In detail Koch, *Die Externalisierungspolitik der Kommission*, 2004. In particular with regard to democracy's deficits Lübbe-Wolff, VVDStRL 2001, 246 (267 ff.).

73 *Planning and Coordination Group on Externalisation*, Externalisation of the management of Community programmes, 2.1.

74 Even as early as 1958 the Court's famous Meroni judgment (Case 9/56 [1958] ECR 9) was characterised by externalisation problems.

75 *Commission*, Communication from the Commission – Externalisation of the management of Community programmes including presentation of a framework regulation for a new type of executive agency, COM (2000) 788 final, p. 3.

76 This consideration seems to be plausible. Despite its wide range of objectives and responsibilities within the European Community consisting of 25 Member States the

professional competence.[77] The executive agency is to replace the so-called Technical Assistance Office (TAO), in particular. These offices were arranged according to various organisational types, and hundreds of them performed tasks for the Commission that were sometimes of great significance – and yet without proper control.

The term 'Executive Agency'

By legal definition, executive agencies are 'legal persons under Community law created by Community decision to which powers can be delegated to implement all or part of a Community programme or project on behalf of the Commission and under its responsibility'.[78] When establishing executive agencies, the Commission is bound by a Council Regulation[79] based on Article 308 of the EC Treaty.[80] This regulation defines the conditions and arrangements for the creation of executive agencies and, to a large extent, provides for the organisation and operational method of this agency. As a consequence, all future executive agencies will only differ – within the meaning of required cohesion – in the area of the Community management of grants in which they perform tasks. In contrast to Community agencies, the legal basis for their creation can be limited to the definition of tasks that are to be delegated to the executive agency.[81]

Creation of the executive agency

An executive agency can only be created by the Commission if a cost-benefit analysis has positive results. The expenditure connected with the establishment and maintenance has to be in due proportion to the quality improvement of the management, which is linked to the creation of a specialised, legally independent institution which is, however, intended for a limited duration.[82] The Commission's expenditure which results from its responsibility to check the executive agency has to be taken into particular consideration. The apparently independent position of the Commission in regard to creating the executive

---

Commission comprises less than 30,000 established posts. This is roughly only three times as much as the staff of the town of Stuttgart.

77 *Craig*, ELRev 2003, 840 (843).

78 Article 55 1. FR 2002.

79 Council Regulation (EC) No. 58/2003 of 19 December 2002 laying down the statute for executive agencies to be entrusted with certain tasks in the management of Community programmes (OJ EC 2003 No. L 11, p. 1 hereinafter: statute for executive agencies).

80 In regard to Article 308 TEC as the basis of an establishment competence *Remmert*, EuR 2003, 134 (137 ff.).

81 The Commission Decision setting up the "Intelligent Energy Executive Agency" (fn. 20), for example, only constitutes two pages in the Official Journal. Five of eight Articles are still restricted to a repetition of rules of the statute for executive agencies (fn. 79).

82 Article 2 1. of the statute for executive agencies (fn. 79); *Craig*, ELRev 2003, 840 (847 f.).

agency is restricted by the fact that it is bound by the strict regulatory procedure of the comitology decision when making a decision.[83] The resolutions involved can only be adopted with the explicit – or at least tacit – approval of the Member States. This indicates the lack of confidence in an independent organisational power of the Commission, which could lead to the development of a more and more differentiated Community organisation of management.

Organisation of the executive agency

After having examined the process of creation of executive agencies, their organisation will now be described in greater detail. They have a similar two-tiered board structure, consisting of a steering committee and a director, similar to the Community agencies.[84]

The steering committee's major task is the adoption of the annual work programme of the executive agency.[85] It also draws up the administrative budget of the institution, decides on its further organisational structure and defines the application rules for the personnel administration.[86] The strategic focus of the executive agency lies, therefore, with the steering committee, which consists of five members that are appointed by the Commission.[87] In contrast, the representatives of the Commission play a minor part in the management boards of the Community agencies, compared to the representatives of the Member States.[88] If their role is considered to be that of securing the Member States' influence on the EC administration,[89] the Commission's representatives represent the element which links the executive agency to the Commission.

Another element in this respect is the fact that the director of the executive agency can be appointed and dismissed by the Commission at any time.[90] The director implements the administrative budget and the annual work programme. He is also in charge of the executive agency's staff,[91] and so he is responsible for

83 Article 5 of the comitology decision (fn. 34); compare Wichard, in: Calliess/Ruffert (eds.), EU/EC Treaty, 2nd ed. 2002, Art. 202 TEC mn. 17.

84 Cf. Fischer-Appelt, *Agenturen der Europäischen Gemeinschaft*, 1999, 221.

85 Article 9 2.1. of the statute for executive agencies (fn. 79).

86 Article 9 3., 5., Article 18 3. of the statute for executive agencies (fn. 79).

87 Article 8 1. of the statute for executive agencies (fn. 79). The Commission has appointed only high-ranking officers from the Directorates-General with subject relevance to the Steering Committee of the 'Intelligent Energy Executive Agency', see 'Communication from the Commission of 26 March 2004 concerning the appointment of the five members of the Steering Committee of the Intelligent Energy Executive Agency' (OJ 2004 No. C 79, p. 12).

88 *E.g.* Article 26 1. of the Regulation (EC) No. 881/2004 of the European Parliament and of the Council of 29 April 2004 establishing a European Railway Agency (OJ 2004 No. L 164, p. 1): one representative of each Member State and four representatives of the Commission have voting rights.

89 Schmidt-Aßmann, in: FS für Häberle (fn. 22), 395 (401).

90 Article 10 of the statute for executive agencies (fn. 79).

91 Article 11 3. 1., 4., 6. of the statute for executive agencies (fn. 79).

the daily operations. This is also the case concerning the directors of Community agencies,[92] but the latter are appointed and dismissed by the management boards and are thus predominantly on the basis of approval by the Member States' representatives.[93]

Control by the Commission

The close connection with the Commission can also be identified with regard to the activity of the executive agency. On the one hand, the adoption of the annual work programme requires the Commission's approval.[94] And on the other hand, it can influence the daily management to a large extent. In the event of a complaint by third parties, the Commission has to verify the legality of the executive agency's actions. However, the third party, has generally to be individually and directly affected by the action concerned. The conditions for the right to lodge a complaint are thus designed according to those of the rules for bringing proceedings defined in Article 230(1) of the EC Treaty.[95] The right to lodge a complaint does not stop the Commission from scrutinising the executive agency's activities extensively. Officially, it also has the right to get involved in every possible activity of the executive agency and, where appropriate, issue instructions for changing the activity.[96] While a procedure for submitting a complaint before the Commission is also partly provided for Community agencies[97] which do not have their own Boards of Appeal,[98] an extensive legal supervision of the Commission exists only over the executive agencies. The Commission decisions made in the context of complaint procedures are also not exclusively supervisory tools. They also serve as indirect access to the courts against actions of the executive agencies.[99]

Finally, a highly interesting rule will be examined. For the management of the programme, no operational resources are allocated to the executive agency, which only has an administrative budget. For this purpose, the responsible

92 Fischer-Appelt, Agenturen (fn. 84), 238 f.

93 E.g. Article 31 1. of the Regulation (EC) No. 881/2004 (fn. 88).

94 Article 9 2. 1. of the statute for executive agencies (fn. 79).

95 Compare Röhl, Jura 2003, 830 (832 ff.).

96 Article 22 2., 3. of the statute for executive agencies (fn. 79).

97 E.g. Article 22 Council Regulation (EC) No. 2062/94 of 18 July 1994 establishing a European Agency for Safety and Health at Work (OJ 1994 No. L 216, p. 1). Fischer-Appelt, Agenturen (fn. 84), 309 ff.

98 Boards of Appeal are currently planned for three Community agencies which have independent decision-taking powers compared to a third party; e.g. Article 31 ff. Regulation (EC) No. 1592/2002 of the European Parliament and of the Council of 15 July 2002 on common rules in the field of civil aviation and establishing a European Aviation Safety Agency (OJ 2002 No. L 240, p. 1). In regard to the Office for Harmonisation in the Internal Market and the Community Plant Variety Office Dammann, *Die Beschwerdekammern der europäischen Agenturen*, 2004.

99 Cf. Fischer-Appelt, *Agenturen* (fn. 85), 311 f.; Craig, ELRev 2003, 840 (850 f.).

director is the Commission's authorising officer by delegation ex officio,[100] and, in this capacity, he directly implements a subsection of the Commission. In doing so, he is bound by the rules regulating the budgetary implementation which apply to the Commission[101] and is hence subject to supervision by the Internal Auditor. Payments are no longer made within the organisational framework of the executive agency but by the Commission's accounting officer.[102] The Commission integrates the director, a member of a legally independent Community institution, in its own budget implementation. This does not represent, however, a delegation of tasks relating to the budget implementation to third parties.[103]

Conclusion

This survey of the executive agencies' organisation and activities should have already made it obvious that it is their extremely close connection to the Commission that characterises them in particular.[104] In this way, the executive agencies actually represent subordinated authorities of the Commission – despite their legal independence and, in this respect, they differ dramatically from the Community agencies.[105]

3.4. SHARED MANAGEMENT OF FUNDS

3.4.1. Introduction

Most grants within the scope of the Common cohesion and agricultural policy are managed on a shared basis. In these policy areas, the major Community funds serve as financial instrument: the European Agricultural Guidance and Guarantee Fund (EAGGF), based on Article 34(3) of the EC Treaty, the European Social Fund (ESF), based on Article 146 of the EC Treaty, the European Regional Development Fund (ERDF), based on Article 160 of the EC Treaty and the Cohesion Fund, based on Article 161(2) of the EC Treaty. These funds have no legal character but are part of the overall budget.[106] For this reason the

---

100 Article 11(3)(3), Article 16 2. of the statute for executive agencies (fn. 79). On the powers of authorising officer see above fn. 68.

101 Craig, ELRev 2003, 840 (849).

102 Article 82 FR 2002.

103 See above 3.2.3.

104 Koch, *Externalisierungspolitik* (fn. 72), 82 f.

105 Schmidt-Aßmann, in: FS für Häberle (fn. 22), 395 (401 with n. 31a); *id.*, ZHR 168 (2004), 125 (128 with fn. 16).

106 *Cf.* Article 268 1. TEC. The fact that only the ESF appears in this regulation can be explained as follows: The content of Article 268(1) TEC has not been changed since the EEC Treaty came

Commission is, pursuant to Article 274(1)(1) of the EC Treaty, responsible for budget implementation with regard to expenditure financed by these funds.

Actions within the agricultural market policy are financed predominantly by the Guarantee Section of the Agricultural Fund (EAGGF Guarantee Section) whereas actions within the agricultural structure policy are financed by the Guidance Section (EAGGF Guidance Section). This is the reason why the EAGGF Guidance Section is included, along with the ESF and the ERDF, in the group of Community Structural Funds under primary law (Article 159(1)(3) of the EC Treaty). The way in which the funds work is defined in two major regulations[107] and numerous other legal provisions.

3.4.2. Management structures of the expenditure on the agricultural market and the Structural Funds

Similarities and differences

With regard to both areas, agricultural market and Structural Fund expenditures, the Member States decide on the funding of a concrete measure by Community resources and pay out the amounts. For this purpose, the Community provides the required funds. This represents the major similarity of these two areas of expenditure, that is, the characteristic of shared management of funds.

However, apart from this, only few similarities can be found. As regards the area of agricultural market expenditure, decisions can be based on secondary law, whereas those concerning the area of expenditure on Structural Funds are preceded by fundamental provisions by the Commission[108] and in particular by an extensive project design phase.[109] The programming, the process of organisation, decision-making and financing in several stages intended to implement, on a multi-annual basis, the joint action by the Community and the Member States'[110] constitutes the wide difference compared to the management of agricultural market expenditure. The necessity of joint coordination between Community and Member State is due in particular to the principle of

into force. In the original EEC Treaty, however, only the establishment of the ESF was intended to be obligatory.

107 As for the EAGGF Guarantee Section Council Regulation (EC) No. 1258/1999 of 17 May 1999 on the financing of the common agricultural policy (OJ 1999 No. L 160, p. 103); as for the Structural Funds Council Regulation (EC) No. 1260/1999 of 21 June 1999 laying down general provisions on the Structural Funds (OJ 1999 No. L 161, p. 1).

108 In detail Schöndorf-Haubold, *Die Strukturfonds der Europäischen Gemeinschaft*, 2005, 144 ff.

109 Accordingly the sentence starting the previous passage could be specified as follows: Community aid decisions of the Member States within the area of agricultural expenditure are reached for the purpose of implementing acts of secondary legislation, those within the area of structural funding for the purpose of implementing the drawn up budget.

110 Article 9 lit. a Council Regulation (EC) No. 1260/1999 (fn. 107); Holzwart, *Der rechtliche Rahmen für die Verwaltung und Finanzierung der gemeinschaftlichen Strukturfonds am Beispiel des EFRE*, 2003, 197 ff.; Schöndorf-Haubold, *Strukturfonds* (fn. 108), 158 ff.

co-financing. When both, the Community and a Member State and/or one of its subdivisions, fund actions jointly, they both have to be conceded significant influence on the character of the funded activities. In contrast, the principle of exclusive Community funding is applied to agricultural market expenditure.[111] The Member States only have an influence on the type of funded action by means of the Council which, in turn, acts as Community body.

The authorities involved

With regard to the area of agricultural market expenditure,[112] the Member States inform the Commission about the services and institutions that are authorised to pay the expenditure as so-called paying agencies:[113] these services or institutions have to meet considerable requirements of Community Law, in particular in terms of their financial management.[114] The paying agency's major task is to grant and make the payments,[115] but, under strict conditions, the granting task may also be transferred to other bodies.[116]

Paying agencies also have to be appointed by Member States for the purpose of expenditure on Structural Funds.[117] In the first instance, they transfer the payments made by the Commission to the beneficiaries. However, the so-called management authority is the centre of the implementation of the concerned finalised programme planning forms,[118] but this authority does not necessarily award the grants: this can be done by certain institutions that are authorised by national law.[119] However, the management authority is responsible for the implementation of the programme and the effective management in accordance

111 Cf. ECJ, case C-239/01 – Germany *v* Commission, [2003] ECR I-10333 (mn. 69 ff.); Busse, VerwArch 2003, 483 ff.

112 See also Craig, ELRev 2003, 840 (859 ff.).

113 Article 4 1. lit. a Council Regulation (EC) No. 1258/1999 (fn. 107). Overview of the paying agencies in the EU-15 in *Court of Auditors*, Annual Report concerning the financial year 2002, OJ EU 2003 No. C 286, p. 1 (123).

114 See Article 1(3)(2) and the appendix of Commission Regulation (EC) No. 1663/95 of 7 July 1995 laying down detailed rules for the application of Council Regulation (EEC) No. 729/70 regarding the procedure for the clearance of the accounts of the EAGGF Guarantee Section (OJ EC 1995 No. L 158, p. 6); as regards the binding nature of these 'guidelines for a paying agency's accreditation criteria' Mögele, *Die Behandlung fehlerhafter Ausgaben im Finanzierungssystem der gemeinsamen Agrarpolitik*, 1997, 53 f.

115 Article 4 2., 3. Council Regulation (EC) No. 1258/1999 (fn. 108), No. 2 appendix of Commission Regulation (EC) No. 1663/95 (fn. 114).

116 *Cf.* §29d para. 1 of the Landwirtschafts- und Landeskulturgesetz des Landes Baden-Württemberg: The *Ministerium für Ernährung und Ländlichen Raum* as approved paying agency can delegate its authorisation function to the subordinated agricultural authorities.

117 Article 9 lit. o Council Regulation (EC) No. 1260/1999 (fn. 107).

118 Article 9 lit. n Council Regulation (EC) No. 1260/1999 (fn. 107).

119 Schöndorf-Haubold, *Strukturfonds* (fn. 108), 260; Holzwart, *Gemeinschaftliche Strukturfonds* (fn. 110), 283.

with the rules.[120] It is supervised by a monitoring committee designated by the management authority and thus attached at Member State level. The monitoring committee is joined by a representative of the Commission who participates in an advisory capacity.[121]

This brief overview has already made it obvious that it is not only the definition of tasks of the Structural Funds which are far more complex than those of the agricultural funds but also the administrative structure.[122] However, Community law has a considerable bearing on the Member States' administrative structures of both areas by means of many provisions concerning even tiny details. A principle of organisational autonomy of the Member States in respect of the implementation of Community law would not only be affected in its marginal area adversely but also deep at its core.

3.4.3. Clearance-of-accounts procedures and procedures for making financial corrections

The Member States' competence to decide on the funding of a specific action by Community resources and to make the payments on the one hand, and the Commission's responsibility for the implementation of the budget according to Article 274(1)(1) of the EC Treaty on the other hand, need to be harmonised.[123] The instrument provided by Community Law for this purpose is the clearance-of-accounts procedure concerning the area of agricultural market expenditure[124] and the Community procedure for making financial corrections concerning the area of expenditure on Structural Funds.[125] This connection is also expressed clearly in the new Financial Regulation.[126]

Both mechanisms are administrative procedures of the Commission towards a Member State. They result in a decision within the meaning of Article 249(4) of the EC Treaty.[127] For the conformity decision within the context of the clearing of accounts, the Commission only has to consult the EAGGF committee consisting of Member State representatives.[128] For the financial correction decision no committee involvement is intended. Thus, the Commission defines

120 Article 34 1. Council Regulation (EC) No. 1260/1999 (fn. 107).

121 Article 35 1., 2. Council Regulation (EC) No. 1260/1999 (fn. 107).

122 Cf., e.g. 'Einziges Programmplanungsdokument für die Gebiete Baden-Württembergs 2000–2006', 8.1.

123 See above B.I.2.b).

124 Article 7 Council Regulation (EC) No. 1258/1999 (fn. 107).

125 Article 39 3. Council Regulation (EC) No. 1260/1999 (fn. 107). When implementing structural funds programmes the Member States also and in the first instance make financial corrections (Art. 39 1 subparagraph. 1 of the Council Regulation (EC) No. 1260/1999); Therefore it is stated here as "Community" financial correction procedure.

126 In particular Article 53 5. FR 2002. See also Nicolaysen, *Europarecht I*, 2nd ed. 2002, 259.

127 In regard to the Community financial correction decision Schöndorf-Haubold, *Strukturfonds* (fn. 108), 339.

128 Article 7 1. Council Regulation (EC) No. 1258/1999 (fn. 107).

the decision's content autonomously. An order of committee involvement beyond a mere consultation would also not have been allowed due to the connection of both procedures with Article 274(1)(1) of the EC Treaty.

Regarding the agricultural market expenditure, the Commission monthly reimburses the amounts that were pre-financed by the Member States.[129] However, the payments are always made subject to the definite decision on the actual eligibility, that is, to the conformity decision concerning a certain financial year. By means of this decision, the Commission excludes expenditure from Community funding which has not been paid in accordance with Community rules by the Member States.[130] In the event that certain tasks are excluded from Community funding by the conformity decision the Member State is obliged to refund the Community the amounts assigned in the decision. If the Member State does not succeed in reclaiming wrongly made payments from the beneficiaries, it bears the financial risk itself.

Together with the approval of a programme, the Commission decides on the amount of the Community contribution the Member State can use for expenditure on Structural Funds. The Member State can use these funds to finance specific projects. By means of reducing or cancelling grants, Community law requires the Member State to control and, where appropriate, to make financial corrections. But as the programme does not yet include concrete projects, the Member State can cancel the Community contribution for a project which does not meet the conditions for Community funding and transfer it to another project.[131] That is the reason why even an irregularity detected through the Commission's controls[132] does not necessarily result in a reduction of the amount granted to the Member State by the Community. In fact, the Member State can use the Commission's detection as an opportunity for such a reallocation so that a Community financial correction decision resulting in a reduction or cancellation of the Community contribution to a programme is only required in exceptional cases. Moreover, compared to the area of agricultural market expenditure, it is much more difficult to identify a conflict with Community law given the inexact wording in the approved programmes.

Thus, the conformity decision represents, in principle, the Commission's consistent reaction to an expenditure which has been paid wrongly by the Member State, whereas a Community financial correction decision is the reaction to a, from the Commission's point of view, fundamentally non-compliant Member State which does not make the required financial corrections itself.

In practise, only the clearance-of-accounts procedure has played a role so far. The Member States regularly take legal action against the conformity decisions

---

129 Article 5, Article 7 2. Council Regulation (EC) No. 1258/1999 (fn. 107).

130 *Cf.* Article 7 4. subparagraph 1 of the Council Regulation (EC) No. 1258/1999 (fn. 107).

131 Article 39 1. subparagraph. 2 Council Regulation (EC) No. 1260/1999 (fn. 108).

132 On this system of first and second line controls David, *Inspektionen im Europäischen Verwaltungsrecht,* 2003, 102 f.

directed at them. However, the proceedings show that the Commission benefits considerably from the entire structure of the proceedings as well as from the distribution of the burden of proof.[133] Hence, it can fully fulfil its budgetary responsibility within the area of agricultural market expenditure. Besides, the clearance of accounts procedure has proved to be an effective instrument of the Commission's 'factual legal supervision' over the Member States' administration.[134]

4. CONCLUSION

With good reason, the allocation of grants has increasingly been the focus of scientific attention in recent years.[135] The sheer amount of allocated funds is substantial. Besides, the European administrative law has lately undergone highly important changes with the codification of general grant management law. The clearance of accounts procedure and the Community procedure for making financial corrections represent specific Community mechanisms of management for the purpose of securing the assumption of the Commission's budgetary responsibility. They are models of a continuously developing administrative law. The legislative proposals[136] for the next phase of financing starting in 2007 foreshadow other new fundamental changes.

---

133 Cf. Craig, ELRev 2003, 840 (862 ff.).

134 See Priebe, in: Hill/Pitschas (eds.), *Europäisches Verwaltungsverfahrensrecht*, 2004, 337 (343); Schmidt-Aßmann, in: FS für Steinberger (fn. 3), 1375 (1398 f.).

135 See the area-specific essays from Mögele, *Behandlung fehlerhafter Ausgaben* (fn. 114); Pfeiffer, *Forschungspolitik* (fn. 66); Holzwart, *Gemeinschaftliche Strukturfonds* (n. 110); Schöndorf-Haubold, *Strukturfonds* (fn. 108); see also the more comprehensive approach from Rodi, *Die Subventionsrechtsordnung*, 2000.

136 In particular, Commission, Proposal for a Council Regulation on the financing of the common agricultural policy COM (2004) 489 final; id., Proposal for a Council Regulation on support for rural development by the European Agricultural Fund for Rural Development (EAFRD), COM (2004) 490 final; id., Proposal for a Council Regulation laying down general provisions on the European Regional Development Fund, the European Social Fund and the Cohesion Fund COM (2004) 492 final.

C. ADMINISTRATIVE STRUCTURES AND LEGAL PROTECTION

XVII. THE VOIDABLE DECISION ACCORDING TO ARTICLE 230(4) OF THE TREATY ESTABLISHING THE EUROPEAN COMMUNITY AS A FORM OF LEGAL PROTECTION*

Hans Christian Röhl

1. INTRODUCTION: EUROPEAN PROCEDURAL LAW BETWEEN CONVERGENCE AND DIFFERENCE

The question how to provide judicial protection for the "administration in the Community area" can be answered differently according to the different national legal systems. In the light of uniform problems, the need for a search for a convergence of the administrative judicial protection is obvious.[1] The contrary is true for the judicial protection according to the rules of the EC Treaty, since in that case, different approaches of interpretation have to be revealed for uniformly applied rules about judicial protection and its institutions. Those approaches can be characterized by contradictory basic understandings of the Member States' legal systems, in particular.

Such a contradiction is represented by the thinking in German administrative law, which is oriented towards legal forms, compared to the approach of the Romanic systems which is directed more towards forms of judicial protection, especially the doctrine of French administrative law:

- The German administrative law doctrine allocates a "storage function"[2] to its legal forms, and especially to the administrative act. The qualification of an

---

* Revised and updated version of Röhl, *ZaöRV 60 (2000)*, 331 ff.

1 Groß, DV 2000, 415; Spilitopoulos (ed.), *Towards a unified judicial protection of citizens in Europe* (?), London 2000.

2 Ossenbühl, JuS 1979, 681 ff.; Pauly, in: Becker-Schwarze/Köck/Kupka/v. Schwanenflügel (eds.), *Wandel der Handlungsformen im öffentlichen Recht*, 1991, 25 (35–37); v. Danwitz, *Verwaltungsrechtliches System und Europäische Integration*, 1996, 35, 67 ff.; Schmidt-Aßmann,

administrative action as an administrative act invokes procedurally the action for annulment and the institute of the formal stability, legally the regulations of §§9 ff. VwVfG and substantively, e.g., the rescinding regulations of §§48 ff. VwVfG. However, the question of whether judicial protection is provided against an action is independent of its legal nature.
- In contrast, the term *décision* in French administrative law is a procedural concept only. By the qualification of an action as *décision*, which leads to the *recours pour excès de pouvoir,*[3] judicial protection is invoked. Other actions than *décisions* basically cannot become subject of judicial control aiming at the rescission or abolition of the action. However, procedural and substantive consequences are not linked to this qualification, but, e.g., to sub-categories, such as the differentiation into *actes réglementaires* and *actes individuels.*"[4]

This differentiation is reflected in the interpretation of Article 230(4) of the EC Treaty. Therefore, the "decision" according to the EC Treaty is considered as being a pendant to the administrative act and therefore being a legal form term, by a part of the German doctrine. Article 230(4) of the EC Treaty and Article 249(4) of the EC Treaty seem to build the basis of a uniform legal form.[5] However,

---

Das allgemeine Verwaltungsrecht als Ordnungsidee, 2nd edition, 2004, chapter 6, marginal number (=mn.) 34.

3 Chapus, *Droit administratif général*, T 1 15th edition, Paris 2001, No. 670. This legal remedy accords with an action of avoidance and represents, besides the action for damages, the central legal remedy of the French administrative procedural law, cf. Pacteau, in: Spiliotopoulos, *Judicial Protection* (fn. 1), 290 (330 ff.); Koch, *Verwaltungsrechtsschutz in Frankreich*, 1998, 104 ff.

4 Ladenburger, *Verfahrensfehlerfolgen im französischen und im deutschen Verwaltungsrecht*, 1999, 196 ff.

5 Ule, *Gutachten für den 46.* DJT, 1966, Vol. 1 Part 4, 12; Thierfelder, *Die Entscheidung im EWG-Vertrag*, 1968, 94, 135; Daig, *Nichtigkeits- und Untätigkeitsklagen im Recht der Europäischen Gemeinschaften* 1985, mn. 21, 101 (which only discusses the assignment to the regulation within the scope of these implementations; further, however, mn. 32 ff.); Dauses, *Gutachten D für den 60,* DJT, 1994, D 21; W. Cremer, *Forschungssubventionen im Lichte des EGV*, 1995, 206 ff.; Oppermann, *Europarecht*, 2nd edition, 1999, mn. 725. Also discussed, e.g., by Junker, *Der Verwaltungsakt im deutschen und französischen Recht und die Entscheidung im Recht der Europäischen Gemeinschaften*, Dissertation Münster 1990; Dörr, in: Sodan/Ziekow (eds.), *Nomos-Kommentar zur VwGO*, Lsbl. Stand January 2003, EVR, mn. 105: The appealed legal actions would have "to represent substantive decisions in terms of Article 189(4) of the EC Treaty". (Accentuation there); now also Borowski, EuR 2004, 879 (882 with fn. 21).
However, a larger number of opinions indicate that it is an identical term: Burgi, in: Rengeling/Middeke/Gellermann (eds.), *Handbuch des Rechtsschutzes in der Europäischen Union*, 2003, §7 mn. 37; Gaitanides, in: von der Groeben/Schwarze (eds.), *EU-/EG-Vertrag*, 6th edition, 2004, Article 230 mn. 13; Booß, in: Grabitz/Hilf (eds.), *EUV/EGV*, Lsbl. Stand 2004, Article 230 EGV mn. 12, 16, 47, 55; Ehlers, VerwArch 84 (1993), 139 (150); Schmidt-Aßmann, in: Schoch/Schmidt-Aßmann/Pietzner (eds.), VwGO, Lsbl. Stand 2003, Introduction mn. 116; Commentaire Mégret, Le droit de la CEE, Vol. 10, 2nd edition., Brussels 1993, Art. 189 No. 72; Lenaerts/Arts, *Procedural Law of The European Union*, London 1999, No. 7-009.

this perception is unfounded.[6] It is not possible to extract a definite statement in favour or against a uniform legal form out of the text of the Treaty (see 2.). Also the jurisdiction of the European Court of Justice has distanced itself from the uniform term of legal form (see 3.), especially because the term "decision" of Article 230(4) of the EC Treaty provides the only possibility for judicial protection. The amendments of the Lisbon Treaty confirm this result by abandoning the term of decision entirely.

The analysis according to the perspective presented by the doctrine of legal form remains significant due to two different aspects. A mere procedural understanding of the voidable decision in terms of Article 230(4) of the EC Treaty cannot solve the problems of the European procedural law concerning the adjustment with substantive law, which can be demonstrated clearly in the figure of stability (*Bestandskraft*) (see paragraph 4). On the other hand, it becomes obvious that the doctrine of the legal forms of the administrative actions cannot easily be applied to the administrative law of the EC Treaty[7] (see paragraph 5).

2. ABOUT THE CONCEPT OF THE DECISION IN THE EC TREATY

2.1. INTRODUCTION

At first sight, the phrasing of the EC Treaty suggests an identity of the legal forms mentioned in Article 249, with the actions covered by Article 230. However, a more careful analysis invokes doubts (see para. 2.2), which has encouraged a recent treaty amendment (see para. 2.3). Considerations concerning judicial protection, in particular, exclude a formal understanding of the procedural decision term of the EC Treaty (see 2.4). The version of the article concerning judicial protection in the Lisbon Treaty confirms this development (see para. 2.5).

6 Indication here on Bleckmann, *DÖV* 1993, 837 (844). More optimistic about a manageable term of decision Schmidt-Aßmann, *Ordnungsidee* (Fn. 2), chapter 7 mn. 48, 50, also chapter 6 mn 34 at Fn. 86; Kadelbach, *Allgemeines Verwaltungsrecht unter europäischem Einfluss*, 1999, 326 f.; about the decision in terms of Article 249(4) of the EC Treaty also see *Vogt*, in this volume, p. 341.

7 A continuative analysis of the forms of action of the EC Treaty v. Bogandy/Bast/Arndt, *ZaöRV* 2002, 78, and Bast in: v. Bogandy/Bast (eds.), *Europäisches Verfassungsrecht*, 2nd ed. 2009, 489.

2.2. THE TERM OF ARTICLE 230(4) OF THE TREATY ESTABLISHING THE EUROPEAN COMMUNITY

Article 230(1) of the EC Treaty opens the possibility for the institutional complaints of paragraph 2, for a claim against all acts[8] which are not opinions or recommendations. This phrasing does not definitely refer to the catalogue of Article 249 of the EC Treaty. Therefore, a statement in favour or against an identity thesis cannot be derived from this rule. Accordingly, the case law extends Article 230(1) of the EC Treaty to

> "any measures adopted by the institutions, whatever their nature or form, which are intended to have legal effects".[9]

Article 230(4) of the EC Treaty, which is relevant for private claimants, uses the same expression as Article 249(4) of the EC Treaty: only a *decision*[10] is voidable. The original case law of the European Court of Justice assumed the equivalence of the terms.[11] It would be "inconceivable that the term 'decision' would be used in Article 173 in a different sense from the technical sense as defined in Article 189." This case law forms the main basis for the argument for a uniform decision term within the literature.[12] This seems to be approved by a continuation of the case law.[13] However, this only applies for the differentiation of the provision of a particular case from the general provision, and thus for the regulation, especially. To this end the Court applies the criterion of the "general application",[14] which originates from Article 249(2) of the EC Treaty. This statement does not provide

---

8 French: "actes"; Italian: "atti"; Dutch: "handelingen"; German: "Handlungen".

9 ECJ, case 22/70, European Court reports 1971, 263 (277 mn. 38/42) – AETR; ECJ, case 366/88, European Court reports 1990, I-3571 (3598 f. mn. 89) – France *v* COM.

10 French: "décisions"; Italian: "decisioni"; Dutch: "beschikkingen"; German: "Entscheidungen".

11 ECJ, case 16 and 17/62, European Court reports 1962, 471 (478) – Conféderation nationale des producteurs de fruits et légumes. Also AG Roemer in ECJ, case 8–11/66, European Court reports 1967, 99 (133) – Cimenteries B.D.R. et. al. /Noordwijks Cement Accoord.

12 Thierfelder, *Entscheidung* (fn. 5), 94; Schwarze, in: *FS für Schlochauer*, 1981, 927 (930); Allkemper, *Der Rechtsschutz des einzelnen nach dem EG-Vertrag*, 1995, 61; Bockey, *Die Entscheidung der Europäischen Gemeinschaft*, 1998, 160; Lengauer, *Nichtigkeitsklage vor dem EuGH*, 1998, 94 f., who wants to answer to the problem of "atypical" legal acts (see l.c., 56–61) with a reinterpretation into a decision (95).

13 ECJ, case C-298/89, European Court reports 1993, I-3605 (mn. 15 f.) – Gibraltar I; case C-336/90, European Court reports 1992, I-3971 (mn. 14) – Gibraltar II; case C-397/92, European Court reports 1993, I-3981 (mn. 13) – Gibraltar III, case C-10/95 P, European Court reports 1995, I-4149 (mn. 28) – Asocarne; case C-87/95, European Court reports 1996, I-2003 (mn. 33) – CNPAAP; CFI, case T-116/94, European Court reports 1995, II-1 (mn. 22) – CNPAAP; cf. also CFI, case T-472/93, European Court reports 1995, II-421 (mn. 29) – Isoglucose; at last CFI, case T-166/99, European Court reports 2001, II-1857 (mn. 35); case T-17/00, European Court reports 2002, II-579 (mn. 58 f.) – Rothley et al.; case T-45/02, European Court reports 2003, II-1973 (mn. 31) – DOW AgroSciences.

14 French: "une portée générale"; Italian: "portata generale"; Dutch: "een algemene strekking"; German: "allgemeine Geltung".

for complete equivalence. Rather more Article 230(4) of the EC Treaty itself already includes within its second alternative – at least in the German version – a hint of a not just formal concept of "decision".[15] It mentions a decision, which "although in the form of a regulation, is of direct and individual concern to the former".[16] This material criterion has therefore become the most important forum for the discussion about the subject of the action for annulment.[17]

2.3. THE DEFENDANT POSITION OF THE EUROPEAN PARLIAMENT

An earlier amendment of the Treaty has confirmed that the subject of the action for annulment according to Article 230(4) of the EC Treaty can exceed the scope of Article 249(4) of the EC Treaty. By adopting the case law of the European Court of Justice,[18] the Maastricht Treaty has amended Article 173(1) (now: 230) of the EC Treaty, by one further alternative. According to this, acts of the European Parliament that are *intended* to produce legal effects *vis-à-vis* third parties can be object of an action for annulment.[19] Due to the case Les Verts *v* Parliament, which was the cause of the amendment to the Treaty, this can also be applied to the individual action of paragraph 4. Action against the appealed legal acts of the European Parliament was undertaken not only by the fractions represented in Parliament, but also by other political groups. Therefore, it was not permitted to equate this with the privileged claimants of paragraph 1.[20] The entitlement of the action could only be derived from the former paragraph 2, today's paragraph 4. Therefore, if Article 230(1), 3rd alternative of the EC Treaty mentions actions with a legal effect towards third parties as a subject to a control of legality by the ECJ, this can also be applied to the non-privileged claimants of paragraph 4. However, the actions, for which the opportunity of judicial review should be provided, do not – as the voidable decision of parliament – represent a

---

15 As well Vandersanden, CDE 31 (1995), 535 (546 No. 24).

16 "Bien que prises sous l'apparence d'un règlement (…), la concernent directement et individuellement"; "le decisioni, che, pur apparendo come un regolamento (…), la riguardano dirretamente ed individualmente"; "beschikkingen, die, hoewel genomen in de vorm van een verordening, (…), hem rechtstreeks en individueel raken"; "Entscheidungen, die, obwohl sie als Verordnung (…) ergangen sind, sie unmittelbar und individuell betreffen".

17 Cf. below para. 3.5.

18 ECJ, case 294/83, European Court reports 1986, 1339 (1365 f. mn. 23–25) – Les Verts/EP; case 78/85, European Court reports 1986, 1753 (mn. 10) – Groupe des droites Européennes/EP.

19 Cf. the other language versions, which – compared to the German version – do not describe a relation concerning the claimant, but only an attribute of the legal act: "*destinés* à produire des effects juridiques vis-à-vis des tiers"; "*destinati* a produrre effetti giuridici nei confronti dei terzi"; "handelingen van het Europees Parlement die *beogen* rechtsgevolgen ten aanzien van derden te hebben"; "Handlungen des Europäischen Parlaments sind mit Rechtswirkungen gegenüber Dritten anfechtbar". The italics are made by the author.

20 Opinion AG Mancini, 1353.

formal decision in terms of Article 249 of the EC Treaty. This already results from the fact that the Parliament is not mentioned as the only author of the legal acts. This indicates once more that the term 'decision' of Article 230(4) of the EC Treaty is not to be understood in a formal sense.[21]

2.4. THE JUDICIAL PROTECTION FORM AND THE JUDICIAL PROTECTION MANDATE

Making judicial protection dependent on the existence of an objectively assignable cause of action is hardly compatible with the mandate of individual judicial protection of the courts. In German administrative procedural law therefore, the objective provision governing access, as it was present in the principle of enumeration, has been overcome by the general clause of §40 VwGO. For actions for annulment or abolition, under the procedural law of the EC Treaty, on the other hand, there is, as in French law, only one remedy, which obviously has to affect the definition of the cause of action.

The question about the formal qualification of the legal act within the scope of the admissibility conditions is also known in German administrative procedural law. It distinguishes the cause of action from the right to sue, i.e. a relation of the cause of action to the claimant. Different causes of action are allocated to different forms of actions and those are linked to special procedural requirements. Only, the "if" of the admission to the courts is not linked to the cause of action,[22] which would be prohibited by the constitution any way. If an administrative measure, of whatever nature, interferes with the subjective rights of the claimant, the judicial protection has to be provided under Article 19(4) of the German Constitution.[23] Since this is the reason that the qualification of the cause of action does not determine whether judicial protection exists,[24] the legal forms can be defined more precisely and, at the same time, linked to procedural and substantive consequences.

21 Also now Arnull, CMLR 38 (2001), 7 (14 f.).

22 Erichsen, in: id. /Ehlers (eds.), *Allgemeines Verwaltungsrecht*, 12th edition 2002, §12 mn. 3.

23 Pietzcker, in: Schoch/Schmidt-Aßmann/Pietzner, *VwGO* (fn. 5), Vorb. §42 mn. 21. This has to be and can possibly be called against non-legislative legal rules due to a lack of admissible judicial review by an action for a declaratory judgement, Gerhardt, in: Schoch/Schmidt-Aßmann/Pietzner, VwGO (fn. 5), Vorb. §47 mn. 10.

24 About the administrative act with references BVerwGE (= Decision of the German Federal Administrative Court) 60, 144 (148 f.); E 77, 268 (274 f.).

2.4.1. *About French administrative procedural law: The décision as subject matter of an action*

In the French annulment process of the *recours pour excès de pouvoir*, the judicial protection depends on the existence of a *décision*. Basically, French administrative procedural law requires a decision prior to calling the administrative courts.[25] As a procedural instrument, the so-called *décision* cannot be exclusively defined by formal criteria, but receives a further application area.[26] However, not all administrative actions are covered. The *décision* is understood as being a legal action, which is aimed at the amendment or the confirmation of a legal situation. Mere factual actions are not decisions in this regard.[27] In this case, judicial protection would have to be sought in a claim for government liability.

Since largely every regulating action of the administration is subject to action for annulment in French law, it is difficult to establish a clear separation between the cause of action and the relation of the cause of action towards the claimant within the admissibility conditions. On the one hand, the perspective of judicial protection argues for an extension of the term decision. Since the *décision*, within the scope of the *recours pour excès*, thus only covers a procedural function, it is, on the other hand, largely insignificant, whether a subjective requirement is added to the definition of the cause of action or this subjective requirement is understood as an element of further admissibility requirements.

2.4.2. *The judicial protection mandate of Article 220 of the Treaty establishing the European Community*

If the aim of the administrative process is the protection of the claimant's rights, the possibility for an action against infringements of these rights has to be provided by all means. Accordingly, the Spanish administrative procedural law, e.g., which has followed the French model for a long time now – probably under the influence of the constitutional legal guarantee of judicial protection – abandoned the annulment model. In Spain, it is not the existence of a decision which is a requirement for judicial protection, but judicial protection is also available for other actions of the administration (*actuaciones materiales*).[28] For European procedural law, the judicial protection mandate of Article 220 of the EC Treaty should also prohibit the granting of judicial protection depending on a formal qualification of the contested measure.[29] With reference to this

---

25 Chapus, *Droit du contentiuex administratif*, 10e ed., Paris 2002, No. 629 ff.

26 In detail see par. 3.

27 Chapus, *Droit administrative général* (fn. 3), No. 670, 695.

28 Article 25 of the Ley 29/1998, reguladora de la Jurisdicción Contencioso-administrativa (B.O.E. of 14 July 1998), thereto González-Varas, *DÖV 2000*, 240 (240 f.).

29 This dilemma is mentioned by Vandersanden, *CDE 31* (1995), 535 (537 Nos. 8 f. and 546 Nos. 25 ff.); also Lenaerts/Arts, *Procedural Law* (fn. 5), No. 7–009.

regulation, the ECJ defined the term of the voidable measure widely in the IBM case. According to this "any measure the legal effects of which are binding on, and capable of affecting the interest of, the claimant by bringing about a distinct change in his legal position is an act or decision which may be subject of an action under Article 173 of the EC Treaty for a declaration that it is void. However, the form in which such acts or decisions are cast is, in principle, immaterial as regards the question whether they are open to challenge under that Article".[30] However, this wide formula, which is based on case law, only describes a consequently continued position of the case law of the ECJ. Greater differentiation can be applied to the entire picture presented in case law, and this will be explained in more detail in paragraph 3.

2.5. THE INDIVIDUAL JUDICIAL PROTECTION ACCORDING TO THE DRAFT TREATY ESTABLISHING A CONSTITUTION FOR EUROPE

Article 263 of the Treaty on the Functioning of the European Union implements the final separation between legal form and the judicial protection form. Article 288 TFEU enumerates, according to Article 249 of the EC Treaty, the possible legal forms, which are available to the organs of the Union, on the basis of single terms.[31] However, they are not included in the judicial protection Article 263 TFEU. Therefore, there is a greater possibility for an action against all "acts".[32] The qualification of the measure has no importance for the action's admissibility anymore, apart from the special case of "a regulatory act which is of direct concern to them and does not entail implementing measures".

30 ECJ, case 60/81, European Court reports 1981, 2639 (2651, mn. 9) – IBM; CFI case T-3/93, European Court reports 1994, II-121 (149, mn. 43, 57) – Air France; case T-452/93 et al., European Court reports, II-229 (mn. 29) – Pevasa; case T-377/00 et al., European case reports, II-1 (mn. 76 f.) – Philip Morris et al.

31 Regulation, directive, decision.

32 According to paragraph 1, one would have to add: "(...) other than recommendations and opinions".

3. THE VOIDABLE DECISION ACCORDING TO ARTICLE 230(4) OF THE TREATY ESTABLISHING THE EUROPEAN COMMUNITY IN THE JURISDICTION OF THE EUROPEAN COURT OF JUSTICE

3.1. INTRODUCTION

The case law of the ECJ concerning the voidable decision in terms of Article 230(4) of the EC Treaty has distanced itself obviously from the idea of a uniform legal form. This shall be shown following the different necessary elements which can be extracted from the jurisdiction of the ECJ concerning the existence of a voidable decision. There has to be an action of an EC Institution (see 3.2), which has a compulsory effect (see 3.3) and which has not been made in a contractual relationship (see 3.4). It has to concern the claimant individually (see 3.6) and directly (see 3.7). On the other hand, it is unimportant whether the action is generally applicable (see 3.5).

3.2. ACTIONS OF AN EC INSTITUTION

Voidable decisions basically have to be issued by one of the institutions mentioned in Article 230(1) of the EC Treaty.[33] However, the ECJ has – for reasons of judicial protection – also admitted actions against other institutions, if their acts were able to affect the claimant's rights.[34] Also independent acts of inferior institutions have been categorised as voidable decisions.[35] Finally, actions can possibly be assigned to the Commission, which are made by institutions created by the Commission[36] or by institutions which are in contractual relationship with the Commission.[37]

On the other hand, for (in the following so-called) formal decisions in terms of Article 249(4) of the EC Treaty, other institutions than those mentioned

33 On this, Booß, in Grabitz/Hilf, *EUV/EGV* (fn. 5), Article 230 mn. 6; CFI, case T-13/89, European Court reports 1990, II-797 (820 mn. 81) – Nefarma.

34 As in ECJ, case 87/193, European Court reports 1989, 1045 (mn. 41 ff.) – Maurissen, for a clerk's action against the president of the Court of Auditors, and Les Verts against the Parliament (cf. above fn. 18).

35 Cf. already ECJ, case 8–11/66, European Court reports 1967, 99 (122 ff.) – Cimenteries: "Information" of the Commission according to Article 15 6. Regulation Nr. 17 as voidable decision, even though not engrossed by a Commission member. Therefore, AG Roemer assumed the inexistence of a decision (Opinion, 145). Thereto Commentaire Mégret (fn. 5), Article 173 No. 11. Similar, CFI, case T-84/97, European Court reports 1998, II-795 (LS 3) – BEUC II.

36 ECJ, case 32 et al. /58, European Court reports 1958/59, 287 (312) – SNUPAT.

37 CFI, case T-369/94 et al., European Court reports 1998, II-357 (mn. 53) – DIR Int. Film.

cannot be considered as authors. Formal decisions of the Commission, e.g., require the decision-making of the Commission as a collegial board. A delegation is only permissible for definitely described measures of the executive board and the simple ongoing routine of the administration,[38] but, on the other hand, not for the more important decisions, in particular, the final decision of an administrative procedure.[39]

This differentiation between judicial protection form and legal form becomes more obvious in the Lisbon Treaty. The authorship of the legal forms mentioned in Article 288 TFEU is precisely assigned to the single institutions in the following Articles; judicial protection, on the other hand, is also provided against actions of the institutions, departments and agencies in Article 263 TFEU.

3.3. COMPULSORY LEGAL EFFECTS

The action for annulment of Article 230 of the EC Treaty is only directed at acts that can constitute a compulsory legal effect.[40] Therefore, a material criterion is important and not a form or description of the measure.[41] On the basis of this criterion, the voidable decision is being separated from mere preparatory acts and factual acts (*Realhandeln*). The classification of this characteristic as part of the definition of a voidable decision does not – as already in the case of the characteristic of the direct effect mentioned below – work completely selectively, since it can be understood as an objective characteristic of the action or a relation towards the claimant. Because of the only qualification aim, the admissibility of

38 ECJ, case 5/85, European Court reports 1986, 2585 (mn. 37) – Akzo; CFI, case T-450/93, European Court reports 1994, II-1177 (1191 f., mn. 34 ff.) – Lisretal.

39 CFI, case T-80/89 et al., European Court report 1995, II-729 (mn. 95–107) – BASF et al./KOM, confirmed by ECJ, case C-137/92 P, European Court reports I-2555 (mn. 69 ff.) – BASF: Decisions according to Article 81 (85 old version) of the EC Treaty; CFI, case T-435/93, European Court reports 1995, II-1281 (mn. 102 ff.) – ASPEC; decision according to Article 88 3. (93 old version) of the EC Treaty. Hereto Ritter, in: Immenga/Mestmäcker, *EG-Wettbewerbsrecht*, volume II, 1997 ff.; VO Nr. 17 Art. 3, mn. 27 ff.

40 ECJ, case 133/79, European Court reports 1980, 1299 (1309 mn. 15) – Sucrimex; CFI, case T-130/02 – Kronoply; case T-377/00 et al., European Court reports 2003, II-1 (mn. 76 f.) – Philip Morris et al.; case T-93/00, European Court reports 2003, II-1635 (mn. 59 ff.). Hereto detailed, Kirschner, *Die Abgrenzung des Verwaltungsaktes von anderen behördlichen Handlungen, vor allem zur Beeinflussung wirtschaftlicher Abläufe, in der Rechtsprechung des Gerichtes erster Instanz der EG*, 1991; Booß, in Grabitz/Hilf, *EUV/EGV* (fn. 5), Art. 230 EGV mn. 16 ff.

41 Commentaire Mégret (fn. 5), Article 173 No. 11. The ECJ denied attempts of the High Authority of the ECSC, to introduce formal criteria for the qualification of the decision according to the ECSC Treaty (Decision of the Commission No. 22/60, OJ 1960, p. 1248 and the thereto published notification, OJ 1960, p. 1250), ECJ, case 23 et al./63, European Court reports 1963, 439 (454) – Henricot, thereto Commentaire Mégret, l.c., 113; cf. also ECJ, case 275/80 et al., European Court reports 1981, 2489 (fn. 8) – Krupp.

the action, this indistinctness within the understanding of the term has not led to any practical consequences.

Basically, no binding legal effects are resulting from preparatory or procedural measures of the Commission.[42] Origin of this fact is the thought of a functional coordination between the process and judicial control. Usually, the court should not intercept an ongoing process.[43] However, there are some exceptions to this basic rule.

- Voidable are decisions in the procedure which include a final gravamen, especially since they concern procedural rights. This applies for measures, by which access to the procedure is denied[44] or under which access to the claimant's records is granted to third parties.[45] In this case it is not important whether the avoided measure is a formal decision in terms of Article 249(4) of the EC Treaty, or whether such a decision had been made prior to such a formal decision.
- Interim measures with temporary regulatory effect are also voidable, which can be issued by the Commission during the preparatory procedures.[46] Usually, the persons being affected can take the action for annulment, even though there is not a formal decision in terms of Article 249 of the EC Treaty.

The border between not-voidable real acts and voidable decisions is especially important for statements of the Commission within EC law. Basically, mere announcements as real acts are not voidable.[47] If there is no legal basis for the Commission's actions, it is furthermore assumed that no legal effect has been

42 ECJ, European Court reports 1981, 2639 (2651–2654 mn. 8–24) – IBM: The opening of a process and notification of the catalogue of complaints in the antitrust suit; CFI, case T-64/89, European Court reports 1990, II-367 (381 ff. mn. 42–58) – Automec: Letter to the appellant in an anti trust supervising procedure; CFI, case T-37/92, European Court reports 1994, II-285 (mn. 34 ff.) – BEUC I, CFI, case T-596/97, European Court reports 1998, II-2383 (LS 3) – Dalmine: Penalty payment assignment according to Article 16 q. Regulation No. 17, since the Commission has to declare the entire amount of the penalty payment.

43 CFI, case T-64/89, European Court reports 1990, II-367 (381 ff. mn. 46) – Automec. Likewise, mere institution-internal measures are not voidable: ECJ, case 78/85, European Court reports 1986, 1753 (mn. 10) – Groupe de droites Européenes/EP: Appointment of an investigation committee.

44 CFI, case T-84/97, European Court reports 1998, II-795 (LS 3) – BEUC II: the claimant is notified that he will not be called in to the proceedings and therefore will not access the records.

45 ECJ, case 53/85, European Court records 1986, 1965 (1989 f.) – AKZO.

46 ECJ, case 8–11/66, European Court reports 1967, 99 (122 ff.) – Cimenteries; CFI, case T-19/91, European Court reports 1992, II-415 (mn. 16) – Vichy: "Notification" of the Commission according to Article 15(6) Regulation No. 17; case T-120/96, European Court reports 1998, II-2571 (mn. 54) – Lilly Industries Ltd; case T-241/97, European Court reports 2000, II-309 (mn. 49 ff.) – Stork.

47 To the following Daig, *Nichtigkeitsklagen* (fn. 5), mn. 32 ff.

intended.[48] Also the isolated grounds of a decision cannot become subject to an action for annulment.[49] Often, notifications can already reveal the Commission's decision behind it.[50] Therefore, also oral statements can represent voidable decisions if they have the effect of closing the legal procedure.[51] Formal decisions in terms of Article 249(4)of the EC Treaty, on the other hand, can only be enacted in writing[52] and have to be disclosed to the addressees, i.e. "those to whom they are meant for", and not to everyone who is directly and individually concerned.[53] A publication in the Official Journal is not necessary in every case, according to Article 254(1) and (2) of the EC Treaty. However, some regulations do require it, e.g. Article 26 of the Aid Procedural Regulation.[54]

Also it can also be shown on the basis of the criterion of the compulsory legal effects that the voidable decision according to Article 230(4) of the EC Treaty and the formal decision according to Article 249(4) of the EC Treaty are focused on two different subjects.[55] The decisive argument of the ECJ results from Article 220 of the EC Treaty. It would be inconsistent to interpret restrictively the conditions under which the action is admissible by limiting its scope merely to the categories of measures referred to in Article 249 of the EC Treaty.[56] Since the qualification as a decision – parallel to other countries, which only have one annulment system – opens the way for judicial protection,[57] the ECJ also admits actions which are not decisions in terms of Article 249 of the EC Treaty.[58] Article

---

48 E.g. ECJ, case 182/80, European Court reports 1982, 799 (mn. 16 f.) – Gauff.

49 CFI, case T-138/89, European Court reports 1992, II-2181 (mn. 31) – NBV.

50 ECJ, case C-135/92, European Court reports 1994, I-2885 – Fiskano. A Swedish fishing vessel is being excluded from the catching licensing in Community waters for one year. The action is brought against the letter of the Commission, which informed the State of Sweden.

51 ECJ, case 316/82 et al., European Court reports 1984, 641 (656 mn. 9) – Kohler: the claimant was informed orally that the selection procedure she participated in and in which she took the first place on the employment list would be aborted without any employment. According to the ECJ's opinion, neither general legal provisions nor special clauses of the civil service status would exclude the possibility of taking action against a nuncupative decision. CFI, case T-3/93, European Court reports 1994, II-121 (149, mn. 43, 57) – Air France: The Commission's statement which is communicated by a press spokesman, stating that the Commission is not competent for non-declared fusions, since the fusion-control regulation does not apply to the fusion in question, is voidable.

52 See G. Schmidt, in: v.d. Groeben/Schwarze, *EU-/EG-Vertrag* (fn. 5) Art. 254 mn. 18.

53 G. Schmidt, in: v.d. Groeben/Schwarze, *EU-/EG-Vertrag* (fn. 5) Art. 254 mn. 17.

54 Council Regulation No 659/1999 of 22 March 1999 "laying down detailed rules for the application of Article 93 of the EC Treaty", OJ L 83, 27 March 1999, p. 1.

55 Other opinion Borowski, *EuR 2004*, 879 (883): Article 249(4) of the EC Treaty has to be interpreted in view of Article 230(4) of the EC Treaty.

56 ECJ, case 60/81, European Court reports 1981, 2639 (2651 mn. 8) – IBM; however, in the end, this statement was not decisive, since the action was impermissible. Schweitzer, in: *FS für F. Klein*, 1994, 85 (100).

57 Bleckmann, *Europarecht*, 6th edition 1997, §7 mn. 462.

58 Schwarze, *Europäisches Verwaltungsrecht*, 1988, Band 2, 934; Schmidt-Aßmann, JZ 1994, 832 (835 f.).

263 TFEU, which provides judicial protection against every "act", assimilates this case law consequently.

3.4. ACTIONS BEYOND CONTRACTUAL RELATIONSHIPS

According to Article 288(1) in conjunction with 240 of the EC Treaty, the responsibility over contractual disputes usually lies with the courts of the Member State concerned, as long as there has not been a jurisdiction agreement according to Article 238 of the EC Treaty.[59] Therefore, the ECJ does not permit an action being brought in objection to public or private contracts of the European Community, despite the wide understanding of the voidable decision. Other measures with regulatory effect or content which are also excluded from the annulment by the contractual partner include those of the Commission which are issued within the scope of these contractual relationships, such as admonitions and payment requests etc.[60] Due to its EC Treaty basis, such a decision is reserved for the national courts in their function as a EC Treaty applying judge. Thus, voidable decisions are only one-sided actions beyond contractual relationships.[61]

The judicial protection in connection with the contracts according to Article 230(4) of the EC Treaty thus follows the French model. Accordingly, a voidable decision can exist, if one-sided actions can be identified which are not part of a contractual relationship. This is assumed for the decision to draw up a contract, e.g. about the funding of a research project or the allocation of employment and thereby implicitly exclude other applicants. As in French administrative procedural law, this action can be qualified as separate from the contract and therefore as voidable.[62] Those decisions, implicitly combined in contractual

---

59 The Lisbon Treaty does not change anything about this, cf. Article 288, 238 and 240 TFEU.

60 ECJ, case 43/84, European Court reports 1985, 2581 (mn. 26) – Maag; case 251/84, European Court reports 1986, 217 – CMA; case C-142/91, European Court reports 1993, I-553 (mn. 18) – Cebag; CFI, case T-44/96, European Court reports 1997, II-1331 (1343 ff. mn. 36 ff.) – Oleifici Ilaiani; case T-186/96, European Court reports 1997, II-1633 (1644 mn. 45–52) – Mutual Aid II. About the parallel legal situation in France Chapus, *Contentieux administratif* (fn. 25), No. 825 ff.

61 Booß, in: Grabitz/Hilf, *EUV/EGV* (fn. 5), Art. 230 EGV mn. 18. Bockey, *Entscheidung* (fn. 12), 31 f. proposes for the denotation of this requirement the formulation introduced in Article 4(5) of the Community Custom Code, for the decision in custom law of "hoheitliche Maßnahme". Other language versions of the Code (French, Italian and English), however, do not include any similar expression, e.g. in the English version the expression is described as "any official act by the custom authorities".

62 ECJ, case 23/76, European Court reports 1976, 1807 (1820 f. mn. 23/25 and 26/30) – Pellegrini, cf. also there p. 1827 the statements of AG Mayras; ECJ, case 56/77, European Court reports 1978, 2215 (mn. 12) – Agence européenne; case C-48/96 P, European Court reports, 1998, I-2873 (mn. 16 f.) – Windpark Groothusen; CFI European Court reports 1998, II-357 (mn. 22) – DIR Int. Film.

actions, are rarely formally expressed and are usually not founded, as would be necessary for a formal decision in terms of Article 249(4) of the EC Treaty. However, according to ECJ case law, it does not affect their legality.[63]

3.5. THE MEANING OF THE LEGAL FORM FOR VOIDABILITY

3.5.1. Introduction

In an unbiased reading of Article 230(4) of the EC Treaty, the decision-like character of the voidable measure seems to represent a further condition for admissibility of the action for annulment. This would exclude the voidability of normative actions of the European Community, especially in the form of the regulation.

3.5.2. The problem of the voidability of acts of a general nature

The voidability of regulations is one of the most intensively discussed questions in European procedural law.[64] Finding a uniform and also systematically satisfying answer is difficult, since the lack of a norm hierarchy in EC law[65] implies that, under the categories of regulations and directives, legal acts with wide-reaching implications, which have been enacted with the cooperation of Parliament, the Council and the Commission, can be found alongside insignificant codes of practice of the Commission. Fundamentally, an exclusion of the voidability of normative acts can be deduced from Article 230(4) of the EC Treaty. This can be seen in its purport on a historical basis, on the one hand, and on the other hand from a comparison with the earlier created rule of Article 33(2) ECSC, which had provided for a voidability of normative acts – albeit limited – of the High Authorities of "decisions with a general character." Such a

---

63 ECJ, European Court reports 1978, 2215 (mn. 12) – Agence européenne; ECJ, European Court reports 1998, I-2873 – Windpark Groothuisen.

64 References by Nihoul, *RTDE 1994*, 171 (187 N. 41). Further Waelbroek/Verheyden, *CDE 31* (1995), 399 ff.; Vandersanden, *CDE 31* (1995), 535 ff.; Sedemund/Heinemann, *DB 1995*, 1161 (1162 f.); Nettesheim, in: Micklitz/Reich (eds.), *Public Interest Litigation before European Courts*, 1996, 225 ff.; Hedemann-Robinson, EPL 2 (1996), 127 ff.; Cooke, *Conflict of Principle and Pragmatism – Locus standi under Article 173(4) ECT*, 1996; Craig/de Búrca, *EU Law*, 3rd ed., Oxford 2003, 493 ff.; W. Cremer, in: Calliess/Ruffert (eds.), *Kommentar zu EU-Vertrag und EG-Vertrag*, 2nd edition 2002, Art. 230 mn. 27–36. From the legal-political aspect Börner, in: *Referat 46. DJT*, G 32 ff.; against Matthies, in: *Referat 46. DJT*, G 62 ff.

65 On this H. Hofmann, *Normenhierarchien im europäischen Gemeinschaftsrecht* [Norm Hierarchies in European Community Law], 2000. Cf. also Waelbroeck/Verheyden, *CDE 31* (1995), 399 (436 ff. No. 61 ff.).

voidability, in particular, should not be included in the EC Treaty.[66] The judicial protection mandate of Article 220 of the EC Treaty has been referred to in demands for a more liberal interpretation of Article 230(4) of the EC Treaty.[67] On the other hand, it has been pointed out that the importance and general application of regulations means that they cannot be exposed to the disposition of an inestimable number of private claimants, seeking judicial protection.[68] Furthermore, there is a reference to other possibilities for judicial protection, which can be used with regard to normative acts,[69] namely and first and foremost – because of the primarily Member State execution – the preliminary ruling procedure according to Article 234 oµf the EC Treaty, further the integrated control enabled by Article 241 of the EC Treaty and the action for damages which is independent of the action for annulment according to Article 288(2) of the EC Treaty. However, there are a number of disadvantages attached to the possibility of actions being brought in national courts and the preliminary ruling referred to here. They make it appear doubtful whether this possibility really represents an adequate equivalent of the possibility of actions before the European Courts.[70]

Even though this criticism has been explicitly repeated in the elaborately substantiated opinions of Attorney General Jacobs,[71] and the Court of First Instance also joined in in urging a change of the jurisdiction in the Jégo-Quéré case,[72] the ECJ stayed with its conventional case law in the UPA case. The central

---

66 On this, Börner, *Die Entscheidungen der Höhen Behörde*, 1965, 114–117; Schwarze, in: *FS für Schochauer*, 1981, 927 (930). This Argument in ECJ, case 16 and 17/62, European Court reports 1962, 963 (978) – Confédération nationale des producteurs de fruits et légumes; critically Erichsen/Weiß, *Jura 1990*, 528 (532 f.).

67 In detail with legally comparing references Walbroeck/Verheyden, *CDE 31* (1995), 399 ff. Recently, especially the opinions of AG Jacobs, in: *ECJ*, case C-50/00 P, European Court reports 2002, I-6677 – Unión des Pequeños Agricultores.

68 Approving Schwarze, *FS für Schlochauer* (fn. 66), 927 (932), further Classen, *Die Europäisierung der Verwaltungsgerichtsbarkeit*, 1996, 68; J.-P. Schneider, *AöR 119* (1994), 294 (303).

69 Schwarze, *FS für Schlochauer* (fn. 66), 927 (938 ff.); Dauses, *DJT-Gutachten* (fn. 5), D 109, Classen, *Europäisierung* (fn. 68), 68 f.

70 On this, e.g., AG Jacobs, in: ECJ, case C-358/89, European Court reports 1991, I-2501 – Extramet, there mn. 69–74; id., in the opinions UPA (mn. 68), there mn. 38 ff.; v. Burchard, *EuR 26* (1991), 140 (144 f.); Allkemper, *Rechtsschutz* (fn. 12), 205 ff.; v. Danwitz, *NJW 1993*, 1108 (1112 f.); Sedemund/Heinemann, *DB 1995*, 1161 (1163 f.); Rengeling, in: *FS für Everling*, Vol. 2, 1995, 1187 (1192–1197); Waelbroeck/Verheyden, *CDE 31* (1995), 399 (433 ff.). Against those arguments, on the other hand, Nihoul, *RTDE 1994*, 171 (188–193), who, in my opinion, evaluates the practical difficulties and the duration of the submission process, in particular, too little.

71 ECJ, case C-50/00 P, European Court reports 2002, I-6677 – Unión des Pequeños Agricultores *v* Council; on this inter alia Nettesheim, *JZ 2002*, 928; Wölker, *DÖV 2003*, 570; Röhl, *Jura 2003*, 830; Gillaux, *CDE 2003*, 177; Ragolle, *ELRev* 28 (2003), 90; about the realisation of the resultant requirements of judicial protection in German law Lenz/Staeglich, *NVwZ 2004*, 1428.

72 CFI, case T-177/01, European Court reports 2002, II-2365 – Jégo-Quéré et Cie SA *v* Commission; consequently repealed by the ECJ, case C-263/02 P – Commission *v* Jégo Quéré

point of the decision is the idea that the gap in judicial protection referred to by the Attorney General and the CFI does not exist. The EC Treaty provided an absolute judicial protection system, which resulted from the interaction of the courts of the Member States and those of the Community. Closing any eventual gaps of judicial protection was the task of the Member States. The latter would have to provide adequate remedies and would have to apply their inner-state judicial protection system in such a way that the integrated control of European norms is provided for, in all cases. According to the ECJ, a new interpretation of Article 230(4) of the EC Treaty would exceed the competence of the Community judges, since it would lead to the abolition of the requirement of individual interest and would therefore equal an alteration of the Treaty, which could only be done by the Member States.

3.5.3. The Separation of legal form and legal effect

The lack of a categorical separation[73] of legal form and legal effect also burdens the discussion about the voidability of normative acts within the scope of Article 230(4) of the EC Treaty, especially in connection with the question about individual and direct concern.[74]

On the one hand with this term the character of an act having a regulating effect is indicated – i.e. a character, which would rather be assumed to be part of the cause of action – on the other hand, its effect on the judicially protected position of the claimant, which is rather part of the question about the relation to the subject of the action.[75] On the basis of a classification of regulations and norms in individual cases, this ambiguity might be historically based on a shift of ideas from the ECSC to the ECT: Article 33(3) of the ECSC mentions the annulment of individual decisions, which concern the claimant: "un recours contre les décisions et recommandations individuelles les concernant", i.e. refers to the "caractère individuel" of Article 15(2) ECSC.[76] On the other hand, Article 230(4) of the EC Treaty uses the character of the individual interest in order to

et Cie SA; discussion by Röhl, *GPR 2004*, 178.

73 Also British authors summarise the permissibility condition "locus standi", the question about the character of the decision as well as about the individual and direct concern; e.g., Hartley, *The Foundations of European Community Law*, 5th ed., Oxford 2003, 355 ff.

74 Cf. the differentiation between "form" and "substance" in Nettesheim, in: Micklitz/Reich, *Public Interest Litigation* (fn. 64), 225 (226).

75 Against the twofold application of the individuality criterion, see Matthies, in: *Referat 46. DJT*, G 60 f.; now definitely also Arnull, *CMLR 38* (2001), 7 (40 f.).

76 The German translation of the Treaty: "Klage gegen die sie individuell betreffenden Entscheidungen und Empfehlungen", on the other hand, refers the criterion "individuell" incorrectly to the relation of the annulled legal act to the claimant; Erichsen/Weiß, *Jura 1990*, 528 (532); Drewes, *Entstehen und Entwicklung des Europäischen Rechtsschutzes vor den Gerichten der Europäischen Gemeinschaften*, 2000, 65, 80; clarifying, ECJ, case 7/54 et al.; European Court reports 1955/56, 51 (87) – Groupement des Industries Sidérurgiques Luxembourgeoises.

describe a relation to the claimant. By linking the interpretation of the criterion of the individual interest according to the CFI to the jurisdiction concerning the distinction between individual and general decisions according to the ECSC, the ECJ merged arguments, which serve the distinction between normative legal acts and regulations in individual cases, and therefore the question concerning a general character of the annulled legal act, and used them for the category of individual interest and therefore the question about the relation to the claimant.[77] Since the differentiation between the normative legal act and the regulation in individual cases only leads to consequences concerning the question of the admissibility, this shift did not attract attention immediately.[78]

3.5.4. *The action for annulment against regulations*

The problem with the admissibility of actions against normative acts is usually apparent with regulations. The basic statement of the case law used to be definite: "*actual*" regulations would not be subject to annulment. They could not be understood as decisions in terms of Article 230(4) of the EC Treaty; this statutory provision would only provide the voidability of "decisions", which – according to Article 249(4) of the EC Treaty – have to be differentiated from the regulations because of their general character.[79] However, it depends on the individual contested provision and it could therefore be the case that a legal act enacted as a regulation could include single provisions with a decision-like character, which could be subject to an action for annulment in individual cases.

"Pseudo" – regulations and retroactivity cases

According to the second alternative of Article 230(4) of the EC Treaty, decisions "in the form of a regulation"[80] can also be annulled. This denotes provisions, which subjectively represent decisions in individual cases, but which appear in the form of a regulation. The statement of the ECJ refers to this: institutions could not deny judicial protection by their choice of legal form.[81] The ECJ has qualified, in particular, those decisions which appear in the form of a regulation and which refer ascertainably to many completed cases but it has not qualified those acts as decisions where the individuals involved can be ascertained but

---

77 Critically Matthies, in: *Referat 46. DJT*, G 60 f.

78 Critically already Börner, in: *Referat 46. DJT*, G 23–32 about the jurisdiction, who declares by the criterion of the individual interest, also the action against decisions with normative effect, as inadmissible. Similarly Hedemann/Robinson, *EPL 2* (1996), 127 (136–140) and Craig/de Búrca, *EU Law* (fn. 64), 487.

79 ECJ, case 16 and 17/62, European Court reports 1962, 963 (978) – Confédération nationale des producteurs de fruits et légumes; approved by ECJ in the cases above fn. 13.

80 More clearly in the French version: "sous l'apparence d'un règlegement".

81 E.g., ECJ., case 789/80, European Court reports 1980, 1949 (mn. 7) – Calpak; CFI, case T-476/93, European Court reports 1993, II-1187 (mn. 19) – FRSEA.

whose numbers are not limited. However, this line of the jurisdiction was interrupted, when regulations were declared as voidable, *as far as* they refer to completed cases.[82] A special treatment of this retroactivity problem, also known in German law, should be indicated. However, those cases of an *also* individual effect can only hardly be included in a concept of Article 230 of the EC Treaty determined as a legal form, which requires a non-ambiguous qualification.[83] The fact, that this jurisdiction had been limited to special cases, has possibly prevented the reflection about its meaning within the scope of Article 230 of the EC Treaty.

Regulations with (also) individual effects

The anti-dumping cases lead to a noticeable rejection of an understanding of Article 230 of the EC Treaty as legal form.[84] Here, the ECJ declared regulations as voidable: it attributed a normative *character*, and an individual *effect*[85] to its provisions. Thus, it was not the case that single provisions arising from a regulation with general effect were given the character of a decision. Predominantly, the capacity to bring actions according to Article 230(4) of the EC Treaty was granted to those corporations, who were the target of anti-dumping investigations. An important factor was mainly connected with the fact that the corporations had no other possibility of judicial protection when exporting to the Community,[86] since the anti-dumping tariffs were imposed on the importers.[87] Therefore it was also clear for the anti-dumping law that

82 ECJ, case 62/70, European Court reports 1971, 908 (908 mn. 10) – Bock; case 11/82, European Court reports 1985, 207 (242 ff., mn. 12–31) – Piraiki-Patraiki; case C-152/88, European Court reports 1990, I-2477 (2507 mn. 10–12) – Sofrimport; Scherzberg, in: Siedentopf (ed.), *Europäische Integration und nationalstaatliche Verwaltung*, 1991, 17 (23 f.); Hedemann-Robinson, *EPL 2* (1996), 127 (133–135).

83 "A single provision cannot at one and the same time have the character of a measure of general application and of an individual measure", ECJ, case 45/81, European Court reports 1982, 1129 (1144 mn. 18) – Moksel.

84 Allied Corporation I and II, ECJ, case 239 et al./82, European Court reports 1984, 1005; case 53/83, European Court reports 1985, 1621; CFI, case T-2/95, European Court reports 1998, II-3939 (mn. 49–52) – Industrie des Poudres Squériques; on this amongst others Rabe, *EuR 26* (1991), 236 ff.

85 Waelbroeck/Verheyden, *CDE 31* (1995), 399 (401).

86 Allied Corporation I (fn. 85), mn. 13. The same applies to the concerned rival firms within the Community in case of the rejection of an anti-dumping regulation (ECJ, case 264/82, European Court reports 1985, 849 (865 f., mn. 11–16) – Timex), but also for the corporations within the Community, who have an interest in the low priced purchase of the goods. About the concept of judicial protection as basis for the permissibility, Scherer/Zuleeg, in: Schweitzer (ed.), *Europäisches Verwaltungsrecht*, 1991, 197 (213 f.); Lenaerts/Arts, *Procedural Law* (fn. 5), No. 7–067.

87 Accordingly, those importers do not have the right to take action, since they can incidentally invoke a control of the regulation by the rescission of the notice of assessment, ECJ, Allied Corporation I (fn. 85), mn. 15.

provisions with a normative character can also concern single parties individually and can therefore provide the right to take an action for annulment.[88]

This jurisdiction has been applied to other areas of Community law when the ECJ, for instance, permitted the action against a genuine regulation in the Codorníu case.[89] Here, the rule was confirmed and generalised that the action of annulment to a legal act with a normative content need not be a priori inadmissible because of its legal nature, but that the question of individual concern is predominantly important.[90] This basic statement has been repeated in subsequent cases, initially without declaring a regulation as voidable.[91] It was only at a later stage that the CFI also permitted an action for annulment against a regulation, the character of which the court explicitly qualified as normative and therefore the regulation could not be categorised as a decision in terms of Article 230(4) of the EC Treaty.[92] In general, then, real regulations are also voidable, if they concern several parties individually. The fundamental reason for this is the judicial protection mandate of the ECJ manifested in Article 220 of the EC Treaty.[93]

3.5.5. The voidability of guidelines

Since, unlike regulations, directives need to be enacted by the national legislator, the claimant is usually granted judicial protection on a national level in coaction with the preliminary proceedings (*Vorlageverfahren*).[94] At first sight, on the basis of directives a differentiation according to form seems to be sufficient. However, also in this matter, the case law of the ECJ seems to be inconsistent.[95] Anyway in

88 ECJ, case C-358/89, European Court reports 1991, I-2501 – Extramet.

89 ECJ, case C-309/89, European Court reports 1994, I-1853 – Codorníu. Mn. 19 of the decision: "Although it is true that according to the criteria in the second paragraph of Article 173 of the Treaty the contested provision is, by nature and by virtue of its sphere of application, of a legislative nature in that it applies to the traders concerned in general, that does not prevent it from being of individual concern to some of them."

90 Cf. above Fn. 91 Hedemann-Robinson, *EPL 2* (1996), 127 (151); Neuwahl, *EL-Rev 21* (1996), 17 (22 f.).

91 ECJ, case C-142/00, European Court reports 2003, I-3483 – Nederlandse Antillen. CFI, case T-116/94, European Court reports 1995, II-1 (mn. 26) – Cassa nazionale di previdenza ed assistenza; case T-481 et al./93 European Court reports 1995, II-2941 (mn. 50) – Vereniging van Exporteurs in Levende Varkens et al.; case T-482/93, European Court reports 1996, II-609 (mn. 56) – Weber; case T-158/95 (mn. 56) – Eridania. Used as argument in ECJ, case C-68/95, European Court reports 1996, I-6065 (mn. 59) – T. Port. Lenaerts/Arts, *Procedural law* (Fn. 5), No. 7–043.

92 CFI, case T-125/96 et al. (mn. 161–169, especially 162 f.) – Boehringer.

93 Cf. AG Jacobs in: ECJ, case C-358/89, European Courts reports 1991, I-2501 (mn. 34 ff., especially 50.53) – Extramet; Nettesheim, in: Micklitz/Reich, *Public Interest Litigation* (fn. 64), 225 (230).

94 Detailed J.-P. Schneider, *AöR 119* (1994), 294 (302–308).

95 Left open in ECJ, case C-10/95, European Court reports 1995, I-4149 (mn. 31 f.) – Asocarne, on this Klüpfel, *EuZW*, 1996, 393 ff. About the entire affaire Vandersanden, *CDE 31* (1995), 535 (541 f. No. 17–19); W. Cremer, *EWS* 1999, 48 (50 f.) and *id.* in: Calliess/Ruffert, *EUV/EGV*

more recent case law, the CFI seems to proceed under the assumption of the possibility of an appeal to "actual" directives, which are therefore not "pseudo-directives", on condition of the existence of individual and direct concern.[96]

3.5.6. Decisions with the character of a legal rule addressed to the Member States

According to the case law of the ECJ, the category of legal acts with a normative effect towards the claimant should also include decisions, especially if they are addressed to one or more Member States and concern the validity or admissibility of national legal norms. The Plaumann case represents the basic case in this constellation of a decision to a Member State referring to a national norm.[97] In this case, the Federal Republic of Germany was denied the approval of an alteration in custom tariffs. An economic operator, who would have benefited from such an alteration brought an action against it. In other cases too,[98] the ECJ initially denied the admissibility of the action of opposition, because of the general application of the contested legal act, whereas the differentiation from provisions in single cases was made by means of the criterion of "general application", similarly to differentiation from the regulation. The exceptions to this basic rule developed parallel to the case law concerning regulations. The provision was considered voidable, when in the special circumstances of the case by its issuance, the party concerned has already been identified,[99] and therefore once again in cases of retroactivity.[100] In addition to this, an individual concern was also accepted in other cases, especially of process participation.[101] In current case law the provision's qualification is no longer decisive, according to the basic line of the reasoning mentioned above, but it is merely asked whether the claimant is individually and directly concerned.[102]

(fn. 64), Art. 230 Rn. 37–43. For an analogous application of Article 230 4. of the EC Treaty Allkemper, *Rechtsschutz* (fn. 12), 95 ff. with further references in Fn. 374.

96 CFI, case T-135/96, European Court reports 1998, II-2335 (mn. 68 f.) – UEAPME, there, rejected because of lacking individual concern; CFI, case T-172/98 et al., European Court reports 2000, II-2487 (mn. 27 ff.) – Salamander; Lenaerts/Arts, *Procedural Law* (Fn. 5), No. 7–044.

97 ECJ, case T-135/96, European Court reports 1963, 215 – Plaumann; confirming ECJ, case 67 et al./85, European Court reports 1988, 219 (267 f., mn. 14 f.) – van der Kooy. Critically about such an interpretation of the character of the individual concern Börner, in *Referat 46. DJT*, G 23–32.

98 Symptomatically ECJ, case 206/87, European Court reports 1989, 275 (289 mn. 12–19) – Lefebvre, which is about the approval concerning France's exclusion of bananas from the dollar area from the Community treatment.

99 ECJ, case 106 et al. /63, European Court reports 1965, 548 – Töpfer.

100 So called by ECJ, case 206/87, European Court reports 18989, 275 (289 mn. 17) – Lefebvre.

101 ECJ, case 67 et al. /85, European Court reports 1988, 219 (268 f., mn. 20–25) – van der Kooy.

102 ECJ, case C-390/95 P, European Court reports 1999, I-769 (mn. 25–28) – Antillean Rice Mills; CFI, case T-480/93, European Court reports 1995, II-2305, case T-481/93, European Court reports 1995, II-2941 – Vereniging van Exporteurs in Levende Varkens et al; case T-398/94, European Court reports 1996, II-477 (mn. 38) – Kahn Scheppvaart; case T-482/93, European

3.5.7. The legal form as a mere preliminary question

This result from the voidability of normative acts can only be justified in theory by relinquishing an identity of the decision in terms of in Article 230(4) and Article 249(4) of the EC Treaty. On the other hand, changing the qualification of the voidable normative act into a decision is also excluded, if the definition in Article 249(4) of the EC Treaty were to be included.[103] If the latter applies, for example regulations which also concern single parties individually would not have to be published in the Official Journal, Article 254(2) of the EC Treaty. A mere redefinition of the measure, on the other hand, does not lead to greater effectiveness. Some have proffered the opinion of a double nature of the legal act: such cases represent, for example, a regulation and a decision, at the same time.[104] However, such an approach has proved to be systematically dissatisfying. It would only realise an adaptation to the wording of Article 230(4) of the EC Treaty without, however, effecting the sense of the definition of the wording, which was the result intended by the legislator. It would have achieved little, since the term decision has been expanded anyway with regard to preparatory and procedural measures (above paragraph 3.5.3).

As a reasonable result, it can only be concluded that the ECJ waived the requirement of a decision in terms of Article 230(4) of the EC Treaty, as a condition for an action for annulment also with regard to the differentiation from normative legal acts, while only the individual and direct concern of the claimant is required.[105] Through this, the action for annulment according to Article 230 of the EC Treaty has no proper section on examination for "cause of

---

Court reports 1996, II-609 – Weber; case T-70/94, European Court reports 1996, II-1741 – Comafrica; case T-298/94, European Court reports 1996, II-1531 – Roquette Frères; case T-60/96, European Court reports 1997, II-849 (mn. 5) – Merck et al.; case T-86/96, European Court reports 1999, II-179 (mn. 45) – ADL.

103 Against Allkemper, *Rechtsschutz* (fn. 12), 61 and 99; Gesser, *Die Nichtigkeitsklage nach Artikel 173 EGV*, 1995, 29; Lengauer, *Nichtigkeitsklage* (fn. 12), 95.

104 As CFI, case T-481 et al./93, European Court reports 1995, II-2941 (2961 mn. 50) – Levende Varkens; case T-47/95, European Court reports 1997, II-481 (494 mn. 43) – Terres Rouges; case T-122/96, European Court reports 1997, II-1559 (1580 f. mn. 58) – Federolio. Against AG Jacobs, in: ECJ, case C-358/89, European Court reports 1991, I-2501 (2517 mn. 39–49) – Extramet; AG Lenz, in: ECJ, European Court reports 1994, I-1835 (1865 mn. 33) – Codorníu; Sedemund/Heinemann, *DB 1995*, 713 (717); Arnull, *CMLR 32* (1995), 7 (24); Nettesheim, in: Micklitz/Reich, *Public Interest Litigation* (fn. 64), 225 (228). Different ECJ, case 45/81, European Court reports 1982, 1129 (1144 mn.18) – Moksel, cf. above fn. 84.

105 AG Jacobs, in: ECJ, case C-358/89, European Court reports 1991, I-2501 (2517 mn. 50–53) – Extramet; AG Lenz, in: ECJ, European Court reports 1994, I-1835 (1865 mn. 32–37) – Codorníu; clearly also Ehlers, *VerwArch 84 (1993)*, 139 (150 f.); Arnull, *CMLR 32* (1995), 7 (39 f.); Sedemund/Heinemann, *DB 1995*, 1161 (1165); Waelbroeck/Verheyden, *CDE 31 (1995)*, 399 (412 No. 16); Vandersanden, *CDE 31 (1995)*, 535 (547 f., No. 28 f.); Neuwahl, *ELRev 21* (1996), 17 (19–23, 31); Cooke, *Principle and Pragmatism* (fn. 64), 25–29, 33; Nettesheim, in: Micklitz/Reich, *Public Interest Litigation* (fn. 64), 225 (230); Arnull, *CMLR 38 (2001)*, 7 (14 ff.); about the same result also Borowski, *EuR 2004*, 879 (888).

action", which is linked to the legal forms of Article 249(4) of the EC Treaty and which would have to be separated from the subjective entitlement to bring an action, which would have to be deduced from the characteristic of the individual and direct *concern*.[106] In this context, the qualification of the legal act is only important in so far as a claimant, unlike in regard to regulations or directives, does not have to prove a direct and individual concern for a decision addressed to him.[107] For a regulation, directive or a decision with normative effect being addressed to the Member State, on the contrary, an examination concerning individual and direct concern is necessary, and this will lead to admissibility only in exceptional cases while the exclusion of the annulment cannot be supported solely by such a qualification.[108] A proper theoretical content is not achieved by a classification under a legal form.[109] The decoupling of the judicial protection from the forms of action in the Lisbon Treaty completes this development.[110]

3.6. REGARDING THE CLAIMANT – THE INDIVIDUAL CONCERN

For normative acts as well as for decisions addressed to third parties, the admissibility of the action requires that there is proof of the claimant's individual concern. In detail, the court considers the relevant matter of the individual application, but some general characteristics can be discerned, which form the basis on which the ECJ determines the individual concern for both normative acts and third party actions.[111] They describe the relationship of the cause of action towards the claimant, and can therefore not be considered as an element of a cause of action which has to be objectively determined, respectively.

The most important criterion in detecting the individual concern is the participation of the claimant in the administrative procedure. If the claimant's performance was the topic of an administrative procedure or if he was entitled to procedural rights during the administrative procedure because of normative

---

106 Booß, in: Grabitz/Hilf, *EUV/EGV* (fn. 5), Art. 230 EGV mn. 55 f. Indicated as a tendency by Sedemund/Heinemann, *DB 1995*, 713 (719); different, e.g., AG Warner, in: ECJ, case 789/79 et al., European Court reports 1980, 1949 (1970 f.) – Calpak; *Erichsen/Weiß, Jura 1990*, 528 (531); Scherzberg, in: Siedentopf, *Europäische Integration* (fn. 83), 17 (23); *Allkemper, Rechtsschutz* (fn. 12), 57 ff.; Dörr, in: Sodan/Ziekow, *VwGO* (fn. 5), EVR mn. 111; *W. Cremer, EWS 1999*, 48 ff.; Burgi, in: Rengeling/Middeke/Gellermann, *Handbuch des Rechtsschutzes in der EU* (fn. 5), §7 mn. 49: "dogmatically actually prior provision of the legal nature". Ignoring the differentiation Schwarze, in: id. (ed.), *EU-Kommentar*, Art. 239 mn. 12 at the end.

107 Neuwahl, *ELRev 21* (1996), 17 (22 f.).

108 As Neuwahl, *ELRev 21* (1996), 17 (22 f.).

109 Also Booß, in Grabitz/Hilf, *EUV/EGV* (fn. 5), Art. 230 EGV mn. 12, 16, 47, 55; Bast, in: v. Bogdandy, *Europäisches Verfassungsrecht* (fn. 7), 521.

110 Above 2.5.

111 Lenaerts/Arts, *Procedural Law* (fn. 5), No. 7–059 ff.

allocation, respectively – as in the subsidy law[112] – on the basis of general principles of law, he is usually also entitled to an action for annulment of the legal act which has been enacted on the basis of the procedure. It is doubtful whether a factual concern can suffice as adequate individualisation.[113] The extent to which Community civil rights or other material legal positions could facilitate a sufficient standing cannot be adequately deduced from the case law.[114] The ECJ expresses itself quite restrictively in the end. This might be due – especially in the case of normative acts – to the fact that otherwise the principle of its non-admissibility under Article 230(4) of the EC Treaty would be reversed completely. Therefore, the obstacle of the non-admissibility for normative acts usually cannot be overcome.[115] However, this is not because these rules would not fall under the action of annulment on the basis of their legal form, but because the ECJ is only willing to assume an individual concern in exceptional cases.[116] If this restrictive attitude is completely compatible with a concept of judicial protection, which the ECJ wants to deduce abstractly from Article 220 of the EC Treaty, appears to be uncertain.

3.7. THE PRINCIPLE OF DIRECT CONCERN

The voidable legal act also has to concern the claimant "directly".[117] This criterion, being especially applied in relation to decisions, is comparable to the requirement of the "direct legal effect to the outside" in §35, first sentence, VwVfG. Its purpose is the correct allocation of the jurisdiction competences in the face of the cooperation of various administrative authorities. The characteristic of direct concern therefore has a significant influence on the allocation of competences in the European judicial protection system. However, it refers to the meaning of an act for the claimant and therefore contains nothing specific concerning the cause of action.[118]

---

112 Now because of Article 20, Article 6(1) (2), Article 1 lit h) of the Regulation No 659/1999, cf. above fn. 54.

113 As Classen, *Europäisierung* (fn. 68), 83, also Schwarze, *RIW 1996*, 893 (897).

114 Approving, e.g. W. Cremer, *EWS 1999*, 48 (52); see already Ule, *46. DJT-Gutachten*, 21 f.

115 Craig/de Búrca, *EU Law* (fn. 64), 510 ff., justify the retentive admission of actions against normative acts with consideration to formal arrangements of the Community legislator and the multitude of possible actions. According to the German point of view, the arguments used there would have to be treated within the scope of subjective public law.

116 In the leading decision UPA (above, fn. 71) approved once again. Detailed analysis by Lenaerts/Arts, *Procedural Law* (fn. 5), No. 7–052 – 7–074 and Craig/de Búrca, *EU law* (fn. 64), 500 ff.

117 On this Daig, *Nichtigkeitsklagen* (fn. 5), mn. 131–134.

118 That, in contrast to this, the criterion of §35, first sentence, VwVfG refers to an objective characteristic, does not consider, who assumes the possibility of a double nature, correctly arguing this: *Stelkens/Stelkens*, in: Stelkens/Bonk/Sachs (eds.), *Verwaltungsverfahrensgesetz*, 6th edition 2001, §35 mn. 19.

4. PROBLEMS OF A PURE PROCEDURALLY-DETERMINED CONCEPT OF DECISION

4.1. INTRODUCTION

Article 230(4) of the EC Treaty is not linked to a legal form defined in another place, but uses its own, at first sight merely procedural concept of the decision. However, the experiences with the German doctrine of legal forms make it a matter for debate whether a merely procedural understanding which leaves out procedural and substantive implications could be maintained. This can be illustrated on the basis of the figure of stability.

4.2. PERIOD FOR ANNULMENT

An important procedural consequence of the classification of an action as a voidable decision is the applicability of the provision specifying a period of time of Article 230(5) of the EC Treaty: the action for annulment is only permissible within two months after the notification or announcement of the action or from the moment when the claimant has learnt of the action and its essential reasons. In contrast to German law, the short two-months-period without any remedy instruction[119] does not only run from the moment of the notification. If there has not been a notification,[120] the knowledge of the existence of a legal act concerning the claimant can in itself be sufficient to invoke the consequences of the time period.[121]

4.3. EFFECTIVENESS AND STABILITY

4.3.1. Introduction

The qualification of a measure as voidable in terms of Article 230(4) of the EC Treaty implies in reverse that, without repeal, it will remain effective without a

119 Approved in: ECJ, case C-153/98 P, European Court reports 19999, I-1441 – Guérin.

120 In this case, the period does not start to run until this moment. CFI, case T-100/97 (mn. 41 ff.) – Kneissl; case T-14/96, European Court reports 1999, II-139 (mn. 32 ff.) – BAI; even though this is not mandatory or constant practice, CFI, case T-264/03 (mn. 51 ff.).

121 ECJ, case 236/86, European Court reports 1988, 3761 (mn. 14) – Dillinger Hüttenwerke; case C-180/88, European Court reports 1990, I-4413 (mn. 22–24) – Wirtschaftsvereinigung Eisen- und Stahlindustrie; case C-102/92, European Court reports 1993, I-801 (mn. 18) – Ferriere Acciaierie Sarde; CFI, case T-465/93, European Court reports 1994, II-361 (mn. 29) – Murgia Messapica; case T-155/95, European Court reports 1998, II-2751 – LPN.

judgment modifying its legal status, or that its effectiveness is assumed.[122] This also implies that other authorities and especially the national courts are bound by such an act.

A significant consequence of this effectiveness is the possibility that voidable decisions can develop stability, if they have not been rescinded within the period of Article 230(5) of the EC Treaty.[123] Such a stability,[124] i.e. the exclusion of admissibility, would be unproblematic, if this was the only procedural consequence. Due to the link with the substantive consequences, i.e. the effectiveness of the decision, the failure to observe the time-limit has consequences in those cases, in which the voidable action represents the preliminary question for a court's or authority's decision. Related to proceedings in front of national courts, this problem invokes processes in form of the ECJ within the scope of proceedings or of government liability, since this is the only measure for declaring legal acts of the EC-institutions as void.[125]

4.3.2. The Deggendorf case law

Apparently in the Rau case, the ECJ still assumed an independence of the preliminary procedure and the action of annulment referring to one and the same decision and therefore has imputed merely procedural consequences to the failure to observe the time-limit according to Article 230(5) of the EC Treaty.[126] The acceptance of a material effect of the stability has been found by the ECJ in the case of "Textilwerke Deggendorf".[127] A subsidy beneficiary had not challenged the Commission's reclaim decision being addressed to the Member

---

122 Gaitanides, in: v. d. Groeben/Schwarze, *EU-/EG-Vertrag* (fn. 5), Art. 230 mn. 5, Art. 231 mn. 2. Annacker, Der fehlerhafte Rechtsakt im Gemeinschafts- und Unionsrecht 1999, 79 f.; ECJ, case 7/56 et al., European Court reports 1957, 85 (126) – Algera; case 101/78, European Court reports 1979, 623 (mn. 5) – Granaria; case 15/85, European Court reports 1987, 1005 (1036); ECJ, case C-137/92, European Court reports 1994, I-2555 (mn. 48) – KOM/BASF.

123 Cf. especially ECJ, case 20/65, European Court reports 1965, 1112 (1117) – Collotti; case 156/77, European Court reports 1978, 1881 (mn. 21/24); case C-183/91, European Court reports 1993, I-3131 (mn. 9 f.); case C-310/97 P, European Court reports 1999, I-5363 (mn. 57–61) – AssiDomaen Kraft Products.

124 On this Kamann/Selmayr, *NVwZ 1999*, 1041.

125 ECJ, case 314/85, European Court reports 1987, 4199 (mn. 20) – Foto-Frost.

126 ECJ, case 133 et al. /85, European Court reports 1987, 2289 (2338, mn. 11 f.) – Rau. However, in European Court reports 1994, I-833 (mn. 20) – Deggendorf and European Court reports 1997, I-585 (mn. 22) – Wiljo, the ECJ explains that the question being mentioned in the following concerning a material stability has not been asked, since the decisions presented in a procedure in terms of Article 230 of the EC Treaty could not develop stability because of an opportune rescission. Cf. also already ECJ, case 156/77, European Court reports 1978, 1881 (mn. 25).

127 ECJ, case C-188/92, European Court reports 1994, I-833 – TWD Textilwerke Deggendorf. Having been approved in the following time: ECJ European Court reports 1997, I-585 (mn. 19–23) – Wiljo NV; CFI, case T-227/95, European Court reports 1997, II-1185 (mn. 58) – Zellstoff II. This jurisdiction is also accordingly applied to the Member States, ECJ, case C-241/01, European Court reports 2002, I-9079 (mn. 34 ff.) – National Farmers Union.

State according to Article 88(2) of the EC Treaty within the time period according to Article 230(5) of the EC Treaty, even though the beneficiary would have been entitled and able to do so. In a later procedure against the decision of the national authorities, the objection of the beneficiary that the Commission's decision had been unlawful was not heard. The procedural consequence was that the national court was not able to submit the question concerning the validity of the Commission's decision according to Article 234 of the EC Treaty to the ECJ, anymore. This consequence can only be drawn if the voidable decision is considered as having a regulatory effect and can therefore invoke material effects in subsequent proceedings. In theory, this represents the acceptance of a material stability for voidable decisions.

4.3.3. Procedures covered by stability

The stability of voidable decisions extends to procedures before the European courts as well as the national courts in cases concerning the validity of a provision in question. Actions for damages based on Article 288(2) of the EC Treaty are independent and represent an autonomous remedy, according to the consistent case law of the ECJ.[128] Therefore, that a decision may for reasons of stability not be challenged directly does not hinder an action for damages,[129] if it does not serve as evasion of the inadmissibility of an action for annulment.[130] This would comply with the legal situation in France.[131]

4.3.4. Legal actions covered by stability

In cases where voidable actions can develop stability with its material consequences, the approval of the possibility of annulling other than formal decisions of Article 249(4) of the EC Treaty can itself prove to be a Trojan horse.[132] On the one hand, this applies for non-formal decisions (a) and on the other for normative actions of the EC institutions (b).

---

128 ECJ, case 281/82, European Court reports 1984, 1969 (1982 mn. 11) – Unifrex. On this van der Woude, in: Heukels/McDonnell, *The Action for Damages in Community Law*, The Hague 1997, 109 (116).

129 ECJ, case 4/69, European Court reports 1971, 325 (336 mn. 6) – Lütticke: about the action against the failure to act. ECJ, case 5/71, European Court reports 1971, 975 (mn. 3) – Schöppenstedt: Damages also for normative acts, insofar independent of the action for annulment, especially ECJ, case 175/84, European Court reports 1986, 753 (770, mn. 32) – Krohn. Different still ECJ, case 4/67, European Court reports 1967, 487 (498) – Collignon.

130 CFI, case T-541/93, European Court reports 1995, II-624 (mn. 59) – Cobrecaf, case T-72/99, European Court reports 2000, II-2521 (mn. 36). On this van der Woude, in: Heukels/McDonnell, *Action for Damages* (fn. 129), 109 (116).

131 Auby/Drago, *Contentieux administratif*, 3e ed., 1984, T. 1, No. 798, 946.

132 Cf, already Börner, *Entscheidungen* (fn. 66), 51 ff.; and Daig, *Nichtigkeitsklagen* (fn. 5), mn. 46; also Röben, *Die Einwirkung der Rechtsprechung des Europäischen Gerichtshofs auf das Mitgliedstaatliche Verfahren in öffentlich-rechtlichen Streigkeiten*, 1998, 72.

Other legal actions

In the case of Windpark Groothusen[133] the claimant attempted to claim financial support from the Commission. However, the claimant did not receive the information in one of the many notifications from the Commission concerning the progress of the procedure, that a decision has already been made declaring the final exclusion of the proposed project. Accordingly, the time period to apply for an annulment expired. The ECJ adhered to the content of the now static decision. It would also be possible that the Commission transfers the documents to a national authority. If the claimant in the procedure against the national authority now claims that knowledge from these documents was subject to a prohibition of application, since the Commission had not been entitled to transfer or raise them, the question arises whether the collection of data or the transfer of documents represented a voidable action and therefore – when the time period had expired – the national court was limited in its possibility of judicial review in this regard.[134]

Normative Actions

In case the voidability is expanded to include normative legal acts, e.g. regulations, the party concerned is threatened by a possible stability to that extent. In French law however, the principle that the objection of the illegality of an administrative action against *actes réglementaires* is always possible applies – even though, a potential time period to take an action might have expired.[135] In European procedural law, the search for an answer at first leads to Article 241 of the EC Treaty, which seems to basically exclude a stability of regulations, as well. However, the jurisdiction has expanded Article 241 of the EC Treaty by one material criterion. For reasons of judicial protection, it has declared this provision as applicable for all legal actions of a general character, which have the same effects as regulations and for which private parties do not have a possibility to rescind.[136] The downside of this material criterion can be seen in the statement of the Attorney General in the Deggendorf case,[137], when he says: "The Court' s judgment in Simmenthal v Commission (4) suggests that Article 184 may be invoked only against normative measures which natural and legal persons would not be able to attack under Article 173."

---

133 ECJ, case C-48/96 P, European Court reports 1998, I-2873 – Windpark Groothusen.

134 Investigated in detail for cases of inter-administrative relations by J. Hofmann, *Rechtsschutz und Haftung im Europäischen Verwaltungsverbund*, 2004, 219 ff.

135 Auby/Drago, *Contentieux administratif* (fn. 132), No. 799, 947 f.; Pacteau, in: Spiliotopoulos, *Judicial Protection* (fn. 3), 327; however, now restrictions apply, e.g. for local plans.

136 ECJ, case 92/78, European Court reports 1979, 777 (mn. 35–43) – Simmenthal; cf. also ECJ, European Court reports 1994, I-833 (mn. 23) – Deggendorf. Already Börner, in: *Referat 46. DJT*, G 38.

137 There mn. 14.

Accordingly, the ECJ has not categorically excluded the stability of regulations or other legal actions being declared as voidable but which are not formal decisions. Rather more, the stability should depend on the fact whether the admissibility of an action has been "evident" or "undisputed".[138] Thus, this is usually not the case for regulations[139] and directives.[140] Exceptions are possible, as shown by the anti-dumping Regulations, which can develop stability despite their normative character.[141] The criterion of publicity cannot be used as the connecting factor for the time periods.[142] In general this shows how difficult it is to combine substantive consequences with the concept of the voidable decision defined by the need for judicial protection.

5. SUMMARY, RESULT AND PROSPECT

5.1. SUMMARY

This work dedicated to the concept of the voidable decision according to Article 230(4) of the EC Treaty dealt with the question of the model followed by the procedural law of the EC Treaty: The legal-form oriented approach of the German law of administrative procedure or the way of French law, which is more oriented towards forms of legal protection. In support of "decision" as a legal-form term according to the EC Treaty, one could mention that the provisions of Article 230(4) of the EC Treaty and Article 249(4) of the EC Treaty always require the existence of a "decision". However, a more detailed analysis of the Treaty text lead to doubts concerning such a uniform understanding (above B). The ECJ's jurisdiction concerning the voidable decision according to Article 230(4) of the EC Treaty, in particular, does not use a uniform legal-form concept. The ECJ, following French administrative procedural thinking, concentrates on the classification of an action as voidable decision in terms of Article 230(4) of the EC Treaty. This is also necessary, since the term decision opens the possibilities of judicial protection. However, such an understanding of the decision as a form of judicial protection can lead to difficulties concerning coordination with material law, which can be shown by the institute of stability.

138 Negating the contradiction to Article 241 of the EC Treaty, completely, ECJ, case 11/00, European Court reports 2001, I-7147 (mn. 72 ff.) – Commission *v* ECB.

139 Thereto, ECJ, case C-241/95, European Court reports 1996, I-6699 (mn. 15) – Accrington Beef. Because of this, against a transfer of the Deggendorf jurisdiction to regulations also *Gröpl*, EuGRZ 1995, 583 (588).

140 Thereto, ECJ, case C-408/95, European Court reports 1997, I-6315 (mn. 29) – Eurotunnel; there also Attorney General Tesauro, mn. 17–21.

141 ECJ, case C-239/99, European Court reports 2001, I-1197 – Nachi.

142 More positive Kamann/Selmayr, NVwZ 1999, 1041 (1045).

5.2. ABOUT THE DOCTRINE OF LEGAL FORM IN A EUROPEAN ADMINISTRATIVE LAW

For the carrying out of the mandate of judicial protection according to Article 220 of the EC Treaty, since the decision in the IBM case, one has to assume a wide interpretation of the term "voidable decision" in terms of Article 230(4) of the EC Treaty. The only direct judicial protection against acts of the EC-institutions stands and falls with the qualification as voidable in terms of this provision. In this function as opening to judicial protection, the meaning of the voidable decision in terms of Article 230(4) of the EC Treaty undermines itself, in a similar way to the *décision* in the French judicial protection system. Further dogmatic meanings for procedural or substantive questions ("saving function") are not included. This interpretation conforms to tendencies of former legal practices in Germany, which treated the qualification as an administrative act as an opening for judicial protection and therefore had to also deal with the term of administrative act extensively.

The term of the voidable decision according to Article 230(4) of the EC Treaty, especially, differs from the term of the legal form of the decision according to Article 249(4) of the EC Treaty and has to be determined independently from it. Legal consequences, which result from the qualification of a measure as a legally formal decision in terms of Article 249(4) of the EC Treaty, cannot be used as arguments during the differentiation of voidable decisions in terms of Article 230(4) of the EC Treaty from not voidable actions. Inversely, the jurisdiction of the ECJ concerning the definition of the voidable decision according to Article 230(4) of the EC Treaty cannot be used for the interpretation of Article 249(4) of the EC Treaty. Since the qualification as a voidable decision only bears procedural consequences, one does not have to focus on the precise differentiation of the level of the cause of action towards the right of action.

Therefore, in dogmatic terms, the "decision" as a legal form in EC law does not carry the same importance as does the administrative act in German law. Both procedural and procedure legal provisions or legal principles are not linked to the identification of a legal form, but primarily to material criteria, such as the individual and direct concern in particular.[143] Such an approach does not allow access to a storage function, as it is allowed by the terms of the German doctrine of action forms. In the light of the different functions of the term decision in the different provisions of the EC Treaty, it is impossible to develop an "objection-

---

143 Arnull, *CMLR 32* (1995), 7 (16). Cf., e.g. AG Cosmas in ECJ, case C-48/96 P, European Court reports 1998, I-2873 (mn. 70 ff.) – Windpark Groothusen: No hearing, since no intervention of rights, thus only refusal of a benefit. CF, also there mn. 73 fn. 37: "This is a separate question from the question whether the conditions for initiating proceedings against the decision are fulfilled under Article 173(4) of the Treaty". Also decision, mn. 47.

free and appropriate doctrine of action forms".[144] On the other hand, such a procedure serves for a more flexible assignment of general legal principles. By linking procedural principle with the legal forms of the administrative act and the public-legal contract, an application of the general legal principles being subject to these provisions to other actions, became more complicated through the command of substantiation for analogies.[145] Finally, the theoretical separation of Article 230(4) of the EC Treaty and through this the attachment to a single-case decision also allows the theoretical development of the decision of Article 249(4) of the EC Treaty as a form of action.[146]

The procedural law of the EC Treaty, but also some of the procedural provisions of other Member States, an example of which is French law, do not allow the identification of legal forms at the level of European administrative law.[147] Therefore, the doctrine of legal forms of administrative actions cannot easily be transferred to European administrative law. After all, European administrative law could be inspired by the idea of the doctrine of legal forms as an analytic concept. On the basis of this approach, this investigation wanted to show that the expansion of the action for annulment according to Article 230(4) of the EC Treaty, including normative legal acts, is no single-case of case law. By this means methodical counter-arguments[148] could be invalidated. In addition, it was possible to call attention to the weak points of a concept of decision which was defined purely in procedural terms. However, in order to also assert this systematizing performance of the doctrine of legal forms in European case law, there must be further definition of its profile to the inside and a more open presentation to the outside world.[149]

5.3. ABOUT THE NORMATIVE BASIS OF EC PROCEDURAL LAW

A basic reason for the interpretational difficulties within the scope of the EC procedural law, is the insufficient and inadequate normative basis of EC

144 Scherzberg, in: Siedentopf, *Europäische Integration* (Fn. 48), 17 (42). From his appropriately analysed tendency concerning the ECJ, to qualify the dependence of the form of action of the action for annulment, Scherzberg concludes the need for a uniform term of the decision, but not one solely oriented towards Article 249 of the EC Treaty. He wants to develop it from the synopsis of all provisions referring to the form of action (l.c., 26).

145 As, e.g. for the §§28, 29 and 39 VwVfG Stelkens/Schmidt, in: Stelkens/Bonk/Sachs, *VwVfG* (Fn. 120), §1 mn. 280.

146 See also Vogt, in this volume, p. 341.

147 Against v. Danwitz, *Verwaltungsrechtliches System* (fn. 2), 67 ff., 168 ff. Cf. but now the development in the Spanish procedural administrative law, see above fn. 28.

148 E.g. W. Cremer, *EWS 1999*, 48 (50) and *id.*, in: Calliess/Ruffert, EUV/EGV (fn. 64), Article 230 mn. 36.

149 Important contributions also by v. Bogdandy/Bast/Arndt, *ZaöRV 2002*, 78 and Bast, in: v. Bogdandy/Bast (eds.), *Europäisches Verfassungsrecht* (fn. 7); Vogt, in this volume, p. 341.

procedural law and EC administrative law (*EG-Eigenverwaltungsrecht*). With the procedural instruments of the EC Treaty, and the increasing activities of the EC institutions, especially the Commission, it is impossible to proceed without having systematically dissatisfying results or an obvious infringement of the borders of case law. This will not change, as long as the basic contents of the EC procedural law are to be derived from the text of the EC Treaty and have a similar status. Again, it would be reasonable to adopt only the basic "procedural" provisions concerning the judicial protection mandate, the judicial protection guarantee and further constitutional requirements in the Treaty text. Furthermore, provisions about a judicial review for such legislative acts, which are enacted by the Council in cooperation with the Parliament, could be added. According to the wording of the Lisbon Treaty, these would be legislative acts (Article 289(3) TFEU). For all further questions, a more flexible and differentiated solution at secondary-law level would be required in the form of a general EC-administrative procedural and proceedings law. Since the Lisbon Treaty has not provided relief so far, the effort of interpretation will continue in the years to come. After all, Article 263 TFEU has been clear in so far that it is now certain that the judicial protection in front of the European courts will not follow a concept referring to legal form.

XVIII. LEGAL PROTECTION AND LIABILITY IN THE EUROPEAN COMPOSITE ADMINISTRATION*

Jens Hofmann

1. THE EUROPEAN COMPOSITE ADMINISTRATION

1.1. THE CONCEPT

For a long time, the concept of administration in the European Community used to be described from a dichotomising perspective. Accordingly, legal scholarship distinguished between the execution of EC law by the Member States ("indirect execution")[1] and the execution by the European Commission ("direct execution").[2] The concept of administration in the European Community was characterised as *dualistic* and *local* because the national authorities are mainly competent for the execution and application of EC law.

However, a concept of execution that is only influenced by the idea of separation no longer presents a true picture of the reality of administration in the European Community. If the concept of European Administration is viewed not only from an organisational perspective but also from a functional one, the nexus between the organisationally separated administrative entities becomes clearer, since the cooperation of administrative authorities is the most important

* This contribution is based on the author's thesis called *Rechtsschutz und Haftung im Europäischen Verwaltungsverbund*, [Legal Protection and Liability in the European Composite Administration] 2003. A first version (in German) was published in: Eberhard Schmidt-Aßmann and Bettina Schöndorf-Haubold, Der Europäische Verwaltungsverbund, Mohr Siebeck, Tübingen 2005, p. 353–381. The editors of this book have chosen the term "European Composite Administration" as translation of "Europäische Verwaltungsverbund."

1 Stettner, in: Dauses (ed.), *Handbuch des EU-Wirtschaftsrechts* [Handbook of EU Economic Law] B III., No. 11.

2 Pühs, *Der Vollzug von Gemeinschaftsrecht* [The Execution of Community Law], 1997, 73 ff.; Sydow, DV 34 (2001), 517 ff. (542); Nehl, *Europäisches Verwaltungsverfahren und Gemeinschaftsverfassung,* 2002, 30 ff.; Hegels, *EG-Eigenverwaltungsrecht und Gemeinschaftsverwaltungsrecht,* 2001, 27 ff.

instrument in securing an effective and uniform application of Community law.[3]

To secure an effective execution of EC law, the administrative entities within the EC are connected by inter-administrative ties, which range from an information exchange[4] to joint decision-making processes[5] and a joint concept development.[6] Administrative ties are not only to be found in a vertical direction between the national administrations and the EC administration, but also in a horizontal direction between the national administrations themselves.[7]

The two organisational principles of the European administration – "separation" and "conjointness" – are completed by the principle of *supranational hierarchy*.[8] The complex arrangement that is structured according to these three principles can be labelled as "European Composite Administration" (*Europäischer Verwaltungsverbund*)[9] and also explains why the dualistic model of European administration lays too much stress on the differentiation between the EC administration and the administration of the Member States. This no longer complies with reality.[10] This perception links up with the term "Network of States" (*Staatenverbund*) created by the German Constitutional Court (*Bundesverfassungsgericht*)[11] and reveals, on the one hand, that the European Administration is not a unique bloc but, on the other, that it does not consist of entities which are working separately alongside each other. The term Network has now been adopted by the European Commission as a translation of "Verbund".[12]

3 Communication from the Commission to the Council "Making the most of the Internal Market": Strategic Programme, COM/93/632FINAL, 2.

4 Example: Article 3 ff. Reg. (EEC) No. 595/91, OJ 1991 No. L 67, 11.

5 Example: the procedure under Article 7, 13 Reg. (EC) No. 258/97, OJ 1997 No L 43, 1 (Novel-Food Regulation).

6 E.g. the setup of the coherent European ecological network "Natura 2000" under Dir. 92/43/EWG, OJ EC 1992 No. L 206, 7 (Flora-Fauna-Habitat Directive).

7 To give examples: the mutual assistance on customs and agricultural matters under Article 4 ff. Reg. (EC) No. 515/97, OJ 1997 No. L 82, 1, or the participation of the authority of destination in the authorisation of a shipment of waste under Article 4 Reg. (EEC) No. 259/93, OJ 1993 No. L 30, 1.

8 Cf. to the development of hierarchies in the EC: Eekhoff, *Die Verbundaufsicht*, 2006; Schmidt-Aßmann, in: *Festschrift für Steinberger*, 2002, 1375 ff. (1383); Gil Ibáñez, *The Administrative Supervision and Enforcement of EC Law*, 1999, 251 ff.; Möllers, EuR 2002, 483 ff. (505 ff.); Pühs (fn. 2), 293.

9 Cp. Schmidt-Aßmann (fn. 8), 1375 ff. (1381); *idem.*, in: Schmidt-Aßmann/Hoffmann-Riem (ed.), *Verwaltungsverfahren und Verwaltungsverfahrensgesetz*, 2002, 429 ff. (445ff.); Sydow (fn. 2), 517 ff.

10 Cp. Sydow (fn. 2), 517 ff. (542) and Nehl (fn. 2), 30 ff.

11 BVerfGE 89, 155 ff. (182 ff.); also: Kirchhof, in: v. Bogdandy (ed.), *Europäisches Verfassungsrecht*, 2003, 893 ff. (particularly 904 ff.).

12 The Commission speaks of "Verbundverwaltung" in the German version and of "Networks" in the English version of the Communication "Management of Community programmes by networks of national agencies" COM 2001/648FINAL, 4 ff.

1.2. INTER-ADMINISTRATIVE TIES

1.2.1. The term

Jural links between administrative entities of different categories of international law can be termed "inter-administrative ties".[13] They function not only as the materialisation of one of the organisational principles of the European administration concept, but they are also the significant element in the European Composite Administration. In German juridical discussion, this phenomenon is also described with terms like *Verwaltungskooperation* (administrative cooperation)[14] or *Mischverwaltung* (mixed administration)[15] or even *Netzwerkbildung* (setup of networks).[16]

The variety of the terms used reveals that European case law[17] is still looking for an apt description of the phenomenon of conjointness but without making the effort to seek a definite term, which would be indispensable for juridical systematisation.[18] In this analysis, the circumscription "inter-administrative ties" has been chosen because this term is the most comprehensive term, which covers every kind of cooperation and interaction. It comprises, in particular, legal supervision which can hardly be characterised as a cooperative relationship because of the given conflict of interests, such as in the field of supervision of new aids granted by Member States under Article 88(2) EC Treaty. Also these arrangements cause problems for the systems of legal protection and the liability which are structured similarly like problems caused by constellations which can be characterised as cooperative.[19]

---

13 In detail cp J. Hofmann *(*fn. *), 1. Part B. I.

14 Cp. Schmidt-Aßmann, EuR 1996, 270 ff.; Sommer, *Verwaltungskooperation am Beispiel administrativer Informationsverfahren im Europäischen Umweltrecht*, 2003, 13 ff.; Trute, in: von Mangoldt/Klein/Starck, *Bonner Grundgesetz*, vol. 3, 4th edition, 2001, Article 83, No. 68 ff.

15 Schreiber, *Verwaltungskompetenzen der Europäischen Gemeinschaft*, 1997, 40 ff.; Stettner, in: Dauses (fn. 1), B. III. 3. d); Kadelbach, *Allgemeines Verwaltungsrecht unter europäischem Einfluss*, 1999, 19; Priebe, in: Schmidt-Aßmann/Hoffmann-Riem (ed.), *Strukturen des Europäischen Verwaltungsrechts*, 1999, 71 ff. (97); Galetta, in: Magiera/Sommermann (ed.), *Verwaltung in der Europäischen Union*, 2001, 63 ff. (69, 75).

16 Schmidt-Aßmann, in: Schmidt-Aßmann/Hoffmann-Riem (fn. 9), 429 ff. (445 ff.).

17 As well as the political science (keyword: "Regieren in Mehrebenensystemen" i.e. "governing in multi-level systems"). Cp. Jachtenfuchs/Kohler-Koch, in: idem. (ed.), *Europäische Integration*, 1996, 15 ff.; also Wessels, *Die Öffnung des Staates*, 2000, 53 ff.

18 Cp. Möllers, VerwArch. 93 (2002), 22 ff. (37 ff.); *idem*, VerwArch 90 (1999), 187 ff.

19 Cp. ECJ, Case C-188/92, ECR 1994, I-833 ff. (Textilwerke Deggendorf/Germany).

1.2.2. The relation to transnational administrative acts

Since the "transnational administrative act" (*transnationaler Verwaltungsakt*) is often linked to the cooperation of administration in Europe,[20] the relation between inter-administrative ties and "transnational measures" of administrative authorities needs to be clarified. A transnational measure can be defined as an activity of a state which not only has effect within a state's own territory but which crosses the national border and also has effect in the territory of another state.[21] Together with the supranational measures of the European Community – which are effective in vertical direction – and the national measures of the Member States – which are limited to their own territories – the transnational measures supplement the options of acting sovereign powers within the European Composite Administration.[22] Whereas inter-administrative ties are organisational or procedural links between administrative entities, "transnational measures" are characterised by the cross-border effects of sovereign powers. Like supranational measures, they are ruled by their own dogma, even if they frequently occur in combination with inter-administrative ties and even if some points of law raised by them are similar to those points of law brought up by inter-administrative ties, e.g. the question whether the referral to a foreign court is just and reasonable.[23]

1.2.3. Typology

In nearly all fields of European Administration inter-administrative ties can be identified, for example, in the field of agricultural and customs administration, of tax administration, of the Structural Funds, of the measures to counter fraud affecting the financial interest of the Community, of the supervision of aids granted by states, of the implementation of the rules on competition, of the licensing procedures affecting the rights of free movement or in the field of the setup of the coherent European ecological network "Natura 2000".[24] Inter-administrative ties can be classified as organisational, procedural or operational.

---

20 Schmidt-Aßmann, in: Schmidt-Aßmann/Hoffmann-Riem (fn. 9), 429 ff. (446); Fastenrath, DV 31 (1998), 277 ff. (299); Becker, DVBl. 2001, 855 ff.

21 See: *Ehlers,* Die Europäisierung des Verwaltungsprozeßrechts, 1999, 8 ff.; Ruffert, DV 34 (2001), 453 ff. (455, 457); Fastenrath (fn. 20), 277 ff. (299, 301).

22 Schmidt-Aßmann, in: *Verfassung im Diskurs der Welt,* Liber Amicorum für Peter Häberle, A. Blankenagel/I. Pernice/H. Schulze-Fielitz (ed.), 2004, 395 ff.

23 For more details cp. J. Hofmann (fn. *), 1. Part B. III. 3. *Mutatis mutandis* you find the problems caused by public activities with cross-border effects or by inter-administrative ties in federal states. Cp. §§78, 79 Polizeigesetz für Baden-Württemberg and the case of an exterritorial hearing: BVerwG, DVBl. 2002, 1118 ff. (1121); *Kersten,* UPR 2001, 405 ff.

24 For more details compare J. Hofmann (fn. *), 1. Part C. For more details to the typology and structures of inter-administrative ties cp. 1. Part D.

The latter are usually joint training measures which have no jural influence upon a decision.

Organisational inter-administrative ties affect legal protection and liability only in a limited way. Such ties can be found, in particular, in committees, at EU level for example, in the committees in the procedures known as "Comitology"[25] or at national level, for example, in the monitoring committees for the common administration of the Structural Funds.[26] Provisions which regulate the handling and demarcation of different competences of authorities – either in vertical or horizontal direction – also establish organisational inter-administrative ties, e.g. in the case of the implementation of the rules of competition laid down in Articles 81 and 82 EC Treaty.[27]

However, most inter-administrative ties are *procedural*. They also lead to the most discussion on the most intricate points of law concerning legal protection and liability. One important procedural inter-administrative tie has been established by the rules of mutual administrative assistance.[28] Possible assistance measures range from a simple exchange of information over the delivery of decisions to carrying out enquiries. The exchange of information does not necessarily need a request: sometimes it can be managed by a central data bank, as in the case of the Customs Information System (CIS)[29] or in the case of Eurodac.[30] Extensive provisions for legal protection and liability are provided within the framework of these two data exchange systems. Further ties can be identified within procedures serving the supervision and coordination of the activities of the Member States. Normally, the Member States have to deliver information in such cases. Sometimes the Commission can give an opinion or make a decision, such as within the framework of the supervision of aids[31] or under Article 13 of the Directive on general product safety.[32] Different kinds of inter-administrative ties may be found within multi-stage decision-making procedures, such as within the framework of the authorisation procedure on medicinal products for human use.[33] There, one Member State acting as reference authority manages the authorisation procedure, but the other Member States can raise objections. If they fail to reach agreement, the Commission makes the final decision. In the context of supra- and transnational or even national enquiries, there are often some special inter-administrative ties such as the option of

25 Schmidt-Aßmann (fn. 22), 403.
26 Article 35 Reg. (EC) No. 1260/1999, OJ 1999 No. L 161, 1.
27 Article 4 ff. Reg. (EC) No. 1/2003, OJ 2003 No. L 1, 1.
28 Cp. Wettner, *Die Amtshilfe im Europäischen Verwaltungsrecht*, 2005.
29 Article 23 ff. Reg. (EC) Nr. 515/97 (fn. 7).
30 Reg. (EC) No. 2725/2000, OJ 2000 No. L 316, 1.
31 Articles 4, 7, 10 Abs. 3, 11, 13 and 14 Reg. (EC) No. 659/1999, OJ No. L 83, 1.
32 Dir. 2001/95/EC, OJ 2001 No. L 11, 4.
33 Dir. 2001/83/EC, OJ 2001 No. L 311, 67.

participating in an enquiry, the request to carry out an enquiry or to render mutual administrative assistance during the enquiry.[34]

2. THE CHALLENGE FOR THE EFFICIENCY OF LEGAL PROTECTION

2.1. THE BASIS: THE PRINCIPLE OF SEPARATE JURISDICTIONS

Although "European Composite Administration" has now become a better description of the concept of administration in the Community in place of a dualistic system, such a change of perspective has not yet been made with regard to the system of legal protection. The concept of legal protection is still determined by the differentiation between the administrative execution of EC law by the Community ("direct execution") and by the Member States ("indirect execution") and therefore it still has a dualistic angle.[35] If a person feels concerned by an executive measure of an EC authority, he has to appeal to the European courts; if he feels concerned by an executive measure of a Member State, he has to take legal proceedings before the courts of the Member State concerned (*principle of separate jurisdictions*).[36] In principle, executive measures of a Member State or the Community are not attributed to another authority, so that there is no forum dislocation. An exception is the case when the Commission gives a mandate to a Member State's authority.[37]

The *vertical demarcation of jurisdictions*[38] between the Community and the Member States follows Articles 220 et seq. EC Treaty, which set out the exclusive competences of the European courts. In relation to the scope of these competences, the Member State's courts are, in principle, not able to exercise jurisdiction on measures of the Community. They have no jurisdiction to determine that acts of Community institutions are invalid.[39] Except in cases

34 Compare J. Hofmann (fn. *), 1. Part D. I. 2. i).

35 Cp. Dörr, in: Sodan/Ziekow (ed.), VwGO, EVR, No. 353 ff.; Schmidt-Aßmann, in: Schoch/Schmidt-Aßmann/Pietzner (ed.), VwGO, Einleitung, No. 102.

36 Cp. Ehlers (fn. 21), 16 ff.

37 Examples: Court of First Instance, Case T-94/95 (Landuyt/Commission), ECR 1998, II-213 ff., para. 33 ff.; Case T-93/95 (Laga/Commission), Report 1998, II-195 ff., para. 33 ff. See for further information on the item of attribution of measures J. Hofmann (fn. *), 3. Part A. I. 1. b).

38 For more details see J. Hofmann (fn. *), 3. Part.

39 ECJ, Case C-314/85 (Foto-Frost/HZA Lübeck-Ost), ECR 1987, 4199 ff., para. 12 ff.; Case C-461/03 (Gaston Schul/Minster von Landbouw), ECR 2005, I-10513 ff., para. 17 ff. The legal situation within the framework of the Convention on the Grant of European Patents (EPC – BGBl. II 1976, 826 ff.) is partly different. In spite of existing possibilities to get legal protection at the supranational level of the European Patent Organisation, it is expressly allowed by Article 138 EPC that European Patents are ruled as invalid by Courts of Member States, but

where jurisdiction is conferred on the Court of Justice by the EC Treaty, disputes to which the Community is a party are not excluded from the jurisdiction of the courts or tribunals of the Member States on that ground.[40] The distribution of jurisdiction laid down in the EC Treaty is a distribution of public or "sovereign" power and in this it differs from the demarcation of competences between courts within a state.

Within the vertical relationship between the Community and the Member States, the principle of separate jurisdictions is not only valid with regard to the object of an action. It also governs the demarcation of jurisdictions on judicial precedents of different Member States or Community institutions.[41] Inter-administrative ties set legal precedents when their illegality or their existence or their validity is decisive for the decision of a court on a different object.[42] With the exception of void acts or cases of evidently irrelevant acts of a Member State, the Community courts have no jurisdiction to rule on acts of a Member State which set a legal precedent in a case. This statement is also valid mutatis mutandis for the Member State courts in so far as Community acts are a precedent in a case. Further exceptions to the principle of separate jurisdictions are given in the case of Article. 68(1) EC Treaty and are restricted by time in the case of interim reliefs.[43] The German Constitutional Court (*Bundesverfassungsgericht)* claims moreover to exercise jurisdiction on acts of a Community institution if a minimum standard of protection of the fundamental rights granted by the German constitution (*Grundgesetz)* is not guaranteed by the European courts or if the limit of the EC or EU Treaty is exceeded.[44] Beyond these powers, the courts or tribunals of the Member States are obliged, by Article 234 EC Treaty, to request the European Court of Justice to give a preliminary ruling on the validity or legality of an act of a Community institution which could set a legal precedent. However, this referral is inadmissible if the individual concerned has failed to institute proceedings against the act of a Community institution under Article 230(4) EC Treaty although this person had evident opportunity to do so and consequently the act has now become definitive.[45]

---

the effects of such a ruling are limited to the territory of the Member State concerned. In contrast to that is the claim to be included on the list of professional representatives that intend to receive authorisation as a European Patent attorney. Therefore, you are in principle only able to sue at the level of the European Patent Organisation (cp. BVerfG DVBl. 2001, 1130 ff.).

40 Article 240 EGV.

41 Cp. e.g. ECJ, Case C-6/99 (Association Greenpeace France/Ministère de l'Agriculture et de la Pêche et al.), ECR 2000, I-1651 ff., para. 48 ff.

42 ECJ, Case C-6/99 (fn. 41), para. 48 ff. (55) and Opinion of Advocate-General Mischo, para. 106 ff. For further examples of judicial precedents see in: J. Hofmann, (fn. *), 3. Part A.II.1.

43 Cp. J. Hofmann (fn. *), 3. Part A. II. 2. a) bb), b) and 3. b). In particular to interim relief cp. ECJ, Case C-465-/93 (Atlanta Fruchthandelsgesellschaft/Bundesamt für Ernährung und Forstwirtschaft), ECR 1995, I-3761 ff., para. 19 ff.

44 BVerfGE 102, 147 ff.

45 ECJ, Case C-188/92 (fn. 19), para. 10 ff.

If you consider the relationship between the Member States – *the horizontal relationship* – you will find that the principle of separate jurisdictions bars the Member States from allowing an act of another Member State being the object of a legal proceeding, insofar as the state immunity limits the jurisdiction of the courts. However, an act of a Member State which only sets a legal precedent is, in contrast, not excluded from a legal review by the principle of state immunity.[46] In this case, the courts or tribunals of a Member State have the jurisdiction to refuse recognition of an act of another Member State. Accordingly, the *Conseil d'État* of France was allowed to review and override an alert which had been issued for the purposes of refusing entry made by one Member State. This set a legal precedent within proceedings arising from the refusal to grant a visa because of a false alert in the Schengen Information System.[47] But this power of refusing recognition of an act by a Member State only exists under EC law where acts without a regulatory character are concerned. Transnational administrative acts and other acts of a regulatory character cannot be refused, because they are valid decisions and therefore binding by EC law. The consequence in this case is that separate proceedings have to be instituted against this act in the Member State in question, if it sets legal precedent for a different action.[48]

2.2. VERIFICATION OF THE EFFICIENCY OF LEGAL PROTECTION

2.2.1. Concerning the demarcation of jurisdictions on the object of a proceeding

There must be verification whether the demarcation of jurisdictions on the object of an action which is basically – as shown above – only seen from the perspective of the principle of separate jurisdictions can satisfy the standards of the right to an effective remedy which is guaranteed by the German Constitution (*Grundgesetz*), Community Law and the European Convention on Human Rights. Particular consideration can be given to the aspects of "access to court" (a) and "the precept of a clear demarcation of jurisdictions" (b).

Access to court

The right to an effective remedy requires that a person who is affected by a public measure must, in principle, have access to court. In this case, the remedy must

46 Seidl-Hohenveldern/Stein, *Völkerrecht*, 10th edition 2000, para. 1487 ff.; K. Ipsen, *Völkerrecht*, 4th edition 1999, §26, para. 10.

47 CE No. 224877 of 13 December 2002; CE No. 220419 of 13 December 2002.

48 For more details see J. Hofmann (fn. *), 279 ff.

be practical and effective, and must not be limited unreasonably.[49] The European Court of Justice grants a legal protection against acts of Community institutions, under Article 220 et seq. EC Treaty, which basically satisfies these requirements. It is largely comparable to the right guaranteed by Article 19(4) of the German Constitution (Grundgesetz).[50] The same is true for the legal protection granted by the courts of the other Member States.[51] It is also in line with Article 6(1) ECHR, which states that the right to a court is granted by a Court of the international organisation and not by the courts of the home country of the affected person, where states establish international organisations in order to pursue or strengthen their cooperation in certain fields of activities, and where they attribute to these organisations certain competences and accord them immunities.[52]

However, the referral to the courts of another Member State or to the European Court of Justice is a limitation of legal protection compared with the protection received from an individual's home forum. The referral causes practical difficulties for an individual which – if he is a private person and not a company – might make him refrain from seeking legal protection abroad. Problems which need to be considered include the following aspects: inability to speak the official language, unfamiliarity with procedural rules, large distances and difficulties in finding an advocate.[53] And what is more, the individual might not receive the same standard of legal protection there, compared to that in his home country but might only receive a largely comparable one.[54]

These limitations of legal protection have indeed to be measured against the requirements of proportionality and reasonableness set out by Article 6(1) ECHR. These requirements are fulfilled here. The immunity of the European Community

49 See to Article 19(4) Grundgesetz: Schmidt-Aßmann, in: Maunz/Dürig, GG, vol. 2, Article 19(4), No. 230 ff.; BVerfGE 57, 9 ff. (22). To the right to an effective remedy in Community Law: ECJ, Case 178/84 (Commission/Germany), ECR 1987, 1227 ff., para. 4; ECJ, Case C-340/89 (Vlassopoulou/Justiz- und Europaministerium Baden-Württemberg), ECR 1991, 2357 ff., para. 22. Cp. to Article 6 ECHR: European Court of Human Rights, Judgement of 28 May 1985, No. 8225/78 (Ashingdane/UK), Series A 93, §57; Judgement of 16 December 1992, No. 12964/87 (Geouffre de la Pradelle/France), Series A 253 B, §§27 ff. (28); *Meyer-Ladewig*, EMRK, 2003, Article 6, No. 20 ff.

50 BVerfGE 102, 147 ff. ("Common market of bananas"); BVerfGE 89, 155 ff. ("Maastricht").

51 The right to an effective remedy is also part of the constitution or of equivalent provisions there, cp. Schmidt-Aßmann, in: *Festschrift für Bernhardt*, 1995, p. 1283 ff. (1285). Tonne, *Effektiver Rechtsschutz durch staatliche Gerichte als Forderung des Europäischen Gemeinschaftsrechts*, 1997, 47 ff., provides state by state evidence for that.

52 European Court of Human Rights, Judgement of 18 February 1999, No. 26083/94 (Waite and Kennedy/Germany), NJW 1999, 1173 ff., §67; Judgement of 18 February 1999, No. 28934/95 (Beer and Regan/Germany), §57, to find under www.echr.coe.int.

53 Harings, *Grenzüberschreitende Zusammenarbeit der Polizei- und Zollverwaltungen und Rechtsschutz in Deutschland,* 1998, 340 ff.; Beyerlin, *Rechtsprobleme der lokalen grenzüberschreitenden Zusammenarbeit*, 1988, 262 ff.

54 Baldus, *Transnationales Polizeirecht*, 2001, 349 ff., holds the opinion that Article 19(4) GG demands even the guarantee of an equivalent legal protection abroad.

concerning the jurisdiction of the Member States secures its proper functioning free from unilateral interference from individual Member States. This is a legitimate aim[55] which has been laid down in the EC Treaty. The circumstance that the Community Treaties maintain the immunity of the Member States also serves the legitimate aim of their autonomy. The relegation of a case to the forum of another sovereign power is an appropriate instrument to achieve this aim. It is true that a fictitiously maintained possibility of having a remedy before the courts of the home country connected to a parallel legal protection granted abroad would take away the problems for the individual that are caused by proceedings abroad. Such a solution can be found as part of the framework of the Eurodac[56] and CIS[57] database systems". The Council of Europe has also proposed this for the trans-frontier cooperation between territorial communities or authorities.[58] If this solution is applied in all other cases with inter-administrative ties, it would raise the question which law should be applied. If this hypothesis was taken seriously, this would be the law of the forum state.[59] Things would then become complicated. If the acting state has to recognise the judgments pronounced against the forum state which is fictitiously responsible, its authorities would be measured by the law of a foreign state instead of by its own rules, which it had had to follow during its actions.[60] This would not be consistent with the concept of transnational and supranational measures within the Community law. Moreover, it would intervene too much in the autonomy of the acting authority. Therefore, the relegation of a remedy to a foreign state is in principle necessary. It is also just and reasonable if the legal protection abroad is largely comparable to the protection granted in the home country. But there should be some restriction of the above mentioned limitations on legal protection which might prevent some people from instituting proceedings abroad. Appropriate instruments for this are detailed instructions within the administrative acts about legal remedies available abroad and the general availability of information about the different legal protection systems.

---

55 European Court of Human Rights, Judgement of 18 February 1999, No. 26083/94 (fn. 52), §63 ff.

56 Article 18 Reg. (EC) No. 2725/2000 (fn. 30).

57 Article 36 Reg. (EC) No. 515/97 (fn. 7).

58 Article 3(4) of the Model inter-state agreement on contractual transfrontier co-operation between local authorities (No. 1.4 of the Appendix to the European Outline Convention on Transfrontier Co-operation beteween Territorial Communities or Authorities), BGBl. II (German official journal part II) 1981,965 ff. (982). Compare also Harings (fn. 53), 341 ff.

59 With a similar approach: Beyerlin (fn. 53), 264.

60 Cp. Royla, *Grenzüberschreitende Finanzmarktaufsicht in der EG*, 2000, 157 ff.; Burbaum, *Rechtsschutz gegen transnationales Verwaltungshandeln*, 2003, 59 ff.

In particular: the precept of clear demarcation of jurisdictions

If the individual is not able to identify the administrative authority which is responsible for the measure affecting him, the right to an effective remedy requires special provisions changing, bypassing or attenuating the principle of separate jurisdictions. Since in those cases where the individual is not able to identify the acting body – e.g. in the case of a database system – it is nearly impossible for him to choose the proper opponent and the competent forum for the proceedings. The lack of clear demarcation of responsibilities causes a lack of clear demarcation of jurisdictions.[61] Thus, in some of these cases – the CIS and Eurodac database systems – there are special provisions for bypassing or attenuating the principle of separate jurisdictions.[62] These provisions give a right of information concerning the data recorded on the individual, a right of correction and a right of erasure against every partner in the database system and not only against the partner which has recorded the inaccurate data and which would normally be responsible for the failure. In these special cases, it is possible to bypass the principle of separate jurisdictions since they do not raise the problem above that the acting authority would be measured against a foreign law, since the applied provisions are harmonised.[63]

All things considered, it must be stated that a clear demarcation of responsibilities concerning administrative measures leads to clarity concerning the demarcation of jurisdictions. In contrast, attributing acts to another administrative authority would not improve the clearness of responsibilities because then responsibility would be shifted. If, exceptionally, there is an attribution to another authority, an instruction on the proper forum is necessary. In the other cases, the principle of separate jurisdictions provides a clear demarcation of jurisdictions with a simple instruction: the individual shall institute proceedings against that authority by whose measure he feels that he is affected. A different problem for the right to an effective remedy arises when an act sets a legal precedent for the object of an action. This will be discussed in the following section.

---

61 See to the precept of clear demarcation of responsibilities: Schmidt-Aßmann (fn. 14), 270 ff. (296 ff.). Also: Royla (fn. 60), 170 ff.

62 Compare: Article 36 Reg. (EC) No. 515/97 (fn. 7), Article 18 Reg. (EC) No. 2725/2000 (fn. 30).

63 Compare the provisions concerning CIS: Article 36 Reg. (EC) No. 515/97 (fn. 7) and Dir. 95/46/EC, OJ 1995 No. L 281, 31 (personal data protection by the Member States) respectively Reg. (EC) No. 45/2001, OJ 2001 No. L 8, S. 1 (personal data protection by the Commission). Compare as far as Eurodac is concerned: Article 18(2–12) Reg. (EC) No. 2725/2000 (fn. 30) and Dir. 95/46/EC.

2.2.2. Concerning the demarcation of jurisdictions on legal precedents

Access to court

The right to an effective remedy requires the possibility of a complete judicial review of each affecting administrative measure.

Improvements by changes concerning jurisdiction

It is necessary to evaluate whether the right to a complete judicial review demands that the courts have the jurisdiction to review the legality of all judicial precedents within an action and to set them aside if they are illegal. In the *horizontal relationship* between the Member States, this question only arises in the case of inter-administrative ties of a regulatory character, notably for transnational administrative acts since – as we have seen above – the courts are allowed to review and overrule administrative measures which do not have a regulatory character. But the answer to this question is negative. Basically, it corresponds with the right to a complete judicial review if an act setting a legal precedent is binding by law and is therefore not subject to examination by the courts.[64] But in this case it is presupposed that the individual had the possibility of instituting proceedings against the act setting the precedent in fulfilment of the requirements of the right to an effective remedy. Accordingly, in Germany the courts are only allowed to overrule measures of internal administrative cooperation between authorities[65] because there are procedural uncertainties concerning the admissibility of an action against them,[66] but they are not able to overrule administrative acts setting a legal precedent.[67]

In cases of *vertical inter-administrative ties,* an overruling judicial decision is not possible because under the EC Treaty the jurisdiction of the courts is limited concerning the acts of the public authority they belong to.[68] One exception to the binding character of an administrative act is the construction of "complex

64 Schmidt-Aßmann, in: Schoch/Schmidt-Aßmann/Pietzner (fn. 35), No. 183; BVerfGE 78, 214 ff. (226); European Court of Human Rights, Judgement of 28 June 1990, No. 11761/85 (Obermeier/Austria), Series A 179, §70; Peukert, in: Frowein/Peukert, EMRK, 2. edition., 1996, Article 6, No. 61.

65 For example the consent of a municipality to a building licence under §36 BauGB or of the *oberste Landesstraßenbaubehörde* under §9 para. 2 and 3 Bundesfernstraßengesetz. Compare to the questions of legal protection hereby: Engelhard, *Der mehrstufige Verwaltungsakt und seine prozessuale Behandlung,* 1974, notably 55 ff.

66 An action for annulment (*Anfechtungsklage)* is not possible. You can consider an action for performance or a suit for a declaration (*Leistungsklage* respectively *Feststellungsklage)* which both could be inadmissible because of §44a VwGO. Compare: *Kopp/Schenke*, VwGO, 14th edition, 2005, §44a, No. 6; *Lasotta*, Das Einvernehmen der Gemeinde nach §36 BauGB, 1998, 49 ff.

67 For example §9 para. 8 Bundesfernstraßengesetz.

68 Cp. J. Hofmann (fn. *), 2. Part B.

decision" which is used in cases of the appointment of EC-staff. In order to provide an effective remedy, the European courts have reviewed decisions which have been taken in an early stage of an action if these decisions are closely connected with the object of the action. Otherwise, staff members had to institute as many proceedings as there were acts within the procedure affecting them.[69] Such a solution is only possible in this kind of case, because the objects at issue all derive from EC institutions, thus from the same public power as the court. In contrast to this, the demarcation of jurisdictions laid down in Article 220 et seq. EC Treaty would be violated if it was assumed that the courts have the jurisdiction to review and overrule inter-administrative ties within the EC – Member State relationship. Such an interpretation of the EC Treaty would be in particular conflict with the limit set by the text and the systematics set by Article 234(1b) EC Treaty.[70] The right to an effective remedy which is guaranteed by EC law is, in principle, not able to restrict the principle of exclusive jurisdiction of the European Court of Justice to review EC acts, because this principle is at the same level as the provisions of the EC Treaty referred to. An exception to this could only be made if an effective remedy would otherwise not be granted completely. The inverse penetration of the principle of separate jurisdictions is not possible. It would infringe the principle of limited conferment of powers (Article 5(1) EC Treaty) if the European Court of Justice had the power to overrule decisions of the Member States.[71] Actually, the right to access to court does not force restriction of the principle of separate jurisdictions, since the right to a complete judicial review is also granted if it is possible to institute proceedings directly against each act setting a precedent. The same is true for the right of access to court guaranteed by Article 6 ECHR and Article 19(4) GG.

Improvements by better procedural cooperation

Preliminary rulings

The limiting conditions for the admissibility of a preliminary ruling have also to be measured against the right of access to court.[72] There may be criticism of the fact that the individual only has limited possibilities of enforcing a referral under Article 234 EC Treaty. The national court is obliged to request the European

---

69 ECJ, Case 448/93 P (Commission/Noonan), ECR. 1995, I-2321 ff., para. 17; H.C. Röhl, ZaöRV 60 (2000), 331 ff. (360); David, *Inspektionen im Europäischen Verwaltungsrecht*, 2003, 350 ff.

70 Klepper, *Vollzugskompetenzen der Europäischen Gemeinschaft aus abgeleitetem Recht*, 2001, 210 ff., wants to enable the courts of the Member States to overrule decisions of the Commission and to limit the exclusive jurisdiction of the European Court of Justice on regulations.

71 For more details see J. Hofmann (fn. *), 2. Part C. II. 2.

72 Compare the requirements of Article 6(1) ECHR concerning this matter: European Commission of Human Rights, Decision of 12 May 1993, No. 20631/92 (Divagsa S.A./Spane), Decisions and Reports (D.R.) vol. 74, 274.

Court of Justice if it deems an act of an EC institution to be invalid.[73] The plaintiff himself cannot apply for a referral for a preliminary ruling. In Germany the plaintiff can only suggest it to the court.[74] Unlike the decision on referral there is – at least in Germany – no separate decision of the court to which an objection could be lodged if the court refused to submit the request to the European Court of Justice.[75] In Germany, only the normal remedies are available against the decision on the action and, under special circumstances, the constitutional objection if the right to a competent court is infringed (Article 101(1) GG). The German Constitutional Court (*Bundesverfassungsgericht*) considers the right to the competent court has only been infringed if the courts have handled the provisions imposing a referral to the European Court of Justice arbitrarily, i.e. evidently unsustainably.[76] In the past, the German Constitutional Court has reviewed the upholding of the refusal of the courts restrictively.[77] Now it demands from the courts that they take sufficient notice of EC law[78] and that they prove that by referring to EC legal sources.[79] Moreover, the German Constitutional Court has strengthened its model of a "cooperation in matters of fundamental rights"[80] as well as the legal protection provided for in individual cases because the court holds a reference necessary when a Community act possibly infringes fundamental EC rights.[81] When all things are considered, the fact that preliminary ruling proceedings have not been created as remedy proceedings, must be regarded as an impairment of legal protection as well as the fact that assessment of the necessity of a preliminary ruling is left only to the Member State's courts.[82] It would be desirable if the interpretation of Article 234 EC Treaty gave greater consideration to the right to an effective remedy so that a referral would be obligatory where the plaintiff conclusively claims that a Community act creating a legal precedent was invalid.[83]

Introduction of new preliminary rulings and stays of proceedings

In cases with vertical inter-administrative ties in which the preliminary ruling under Article 234 EC Treaty does not apply – notably in the case that a European

73 ECJ, Case C-314/85 (fn. 39), para. 11 ff.

74 BVerwGE 73, 369 ff.

75 Kopp/Schenke (fn. 66), §94, para. 22.

76 BVerfGE 82, 159 ff. (194 ff.); BVerfG, NVwZ 1993, 883 (884).

77 Cp. BVerfGE 82, 159 ff. (195 ff.); BVerfG, NVwZ 1997, 481.

78 BVerfG, DVBl. 2001, 720 f., No. 21.

79 Füßer, DVBl. 2001, 1574 ff. (1575).

80 BVerfGE 89, 155 ff.

81 BVerfG, DVBl. 2001, 720 ff., No. 22 ff. Hereunto also: Kube, JuS 2001, 858 ff.; Nowak, in: Nowak/Cremer (ed.), *Individualrechtsschutz in der EG und der WTO*, 2002, 47 ff. (65 ff.).

82 See to this character of the preliminary ruling: ECJ, Case 283/81 (C.I.L.F.I.T./Ministero della Sanita), ECR. 1982, 3415 ff., No. 9; Dauses, in: Dauses (fn. 1), P II., No. 105.

83 Also: Allkemper, *Der Rechtsschutz des einzelnen nach dem EG-Vertrag*, 1995, 171 ff. and 205 ff. Schwarze, DVBl. 2002, 1297 ff. (1304).

court considers an act of a Member State creating a legal precedent as illegal – reveals the need for the introduction of a new proceeding of cooperation between the European courts and the national courts like a preliminary ruling. Analogous proceedings are necessary for the horizontal inter-administrative ties which are binding by law. The courts should at least have the option of staying proceedings until the courts of the forum with jurisdiction to rule on the act setting a legal precedent, have decided. Otherwise there might be divergent decisions or – if the action of the individual was dismissed (preliminarily) because of the binding character of the act creating a legal precedent[84] – the individual would be forced unnecessarily to an appeal or a reopening of the case. Existing provisions for a stay of proceedings[85] should therefore be used more often and – where it is necessary – new provisions for this should be introduced. At Community level in particular, the existing provisions for a stay of proceedings are not sufficient and the Court of First Instance has only very limited possibilities of staying proceedings *ex officio*.[86]

Improvements by changes concerning the admissibility of actions

A further problem for the right of access to court is that actions against acts setting a legal precedent are often not admissible because of their preparatory character. This causes conflicts with the right of access to court if these acts setting a precedent are binding for other authorities or courts. In these cases, therefore, the right of access to court basically demands admissibility of the action.

At Community level

Where the case law of the European Court of Justice is concerned, a preparatory act which is part of a procedure involving several stages is open to review only if it is a measure which will definitively lay down the position of the institution at the end of the proceedings, and not a provisional measure intended to pave the way for that final decision.[87] It stands to reason that this interpretation of Article 230(4) EC Treaty should be modified in line with the Community right to an effective remedy, so that all inter-administrative ties setting a legal precedent

---

84 Gundel, in: Ehlers (ed.), *Europäische Grundrechte und Grundfreiheiten*, 2003, §18, No. 59, fn. 140.

85 E.g. §94 VwGO, Article 77 Rules of Procedure of the Court of First Instance and Article 82a Rules of Procedure of the ECJ.

86 Compare Article 77 Rules of Procedure of the Court of First Instance and Article 54 ECJ Statute. The provisions for the ECJ go farther, cp. Article 82a §1 lit. b).

87 ECJ, Case 60/81 (IBM Corp. /Commission), ECR. 1981, 2639 ff., para. 10; European Court of First Instance, Case T-55/01 R (Asahi Vet SA/Commission), ECR 2001, II-1933 ff, para. 62; Case T-37/92 (BEUC and NCC/Commission), ECR 1994, II-285 ff., para. 27; Case T-277/94 (AITEC/Commission), ECR 1996, II-351 ff., para. 51.

should be considered as "definitive" and concerning the interests of the individual who is subject of the measure which follows from this. The wording of Article 230(4) EC Treaty would not hinder such an interpretation[88] because "decision" in terms of Article 230(4) EC Treaty means something different than "decision" in terms of Article 249(4) EC Treaty.[89]

However, the fact that the European Court of Justice deals with the requirements for an admissible object of a preliminary ruling more generously than it deals with an action for annulment[90] raises the question whether the right to an effective remedy really demands a broad interpretation of the rules of admissibility of the action for annulment or whether a decentralised approach – i.e. proceedings at Member State level combined with a reference under Article 234 EC Treaty – is sufficient.

A *decentralised approach to legal protection*[91] grants in principle the right to an effective remedy, but it derives two weak points from the preliminary ruling procedure.[92] One of these is the lack of a possibility for the individual to initiate and to enforce a referral. The second weak point is the preliminary procedure at the European Court of Justice itself. The plaintiff in the original proceedings can only influence the action and the ruling by submitting a statement and by a hearing during the oral part – presupposing that he applies to set out the reasons why he wishes to be heard.[93] Furthermore, he has neither the possibility of filing a substantive application nor of immediately steering the formulation of the question and the grounds of the referral.[94]

Admittedly, decentralised legal protection combined with preliminary ruling proceedings causes a delay,[95] but the alternative to the preliminary ruling – the action for annulment at the European Court of First Instance and, as the case may be, subsequent appeal to the European Court of Justice – can be extremely time-consuming. In fact, a broad interpretation of the rules of admissibility of the action for annulment can be ambivalent for the plaintiff. If the institution of an action for annulment is evidently possible, his case may be harmed by the case law of Textilwerke Deggendorf Judgement. In this case, the plaintiff would be obliged to sue against preparatory and non-definitive measures if he wanted

88 The Case ECJ, C-50/00 P (Unión de Pequeños Agricultores/Council), ECR 2002, I-6677 ff., para 44, is different as it concerns the question if the right to an effective remedy requires the admissibility of an action against a regulation. The Case C-131/03 P (Reynolds Tobacco Holdings Inc. et al./Commission), Judgement of 12 September 2006, para 79 ff., also does not hinder the interpretation suggested above because it has as very special objective, a Commission's decision to bring proceedings before a court of a non-Member State.

89 Cp. H.C. Röhl (fn. 69), 331 ff. (362 ff.); ECJ, Case 60/81 (fn. 87), para. 9 ff.

90 Cp. J. Hofmann (fn. *), 3. Part A. II.2.b) aa) (4).

91 The term comes from Nowak, EuR 2000, 724 ff. and *idem.* in: Nowak/Cremer (fn. 81), 47 ff.

92 Klepper (fn. 70), 181 ff.

93 Compare Article 23(2) ECJ-Statute, Article 104 §4 Rules of Procedure of the ECJ.

94 Klepper (fn. 70), 182.

95 Klepper (fn. 70), 182 ff.

to prevent the measure from becoming definitive and administratively final.[96] Another disadvantage of the necessity of instituting proceedings against every legal precedent measure is the multiplication of the risk of having to bear the costs of litigation. To sum up, it may be stated that the right to an effective remedy does not demand that the rules on the admissibility of the action for annulment have to be interpreted more broadly if legal protection is available at the decentralised level and if it is combined with preliminary proceedings.[97]

At Member State level

The procedural law of many Member States also restricts the possibility of suing against preparatory measures which are part of an administrative procedure involving several stages. The German administrative courts held that actions were inadmissible against proposals made by the German authorities for sites within Natura 2000 procedures setting up a coherent European ecological network for several reasons.[98] Problematic points of admissibility are those of the right of action [*Klagebefugnis]*, the legal interest in a declaratory judgement [*Feststellungsinteresse*] and the inadmissibility of actions against procedural acts of an authority (§44a VwGO). Spanish, French and Italian procedural law also distinguishes between voidable acts and preparatory measures which do not affect the individual directly and therefore cannot be the object of an action.[99] In cases concerning inter-administrative ties, these provisions can conflict with the right to an effective remedy because Article 6(1) 1 ECHR, in particular,[100] requires that a measure is object of an action if it sets a legal precedent for another case and if it is binding for the courts.

A conflict with Article 6(1) ECHR became apparent in the Oleificio Borelli case.[101] In this case, an oil mill company had submitted an application for aid for the construction of an oil mill. from the EAGGF, Guidance Section, to the Commission through the Italian Government. The regional authorities had issued an unfavourable opinion in respect of that application. Then the Commission informed the plaintiff that it could not grant the aid on the ground

---

96 ECJ, Case C-188/92 (fn. 19); Röben, *Die Einwirkung der Rechtsprechung des Europäischen Gerichtshofs auf das Mitgliedstaatliche Verfahren in öffentlich-rechtlichen Streitigkeiten*, 1998, 72; H.C. Röhl (Fn. 71), 331 ff. (361).

97 Similarly for the legal protection against Community regulations: ECJ, Case C-50/00 P (fn. 88), para 39 ff. and Gundel, VerwArch 92 (2001), 81 ff.

98 BVerwG, NVwZ 2006, 822 ff., VG Oldenburg, NuR 2000, 296 ff.; VG Gießen, NuR 2000, 112 ff.; VG Oldenburg, NuR 2000, 713 ff.; VG Frankfurt a.M., NuR 2001, 414 ff.; VG Schleswig, NVwZ 2001, 348 ff.; VG Oldenburg, NVwZ 2001, 349 ff.; VG Lüneburg, NVwZ 2001, 590 ff.; VG Düsseldorf, NVwZ 2001, 591 ff.; OVG Lüneburg, NuR 2000, 298 ff., 299 and 711 ff.; Kahl/Gärditz, NuR 2005, 555 ff.

99 Röben (fn. 97), 219.

100 European Court of Human Rights, Judgement of 28 June 1990, No. 11761/85 (fn. 64), §70; Peukert, in: Frowein/Peukert (fn. 64), Article 6(61).

101 ECJ, Case C-97/91 (Oleificio Borelli SpA/commission), ECR. 1992, I-6313 ff., para. 7 ff.

that, in view of the unfavourable opinion, the conditions which laid down that effect in the relevant regulation were not fulfilled. Therefore the company instituted an action for annulment against the decision of the Commission. It argued that there was any judicial redress in Italy since the opinion is a preparatory measure against which no action will lie under Italian law.[102] The company would be deprived of an effective remedy if the European Court of Justice failed to annul the decision of the Commission. But the European Court decided that it had no jurisdiction to rule on the lawfulness of a measure adopted by a national authority. This position could not be altered by the fact that the measure in question formed part of a Community decision-making procedure, since it clearly followed from the division of powers in the field of question between the national authorities and the Community institutions. In such circumstances, any irregularity of the opinion could not affect the validity of the decision of the Commission. The Court also decided that it was then for the national courts to rule on the lawfulness of the national measure at issue and to regard an action as admissible even if the domestic rules of procedure do not provide for this in such a case.[103] The Court argued that the requirement of judicial control of any decision of a national authority reflected a general principle of Community law.[104]

This judgement has to be seen in context with other judgements of the European Court of Justice obliging the domestic courts to modify national procedural rules under Article 10 EC Treaty if they render the exercise of rights conferred by Community law virtually impossible or excessively difficult.[105] In the past, this argument was used to adjust domestic procedural rules to European law requirements.[106] In future, it also can be applied, together with the right to an effective remedy,[107] to change domestic procedural law. To some extent, it may be sufficient to interpret national procedural laws in line with the requirements of the right to effective judicial control brought about by the European Composite Administration. For example, shall actions against preparatory measures within the framework of a multi-level administrative procedure be regarded as definitively affecting the individual and thus as a

102 Case C-97/91 (fn. 101), 6318.

103 ECJ, Case C-97/91 (fn. 101), para 9 ff.

104 ECJ, Case C-97/91 (fn. 101), para 14.

105 ECJ, Case. C-213/89 (The Queen/Secretary of State for Transport, ex parte: Factortame Ltd. et al.), ECR 1990, I-2433 ff., para. 19 ff.; joined cases C-6 and 9/90 (Francovich and Bonifaci et al./Italy, ECR. 1991, I-5357 ff., para. 36; Case C-208/90 (Emmott/Minister for Social Welfare and Attorney General), ECR 1991, I-4269 ff., para. 23; Case C-312/93 (Peterbroeck, van Campenhout & Cie. SCS/Belgium), ECR 1995, I-4599 ff., para. 12 ff.; joined cases C-430 and 431/93 (van Schijndel and van Veen/Stichting Pensioensfonds voor Fysiotherapeuten), ECR 1995, I-4705 ff., para. 17 ff.

106 Compare Schoch, *Die Europäisierung des verwaltungsgerichtlichen Rechtsschutzes*, 2000, notably 19 ff.; Ehlers (fn. 21), notably 45 ff.

107 Compare ECJ, Case C-50/00 P (fn. 88), para. 39 ff.

possible object of an action if they set a legal precedent for other authorities or courts.[108] However, the domestic courts are still not allowed to overrule measures of Community institutions because this would exceed the jurisdiction given them in the EC Treaty.

The precept of clear demarcation of jurisdictions

The precept of clear demarcation of jurisdictions is part of the right to access to court. It demands that procedural rules are clearly arranged so that an individual who has access to legal advice is able to choose the correct forum and form of proceedings.[109] In this respect, the efficiency of legal protection against inter-administrative ties is in question.[110] In principle, it is certainly clear that the individual has to institute legal proceedings at the courts which belong to the public power that is responsible for the affecting measure. This is basically true for measures of other public powers which set a legal precedent. Exceptions to this are measures without a regulatory character in the horizontal relationship, and, in the vertical relationship, measures of the Community which can be reviewed in a preliminary ruling. As regards the latter, separate proceedings are only necessary if an action of annulment is evidently admissible because otherwise the measures would become definitive.[111] The evidence criterion of the European Court of Justice can be understood to be a consequence of the precept of the clear demarcation of jurisdictions and should therefore be dealt with specifically.

However, as regards the clear demarcation of jurisdictions it seems to be problematical that the individual often does not know that there have been inter-administrative ties in the context of the decision by which he feels affected. If he knows that other administrative authorities have undertaken preparatory measures, he is often unable to recognise whether their illegality affects the decision by which he feels affected and whether they set a legal precedent. Therefore, clear demarcation of responsibilities is missing in many cases.[112] The plaintiff runs a high risk while interpreting the administrative law of the European Composite Administration. If he fails to institute an action against a

108 Similarly General-Advocate Darmon, Opinion to the ECJ Case C-97/91 (fn. 101), para 32.

109 Schmidt-Aßmann, in: Maunz/Dürig (fn. 49), No. 230 ff.; European Court of Human Rights, Judgement of 16 December 1992, No. 12964/87 (fn. 49), §§27 ff. (34 ff.); Tonne (fn. 49), 167 ff.

110 Schmidt-Aßmann, JZ 1994, 839 ff. (836).

111 ECJ, Case. C-188/92 (fn. 19), para. 10 ff.; Case C-178/95 (Wiljo NV/Belgium), ECR 1997, I-585 ff., para. 21; ECR Case C-241/01 (National Farmers' Union/Secrétariat général du gouvernement), ECR 2002, I-9079 ff., para. 34 ff. See also: Kamann/Selmayr, NVwZ 1999, 1041 ff. and H.C. Röhl (fn. 69), 331 ff. (358 ff.).

112 Also Schmidt-Aßmann (fn. 14), 270 ff. (296); Royla (fn. 60), 170 ff.; Winkelmüller, *Verwaltungskooperation bei der Wirtschaftsaufsicht im EG-Binnenmarkt*, 222 ff.; Franchini, Dir. Amm. 2000, 81 ff. (88 ff.); Gundel, in: Ehlers (fn. 84), §18, No. 59.

measure, it might become definitive.[113] Conversely, he runs the risk that his action will be dismissed and he will have to bear the costs. This dilemma can be solved if the authority which makes the decision concerning the individual gives instructions about the preceding inter-administrative ties,[114] and also gives instructions about legal remedies available.

Legal protection within a reasonable timeframe

The existence of two courses of law leads to a considerable delay when the individual has to take both, perhaps as far as the court of the last instance, since, in most cases, both proceedings are not instituted as parallels but as stages. In all likelihood, the courts of one forum will stay proceedings until the courts of the other forum have decided on the measure which sets a legal precedent. In some cases, it is even possible that the European Court of Justice will be involved twice. If you consider a case like the above Oleificio Borelli case,[115] it has been said that the individual has to sue against the measure of the domestic authorities setting a legal precedent. During this action, the court may find that it wants to refer the case to the European Court of Justice under Article 234 EC Treaty on the question whether the unfavourable opinion of the domestic authority forces the Commission to refuse to grant the aid the individual has applied for and whether the authority has to modify its domestic procedural law. Parallel to this, the individual has to institute an action for annulment against the decision of the Community at the Court of First Instance within the time limit of two months laid down by Article 230(5) EC Treaty. Until the proceedings on the legal precedent measure have been completed in the domestic courts, the proceedings at the Court of First Instance should be stayed under Article 77(c) Rules of Procedure of the Court of First Instance. It is only after this that it can be continued in possibly two instances.

Admittedly, the course of proceedings outlined above is not necessarily the normal one, but it is also not an improbable one. The case clearly shows that the existent concept of legal protection within the European Community may come into conflict with the right to a decision within a reasonable time limit. The danger of a conflict with this right increases when the authorities of several Member States are involved in addition to the Commission.

The danger of an infringement of the right to a decision within a reasonable time limit could be reduced by introducing further preliminary proceedings, notably in the horizontal relationship and for the European courts before the domestic courts. It would also be necessary and reasonable if the courts had the

113 ECJ, Case C-188/92 (fn. 19), para. 10 ff.

114 Similarly: Conseil d'État No. 198344 of 9 June 1999, InfAuslR 2000, 166 ff.; Klepper (fn. 70), 210.

115 ECJ, Case C-97/91 (fn. 99) and above.

possibility of overruling measures of the Community, or of the Member States, respectively, setting legal precedent, not only in the horizontal but also in the vertical relationship. This power should be limited with regard to measures without a regulatory character and to decisions of the Commission addressed to a Member State. Exception should be made for administrative acts or Commission decisions addressed to an individual which are definitive and binding by law. Such an enlargement of jurisdiction affects the principle of separate jurisdictions and therefore requires an amendment of the EC Treaty.

As a result, we can state that an improvement of the existent situation of legal protection is required by the right to an effective remedy. The European Court of Human Rights has nevertheless expressly demanded that the Member States of the European Convention on Human Rights have to arrange their procedural rules in such a way that the right to a decision within a reasonable time limit is granted.[116]

This result cannot be achieved by the courts' merely interpreting the EC Treaty, because the principle of separate jurisdictions is laid down in the EC Treaty and has the same standing as the right to an effective remedy. The principle of separate jurisdictions can only be infringed in extreme cases and must take account of the immunity of the Community.[117] Moreover, the right to a decision within a reasonable period of time – because of its content – cannot generally change the principle of separate jurisdictions. Whether it is infringed can only be stated at the end of legal proceedings, despite the structural insufficiency of the concept of legal protection concerning cases dealing with inter-administrative ties. Moreover, it would not lead to greater clearness concerning the appropriate forum and to more legal certainty, if the courts were allowed to enlarge their jurisdiction case by case on the basis of a prognosis whether the right to a decision within a reasonable period of time was going to be infringed or not. Instead of the courts, it is up to the Member States, as the contracting parties, to improve the concept of legal protection.

Results

We have seen that the limited jurisdiction concerning measures setting a legal precedent within the European Composite Administration leads to less efficiency of legal protection. Therefore, the Member States should alter the EC Treaty and restrict the principle of separate jurisdictions. In the vertical relationship, the courts should assume the jurisdiction to overrule – as in the horizontal relationship – measures with a non-regulatory character and Community decisions addressed to the Member States which they have to execute. An

116 Judgement of 24 August 1993, No. 12986/87 (Scuderi/Italy), Series A, 265-A, §16; Judgement of 26 November 1992, No. 11519/85 (Francesco Lombardo/Italy), Series A 249-B, §23.

117 More details see J. Hofmann (fn. *), 2. Part C.I.1., II.2 and III.1.c).

appropriate alternative would be the introduction of new preliminary ruling proceedings, such as the proceedings under Article 234 EC Treaty, for other cases of vertical inter-administrative ties and for transnational acts. In addition to this, the plaintiff in proceedings before the domestic courts should be given a right to initiate a referral to the European Court of Justice. In addition to this, the domestic procedural rules have to be interpreted and applied by now in such a way that proceedings against inter-administrative ties creating a legal precedent are in principle admissible. If such a measure has been included in the run-up to a decision addressed to an individual, he has to be informed about it and instructed about the legal remedies available.

3. THE CHALLENGE FOR THE EFFICIENCY OF THE LIABILITY SYSTEM

3.1. THE BASICS OF DEMARCATION OF JURISDICTIONS

The demarcation of jurisdictions on liabilities in the vertical relationship between Member States and Community institutions adheres to the principle of separate jurisdictions.[118] Under Articles 235 and 288(2) EC Treaty, the European Court of Justice has exclusive jurisdiction to rule on non-contractual liability for damages caused by the Community institutions or their servants in the performance of their duties.[119] For example, Member States are even excluded from ordering proceedings for an expert report whose purpose is to determine the role of the institution in question in events which are alleged to have caused damage, for the purposes of subsequent proceedings against the European Community to establish the non-contractual liability of the European Community.[120] Conversely, the European Court of Justice has no jurisdiction to rule on damage claims made by individuals against a Member State.[121]

The criterion for the demarcation of jurisdictions laid down in the EC Treaty is the "direct causation" (in terms of an attribution) by a Community institution or a Member State.[122] If the damage was directly caused by an EC institution, the

---

118 Compare ECJ, Case C-275/00 (EC/First NV and Franex NV), EuZW 2003, 54 ff., para. 43 ff. and Advocate-General Léger, Opinion to this case, para. 44 ff.; also ECJ, Case C-97/91 (fn. 101), para. 20 ff.

119 ECJ, Case C-55/90 (Cato/Commission), ECR 1992, I-2533 ff., para. 17; joined cases 106–120/87 (Asteris AE et al. /Greece and EEC), ECR 1988, 5515 ff., para. 14 ff.; Case 281/84 (Zuckerfabrik Bedburg AG et al. /Council and Commission), ECR 1987, 49 ff., para. 12.

120 ECJ, Case C-275/00 (fn. 118), para. 43 ff.

121 ECJ, joined cases 106–120/87 (fn. 119), para. 15; Oliver, in: Heukels/McDonnell (ed.), The Action for Damages in Community Law, 1997, 285 ff. (286 ff.).

122 Compare Meij, in: Heukels/McDonnell (fn. 121), 273 ff. (284) and Koenig/Pechstein/Sander, EU-/EG-Prozessrecht, 2nd ed., 2002, para. 688 ff.; v. Bogdandy, in: Grabitz/Hilf (ed.), Das Recht der Europäischen Union, Article 288 EGV, No. 48.

European Court of Justice is competent. Otherwise, a Member State court is the only appropriate forum. The generally agreed decisive question for the attribution of the damage is who the legal system obliges to compensate the damage.[123] Guidelines from case law can be used to demarcate the liabilities in detail.[124] The main guideline is, however, that the authority in question shall be liable for damage which definitively determines the content of an action brought by several involved entities. This is not necessarily the authority which is acts with an external effect to the individual; it can also be the authority which has made definitive presettings for the authority acting outwards.[125]

If the same damage can be attributed to several entities, such as, for example, in the case where the Commission supervising the Member States authorises the illegal measure of a Member State,[126] both entities are liable. The rivalry of liability generated in this way cannot be solved by a liability *pro rata* or by primary and secondary liability but by the common rules of joint liability.[127]

Within the horizontal relationship, the demarcation of jurisdictions follows the principle of separate jurisdictions and thus the criterion of attribution. The courts of a Member State only have jurisdiction to rule on the liability of the authorities of its own state.[128] The statements made on the demarcation of liabilities and the solution of the problem of liability rivalry regarding the vertical relationship are *mutatis mutandis* also valid for the relationship between the Member States.[129]

3.2. PROBLEM: LACK OF A CLEAR DEMARCATION OF JURISDICTIONS

As regards liability claims, the guarantee of Article 6(1) ECHR also demands that access to the courts is not unreasonably difficult but practical and effective.[130] Legal proceedings have to be arranged so clearly that the individual is able to find the right forum (precept of clear demarcation of jurisdictions).[131]

---

123 Detterbeck, AöR 125 (2000), 202 ff. (251).

124 See J. Hofmann (fn. *), 3. Part B. I. 1. c).

125 ECJ, Case 175/84 (Krohn & Co. Import-Export/Commission), ECR 1986, 753 ff., para. 16 ff.; European Court of First Instance, Case T-30/99 (Bocchi Food Trade International GmbH/ Commission), ECR 2001, II-943 ff., para. 31; v. Bogdandy, in: Grabitz/Hilf (fn. 122), Article 288(56) EGV.

126 ECJ, joined cases 5, 7, 13–24/66 (Kampffmeyer et al./Commission), ECR 1967, 331 ff.

127 See J. Hofmann (fn. *), 3. Part B. I. 2.

128 Also Royla (fn. 60), 162 ff.; David (fn. 69), 370 ff.

129 For more details see J. Hofmann (fn. *), 3. Part B. II.

130 European Court of Justice, Judgement of 8 July 1987, No. 10092/82 (Baraona/Portugal), Series A 122, 18, §44; Judgement of 27 April 1989, No. 11213/84 (Neves e Silva/Portugal), Series A 153-A, 14, §§35 ff.; Peukert, in: Frowein/Peukert (fn. 64), Article 6, No. 22.

131 European Court of Human Rights, Judgement of 16 December 1992, No. 12964/87 (fn. 50), §§27 ff. (34 ff.).

There are no problems with regard to the precept of clear demarcation of jurisdictions as far as several entities are jointly liable, since under the common principles of joint liability the full compensation of damage can be claimed from each authority. Therefore the individual is free to institute an action against the authority whose acts affect him. The cases of exclusive liability are much more difficult. In these cases the injured party often does not know that another Member State or the Commission was involved in the proceedings before. This problem can be solved if the authority whose acts affect the individual reveals the participation of another authority in the grounds of its decision and if it informs him about the content of the foregoing measure. Both of these solutions have already been implemented to some extent.[132] But even if this was so, it would be difficult for the claimant to identify the liable administrative authority on the basis of the above guidelines developed from case law. The reason for this lies, first of all, in the fact that the attribution of liability on the basis of the above criteria is very dependent on the importance of the respective inter-administrative tie in its procedural context. It must be evaluated whether the inter-administrative tie was legally binding, if it obliged another authority to a certain behaviour or if the executing authority had discretionary power. The qualification of a cooperative measure as legally binding or as a non-binding expression of opinion, in particular, can be extraordinarily sophisticated. If the term "decision" is not used expressly by the Community law, a complex interpretation of system and purpose of the provision might be necessary.[133] Procedural internals may be also of relevance for the attribution of the damage, as in the case that the executing authority knows that the submitted facts are wrong.

The binding determination of behaviour is basically an appropriate criterion of attribution so that the appropriate authority can be identified as being responsible for the injuring measure and as being liable for the damage. But it cannot reasonably be expected of the individual – even if he consults a lawyer – to search every corner of the procedure causing the damage to find out which authority is more liable for the damage, the domestic authority or the Commission.[134] Since even the European Court of Justice sometimes experiences difficulty in finding the liable entity, as it can be seen in the measures of the Commission in question which are *de facto* binding.[135] Thus clearness of liability

132 Compare ECJ, Case 175/84 (fn. 125); joined cases C-121/91 and C-122/92 (CT Control BV et al./Commission), ECR 1993, I-3873 ff., para. 10. Partly the duty to publish foregoing measures in the Official Journal already exists as under Article 26 Reg. (EC) No. 659/1999 (fn. 31).

133 Compare ECJ, Case 175/84 (fn. 123), 753 ff.

134 Advocate-General Mancini, Opinion to the Case 175/84 (fn. 125) delivered on 19 November 1985, 753 ff. (761).

135 Compare ECJ, Case 133/79 (Sucrimex S.A. et al./Commission), ECR 1980, 1299 ff., para. 20 ff.; ECJ, Case C-146/91 (KYDEP/Commission), ECR 1994, I-4199 ff., para. 16; European Court of First Instance, Case T-54/96 (Oleifici italiani et al./Commission), ECR 1998, II-3377 ff., para 67, and J. Hofmann (fn. *), 3. Part B. I. 1. c) aa) (3).

is not a feature of the present concept of liability and this in its turn causes some vagueness concerning jurisdiction and legal certainty.[136]

3.3. POSSIBLE SOLUTIONS

There is a solution for the problem of the lack of clarity concerning jurisdiction of liability which does not require the restriction of the principle of separate jurisdictions or the modification of the EC Treaty. The model of a *locum tenens* liability that is already applied in some data exchange systems as in the CIS[137] and within the third pillar of EU law as in the SIS[138] or as in the framework of Europol[139] should be transferred to all the other cases with inter-administrative ties. This means that, in addition to the actually liable authority to which the damage can be attributed according to the above criterion of determination, the authority should also be (jointly) liable as *locum tenens* whose act has affected the individual.

This result can by achieved by a wider interpretation of the criterion of attribution of liability. The damage has to be attributed to the person who has to bear it under the legal system. The right to an effective remedy is part of the legal system. But this right is not sufficiently taken into account if the damage is only attributed to the authority which has determined the damaging behaviour, since this rule causes unclearness concerning jurisdiction. In contrast to this, it would lead to a maximum of simplicity and clearness concerning jurisdiction if the authority acting towards the individual was always held liable.[140] The law applicable on the liability would be the law of the authority concerned. But it is clear that such provisions which render the attribution of the damage virtually impossible or excessively difficult must be left unapplied, and this is required for the right to an effective remedy although it is actually not liable.[141] Such provisions are the requirement of fault (§839(1) BGB), for example, or – concerning the right to reparation under Community law – and the requirement of an adequately qualified breach of EC law.

---

136 Also General-Advocate Mancini, Opinion to the Case 175/84 (fn. 125) delivered on 19 November 1985, 753 ff. (761) and: Grévisse/Combrexelle/Honorat, in: *Estudios en homenaje al Don Manuel Díez de Velasco,* 1993, 933 ff. (943 ff.), David (fn. 69), 372.

137 Article 40 Reg. (EC) No. 515/97 (fn. 7).

138 Article 116 Übereinkommen zur Durchführung des Übereinkommens von Schengen [Convention on the Application of the Convention of Schengen], BGBl. II (German official journal part II) of 23 July 1993, 1013 ff.

139 Article 38 ff. Europol Convention, OJ 1995 No. C 316, 2 ff., as amended by the Council act of 28 November 2002, OJ EC 2002 No. C. 312, 1 ff.

140 Similarly General-Advocate Mancini, Opinion to the Case 175/84 (fn. 125) delivered on 19 November 1985, 753 ff. (761).

141 ECJ, Case C-228/96 (Aprile Srl i. l. /Amministrazione delle Finanze dello Stato), ECR 1998, I-7141 ff., para. 13 ff.; Case C-336/00 (Austria/Huber), ECR 2002, I-7699 ff., para. 60 ff.; Case C-255/00 (Grundig Italiana SpA/Ministero delle Finanze), ECR 2002, I-8003 ff., para. 33 ff.

As a consequence of this, a rivalry is generated between two liable entities which can be solved by the rules of joint liability deriving from a common principle of Community law.[142] Accordingly, the authority which had to bear the damage without being liable under the above criterion of attribution can obtain redress from the authority which is liable in terms of this criterion. The European Court of Justice should adjust its ruling correspondingly to grant effective legal protection.

4. SUMMARY

To sum up, it may be stated that on the basis of the principle of separate jurisdictions an effective legal protection can also be granted. It must not be rejected totally. But there is a need for some substantial adjustment. Until the required provisions are issued, it is up to European jurisprudence as well as to the European and Member State courts to provide for more clearness of responsibilities by an analysis which would give a systematic classification of the European Composite Administration and by an interpretation of the existing rules modifying the concept of legal protection in the light of the right to an effective remedy as far as possible so that the legal protection can cope with the challenge of the European Composite Administration. In future however, it is an irrefutable requirement that enhancements have to be made concerning the European concept of legal protection: The dualistic system has to be altered into a network system.

142 See: J. Hofmann (fn. *), 3. Part B. I. 2 b) und II. 2.

XIX. THE EUROPEAN CONVENTION ON HUMAN RIGHTS AND TRANSNATIONAL COOPERATION IN CRIMINAL MATTERS

Aukje van Hoek and Michiel Luchtman*

1. INTRODUCTION

Sometime between April 1993 and January 1994 a number of employees of the *Kredietbank Luxembourg* (KB Lux) stole microfiches, documents and money from their employer. Thus, they obtained sensitive personal data over thousands of Dutch and other foreign accountholders of KB Lux. After the bank had discovered the theft, the microfiches were used as a means of blackmail: only if the bank refrained from reporting the theft to the police, would the employees return the microfiches to the bank. However, if the bank should contact the police, the material would be handed over to foreign authorities. It goes without saying that the latter would not only be awkward for KB Lux, but also in clear violation of Luxembourg banking secrecy. Unfortunately for the bank, this was what happened. In the following events some of the (by then former) employees of the bank were convicted of, *inter alia*, a violation of the Luxembourg banking secrecy legislation.

A few years later criminal investigations were opened in Belgium against Belgian taxpayers for criminal evasion of taxes. The cases were to a very large extent based on data obtained from the microfiches, although these microfiches contained no reference to any bank or other financial institution in particular. The Belgian prosecuting authorities were furthermore not able to account for the

* This contribution was previously published in Aukje van Hoek et al. (eds.), Multilevel Governance in Enforcement and Adjudication, Antwerpen/Oxford: Intersentia 2006. We like to thank Peter Morris for his comments on the use of the English language. We further thank the research group on Cooperation in the field of Justice and Home Affairs of the University of Tilburg and in particular Conny Rijken for her insightful commentary on the paragraph on Joint Investigation Teams. Of course any remaining mistakes are entirely ours. This research was concluded at 1 December 2005. Later developments, such as the decision of the Amsterdam Court of Appeal of 19 January 2006, case no. 03/04509, *LJN* no. AU9845, were not taken into account.

way in which the microfiches had been obtained. One version stated that the former KB Lux employees had themselves handed over the material to the police, while, according to another version, the microfiches were obtained with the use of criminal informants. A third version refers to an illegal search and seizure in Belgium. The Belgian supervisory committee on the police (*Vast Comité voor Toezicht op de Politiediensten*) and some Belgian criminal courts could not bring clarity to the matter. As a consequence, the courts ruled that the material could not be used as evidence. The material was also rejected in a non-criminal tax case.[1]

In the meantime, the KB Lux affair extended its impact beyond the Belgian borders. Based on EC Directive 77/799 on mutual administrative assistance in tax matters[2] the Belgian tax authorities provided the information to other EU countries, including the Netherlands and Germany. The Dutch authorities commenced investigations into the matter. Thousands of Dutch taxpayers were approached and in a considerable number of cases criminal investigation proceedings were started.[3] An issue of central importance in these cases was, of course, the reliability and alleged illegal obtaining of the microfiches in Belgium.[4] The question as to the admissibility of the evidence was raised before the Dutch courts on a number of occasions. What is striking here is the extent to which the different judgments diverge. This is all the more surprising since all Dutch courts refer to the rule of non-inquiry as the starting point of their analyses.[5]

The rule of non-inquiry allows the courts in one country to refrain from investigations into legal, economic and/or social matters of another country. It has its basis in extradition law, but is now also used in other forms of international cooperation. The rationales of the rule are several. In the United States it is often

---

1 District Court of Brussels, 28 June 2002, no. 02/23379, published on www.futd.nl/content/futd/achtergronden/dagbladen/20022872.html (website last visited on 7 July 2005).

2 Council Directive 77/799/EEC of 19 December 1977 concerning mutual assistance by the competent authorities of the Member States in the field of direct taxation, OJ L 336/15, last amended by Council Directive 2004/106/EC of 16 November 2004, OJ L 359/30.

3 The KB Lux affair has given rise to a great deal of debate in the Netherlands; see, among others, *Tijdschrift voor formeel belastingrecht* 2003/04; T.A. van Kempen/L.J. de Rijke, Het achterhalen van niet opgegeven tegoeden door de Belastingdienst; de zaak Kredietbank Luxemburg, *Nederlands Juristenblad* 2003/29, p. 1497–1504; L.C.A Wijsman en A.C. van Aalst, Het protocol inzake het rekeningenproject. Een inventarisatie van rechtsvragen, *Weekblad voor Fiscaal Recht* 2003/832; W.C.A. Valkenburg, Rubriek fiscaal strafrecht, *Tijdschrift voor onderneming en strafrecht* 2004/2, p. 48–52; reference to the website of the Dutch Ministry of Finance is also recommended: www.minfin.nl (search for 'rekeningenproject'; website last visited on 7 July 2005).

4 To our knowledge the provision of the information by the Belgian authorities on the basis of Directive 77/799 (OJ L 336/15) was not as such a very major issue in the Dutch cases.

5 In Dutch: *vertrouwensregel*; in Germany this rule is sometimes referred to as the *formelles Prüfungsprinzip*. The Dutch translation of the rule of non-inquiry is in our view not completely accurate. The term *vertrouwensregel* refers to a principle of mutual trust, to be accredited to foreign legal systems. The *rule of non-inquiry* refers to an unwillingness to investigate or a lack of jurisdiction thereto. See below.

conceived as a direct consequence of the division of powers between the executive and the judiciary.[6] International criminal cooperation, being a part of foreign policy, is a matter that has to be dealt with by the executive (the President or the Secretary of State on his behalf). Therefore, the courts should not – as a rule – entertain questions concerning the legitimacy of the acts of foreign authorities. This does not mean, however, that such types of questions are not dealt with at all. They are on the contrary conducted by the executive powers, which are considered to be better equipped for these kinds of investigation.[7] This is however only one possible explanation for the existence of the rule of non-inquiry.

Another rationale, which seems to have gained the upper hand in (continental) Europe, places emphasis on the mutual trust that underlies every system of legal cooperation between states. In criminal matters this trust can be expressed through the conclusion of treaties on mutual assistance. In this view, the existence of a treaty relationship implies an *a priori* and in-depth investigation by the competent authorities into the legal and social situation of other states.[8] There is thus no need for the courts to conduct their own investigations in individual cases.[9] This is why the rule of non-inquiry and the treaty requirement that exists in international cooperation in criminal matters are often linked. Nowadays, not only treaties that deal specifically with criminal cooperation serve as the basis of such trust, but also treaties on the protection of human rights, for instance the European Convention on Human Rights (ECHR).[10] The logic being that because the Convention offers general guarantees for the protection of human rights in the Member States, the authorities in one state need not check the human rights situation in another Member State in individual cases of cooperation.

---

6 In private international law similar rules exist – for example under the American doctrines of the 'act of state' and the 'political question'; see C.G. van der Plas, *De taak van de rechter en het IPR* (dissertation Nijmegen), Deventer: Kluwer 2005, p. 363 ff and p. 317 ff with references.

7 Cf. Christopher L. Blakesley, National reports – United States of America, in: Albin Eser/Otto Lagodny/Christopher L. Blakesley (eds.), *The Individual as Subject of International Cooperation in Criminal Matters*, Baden-Baden: Nomos Verlag 2002, p. 605–609; see also *in extenso* Alette Smeulers, *In Staat van uitlevering* (dissertation Maastricht): Intersentia 2003, p. 460–486, both authors with references to American case law. This reasoning also carries a risk: the accused's rights might be traded against other interests of foreign policy, such as trade interests.

8 This again could be explained by the division of powers: the executive is responsible for entering into treaties.

9 This rationale is often criticized, because for one thing it makes no distinction between bilateral and multilateral treaties. Especially in the latter case, the signing of a treaty certainly does not always imply an in-depth investigation into the domestic situation of all other treaty partners. Furthermore, sometimes regime changes may occur for the worse. In most cases this does not lead to the treaty being repealed.

10 There are also practical reasons for the rule of non-inquiry, one very important one being that it can be very difficult to (correctly) apply the rules of a foreign legal system. However, this argument is almost never explicitly mentioned by the courts.

So the American rule of non-inquiry would disallow courts from investigating the legitimacy of foreign acts of state based on the separation of powers.[11] The continental rule of mutual trust does relieve the courts (and sometimes the administration) from the duty to do so *ex officio*, but does not preclude the courts from doing so if requested by the defendant. However, in practice the courts may refuse to hear a complaint in all but the most extreme cases, taking the principle of mutual trust one step further. How differently the rule is interpreted, is demonstrated by the following judgments of the Dutch courts in the KB Lux affair:

- the District Courts of Alkmaar[12] and Groningen[13], for instance, accept that the rule of non-inquiry may be left aside, if there are serious indications that the ECHR has been violated and that the suspect's interests have been damaged as a result. So they apply what is known as the *Schutznorm* principle to the case. In their opinion this situation did not occur in the present case. As the investigations in Belgium were directed against a Belgian suspect, the interests of the Dutch suspects were not harmed in any way by the actions of the Belgian authorities. There were also no indications that the Dutch authorities were involved in the alleged irregularities in the Belgian investigation. As a consequence, the materials could therefore be used as evidence;
- the District Court of Leeuwarden[14] also ruled that the irregularities did not harm the suspects' interests. Moreover, since the information was – apparently – only used as a basis for further investigations, there was no need to investigate any further. The District Court of The Hague[15] noted that the defence only questioned the lawfulness of the actions of the Belgian authorities and not the reliability of the evidence. Thus, both courts seem to reduce their investigations to the requirements of Article 6 ECHR;
- a completely different approach was chosen by the District Courts of Breda[16] and Amsterdam.[17] The Breda court ruled that it could not be excluded that the Belgian authorities had not used their investigatory powers in accordance

11 Though also in the American system, the courts do in fact entertain political questions.

12 Rechtbank Alkmaar 19 February 2004, *LJN* no. AO5509, case no. 14.060137-02, to be found on www.rechtspraak.nl.

13 Rechtbank Groningen 16 October 2003, *LJN* no. AM 1882, case no. 18/076010-01, published in Vakstudienieuws 2003, 56.4 and on www.rechtspraak.nl.

14 Rechtbank Leeuwarden 6 December 2004, *LJN* no. AR 7028, case no. 17/029023-01 VEV, to be found on: www.rechtspraak.nl.

15 Rechtbank 's-Gravenhage, *LJN* no. AR5790, case no. 09/755139-02, to be found on: www.rechtspraak.nl.

16 Rechtbank Breda 11 December 2003, case no. 02/003498-01, published in Vakstudienieuws, 2.8 and on www.rechtspraak.nl.

17 In this case the court never reached a final verdict, because of the demise of the suspect; Rechtbank Amsterdam 12 September 2002, *LJN* no. AE7569, case number 13/120067-01, published in Vakstudienieuws, 2002, 45.7 and on www.rechtspraak.nl.

with the rights of defence, as laid down in the ECHR, and that the Dutch suspect's interests may also have been harmed by this. Although at the start of the Dutch investigation the Dutch authorities could rely on the information provided by the Belgian authorities, this does not mean the information may also be used as evidence. On the contrary, due to the fact that the origin of the microfiches could not be retrieved and there were no further indications that the Belgian authorities would be prepared to clarify certain matters,[18] the material was not allowed as evidence.

It is striking to see how differently the responsibilities of the Dutch authorities in a transnational context are weighed by the courts. The application of the principle of mutual trust, combined with a strict interpretation of the *Schutznorm*, in some of the cited judgments places the defence in a position that is not to be envied. These courts apparently limit the responsibility of the Dutch authorities to the actions in which they were directly involved. Since they were not involved in *acquiring* the data, apparently no separate issue under Article 8 arose. To us, this is surprising. Does not the *subsequent use* of those data, covered by banking secrecy, indeed raise separate questions under Article 8? And considering that banking secrecy is often meant to protect the privacy of bank clients, why – according to some courts – are the interests of Dutch account holders therefore not harmed?[19] These questions were now totally ignored, thereby depriving the Dutch defendant of a legal remedy, whereas Belgian account holders in a similar position did have such a remedy. Should not the Dutch courts at the very least have examined these aspects, possibly referring to the defendants in the Belgian courts? Or do transnational investigations bring about inherent limitations in legal protection?

The KB Lux affair is a fine illustration of the questions that may rise when states are confronted with transnational elements in criminal investigations. They deal with ever-increasing cooperation within the European Union that strongly affects the legal position of citizens in a horizontal, interstate relationship. Are individuals, as was the case for decades, still considered to be the mere *object* of cooperation or could we speak of a tendency that places the individual on a more equal footing with states, thereby stressing that legal protection is not merely an issue that needs attention in the vertical relationship between an individual and a state, but also in the horizontal relationship between

18 A salient detail was that the Dutch request for mutual assistance in criminal matters was turned down by the Belgian authorities on the basis of Article 2 (national interest of the requested state) of the 1959 European Convention on Mutual Assistance in Criminal Matters (ECMACM), European Treaty Series 030.

19 See on banking secrecy in general the OECD survey *Improving access to Bank Information for Tax Purposes*, 2000: OECD and also ECJ 10 December 2002, Case C-153/00, *ECR* 2002, p. I-11319 (*Paul der Weduwe*).

states?[20] To an ever increasing extent this question draws attention in legal doctrine.[21] The KB Lux affair however suggests that it is not yet accepted in practice. Although in an internal, national context state authorities are completely bound by the European Convention, there is a danger that in a transnational context states play (and are allowed to play) a game of 'hide and seek'[22], leaving their citizens without effective protection against infringements of Convention rights.

In this article we will try to pinpoint the responsibilities of states involved in transnational criminal cooperation within the EU framework, with respect to the effective enforcement of the European Convention on Human Rights. What responsibilities do the requested and the requesting state have? What are the risks for this effective enforcement under the current system of transnational cooperation (based on mutual trust) and how, if at all possible, are these risks to be countered, without undermining the cooperation itself? We will therefore continue this contribution with discussing the case law of the European Court of Human Rights on transnational cooperation in *sensu lato* in order to create an overview of state responsibility under the Convention (paragraph 2). Having done this, we will confine ourselves to the articles of the Convention which were involved in the KB Lux case and which are – in our opinion – the most pertinent to mutual assistance in criminal matters: Articles 6 and 8. The focus will be on cooperation within the EU, so as to be able to take into account the special features of cooperation under the EU Treaty. Therefore, (possible) accession to the ECHR will also be considered. In paragraph 3, we will discuss three forms of cooperation that are currently used or being developed within the EU framework, namely the classical concept of mutual assistance in criminal matters, the so-called joint investigation teams (JIT) and the proposal for a European evidence warrant (EEW).

---

20 Compare the reference to 'transnational justice' in the contribution by J.A.E. Vervaele to this book.

21 See, among others, Albin Eser/Otto Lagodny/Christopher L. Blakesley (eds.), *The Individual as Subject of International Cooperation in Criminal Matters*, Baden-Baden: Nomos Verlag 2002; Peter Popp, *Gründzüge der internationalen rechtshilfe in strafsachen*, Basel/Genf/Munich: Helbing und Lichtenhahn; Munich: Beck 2001; Van den Wyngaert, 'Rethinking the law of international criminal cooperation: the restrictive function of international human rights through individual-oriented bars', in: Albin Eser/Lagodny/Blakesley (eds.) (2002) and Otto Lagodny, *Principles and Procedures for a new Transnational Criminal Law*, Freiburg im Breisgau: Ed. iuscrim, Max-Planck-Inst. für ausländisches und Internat. Strafrecht 1992.

22 A. Smeulers, 'The position of the individual in international criminal cooperation', in: J.A.E. Vervaele (ed.), *European Evidence Warrant – Transnational Judicial Inquiries in the EU*, Antwerpen/Groningen/Oxford: Intersentia Law Publisher 2005 (hereafter Smeulers (2005)).

2. THE CASE LAW OF THE EUROPEAN COURT OF HUMAN RIGHTS

2.1. INTRODUCTION: THE EXTRATERRITORIAL AND/OR INDIRECT APPLICABILITY OF THE CONVENTION

Article 1 of the Convention provides that 'the High Contracting Parties shall secure to everyone within their jurisdiction the rights and freedoms defined' therein. This provision is interpreted as a territorial restriction on the scope of application of the convention.[23] But, as is well known in both international criminal law and private international law, the principle of territorial application does only provide the beginning of an answer to the question of application in international cases. It is unequivocal that the Convention applies in purely domestic situations affecting a single Contracting State. But it is less clear where the responsibility of Contracting States ends in international or transnational situations. This problem is often referred to as the problem of the Convention's indirect or extraterritorial effect.

In the case law of the ECtHR the problems regarding the application of the Convention in international situations take different shapes, sometimes referred to as the applicability ratione loci (which refers to responsibility over territory) and the applicability ratione personae (responsibility towards persons 'within the jurisdiction' of the Contracting State). These two concepts are linked through the fact that the jurisdiction of states is predominantly territorial in character.[24] States, as a rule, exercise control over their territory. This is the most widely recognized basis for jurisdiction. According to the Human Rights Court all other, extraterritorial, grounds for jurisdiction are conditional on assent from the state having territorial jurisdiction.[25] So, those persons inside the territory

---

23 *Soering* v. *UK*, Appl.no. 14038/88, Court (Plenary), Judgment (Merits and just satisfaction) 7 July 1989, Series A no. 161, para. 86 'Article 1 sets a limit, notably territorial, on the reach of the Convention.'

24 *Bosphorus Hava Yollari Turizm ve Ticaret Anonim Sirketi* v. *Ireland*, appl. no. 45036/98, Merits, Grand Chamber 30 June 2005 para. 138 (further referred to as *Bosphorus*); *Bankoviç e.a.* v. *Belgium* and 16 other States, Appl.no. 52207/99, Court (Grand Chamber), Admissibility decision 12 December 2001, *RJD* 2001-XII, para. 59–61; *Gentilhomme, Schaff-Benhadji, Zerouki* v. *France* Appl.no. 48205/99, 48207/99 and 48209/99, Court (Second Section), Judgment (Merits and just satisfaction), para. 20 (available in French only); *Assanidze* v. *Georgia*, Appl. no. 71503/01, Court (Grand Chamber), Judgment (Merits and just satisfaction) 8 April 2004, para. 137. Compare ICJ Advisory Opinion of 9 July 2004 on the legal consequences of the Construction of a Wall in the Occupied Palestinian Territory, General list no. 131, www.icj-cij.org, decisions 2003, para. 109.

25 Bankoviç para. 59–60 and 67, *Öcalan* v. *Turkey*, Appl. no. 46221/99, Court (first section), Judgment (Merits and just satisfaction) 12 March 2003, para. 93. The Court seems to have a very strict view on the exercise of extraterritorial jurisdiction: Any exercise of extraterritorial jurisdiction would be dependent on permission of the territorially involved state. In taking this position, the Court seems to focus mainly on the jurisdiction to enforce (perform state

usually fall within the jurisdiction of the state involved, while those outside the territory of a contracting state usually fall outside that state's jurisdiction and hence outside the protective scope of the convention.[26] This general rule has several exceptions, some linked to the notion of territory, others linked to jurisdiction.

2.2. APPLICATION OR NON-APPLICATION RATIONE LOCI[27]

The issue of locus is raised when sovereignty over a territory is in dispute[28] or when a Contracting State is claimed to assert effective control over a territory outside its internationally recognized boundaries.[29] But the Convention's territorial scope of application is also at issue in those cases where Contracting States perform government acts outside their territory e.g. by partaking in the penal court system[30], or by arresting a suspect on foreign territory.[31] Is such behaviour still 'within the jurisdiction' of the state involved? Under international

acts) and not so much on the jurisdiction to prescribe (apply one's laws) and/or adjudicate (consider an issue to be within the competence of the national courts). Because only in the case of enforcement permission is needed from the state in which the public act will be carried out.

26 Compare *Ilascu and others* v. *Moldova and Russian Federation*, Appl. no. 48787/99, Court (Grand Chamber), Judgment (Merits and just satisfaction) 08 July 2004, para. 311; *Assanidze* v. *Georgia*, Appl. no. 71503/01, Court (Grand Chamber), Judgment (Merits and just satisfaction) 8 April 2004, para. 137–139.

27 The issue discussed here coincides to a large extent with the issue of attribution under international law – when can an internationally wrongful act (e.g. the breach of a conventional obligation) be attributed to a Member State? In international law an important source of information and inspiration on state responsibility are the Articles on the responsibility of states for internationally wrongful acts prepared by the International Law Commission and presented to the General Assembly of the UN at its 56th meeting (see resolution 56/83 of 12 December 2001). The documentation with regard to the Articles can be found on the website of the UN: www.un.org. The Articles are – to a large extent – considered to be a codification of customary international law. Compare ICJ Advisory opinion of 9 July 2004 on the legal consequences of the construction of a wall in the occupied Palestinian territory, General list no 131, www.icj-cij.org, para. 140 on the defence of 'necessity' in Article 25 of the ILC articles, with reference to its earlier judgment on the Gabcikovo Nagymaros Project (Hungary/Slovakia) ICJ Reports 1997. See also W. van Genugten, 'Staatsaansprakelijkheid', *NJB* 2003, p. 1336; M. Noortmann, 'De ontwerpartikelen inzake staatsaansprakelijkheid van de VN-Commissie voor Internationaal Recht', *NJB* 2003/17 p. 882 and P.H. Kooijmans, 'Internationaal publiekrecht in vogelvlucht', Deventer: Kluwer 9th ed. 2002, p. 110.

28 *Ilascu and others* v. *Moldova and Russian Federation*, Appl. no. 48787/99, Court (Grand Chamber), Judgment (Merits and just satisfaction), EHRC 2004-9 p. 862–866 note M. Gondek, para. 312, *Assanidze* v. *Georgia*, Appl.no. 71503/01, Court (Grand Chamber), Judgment (Merits and just satisfaction) 8 April 2004, para. 138.

29 Bankoviç para. 59; Ilascu para. 314.

30 See the facts in *Drozd and Janousek* v. *France and Spain*, Appl. no. 12747/87, Court (Plenary), Judgment (Merits) 26 June 1992, Series A no. 240.

31 See the facts in Öcalan.

law, a State is held accountable for any breaches of its international obligations which can be attributed to that State.[32] Acts of state organs and government officials acting within their official capacity will, as a rule, be attributable to the State they represent. This rule can be applied regardless of the locus of the act.[33] But under the ECHR such extraterritorial liability is rare, as is demonstrated by and explained in the Bankoviç judgment.[34] This case concerned the death of four Yugoslav citizens and the injuries inflicted on one Yugoslav citizen during an attack by NATO forces on a radio and television station in Belgrade.[35] At the relevant time, (the former) Yugoslavia was not a party to the Convention.[36] The relatives of the deceased and the injured party claimed a breach of – inter alia – Article 2 of the Convention (the right to life) by the European NATO partners taking part in the operations. In its decision of 12 December 2001 the Grand Chamber declared that the complaint was inadmissible because 'the impugned action of the respondent States does not engage their Convention responsibility'. According to the Court the Convention forms part of the European *ordre public* and has a regional vocation only.[37] It operates within the *espace juridique* created by the Contracting States and does not – in principle – apply outside the ambit of the Council of Europe. The fact that a Contracting State asserts control over certain behaviour, e.g. the attacks on Serbian targets, does not overcome this territorial restriction imposed on the treaty obligations themselves.[38]

In its judgment the court specifically rejected the control theory under which contracting states are held responsible for all actions within their control. The court distinguished the Bankoviç case from the Cyprus case, in which Turkey was held responsible for breaches of Convention rights in Northern Cyprus, by

32 Compare UN General Council Resolution 56/83 of 12 December 2001 and International Law Commission – draft articles on state responsibility Article 2; I. Brownlie, State responsibility: the problem of delegation, in Völkerrecht zwischen normativem Anspruch und politischer Realität, Ginther K. et al. eds., 1994, p. 299.

33 Compare ICJ Advisory opinion of 9 July 2004 on the Israeli/Palestinian wall, para. 109. When a State is held responsible for omissions, however, it is necessary first to create a duty to act. The ECHR contains such a duty – a duty to guarantee to anyone within the jurisdiction the enjoyment of Convention Rights. Compare also I. Browlie, *l.c.*, p. 300 and 306.

34 Bancoviç, para. 71–74.

35 The total number of casualties was higher, but only five of them were represented by the applicants.

36 See para. 80.

37 See para. 80.

38 In a later judgment the ECtHR seems to have slightly expanded the scope of the convention, to include the situation in which a Member State has effective control over territory not normally falling within the ambit of the Convention. But actions by government officials are still in themselves not enough to establish liability outside the convention's territorial reach. ECtHR 16 November 2004 *Issa e.a.* v. *Turkey*, Appl.no 31821/96, Court (Second Section), Judgment (Merits), *EHRC* 2005-1 p. 29–31 note M. Gondek. However, the apprehension of a suspect on foreign territory with a subsequent transfer to Turkey does bring a suspect within the jurisdiction of Turkey, as is demonstrated by the Öcalan case. Compare on the issue of effective control the Namibia case of the ICJ, ICJ Reports 1971, p. 54 and I. Brownlie, *l.c.*, p. 300.

recollecting that, but for the special circumstances, the Convention would have applied to Northern Cyprus. After all, at the relevant time Cyprus was a party to the Convention.[39] So the Convention's scope of application was not extended by the application thereof to Northern Cyprus. Imputating responsibility to Turkey was necessary to avoid a legal vacuum.

We will not go into the criticism which is possible concerning the territorial restriction of the Convention's applicability from the point of view of both international law and human rights.[40] What is of interest to us here is the positive element of the Court's territorialism: based on the case law of the ECtHR it could be argued that the Convention is meant to apply without exception within the ambit of the *espace juridique*. This rule of territorial application is only subject to an exception in cases of total loss of control over the territory due to foreign occupation and/or insurgency.[41] Transnational or international peculiarities and/or arrangements should not detract from the guarantees offered by the convention.

2.3. TRANSFER OF POWERS AND IMMUNITIES

So, the Contracting States have a duty of care which is mainly territorial in character. But sometimes situations that are clearly localized within the territory of a Contracting State are nevertheless not within their (full) jurisdiction because the power involved is delegated to an international organisation. In international law, the rules on the liability of international organisations and the relationship thereof with the liability of their Member States are still underdeveloped.[42] It seems to be a common understanding however, that on the one hand Member States are not ipso facto liable for the actions of the international organisations of

39 See Court in Bankoviç, para. 80.

40 Compare the extraterritorial reach of the International Convention on Civil and Political Rights, accepted by the ICJ in para. 109–111 of the advisory opinion of 9 July 2004 on the Israel-Palestinian wall.

41 Loss of control over part of the territory does not absolve a contracting state of all its obligations *vis-à-vis* the territory and its inhabitants. The state still 'has a duty to take all the appropriate measures which it is still within it powers to take.' ECtHR 8 july 2004, *Ilascu and others* v. *Moldova and Russian Federation*, Appl. no. 48787/99, Court (Grand Chamber), Judgment (Merits and just satisfaction), *EHRC* 2004-9 p. 862–866 note M. Gondek, paras 313 and 333. See also *Assanidze* v. *Georgia*, Appl. no. 71503/01, Court (Grand Chamber), Judgment (Merits and just satisfaction) 8 April 2004, para. 139–140/144. In para. 144 ff of that judgment the court distinguishes responsibility (being within the jurisdiction of state X) and imputability (being effectively within the powers of authority Y).

42 Compare IDI resolution on the legal consequences for Member States of the non-fulfilment by international organizations of their obligations toward third parties, Session of Lisbon 1995, ILC, 55th session of the GA 2003; First report on responsibility of international organizations by Mr. Giorgio Gaja, Special Reporter, A/CN.4/532. ILA International Committee on the accountability of international organisations, report to the Berlin Conference 2004, part III, p. 25–26.

which they are members[43] while on the other a State cannot discharge itself of its international obligations by transferring the relevant power to an international organisation.[44] The ECHR has not decided with any clarity on the first issue[45] whereas the case law on the second issue seems to be in line with the general understanding in international law.[46]

Two sets of case law can be distinguished, one dealing with of international organisations' immunity from jurisdiction, the other with the transfer of powers to the EC. According to the principle of immunity, international organisations cannot be sued before the courts of the host state.[47] By granting immunity to the organisation, the host state denies access to its courts to individuals instigating a claim against the organisation. Thus, immunity from jurisdiction touches upon the rights guaranteed by Article 6 of the Convention.[48] In older decisions, the

---

43 Compare IDI resolution article 6, CFDT v. 1) European Communities; 2) Member States jointly and/or severally, Appl.no. 8030/77, Admissibility decision 10 July 1978, DR 13, 231, Compare also *Viron Xhavara and 15 others* v. *Italy and Albania*, ECtHR Admissibility Decision 11 January 2001, appl.no. 39473/98 (en droit, para. 1): 'Le fait que l'Albanie est partie à la Convention italo-albanaise ne saurait, à lui seul, engager la responsabilité de cet Etat au regard de la Convention pour toute mesure adoptée par les autorités italiennes en exécution de l'accord international en question'.

44 R.A. Lawson, *Het EVRM en de Europese Gemeenschappen: bouwstenen voor een aansprakelijkheidsregime voor het optreden van internationale organisaties*, Deventer: Kluwer 1999, p. 420.

45 See on this issue the party statements made in *Senator Lines GmbH* v. *Austria e.a.* (the 15 Member States of the EC), appl. no 56672/00, ECtHR Admissibility Decision 10 March 2004. The question was raised in several cases, amongst which were CFDT v. 1) European Communities; 2) Member States jointly and/or severally, Appl. no. 8030/77, Admissibility decision 10 July 1978, DR 13, 231; *Dufay* v. *the EC and its Member States*, appl. no 13539/88, Commission admissibility decision 19 January 1989, *Heinz Heinz* v. *Contracting States to the European Patent Convention*, Appl. no. 21090/92, Commission (Plenary), Admissibility decision 15 October 1992, DR 76-A,125; *Garzilli* v. *Etats members de l'Union Eurpéenne*, Appl. no. 32384/95, Commission (Premiere Chambre), Decision 22 October 1998 and most recently *Senator Lines GmbH* v. *Austria and the other Member States of the EC*, Appl. no. 56672/00, Court (Grand Chamber), Admissibility decision 10 March 2004, but in most cases it did not have to be answered since the complaint was inadmissible for other reasons. Only in CFDT did the Commission specifically reject the complaint against the Member States as such since in the instant case they had not by taking part in the decision of the Council of the European Communities exercised their jurisdiction within the meaning of Article 1 of the Convention. (The Law, para. 7). Compare Kranenborg/Lawson, 'Grondrechten in de Europese Grondwet: wat levert het ons eigenlijk op?', *AAe* 2005, vol. 54, no. 4, p. 219.

46 See i.a. *Matthews* v. *UK*, Appl. no. 24833/94, Court (Grand Chamber), Judgment (Merits and just satisfaction) 18 February 1999, RJD 1999-I and *Heinz* v. *Contracting States party to the European Patent Convention*, Appl. no. 21090/92, Commission admissibility decision 15 October 1992.

47 In private international law this is called immunity from jurisdiction, to be distinguished from immunity from execution. See J. Spiegel, *Vreemde staten voor de Nederlandse rechter*, dissertation Free University Amsterdam, W.E.J. Tjeenk Willink 2001; L.J. Bouchez, 'The Nature and Scope of State Immunity from Jurisdiction and Execution', *NYIL* 1979, pp. 3–33.

48 Though it has been argued that Article 6 does not apply to conflicts between the international organisation and its officials. Compare Lawson p. 446 and *Dufay* v. *the EC and its Member States*.

Commission viewed the granting of immunity as pertaining to Article 1: claims covered by immunity were outside the jurisdiction of the host state. In later decisions, the court based its reasoning solely on Article 6: immunity is a restriction on the access to justice guaranteed by Article 6.[49] Under both lines of reasoning, however, the host state is held responsible for assuring that the immunity does not leave the claimants without any means of recourse.[50] Before granting immunity, the host state should ensure that the internal grievance procedure of the international organisation complies with Article 6.[51] This check, to be carried out before referral, is by necessity general and abstract in nature.[52]

A similar duty lies on the Member States of the EU/EC. Member states cannot absolve themselves from their responsibility by transferring certain government functions to an international organisation. This basic tenet of international law creates an uncomfortable relationship between the two major European courts – the ECJ and the ECtHR. This relationship will be discussed in more detail below. Here we will only prelude on that discussion with the case of *M. & Co v. the Federal Republic of Germany.*[53] This case dealt with the rights of defence in European antitrust cases. The applicant was fined by the European Commission for anticompetitive behaviour. The fine was executed in Germany, under German law in accordance with Article 192 of the EC Treaty (as it then stood). The company claimed a breach of its right of defence and took action against its home state Germany before the human rights court in Strasbourg. The Commission found that Germany was under a duty to ensure that the EC procedures for imposing a fine met with the criteria laid down in Article 6. But it continued by stating that as a rule the European procedure does comply with this provision. Accordingly, Germany could transfer its powers in this field to the EC and it was not considered necessary to check in every individual case whether or not a breach of Article 6 has taken place.

---

49 Compare on the issue of parliamentary immunity the recent case of *De Jorio* v. *Italy*, Appl. no. 73936/01, Court (first section), Judgment (Merits and just satisfaction) 3 June 2004.

50 The issue is more acute in the case of immunity of international organisations, as in these cases there is no alternative access to an independent court system of another state, as is the case with state immunities.

51 The District Court of The Hague (Rb Den Haag) 28 November 2001 *NJ Kort* 2002, 1; *NIPR* 2002, 127 applied this reasoning in a (interim) judgment on the granting of immunity to the International Service for National Agricultural Research.

52 Unless of course the courts are seized after the internal grievance procedure has taken its course: compare *Lenzing AG* v. *UK*, Appl. no 38817/97, Commission (First Chamber), ECtHR Admissibility Decision 9 September 1998. Here the Commission checked *in concreto* the fairness of the internal grievance procedure of the European Patent Board. Compare Lawson 1999, p. 450.

53 *M & Co* v. *Germany*, Appl. No 13258/87, Commission (admissibility decision) 9 February 1990.

Although the first half of the conclusion makes sense and matches the one on immunity, in our opinion the latter is rather surprising.[54] It is understandable that a check at the stage of transfer, which occurs 'before the fact' can only be general. And it is true that the EC as an international organisation has a well-developed system of legal protection, including the right of review by an independent tribunal (the ECJ). Moreover, the ECHR is part of the European legal system, as recognized by the ECJ.[55] So in a sense, with regard to the rights contained in Article 6 ECHR, the EC is more or less comparable to its Member States. Referral to the European court system need not be more burdensome to the citizen than referral to the court system of another Member State.[56] But with regard to both the Member States and the EC itself, the situation is different at the stage of execution: by then a breach of Article 6 has or has not materialised. A more detailed control in the individual case is not only possible, but is indeed indicated. At least only that conclusion seems to be in line with the judgment in the Pellegrini case discussed in the next section.

2.4. RECOGNITION AND ENFORCEMENT OF JUDGMENTS

In the Pellegrini case,[57] the court dealt with the recognition by Italy of a decision by the Rota, the Vatican court, to annul the marriage between Ms Pellegrini and her husband of 25 years. This recognition is based on the Concordat between Italy and the Holy See. The Holy See is a recognized entity in public international

54 This is sometimes ascribed to a tendency of the ECtHR to respect the internal legal order of the EC. However, the Matthews case shows that, if need be, the court is willing to interfere in European matters. In this case, the UK was convicted for the fact the inhabitants of Gibraltar could not vote in the elections for the European Parliament. Appl. no 24883/94, Court (Grand Chamber) Judgment (merits and just satisfaction) 19 February 1999 RJD 1999-I. Again in the case of *Senator Lines GmbH* v. *the 15 Member States of the EC*, the injured party tried to indict the Member States for a breach of fair trial by the European Commission in an anti-trust case. It relied on the Matthews case to hold each Member State 'individually and collectively responsible for the acts of the Community'. The claim failed due to lack of *ius standi*. Compare also the case of *Heinz* v. *the Contracting Sates Party to the European Patent Convention* insofar as they are High Contracting Parties to the ECHR, appl no 21090/92 admissibility decision 1 October 1994.

55 See e.g. C-94/00, Roquette Frères SA, ECJ 22 October 2002, *ECR* I-09011, para. 23.

56 Which as a rule is not checked by the ECtHR either – Compare Prince Hans Adam II of *Liechtenstein* v. *Germany*, Appl. no 42527/98, Court judgment (merits) 12 September 2001, *RJD* 2001-VIII.

57 *Pellegrini* v. *Italy*, Appl. no 30882/96, Court 2e section, Judgment (Merits and just satisfaction) 10 July 2001, *RJD* 2001-VIII. See for comments J-P Costa, *Revue Trimestrielle des droits de l'homme,* 2002/463, p. 470–476; E. Dieni, L'arrêt Pellegrini contre Italie de la Cour Européenne des Droit de l'Homme, *Revue de Droit Canonique* 50/2, 2000, p. 141–161; C. Focarelli, Equo processo e riconoscimento di sentenze straniere: il caso Pellegrini, *Rivista di diritto internazionale,* 2001, 84/4, p. 955–977; N. Mole, 'From Rome to Brussels via Strasbourg – Pellegrini v. Italy and Brussels II', *IFL* 2002, p. 9–15.

law. Although situated within European territory[58], it is not a party to the European Convention.[59] The procedures before the Rota are based on canon law and do not fully comply with the requirements of Article 6.[60] In the specific case, Ms Pellegrini had claimed a violation of her right to a fair trial both in the procedure before the Rota and before the Italian courts. Her claim was rejected in both instances. She subsequently filed a complaint against Italy with the ECtHR. In its judgment the ECtHR decided that the procedure before the Rota had indeed violated Ms. Pellegrini's defence rights.[61] But as the Holy See itself is not bound by the Convention, only Italy could be called upon to uphold these rights. According to the Court, the Italian courts had the duty to duly satisfy themselves, before they authorised the enforcement of the decision annulling the marriage, that the relevant proceedings fulfilled the guarantees of Article 6. A review of that kind is required where a decision in respect of which enforcement is requested emanates from the courts of a country which does not apply the Convention. Such a review is especially necessary where the implications of a declaration of enforceability are of paramount importance to the parties.[62]

So the court should have embarked on a full scrutiny of the ecclesiastical proceedings to decide whether in the individual case the requirements of Article 6 had been met. This duty seems to be motivated by the grave consequences of recognition for the parties involved. The court specifically mentioned that in this case the court which delivered the original judgment was not itself bound by the convention. This suggests that a similar test is not warranted if judgment is rendered by a court of a contracting state. This element of the decision will be discussed further below.

What should be kept in mind when analysing the Pellegrini case is the fact that this was, for all means and purposes, a *domestic* case. Both Ms Pelligrini and her husband were Italian citizens resident in that country. They had celebrated their marriage there and spent their conjugal life in that country. The 'external' element is introduced in the marriage through the status of the Holy See and its involvement with the family life of Italian Catholics. The annulment of Catholic marriages by the Vatican courts is based on an agreement between the Italian state and the Holy See, granting the latter concurrent jurisdiction over these matters.[63] Poland and Spain have similar agreements with the

58 As far as one can say that the Holy Church is situated in any specific place.

59 The Holy See has held observer status within the Council of Europe since 7 March 1970, but is not a party to the ECHR. See www.coe.int.

60 Dieni, *l.c.*, p. 154 nt 30.

61 In this the Human Rights Court's assessment differs from the one by the Italian Courts, which did not find the canon procedure to be in breach of the right to a fair trial (as protected by the public policy clause).

62 Pellegrini, para. 40.

63 The agreement deals only with the civil effects of such an annulment. The religious meaning of marriage and divorce is the sole provenance of the church. On the interaction between canon law and civil law in Italy, see E. Dieni, p. 141–161.

Vatican.[64] The agreement between the Holy See and Portugal even grants the Vatican *exclusive* power over this specific issue. So the relationship between the Catholic states and the Vatican contains an element of (quasi-) transfer of competences in the area of family law. This might explain the strictness of the duty imposed on Italy: the Rota decision was measured in full against the requirements of Article 6 whereas a different standard is used in the case of *Drozd v. France*.

The Drozd case involved the criminal justice system of Andorra. This state, which at the relevant time was not a party to the Convention[65], has only a limited judicial and penal capacity. It makes use of French and Spanish lawyers to sit on the criminal bench.[66] Anyone sentenced to incarceration for a period longer than three months, is transferred to either Spain or France – at the choice of the convicted person – for the execution of the sentence.[67] In the Drozd case the court had to answer the question whether violations of Convention rights by the Andorran justice system are imputable to France. The court stated that though the French government is involved in the Andorran justice system, it bears no direct responsibility for the results thereof.[68] The fact that the sentence is executed in France, however, gives that country an independent responsibility *vis-à-vis* the convicted. This responsibility is based on Article 5 section 1, guaranteeing the right to liberty and the security of the person.

Mr. Drozd claimed that his detention was unlawful as he was convicted without a fair trial. The Court admitted that the proceedings in Andorra can affect the legality of the detention in France. However, 'as the Convention does not require the Contracting Parties to impose its standards on third States or territories, France was not obliged to verify whether the proceedings which resulted in the conviction were compatible with all the requirements of Article 6 of the Convention. To require such a review of the manner in which *a court not bound by the Convention* had applied the principles enshrined in Article 6 would also thwart the current trend towards strengthening international cooperation in the administration of justice, a trend which is in principle *in the interests of the persons concerned (emphasis added AH/ML)*. The Contracting States are, however, obliged to refuse their co-operation if it emerges that the conviction is the result of a flagrant denial of justice.' A similar position was taken in the case

64 Brussels II Regulation Article 40, Mole *l.c.*, p. 11–13.

65 Judgment para. 84 ff. Andorra became a member of the Council of Europe in 1994 and acceded to the ECHR. The Convention entered into force on 22 January 1996.

66 Judgment para. 52.

67 Judgment para. 55–56.

68 There is no jurisdiction *ratione loci*, because Andorra is not an area which is common to France and Spain, nor a Franco-Spanish condominium. Hence it cannot be regarded as French territory (para 89). There is no jurisdiction *ratione personae* because the French judges in the Andorran courts are not acting on behalf of France, but rather on behalf of Andorra. Moreover, there was no any active involvement on the part of France in the specific cases (paras 96–97).

of *Iribarne Perex v. France*, which also involved the execution of an Andorran criminal conviction in France.[69]

Several elements of this judgment merit specific attention. First the Court mentioned, yet again, that the Convention is meant to regulate the behaviour of its Contracting states and has no external ambitions. One should note that the 'external element' in this case is extraterritorial in character. In this respect the Drozd case differs from the Pelligrini case, where the external element was of a religious, rather than a territorial nature. Second, the court seemed to attach a great deal of weight to the fact that transnational cooperation in the case of the transfer of convicted persons is in the interest of the individuals concerned.[70] Demanding strict compliance with Article 6 in those cases would, by blocking such a transfer, thwart the effective protection of the convicted person. Again, the situation was different in the Pellegrini case. Ms Pelligrini derived no benefit from the recognition of the foreign judgment. On the contrary, her legal position *vis-à-vis* her husband was thereby severely worsened. This might explain the different standard used. Whereas in the Pellegrini case all the requirements of Article 6 had to be met, in the Drozd case cooperation only had to be refused in the case of a flagrant denial of justice. Apparently in those extreme cases the protection of public policy prevails maybe even over the interests of the individual.[71]

In both the Pellegrini case and the Drozd case, the court specifically mentioned that the court delivering judgment is not itself bound by the Convention. But whereas in Pellegrini this argument seemed to underlie the duty to check fully for compliance with Article 6, the argument was used in the Drozd case to mitigate the duty of the recognizing state with regards to Article 6. In our opinion, it should not make any difference as to the standard to be applied whether a judgment is rendered by a co-Member State or not.[72] Being a Member State to the ECHR is not in itself a guarantee against breaches of Convention Rights, the case law of the ECtHR contains ample evidence of this. The standard to be used is however linked to and is complicated by the issue of 'local remedies' with regard to the enforcement of judgments and Article 6. By this term we refer to the duty, sometimes imposed on the individual objecting to recognition and enforcement, to seek remedies in the country of origin of the litigious decision. The doctrine of local remedies (as used in this sense) lies at the heart of recent Community instruments dealing with recognition and enforcement in both

69 *Iribarne Pérez* v. *France*, Appl. No. 16462/90, Commission (admissibility decision) 19 January 1994.

70 Compare ECtHR, *Veermäe* v. *Finland*, Appl. no. 38704/03, Court (4th section) 15 March 2005 (admissibility decision).

71 See also *Iribarne Perez* v. *France*.

72 Compare in this respect the case of *T.I.* v. *UK* (Court (Third Section), Admissibility decision, 7 March 2000, RJD 2000-III) discussed in the next section.

criminal matters and commercial and civil matters.[73] Older European instruments on recognition of civil law judgments (e.g. the Brussels Convention and Regulation) as well as instruments operating outside the EU context contain a ground of refusal which can be used in the case of a breach of Article 6 rights – the public policy exception. This public policy exception has been omitted from the new EU instruments, partly for political reasons (criminal law) partly because it was rarely used (civil law). In the thus created system of automatic recognition, the complainant is referred to the country of origin of the judgment or court order when there are (alleged) violations of his defence rights. However, a duty to recognize and enforce judgments and court orders given in violation of Article 6 seems to be at odds with the duty of the Member States under the ECHR.[74] So, several authors (and some courts of well) would reintroduce an Article 6 test at the execution stage.[75]

---

73 The Brussels I Regulation in its rules on recognition and enforcement leaves room for refusal based on violations of Article 6, but refers to the country of origin in the case of a faulty notification (Article 34 section 2). The Regulation establishing a European Enforcement Order does not (seem to) leave any room for refusing enforcement in the country of execution, any disputes on the validity of the EEO being referred to the country of origin. Likewise the proposal for a regulation establishing a European Small Claims Procedure, COM(2005)87 final contains a system of automatic recognition with review in the country of origin. For criminal law, see inter alia the Framework Decision of 13 June 2002 on the European arrest warrant and the surrender procedures between Member States, OJ L 190/1 and the Proposal of 14 November 2003 for a Council Framework Decision on the European Evidence Warrant for obtaining objects, documents and data for use in proceedings in criminal matters, COM (2003) 688.

74 AIDC Resolution II-2: 'When confronted with conflicting obligations under public international law pursuant to conventions on the protection of human rights on the one hand and on international co-operation in criminal matters on the other hand, States should let their obligations with respect to human rights prevail, either by refusing assistance or by imposing conditions on the other State involved', International Review of Penal Law, vol. 65 nr. 1–2, 1994 p. 604–605.

75 Compare for the European Enforcement Order: A. Stadler, Das Europäische Zivilprozessrecht – Wie viel Beschleunigung verträgt Europa?, *IPRax*, vol. 24, no. 1, 2004, p. 2–11 and K. Stoppenbrink, 'Systemwechsel im internationalen Anerkennungsrecht', *European Review of Private Law*, vol. 10, no. 5, 2002, p. 664 ff. In private law circles there is little objection to the abolition of the public policy clause. See R. Hüsstege, 'Braucht die Verordnung über dem europäischen Vollstreckungstitel eigene ordre-public-Klausel?' in: H.-P. Mansel e.a., *Festschrift für Erik Jayme*, Band 1, München: Sellier European Law Publishers, 2002, p. 371–385; A. Stein, 'Der Europäischen Vollstreckungstitel für unbestrittene Vorderungen tritt in Kraft', *IPRax*, vol. 24, no. 3, 2004, p. 181–191 and M. Zilinsky, *De Europese Executoriale Titel*, Deventer: Kluwer, 2005, p. 188–191. This is different for the European Arrest Warrant, see P. Garlick, 'The European Arrest Warrant and the ECHR', in: R. Blekxtoon e.a. *Handbook on the European Arrest Warrant*, The Hague: T.M.C. Asser Press 2005, p. 167–194, i.a. 175 and 177 ff; N. Keijzer, 'Extradition and human rights: a Dutch perspective' in: R. Blekxtoon e.a. (2002) p. 183–194, 193; N. Rozemond, 'Een evaluatie van de Nederlandse overleveringswet, Preadvies voor de Vereniging voor de vergelijkende studie van het recht in België en Nederland 2005', to be published in *Delikt & Delinkwent* February 2006. For European executory titles under Article 256 (former Article 192) see the authors mentioned by I. Pernice, 'Vollstreckung gemeinschaftsrechtlicher Zahlungstitel und Grundrechtsschutz' *RIW* 1986 Heft 5 p. 354; H.H. Rupp, 'Materielles Prüfungsrecht bei Erteilung der europarechtlichen Vollstreckungsklauseln?'

However, even then the existence of local remedies may play a role at the stage of recognition and enforcement through the doctrine of estoppel. The Dutch Supreme Court, for one, accepted such an effect in a ruling rendered in 2002. It that case the party opposing recognition claimed breaches to his right to be heard in the country of origin of the judgment. But he had not contested the judgment at first instance by means of an appeal or any other means of recourse available to him. According to the Supreme Court, in those circumstances the court did not have to entertain his claim with regard to Article 6.[76] Likewise, the Brussels I Regulation in its rules on recognition and enforcement, although leaving room for refusal based on violations of Article 6 ECHR, refers to the country of origin in the case of a faulty notification (Article 34 section 2). Whether under the Human Rights Convention the applicant is required to introduce his complaint in the original proceedings and to use the available appeal options, is as yet unclear.[77] So is the position of the ECJ, which dealt with violations of the ECHR and the public policy exception in the Brussels Convention in the Krombach

---

NJW 1986, Heft 10, p. 640–641; N.A. Schoible, 'Die "Execution auf Grund von akten und Urkunden supranationaler Organisationen" in Őstereich', in: FS. Geimer, *Einheit und Vielfalt des Rechts*, Munich: Beck, 2002, p. 980–1011.

76 HR 5 maart 2002, *NJ* 2004, 170 (note P. Vlas) Likewise, in cases concerning extradition to other Convention states, the Dutch Supreme Court will refer a complainant to the local remedies of the requesting state for any complaints on fair trial. Keijzer *o.c.*, p. 191–192; HR 11 March 2003, *NJ* 2004, 42, and 20 May 2003, *NJ* 2004, 41 (note Y. Buruma). We would argue however, that in these cases, the doctrine works differently. At the stage of recognition of judgments or measures (which is described here) the alleged breach has already occurred, but could have been remedied locally. In extradition cases, courts are mostly confronted with potential future breaches of Convention rights. But in extradition cases, several special issues may arise. In the Dutch system the availability of a local remedy is a precondition for extradition in the case of a criminal conviction in absentia. The issue is also raised in cases of extradition for the purpose of execution of a criminal sentence, when the person to be extradited claims a breach of the requirement of trial within a reasonable time (Art. 6 ECHR). In the latter case the Dutch Supreme Court also referred to local remedies: the person to be extradited should challenge the execution in the requesting state, *after* being extradited (HR 11 March 2003, *NJ* 2004, 42). One could argue however, that if the execution is time-barred under Article 6, so is the extradition either because there is no longer a valid title to execute or because extradition is in itself an act of execution/prosecution. The District Court of Amsterdam, in a decision of 1 July 2005 (cited by N. Rozemond) relies on the argument that in case of a flagrant breach of the right to trial within a reasonable time, there is no *effective* remedy possible, hence extradition should be refused. In the English law of extradition a distinction is made between fair trial issues which are best decided during trial (in the requesting state) and issues leading to a refusal to extradite (by the requested state) – see *Ramda* v. *Secretary for the Home Department* [2002] EWHC 1278 (admin), discussed in Garlick *l.c.*, p. 179.

77 A minor indication to this effect might be derived from the case of *Dufay* v. *the EC and its Member States*, in which Ms Dufay filed a complaint regarding her dismissal by the EC. The complaint against the Member States was declared inadmissible because she had not exhausted the available EC remedies. It could also be argued that the judgment in the Bosphorus case (discussed in section 2.10) should mainly be explained as a local remedies issue. See below.

case.[78] Thus far neither court has been obliged to decide on the matter: in both the Pellegrini case and the Krombach case the applicants had exhausted the local remedies. But we would suggest that the recognizing court does not have to perform a full scrutiny of a foreign judgment when local remedies were available – both in law and in fact[79] – but remained unused. After all – people can forego their rights under Article 6. Even in those cases, however, recognition should be refused in case of a flagrant denial of justice – because then the public policy element of the refusal ground really kicks in.

2.5. EXTRADITION

In the Drozd case, the Court underpinned its reasoning by referring to the Soering case.[80] This case forms the benchmark case for all cases concerning international cooperation in criminal matters. It dealt with extradition.

In the Soering case, the ECtHR decided on the application of the Convention (and more specifically Articles 3 and 6) to the extradition of a German citizen to the USA, a non-member state. The point at issue was that the person to be extradited to the USA was accused of a crime carrying the death penalty in the State of Virginia.

After stating the law in the several states involved, the Court reiterated its earlier case law that extradition may affect the enjoyment of Convention rights and hence may be subject to the scrutiny of the Court. The present case involved the right not to be subjected to torture and inhuman or degrading treatment or punishment (Article 3).[81] This right, violated by the American death row system, is of a very fundamental nature. Yet, the Convention standards do not apply in full to the issue. The Convention does not govern the actions of States not Parties to it, nor does it purport to be a means of requiring the Contracting States to impose Convention standards on other States (para. 86). Contracting states incur liability under the Convention in a more indirect way. In this case the UK could

78 Case C-7/98 *Krombach* v. *Bamberski*, ECJ 28 March 2000, *ECR* I-1395, note A.A.H. van Hoek *Common Market Law Review*, vol. 38, no. 4, 2001, p. 1011–1027.

79 Settled case law, see inter alia *Djavit An* v. *Turkije*, Appl. no. 20652/92, Court (third section), Judgment (Merits and just satisfaction) 20 February 2003, *RJD* 2003-III, paras 28–29. The latter requirement also refers to the element of notification – there must have been a real opportunity to lodge an appeal, after gaining knowledge of the judgment and its reasoning.

80 *Soering* v. *UK*, Appl. no. 14038/88, Court (Plenary), Judgment (Merits and just satisfaction) 7 July 1989, Series A no. 161.

81 In later cases the court referred directly to the 6th protocol, abolishing the death penalty, see e.g. *Nivette* v. *France*, Appl. no. 44190/98, Court (1st Section), Admissibility decision 14 December 2000, *RJD* 2001-VII.

be held responsible for the fact that its actions have as a direct consequence the exposure of an individual to proscribed treatment.[82]

In the process the Court had to overcome the fact that it normally does not hear cases on future potential violations of Convention rights. It did so by pointing out the serious and irreparable consequences of extradition for the rights of the person concerned. In order to activate the liability of the extraditing state there must be substantial grounds for believing that the person to be extradited faces a real risk of being subjected to torture or to inhuman treatment. In subsequent cases it became apparent that the burden of proof in such cases is rather high: general safety risks or poor prison condition do not suffice, the person to be extradited will have to substantiate a personal risk with regard to the proscribed treatment.[83]

In determining whether extradition would lead to a violation of the Convention, the Court weighs the interests of the effective protection of the rights involved against the legitimate interests of transnational cooperation in criminal matters. In this weighing process, extradition is seen as a tool to combat the evasion of justice and hence as primarily serving a public interest. The Court also addresses the proportionality issue by pointing out that in the specific case of Soering the public interest of law enforcement could have been protected by the lesser means of extradition to Germany – a Member State willing to prosecute but not applying the death penalty.

With regard to a claim under Article 6, the court 'does not exclude that an issue might exceptionally be raised under Article 6 by an extradition decision in circumstances where the fugitive has suffered or risks suffering a flagrant denial of a fair trial in the requesting country. However, the facts of the present case do not disclose such a risk.'[84]

The Soering case was followed by several others, both on the extradition of criminals and on the expulsion of aliens. An interesting case from the point of view of co-operation within the EU is the case of *T.I. v. UK*.[85] This case dealt with the expulsion of a so-called Dublin claimant from the UK to Germany, the

---

82 See recently *Mamatkulov and Abdurasulovic* v. *Turkey*, Appl. no 46827/99 and 46951/99, Court (first section), Judgment (Merits and Just Satisfaction) 6 February 2003 para. 68. In the Ilascu case, the Court phrased it slightly differently and referred to government acts with 'sufficiently proximate repercussions on rights guaranteed by the Convention', which attract a state's liability even if those repercussions occur outside its jurisdiction – *Ilascu and others* v. *Moldova and Russian Federation*, Appl.no. 48787/99, Court (Grand Chamber), Judgment (Merits and just satisfaction), *EHRC* 2004–9 p. 862–866 note M. Gondek, para. 317.

83 Mamatkulov Appl. no 46827/99 and 46951/99, Court (1st section), Judgment (Merits and Just Satisfaction) 6 February 2003 para. 66. Mamatkulov Appl. no 46827/99 and 46951/99 Court (Grand Chamber), Judgment (Merits and just satisfaction) 4 February 2005 para. 69 ff.

84 Soering Para. 113; Mamatkulov 1st section para. 85 ff. See on this issue Trechsel, 'The Role of International Organs Controlling Human Rights in the Field of International Co-operation', in: Albin Eser and Otto Lagodny, *Principles and Procedures for a new Transnational Criminal Law*, Freiburg im Breisgau: Max-Plank Institut 1992, p. 658–659.

85 Court (Third Section), Admissibility decision, 7 March 2000, *RJD* 2000-III.

country of first entry. In this case the court found 'that the indirect removal in this case to an intermediary country, which is also a Contracting State, does not affect the responsibility of the United Kingdom to ensure that the applicant is not, as a result of its decision to expel, exposed to treatment contrary to Article 3 of the Convention. Nor can the UK rely automatically in that context on the arrangements made in the Dublin Convention concerning the attribution of responsibility between European countries for deciding asylum claims. Where states establish international organisations, or mutatis mutandis international agreements, to pursue co-operation in certain fields of activities, there may be implications for the protection of fundamental rights. It would be incompatible with the object and purpose of the Convention if Contracting States were thereby absolved from their responsibility under the Convention in relation to the field of activity covered by such attribution.[86] The Court notes the comments of the UNHCR that, while the Dublin Convention may pursue laudable objectives, its effectiveness may be undermined in practice by the differing approaches adopted by Contracting States to the scope of protection offered.' Again, Contracting States are held fully responsible for the international obligations which they adopt. It is also worth noting, that the fact that expulsion took place to another Contracting State does not seem to affect the responsibility of the UK. Apparently the Court – in this case at least – did not operate on the assumption of conformity, which lies at the heart of the mutual trust concept in national law.

When extradition is requested with a view to prosecution, the claim against the extraditing state is most often based on the risk of being exposed to the death penalty and/or inhuman treatment, combined with the risk of not receiving a fair trial. These risks have not yet materialized, but are expected to after extradition. An exception is the case of *Chinoy v. UK*.[87] In that case the person to be extradited claimed a breach of his right to privacy (Article 8) by the investigation authorities of the requesting state. This breach could, according to the applicant, lead to a separate breach of Article 8 by the requested authority. Also it could result in the detention for reasons of extradition being unlawful (Article 5). This case, in which the extraterritorial breach of Convention rights had already taken place, will be discussed below.

2.6. TRANSNATIONAL COOPERATION IN CRIMINAL MATTERS

Transnational cooperation in criminal matters, used in the present limited sense, refers to cooperation between investigating and prosecuting authorities, mostly

86 See e.g. *Waite and Kennedy* v. *FRG*, Appl. no. 26083/94, Court (Grand Chamber), Judgment (merits) 18 February 1999, *RJD* 1999-I, para. 67.

87 Chinoy v. UK, Appl. No. 15199/89, Commission applicability decision 25 June 1991.

in order to prepare a future criminal charge. It consists of the exchange of information, search and seizures and the hearing of witnesses. This kind of cooperation poses specific problems with regard to the protection of human rights. The actions of the authorities are often unknown to the investigated person – sometimes until they are entered as evidence. Also the separate actions of the authorities can not always be judged on their own, but contribute to a single goal – the criminal investigation and prosecution. This may make it more difficult for the states involved to identify and fulfil their separate responsibility. The person claiming a violation may find it more difficult to pinpoint the breach and the authority responsible for it. Before discussing the system of transnational cooperation in criminal matters in more detail in paragraph 3, we will finish our discussion of the case law of the ECtHR on the types of cooperation described here. Case law is available on all three types of cooperation.

2.6.1. Exchange of information

The case of *Chinoy v. UK*[88] though on the face dealing with extradition, does in fact concern the field of mutual assistance in criminal matters. In the case at hand, Mr. Chinoy was indicted by a US federal grand jury with charges of several drugs-related crimes.[89] The US authorities requested the UK government to extradite him under the US-UK extradition treaty. The request was substantiated by evidence including the transcripts of conversations by the defendant and others intercepted by the US authorities in France. Chinoy complained about the illegal character of the recordings, both before a French *magistrat* and in the English extradition proceedings. When both complaints had no effect, he turned to the Human Rights Commission claiming the UK violated his Convention rights in handling the offensive information. Both the acceptance and storage of the information and the subsequent use made thereof in assessing his case, he claimed, constituted a breach of Article 8 of the Convention. Moreover, the illegal evidence corrupted the legal basis for his detention, resulting in a breach of Article 5.

In order to judge the responsibility of the UK in the present case, the Commission considered the use made by UK officials of the (allegedly) illegal information. This consisted of the acceptance of the materials from the US, an examination as to its relevance and the production of the relevant parts as evidence in the proceedings. In the circumstances of the case, the Commission did not find a breach of Article 8. This conclusion seems to be based on a weighing of interests amongst which the importance of international cooperation in the international campaign against drugs trafficking. The Commission seemed to balance the uncertainty with regard to the unlawfulness of the information

88 Appl. no. 15199/89, Commission applicability decision 25 June 1991.

89 Possession of drugs with the intention to distribute as well as money laundering.

against the clear relevance of the same to the extradition proceedings. In this respect it noted that the transcripts and tapes which were used in open court related solely to business matters and hence did not invade the privacy of the complainant's family life.

So the Commission attached no relevance to the acceptance, storage and internal use of the material by the British authorities, although these aspects were specifically raised by the applicant. Thus, it seems that the lawfulness of receiving, storing and processing information is not tainted by the breach of privacy at the stage of information gathering. This seems to contradict the findings of the Court in the Leander case.[90] In its judgment, which predates Chinoy, the Court ruled that the storage and the exchange of personal data give rise to separate responsibilities under Article 8.

With regard to the breach of Article 5, the decision hinged on the admissibility of unlawfully obtained evidence. In this respect the Commission recalled that the Convention contains no express or implied requirement that evidence obtained unlawfully under domestic law must be ruled inadmissible. Neither did the fact that the information was obtained in breach of French law, bar it from being included in the evidence under English law. So, there was a legal basis for detention under English law. Moreover, the Commission found no indication of arbitrariness in the decision of the UK courts to admit the evidence.

The Commission based its decision on the assumption that *some doubt existed* as to the lawfulness of the recording under the Convention and under French law whereas Chinoy had stated that the recordings had been made in *flagrant breach* of French law. However, the French courts had refused to hear his arguments on this issue. As a result of this refusal his position was severely weakened, both before the English courts and before the Commission. This element was ignored by the Commission, as the complaint was not directed against France.[91]

The reasoning in Chinoy is built upon in the case of *Echeverri Rodriguez v. the Netherlands*.[92] In this case, concerning illegal telephone taps made in the US and used in Dutch criminal proceedings, the Court decided that 'Questions concerning the admissibility of evidence are primarily a matter for regulation by national law... The task of the Court under the Convention is to ascertain whether the proceedings as a whole, including the way in which evidence was taken, were fair.

---

90 ECtHR 26 March 1987 (judgment on the merits), appl. No. 10/1985/96/144, Publ. ECHR Series A vol. 166 (*Leander* v. *Sweden*), later confirmed in ECtHR 16 February 2000, appl. No. 27798/9 (*Amann* v. *Switzerland*); see also the 1981 Convention for the Protection of Individuals with regard to Automatic Processing of Personal Data of the Council of Europe, ETS 108.

91 Decision, 'The law', para. 1.

92 ECtHR (1st section) 27 July 2001 (admissibility decision), Appl. no. 43286/98, *NJ* 2002/102 (note Sch).

… The Court considers that the Convention does not preclude reliance, in the investigating stage, on information obtained by the investigating authorities from sources such as foreign criminal investigations. Nevertheless, the subsequent use of such information can raise issues under the Convention where there are reasons to assume that in this foreign investigation defence rights guaranteed in the Convention have been disrespected. However, the applicant has not substantiated in any way that such reasons existed in the instant case.'

Again, the court seems to distinguish between the use of unlawfully obtained information during the investigation and its introduction into evidence. And again, in the latter case the test applied is stricter. However, a complaint only has a possibility of success if the applicant can gather enough information to prove unlawfulness and/or breaches of convention rights during the investigation. In most cases this is not a simple matter: the source of the information might not be known, or the authorities involved may not be subject to any effective scrutiny – compare the unwillingness of France to investigate into the illegal American investigations within its territory. This jeopardizes the right to an effective remedy. It is standard case law, that the rights protected by the Convention should be practical and effective, not theoretical and illusory.[93] In our opinion, the right to an effective remedy – with regard to both Article 6 and Article 8 – requires the disclosure of the source of the information under dispute unless there are compelling reasons to the contrary.[94] This is necessary both to identify the party responsible for a breach of privacy and to be able to challenge the evidence in court.[95] Information should not be used if the provenance thereof is unknown and can't be identified. This requires a willingness on the part of the co-operating authorities to disclose the necessary information.

2.6.2. Search and seizures on behalf of another state

In the case of *S. v. Austria*, Austria had searched of the premises of S in Austria and seized several documents. These activities were carried out at request of the German authorities.[96] In the admissibility decision the search, being a violation of private and family life, home and correspondence (Article 8 sub 1) was tested against the requirements of Article 8 sub 2. In this case the mutual assistance was based upon a specific provision under Austrian law. Hence the search had a legal basis. The restriction so imposed also served a legitimate aim which was 'the prevention of crime'. This term refers to crime in general, both within and

93 See most recently Mamatkulov, Grand Chamber, 4 February 2005, para. 121.

94 Compare Leander para. 84.

95 The complainant needs to be able to raise an 'arguable claim' – see for example Leander para. 77.

96 *S. v. Austria* Appl. No. 12592/86 Commission, Admission Decision 6 March 1989.

outside the territory of the contracting state.[97] The final requirement under the convention is that the particular search was necessary, appropriate and proportionate. This element however, could not be tested by the Austrian courts. Under Austrian law it was delegated to the requesting authorities, which in this case were German. According to the Commission, the impossibility under Austrian law to independently judge the proportionality of the measure does not in itself constitute a breach of the Convention. In the present case, there were no indications that the search carried out was in fact objectively unjustified and disproportionate. Therefore, the Commission found neither a violation of Article 8 nor of Article 13. So the applicant was left without any effective remedy. Yet on paper nothing is lost. Austria is still responsible for the proportionality and necessity of any search it carries out. The mutual trust provision in its law does not absolve the state of its responsibility. But shouldn't this responsibility entail the possibility to check for conformity, preferably beforehand? In several cases the ECtHR has stressed the need to prevent breaches of Convention rights.[98] Such preventive action presupposes, yet again, a willingness to share the necessary information.

This is demonstrated in the judgment of the ECJ in the Roquette Frère case in 2002. This case dealt with the respective responsibilities of the Commission and the Member States with regard to the legitimacy of searches carried out by national authorities in anti-trust cases.[99] According to the ECJ, the Commission is responsible for the decision to investigate. This decision, and the procedure followed, may be tested before the European Courts. It is not open to scrutiny in the national courts. However, a Member State that is asked to assist in acquiring evidence has an independent duty to assure the respect of basic rights, especially the privacy rights embedded in Article 8 ECHR. In practice this check revolves around the third requirement mentioned above: a search and seizure measure should not be disproportionate and arbitrary.[100] The provision on community loyalty in the EC Treaty does not force the Member States to blindly accept and honour all requests, but rather obliges the Member States and the European Commission to cooperate. So the EC has to provide the national court with all

97 'The Commission observes that Article 8 para. 2 authorises interferences with the rights guaranteed by paragraph 1 of the same Article, inter alia, 'for the prevention of crime'. And in this respect it does not distinguish between measures taken in connection with criminal proceedings in the State concerned or a foreign State'.

98 Compare Mamatkulov Grand Chamber para. 124: 'The notion of an effective remedy under Article 13 requires a remedy capable of preventing the execution of measures that are contrary to the Convention and whose effects are potentially irreversible.' Although this admittedly holds true especially with regards to deportation and extradition measures which may lead to irreparable harm to basic Convention rights, it seems to be a venerable starting point in all cases of transnational co-operation. Compare also ECHR *Chappel* v. *UK*, appl. no. 10461/8330, Court (Chamber), Judgment (Merits) March 1989, Series A 152-A.

99 C-94/00, ECJ 22 October 2002, *ECR* 2002, p. I-9011.

100 The legal basis is provided for in the European regulation and national law; the legitimate aim is law enforcement.

the information which the latter needs to check for conformity with Article 8. The Member States in their turn have to respect the independent responsibilities of the EC.

2.6.3. Hearing of witnesses

In the case of *P.V. v. FRG*,[101] P.V. complained that in criminal proceedings against him the German court had made use of evidence obtained by commission rogatory in Turkey although he had been unable to cross-examine the witness thus questioned. The Court pointed out that 'the German authorities cannot be held responsible for the non-observance of provisions of the Turkish law by a Turkish court'.[102] But this does not exclude a separate responsibility of the German courts under Article 6: 'although this court was not responsible for the examination of C on commission it is in principle conceivable that the use of the evidence thereby contained could be contrary to that provision' (Article 6.3.d). But in the present case, and according to the Court, Article 6 had been complied with. This finding was based on an analysis of Article 6 itself. Although this provision (and notable Article 6.3.d) protects the right of a suspect to counter the evidence put forward, it does not contain an absolute right to cross-examine all witnesses. Article 6 is also respected if the accused and his counsel can put questions to the witness through the court. 'Especially, this holds true if witnesses are to be examined on commission (cf. No. 5049/71)'.

So the court which allows the introduction of evidence gathered abroad, has an independent duty under Article 6 as regards the way in which the evidence was gathered. However, in the present case the contents of the convention rights themselves were quite explicitly adapted to the transnational circumstances.

2.7. TRIAL WITHIN A REASONABLE TIME

The case of *Sari v. Turkey and Denmark*[103] concerned the transnational complication in the criminal proceedings against Mr Sari, a Turkish citizen, who was accused of the homicide[104] of a Danish citizen in Denmark. He fled the jurisdiction and was later found to be present in Turkey. Denmark requested his extradition but left open the possibility of transferring the proceedings. A long

101 *P.V.* v. *FRG*, Appl. no. 11853/85, ECHR Admissibility decision 13 July 1987.
102 Decision para. 4c.
103 *Sari* v. *Turkey and Denmark*, Appl. No. 21889/93, Court (Fourth Section), Judgment (Merits) 8 November 2001, available in French only.
104 '*Homicide volontaire*'. See para. 10 of the judgment.

exchange ensued.[105] In 1998, some eight years after the fact,[106] the proceedings against Sari ended in a final conviction, and a sentence of five years imprisonment in Turkey. At the ECtHR Sari complained of the length of the criminal proceedings against him, claiming a violation of Article 6, para. 1.

The court started by stating that the reasonable time in Article 6 para. 1 refers to the proceedings in their entirety.[107] So, the period in the present case runs from the first charges in Denmark to the final conviction in Turkey. Of this period, Denmark was involved for the first four years[108], Turkey for almost eight years.

As to the question of reasonableness of the delay, this is weighed against (inter alia) the complexity of the case and the comportment of both the accused and the authorities involved. In the present case, the applicant had referred to the lack of complexity of the crime with which he was accused: a simple homicide.[109] However, the court estimated that the transnational element of the case caused serious complications.[110] These complications had been caused by the applicant himself, as he chose to flee the jurisdiction of Denmark.[111] Moreover, for two years he escaped arrest altogether. As a result, the delay was for a considerable part attributable to the applicant himself. As for the remainder, the whole process of transnational cooperation might have been slow, but this was attributable to neither Denmark nor Turkey individually. Rather, the two states had joint responsibility for any lack of promptness in their cooperation. This joint responsibility was mitigated by the fact that the court seemed to accept that the system of transnational cooperation in criminal matters is at present slow and complicated. In the end, the court found no violation of Article 6.

This case is interesting in that the court looked at the individual responsibility of the States for any tardiness on their part, but also recognized the joint responsibility for the cooperation itself. However, in several ways the right protected by Article 6 is watered down in international cases. The court admitted that the need for transnational cooperation enhanced the complexity of the case, thereby extending the 'reasonable' time-limits. Furthermore, the court accepted

---

105 The long duration was in part caused by the reluctance of the Danish authorities to yield jurisdiction to the Turkish authorities. This reluctance was caused by the fact that the crime committed in Denmark carried the death penalty in Turkey.

106 8 years, 7 months and 22 days to be precise. See para. 68 of the judgment.

107 In this conclusion the Court seemed to deviate from its earlier decision in *Pafitis* v. *Greece* (app. No. 20323/92, Commission appl.dec. 4 September 1996, judgment February 1998). In that case, the time involved in the preliminary procedure before the ECJ was not taken into account in deciding on the reasonable time delay in a Greek procedure.

108 The period ran from the first indictment to the complete transfer of the file to Turkey. See para. 70 of the judgment.

109 Para. 73.

110 Para. 78.

111 From then on, the case involved not only the proceedings in the matter itself, but also an extradition request and the transfer of proceedings (para 79). Hence the case was made relatively complex (para. 78) by the behaviour of the applicant himself (para. 79).

that transnational cooperation is at present slow and problematic, further extending the leeway granted to the states involved. Read together with the cases discussed above, it seems that the problem of applying the Convention to international cooperation in criminal matters does not lie in the difficulty of extraterritorial application. Nor is the problem caused by questions of the division of liability between the states involved. Rather, effective protection is hampered by the watering down of rights in transnational cases and by the burden put upon the applicant to state and proof the violation of his rights.

2.8. ORGANLEIHE UNDER THE ECHR

The German term 'Organleihe' refers to the situation in which a public authority or public official of a state is placed at the disposal of another state to partake in government functions there.[112] In this scenario, the question may be raised which state is responsible for the acts performed by the authority concerned. This issue was addressed in several cases, two of which will be discussed here. The first concerns the case of *X and Y v. Switzerland*, Appl. no. 7289/75 & 7349/76, Adm.dec. 14 July 1977, Decisions & Reports IX, March 1978, p. 57.

In this case, the main complainant was a German citizen who when staying in Liechtenstein with his second, out-of-wedlock, family was ordered by the Swiss aliens' police to leave the Swiss-Liechtenstein area and not to return. He cited Switzerland for inter alia the violation of his family life. At the relevant time, Liechtenstein was not a party to the Convention.[113]The part of the judgment which interests us, concerns the responsibility of Switzerland for measures concerning the status of aliens in the Swiss/Liechtenstein customs territory. In 1923, by bilateral agreement, Liechtenstein was included in the Swiss custom territory subject to the condition that it adopted the Swiss laws on the position of third country nationals. This cooperation was elaborated upon by treaties on cooperation in matters of aliens' police, the one in force at the time of the alleged infringement having been concluded in 1963. According to the 1963 treaty, on this specific issue the Swiss laws would apply to the Liechtenstein territory, and Liechtenstein would delegate certain functions of the aliens' police to the Swiss federal authorities. Based on this international arrangement, Liechtenstein territory was treated in a similar fashion to a Swiss canton. Accordingly, when the complainant was ordered to leave the territory because of gross violations of the regulations applicable to aliens (illegal residence and failure to report to the authorities), the order was issued by the Swiss police and was based on Swiss law.

112 Alternatively, organs of international organisations are placed at the disposal of (Member) States and vice versa.

113 Liechtenstein joined the Council of Europe in 1978, the ECHR entered into force on 8 September 1982.

In their admissibility decision, the Commission had to address the question of whether the Swiss order was imputable to Switzerland, or was rather an act performed on behalf of the Liechtenstein government for which the latter bore sole responsibility. In its answer, the Commission attached great importance to the fact that the Swiss authorities, when acting for Liechtenstein, do not differentiate from their national competences, but act exclusively in conformity with Swiss law. It is only the effect of the act which is automatically extended to the Liechtenstein territory under the treaty. A prohibition on entering the territory cannot be mitigated or repealed by the Liechtenstein authorities. In that case, the Commission decided that 'acts by Swiss authorities with effect in Liechtenstein bring all those to whom they apply under Swiss jurisdiction within the meaning of Article 1 of the Convention'. So Switzerland was held responsible for the acts of its officials pertaining to Liechtenstein.

The Court reached the opposite conclusion in the case of *Drozd and Janacek v. France* (discussed above). Again, the case concerns one of the European mini-states, in this case Andorra, which needs assistance help from its neighbours in performing certain government functions. Again, the neighbours coming to the country's aid – in this case Spain and France – are party to the Convention whereas the mini-state itself is not.[114] The relevant government functions concern the criminal justice system and the penal system. French and Spanish judges sit on the bench of the Andorran criminal court. Longer prison sentences are served in either France or Spain. As is discussed *in extenso* in section 2.5, Spain and France are responsible for the execution of prison sentences within their territory. However, as is mentioned only in passing there, neither state was held responsible for the judgment itself, notwithstanding the fact that the judgment was pronounced with the involvement of Spanish and French judges. The court applied the following reasoning. Andorra is neither a part of Spain nor of France, but is an entity in its own right. So there is no jurisdiction ratione loci. Yet, Spain and France can be held responsible for actions outside their territory when complainants fall within the jurisdiction of the said states. The Court denied such responsibility: 'Whilst it is true that judges from France and Spain sit as members of the Andorran courts, they do not do so in their capacity as French of Spanish judges. Those courts, ... exercise their functions in an autonomous manner; their judgments are not subject to supervision by the authorities in France or Spain. Moreover, there is nothing in the case-file which suggests that the French or Spanish authorities attempted to interfere with the applicant's trial'.[115]

---

114 The judgment notes that Andorra was not at the time a member of the Council of Europe and had not applied for associate member status (para. 89). Andorra joined the Council of Europe in 1994, the ECHR entered into force in 1996.

115 Para. 96.

So apparently in a horizontal context – of cooperation between states – a state (A) can be responsible for certain acts performed by its authorities even when these acts are performed in service of another state (B). This will be the case if A's officials apply the law of A and remain within their normal competences. However, if an official from A, placed at the disposal of state B, is totally embedded in the system of state B, applying its laws and operating under its supervision and control, the acts of the official are no longer imputed to state A.[116] This finding is in line with the current doctrine in international law, as is evident (inter alia) from the Articles on the responsibility of states for internationally wrongful acts, presented by the International Law Commission of the UN to the General Assembly in 2001. Article 6 of the latter instrument states that 'the conduct of an organ placed at the disposal of a State by another State shall be considered an act of the former State under international law if the organ is acting in the exercise of elements of the governmental authority of the State at whose disposal it is placed'.[117]

The case law described here only deals with the liability of the state lending out its officials and not with the responsibility of the state receiving the assistance. Would Liechtenstein, if it had been party to the ECHR at the relevant time, have been liable for the actions of the Swiss police? In all likelihood it would, either because of the territorial responsibility it carries or because of the legal effects it attaches to the orders of the Swiss authorities. A similar logic can be applied to the acts of international organisations. Under international law, the attribution of liability to an international organisation or rather to one of its Member States seems to hinge on the actual power of control over the organ/official which acted in breach of international law.[118] In the case law of the ECtHR however, the basic rule is that states have a duty of care with regard to their own territory. This duty can not be detracted from by international arrangements.[119] Whether this rule still fits the current developments in European law, is discussed below.

2.9. THE COURT'S BALANCING ACT

The case law on extraterritorial application shows clearly that, according to the Court and the Commission, the European Convention is drafted so as to provide minimum norms for the European states which are party thereto. It does not

---

116 Notice that neither decision contains information on the liability of state B under the Convention.

117 Annex to Resolution 56/83. Other Articles confirm that States can be held responsible for acts committed by others under their direction and control: Article 8 and Articles 16 ff.

118 First report on responsibility of international organizations by Mr. Giorgio Gaja, Special Reporter, A/CN.4/532. ILA International Committee on the accountability of international organisations, report to the Berlin Conference 2004, p. 27–30.

119 See section 2.3, above.

have a universal vocation. Yet within the Member States it is meant to apply in full. International complications should not detract from the protection thus offered. This is evident from the case law on Northern Cyprus as well as the case law on the transfer of powers to international institutions.

The protection of convention rights is always balanced against (other) national interests.[120] In several cases, both the Court and the Commission have stressed the importance of transnational cooperation in criminal matters for the effective enforcement of criminal laws. Although, in theory, the existence of international agreements and transnational institutions do not affect the responsibility of the Contracting States, in transnational cases a certain loss of rights seems to be taken for granted.[121] This *effet atténué*[122] is most prominent in cases concerning fair trial. Sometimes the adjustments are based on the international complications of the case as such, for example with regard to trial within a reasonable time and the right to challenge the testimony of witnesses. The most common use for the term 'effet atténué', however, is to describe the cases in which the Court sanctions only 'flagrant denials of justice' and does not test against the requirements of Article 6 in full. In this respect, famous cases are the Soering case on extradition and the Drozd case on the transfer of sentenced persons. In the first case the limited supervision can be explained by the fact that Soering had asked to be protected against a possible future infringement of Convention rights by a non-convention state. Future infringements do not, as a rule, fall within the jurisdiction of the ECtHR. In the latter case the marginal control of the requirements of Article 6 can be explained by the fact that the transnational co-operation benefited the person whose convention rights were involved.[123] The judgment can be explained by the desire to avoid the situation where the abstract protection of convention rights actually damages the overall position of the person thus protected. So the lowering of the standard of review in international cases is not unequivocal. In the case of Pellegrini against Italy the recognition by Italy of a non-convention judgment was tested in full against the requirements of Article 6. And, in our opinion, the case law does not show an 'effet atténué' as regards the other convention rights, e.g. the right to life and the protection against torture and inhuman and degrading treatment.

---

120 See also F.J. Bruinsma, 'Judicial identities in the ECHR', published in this book.

121 And/or to be contributed to the applicant himself – see the case *Sari* v. *Turkye and Denmark*, discussed above.

122 This term is also used to describe the difference between domestic and international public policy in private international law: Mandatory provision and constitutional rights are not applied in full to international situations, but have a 'effet attenué'. Compare ECJ *Krombach* v. *Bamberski*.

123 Cf. H.G. van der Wilt, 'Volkenrechtelijke aspecten van internationale rechtshulp', in: A.H.Klip, A.H.J. Swart and H.G. van der Wilt (eds.), *Het Wetboek van Strafvordering; Internationale en Interregionale samenwerking in strafzaken*, Deventer: Kluwer (loose leaf), par. I.4.1, nr 6.

This does not mean, however, that the protection of Convention rights is – at the time – sufficiently guaranteed in transnational cases. Several cases show that effective protection can be frustrated by a lack of information on the side of the complainant. Facts are needed, not only to substantiate the allegation that a violation of Convention rights has taken place, but also to pinpoint the responsible state. Especially in cases of mutual assistance in criminal matters, it might prove difficult to trace the source of information – which in turn might make it difficult to assert one's rights under Article 6 and Article 8. In the next part of this article, we will look more deeply into these issues and try to develop a system which will honour both the legitimate need for cooperation and the convention rights of the individuals concerned.

2.10. THE POSITION OF THE EC/EU AND ITS MEMBER STATES

At several instances we have already hinted at the complications caused by the existence of the EC/EU when it comes to allotting responsibility for cooperation in the field of justice and home affairs. Here we look into this aspect in more detail. The interaction between the EU/EC and its Member States is to a large extent based on the model of cooperative federalism. This means that the European Union and Community often have to co-operate with the member states for the full implementation of their laws and policies.[124] Directives and Framework decisions have to be transposed into national law before they become binding on the citizens. In those cases, it will be *national* law which affects the position of the individual. Likewise, the enforcement of Community law is to a large degree left to the national legal systems.[125] National courts have sole competence in conflicts amongst private individuals and in conflicts between individuals and Member State authorities. The ECJ might become involved in such disputes by way of preliminary questions, but only if the national courts so decide. The ECJ is only called upon to explain the European rule and/or to rule on its validity. The final judgment – in which the abstract rule is applied to the individual case – is delivered by the national courts.[126] This separate responsibility of the Member States for the enforcement of European law is enhanced by the fact that the Member States retain a large (albeit shrinking)

124 Within federal systems this model is known as co-operative federalism. See W.T. Eijsbouts, J.H. Jans, F.O.W. Vogelaar, *Europees Recht; Algemeen Deel*, Groningen: Europa Law Publishing 2004, p. 356 ff.

125 Compare Article 256 EC Treaty; Pernice *l.c.*, RIW 1986, p. 354; N.A. Schoible, 'Die "Execution auf Grund von akten und Urkunden supranationaler Organisationen" in Österreich', In: FS. Geimer, *Einheit und Vielfalt des Rechts*, Munich: Beck, 2002, p. 985.

126 In practice the ECJ might explain in so much detail that the national courts can only apply the ECJ ruling. Likewise, directive can be very precise in their requirements, leaving the national legislator no discretion whatsoever.

autonomy in procedural and enforcement matters. Finally, as the EU has limited powers in the field of policing and criminal justice, the cooperation in the area of interest here will most often be carried out by Member State authorities under their national law.[127] This means that these national authorities are not (yet) organs of the EU (nor of the Member States with which they cooperate) to the extent necessary under the case law on *Organleihe*, described above.[128] In that case, the question arises 1) whether the EU bears responsibility for the implementation and enforcement at national level, 2) whether the Member States themselves are liable for their actions if these actions were taken in order to comply with European law. We will focus on the latter question, as only that is of direct relevance to the subject discussed here.

Both the Human Rights Commission and the Court have had occasion to struggle with the question described above – but this case law has still left questions unanswered. The position of the Court on this issue is most recently explained in the case of *Bosphorus v. Ireland*.[129] The majority judgment of the Grand Chamber was accompanied by a joint concurring opinion of six judges and a separate concurring opinion of Judge Ress.

The case concerned the impounding of an aircraft by Ireland following the proclamation of sanctions against the Former Republic of Yugoslavia. These sanctions were proclaimed by the UN Security Council and implemented in the EC by means of an EC regulation. The actions of the Irish Republic were based on this European regulation. The impounded aircraft belonged to JAT, a Yugoslav corporation, but was dry leased[130] to a Turkish company for four years. As a result of the Irish measures, the Turkish company was unable to use the aircraft and sustained considerable losses. Both in the national procedure and in Strasbourg, it claimed a violation of its property rights under Article 1 of Protocol 1.

---

127 See for the problem of Joint Investigation Teams below, section 3.3.

128 Although several authors stress the importance of national courts as keepers of European law and call the national courts in this respect 'organs' of the EC, this does not necessary imply that they are 'organs' of the EC with regard to international liability regimes. See for example W.T. Eijsbouts, J.H. Jans, F.O.W. Vogelaars, *Europees Recht; Algemeen Deel*, Groningen: Europa Law Publishing 2004 p. 50; P.A.M. Meijknecht, 'Europees bevoegdheids- en executierecht op weg naar de 21e eeuw; Preadvies Nederlandse Vereniging voor Internationaal recht; *Mededelingen* no. 105; Deventer, 1992 p. 1–49. The difference between classical models of international cooperation (*Amtshilfe* and *Rechtshilfe*) and *Organleihe* is elaborated upon by Florian Wettner, 'Das allgemeine Verfahrensrecht der gemeinschaftlichen Amtshilfe', in: Eberhard Schmidt-Aßmann/Bettina Schöndorf-Haubold (eds.), *Der Europäische Verwaltungsverbund – Formen und Verfahren der Verwaltungszusammenarbeit in der EU*, Tübingen: Mohr Siebeck 2005, pp. 125–146 (and more specifically p. 128 – note 24 and p. 130); id., in this volume, p. 313 et seq.

129 *Bosphorus Hava Yollari Turizm ve Ticaret Anonim Sirketi* v. *Ireland* (hereafter Bosphorus) appl.no. 45036/98, Merits, Grand Chamber 30 June 2005.

130 This means that JAT only provided the aircraft, which was then equipped, staffed and operated by the Turkish company. During the dry lease the plane was registered in the Turkish register.

The first step which the Court took was to state that the acts implemented by the Irish authorities on Irish territory following a decision by the Irish Minster for Transport were within the jurisdiction of Ireland within the meaning of Article 1 of the Convention. Whether or not Ireland can be held responsible for implementing EC measures is not a question which concerns the scope of the Convention, but is considered under the merits of the case. As was mentioned earlier in section 2.3, the Court at an earlier stage took a similar position with regard to the granting of immunity. The effect of this shift in focus (from preliminary issue to an issue of merits) seems to be that it stresses the responsibility of the state involved and gives slightly more control to the ECtHR over the outcome of the deliberation.[131]

After this preliminary issue the attention shifted to Article 1 of the first protocol. It is not disputed that there was interference with the applicant's possessions.[132] So the Court mainly concerned itself with the legitimacy of this interference. Firstly, the question was addressed whether there is a legal basis for this interference. The Court noted that the measure is based directly on the EC Regulation.[133] A regulation has direct effect within the legal order of the Member States. The Member States are under a duty to comply with European law. In this case, the Irish authorities had no real discretion to exercise. So the legal basis for the impugned actions is to be found exclusively in EC law. Does this legal basis justify the actions taken? The Court noted that there seems to be a conflict of interests at stake. On the one hand, the Member States have a legitimate interest in fulfilling their international obligations. On the other hand, the Member States are still responsible for fulfilling their obligations under the Convention. The balance between those two interests should be struck as follows: 'In the Court's view, State action taken in compliance with such legal obligations is justified as long as the relevant organisation is considered to protect fundamental rights, as regards both the substantive guarantees offered and the mechanisms controlling their observance, in a manner which can be considered at least equivalent to that for which the Convention provides.'[134] 'If such equivalent protection is considered to be provided by the organisation, the presumption will be that a State has not departed from the requirements of the Convention when it does no more than implement legal obligations flowing from its membership of the organisation. However, any such presumption can be rebutted if, in the circumstances of a particular case, it is considered that the protection of Convention rights was manifestly deficient.'[135] Next, the Court tested the

131 See also the joint concurring opinion, p. 49 of the judgment.

132 Para. 139. This interference was deemed by the court to amount to a control of the use of property (rather than deprivation of property).

133 The fact that the EC regulation is in its turn a direct implementation of the UNSC resolution, is deemed to be irrelevant, as the UNSC resolution has no direct effect.

134 Para. 155.

135 Para. 156.

protection offered within the EC system, albeit exclusively with regard to procedural protection, and found it to be equivalent to that of the Convention system. In the present case, the court found no disfunctioning in the control mechanisms (again, a procedural test), so the assumption of conformity is not rebutted. Hence, the Court found no violation of Article 1, Protocol 1.

In its judgment the ECtHR did not compare the EC to a Member State, but rather placed the ECJ on par with itself. The joint concurring opinion departs from the majority mainly on this latter point. First, attention is drawn to the incomplete system of direct appeal to the ECJ, which grants only limited access to individuals. Then the judges remark that the system of preliminary rulings is not equivalent to the system of appeal to the ECtHR, because it has an a priori character and any judgment given still needs to be implemented in the national legal system. In order to prevent the coming into existence of a double standard of human rights protection (one applying to EC Member States and one to other states parties to the Convention), the possibility to carry out a case-by-case check is deemed vital. The concurring opinion of Judge Ress joined his fellow concurring members in being concerned as regards double standards and the importance of a case-by-case check. But he went beyond that and tried to elaborate criteria to decide whether the European protection in a specific case is 'manifestly deficient'. The review by the ECJ is manifestly deficient – according to Judge Ress – when there has been no adequate review, for example because the complainant is denied access to the ECJ. In this Ress referred to the case of Segi[136] and that of Gestoras Pro-Amnistía[137] which are discussed in the contribution of I. Tappeiner to this book. But the review can also be manifestly deficient on substantive grounds; when the ECJ obviously misinterprets or misapplies the Convention. If we follow this latter interpretation, the judgment of the ECtHR can be understood as (mainly) creating a local remedies rule for EC cases which would force complainants to first exhaust the review possibilities offered by the EC system itself.

This latter effect is evident when we take a closer look at several possible scenarios in which the compatibility of EC law with the Convention is at stake. Firstly, the case of M & Co is brought to mind in which an administrative decision with regard to a specific company is taken by the EC authorities. The involvement of the Member States is limited to the execution of the decision against the assets of the complainant, the Member States do not apply or implement any EC legislation as such. In such cases the individual has (as a rule) access to the ECJ. He or she should avail him/herself of this remedy before complaining of a breach of Convention rights in the Member State executing the order. The similarity with the local remedies rule as described in section 2.4 is

136 Court of First Instance Order of 7 June 2004, T-338/02, appeal brought on 17 August 2004, C-355/04.

137 CFI 7 June 2004, T 333/02; Appeal C-354/04.

obvious.[138] The executing state only has to ascertain that the complainant had access to the ECJ and that the ECJ did not manifestly disregard the guarantees of the Convention. The system proclaimed in Bosphorus can be applied relatively easily.

Matters become slightly more complicated in cases where the European activity consists of lawmaking rather than administration. As mentioned above, regulations apply directly in all Member States. However, conformity with Convention standards as regards their application in individual cases cannot be raised directly before the ECJ by the individuals concerned. The ECJ only becomes involved when the national court places the matter before it, by way of a preliminary question. Accordingly this system will not only malfunction when the ECJ manifestly misinterprets the convention standards, but also when the national courts fail to put the question to the ECJ. This latter malfunctioning – which seems to have been (intentionally?) overlooked by the ECtHR – will definitely attract Member State responsibility![139]

The EC does not only create norms by way of regulations, but it also (and in some fields exclusively) uses directives. Directives are only binding as to their result, leaving the Member States with some discretion as to the means by which to attain the end-result. They need to be transposed into national law. This attracts the responsibility of the Member States for the use which they make of their discretionary powers. Moreover, in several instances, the directive only imposes minimum standards, leaving the Member States the option to take additional, more stringent measures. Again, the Member States are fully responsible for the use made of this possibility. With regard to the hard core of the EC law obligations, however, the system of Bosphorus would apply. So, where national elements of the implementing legislation are concerned, the national remedies apply as to the possible infringement of Convention rights. The elements of the same legislation which are based directly on the directive, however, have to be placed before the ECJ. The final judgment on application in the individual case will, however, in all cases be given by the national courts. According to Judge Ress, the national courts should not apply the ECJ ruling if the latter manifestly contradicts the case law of the ECtHR.

So, one has to distinguish between administrative acts and regulatory activities. Again, a distinction has to be made between measures which do and

138 In the case of *Dufay* v. *the EC and its Member States*, which involved the dismissal of an EC official, the Commission in its admissibility decision explicitly mentioned the non-exhaustion of EC remedies as a reason to dismiss the complaint. *Dufay* v. *the EC and its Member States* (appl. No. 13539/88, Commission adm.dec 19 January 1989).

139 The ECtHR seemed to work on the premise that in the Bosphorus case the ECJ had become involved by way of interpretation – which would leave the national courts more freedom to refrain from asking questions. However, it is altogether feasible that the question raised in the national procedure is one of validity – the EC measure itself being void because of its incompatibility with Convention standards. In that case also the lower courts are under a duty to refer to the ECJ (ECJ 1987, case 314/85, Foto-Frost).

measures which do not leave the implementing Member State a margin of discretion.[140] The Court further distinguished between secondary EC-law and measures taken by separate treaty.[141] Yet there is another distinction which in our opinion is relevant with regard to the responsibilities of national courts *vis-à-vis* the ECJ. This is the distinction between regulations dealing with substantive issues and regulations dealing with mutual assistance (in its widest sense). In the latter type of regulations the Member States are ordered to cooperate with other Member States and/or to give effect to administrative or judicial decisions originating in other Member States. In those cases, the protection of Convention standards by the originating authorities is not guaranteed by the EC system, but rather by the national systems of the cooperating states. The role of the ECJ is limited to interpreting the regulation. This should be done in the light of human rights protection. In our opinion the ECJ can come to no other conclusion than to find that all regulations on mutual assistance contain an (explicit or inherent) ground for refusal which allows the Member States not to cooperate if such cooperation would contribute to a violation of Convention rights in a relevant way. Such a duty to refuse cooperation flows directly from the case law of the ECtHR, as is amply demonstrated above. If the ECJ does not recognize this duty of the individual Member States under the Convention, this amounts to a manifest disregard of the case law of the ECtHR, which would rebut the presumption of equivalent protection.

How will the system developed in Bosphorus be influenced (if at all) by a future accession of the EC/EU to the ECHR?[142] A major change will be that the EC/EU itself can be summoned before the ECtHR. In cases like M & Co this opens up a direct review possibility.[143] Interestingly enough, accession would also change the relationship between the two courts, which now seem to operate

---

140 Through this the Court distinguished the Cantoni case (*Cantoni* v. *France*, appl.no 17862/91, Court (Grand Chamber), Judgement (Merits) 15 November 1996, Reports 1996-V, p. 1614) from the present case. See para. 157 of the judgment.

141 Through this the Court distinguished the Matthews case (*Matthews* v. *UK*, Appl.no. 24833/94, Court (Grand Chamber), Judgment (Merits and just satisfaction) 18 February 1999, RJD 1999-I) from the present case. See para. 157 of the judgment.

142 In the Treaty establishing a Constitution for Europe the Member States lay the basis for the accession of the EU to the ECHR (Article I-9 para. 2; Compare S.C. van Bijsterveld/E.M.H. Hirsch Ballin, *De integratie van het handvest van de grondrechten van de Europese Unie in de Constitutie van de Europese Unie*, WRR rapport, p. 91). This accession had been blocked by the 1996 opinion of the ECJ denouncing the right of the EC to accede on its own behalf to the European Convention (Opinion 2/94, 28 March 1996, *ECR* 1996, p. I-1759). At present, the fate of the European Convention is unclear, due to the double NO resulting from the French and Dutch referenda.

143 It will be more complicated to directly challenge EC/EU law in other instances. The ECtHR only hears individual cases, and both the European legislation and the preliminary rulings of the ECJ operate on an abstract level – their application mostly takes place at the national level. On the position of certain institutions operating within the EU framework but not mentioned as such in the treaties, see D.M Curtin, 'Unidentified international organisations and human rights protection', in: Brants/Kelk/Swart, *Er is meer: opstellen over mensenrechten in*

on the basis of parity.[144] After all, accession would submit the European legal order and its component parts – including the ECJ – to the jurisdiction of the ECtHR.[145] This might shift the standard of review currently used in EC/EU cases and make it more comparable with the standards applying in cases of cooperation between states. What accession does not change, however, is the division of powers between the EC/EU and its Member States. This means that with regard to cooperation between the authorities of the Member States we would still hold the Member States responsible for any breaches of Convention rights by their authorities.[146]

3. MODELS OF COOPERATION

3.1. INTRODUCTION

The emphasis which the ECtHR places on the individual responsibility of states for actions that take place within their territory is certainly of relevance for international cooperation in the field of evidence gathering. The question is to what extent this starting point is in line with present-day concepts of mutual assistance in criminal matters. A scheme may be drawn that distinguishes four models for transnational evidence gathering according to the types of state action involved:

1. The most common model leaves the state that receives a request for assistance for the gathering of evidence within its territory (the requested state) a relatively wide margin of appreciation to turn down a request for assistance. This state usually applies its own laws, when executing a request (*locus regit actum*), even though the information obtained is to be used in another country. In German legal doctrine this concept is known as *Rechtshilfe*.
2. A second model that may be distinguished only gradually differs from the first model. Here the wide margin of appreciation of the requested state is strongly reduced or even abandoned. Under this model the 'requested' state – it might be more appropriate to refer to it as the 'executing' state – is obliged

internationaal en nationaal perspectief, Deventer: Gouda Quint/Utrecht: Willem Pompe Instituut, 1996, p. 71–73.

144 Compare the Study of technical and legal issues of a possible EC/EU accession to the European Convention on Human Rights, Report adopted by the Steering Committee for Human Rights (CDDH) at its 53rd meeting (25–28 June 2002), DG-II(2002)006, CDDH(2002)010 Addendum 2, Council of Europe, Strasbourg, 28 June 2002, p. 18 para. 82 in which the relationship between the ECJ and the ECtHR is likened to the relationship between the several highest federal courts in Germany.

145 Compare CDDH Report p. 11–12, paras. 48–49 and p. 17, para. 77.

146 See on the possibility of the joint liability of the EC/EU and its Member States (or rather on a position of co-defendants) the CDDH Report, p. 13–14, paras 57–62.

automatically to execute the other state's request. However, like under the first model, the state that issues the request has no say over the actions of the executing state. The latter remains responsible for its actions, while applying its own laws.

3. In a third model the state that provides assistance effectively lends out its own authorities to the other state (compare the Drozd and Janousek case). The requested state loses control over its authorities, which act as the extended arm of the state seeking assistance. They operate within the framework of the foreign laws. This lending out of officials may occur both within and outside the territory of the requested state. With reference to German legal doctrine we may refer to this concept as *Organleihe* (see supra section 2.8).
4. At the other end of the scale the requested state permits the state seeking assistance to investigate directly on its territory. In this concept the role of the state providing assistance is limited to tolerating these actions. Beyond that, it has no say over the foreign authorities acting on its territory. It loses control over its territory, where foreign officials act with foreign competences, applying foreign laws.

In the remainder of this article, the systems of cooperation in the field of transnational evidence gathering are explored against the background of the case law of the ECtHR. Our focus is on the question of whether and to what extent they are compatible with this case law. In the next section we will start with the prevailing form of mutual assistance (which at present answers the description of model 1 above). It is based on the European Convention on Mutual Assistance in Criminal Matters (ECMACM).[147] However, within the framework of the EU new concepts of cooperation are currently being developed. Placed against the background of the four models introduced, we will also discuss the so-called joint investigation teams (infra section 3.3) and the (EU proposal for a) European evidence warrant (EEW) (infra section 3.4). Both concepts are intended as an alternative to the 'classic' *Rechtshilfe* model and aim to enhance the transnational gathering of evidence. Although there is at this point in time little practical experience with these new concepts, they are certainly worth briefly exploring. In particular it is interesting to see how these new concepts fit into the models just described and whether they give rise to special problems in the light of the ECtHR's case law discussed earlier. The fourth model has been put into practice in Switzerland, where cantonal authorities are allowed to investigate on the territory of another canton subject to the application of their own laws.[148] In

147 European Treaty Series 030.

148 See on this model the *Konkordat vom 5. November 1992 über die Rechtshilfe und die interkantonale Zusammenarbeit in Strafsachen* published in *Amtliche Sammlung* 1993, 2876; also C. Siebert, 'L'Évolution du modele Suisse de l'entraide judiciare et de la cooperation intercantonale en matière pénale', in: J.A.E. Vervaele (ed.), *European Evidence Warrant – Transnational Judicial Inquiries in the EU*, Antwerp/Groningen/Oxford: Intersentia Law Publisher 2005, p. 18–210.

international law, however, it is relatively unknown. Elements of this model may be recognized in transnational police cooperation (for instance cross-border observation or hot pursuit)[149] and in some European directives concerning financial supervision.[150] But for the sake of conciseness, we will not discuss the fourth model any further here.

3.2. MUTUAL ASSISTANCE IN CRIMINAL MATTERS

3.2.1. The concept of mutual assistance in criminal matters

In our view, the first concept of the model as introduced above is, at least in theory, compatible with the doctrine of state responsibility as is given shape by the ECtHR. Under this classical[151] concept of mutual assistance in criminal matters judicial authorities may ask authorities from other states to gather and provide evidence that is needed in a criminal investigation. Although this regime introduces an obligation to cooperate in criminal matters, this obligation is by no means absolute. It leaves states with enough room to refuse the execution of a request for assistance if there are indications that it may lead to a breach of the ECHR. First of all, under the 1959 Convention on mutual assistance, just as under its supplements in subsequent treaties,[152] states are left with a considerable amount of discretion to refuse assistance if human rights are in danger in the requesting state or due to the provision of assistance itself.[153] Second, the requesting authorities have no say whatsoever concerning the actions of the

---

149 Cf. Articles 40 and 41 of the 1990 Schengen Implementation Agreement; see, amongst others, André Klip, Extraterritorial investigations, in: Bert Swart and André Klip (Eds.), *International Criminal Law in the Netherlands*, Freiburg im Breisgau: Ed. iuscrim, Max-Planck-Inst. für ausländisches und Internat. Strafrecht 1997.

150 Cf. Article 57 of Council Directive 2004/39/EC of 21 April 2004 on markets in financial instruments amending Council Directives 85/611/EEC and 93/6/EEC and Directive 2000/12/EC of the European Parliament and of the Council and repealing Council Directive 93/22/EEC, OJ L 2004 145/1; see also Annette Althaus, *Amtshilfe and Vor-Ort-Kontrolle*, Bern: Stämpfli Verlag 2001.

151 'Classical' compared to the two new forms of cooperation discussed in section 3.3 and 3.4. Of course, mutual assistance in criminal matters is at this point in time by far the most dominant model.

152 Via Article 26 ECMACM 1959 the treaty was amended by, *inter alia*, the 1990 Schengen agreement and more recently by the Convention on Mutual Assistance in Criminal Matters between the Member States of the European Union, OJ 2000 C 197, and the Protocol established by the Council in accordance with Article 34 of the Treaty on European Union to the Convention on Mutual Assistance in Criminal Matters between the Member States of the European Union, OJ 2001 C 326.

153 Article 2 of the ECMACM 1959, for instance, provides the following ground for refusal: 'Assistance may be refused: (...); b. if the requested Party considers that execution of the request is likely to prejudice the sovereignty, security, ordre public or other essential interests of its country.'

requested authorities.[154] The latter remain completely responsible for their actions. Requests for assistance are carried out under their own laws (*locus regit actum*).[155] Newer forms of transnational cooperation may alter these elements to a certain extent via the application of the *procedural* rules of the requesting state (*forum regit actum*), but this alteration does not tamper with the full control of the requested party over its own actions and its own *Kompetenzordnung*.[156] Breaches of fundamental rights, for instance, still require a basis in national law. Furthermore, the requesting authorities do not gain control over the requested authorities; the latter remain responsible.

However, as clear-cut as the responsibilities of the requesting and requested state may be in theory, in practice things are less clear. The Court's (and the Commission's) case law which we have discussed above surely demonstrates this, even though the case law on this point is relatively rare. In the *Chinoy* case for instance, the plaintiff found it almost impossible to establish whether or not the gathering of evidence in his case was illegal. Also in the case of *Sari v. Turkey and Denmark* the international complications of the case led to a watering down of Convention standards. This is not surprising. Within the framework of mutual assistance it is difficult to pinpoint the exact scope of state responsibility under the Convention.[157] This has to do with the fact that the assistance requested often cannot be isolated from the main proceedings in the requesting state. It forms an integral part of those proceedings. For instance, evidence obtained by means of letters rogatory is often directly used in a court of law in another state. Alleged irregularities in the requested state may directly affect the fairness of the procedure in the requesting state. One might say that this is different in extradition cases, where the act of extradition can relatively easily be distinguished from the actual trial in the requesting state. As a rule, it is less difficult to isolate each state's responsibilities under the Convention.[158] In the following two section we will try to define the separate responsibilities of the requested (providing) state and those of the requesting (receiving) state. After all, this is the approach which the ECtHR also follows.

---

154 Cf. Jan M. Sjöcrona, *De kleine rechtshulp* (diss. Leiden), Arnhem: Gouda Quint 1990, p. 68 and 70–71.

155 Cf. Article 3 of the ECMACM 1959.

156 Cf. Article 4 of the 2000 EU Convention; see also Florian Wettner, 'Das allgemeine Verfahrensrecht der gemeinschaftlichen Amtshilfe', in: Eberhard Schmidt-Aßmann/Bettina Schöndorf-Haubold (eds.), *Der Europäische Verwaltungsverbund – Formen und Verfahren der Verwaltungszusammenarbeit in der EU*, Tübingen: Mohr Siebeck, 2005, p. 132–133; id., in this volume, p. 313 et seq.

157 Cf. H.G. van der Wilt, 'Volkenrechtelijke aspecten van internationale rechtshulp', in: A.H.Klip, A.H.J. Swart and H.G. van der Wilt (eds.), *Het Wetboek van Strafvordering; Internationale en interregionale samenwerking in strafzaken*, Deventer: Kluwer (loos leaf), para. I.5.1, no. 3; André Klip, 'The decrease of protection under human rights treaties in international criminal law', *International review of penal law* (Vol. 68), p. 292 (hereafter referred to as Klip (1997)).

158 Klip (1997), *o.c.*, p. 292.

3.2.2. *Responsibilities of the requested/providing state*

A state providing information or documents to another state will first and foremost have to deal with possible infringements of Article 8 of the Convention (protecting privacy and family life). Actions taken, such as the *gathering* of evidence on behalf of another state and the following *provision* of the (personal) data to that state, readily entail obligations under that article. One only has to think of search and seizures or the (compulsory) interrogation of witnesses to realize that mutual assistance may lead to severe infringements of personal and/or family life. Such infringements must fulfil the requirements of the second section of Article 8. This means that interference in the exercise of this right will at the very least have to be in accordance with the law and necessary in a democratic society in the interests of, *inter alia*, the prevention of disorder or crime. According to the standard case law of the Court, such infringements must not only be accessible and foreseeable, but also proportionate. Furthermore, safeguards against the arbitrary use of investigation powers must be provided for.[159] The precise interpretation of these safeguards is often left to the discretion of the Contracting States. A requirement may for instance be that it has to be beyond reasonable doubt that the suspect has in fact committed the crime, that a crime has been committed and/or that the requested documents are present at the indicated location. Sometimes, especially in cases of serious infringements, such as search and seizure, coercion measures are only permitted for serious types of crime and/or after judicial approval.

On a transnational level, it is this national autonomy with respect to the organisation of criminal law and procedure and the consequent relatively large margin of appreciation that easily results in an individual becoming trapped between two criminal justice systems in cases of international cooperation. In 1983 the Dutch lawyer (now judge) A.M.M. Orie referred to this phenomenon as the crack in the system of international cooperation in criminal matters (in Dutch: *systeembreuk*).[160] Although each system may in isolation be perfectly in line with the demands and requirements of Article 8, a combination of the two (or more) systems may cause problems. Guarantees against abuses, such as hierarchical supervision and/or judicial scrutiny *before* (for instance by means of

159 Cf. ECtHR, *Funke* v. *France*, appl. no. 10828/84, Court (Chamber), Judgment (Merits and Just Satisfaction) 25 February 1993, *Series* A 256-A, with regard to house searches, and ECtHR, Klass and others v Germany, Court (Plenary), Judgment (Merits) 6 September 1978, *Series* A28, with respect to the surveillance of telecommunications.

160 A.M.M. Orie, 'De verdachte tussen wal en schip òf de systeem-breuk in de kleine rechtshulp', in: E. André de la Porte (et al.) (eds.), *Bij deze stand van zaken – Bundel opstellen aangeboden aan A.L. Melai*, Arnhem: Gouda Quint 1983, p. 351–361; see also A.H. Klip, *Criminal law in the European Union* (inaugural lecture Maastricht), Deventer: Kluwer 2005, p. 64 (hereafter referred to as Klip (2005)); G.J.M. Corstens, 'Europeanisering van het strafrecht', in: G.J.M. Corstens, W.J.M. Davids, M.I. Veldt-Foglia (eds), *Europeanisering van het Nederlands recht – Opstellen aangeboden aan Mr. W.E. Haak*, Deventer: Kluwer 2004.

judicial approval) and/or *after* the investigations (for instance by means of a special legal remedy or during the trial phase) do not always function properly in the international context. One country may, for instance, rely on judicial scrutiny after the fact, while another may ask for judicial approval beforehand. When these two systems are combined, the result may be a double-check, but also a legal vacuum. Furthermore, the usual supervision of the public prosecutor in national inquiries has no or little effect in transnational investigations, since he – as a representative of the requested state – is not informed about the facts and circumstances of the foreign investigation. Although most countries have for this reason developed special legal remedies in the field of international cooperation, this is still not always enough. For one thing, the scope of review is often limited, as we will point out below, and, secondly, these measures are taken on a national level and are therefore not necessarily in line with measures from other states.[161]

Differences in legal systems and legal protection are not the only problem. One of the essential aspects of rendering legal assistance is that the requested authorities are not informed of the circumstances of the case in any detail. After all, instead of fulfilling their own tasks, they are assisting others. Some reliance on the other party is therefore necessary. In current interstate practice, this element brings about some (in our view questionable) limitations with respect to the responsibilities of the requested state. In fact, the case of *S. v. Austria,* mentioned above, is a perfect example of this. As we saw, the Austrian courts were only willing to look into the admissibility of the act requested under Austrian law. They refused to assess its necessity, appropriateness and proportionality, since it was not considered to be their task to do so. The underlying rationale of this approach is an (otherwise implicit) international division of labour between the requesting and requested authorities. It is considered not to be up to the authorities of the requested state to establish guilt and to safeguard the principle *in dubio pro reo.*[162] This is considered to be a task for the requesting party. Moreover, the latter has often already tested this on the basis of the evidence available to it. Testing the evidence again would boil down to demonstrating considerable distrust in the requesting authority's capabilities.[163] But then, when an independent appraisal of the evidence is improper, there is no need to hand over the material evidence of the case either;

---

161 Cf. Bert Swart, in: *Revue internationale de droit penal*, 1e et 2e trimestres 1994 Erès, p. 391.

162 Otto Lagodny,' Comparative Overview', in: Albin Eser/Otto Lagodny/Christopher L. Blakesley (eds.), *The Individual as Subject of International Cooperation in Criminal Matters*, Baden-Baden: Nomos Verlag 2002, p. 746 ff and p. 763.

163 The Swiss Bundesgericht, *Bundesgerichtsentscheid* (BGE) 110 Ib 173 – 184 (180), for instance, explicitly refers to the existence of a rule of non-inquiry, by stating that: 'Die Schweizerische Behörde hat sich beim Entscheid über ein Rechtshilfebegehren nicht über das Bestehen der angeführten Tatsachen auszusprechen. Sie ist an die Darstellung des Sachverhaltes im Begehren des ersuchenden Staates gebunden, soweit diese nicht offensichtliche Fehler, Lücken oder Widersprüche enthält.' However, in fiscal matters things are somewhat different, due to

a description of the facts is enough. This, in turn, simplifies the system of transnational cooperation to a considerable extent and lowers the threshold to request information from other states, as it is not necessary to disclose the information gathered in the case to the requested authorities. It remains unclear what the Court's opinion in this matter is. In *S. v. Austria* the EComHR did not answer the applicant's objections to this interstate practice, although it noted that although the question as to the admissibility of the search was left to the appreciation of the German authorities, this did not mean that the search actually lacked the necessary requirements.

Although there is some logic behind this approach, questions arise as to the testing of the proportionality of the measures. This test, in our opinion, lies at the heart of Article 8 ECHR. Even though most countries do provide (at least as far as coercive measures are concerned) for remedies against the gathering of evidence and its provision to another state, the material object of litigation in those procedures is mostly limited to formal aspects of the (execution of the) request, such as the fulfilment of the requirement of double criminality; the *locus regit actum* principle being only applied to the procedural aspects of the case.[164] The proportionality check *sensu lato* is left to the requesting state. As we stated above, this approach is in our view not in line with the responsibilities of the requested state under Article 8. After all, the requesting party has no say whatsoever over the actions of the requested state.[165] Accepting this starting point on the one hand, but refusing to test its proportionality on the other, seems, to us, to be self-contradictory. Current interstate practice thus creates a gap in legal protection that does not exist in purely national cases. Either an individual has to file a complaint against the proportionality of a requested measure (if at all possible) in the state that is not responsible for the execution thereof, or he files a complaint in the state that is responsible, but refuses to assess the proportionality of the requested measure. Both options do not seem to lead to an adequate level of protection.

Of course, if current interstate practice does not suffice, the question arises how states should alter their practice. In our view, two things are of importance here. Our premise is that states must live up to the individual responsibility which they have under Article 8 when executing a request for mutual assistance. Therefore, first and foremost a significant reduction of the scope of the rule of

---

the Swiss approach to criminal tax matters: *BGE* 115 Ib 78; see also Peter Popp, *o.c.*, p. 123–124 and 159 ff.

164 Cf. Arnhem Court of Appeal 11 June 1997, *Nederlandse Jurisprudentie* 1997, 617; Karl Friedrich Nagel, *Beweisaufnahme im Ausland*, Freiburg im Breisgau: Ed. iuscrim, Max-Planck-Inst. für ausländisches und Internat. Strafrecht 1988, p. 152; Suzanne Scheller, *Ermächtigungsgrundlagen für die internationale Rechts- und Amtshilfe zur Verbrechungsbekämpfung*, Freiburg im Breisgau: Ed. iuscrim, Max-Planck-Inst. für ausländisches und Internat. Strafrecht 1997, p. 64–65; Peter Popp, *o.c.*, p. 159 ff.

165 Cf. Wettner, *o.c.*, pp. 128–130.

non-inquiry is necessary in order to make a proportionality check possible. Especially within the European Union and its area of freedom, security and justice, strict interstate courtesy and self-imposed restraint seem to be increasingly inappropriate.[166] With an ever closer European Union, one could question what the difference is between a check by a Berlin district court as to the lawfulness of investigation measures by the Frankfurt police and the same kind of check by the same court concerning an investigation by the Amsterdam police.[167] After all, the creation of a legal area indicates that this is no longer the domain of foreign affairs, but rather that of the judiciary. This was also emphasized by the Court of Justice in the *Brügge* and *Gözütok* cases.[168] But then, where the rule of non-inquiry is reduced in scope, other states should provide all the necessary information in order to carry out the proportionality test. This might also be derived from the duty of loyal cooperation that was recently established in the third pillar of the EU structure.[169]

A second requirement is that breaches of the convention should, if possible, be prevented.[170] In our view this requirement especially forces states to assess the (proportionality of) measures requested beforehand.[171] After all, only then can a sensible judgment be rendered in the case; it makes no sense to judge the proportionality of a criminal investigation measure *after* the fact, because then the damage might already have been done. So, when *gathering* evidence in national criminal or transnational cases at the very least an *a priori* assessment has to be made, weighing the interests of the requesting state, those of the requested state and the right to privacy of the suspect or third parties involved. The same holds true for the actual *provision* of information to the requesting state.

Having stressed the responsibility of the requested state for the actions it takes on its own territory, it still has to be decided how intrusive the test must be. Should it take place *ex officio* or only on request? Should it contain a full test of the material evidence in the case or merely checking the facts, as laid down in the request for assistance? What if information from abroad is necessary, but other states are unwilling to provide this? In our view the approach which the

---

166 Cf. Paul Garlick, The European arrest warrant and the ECHR, in: R. Blekxtoon and W. van Ballegooij (eds.), *Handbook on the European Arrest Warrant*, The Hague: TMC Asser Press 2004, p. 169; Klip (1997), *o.c.*, p. 307.

167 Cf. J.M. Sjöcrona and A.M.M. Orie, *Internationaal strafrecht vanuit Nederlands perspectief*, Deventer: Kluwer 2002, p. 208.

168 C-187/01 and C-385/01, ECJ 11 February 2003 (*Brügge and Gözütok*); see on these cases the contribution by Vervaele in this volume, p. 541 et seq.

169 C-105/03, ECJ 16 June 2005 (*Pupino*).

170 Cf. A. Smeulers (2005), p. 79–102, who rightly states that the primary aim should be to prevent breaches. Therefore, it is not relevant that breaches can later be rectified in the trial state.

171 Cf. ECtHR 30 March 1989, *Series* A 152-A, *Ian Chappell* v. *the United Kingdom*, with respect to house searches.

European Court of Justice adopted in the case of *Roquettes Frère SA*[172] offers a fair starting point for answering these questions. In that case, which dealt with (suspected) infringements of competition law, the Court of Justice determined the lines along which responsibilities between the European Commission (and supervision by the Court) and national authorities are divided in case coercive measures are needed in one of the EC Member States (in this case France).[173] In short, the Court made a distinction between, on the one hand, verification that the coercive measures sought in pursuance of a request by the Commission are *not arbitrary* or *disproportionate* to the subject-matter and, on the other, a review of the justification of those measures that go beyond this test (for instance, the necessity of the measures). The latter is reserved for the European Commission which in this matter acts under the scrutiny of the Court of Justice. The first question, however, is to be decided by the national authorities (if the national law – as was the case in France – prescribes this). For the Commission there is the task to make clear to the national court, *inter alia*, that it is in possession of information or evidence providing reasonable grounds for suspecting an infringement of competition rules.[174] The Commission does not need – as is also the case in mutual assistance in criminal matters – to hand over the material evidence, since this would be highly ineffective and possibly dangerous for the ongoing investigation. National courts may therefore not request the evidence on which the Commission's evidence is based. The same approach could be used in current interstate practice. Nothing stands in the way of individual countries already applying this test.

The question remains, however, whether this solution goes far enough. For instance, also under this regime the interpretation of the facts of the case remains in the hands of the requesting party. Furthermore, (severe) irregularities in the requesting or, as was the case in the *Chinoy* case, a third state are still not likely to be discovered. What if the defence or third parties raise these questions? Should the requested state answer them? We think that it should. Their outcome may affect, for instance, the reasonableness of a suspicion and thereby make the requested measure arbitrary or disproportionate. Therefore, a duly substantiated

172 C-94/00, ECJ 22 October 2002, *ECR* 2002, p. I-9011; see also supra note 55.

173 One might argue that a comparison with the approach in EC competition law does not stand up to scrutiny, since the Commission is an administrative authority. Within the framework of mutual assistance, however, judicial authorities are responsible. This would explain a more lenient attitude. In our view this approach is not to be followed. First of all, it is to be doubted that all 'judicial authorities' qualify as 'judicial'. To an ever increasing extent administrative authorities, such as, for instance, customs or tax authorities may make use of judicial channels. Article 24 of the 1959 European Convention leaves it to the states to decide on this matter; see John Vervaele and André Klip (eds), *European Cooperation between Tax, Customs and Judicial Authorities*, The Hague/London/New York: Kluwer 2002, p. 291. Secondly, and even more importantly, this line of reasoning still does not discharge the requested authority from its own obligations under the ECHR as we stressed above.

174 See §61 of the judgment.

defence would in our view require an answer by the requested authorities, based on a full scrutiny of all the facts of the case. Not only does this solution imply a reduction in the scope of the rule of non-inquiry, but it also presupposes a willingness on the part of other states to mutually provide each other with the relevant information in order to carry out this test. The logical consequence of this approach would be that if the requesting state (or a third EU state) is unwilling or unable to provide additional information, the request should be turned down.[175]

In practice it is uncertain how often situations like these occur. After all, one of the main problems is exactly the problem individuals have in substantiating their claim. The international elements of a case certainly cause additional problems, as the *Chinoy* case demonstrates, and confront the defence or third parties with a *probatio diabolica*, i.e. the burden of proof concerning facts of which they are not (yet) aware. We are afraid that this issue cannot be easily resolved. It might be for this reason that some authors propose that the countries involved should be summoned jointly before the ECtHR in the case of alleged violations.[176] We subscribe to the underlying rationale that it should not be the responsibility of the complainant to determine the exact responsibilities of states which cooperate. Yet even when such joint responsibility is assumed, the question remains how it should be given shape in practice. Joint responsibility *after the* fact does not prevent breaches from occurring. Neither does it help the interested parties to substantiate their claim. It is standard case law that when a complaint is not supported by facts, the ECtHR will dismiss it – be it against a single state or the two cooperating states jointly. One needs a court which is willing and able to look into the facts. Joint liability in itself does not provide such a remedy, although it may be an incentive to the states involved to create one. In the next section, dealing with the responsibilities of the requesting/trial state, we will deal with this further. Before doing so, some remarks have to be made with respect to the responsibilities of the requested state for protecting the right to a fair trial (Article 6).

The responsibilities of the requested state with respect to violations of Article 6 of the Convention are less strict. This has to do with the fact that in most cases mutual assistance is rendered at the pre-trial stage. Irregularities in this phase do not necessarily – according to the Court's case law – render the whole proceedings unfair. This early in the proceedings it is particularly difficult to predict whether a violation of Article 6 has occurred. After all, compensation during a later phase – e.g. the trial stage – may follow. When judging the fairness of the procedure, the Court takes into account the proceedings as a whole.[177]

---

175 Cf. our observations at the end of subsection 2.6.1.

176 Cf. Klip (2005), p. 64–65. He specifically refers to the Sari case, discussed in section 2.7, which dealt with the right to a trial within a reasonable time.

177 Cf. ECtHR 24 November 1993, *Series* A-275, *Imbriosca* v. *Switzerland*.

There is no reason to assume that the Court will apply another test in transnational cases. This leads to the conclusion that – as a rule – it is not the requested/providing state, but the requesting/receiving state that will be in the best position to assess the fairness of a procedure. Some authors advocate the joint responsibility of all states involved in transnational cooperation for the fairness of the resulting trial. After all, the requesting state has only limited powers concerning the investigations conducted in other states.[178] We tend to disagree: it is up to the requesting state to determine what use may be made of the evidence provided by the requested state. The only responsibility which the requested state has concerns its own involvement. And this responsibility is largely limited to the procurement and provision of the information as such and hence pertains to Article 8.

3.2.3. Responsibilities of the requesting/receiving/adjudicating state

If foreign information is used in evidence in a criminal procedure, the responsibilities of the receiving/trial state under Article 6 are of a completely different nature. This state is responsible for the fairness of the proceedings in general and the use of such information in particular. This means that essential notions of 'fairness', such as the equality of arms and the adversarial character of the proceedings, will have to be guaranteed. There seems to be no reason to leave aside or to weaken these requirements in a transnational setting, especially not as far as cooperation between EU Member States is concerned.[179] Recourse to the flagrant denial test which the Court introduced in the *Soering* and the *Drozd & Janousek* cases is out of the question. After all, in the Soering case the test was used for (possible) future infringements of Article 6 resulting from extradition to a non-ECHR Member State. The lower standard of protection is to be explained through the future and uncertain character of any infringement. The Drozd case concerned the transfer of sentenced persons from a non-ECHR Member State to a Member State. Such transfer may generally be regarded as being for the benefit of the convicted person. Those situations cannot be compared to the present situation. The adjudicating state is directly responsible for the fairness of the trial which it conducts itself. The use of foreign evidence is an intrinsic part of that trial. Hence the right to test the evidence should primarily be enforced against the trial state. When the provenance of information is not accounted for, it cannot be tested – neither by the defence, nor by the court – and hence it should not be used in evidence. This would seem to be the simple and straightforward

---

178 Cf. Bart De Smet, *Internationale samenwerking in strafzaken tussen Angelsaksische en continentale landen*, Antwerp – Groningen: Intersentia 1999, p. 17–172.

179 In the case of P.V. v FRG the court allowed a (slight) lowering of (national) safeguards to fit the transnational circumstances of the case; see subsection 2.6.3. The core of the right to question the evidence was however upheld.

consequence of the responsibility of the receiving state for upholding Article 6. This is not so in practice, however.

When discussing the Roquettes Frère case, we noted that the ECJ went into great detail concerning the division of responsibilities between the Community and the national organs. It stressed the fact that although the scope of jurisdiction of the national courts with respect to coercive measures was limited, this certainly did not mean that the Commission was not subject to supervision. On the contrary, this was conceived as a responsibility of the ECJ. It remains to be seen whether the national courts at the trial stage, within the framework of mutual assistance, are also willing to test foreign evidence, for instance if questions relating to Article 6 arise. The KB Lux affair, which we discussed in the introduction, is to a certain extent somewhat ominous here, since some Dutch courts explicitly refused to test the actions of the Belgian authorities, even though irregularities were ascertained in Belgium.[180] In other, mostly civil law, countries a reliance on the rule of non-inquiry is also seen.[181] Moreover, in the KB Lux affair some courts also ruled that the defence's statements need not be examined because the violations of Luxembourg banking secrecy and the consequent use of the information by Belgian and Dutch authorities did not, according to them, harm the suspects' interests (*Schutznorm*). Complaints were dismissed even before looking into the facts. Although the admissibility of evidence is primarily a matter for national law,[182] this rigid approach by the Dutch courts leaves the suspect without any remedy, not only as far as Article 6 is concerned, but also with respect to Article 8.[183] As mentioned before, this creates a gap in the legal protection of all persons involved. The original request for mutual assistance is often not checked by an independent court.[184] The

180 It is not yet clear if the Dutch supreme court will back this approach. This court never explicitly mentioned the rule of non-inquiry in the context of mutual assistance in criminal matters; cf. J. Koers, *Nederland als verzoekende staat bij de wederzijdse rechtshulp in strafzaken* (dissertation Tilburg), Nijmegen Wolf legal publishers 2001, p. 458–480. However, this certainly does not mean that it does not play a role in practice; cf. H.G. van der Wilt, *o.c.*, para. I.5.1, no. 4.

181 Cf. the country reports in the *Revue internationale de droit penal*, 1e et 2e trimestres 1994 Erès.

182 This explains why the application of the *Schutznorm* doctrine is not *ipso facto* in conflict with Art. 6. It might, however, be in conflict with Art. 13 of the Convention in combination with Article 8; cf. A.A. Franken, *Voor de vorm* (inaugural lecture Utrecht), The Hague: Boom Juridische Uitgevers 2004.

183 For that matter, the actual application of the *Schutznorm* by some of the Dutch courts is in our view incorrect. Data protected by banking secrecy are certainly of interest to the persons whose data are protected. This holds true not only for the (illegal) *acquisition* of these data by the Belgian authorities, but also for their *provision* to and subsequent *use* by the Dutch authorities. The use of such information also raises those responsibilities under Art. 8. So, at the very least, the origin of those data should be accounted for. We might even argue that the further use of data obtained irregularly *ipso facto* constitutes a new breach of Article 8.

184 Of course, in the KB Lux affair the information was provided spontaneously via Council Directive 77/799 (mutual assistance in tax matters); supra note2. But this decision was not tested in court either.

requested state does not carry out a complete check *ex officio*, because it relies on the description of the facts provided by the requesting state. So when the trial state, which need not be the requesting state, does not take full responsibility for the way the evidence was attained, no one does. Combined with a defence that is barely in a position to substantiate its claims, the latter has to overcome an almost impossible hurdle. Should not the national courts be of assistance here?

So, again, the question arises whether alternatives to this current interstate practice are available. This time we focus on the trial state's responsibility relating to Articles 6 and 8. Again, we are mainly concerned with the scope of the review by the courts, the 'burden of proof' (whether a full review or not; *ex officio* or not) and with the 'chain of custody' of the materials. Our aim is not so much to provide guidelines for the burden of proof resting on the defence, but mostly to strengthen the position of the trial state, with respect to its access to foreign sources of information with relevance to the fairness of the trial. Closely related to the foregoing is the question whether or not it should *always* be the trial state that offers protection.

Our preferred model resembles to a great extent the test which the authorities of the requested state should apply when executing a request for assistance. We described this in the previous section. This would bring along an *ex officio* check for eminent breaches and a more detailed inquiry into the facts, when substantiated.[185] Since we are now in the trial phase and the investigations have been completed, it seems reasonable to expect that the authorities of that state should account for the origin of the foreign materials in the case file (chain of custody) and – if necessary – to ensure that any additional information with respect to the origin of data or to their reliability can be easily acquired. The implications of this are twofold: the trial state is responsible for the material it uses, and hence for the way this material was obtained, even if this was done by other states (*no rule of non-inquiry*), but, on the other hand, the requested state has a duty to facilitate the trial state (*disclosure*). It must, when requested, provide the trial state with all the necessary information. Such a duty to cooperate could – within the European Union – be derived from the duty of loyal cooperation.[186] Failing to live up to this obligation should, in our view, lead to the exclusion of that material, even when it is the requested authority (and not the trial state) that is unwilling to cooperate.

Legal protection, as far as Article 6 is concerned, is therefore to be concentrated in the trial state.[187] But is this state allowed to refer some aspects of this protection, especially the regularity of investigations in other countries, to other states? After all, under the *Rechtshilfe* model only the requested state has a

185 It is up to the courts what burden of proof rests with the defence. But with a view to the central position of the trial court, in our opinion this court should not be too strict.

186 C-105/03, ECJ 16 June 2005 (*Pupino*).

187 Cf. John Vervaele and André Klip, *o.c.*, p. 290–291.

say over its actions. It is presumably in a better position to assess the facts. A third party in the requested state, confronted with a search of his premises, would presumably concentrate his legal protection in that state. The defendant, on the other hand, might prefer proceedings to be concentrated in the trial state, also with regard to the aspects of the investigations that took place abroad. So the pertinent question is what the effects of local remedies are on the position of the parties at a later stage of the investigations and in the subsequent trial. It goes without saying that the existence and/or the creation of local remedies is an improvement as long as using them is conceived as a *right* of the individual, not as a means for states to 'dodge' their responsibilities.[188]

It does not seem to be in conflict with the ECHR to refer a complaint to another state, as long as the referring state has checked that an effective remedy is indeed provided for.[189] However, we wonder whether this might really help to improve the position of the individual. Even assuming that remedies are available, the requested state is, as we discussed in the previous section, often not in a position to fully test the facts of the case. On the contrary, it is acting at the request of another state. A referral to the requested state does not therefore necessarily provide an *effective* remedy. And yet again we wonder if the applicant will be in a position to substantiate its claim in the requested state. For a remedy to be more than just lip service to upholding the Convention, applicants should at the least have access to the case file. Is the requested state really equipped for this? Finally, the requested state can only test for conformity with Article 8. It has no responsibility as to the fairness of the trial (which will or will not take place at a later date). Guaranteeing a fair trial is the sole responsibility of the trial state. That means that parties cannot be stopped from entering a complaint on the evidence in the trial state because they had failed to exhaust the local remedies. Moreover, even if they did file a complaint in the requested state, the result thereof is not conclusive. If new information on the irregularity of the actions of the requested state (or of the original request) surfaces, a new appraisal is needed as to the admissibility of the evidence thus gathered.[190]

---

188 We take it that this is what André Klip means when he refers to a joint state responsibility: 'In my opinion, this is a sort of joint liability. Before the proceedings are considered as a whole, as the ECHR requires under the convention, a citizen should be able to use legal remedies in every state involved.' See Klip (2005), p. 65.

189 If such a remedy is not provided, a referral to the other state would in our view constitute a breach of the Convention (cf. *M & Co* v. *Germany*, discussed above). See about the local remedies rule also section 2.4.

190 Besides the scope of the test to be carried out by the trial state, the question also arises what laws are to be applied – those of the trial state or those of the requested state? This applies not only with respect to the question *whether* irregularities have occurred in the requested state, but also with respect to the consequences attached thereto. A combination of the rules of the *lex fori* and the principles of the ECHR is nowadays gaining the upper hand. This was also laid down by the AIDP in 1994 during the XVth congress in Rio de Janeiro: 'States where the laws of evidence in criminal proceedings restrict the use of evidence illicitly obtained, should apply the same restrictions with respect to evidence obtained through international assistance

Whereas the trial state is the main if not the sole guardian of Article 6, the situation is less clear-cut as to the responsibilities under Article 8. As the requesting state, it does not itself invade the privacy of the persons involved and hence may not involve responsibility for the breach. As the trial state it could only be liable if the use of the information gathered in breach of Article 8 would constitute a separate breach of Article 8. This could be argued on the ground that the use of personal data also brings along a responsibility for the way in which it was obtained.[191] For the defendant this question appears, at first sight, to be of minor relevance, since his rights are also protected under Article 6. However, as the ECtHR ruled in the Khan case[192], a breach of Article 8 does not necessarily render a trial unfair. A breach of Article 8 would thus call for a separate remedy (Article 13), for instance offering financial compensation. Even more problematic, however, seems to be the position of third parties. After all, these are not a party in the trial phase, whereas the domestic remedies in the requested state – if at all present – only offer limited protection (see the previous section). The changes we proposed do not solve this problem altogether. The disadvantageous position of third parties in substantiating their claims therefore remains problematic. In the end, we are afraid that finding a solution to this problem will require such far-reaching adjustments to the current system that it would leave the whole system ineffective.

3.2.4. Conclusion – A return to KB Lux

It is now opportune to summarize our findings. Under the *Rechtshilfe* model, at first sight the responsibilities of states cooperating in criminal matters are clear-cut. Whereas the requested state is fully responsible for the actions it carries out on behalf of another state and should mainly be concerned with Article 8, the latter is responsible for the consequent use of this material at the trial (Art. 6) or – when personal data are concerned – for the actual use of those data (Art. 8). In practice, this clear division is difficult to uphold. The requested state is not in a

in criminal matters. In all states evidence that has been obtained in disregard of fundamental human rights should be excluded.' This approach has also been chosen by the Dutch Supreme Court (Hoge Raad/HR): HR 18 May 1999, *Nederlandse Jurisprudentie* (NJ) 2000, 107 (4-M case); see also M.C.D. Embregts, *Uitsluitsel over bewijsuitsluiting* (dissertation Tilburg), Deventer: Kluwer 2003, and *in extenso* Koers, *o.c.*, p. 515–608.
In Germany the *gathering* of evidence is apparently governed by the rules of the *lex loci*, while the *consequent use* thereof is determined by German rules, being the *lex fori*; Scheller, *o.c.*, p. 94–101. In article 33, paragraph 2 of the Corpus Juris 2000, this option was also chosen; see M. Delmas-Marty and J.A.E. Vervaele (eds.), *The implementation of the Corpus Juris in the member states*, vol 1, Antwerp/Groningen/Oxford: Intersentia 2000, p. 209–210.

191 In the KB Lux affair the materials (personal data concerning Dutch account holders) were provided spontaneously. Since the materials were consequently accepted and used by the Dutch in criminal proceedings, the same could be argued there.

192 ECtHR, *Khan* v. *the United Kingdom*, appl. no. 35394/97, Court (Third Section), Judgment (Merits and Just Satisfaction) 12 May 2000, *Reports* 2000-V.

position to fully test the facts of the case. Expecting it to do so, would overcharge the system and render it completely ineffective. For this reason, a certain extent of mutual trust is inevitable.

Trust should however never be absolute. Unfortunately, current practice points in a different direction. With respect to Article 8, the responsibilities of the requested state should focus on retaining the proportionality principle in transnational affairs. This implies, first and foremost, an *ex officio* test of the facts of the case, as described in the Roquettes Frère case. A more detailed inquiry is called for whenever the interested party shows a prima facie case of a breach having occurred. The application of the rule of non-inquiry seems to be incompatible with this. The system proposed here will prevent the requested state from violating the ECHR, but will not always prevent breaches of personal rights from occurring. A person harmed may not always be able to show prima facie evidence of a breach, absolving the state of the need to provide a remedy (under the Convention). This problem seems almost impossible to resolve. What other alternatives are there? We could imagine a system that requires legal protection *before* the request is sent to the other state. This would allow the defence to challenge the reasonableness of a suspicion, thereby attacking the proportionality of the measure required and actually *preventing* possible breaches. However, it remains to be seen whether such openness at the pre-trial stage is compatible with the interests of the ongoing proceedings. Another alternative would be a system that offers full disclosure to the authorities of the requested state, providing them with the opportunity to look into the case in detail. This might be a fair solution as it offers full legal protection also to the parties whose right to privacy is directly affected, including third parties. However, this option would also be highly impractical, since it would require the requested state to work out the ongoing criminal proceedings in other states. Moreover, it still remains to be seen if third parties are actually in a position to substantiate their case to the degree required.

With respect to Article 6, it appears most effective to concentrate the main part of legal protection in the trial state, since at that point in time the case file must – as a rule – be disclosed to the defence. Furthermore, then the case file should be complete, allowing interested parties to question both the way in which it was gathered and its reliability. A logical consequence of this would be that if the origin of the material remains undisclosed, it should not be used. We have to admit, however, that in this model third parties in the requested state probably (partly) fall between two stools, since a remedy in the trial state is most likely not provided for them.

Let us at the end of this section return to the KB Lux affair. How is this affair to be appreciated in the light of the foregoing? As we saw in the introduction, the Dutch courts follow the continental approach of mutual trust. It is assumed that Belgium acted in accordance with the ECHR. This starting point is applied rigidly, however. Almost all the courts are of the opinion that testing the Belgian investigations is only appropriate where serious indications exist that the Convention has been breached. In doing so, the Dutch courts adopted too narrow a view with regard to their responsibilities under both Article 6 and 8. In Belgium evidence was excluded both in tax cases and in criminal cases, so the Dutch courts should have looked into the matter *ex officio*. Since the origin of the materials remained unaccounted for, it should not have been used.[193]

The Dutch approach is to a certain extent to be explained by the *Schutznorm*; it is repeatedly stated that the defendant was not harmed in his interests, because the Belgian investigations were aimed against Belgian account holders. We think that this is incorrect. First of all, we disagree with the court on the premise that the breach of Luxembourg banking secrecy and the consequent (irregular) acquisition by the Belgian authorities did not damage the interests of the Dutch account holders. After all, their personal data were stolen.[194] The *Schutznorm* is therefore given too broad a scope. Moreover, even assuming it was applied correctly, still the *Schutznorm* is an issue relating to the *admissibility* of evidence.[195] It is not a means to narrow court control as to the *reliability* and *lawfulness* of evidence used in court.[196] The trial state should at all times be able to account for the materials leading to the evidence it uses. With respect to Article 8, the responsibility for the use of the personal data, obtained by breaching banking secrecy, should also have been examined. The exclusion of the evidence by the Belgian courts in our view constitutes at the very least a *prima facie* case of a breach of Article 8, calling for an answer with respect to the consequent use of these data by the Dutch authorities. Did this use constitute a separate infringement that therefore calls for an effective remedy (Article 13) for Dutch account holders? Again, this matter should have been looked into *ex officio*.

193 Following a request for mutual assistance by the Dutch public prosecutor, the Belgian authorities answered that they were unable to provide further information as to the origin of the information; cf. District Court of The Hague, 5 November 2004, *LJN* no. AR5790, appl.no. 09/755139–02; supra note 15.

194 See also supra note 183.

195 This makes it, according to the standard case law of the ECtHR, primarily a matter for national law; cf. ECtHR *Schenk* v. *Switzerland*, appl. No. 10862/84, Court (Plenary), Judgment (Merits), 12 July 1988, Series A-140; ECtHR *Khan* v. *the United Kingdom*, appl. no. 35394/97, Court (Third Section), Judgment (Merits and Just Satisfaction) 12 May 2000, *Reports* 2000-V.

196 Cf. M.C.D. Embregts, *Uitsluitsel over bewijsuitsluiting* (dissertation Tilburg), Deventer: Kluwer 2003. The position of the Dutch Supreme Court (Hoge Raad) on this issue is not entirely clear. Compare Hoge Raad 6 July 2004, *Nederlandse Jurisprudentie* (NJ) 2004, 469; *Jurisprudentie Online* (JOL) 2004, 382 versus Hoge Raad 30 March 2004, *NJ* 2004, 376.

3.3. JOINT INVESTIGATION TEAMS

After discussing the classical concept of mutual assistance in criminal matters, we will now discuss the impact which joint investigation teams (JIT) might have on transnational human rights protection. Joint investigation teams are investigation teams with operational powers – including means of coercion – that are comprised of officials from several Member States. These officials may very well have different personal statuses; some of them may be part of the judiciary, while others are police officers or members of special investigation offices, for instance customs officers. Joint investigation teams are not necessarily bound to the territory of one Member State. On the contrary, they are allowed to be active on the territories of all the participating states.

The main question is what bearing these developments have on state responsibilities under the ECHR. How are joint teams to be classified under the four different models introduced in section 3.1, and what impact does this have on state responsibility under the ECHR that is based on individual state responsibility? Joint teams may complicate matters, since they consist of officials from a number of states and they may be active in more than one Member State. Article 13 of the EU Convention on mutual assistance illustrates this.[197] This article deals with joint teams and offers several starting points for the determination of the responsible state(s). In the third paragraph of this article it is stated that:

> 'A joint investigation team shall operate in the territory of the Member States setting up the team under the following general conditions:
> (a) the leader of the team shall be a representative of the competent authority participating in criminal investigations from the Member State in which the team operates. The leader of the team shall act within the limits of his or her competence under national law;
> (b) the team shall carry out its operations in accordance with the law of the Member State in which it operates. The members of the team shall carry out their tasks under the leadership of the person referred to in subparagraph (a), taking into account the conditions set by their own authorities in the agreement on setting up the team;
> (c) the Member State in which the team operates shall make the necessary organisational arrangements for it to do so.'[198]

---

197 See also the Council Framework decision of 13 June 2002 on joint investigation teams (2002/465/JHA), OJ L 162/1, that resembles Articles 13 and 16 of the EU Convention. The Framework decision is in force at this point in time, but will be withdrawn when the EU Convention on mutual assistance enters into force. Other treaties also contain provisions with regard to joint teams.

198 In Article 1, paragraph 3 of the Framework decision the same wording is used.

So, the team is set up in one of the Member States in which the main part of the investigations is expected to be carried out.[199] The team leader must be a representative of the state where the investigations take place.[200] He is bound by local national law. Other team members act under his command and responsibility. They (of course) are also bound by the rules of the *lex loci*. Yet, this changes as soon as investigations in other participating states are necessary. For this situation paragraph 7 of Article 13 prescribes:

> 'Where the joint investigation team needs investigative measures to be taken in one of the Member States setting up the team, members seconded [see on this notion the fourth paragraph of Article 13, AH/ML[201]] to the team by that Member State may request their own competent authorities to take those measures. Those measures shall be considered in that Member State under the conditions which would apply if they were requested in a national investigation.'

Joint teams thus offer important advantages over the classical concept of mutual assistance. Instead of the time-consuming granting procedures and relatively wide-reaching grounds for refusal, that are typical of mutual assistance in criminal matters, one may simply ask the seconded members to take investigative measures. Then, responsibility also changes hands, as far as the specific measures in that state are concerned. The authorities of that state are fully and exclusively responsible for the investigations carried out.[202] Members of the team from other countries, if present during the investigations, act under their responsibility. Again, the *locus regit actum* rule applies. The lawfulness of the investigations that were carried out is to be assessed by the laws of the state where the actions took place.

It is interesting to note that joint teams use an entirely different approach to international cooperation as described in the previous paragraph. They are conceived as a bundling of multiple national investigations.[203] Instead of helping other states with their criminal investigations (as is the case under mutual

199 Explanatory report on the Convention of 29 May 2000 on Mutual Assistance in Criminal Matters between the Member States of the European Union, OJ C 379/7, p. 18.

200 This state is not necessarily the state where the trial eventually takes place; see A.H. Klip and A.L. Smeulers, *Opsporing in de Euregio: gemeenschappelijke onderzoeksteams en parallelle opsporing* (not published), Maastricht: 2004.

201 In the fourth paragraph the following is stated: '4. In this Article, members of the joint investigation team from Member States other than the Member State in which the team operates are referred to as being 'seconded' to the team.'

202 Explanatory report on the Convention of 29 May 2000 on Mutual Assistance in Criminal Matters between the Member States of the European Union, OJ C 379/7, p. 18; see also Gert Vermeulen (et al.), *Een nieuwe Belgische wetgeving inzake international rechtshulp in strafzaken*, Antwerp/Apeldoorn: Maklu 2002, p. 155 and A.H. Klip and A.L. Smeulers, *o.c.*

203 See the Dutch *traveaux préparatoires* with respect to the implementation act of the EU Convention on mutual assistance; *Kamerstukken II* 2001–02, 28 351, no. 3, p. 9: 'De achterliggende gedachte is dat het onderzoek van een gemeenschappelijk onderzoeksteam in feite een concentratie van nationale onderzoeken inhoudt.'

assistance in criminal matters), under the joint team regime national interests are directly served. The aim is to equate investigations of joint teams as far as possible with national inquiries and to coordinate them.[204] We could therefore classify the cooperation within joint teams as a mixture of models 2 and 3 discussed above (section 3.1). After all, on the one hand grounds for refusal are excluded once the team is established,[205] and, on the other, the state where the team acts is fully responsible for the team's actions (model 2). Participating members from other states act under their instructions and responsibility (model 3; *Organleihe*). It therefore does not make sense to hold those other states liable as well. This approach is perfectly in line with the demands of the ECtHR, since it is always the state on whose territory actions take place that is responsible.

Although there is little practical experience with joint teams, it might be interesting to explore briefly the changes which this approach may bring with respect to the upholding of human rights. First of all, the way in which cooperation within joint teams is organised suggests that within the team there is no room left for the rule of non-inquiry. After all, information that was brought into the team also serves the purpose of national inquiries.[206] It makes sense that national laws are fully applied, including an assessment of the proportionality of the case and a report on the actions taken. In our view this would be a significant improvement compared to the mutual assistance regime. On the other hand, it is striking to note that grounds for refusal are absent, once the team is established. It is unclear if this reduces the margin to refuse cooperation with a view to the protection of human rights. In our view this is, at least in theory, not the case. On the contrary, grounds for refusal appear unnecessary, because the state that conducts the investigations is (also) serving his own interests and is therefore fully responsible for its actions; other team members have no say over it. This is in line with the concept of joint teams as a bundling of national investigations.

What might be problematic, however, is how this state responsibility is given shape in practice. After all, the competent authorities (referred to in section 7 of Article 13 mentioned above) are not (only) conducting a national investigation under the usual supervision of their superiors and/or after judicial approval. Instead, they are carrying out investigations at the request of a colleague that takes part in a joint team. This is a strictly horizontal situation. Judicial approval is only required if national law so prescribes[207], whereas the team leader (of the state where the team is set up) also has no say over their actions. So, as is the case under the mutual assistance regime, the question arises who effectively supervises

---

204 See the Dutch *traveaux préparatoires* with respect to the ratification of the EU Convention on mutual assistance; *Kamerstukken II* 2001–02, 28 350, no. 3, p. 6.

205 The request to establish a joint team, though, is a 'classical' request for mutual assistance; cf. A.H. Klip and A.L. Smeulers, *o.c.*, p. 10–11.

206 Section 10 of Article 13 does however contain limitations with regard to the use of the information obtained by the team.

207 *Kamerstukken II* 2001–02, 38 351, no. 3, p. 9.

these activities. The essential difference with mutual assistance is however that under the latter regime this question concerns two states[208], whereas under the joint team regime theoretically only one state is involved, namely the state where the investigations are actually carried out (be it the state where the team is set up or another state).

Another issue that needs to be addressed and in fact even gains weight under the joint team regime is that national laws are applied directly, without adjustments to the international setting of the inquiry. We have to keep in mind that the criminal justice system of one state is not necessarily compatible with that of another state (the *systeembreuk*; see section 3.2.2). Under the regime of mutual assistance many countries created special legal remedies for this reason, especially when coercive measures are requested. Although the scope of these remedies may be limited due to the rule of non-inquiry (see section 3.2.2), at least they offer some protection in transnational investigations. Under the joint team regime remedies are only present if they also exist in comparable national investigations.[209] National norms are applied directly without adjustments to the transnational surroundings of the investigations. This easily results in a loss of legal protection, if one regime, for instance, places emphasis on legal protection in the pre-trial stage (with a simultaneous reinforcement of the position of the suspect and/or third parties during that stage), while another state may rely heavily on the trial stage as the most suitable place for offering legal protection. To overcome this problem, much is (again) dependent on the trial state's willingness to ensure the fairness of the proceedings as a whole. But are trial judges willing to investigate (alleged) irregularities in other states or will they rely on the rule of non-inquiry once more?[210] Are they prepared to compensate for flaws in legal protection that have emerged earlier in the investigation in other states? In our view, they should be, since this is the trial state's primary responsibility.[211] National courts, in order to compensate for a loss of legal

208 After all, as we saw in section 3.2.1, current interstate practice is based on a 'division of labour' between the requested and requesting state. The requested authority has to rely on the requesting party, as the latter is in a better position to assess, for instance, the appropriateness of a measure that is requested.

209 The Dutch Act implementing the EU Convention contains a special procedure for the use of materials obtained by – in short – the use of coercive measures (see the proposed Article 552qd of the Dutch Code of Criminal Procedure), because in the Dutch internal legal order, special remedies are provided for in those cases. The provisional use of such evidence within the team, which is based in another state, is permitted. For use as evidence, however, additional judicial approval is needed. According to the Dutch government, this regime would allow (third) parties to effectively exercise their appeal rights; see *Kamerstukken II* 2001–02, 28 351, no. 3, p. 9.

210 Cf. Klip and Smeulers, *o.c.*, p. 24. These authors also mention other practical problems, such as the fact that a joint team might be moved from one country to another during the investigation. Of course, this also hampers effective control over the team and its actions.

211 The Dutch implementation act requires, amongst other things, the Dutch authorities to stipulate that foreign officials are prepared to testify at the trial, if necessary (see the proposed Article 552qa of the Dutch Code of Criminal Procedure; *Kamerstukken II* 2001–02, 28 351,

protection that might occur during the investigation stage, should therefore test the lawfulness (according to the lex loci) of the evidence obtained abroad, if so desired (and substantiated) by the defence.

In short, joint teams offer interesting possibilities for enhancing international cooperation. The word 'joint' suggests an entirely new concept of cooperation and also a joint responsibility of a state for the actions of such teams. This would at first sight create a conflict with the ECtHR's case law. The way such teams are organised seems, surprisingly enough, to be fully compatible with this case law. A great deal of emphasis is placed on the responsibilities of the participating states concerning the actions of the team on their territory, also when officials from other countries participate in the investigations. This also explains why grounds for refusal are absent. On the other hand, the modelling of joint teams as a bundling of multiple national investigations appears to be somewhat artificial. Specific adjustments to the transnational surroundings are not made. In our view this approach places a heavy burden on the trial state, which has to compensate for flaws in legal protection in the investigation stage. This is of course not problematic as long as it concerns actions that have taken place on its own territory. It remains to be seen, however, if states are also prepared to do this, in case investigations have taken place in other participating states. After all, the authorities of the trial state (be it the team leader or the trial judges) seem to have no say over the manner in which investigations in other states are carried out.[212] A closely connected question is who retains control over the actions of the authorities that carry out investigations at the request of joint team members. In our view, this latter issue is the sole problem of the state where the investigations have taken place.

3.4. (PROPOSAL FOR A) EUROPEAN EVIDENCE WARRANT

Like the joint teams, the European evidence warrant aims to improve international cooperation in criminal matters.[213] And again, like the joint teams, this is done by finding alternatives to the more classical approach of mutual assistance. The magic term for this new concept of cooperation is mutual recognition. After this concept was introduced in EU extradition law by means of the European arrest warrant (EAW)[214], the proposal for an European evidence

---

nos. 1–2); sceptical as to (the feasibility of) this requirement; Klip and Smeulers, *o.c.*, p. 27–28.

212 A complication occurs if the team is moved from one state to another during the investigation.

213 See on the EEW, J.A.E. Vervaele (ed.), *European Evidence Warrant – Transnational Judicial Inquiries in the EU*, Antwerp/Groningen/Oxford: Intersentia Law Publisher 2005.

214 Framework Decision of 13 June 2002 on the European arrest warrant and the surrender procedures between Member States, OJ L 190/1; see on this framework decision R. Blekxtoon

warrant (EEW)[215] now introduces it in the field of the mutual assistance. The scope of this proposal is rather limited, but the European Commission has already made it public that similar proposals are likely to follow.[216] These proposals also take the concept of mutual recognition as their starting point. In the Commission's view, the EEW is the first step towards a single mutual recognition instrument that will replace all of the existing mutual assistance regime.[217]

The European Evidence Warrant (EEW) would be directly enforceable in other Member States. The executing State is expected to enforce orders issued by the issuing State, with only limited grounds for refusal.[218] A specific ground for refusal on human rights grounds is not present in the proposal.[219] Under the four different models which we introduced in section 3.1, an EEW would therefore constitute an example of the second model. On the one hand, it leaves the executing state with virtually no space to refuse a 'request' (better: evidence warrant), on the other this state remains responsible for the actions on its territory. As we have repeatedly stated above, this approach might contravene individual state responsibility under the ECHR. Within joint teams grounds for refusal are also not present. However, they are – at least theoretically – not

---

and W. van Ballegooij (eds.), *Handbook on the European Arrest Warrant*, The Hague: TMC Asser Press 2004.

215 Proposal of 14 November 2003 for a Council Framework Decision on the European Evidence Warrant for obtaining objects, documents and data for use in proceedings in criminal matters, COM (2003) 688 final.

216 The proposal applies to objects, documents or data obtained under various procedural powers, including seizure, production or search powers. However, it is not intended to be used to initiate the interviewing of suspects, taking statements, or the hearing of witnesses and victims. The taking of evidence from the body of a person, in particular DNA samples, is also excluded from the scope of the European Evidence Warrant. Thirdly, the European Evidence Warrant is not intended to be used to initiate procedural investigative measures which involve obtaining evidence in real-time such as the interception of communications and the monitoring of bank accounts. Finally, the European Evidence Warrant is intended to be used in order to obtain evidence that can only result from further investigation or analysis. It could therefore not be used to require the commissioning of an expert's report; see COM (2003) 688 final.

217 The steps towards a single instrument could be as follows: a) the proposed European Evidence Warrant, which provides for the obtaining of evidence that already exists and that is directly available; b) to provide for the mutual recognition of orders for the obtaining of other types of evidence. These can be divided into two categories, namely evidence that does not already exist but which is directly available (interviews of suspects, witnesses or experts, and the taking of evidence through the monitoring of telephone calls or banking transactions) and evidence which, although already existing, is not directly available without further investigation or analysis (e.g. evidence from the body of a person or the commissioning of an expert's report); c) to bring together these separate instruments into a single consolidated instrument which would include a general part containing provisions applicable to all co-operation; see COM (2003) 688 final.

218 The influence of the double criminality requirement for instance is strongly reduced; see Article 16 of the proposal.

219 This is much to the regret of organisations like Statewatch; see their comments on the proposal, published on: www.statewatch.org.

necessary, since joint teams are conceived as a bundling of national investigations. The state where the actual investigations take place remains fully in charge, so that it does not need grounds for refusal. It can simply decide not to carry out an investigation if it does not want to. This way a conflict with the ECtHR's case law is – again theoretically – avoided. But is this also the case if the EEW regime were to come into force? This question is dealt with in this section.

The EEW requires a considerable amount of trust in each other's legal systems. After all, it is in principle not up to the executing state to investigate matters, once this has already been done by the issuing authority. On the contrary, according to the principle of mutual recognition, they should 'simply' execute the warrant and provide the issuing state with the requested information. This is stipulated in Article 11 of the proposal:

> 'Except as otherwise provided for in this Framework Decision [see especially Articles 15 and 16 of the proposal, AH/ML], the executing authority shall recognise a European Evidence Warrant, transmitted in accordance with Article 7, without any further formality being required, and shall forthwith take the necessary measures for its execution in the same way as the objects, documents or data would be obtained by an authority of the executing State.'

The recognition of the warrant is made possible due to the rules that are provided for the *issuing* authority. In Article 6 of the proposal the following is stated:

> 'Each Member State shall take the necessary measures to ensure that the European Evidence Warrant is issued only when the issuing authority is satisfied that the following conditions have been met:
> (a) the objects, documents or data sought are necessary and proportionate for the purpose of proceedings in Article 4 [in short, criminal proceedings, AH/ML].
> (b) the objects, documents or data can be obtained under the law of the issuing State in similar circumstances if they were available on the territory of the issuing State, even though different procedural measures might be used.
> (c) the objects, documents or data are likely to be admissible in the proceedings for which they are sought.'

The foregoing presupposes that the issuing state has a decisive say over the manner in which the warrants are executed, even though the competences and powers for the execution thereof are governed by the laws of the executing state. It is, for instance, not up to the executing authority to look into the substantial reasons for the issuing of the warrant (cf. Article 19(2)). Thus far, one could state that there is nothing new compared to the 'old' situation, which we described above in section 3.2; the difference is only gradual in that the margin of appreciation of the executing state is reduced (fewer refusal grounds, no exequatur procedure, etc). One could even maintain that the rule of non-inquiry has now officially been made the cornerstone of EU cooperation in criminal matters.

Yet, against this background it is rather striking that the executing authority is left with a considerable discretion as to the means it chooses to execute the request. This is an important change compared to the 'old' situation, where the request for assistance also served as an important guideline for the requested authority. It also helped to prevent that the latter would take over the tasks of the requesting authority. Indeed, such a takeover would run counter to the *rationales* behind the concept of mutual assistance.[220] Its aim is to support other states in the fulfilment of their tasks. However, under the new regime the executing authority, in order to enhance the effectiveness of the warrant, is almost entirely free in choosing the means of executing the warrant (freezing of evidence, extradition order, search and seizure, et cetera).[221] Only in Article 12 are certain limitations formulated:

> '1. Each Member State shall take the necessary measures to ensure that the European Evidence Warrant is executed in accordance with the following minimum conditions:
> (a) the executing authority shall use the least intrusive means necessary to obtain the objects, documents or data [this provision, however, is restricted by Article 13 of the proposal, AH/ML];
> (b) a natural person shall not be required to produce objects, documents or data which may result in self-incrimination; and
> (c) the issuing authority shall be informed immediately if the executing authority discovers that the warrant was executed in a manner contrary to the law of the executing State.'[222]

This approach is surprising. After all, choosing the means of investigation belongs to the essence of the activities of the authorities of the *issuing* state. Whether or not in a concrete investigation an extradition order to hand over documents will do the trick or that a far more intrusive search and seizure is necessary, can and should only be assessed by the authority that is actually in charge of the investigations, since this is its 'core business'.[223] Furthermore, as we have said, a well-formulated, specific request also guides the state that is

---

220 Cf. Peter Popp, *o.c.*, p. 274.

221 Cf. COM (2003), 688, p. 9: 'For this reason, the proposal for a European Evidence Warrant allows the issuing State to specify only the objective to be achieved (i.e. to obtain specific evidence), and leaves the executing State to obtain the evidence in accordance with its domestic procedural law. Although it is mandatory under the European Evidence Warrant to obtain the evidence, it is left to the executing State to determine, in the light of the information supplied by the issuing State, the most appropriate way to obtain the evidence in accordance with its domestic procedural law.'

222 The second paragraph of Article 12 also contains some (procedural) conditions.

223 Article 13(a) of the proposal limits this discretion of the executing state. In some cases, the executing state may request coercive measures.

executing the warrant. The executing authority is not in a position to assess what measure would be best in a specific case. It is only capable to assess whether one particular measure is appropriate and in accordance with its own laws and the ECHR. Under the new regime this guiding function of what under the 'old' regime would have been a 'request' is now gone. Of course, as Article 12(1a) stipulates, states must use the least intrusive means possible. But how do they know this? Choosing a task *par excellence* is surely a matter for the executing authority?

In the end the question again arises: what state is in charge under the EEW regime and in charge of what exactly? Although it remains to be seen in what direction developments will precisely go, we are not convinced beforehand that the EEW offers sufficient protection for individuals. In our view there is a danger that responsibilities of states will become mingled, since the executing state is left with a great deal of discretion as to the means it chooses for executing the request, whereas at the same time substantial grounds for issuing the request are not to be examined in the executing state, thus taking the principle of mutual trust one step further (cf. Article 19(2)).[224] We are afraid that this not only leaves the parties in the executing state without effective remedies, but also makes it impossible for that state to live up to its obligations under the ECHR. After all, grounds for refusal are practically absent, so the executing state is, should the occasion arise, forced to choose between either the EEW or the ECHR.

Closely connected with the foregoing is, of course, the abolition of national exequatur procedures. This implies that legal remedies that currently exist under the mutual assistance regime (at least as far as coercive measures are concerned; section 3.2.2) are abandoned. Is this indeed what is meant by the proposal? If so, does this not require additional safeguards in the issuing state? In this respect it is interesting to note that Article 19, sections 1 and 2, of the proposal provide the following:

> '1. Member States shall put in place the necessary arrangements to ensure that any interested party, including bona fide third parties, have legal remedies against a European Evidence Warrant executed pursuant to Article 11 using coercive measures, in order to preserve their legitimate interests.
> 2. The action shall be brought before a court in the issuing State or in the executing State in accordance with the national law of each. However, the substantial reasons for issuing the European Evidence Warrant, including whether the criteria in Article 6 have been met, may be challenged only in an action brought before a court in the issuing State.'

[224] This issue will need even more attention, if later (as is the aim of the Commission; see note 216) the scope of the EEW is extended to other forms of evidence gathering, such as the hearing of witnesses. Will the executing state still be free to choose the means of execution?

These provisions seem to introduce a duty for *all* states to create legal remedies for *all* the parties involved (also third parties in the executing state), as far as coercive measures are concerned.[225] We could even argue on the basis of this text that it is up to the individual to decide where he brings his action.[226] Another improvement is laid down in section 4 of Article 19, where it is stipulated that 'if the action is brought in the executing State, the judicial authority of the issuing State shall be informed thereof and of the grounds of the action, so that it can submit the arguments that it deems necessary. (...)' Both states seem to be obliged to assist each other in offering legal protection. However, when substantial issues are involved, the complainant should address the issuing state.

In our view, the foregoing provisions offer some improvement in legal protection. What remains unsaid, however, is how these remedies are to be mutually coordinated. For instance, does the foregoing mean that states should make remedies available *before* the issuing of the warrant or should they offer protection *after* the fact? To what extent are states free to choose? Should they also offer a remedy for actions of the authorities of the other state?[227] Do these remedies have *res iudicata* status in other states? Moreover, since substantial reasons are only to be discussed in the issuing state, how are breaches of Article 8 to be *prevented* by the executing state, since there is virtually no ground for refusal left? These questions remain unanswered at this point in time. The EEW would offer a fair opportunity to mutually coordinate national laws in order to ensure that the individual does not become trapped between two or more criminal justice systems. It is up to the EU and its Member States to fulfil this task.

4. SUMMARY

In this study we have tested the current and proposed systems of mutual assistance in criminal matters against the guarantees of the European Convention on Human Rights.

The first part of the analysis comprises a review of the case law of the ECtHR on the transnational application of the convention. Under this case law the Convention primarily has territorial application. Framed as a positive obligation: the Member States are responsible for maintaining the convention standards

225 This obligation does not exist for information that is already in the possession of the executing authority; COM (2003) 688, p. 27.

226 After all, as Article 19(2) states 'action shall be brought before a court in the issuing State *or* in the executing State in accordance with the national law of each [emphasis added, AH/ML].' As we saw above (subsection 3.2.4), the position of third parties is problematic.

227 What happens, for instance, when the executing state violates Article 12(1a)? Is the issuing state responsible for this, even if it had no say over the choosing of the means of execution (cf. Article 20(1) of the proposal)?

throughout the *espace juridique*. This duty also applies in the case of cooperation. In line with the accepted notions of state liability in international law, Member States cannot dispose of their responsibility by entering into international arrangements. They retain their pre-existent responsibility over their territory and their actions. In the case of international legal cooperation (in its widest sense) Member States are held responsible to the extent that their actions contribute to a violation of Convention rights, be it by other Member States or by non-member states. Whenever cooperation would lead to a violation of convention rights a refusal to cooperate is called for, regardless of the existence of a relevant ground for refusal under the cooperation scheme. In that respect, the current trend towards automatic recognition within the EC/EU area may pose a problem to the local judiciary, leading to a conflict of duties.

The ECtHR has stated repeatedly that the rights granted by the convention should be practical and effective. This means, *inter alia*, that violations should be – firstly – prevented and secondly – remedied. In the context of transnational cooperation, we take this to mean that prevention is preferable, but granting a remedy in the case of a breach is essential. Whenever a claimant shows a *prima facie* case of such a breach, the courts cannot hide behind magical formulas like mutual trust or the rule of non-inquiry. Either they investigate themselves or refer the claimant to a remedy elsewhere (e.g. the country of primary breach). The latter option does not follow directly from the case law, but the method is used by national courts and does not seem to contravene the convention. Thus a 'local remedies rule' for transnational cooperation is created which would require the complainant to first deploy the available remedies in the country of primary breach.

In the second part of the analysis, we take a closer look at the current and coming systems of mutual cooperation in criminal matters (used in a narrow sense as assistance in acquiring evidence). The traditional systems of *Rechtshilfe* create a more or less clear-cut division of labour between the cooperating states – each performing specific functions within the system of criminal justice and each bearing responsibilities for certain decisions and actions. The convention rights which are at stake in this type of cooperation are mainly Article 6 (fair trial) and Article 8 (privacy). When state A requests state B to take measures against X to obtain evidence, Article 8 is involved. In practice it is mainly the requirement of proportionality which poses problems. To judge the proportionality of coercive measures State B has to ascertain *inter alia* the seriousness of the crime and the seriousness of the allegations against the suspect. Such an inquiry presupposes that state B has all the necessary information to make the assessment. In current practice this is not the case. To avoid breaches of the Convention the courts of state B should, in our opinion, carry out a marginal *ex officio* check for proportionality. Any irregularities in the request which are not immediately evident (e.g. when the suspicion is in its turn based on irregularly acquired evidence) should be looked into upon request: whenever an interested party has a *prima facie* case of a breach, a full inquiry is called for. This responsibility of state B can only be mitigated if the interested party has a remedy available to it in state A – but a special remedy against a request for information will usually be absent.

The adjudicating state bears responsibilities under both Article 6 and Article 8. The use of illegally obtained evidence may render a trial unfair. Although this rule is not very strict (irregularity does not *ipso facto* lead to inadmissibility), we still think that the minimum requirement of fair trial would be that any evidence may be challenged both as to content and as to the mode of its acquisition. Evidence the provenance of which cannot be ascertained, should not be admitted. With regard to the right to privacy, the use in open court of information gathered in breach of Article 8 may lead to an independent breach of Article 8. Hence, the adjudicating state should – if necessary – look into the provenance of any evidence used. Again, it might be compatible with the ECHR to refer an investigation into the evidence to the state of origin – provided a local remedy is available there. However, it seems preferable from the point of efficiency to have the trial state decide on any issues involving the legitimacy of evidence. This would require a willingness to share information on the side of the state of origin of the information involved. Within the EC/EU context such willingness could flow from the duty of loyal cooperation – Member States should help one another to prevent breaches of human rights (which are part of the Community legal order).

In short, following the classical approach we hold each state liable for its own contribution to a breach of convention rights. On this basis a model of cooperation is developed in which mutual trust still plays an important rule, but is not absolute. It is overruled *ex officio* in the case of flagrant breaches of Convention rights. A more detailed inquiry is called for whenever the interested party demonstrates a *prima facie* case of breach. The system thus described will prevent a state from violating the ECHR, but will not prevent breaches of personal rights from occurring. A person harmed may not always be able to show *prima facie* evidence of breach, absolving the state of the need to provide a remedy (under the Convention). Moreover, this person might not even be a party to the proceedings in which the test is to be carried out. Both ailments could be cured if, in every case, somewhere along the line, the evidence is tested *ex officio*. However, due to differences between the several systems of criminal law, such an *ex officio* test will not always be carried out in transnational cases. This double burden can only be solved by either the harmonisation of criminal law (providing a remedy at the early stages of the criminal investigations) and/or full disclosure by the cooperating authorities.

Of the new models of cooperation the Joint Investigation Teams operate under a rather classic model of territorial control: the state in which the investigation measures are carried out bears full responsibility even over foreign agents participating in the JIT. At first sight, the system does not pose insurmountable problems with regard to the gathering of evidence. However, the fact that investigations within a JIT are treated as national inquiries may result in a loss of protection as all adaptations to the transnational character of the investigations are lost. The situation is slightly different with the European Evidence Warrant. The system introduced in the current proposal is quite problematic from the point of view of human rights as it obfuscates the separate responsibilities of cooperating states. Only a coordinated system of judicial protection, to be established together with the EEW itself, can remedy this.

XX. THE TRANSNATIONAL *NE BIS IN IDEM* PRINCIPLE IN THE EU

Towards an EU system of general principles and human rights?*

John VERVAELE**

1. INTRODUCTION: THE *NE BIS IN IDEM* PRINCIPLE AS A DOMESTIC GENERAL PRINCIPLE OF LAW

The *ne bis in idem* principle is a general principle of (criminal) law in many national legal orders, sometimes even codified as a constitutional right. It has also been established as an individual right in international human rights legal instruments. The *ne bis in idem* principle has been historically elaborated as a principle that only applies nationally and is limited to criminal justice. Concerning the substance of the principle, traditionally a distinction is made between *nemo debet bis vexari pro una et eadem causa* (no one should have to face more than one prosecution for the same offence) and *nemo debet bis puniri pro uno delicto* (no one should be punished twice for the same offence). Some countries limit the principle to the prohibition of double punishment.[1]

The rationale of the *ne bis in idem* principle is manifold. It is of course a principle of judicial protection for the citizen against the *ius puniendi* of the state and as such is part of the principles of due law and fair trial. On the other hand respect for the *res judicata* (*pro veritate habitur*) of final judgments[2] is of importance for the legitimacy of the legal system and of the state.

* A first version was published in the *Utrecht Law Review*, volume 1, Issue 2, December 2005.

** Professor of Economic and European Criminal Law, Director of the G.J. Wiarda Institute and Vice-Dean, Utrecht University, School of Law; Professor of European Criminal Law, College of Europe, Bruges.

1 In that case, still a double prosecution can be recognized as a violation of the principles of a fair administration of justice.

2 *Interest reipublice ut sit finis litium,bis de eadem re ne sit actio.*

Traditionally, the *ne bis in idem* principle is recognized by the State for application only within its own domestic legal order. A rich set of case law has meanwhile developed in the European States concerning the domestic *ne bis idem* principle. Generally speaking, the principle applies only in the field of criminal law and to final judgments in criminal matters. This means that in many States double prosecution remains fully possible, as does the combination of administrative punitive sanctions with criminal sanctions. It is also possible in many States to combine criminal sanctions with out-of-court settlements. Not only is the reach of the principle limited, its application in the domestic legal orders of the States also still raises quite a few questions.[3] Much of the domestic case law deals with the definitions of *idem* and *bis*. Should the legal definition of the offences be considered as the basis of the definition of the term the same (*idem*), or rather the facts? Does the application of the *ne bis in idem* principle depend on the scope of the offence descriptions or on the legal values which they aim to protect? Is a distinction made between natural and legal persons for the application of the principle? It can safely be concluded that national case law has not yet produced a common standard concerning the scope and the application of the *ne bis in idem* principle in the domestic legal orders.

Meanwhile the EU, since the coming into force of the Treaty of Amsterdam, has been actively realizing a common area of Freedom, Security and Justice. The classical inter-State cooperation in criminal matters has been replaced by enhanced judicial cooperation directly between the actors of the criminal justice system. Moreover, these now have to recognize each other's judicial decisions based on the principle of mutual recognition. As a result, essential aspects of the functioning of the criminal justice system are now taking place in a European area without internal borders, a transnational judicial area. By several framework decisions the mutual recognition principle has been elaborated for pre-trial judicial decisions, such as seizure, evidence gathering and arrest. Judicial decisions in one Member State have legal effect in the legal area of the EU. The most famous framework decision in this context must certainly be the European Arrest Warrant which replaces the classic extradition procedure. Mutual recognition of each other's arrest warrants not only leads to the quicker surrender of suspects within the EU, but also to the fact that legal principles such as the *ne bis in idem* principle have to be applied transnationally. This transnational application presumes that the scope and the application of the *ne bis in idem* principle in the EU rely on a common standard.

The main questions are therefore: how may we achieve such a common standard, what transnational function should it fulfil and what would be the content of this function? This article analyses (in Section 2) whether and to what extent the ECHR has contributed and may contribute to the development of such

3 See for instance the Report of the UK Law Commission on double jeopardy, 17.24.01, www.lawcom.gov.uk/.

a common *ne bis in idem* standard in Europe. It is also examined whether the application of the *ne bis in idem* principle in classic inter-state judicial cooperation in criminal matters in the framework of the Council of Europe is able to make a contribution as well. The transnational function of the *ne bis in idem* principle is discussed in Sections 3 and 4. First it is analysed how this 'transnationalness' has developed in EC law and in the pre-Maastricht judicial integration. Then a detailed analysis is given of how the Court of Justice has further defined the principle in the framework of the area of Freedom, Security and Justice. Finally, this is tested in Section 5 against the meaning of the *ne bis in idem* principle in the framework decision on the European Arrest Warrant, as an example of the inherent tension between mutual recognition and the protection of human rights in transnational justice. In the concluding Section 6 a summary is given of the findings.

2. THE *NE BIS IN IDEM* PRINCIPLE IN INTERNATIONAL RELATIONS AND AS AN INTERNATIONAL HUMAN RIGHT

Are States willing to accept the operation of an international *ne bis in idem* principle between them? Very few countries recognize the validity of foreign judgments in criminal matters for execution or enforcement in their national legal order lacking a treaty basis. States consider their *ius puniendi* and the full exercise of it as essential to their sovereignty. Even the recognition of *res judicata* in respect of a foreign criminal judgment is problematic, certainly when it concerns territorial offences. Besides arising from self-interest, this may result from the fact that States do not always have sufficient confidence or trust in the way in which other States administer justice. Recognition of foreign *res judicata* means that prosecuting or punishing anew is no longer possible (negative effect) or that the decision has to be taken into account in the context of other cases to be decided (positive effect). A refusal to recognize the validity of foreign judgments leads to multiple prosecution, which is certainly problematic for the individual, but can also cause problems in the international relations between states. Most common law legal systems actually do recognize the *res judicata* effect of foreign judgments, and of the civil law family the Netherlands have the most far-reaching and liberal provisions. The Dutch Criminal Code contains a general *ne bis in idem* provision that is applicable to both domestic and foreign judgements, regardless of where the offence was committed.[4] However, the Netherlands stand quite alone in this respect.

4 For a comment on the Dutch *ne bis in idem* in Art. 68 of the Criminal Code, see P. Baauw, 'Ne bis in idem', in B. Swart et al. (eds.), *International Criminal Law in the Netherlands*, 1997, pp. 75–84.

There is no mandatory rule of international law (*ius cogens*) imposing a duty to respect the *ne bis in idem* principle between States. The application of the principle depends on the content of international treaties. We do find treaty-based *ne bis in idem* provisions, both in human rights treaties and in bilateral or multilateral treaties dealing with judicial cooperation in criminal matters.

The *ne bis in idem* principle is established as an individual right in international human rights legal instruments, such as the International Covenant on Civil and Political Rights of 19 December 1966 (Article 14(7)). The European Convention on Human Rights (ECHR) does not contain such a provision and the former European Commission on Human Rights[5] denied the existence of the principle as such under Article 6 of the ECHR, without however precluding in absolute terms that certain double prosecutions might violate the fair trial rights under Article 6 ECHR. The provision has meanwhile been elaborated in the Seventh Protocol to the ECHR (Article 4), but only a minority of the 25 EU Member States have ratified Protocol no 7. Can we derive from the case law of the ECtHR a common standard? Most of the cases deal with one aspect of *ne bis in idem*, namely the definition of *idem*. After some contradictory judgments[6] on the application of Article 4 of Protocol 7, the ECtHR followed its judgment in the *Franz Fischer v. Austria* decision,[7] based on *idem factum*. However, in the case of *Göktan v. France*,[8] the Court again seemed to rely on the legal *idem*. Although the case law is limited, some conclusions can be derived from it. The ECtHR only deals with the national *ne bis in idem*, meaning the principle as it operates within the domestic legal orders of the Party States, and it does not deal with the international or transnational *ne bis in idem*. This is in line with the application of Article 14(7) of the UN International Covenant on Civil and Political Rights.[9] It is also clear from the Strasbourg case law that the *ne bis in idem* principle is

5 European Commission on Human Rights, 13 July 1970, no. 4212/69, CDR 35, 151.

6 *Gradinger v. Austria*, judgment of 23 October 1995, Series A no. 328-C and *Oliveira v. Switzerland* judgment of 30 July 1998, *Reports of Judgments and Decisions* 1998-V, p. 1990.

7 *Franz Fischer v. Austria of 29 May 2001*, Series A no. 312 (C), confirmed in *W.F. v. Austria*, judgment of 30 May 2002 and *Sailer v. Austria*, judgment of 6 June 2002. See www.echr.coe.int/ for these decisions.

8 *Göktan v. France*, Judgment of 2 July 2002, www.echr.coe.int/.

9 The Human Rights Committee ruled that Article 14(7) does not apply to foreign *res judicata*, UN Human Rights Committee 2 November 1987. The Netherlands has formulated the following reservation:

> 'Article 14, paragraph 7
>
> The Kingdom of the Netherlands accepts this provision only insofar as no obligations arise from it further to those set out in article 68 of the Criminal Code of the Netherlands and article 70 of the Criminal Code of the Netherlands Antilles as they now apply. They read:
>
> 1. Except in cases where court decisions are eligible for review, no person may be prosecuted again for an offence in respect of which a court in the Netherlands or the Netherlands Antilles has delivered an irrevocable judgement.
>
> 2. If the judgement has been delivered by some other court, the same person may not be prosecuted for the same offence in the case of (I) acquittal or withdrawal of proceedings or (II) conviction followed by complete execution, remission or lapse of the sentence.'

not limited to double punishment, but also includes double prosecution, which means that the accounting principle is not enough to respect the principle of *ne bis in idem*. This underlines the importance of cooperation at the level of the inquiry and of preferably introducing *una via* provisions rather than anti-cumulation of sanctions. In addition, the element of *bis* also includes the combination of two criminal charges in the sense of Article 6, for instance, the imposition of a criminal punitive sanction and an administrative punitive sanction.[10] Case law provides some important guidance here, but falls short of producing a solid common standard. Moreover, very few States have ratified Protocol 7.

The *ne bis in idem* principle is also important as a ground for refusing to cooperate in the framework of international treaties dealing with judicial cooperation in criminal matters. The *ne bis in idem* principle was included in the milestone multilateral treaty on Extradition of the Council of Europe of 13 December 1957. Article 9 provided not only for the classic formulation of the *ne bis in idem* principle dealing with final judgments (*res judicata*), but also included final decisions of a procedural character. The former ground for refusal ground is mandatory, however, whereas the latter is only optional:

> 'Extradition shall not be granted if a final judgement has been passed by the competent authorities of the requested Party upon the person claimed in respect of the offence or offences for which extradition is requested. Extradition may be refused if the competent authorities of the requested Party have decided either not to institute or to terminate proceedings in respect of the same offence or offences.'

Article 8 also provides an optional ground for *ne bis in idem* refusal in the case of *lis pendens*:

> 'The requested Party may refuse to extradite the person claimed if the competent authorities of such Party are proceeding against him in respect of the offence or offences for which extradition is requested.'

Article 7 even concerns a prior phase, accepting the preponderance of sovereign interests:

> 'The requested Party may refuse to extradite a person claimed for an offence which is regarded by its law as having been committed in whole or in part in its territory or in a place treated as its territory.'

---

10 The double jeopardy clause in the Fifth Amendment is not limited to criminal law, but includes civil and administrative punitive sanctions. However, the leading case, *United States v. Halper*, 490 U.S. 435 (1989), has recently been again restricted in *Hudson v. U.S.*, 522 U.S. 93 (1997); See also J. Vervaele, 'La saisie et la confiscation à la suite d'atteintes punissables au droit aux Etats-Unis', 1998 *Revue de Droit Pénal et de Criminologie*, pp. 974–1003.

The Extradition Convention deals with *ne bis in idem* in a classic intergovernmental setting between the requesting and requested State, but the additional Protocol of 15 October 1975 supplements Article 9 of the Convention with the following paragraphs 2 and 3 which also cover other Contracting Parties:

> '2. The extradition of a person against whom a final judgement has been rendered in a third State, Contracting Party to the Convention, for the offence or offences in respect of which the claim was made, shall not be granted;
> a) if the afore-mentioned judgment resulted in his acquittal;
> b) the term of imprisonment or other measure to which he was sentenced:
> I) has been completely enforced;
> II) has been wholly, or with respect to the part not enforced, the subject of a pardon or an amnesty;
> c) if the court convicted the offender without imposing a sanction.
> 3. This mandatory refusal ground can however be set aside (optional) by calling in exceptions based on territoriality principle, vital interest in jeopardy or the implication of own civil servants:
> a) if the offence in respect of which judgment has been rendered was committed against a person, an institution or any thing having public status in the requesting State;
> b) if the person on whom judgement was passed had himself a public status in the requesting State;
> c) if the offence in respect of which judgement was passed was committed completely or partly in the territory of the requesting State or in a place treated as its territory.'

Ne bis in idem provisions are not limited to extradition, but have been included in many Council of Europe Conventions concerning judicial cooperation in criminal matters. In Europe, in the framework of the Council of Europe, efforts have been made since the 1970s to introduce a regional international *ne bis in idem* principle. In this cooperation framework the *ne bis in idem* principle only applies *inter partes*, which means that it can be or must be applied between the contracting States in case of a concrete request. It is not considered to be an individual right *erga omnes*. *Ne bis in idem* is provided for under the 1970 Convention of the Council of Europe on the International Validity of Criminal Judgements (Articles 53–57) and under the 1972 Convention on the Transfer of Proceedings in Criminal Matters (Articles 35–37) as mandatory. However, both Conventions have a rather poor ratification rate and contain quite a number of exceptions to the *ne bis in idem* principle. In the 1990 Convention on Laundering, Search, Seizure and Confiscation of the Proceeds from Crime (Article 18, paragraph 1e), which is very well ratified, it is optional, but some Contracting States did include it in their ratification declaration as a ground for refusal for cooperation requests. The Council of Europe Convention of 15 May 1972 on the transfer of Proceedings in Criminal Matters provides in Part V (Articles 35–37):

> ***Article 35.*** 1. A person in respect of whom a final and enforceable criminal judgment has been rendered may for the same act neither be prosecuted nor sentenced nor subjected to enforcement of a sanction in another Contracting State:
> a) if he was acquitted;
> b) if the sanction imposed:
>   i) has been completely enforced or is being enforced, or
>   ii) has been wholly, or with respect to the part not enforced, the subject of a pardon or an amnesty, or
>   iii) can no longer be enforced because of lapse of time;
> c) if the court convicted the offender without imposing a sanction.
> 2. Nevertheless, a Contracting State shall not, unless it has itself requested the proceedings, be obliged to recognise the effect of ne bis in idem if the act which gave rise to the judgment was directed against either a person or an institution or any thing having public status in that State, or if the subject of the judgment had himself a public status in that State.
> 3. Furthermore, a Contracting State where the act was committed or considered as such according to the law of that State shall not be obliged to recognise the effect of ne bis in idem unless that State has itself requested the proceedings.
>
> ***Article 36.*** If new proceedings are instituted against a person who in another Contracting State has been sentenced for the same act, then any period of deprivation of liberty arising from the sentence enforced shall be deducted from the sanction which may be imposed.
>
> ***Article 37.*** This Part shall not prevent the application of wider domestic provisions relating to the effect of *ne bis in idem* attached to foreign criminal judgments.

In these Conventions the *ne bis in idem* principle has as its objective the avoidance of double punishment, not of double prosecution or investigation. That is the reason why we do not find *ne bis in idem* provisions in the Council of Europe Convention of 20 April 1959 on mutual assistance in criminal matters or in the additional protocols dealing with judicial letters rogatory.

Even if states recognize the international *ne bis in idem* principle, problems may arise in transnational settings because of the different interpretations of the principle as to the meaning of *idem*, *bis*, etc. The main questions here are whether the ECtHR can deal with these matters and whether individuals may claim the application of the *ne bis in idem* principle as a subjective right or even a human right? Does *ne bis in idem* serves as an impediment to international cooperation in general and to the surrender of suspects in particular or is it a human right of the accused? As we have seen, the principle operates *inter partes*, rather than *erga omnes*. However, the state-to-state approach has begun to be affected by the case law of the ECtHR.[11] In the *Soering* case,[12] the ECtHR decided on the application of Articles 3 and 6 ECHR to the extradition of a suspect to the USA. It ruled that although Article 1 of the ECHR, which provides that 'the High Contracting Parties shall secure to everyone within their jurisdiction the rights and freedoms defined in Section I of this Convention' cannot be read as justifying a general principle to the effect that a Contracting State may not surrender an individual unless satisfied that the conditions awaiting him in the country of destination are in full accordance with each of the safeguards of the Convention, this does not absolve the Contracting Parties from responsibility under that Convention for all and any foreseeable consequences outside their jurisdiction.[13] From this decision it is quite clear that the rule of comity and non-inquiry does not apply in the case of possible flagrant violations of human rights. The requested State has the duty to scrutiny as to whether the requesting State properly respects their rights. Further the respect of human rights is a joint responsibility of both States, and citizens have the right to an effective remedy in this field. This means that the extradition procedure not only affects State to State relations, but also the subjective rights of citizens. In the cases *Drozd v. France and Spain*[14] and *Iribarne Perex v. France*,[15] which both concerned the transnational execution of criminal convictions, the ECtHR ruled that Contracting States are obliged to refuse cooperation if it emerges that the conviction is the result of a flagrant denial of justice.[16]

From the analysis above it is clear that the ECtHR has not yet elaborated a common standard concerning the scope and the application of the *ne bis in idem* principle. Concerning the application of human rights in interstate judicial cooperation, the ECtHR has imposed duties upon the States. Due to a lack of relevant case law, it remains unclear, however, whether the notion of flagrant violation of human rights also applies to a failure to respect the *ne bis in idem* principle as such.

In conclusion therefore state practice in the Member States and the case law of the ECtHR only give us limited guidance for the elaboration of a common transnational *ne bis in idem* standard in a regional integration setting.

---

11 See P. Garlick, 'The European Arrest Warrant and the ECHR' and N. Keijzer, 'Extradition and Human Rights: a Dutch Perspective', in R. Blekxtoon et al. (eds.), *Handbook on the European Arrest Warrant*, 2005, pp. 167–194.

12 ECtHR, 7 July 1989, *Soering v. U.K*, A 161.

13 Para. 86.

14 ECtHR, 26 June 1992, *Drozd v. France and Spain*.

15 ECtHR, 24 October 1995, *Iribarne v. France*.

16 For further analysis see A. van Hoek et al., 'Transnational cooperation in criminal matters and the safeguarding of human rights', 2005 *Utrecht Law Review*, no. 2, www.UtrechtLawReview.org.

3. REGIONAL INTEGRATION IN THE EU AND THE TRANSNATIONAL APPLICATION OF THE *NE BIS IN IDEM* PRINCIPLE

The economic integration process in the framework of the EC stumbled upon the issue of transnational application of the *ne bis in idem* principle when dealing with punitive administrative sanctioning. This means that the principle played a role in EC law even before the coming into force of the Treaty of Maastricht.

The EC has administrative sanctioning powers in the field of competition and far-reaching powers to harmonize national administrative sanctioning in many EC policies. The ECJ has had occasion to address the issue of *ne bis in idem* in the field of competition.[17] Already in 1969, the ECJ held in *Wilhelm v. Bundeskartellamt*[18] that double prosecution, once by the Commission and once by the national authorities, was in line with regulation 17/62[19] and did not violate the *ne bis in idem* principle, given the fact that the scope of the European rules and the national rules differed. However, if this would result in the imposition of two consecutive sanctions, a general requirement of natural justice demands that any previous punitive decisions be taken into account in determining any sanction which is to be imposed (*Anrechnungsprinzip*). It is now fixed case law of the ECJ to confirm the *ne bis in idem* principle as a general principle of Community law,[20] which means that it is not limited to criminal sanctions, but that it also applies in competition matters. However, the ECJ seems to limits the *ne bis in idem* principle to double punishment and still accepts the accounting principle. This problem has not been solved by the new competition regulation 1/2003.[21] This regulation provides that, besides the European Commission, national competition authorities will also apply European competition rules, including the rules concerning enforcement (Article 35). The European Commission and the national authorities will form a network based on close cooperation. In practice, conflicts of jurisdiction and problems regarding *ne bis in idem* should be avoided through best practices of cooperation, after which competition authorities can suspend or terminate their proceedings (Article 13).

17 W. Wils, 'The principle of '*ne bis in idem*' in EC Antitrust Enforcement: a Legal and Economic Analysis', 2003 *World Competition*, no. 2.

18 Judgment of 13 February 1969, [1969] *ECR* 3.

19 Regulation no. 17/62, OJ P 013, 21 February 1962, p. 0204–0211, English special edition: Series 1 Chapter 1959–1962 p. 0087.

20 See for instance Judgment of 14 December 1972, *Boehringer Mannheim/Commission* (Rec.1972, p. 1281) (DK1972/00323 GR1972–1973/00313 P 1972/00447 ES1972/00261 SVII/00061 FIII/00059) and Judgment of the Court of 15 October 2002. *Limburgse Vinyl Maatschappij NV (LVM)* (C-238/99 P), *DSM NV and DSM Kunststoffen BV* (C-244/99 P), *Montedison SpA* (C-245/99 P), *Elf Atochem SA* (C-247/99 P), *Degussa AG* (C-250/99 P), *Enichem SpA* (C-251/99 P), *Wacker-Chemie GmbH and Hoechst AG* (C-252/99 P) and *Imperial Chemical Industries plc (ICI)* (C-254/99 P) *v. Commission of the European Communities.*

21 Regulation no. 1/2003, OJ L 001, 4 January 2003, p. 0001–0025, in force from 1 May 2004.

There is however no obligation, which means that double prosecution is not excluded as such. It is quite clear that by excluding double prosecution from the *ne bis idem* principle and by accepting the accounting principle the case law of the ECJ concerning international *ne bis in idem* in competition cases is not entirely in line with the ECtHR case law on the national *ne bis in idem* principle.

The *ne bis in idem* rule can be of importance in other sectors in which the EC has sanctioning power, e.g. within the area of European public procurement.[22] The EC has also harmonized sanctioning regimes in the Member States. The package on the protection of the financial interest of the EC is a good example. Member States have to impose administrative and criminal sanctions for irregularities and fraud. Article 6 of Regulation 2988/95[23] provides for suspension of national administrative enforcement during criminal proceedings. However, the administrative proceedings must be resumed when the criminal proceedings are concluded and the administrative authority must impose the prescribed administrative sanctions, including fines. The administrative authority may take into account any penalty imposed by the judicial authority on the same person in respect of the same facts. It is obvious that these provisions do not reflect the full effect of the *ne bis in idem* principle. Article 6 provides only that the reopening of the administrative proceedings after the criminal proceedings can be precluded by general legal principles. The *ne bis in idem* principle should bar such reopening if the same persons and the same facts are involved, but the regulation does not mention this explicitly. We can conclude that the EC has recognized the transnational *ne bis in idem* principle as a general principle of Community law, but accords to it a scope and application that lags behind even the minimal standard set by the ECtHR.

On the other hand, even before the integration of Justice matters in the EU, European Justice Ministers were fully aware that the deepening and widening of European integration would lead to an increase in trans-border crime and of transnational justice in Europe and that concurring prosecution and sanctioning would become an obstacle to Justice integration. In the framework of the European Political Cooperation, before the coming into force of the Maastricht Treaty with its Third Pillar on Justice and Home Affairs, the 1987 Convention on Double Jeopardy was elaborated between the Member States of the EC. This Convention deals with the *ne bis in idem* principle in a transnational setting in the EC. The Convention has been poorly ratified,[24] but its substance has been integrated into the CISA to such an extent that it may qualify with reason as the first multilateral convention establishing an international *ne bis in idem* principle as an individual right *erga omnes*.

22 Regulation no. 1605/2002, Articles 93–96, OJ L 248, 16 September 2002, p. 0001–0048 and Regulation 2342/2002, Article 133, OJ L 357, 31.12.2002, p. 0001–0071.

23 Regulation no. 2988/95, OJ L 312, 23 December 1995, p. 0001–0004.

24 The *ne bis in idem* Convention has been ratified by Denmark, France, Italy, the Netherlands and Portugal and is provisionally applied between them.

Article 54. A person whose trial has been finally disposed of in one Contracting Party may not be prosecuted in another Contracting Party for the same acts provided that, if a penalty has been imposed, it has been enforced, is actually in the process of being enforced or can no longer be enforced under the laws of the sentencing Contracting Party.

Article 55. 1. A Contracting Party may, when ratifying, accepting or approving this Convention, declare that it is not bound by Article 54 in one or more of the following cases:

a) where the acts to which the foreign judgment relates took place in whole or in part in its own territory; in the latter case, however, this exception shall not apply if the acts took place in part in the territory of the Contracting Party where the judgment was delivered;
b) where the acts to which the foreign judgment relates constitute an offence against national security or other equally essential interests of the Contracting Party;
c) where the acts to which the foreign judgment relates were committed by officials of that Contracting Party in violation of the duties of their office.

2. A Contracting Party which has made a declaration regarding the exception referred to in paragraph 1(b) shall specify the categories of offences to which this exception may apply.
3. A Contracting Party may at any time withdraw a declaration relating to one or more of the exceptions referred to in paragraph 1.
4. The exceptions which were the subject of a declaration under paragraph 1 shall not apply where the Contracting Party concerned has, in connection with the same acts, requested the other Contracting Party to bring the prosecution or has granted extradition of the person concerned.

Article 56. If a further prosecution is brought in a Contracting Party against a person whose trial, in respect of the same acts, has been finally disposed of in another Contracting Party, any period of deprivation of liberty served in the latter Contracting Party arising from those acts shall be deducted from any penalty imposed. To the extent permitted by national law, penalties not involving deprivation of liberty shall also be taken into account.

Article 57. 1. Where a Contracting Party charges a person with an offence and the competent authorities of that Contracting Party have reason to believe that the charge relates to the same acts as those in respect of which the person's trial has been finally disposed of in another Contracting Party, those authorities shall, if they deem it necessary, request the relevant information from the competent authorities of the Contracting Party in whose territory judgment has already been delivered.
2. The information requested shall be provided as soon as possible and shall be taken into consideration as regards further action to be taken in the proceedings under way.
3. Each Contracting Party shall, when ratifying, accepting or approving this Convention, nominate the authorities authorised to request and receive the information provided for in this Article.

> ***Article 58.*** The above provisions shall not preclude the application of broader national provisions on the *ne bis in idem* principle with regard to judicial decisions taken abroad.

The Schengen provisions have served as a model for several *ne bis in idem* provisions in the EU instruments on Justice and Home Affairs.[25] In this sense the Schengen Treaties have served as a testing laboratory. The Convention on the Financial Protection of the European Communities and its several protocols contain several provisions on *ne bis idem,*[26] as does the Convention on the Fight Against Corruption Involving Officials of the European Communities or Officials of Member States of the European Union.[27] The Corpus Juris[28] on European Criminal Law does not provide for a specific transnational *ne bis in idem* provision, but deals with the problem in Article 17 in the framework of concurring incriminations, as far as double criminal sanctioning is concerned, and imposes the accounting principle in case a criminal sanction is imposed after an administrative sanction.

From the above analysis it becomes quite clear that integration – be it economic integration with consequences for law enforcement, or justice integration – and the establishment of common territorial areas automatically usher in the transnational aspect of the *ne be in idem* principle.

4. *NE BIS IN IDEM*, THE ECJ AND THE AREA OF FREEDOM, SECURITY AND JUSTICE

4.1. INTRODUCTION

The CISA has been an important landmark for the establishment of a multilateral treaty-based international *ne bis in idem*. Although the CISA was very much linked with the internal market and the four freedoms, it was an intergovernmental instrument. With the coming into force of the Treaty of Amsterdam, in May 1999, the Schengen provisions were integrated into the EU *acquis*. The *ne bis in idem* Schengen provision was integrated in the Third Pillar provisions of the area of Freedom, Security and Justice. The EU was very much

---

25 H. Kühne, '*ne bis in idem* in den Schengener Vertragsstaaten', 1998 *J.Z.*, pp. 876–880, W. Schomburg, 'Die Europäisierung des Verbots doppelter Strafverfolgung – Ein Zwischenbericht', 2000 *NJW.*, pp. 1833–1840 and C. Van den Wyngaert et al., 'The international non bis in idem principle: Resolving some of the unanswered questions', 1999 *I.C.L.Q.*, pp. 786–788.

26 See Article 7 of the Convention, OJ 1996 C 313/3.

27 OJ 1997 C 195/1, Article 10.

28 M. Delmas-Marty et al. (eds.), *The Implementation of the Corpus Juris in the Member States*, vol. 1–4, 2000–2001.

aware of the necessity to legislate in more detail on the transnational *ne bis in idem* principle in the area of Freedom, Security and Justice. Provisions in international treaties governing the principle were too different and their application in the Member States varies too much. Point 49(e) of the Action Plan of the Council and the Commission on the implementation of the area of Freedom, Security and Justice[29] provides that measures will be established within five years of the entry into force of the Treaty 'for the coordination of criminal investigations and prosecutions in progress in the Member States with the aim of preventing duplication and contradictory rulings, taking account of better use of the *ne bis in idem* principle'. In the Programme of measures to implement the principle of mutual recognition of decisions in criminal matters,[30] the *ne bis in idem* principle is included among the immediate priorities of the EU and reference is *inter alia* made to the problem of out-of-court settlement. In effect it became clear, also through national case law, that national courts were experiencing problems with transactions and the application of the Schengen provisions on the transnational *ne bis in idem* principles.

Apart from the legislative perspective, the Treaty of Amsterdam also introduced the European Court of Justice as an important player in this field. The European Court of Justice had already established a full range of general principles of Community law, including in the area of criminal law and criminal procedure.[31] With the coming into force of the Third Pillar cooperation in Justice and Home Affairs (JHA) under the EU Treaty of Maastricht and the extended jurisdiction of the Court of Justice in Third Pillar issues under the EU Treaty of Amsterdam the ECJ has been given the opportunity to widen the scope of the general principles into new policy areas that touch more directly upon principles of due law and fundamental rights. In the first preliminary questions on the Schengen *acquis*[32] in the joined cases *Gözütok and Brügge*, national courts referred to the ECJ for a preliminary ruling under Article 35 EU on the interpretation of Article 54 of the CISA, raising interesting questions on the validity and the scope of the *ne bis in idem* principle in the EU/Schengen context. National courts asked the ECJ to clarify the scope and application of the transnational *ne bis in idem* principle. As this was a landmark case, we will analyse it in detail below, focusing on the transnational dimension.

---

29 OJ C 19, 23 January 1999.

30 OJ C 12, 15 January 2001.

31 See further Case 80/86, *Kolpinghuis*, [1987] *ECR* 3969. For further comments H. Sevenster, 'Criminal Law and EC Law', 1992 *CMLR*, pp. 29–70.

32 ECJ 11 February 2003, Cases C-187/01 and C-385/01, *Hüseyin Gözütok and Klaus Brügge*, [2003] *ECR* I-5689.

4.2. THE JOINED CASES GÖZÜTOK AND BRÜGGE: FACTS

Mr Gözütok, a Turkish national who had lived in the Netherlands for several years, was suspected of the possession of illegal quantities of soft drugs. In the course of searches of his coffee- and teahouse in 1996, the Dutch police did indeed find several kilos of hashish and marijuana. The criminal proceedings against Mr Gözütok were discontinued because he accepted a financial transaction proposed by the Dutch Public Prosecutor's Office, as provided for in Article 74(1) of the Dutch Criminal Code: 'The Public Prosecutor, prior to the trial, may set one or more conditions in order to avoid criminal proceedings for serious offences, excluding offences for which the law prescribes sentences of imprisonment of more than six years, and for lesser offences. The right to prosecute lapses when the conditions are met'. Mr Gözütok paid the proposed sums of NLG 3,000 and NLG 750. Mr Gözütok subsequently drew the attention of the German authorities after a notification of suspicious transactions by a German Bank to the German financial intelligence unit, which had been set up in the framework of the EC obligations against money laundering.[33] The German authorities obtained further information concerning the abovementioned offences from the Dutch authorities and decided to arrest Mr Gözütok and to prosecute him for dealing in narcotics in the Netherlands. In 1997, the District Court of Aachen in Germany convicted Mr Gözütok and sentenced him to a period of one year and five months' imprisonment, suspended on probation. Both Mr Gözütok and the Public Prosecutor's Office appealed. The Regional Court of Aachen discontinued the criminal proceedings brought against Mr Gözütok inter alia on the ground that under Article 54 of the CISA the German prosecuting authorities were bound by the definitive discontinuance of the criminal proceedings in the Netherlands. In a second appeal by the Public Prosecutor's Office to the Higher Regional Court, the Court decided to stay the proceedings and refer the matter to the ECJ for a preliminary ruling on the basis of Article 35 EU Treaty.

Mr Brügge, a German national living in Germany, was charged by the Belgian prosecution authorities with having intentionally assaulted and wounded Mrs Leliaert in Belgium, which constituted a violation of several provisions of the Belgian Criminal Code. Mr Brügge faced a double criminal investigation, one in Belgium and one in Germany. In the Belgian criminal proceedings, the District Court had to deal with both the criminal and civil aspects of the case, due to the fact that Mrs Leliaert, who became ill and unable to work because of the assault, as a civil party claimed pecuniary and non-pecuniary damages. In the course of the proceedings before the District Court of Veurne in Belgium, the Public Prosecutor's Office in Bonn in Germany offered to Mr Brügge an out-of-court

33 Council Directive 91/308/EEC of 10 June 1991 on prevention of the use of the financial system for the purpose of money laundering, OJ L 166, 28 June 1991, pp. 0077–0083.

settlement in return for payment of DEM 1000, in line with Section 153a in conjunction with Paragraph 153(1), second sentence, of the German Code of Criminal Procedure. The District Court of Veurne decided to stay the proceedings and refer questions to the ECJ for a preliminary ruling on the basis of Article 35 EU Treaty.

4.3. LEGAL BACKGROUND AND THE PRELIMINARY QUESTIONS

The German Higher Regional Court referred to the ECJ the following questions for a preliminary ruling: 'Is there a bar to prosecution in the Federal Republic of Germany under Article 54 of the Schengen Implementation Convention if, under Netherlands law, a prosecution on the same facts is barred in the Netherlands'? In particular, is there a bar to prosecution where a decision by the Public Prosecutor's Office to discontinue proceedings after the fulfilment of the conditions imposed (*transactie* under Netherlands law), which under the law of other Contracting States requires judicial approval, bars prosecution before a Netherlands court?' The Belgian District Court referred to the ECJ the following question for a preliminary ruling: 'Under Article 54 of the Schengen Implementation Convention is the Belgian Public Prosecutor's Office permitted to require a German national to appear before a Belgian criminal court and be convicted on the same facts as those in respect of which the German Public Prosecutor's Office has made him an offer, by way of a settlement, to discontinue the case after payment of a certain sum, which was paid by the accused?' Given the similarity of the substance of the questions, the cases were joined and examined together.

Articles 54 to 58 of the CISA on the application of the *ne bis in idem* rule are incorporated in Title VI of the Treaty on EU (Third Pillar provisions) on the legal basis of Article 34 EU and 31 EU.[34] Article 54 provides: 'A person whose trial has been finally disposed of in one Contracting Party may not be prosecuted in another Contracting Party for the same acts provided that, if a penalty has been imposed, it has been enforced, is actually in the process of being enforced or can no longer be enforced under the laws of the sentencing Contracting Party'. Article 55 stipulates exceptions to the rule of *ne bis in idem*, but they must be formally laid down at the moment of signature or ratification. One of the possible exceptions is that the acts took place in whole or in part in its own territory. Another relevant article in this context is Article 58 that stipulates that national provisions may go beyond the Schengen provisions on *ne bis in idem*, by giving a broader protection.

---

[34] Council Decision 1999/436/EC of 20 May 1999, OJ L 176, 10 July 1999, pp. 0017–0030.

The Treaty of Amsterdam has extended the jurisdiction of the ECJ in Third Pillar matters, inter alia to give rulings on the validity and interpretation of decisions. Member States must accept that jurisdiction in accordance with Article 35(2) and they can, according to Article 35(3) TEU, when accepting choose between granting the power to refer questions for a preliminary ruling either to any of its courts or tribunals or only to those courts or tribunals which give a final decision against which there is no further judicial remedy. Both Germany and Belgium have opted for the full range of courts and tribunals and the questions referred for a preliminary ruling do not affect public order or internal security (Article 35(5) TEU).

4.4. OPINION OF THE ADVOCATE GENERAL (AG)

The AG sticks to a strict interpretation of Article 35(1) TEU, which precludes any view on the application of the *ne bis in idem* principle to the case pending before the national court or with regard to the discontinuance of the criminal action. For this reason the AG expresses that the ECJ must disregard the terms in which the German Higher Regional Court formulates the first of its questions. For that reason the AG reformulates all the preliminary questions into two interpretative questions:

> '1. The first is whether the *ne bis in idem* principle stated in Article 54 of the Convention also applies when in one of the signatory States a criminal action is extinguished as the result of a decision to discontinue proceedings, taken by the Public Prosecutor's Office once the defendant has fulfilled the conditions imposed on him.
> 2. If the reply to the above question is positive, the German court wonders whether it is necessary for the decision taken by the Public Prosecutor's Office to be approved by a court.'

The AG qualifies Article 54 as a genuine expression of the *ne bis in idem* principle in a dynamic process of European integration. It is not a procedural rule but a fundamental safeguard, based on legal certainty and equity, for persons who are subject to the exercise of the *ius puniendi* in a common area of Freedom, Security and Justice. He also is of the opinion that the *ne bis in idem* principle is not only applicable within the framework of one particular legal system of a Member State. A strict application of national territoriality is incompatible with many situations in which there are elements of extra-territoriality and in which the same act may have legal effects in different parts of the territory of the Union. On the other hand the *ne bis in idem* rule is also an expression of mutual trust of the Member States in their criminal justice systems. Penal settlements are not contractual, but an expression of criminal justice. They do exist in many national legal orders, they are a form of administering justice, which protects the rights of the accused and culminates in the imposition of a penalty. Since the rights of the individual are protected, it is irrelevant whether the decision to discontinue the criminal action is approved by a court. A verdict is given on the acts being judged and on the guilt of the perpetrator. It involves the delivery of an implicit final decision on the conduct of the accused and the imposition of penalising measures. The rights of the victims are not affected, while they are not barred from claiming compensation. The phrasing of the Article 54 provision concerning the *res judicata* is in the opinion of the AG not homogenous in the various language versions (finally disposed, *rechtskräftig abgeurteilt*, *onherroepelijk vonnis*, *définitivement jugée*, *juzgada en sentencia firme*...). Member States do not agree on this point. France, Germany and Belgium are in favour of a restrictive interpretation limited to court decisions; the Netherlands and Italy, joined also by the European Commission plead in favour of a more extensive interpretation, including out-of-court judicial settlements. The AG underlines that the terms used by the various versions are not homogeneous and that a strict interpretation, limited to court judgments, may have absurd consequences that are contrary to reason and logic. Two persons suspected of the same offence could face a different application of the *ne bis in idem* principle if the one is acquitted in a final judgement and the other accepts an out-of-court settlement.

The AG concludes:

> 'The *ne bis in idem* principle stated in Article 54 of the Convention implementing the Schengen Agreement on the gradual abolition of checks at the common borders also applies when criminal proceedings are discontinued under the legal system of one Contracting Party as the consequence of a decision taken by the Public Prosecutor's Office, once the defendant has fulfilled certain conditions – and it is irrelevant whether that decision has to be approved by a court – provided that: 1.the conditions imposed are in the nature of a penalty; 2.the agreement presupposes an express or implied acknowledgement of guilt and, accordingly, contains an express or implied decision that the act is culpable; and 3.the agreement does not prejudice the victim and other injured parties, who may be entitled to bring civil actions.'

4.5. THE REASONING AND INTERPRETATIVE ANSWER OF THE COURT[35] AND DE LEGE FERENDA PROPOSALS

The ECJ not only followed the rephrasing of the preliminary questions by the AG, but also subscribed to his main arguments. The discontinuation is due to a

[35] For other comments in literature see M. Rübenstahl et al., 2003 *European Law Reporter*, no. 4, pp. 177–185; K. Adomeit, 2003 *NJW*, pp. 1162–1164; M. Fletcher, 2003 *The Modern Law Review*, pp. 769–780; O. Plöckinger, 2003 *Österreichische Juristenzeitung*, pp. 98–101; N.

decision of the Public Prosecutor's Office, being part of the administration of criminal justice. The result of the procedure penalises the unlawful conduct, which the accused is alleged to have committed. The penalty is enforced for the purposes of Article 54 and further prosecution is barred. The ECJ considers the *ne bis in idem* principle as a principle having proper effect, independent from matters of procedure or form, like the approval by a court. In the absence of an express indication to the contrary in Article 54, the principle of *ne bis in idem* must be regarded as sufficient to apply.

The arguments of Germany, Belgium and France that the wording and the general schema of Article 54, the relationship between Article 54 and Articles 55 and 58, the intentions of the Contracting Parties and certain other international provisions with a similar purpose, preclude Article 54 from being construed in such a way as to apply to procedures barring further prosecution in which no court is involved, fail to convince the ECJ. The ECJ does not find any obstacle in Articles 55 and 58 and considers the intentions of the Contracting Parties as of no value, since they predate the integration of the Schengen *acquis* in the EU. Concerning the Belgian Government's argument of possible prejudice to the rights of the victims, the ECJ follows the Opinion of the AG, underlining that the victim's rights to bring civil actions is not precluded by the application of the *ne bis in idem* principle.

For these reasons the ECJ rules that: 'The *ne bis in idem* principle, laid down in Article 54 of the Convention implementing the Schengen Agreement of 14 June 1985 between the Governments of the States of the Benelux Economic Union, the Federal Republic of Germany and the French Republic on the gradual abolition of checks at their common borders, signed on 19 June 1990 at Schengen, also applies to procedures whereby further prosecution is barred, such as the procedures at issue in the main actions, by which the Public Prosecutor of a Member State discontinues criminal proceedings brought in that State, without the involvement of a court, once the accused has fulfilled certain obligations and, in particular, has paid a certain sum of money determined by the Public Prosecutor'.

The ECJ states explicitly that the area of Freedom, Security and Justice implies mutual trust in each other's criminal justice systems and that the validity of the *ne bis in idem* principle is not dependent upon further harmonization. The ECJ further considers that the intentions of the Contracting Schengen Parties are no longer of value, as they predate the integration of the Schengen *acquis* in the EU. This is as such remarkable, since the Dutch proposal[36] at the time of the conception of Article 54 to include out-of-court transaction settlements was rejected. The intention of the Contracting Parties to exclude transactions from

---

Thwaites, 2002 *Revue de Droit de l'Union Européenne*, pp. 295–298; J. Vogel, 'Europäisches *ne bis in idem*, – EuGH', 2003 *NJW*, p. 1173.

36 As provided for under Article 68(3) of the Dutch Criminal Code.

the *ne bis in idem* principle was clear. However, the integration of the Schengen provisions in the EU, based upon the decision of the IGC and ratified by the national authorities did not only change the conceptual framework of these provisions, but also their meaning and effect. A parallel can be drawn here with the general principles of Community law in the internal market. Community loyalty and non-discrimination, for example, influenced the meaning and effect of several national criminal provisions, without taking into account the intentions of the national legislator. It is typical for an integrated legal order like the EC that the conceptual framework of integration interferes with national sovereignty, also in respect of cooperation and transnational aspects.[37] What happened during the process of market integration in the EC is now repeated in the process of justice integration in the EU. Rights and remedies for the market citizen are transformed into rights and remedies for the Union citizen. National decisions, including criminal decisions, can have an EU-wide effect in a new setting of European territoriality. This is also what makes the European integration process so different from the dual sovereignty in the USA, where the constitutional double jeopardy does not bar double prosecution in several states. When a defendant in a single act violates the 'peace and dignity' of two sovereign powers by breaking the laws of each, in the USA he has committed two distinct offences[38] with two different values to protect. In the EU we have a single area of Freedom, Security and Justice and an integrated legal order in which full effect should be given to fundamental standards.

However, with this decision the ECJ did not solve all the problems of the *ne bis in idem* principle. As mentioned the interpretation of the term final judgment is only one of the problem points. If the legislator does not intervene in due time, the ECJ will certainly receive other requests for preliminary rulings on the interpretation of the *ne bis in idem* principle. Questions that remain fully on the table are of course the problem of the definitions of *idem* and *bis* and the scope of the *ne bis in idem* principle as a whole. The ECJ in the joined *ne bis in idem* cases used the words '(...) discontinues criminal proceedings brought in that State, without the involvement of a court, once the accused has fulfilled certain obligations and, in particular, has paid a certain sum of money determined by the Public Prosecutor', wording that is much wider than the formulation of the AG who spoke of conditions with the nature of a penalty, the decision of guilt and no prejudice to victims. More concretely, the question is whether procedural agreements, such as plea bargaining or full or partial immunity deals for collaboration with the law enforcement authorities fall under the scope of the *ne bis in idem* principle? In some countries these deals can be connected to an out-of-court settlement in the form of a transaction. Another problem is the full

37 See e.g. Judgment of the Court of 2 February 1989, Case 186/87, *Ian William Cowan v. Trésor public*, [1989] *ECR*, p. 00195.

38 *Heath v. Alabama*, 474 U.S. 82 (1985).

application of the *ne bis in idem* rule if the first proceedings were conducted for the purpose of shielding the person concerned from criminal responsibility. Under which conditions can the *ne bis in idem* be set aside and by whom?

In that light it is important to underline that a couple of days after the ECJ ruling in the *Gözütok and Brügge* case Greece submitted a proposal for a framework decision on *ne bis in idem*[39] with the aim to establish common legal rules in order to ensure uniformity in both the interpretation of those rules and their practical implementation. The framework decision would replace Articles 54–58 CISA. The proposal defines criminal offences (Article 1) as offences *sensu stricto* and administrative offences or breaches punished with an administrative fine on the condition that the appeal procedure is before a criminal court. Judgments also include any extra-judicial mediated settlements in criminal matters and any decisions which have the status of *res judicata* under national law shall be considered as final judgments. Article 4 provides for exceptions to the *ne bis in idem* principle if the acts to which the foreign judgment relates constitute offences against the security or other equally essential interest of that Member State or were committed by a civil servant of the Member State in breach of his official duties. Article 3 provides for a consultation procedure and jurisdiction rules in order to avoid double prosecution. The initiative certainly deserves to be welcomed, but its reach is rather too narrow. In fact, excluding punitive administrative sanctioning if not appealable before a criminal court is quite absurd, also in the light of the ECtHR case law, although it does fit in with the German tradition of administrative criminal law (*Ordnungswidrigkeiten*). The draft also contains far too many exceptions to the *ne bis in idem* rule. Finally, the draft does not deal with the applicability of the principle to legal persons. The discussions in the Council are underway but quite difficult on several points, including the issues at stake in the *Gözütok and Brügge* case.

This ECJ judgment on *ne bis in idem* is just the start of an important role for the ECJ in the area of European criminal justice. All this illustrates that there is a real need to sign and ratify the draft Constitution, including the Charter of Fundamental Rights (CFR)[40] as a binding legal text. The CFR refers to the ECtHR as the minimal standard and the EU would also become a party to the ECtHR. The territorial scope of Article 50 CFR[41] dealing with *ne bis in idem* is fully transnational in the EU, but its substantive reach is disappointing due the wording of the text: ‘No one shall be liable to be tried or punished again in criminal proceedings of an offence for which he or she has already been finally

39 Initiative of the Hellenic Republic with a view to adopting a Council Framework Decision concerning the application of the ‘*ne bis in idem*’ principle, OJ C 2003 100/4.

40 Proclaimed in Nice on 7 December 2000, but not legally binding.

41 Council of the EU, Charter of Fundamental Rights of the European Union – Explanations relating to the complete text of the Charter, December 200, available at http://ue.eu.int/df/docs/en/EN_2001_1023.pdf.

acquitted or convicted within the Union in accordance with the law'.[42] By insisting so much on criminal proceedings, this text is not even in line with the current case law of the ECtHR. Moreover, the provision seems to deal only with final judgments. For this reason the Max Planck Institute for Foreign and International Criminal Law set up an expert group to elaborate the so called Freiburg Proposal on Concurrent Jurisdictions and the Prohibition on Multiple Prosecutions in the EU.[43] The text deals with the prevention of multiple prosecutions in international cases through the imposition of forum/jurisdiction rules, the application of transnational *ne bis in idem* and finally, as a safety net, the application of the accounting principle. Concerning transnational *ne bis in idem*, the expert group proposes a *ne bis in idem factum* right for natural and legal persons. The *ne bis in idem* principle should apply to all punitive procedures and sanctions, whether they are of an administrative or a criminal nature, whether they are national or European. The draft proposal uses the term 'finally disposed of' instead of 'finally acquitted or convicted'. This terminology includes every decision taken by prosecution authorities, which terminates the proceedings in a way that makes reopening of the case subject to exceptional circumstances, as for instance the reopening of res judicata cases. This means for example that German or Dutch out-of-court settlements (*Einstellung gegen Auflagen, transactie*) and the French *ordonnance de non-lieu motivée en fait* are included in the definition of *ne bis in idem*. This proposal provides an excellent set of provisions *de lege lata*, both for the legislator and the judiciary, and both at the European and the national level.

Meanwhile the ECJ had to deal with a mainstream of preliminary questions on the ne bis in idem principle. In some cases the ECJ had to define the idem character of ne bis in idem principle. In some Member States the idem is defined by the legal definition of the offence, in other Member States the material identity of the facts committed are decisive for the definition of the idem. Instead of choosing for a idem based on the same material circumstances and the same legal interest (Rechtsgut) to be protected, the ECJ decided for the material criterion only: "the relevant criterion for the purposes of the application of that article is identity of the material acts, understood as the existence of a set of facts which are inextricably linked together, irrespective of the legal classification given to them or the legal interest protected".[44]

The ECJ had also to deal with *ne bis in idem* cases, in which acquittal followed in one country because of the time-bar for the prosecution. The ECJ decided that the *ne bis in idem* principle applies in respect of a decision of a court of a Member State, made after criminal proceedings have been brought, by which the accused

[42] Art. II-50 of the Draft Constitution for the EU.

[43] Www.iuscrim.mpg.de/forsch/straf/projekte/nebisinidem.html.

[44] Case C-436/04, Van Esbroeck, Judgement of the Court, 9 March 2006. See also case C-150/05, Van Straaten, Judgement of 28th September 2006.See also C-367/05, Norma Kraaijenbrink, Judgement of 18 July 2007.

is acquitted finally because prosecution of the offence is time-barred.[45] Finally the ECJ had to deal with the execution of the verdict in the light of the *ne bis in idem* principle. When has a penalty imposed by a court of a Member State been enforced or is actually in the process of being enforced?[46]

5. MUTUAL RECOGNITION, *NE BIS IN IDEM* AND EQUIVALENT PROTECTION: THE EUROPEAN ARREST WARRANT

What does this ECJ preliminary ruling mean for the new set of mutual recognition instruments replacing the classic instruments of judicial cooperation in criminal matters, such as for instance the European Arrest Warrant replacing extradition? It it quite clear that the wave of mutual recognition proposals was mostly driven by thoughts of effectiveness, as was the original proposal of the European Commission[47] for the European Arrest Warrant, which contained a very limited set of provisions on the *ne bis in idem* principle. It is quite clear that in 2001 the importance of the principle in a transnational setting was still underestimated.

> Article 30 *ne bis in idem*
> 1. The executing judicial authority shall refuse to execute a European arrest warrant, if a judicial authority in the executing Member State has passed final judgement upon the person claimed in respect of the offence or offences for which the European arrest warrant has been issued.
> 2. The execution of a European arrest warrant may also be refused if the judicial authorities of the executing Member State have decided either not to institute or to terminate proceedings in respect of the same offence or offences.

However, as a result of the negotiations in the Council these provisions changed substantially when a distinction between final judgments, prosecution and pending proceedings was introduced. The major asset of the new rules is that, in recognizing *res judiciata* as a bar to surrender, they considers final judgments and out-of-court settlements in all Member States of the EU to be on a par with those emanating from the requested State. In the case of final judgments the *ne bis in idem* principle leads to a mandatory ground for refusal. Whenever a final judgment has been passed in a Member State, all other states should abide by this decision. The executing authority will have to assess all prior judgments in respect of the act under scrutiny, irrespective of whether they derive from the

45 Case C-467/04, Gasparini, Judgement of 28th September 2006.
46 See case C-28/05, Jürgen Kretzinger, Judgement of 18 July 2007.
47 Document COM(2001) 522 final, Brussels, September 13th 2001, OJ C 332 E/305.

issuing State, the executing State or another Member State. In fact, for the executing State it is much easier under the European Arrest Warrant regime to bar surrender procedures based on the *ne bis in idem* principle than it was under the extradition Convention of the Council of Europe, which is in line with the mutual trust principle.

Concerning prosecution, what is in fact meant here is the situation of out-of-court settlement. Article 4(3) reads that:

> 'Where the judicial authorities of the executing Member State have decided either not to prosecute for the offence on which the European arrest warrant is based or to halt proceedings, or where a final judgement has been passed upon the requested person in a Member State, in respect of the same acts, which prevents further proceedings.'

Non-execution in this case is optional, which means that cumulative proceedings, like in the case of *Krombach v. Bamberski*,[48] are still possible within the EU, which constitutes a weakening of the CISA provisions as interpreted by the ECJ. The only new aspect compared to the Extradition Convention is that this principle not only plays a role in relation to the issuing State, but in relation to all Member States, i.e. in the whole legal area. It is a pity that this has not been integrated as a mandatory ground for non-execution. Another point of debate could be whether the decision by the Prosecutor must be approved by a court. Furthermore, it is not at all clear who the judicial authorities are and which decisions are covered. Indeed, Article 6(3) states that Member States define who the competent judicial authorities are for the European Arrest Warrant. Article 4(3) refers to the same judicial authorities.

Finally, the European Arrest Warrant includes *lis pendens* proceedings. In line with Article 8 of the Extradition Convention, Article 4(2) defines pending criminal proceedings in the executing Member State as a ground for optional refusal:

> 'Where the person who is the subject of the European arrest warrant is being prosecuted in the executing Member State for the same act as that on which the European arrest warrant is based.'

We can conclude that the final version of the framework decision on the European Arrest Warrant has improved substantially compared to the Commission draft when it comes to the protection offered by the transnational *ne bis in idem* principle. However, the EAW regime also allows for the optional

48 See Case-7/98, *Krombach v. Bamberski*, Judgment of the Full Court of 28 March 2000, [2000] *ECR* I-1395, annotated by A. van Hoek, 2001 *Common Market Law Review*, no. 4, pp. 1011–1027.

application of the *ne bis in idem* principle in the case of out-of-court settlements. Still, the *ne bis in idem* principle has been largely spelled out in the text, which cannot be said of the duty to respect other human rights in a transnational setting: these must be at least flagrantly violated before they may bar the surrender procedure.[49] By contrast, for the principle of *ne bis in idem*, the ECJ has laid the foundation for its transnational application as a human right, which leads to equivalent protection in the common area of Freedom, Security and Justice.

6. CONCLUSION

As has emerged clearly from the analysis above, neither ECtHR practice, nor the application of the *ne bis in idem* principle in the framework of the multilateral treaties in criminal matters of the Council of Europe have led to a common *ne bis in idem* standard in Europe.

In the EU, the traditional *ne bis in idem* principle has developed from a domestic legal principle into a transnational human right. This process began as a result of Schengen integration and has deepened further in the framework of the common area of Freedom, Security and Justice. Classic inter-state cooperation in criminal matters has been replaced by enhanced judicial cooperation, directly between the actors of the criminal justice system. Moreover, these have to recognize each other's judicial decisions, based upon the principle of mutual recognition. Mutual recognition of, for example, each other's arrest warrants does not only lead to speedier surrender of suspects within the EU, but also to the duty of transnational application of legal principles such as the *ne bis in idem* principle. And this transnational operation presumes that the territorial scope and substantive application of the *ne bis in idem* principle within the EU is based on a common standard. This is the only way in which to guarantee equivalent protection. Essential aspects of the operation of the criminal justice system are thus functioning in an European area without internal borders, a transnational judicial area. Member States must be prepared to leave behind their classic, outdated views on sovereignty and accept a vision of shared sovereignty in the common judicial area. Transnational human rights are a substantial part of such a common judicial area.

Despite this, it has clearly emerged from the above analysis that the Union legislator is finding it enormously difficult to give shape and substance to transnational legal principles and this is also true in the case of the *ne bis in idem* principle. It is the ECJ which, through interpretation of the principles of the Community legal order, has to define the legal principles and determine their

49 See Van Hoek et al., *supra* note 16, and Blekxtoon et al., *supra* note 11.

scope and application. The ECJ's preliminary ruling in cases C-187/01 and C-385/01, *Hüseyin Gözütok and Klaus Brügge,* and in near then other cased that followed, has made clear that the ECJ is prepared to play this role, just as it has played it in the process of the integration of the Community. National courts, too, are joining in, as Supreme Courts have submitted several preliminary questions to the ECJ.

Mutual recognition of each other's judicial decisions, such as for instance in the application of the European Arrest Warrant, requires common and equivalent protection of human rights in the area of Freedom, Security and Justice. Common standards of the Rule of Law, at least in line with the minimum standards developed by the ECtHR, are the *minimum minimorum* for mutual trust between States and for mutual trust between the citizens of the EU and thus for the legitimacy of the EU criminal policy as such.

For this reason, it is essential that all the necessary legal guarantees are built in into the new mutual recognition instruments (European evidence warrant, retention of data, etc.) and to allow the ECJ sufficient room to develop transnational legal principles in criminal matters within the EU. If the ECJ is to deal quickly and efficiently with these issues, a specialized chamber would not go amiss.

INDEX

G

H

I

LIST OF AUTHORS

David, Antje, Dr. iur., judge at the Social Court, Social Court Karlsruhe.

Duijkersloot, A.P.W. (Ton), Dr., assistant Professor, Institute of Constitutional Law and Administrative Law, Faculty of Law, University of Utrecht.

Harings, Lothar, Dr., Attorney, partner in the law firm Graf von Westphalen, Hamburg/Brussels.

Hey, Ellen, Prof. Dr., Head of the Department and Professor of Public International Law, Erasmus School of Law, Erasmus University Rotterdam.

Hofmann, Jens, Dr., Judge at the Administrative Court of Karlsruhe.

Jansen, Oswald, Dr., Legal Advisor and attorney of (the municipality of) The Hague, associate professor, Institute for Constitutional and Administrative Law, Utrecht University.

Keessen, Andrea, Dr. assistant Professor, Institute for Constitutional and Administrative Law, Utrecht University.

Knipschild, Klaus, Dr., Attorney, IUR-Realis, Frankfurt.

Luchtman, Michiel, Dr., associate professor at the University of Utrecht, School of Law, Willem Pompe Institute for Criminal Law and Criminology.

Riedel, Daniel, Dr., Regierungsrat, Deputy Head of Division, Federal Ministry of Economics and Technology, Berlin.

Röhl, Hans Christian, Professor Dr., Professor of Public Law at the University Konstanz.

Ruffert, Matthias, Prof. Dr., Professor at the Friedrich Schiller University of Jena, Faculty of Law, Chair for Public Law, European Law and Public International Law.

Schenk, Wolfgang, Dr., Judge (Karlsruhe Administrative Court), at present Research Assistant at the German Federal Constitutional Court, Karlsruhe.

Schmidt-Aßmann, Eberhard, Prof. Dr. Dres. h.c., former director of the Institute for German and European Administrative Law, Professor emeritus at the University of Heidelberg.

Schöndorf-Haubold, Bettina, Dr. iur., Juniorprofessor for Public Law, Justus Liebig University Gießen.

Sommer, Julia, Dr. iur., Attorney, Freshfields Bruckhaus Deringer.

van Hoek, Aukje, Prof. Dr., Professor of Private International Law and Civil Procedure, Faculty of Law, University of Amsterdam.

van Rijswick, Marleen, Prof. Dr., Professor of European and Dutch water law, Institute for Constitutional and Administrative Law, Center for Environmental Law and Policy/NILOS, Faculty of Law, Economics and Governance, Utrecht University.

Vervaele, John, Prof. Dr., Professor in Economic and European Criminal Law, Utrecht School of Law, Willem Pompe Institute for Criminal Sciences.

Vogt, Matthias, Dr., LL.M., trial judge at the administrative court of Lüneburg, Lower Saxony.

Wettner, Florian, Dr., Attorney, associated partner at the law firm Gleiss Lutz, Frankfurt.